P9-CKV-580

The New

Relational Database

Dictionary

*A comprehensive glossary
of concepts arising in connection with
the relational model of data,
with definitions and illustrative examples*

C. J. Date

The New Relational Database Dictionary
by C. J. Date

Copyright © 2016 C. J. Date. All rights reserved.
Printed in the United States of America.

Published by O'Reilly Media, Inc.,
1005 Gravenstein Highway North, Sebastopol, CA 95472

O'Reilly books may be purchased for educational, business, or sales promotional use. Online editions are also available for most titles (*http://safaribooksonline.com*). For more information, contact our corporate/institutional sales department: (800) 998-9938 or *corporate@oreilly.com*.

Revision History:
    2015-12-15   First release.
See *http://oreilly.com/catalog/errata.csp?isbn=9781491951736* for release details.

Nutshell Handbook, the Nutshell Handbook logo, and the O'Reilly logo are registered trademarks of O'Reilly Media, Inc. *The New Relational Database Dictionary* and related trade dress are trademarks of O'Reilly Media, Inc.

Many of the designations used by manufacturers and sellers to distinguish their products are claimed as trademarks. Where those designations appear in this book, and O'Reilly Media, Inc., was aware of a trademark claim, the designations have been printed in caps or initial caps.

While every precaution has been taken in the preparation of this book, the publisher and author assume no responsibility for errors or omissions, or for damages resulting from the use of the information contained herein.

ISBN: 978-1-491-95173-6
[LSI]

About the Author

C. J. Date is an independent author, lecturer, researcher, and consultant, specializing in relational database technology. He is best known for his book *An Introduction to Database Systems* (8th edition, Addison-Wesley, 2004), which has sold some 900,000 copies at the time of writing and is used in several hundred colleges and universities worldwide. He is also the author of many other books on database management, the following among them:

- From Addison-Wesley: *Databases, Types, and the Relational Model: The Third Manifesto* (3rd edition, with Hugh Darwen, 2007)

- From Trafford: *Logic and Databases: The Roots of Relational Theory* (2007) and *Database Explorations: Essays on The Third Manifesto and Related Topics* (with Hugh Darwen, 2010)

- From Ventus: *Go Faster! The TransRelational^{TM} Approach to DBMS Implementation* (2002, 2011)

- From O'Reilly: *Database Design and RelationalTheory: Normal Forms and All That Jazz* (2012); *View Updating and Relational Theory: Solving the View Update Problem* (2013); *Relational Theory for Computer Professionals: What Relational Databases Are Really All About* (2013); and *SQL and Relational Theory: How to Write Accurate SQL Code* (3rd edition, 2015)

- From Morgan Kaufmann: *Time and Relational Theory: Temporal Data in the Relational Model and SQL* (with Hugh Darwen and Nikos A. Lorentzos, 2014)

Mr. Date was inducted into the Computing Industry Hall of Fame in 2004. He enjoys a reputation that is second to none for his ability to explain complex technical subjects in a clear and understandable fashion.

Thy gift, thy tables, are within my brain
Full charactered with lasting memory,
Which shall above that idle rank remain
Beyond all date, even to eternity.
—William Shakespeare: *Sonnet 122*

———— ♦ ♦ ♦ ♦ ♦ ————

"When I use a word," Humpty Dumpty said, in rather a scornful tone,
"it means just what I choose it to mean—neither more nor less."
—Lewis Carroll: *Through the Looking-Glass and What Alice Found There*

———— ♦ ♦ ♦ ♦ ♦ ————

Myself when young did eagerly frequent
Doctor and Saint, and heard great Argument
About it and about; but evermore
Came out by the same Door as in I went.
—Edward Fitzgerald: *The Rubáiyát of Omar Khayyam*

———— ♦ ♦ ♦ ♦ ♦ ————

Lexicographer *A writer of dictionaries, a harmless drudge*
—Dr Johnson: *A Dictionary of the English Language*

———— ♦ ♦ ♦ ♦ ♦ ————

To all keepers of the true relational flame

Introduction

This dictionary contains over 1,700 entries dealing with issues, terms, and concepts involved in, or arising from use of, the relational model of data. Most of the entries include not only a definition as such—often several definitions, in fact—but also an illustrative example (sometimes more than one). What's more, I've tried to make those entries as clear, precise, and accurate as I can; they're based on my own best understanding of the material, an understanding I've gradually been honing over some 45 years of involvement in this field.

I'd also like to stress the fact that the dictionary is, as advertised, relational. To that end, I've deliberately omitted many topics that are only tangentially connected to relational databases as such (in particular, topics that have to do with database technology in general, as opposed to relational databases specifically); for example, I have little or nothing to say about security, recovery, or concurrency matters. I've also omitted certain SQL topics that—despite the fact that SQL is supposed to be a relational language—aren't really relational at all (cursors, outer join, and SQL's various "retain duplicates" options are examples here). At the same time, I've deliberately included a few nonrelational topics in order to make it clear that, contrary to popular opinion, the topics in question are indeed nonrelational (index is a case in point here).

I must explain too that this is a dictionary with an attitude. It's my very firm belief that the relational model is the right and proper foundation for database technology and will remain so for as far out as anyone can see, and many of the definitions in what follows reflect this belief. As I said in my book *SQL and Relational Theory: How to Write Accurate SQL Code* (3rd edition, O'Reilly Media Inc., 2015):

> In my opinion, the relational model is rock solid, and "right," and will endure. A hundred years from now, I fully expect database systems still to be based on Codd's relational model. Why? Because the foundations of that model—namely, set theory and predicate logic—are themselves rock solid in turn. Elements of predicate logic in particular go back well over 2000 years, at least as far as Aristotle (384–322 BCE).

Partly as a consequence of this state of affairs, I haven't hesitated to mark some term or concept as *deprecated* if I believe there are good reasons to avoid it, even if the term or concept in question is in widespread use at the time of writing. Materialized view is a case in point here.

The Suppliers-and-Parts Database

Many of the examples used to illustrate the definitions are based on the familiar (not to say hackneyed) suppliers-and-parts database. I apologize for dragging out this old warhorse yet one more time, but as I've said many times before, I believe that using the same example—or essentially the same example, at any rate—in a variety of different publications can be a help, not a hindrance, in learning. Here are the relvar definitions for that database (and if you don't know what a relvar is, then please see the pertinent dictionary entry!):

```
VAR S BASE RELATION
  { SNO     SNO ,
    SNAME   NAME ,
    STATUS  INTEGER ,
    CITY    CHAR }
  KEY { SNO } ;

VAR P BASE RELATION
  { PNO     PNO ,
    PNAME   NAME ,
    COLOR   COLOR ,
    WEIGHT  WEIGHT ,
    CITY    CHAR }
  KEY { PNO } ;

VAR SP BASE RELATION
  { SNO     SNO ,
    PNO     PNO ,
    QTY     QTY }
  KEY { SNO , PNO }
  FOREIGN KEY { SNO } REFERENCES S
  FOREIGN KEY { PNO } REFERENCES P ;
```

These definitions are expressed in a language called **Tutorial D** (see the section "Technical Issues" below for further explanation). The semantics are as follows:

- Relvar S represents *suppliers under contract*. Each supplier has one supplier number (SNO), unique to that supplier; one name (SNAME), not necessarily unique; one status value (STATUS); and one location (CITY). Attributes SNO, SNAME, STATUS, and CITY are of types SNO, NAME, INTEGER, and CHAR, respectively.

- Relvar P represents *kinds of parts*. Each kind of part has one part number (PNO), which is unique; one name (PNAME); one color (COLOR); one weight (WEIGHT); and one location where parts of that kind are stored (CITY). Attributes PNO, PNAME, COLOR, WEIGHT, and CITY are of types PNO, NAME, COLOR, WEIGHT, and CHAR, respectively.

- Relvar SP represents *shipments* (it shows which parts are shipped, or supplied, by which suppliers). Each shipment has one supplier number (SNO), one part number (PNO), and one quantity (QTY). There's at most one shipment at any given time for a given supplier and given part, and so the combination of supplier number and part number is unique to the shipment in question. Attributes SNO, PNO, and QTY are of types SNO, PNO, and QTY, respectively.

Fig. 1 shows a set of sample values for these relvars. Examples in the body of the dictionary assume those specific values, where applicable.

S

SNO	SNAME	STATUS	CITY
S1	Smith	20	London
S2	Jones	10	Paris
S3	Blake	30	Paris
S4	Clark	20	London
S5	Adams	30	Athens

SP

SNO	PNO	QTY
S1	P1	300
S1	P2	200
S1	P3	400
S1	P4	200
S1	P5	100
S1	P6	100
S2	P1	300
S2	P2	400
S3	P2	200
S4	P2	200
S4	P4	300
S4	P5	400

P

PNO	PNAME	COLOR	WEIGHT	CITY
P1	Nut	Red	12.0	London
P2	Bolt	Green	17.0	Paris
P3	Screw	Blue	17.0	Oslo
P4	Screw	Red	14.0	London
P5	Cam	Blue	12.0	Paris
P6	Cog	Red	19.0	London

Fig. 1: The suppliers-and-parts database–sample values

Alphabetization

For alphabetization purposes, I've followed these rules:

1. Blanks precede numerals.

2. Numerals precede letters.

3. Uppercase precedes lowercase.

4. Punctuation symbols (parentheses, hyphens, underscores, etc.) are treated as blanks.

Technical Issues

1. Keywords, variable names, and the like are set in all uppercase throughout.

2. Coding examples are expressed, mostly, in a language called **Tutorial D**. Now, I believe those examples are reasonably self-explanatory, but in any case that language is largely defined in the dictionary itself in the entries for the various relational operators (projection, join, and so on). A comprehensive description of the language can be found if needed in the book *Databases, Types, and the Relational Model: The Third Manifesto* (3rd edition),

by C. J. Date and Hugh Darwen (Addison-Wesley, 2007). To elaborate briefly: As its subtitle indicates, that book—the *Manifesto* book for short—also introduces and explains *The Third Manifesto*, which is a precise though somewhat formal definition of the relational model and a supporting type theory (including a comprehensive model of type inheritance). In particular, that book uses the name **D** as a generic name for any language that conforms to the principles laid down by *The Third Manifesto*. Any number of distinct languages could qualify as a valid **D**; sadly, however, SQL isn't one of them, which is why coding examples are expressed for the most part in **Tutorial D** and not SQL. (**Tutorial D** is, of course, a valid **D**; in fact, it was expressly designed to be suitable as a vehicle for illustrating and teaching the ideas of *The Third Manifesto*.)

Note: **Tutorial D** has been revised and extended somewhat since the *Manifesto* book was first published. A description of the current version can be found in the book *Database Explorations: Essays on The Third Manifesto and Related Topics*, by C. J. Date and Hugh Darwen (Trafford, 2010)—available online at the *Manifesto* website *www.thethirdmanifesto.com.*[1] What's more, that *Explorations* book also includes some proposals for extending the language still further (e.g., to incorporate explicit foreign key support), proposals that for the purposes of this dictionary I assume to have been adopted.

3. Following on from the previous point, I should make it clear that definitions in this dictionary are intended to conform fully to the relational model as defined by *The Third Manifesto*. As a consequence, you might find certain aspects of those definitions a trifle surprising—for example, the assertion in the entry for **deferred checking** that such checking is logically flawed. As I've said, this is a dictionary with an attitude.

4. The notion of *set* is ubiquitous in the database world. On paper, a set is typically represented by a comma separated list (or "commalist") of items denoting the elements that constitute the set in question, the whole enclosed in braces, as here: {*a,b,c*}. (Blanks appearing immediately before the first item or any comma, or immediately after the last item or any comma, are ignored.) Throughout this dictionary, therefore, I use braces to enclose commalists of items whenever the items in question are meant to denote the elements of some set, implying among other things that (a) the order in which the items appear within that commalist is immaterial and (b) if some item appears more than once, it's treated as if it appeared just once.

5. **Tutorial D** in particular uses braces to enclose the commalist of argument expressions in certain *n*-adic (prefix) operator invocations. If the operator in question is idempotent, as in the case of, e.g., JOIN, then the argument expression commalist truly does represent a set of arguments, and the remarks of the previous paragraph apply unconditionally. For other

---

[1] Actually the *Manifesto* itself has been revised and clarified somewhat since the *Manifesto* book was first published. The current version can be found in that same *Explorations* book.

operators, however, the argument expression commalist represents a *bag* of arguments, not a set—in which case the order in which the argument expressions appear is still immaterial, but repetition has significance (despite the fact that **Tutorial D** and this dictionary do still both use braces in such a context). For example, the operator XOR ("exclusive OR")—meaning the version of that operator defined in this dictionary, at any rate—isn't idempotent. As a consequence, the **Tutorial D** expressions

```
XOR { TRUE , FALSE }
```

and

```
XOR { TRUE , FALSE , TRUE }
```

aren't logically equivalent—the first returns TRUE and the second FALSE.

6. The notion of *logic* is, of course, also ubiquitous in the database world. The relational model in particular is firmly based on logic. More precisely, it's based on conventional two-valued logic ("2VL"), and all references to logic in this dictionary should be taken as referring to that logic specifically, except very occasionally where the context demands otherwise. *Note:* As these remarks suggest, many of the dictionary entries do have to do with concepts from logic. Unfortunately, logic texts (and logicians) vary widely not just in the terminology they use but also, in some cases, in the substance of their definitions. The definitions I give are the ones I find most appropriate myself, but be warned that they're sometimes at odds with others you can find in the literature.

7. *A note on the relational operators:* Perhaps unfortunately, it has become standard practice in the database world to use terms such as projection, join, and so on in two somewhat different senses. To be specific, they're used to refer sometimes to those operators as such and sometimes to the results obtained when those operators are invoked. I've followed this practice myself in this dictionary on occasion, and hope it won't lead to confusion.

8. In fact, it has become standard practice to use terms such as projection, join, and so on in another sense also. By definition, these operators apply to relation values specifically. In particular, of course, they apply to the values that happen to be the current values of relvars. It thus clearly makes sense to talk about, e.g., the join of relvars *R1* and *R2*, meaning the relation *r* that results from taking the join of the current values *r1* and *r2*, respectively, of those two relvars. In some contexts, however (normalization, for example, also view processing), it turns out to be convenient to use expressions like "the join of relvars *R1* and *R2*" in a slightly different sense. To be specific, we might say, loosely but very conveniently, that some *relvar*, *R* say, is the join of relvars *R1* and *R2*—meaning, more precisely, that the value of *R* is equal at all times to the join of the values of *R1* and *R2* at the time in question. In a sense, therefore, we can talk in terms of joins of relvars per

se, rather than just in terms of joins of current values of relvars. Analogous remarks apply to all of the relational operations.

9. Regarding projection in particular, please note that **Tutorial D** treats projection as having very high precedence, in order to reduce the number of parentheses that might otherwise be required in relational expressions. For example, the **Tutorial D** expression

    ```
    SP JOIN S { SNO }
    ```

    is defined to be equivalent to

    ```
    SP JOIN ( S { SNO } )
    ```

    and not

    ```
    ( SP JOIN S ){ SNO }
    ```

10. Talk of projection raises yet another point. Here's the definition from the pertinent dictionary entry:

    > Let relation r have attributes called $A1$, $A2$, ..., An (and possibly others). Then (and only then) the expression $r\{A1,A2,...,An\}$ denotes the projection of r on $\{A1, A2, ..., An\}$, and it returns the relation with heading $\{A1,A2,...,An\}$ and body consisting of all tuples t such that there exists a tuple in r that has the same value for attributes $A1$, $A2$, ..., An as t does.

    Now, if the result has heading $\{A1,A2,...,An\}$, then by definition each of those Ai's is an <attribute name, type name> pair. But in the projection expression $r\{A1,A2,...,An\}$, each of those Ai's is just an attribute name. (The syntax works because attribute names are unique within the pertinent heading and thus imply the associated type names.) So there's a kind of punning going on here: The very same symbol Ai is being used to denote slightly different things in different contexts.

    Generalizing slightly from the foregoing remarks, please understand that the term *attribute* is sometimes used in the body of the dictionary to mean an attribute name rather than an attribute as such; likewise, the term *heading* is sometimes used to mean a set of attribute names rather than a set of attributes as such. I apologize if you find this state of affairs confusing, but once again it's fairly standard practice.

    Note: While I'm on the subject of headings, I should mention that in previous versions of this dictionary, headings were denoted $\{H\}$; in the present version, by contrast, they're denoted simply H (i.e., the enclosing braces have been dropped).

11. There's another convention I need to mention (yet again it's fairly standard, but it's worth spelling out in detail in order to avoid any possible confusion). It's illustrated by, e.g., the entry for **joinable**, which includes the following sentence:

    > Relations $r1, r2, ..., rn$ ($n \geq 0$) are joinable if and only if for all i and j, relations ri and rj are joinable ($1 \leq i \leq n, 1 \leq j \leq n$).

    Consider the opening part of this sentence—"Relations $r1, r2, ..., rn$ ($n \geq 0$) are joinable." Here the case $n = 0$ is to be understood as meaning, not that there exists a relation, not mentioned in the commalist, called $r0$, but rather that the commalist is empty—i.e., there aren't in fact any relations at all.

    Similarly, consider the closing part of the sentence—"relations ri and rj are joinable ($1 \leq i \leq n, 1 \leq j \leq n$)." Here the case $n = 0$ is to be understood as meaning that there aren't any i's or j's, and hence that there are no relations ri and rj.

12. I'd also like to draw your attention to still another standard convention, followed throughout this dictionary (and in fact spelled out explicitly in the pertinent dictionary entries): viz., I use the generic term *update* in lowercase to refer to—among other things— the familiar INSERT, DELETE, and UPDATE operators considered collectively. By contrast, when I want to refer to the UPDATE operator as such, I'll set it in uppercase ("all caps") as just shown.

13. Certain of the definitions and examples make use of a simplified notation for tuples. For example, consider the SP tuple shown in Fig. 1 for supplier S1 and part P1. A formal **Tutorial D** representation of that tuple might look like this:

    ```
    TUPLE { SNO SNO('S1') , PNO PNO('P1') , QTY QTY(300) }
    ```

    In the simplified notation under discussion, however, the same tuple would be represented thus:

    ```
    <S1,P1,300>
    ```

    —or, very occasionally, sometimes even thus:

    ```
    S1   P1   300
    ```

14. This dictionary has almost nothing to say about distributed databases or related matters. The reason is that the whole point about a distributed database as far as the relational model is concerned is that it's supposed to look exactly like a nondistributed database! In other words, all of the problems of distributed databases (and problems there most certainly are)

are, at least in an ideal system, problems of physical implementation, not problems of the logical model.

15. Finally, please note that all references to SQL in this dictionary are to the version of that language defined by the official SQL standard. As you might be aware, however, that standard has been through several versions, or editions, over the years. The version current at the time of writing—and the version on which references to SQL in this dictionary are based—is the 2011 version ("SQL:2011"). Here's the formal reference:

> International Organization for Standardization (ISO), *Database Language SQL*, Document ISO/IEC 9075:2011.

Publishing History and Structure of This Edition

This is the third version, or edition, of this dictionary; the first (with the title *The Relational Database Dictionary*) was published by O'Reilly Media Inc. in 2006, and the second (with the title *The Relational Database Dictionary, Extended Edition*) by Apress in 2008. The following remarks are taken from the introduction to that second edition:

> It's a fact of life that dictionaries always expand from one edition to the next. The first edition of this dictionary had just over 600 entries; this one has over 900—an almost 50 percent increase. New entries include atomic relvar, attribute reference, cardinality constraint, class, computational completeness, connection trap, default, field, Great Divide, overriding, referential cycle, safe expression, stored procedure, and many others. I've also taken the opportunity to improve (and in a few cases correct) several of the existing entries; examples here include derived relation, essentiality, fifth normal form, foreign key, JD implied by superkeys, NAND, NOR, ordering, and pointer. No entries have been removed!
>
> One thing I was slightly surprised to discover in working on this edition was the extent to which database concepts rely, ultimately, on certain mathematical terms and constructs. As a result, I decided to include a few somewhat mathematical entries; examples here include boolean algebra, group, inverse, nonnegative, partial ordering, and mathematical (as opposed to relational model) definitions for relation and tuple. The relevance of such entries might not be immediately apparent, but I felt it was useful to collect them together in one place in order to serve as a convenient reference for anyone who wishes to delve a little more deeply into the precise meaning and origins of a term like relational algebra (or the term relation itself, come to that).

The foregoing remarks, suitably amended, apply to this new edition as well, but with even more force (which is why I decided to use the slightly revised, but I believe merited, title *The New Relational Database Dictionary*). There are now over 1,700 entries in total (an almost 90% increase over the previous edition); new ones include axiom of choice, constant reference, disjoint INSERT, domain of discourse, double negation, exclusive union, individual constant, logical difference, mediator, possibly nondeterministic, primary key attribute, Query-By-Example, repeating field, scalar operator, and tuple product. In addition, numerous existing entries have been expanded and improved (and occasionally corrected), cosmetic improvements have been made throughout, and many more examples have been included.

But the foregoing remarks are far from being the whole of the story. Indeed, the major reason for the increase in size in this edition is that I decided to include, this time around, both (a) definitions arising from the underlying theory of types—including those having to do with the concept of type inheritance in particular—and (b) definitions arising from the use of interval types in particular. Thus, the dictionary is now divided into three parts, as follows:

- *Part I:* Given that relations have attributes and attributes have types (also called domains), it's clear that relational theory does rely on, or assume, a supporting type theory. But nowhere does it say what that theory has to look like. In other words, relational theory and type theory are, at least to a first approximation, completely independent of one another. At the same time, it's quite difficult—certainly less than fully satisfactory, at least—to define and illustrate relational concepts properly without saying something about the underlying theory of types. Thus, Part I of this new dictionary ("Types and Relations"), which effectively subsumes the previous edition in its entirety, now contains numerous entries having to do with that type theory specifically. (Those entries, like the ones having to do with relational theory as such, are all intended to conform to the prescriptions laid down by *The Third Manifesto*. As you'll soon see, however, the inclusion of such entries inevitably led to the inclusion of several further entries dealing with concepts from the world of object orientation (OO). But those entries too are intended to conform to the prescriptions of *The Third Manifesto*, inasmuch as it makes sense for them to do so.)

- *Part II:* As mentioned earlier in these introductory notes, the *Manifesto* book not only defines a theory of types as such, it builds on that theory to define a model of type inheritance ("the *Manifesto* model").[2] Part II of the dictionary ("Inheritance") deals with terms and concepts arising in connection with that model. The definitions and examples in that part of the dictionary are intended to conform to that model specifically. More details can be found in the *Manifesto* book.

- *Part III:* Finally, Part III of the dictionary ("Intervals") deals with terms and concepts arising in connection with the theory of intervals. Interval theory provides the formal underpinnings for the support of data of any of a variety of interval types; in particular, it supports the pragmatically important case of temporal data specifically. The definitions and examples in this part of the dictionary are intended to conform to the theory presented in the book *Time and Relational Theory: Temporal Data in the Relational Model and SQL*, by C. J. Date, Hugh Darwen, and Nikos A. Lorentzos (Morgan Kaufmann, 2014), where further details can be found.

---

[2] Like *The Third Manifesto* itself, the *Manifesto* model of inheritance is revised and extended in the *Explorations* book.

Note: All three parts include a few additional remarks of an introductory nature that are specific to the part in question.

Acknowledgments

This dictionary was Jonathan Gennick's brainchild. Indeed, Jonathan originally intended to write it himself, and I'm very grateful to him for stepping out of the limelight, as it were, and letting me steal his idea and run with it as I've done. Jonathan and I have very different writing styles, and what follows is no doubt a long way from what he originally had in mind; but I hope it at least does justice to his overall vision. I'd also like to thank Apress (publisher of the second edition) for allowing me to return to O'Reilly Media Inc. (publisher of the first edition) with this vastly expanded new version, and my friends and colleagues Hugh Darwen and (for Part III in particular) Nikos Lorentzos for numerous helpful comments and much technical assistance over the past several years. It goes without saying that any remaining errors and infelicities are my own responsibility.

C. J. Date
Healdsburg, California
2015

Part I

Types and Relations

Several of the entries appearing in this part of the dictionary—primarily ones having to do with type theory—are expanded or elaborated on in Part II ("Inheritance"). Such entries are marked "Without inheritance" in what follows (and the corresponding expanded entries in Part II are marked "With inheritance" accordingly).

———— ♦♦♦♦♦ ————

0-adic (*Of an operator or predicate*) Niladic. *Contrast* 0-ary.

0-ary (*Of a heading, key, tuple, relation, etc.*) Of degree zero. *Contrast* 0-adic.

0-place (*Of a predicate*) Niladic.

0-tuple The empty tuple; the tuple of degree zero.

1NF First normal form.

2NF Second normal form.

2VL Two-valued logic.

3NF Third normal form.

3VL Three-valued logic.

4NF Fourth normal form.

4VL Four-valued logic.

5NF Fifth normal form.

6NF Sixth normal form.

———— ♦♦♦♦♦ ————

A   A relationally complete (q.v.), "reduced instruction set" version of relational algebra with just two primitive operators—REMOVE (essentially projection on all attributes but one), q.v., and an algebraic analog of either NOR or NAND, q.v. The name **A** (note the boldface) is a doubly recursive acronym: It stands for *ALGEBRA*, which in turn stands for *A Logical Genesis Explains Basic Relational Algebra*. As this expanded name suggests, the algebra **A** is designed in such a way as to emphasize its close relationship to, and solid foundation in, the discipline of predicate logic, q.v. Further details can be found in the *Manifesto* book. *Note:* That book uses solid arrowheads to delimit **A** operator names, as in (e.g.) ◄NOR►, in order to distinguish those operators from operators with the same name in predicate logic or **Tutorial D** or both, but those arrowheads are deliberately omitted here. More to the point, the *Manifesto* book doesn't actually define either NOR or NAND as a primitive **A** operator; rather, it defines **A** as supporting explicit NOT, OR, and AND operators, q.v. But it then goes on to show that (a) either OR or AND could be removed without loss, and (b) NOT and whichever of OR and AND is retained could be collapsed into a single operator—NOT and OR into NOR, or NOT and AND into NAND—and thus no serious harm is done by thinking of either NOR or NAND (like REMOVE) as a primitive operator of **A**.

abelian group   *See* group (mathematics). *Note: Abelian* (after the mathematician Niels Henrik Abel) is pronounced "ah beel´ ian," with the stress on the second syllable.

ABS   A scalar operator that returns the absolute value of its argument (which must be of some numeric type).
　　Examples: The expressions ABS(+5) and ABS(−5) both denote ABS invocations, and they both return the absolute value 5.

absolute complement   *See* complement (set theory).

absorption   Let *Op1* and *Op2* be dyadic operators, and assume for definiteness that they're expressed in infix style. Then *Op1* absorbs *Op2* if and only if, for all *x* and *y*, *x Op1* (*x Op2 y*) = *x*.
　　Examples: In logic, each of OR and AND absorbs the other, because *x* OR (*x* AND *y*) and *x* AND (*x* OR *y*) both reduce to—i.e., are logically equivalent to—just *x*. Analogously, in set theory and relational algebra, each of union and intersection absorbs the other.

abstract algebra   *See* algebra.

abstract data type   Same as abstract type, in any of the senses of this latter term.

abstract type   (*Without inheritance*) Type. *Caveat:* The term is sometimes used to refer to some specific kind of type (especially one that isn't built in), but a strong case can be made that all types are or should be "abstract," at least in the sense that their physical representation is hidden from the user.

access path   Usually a physical access path, q.v. The term is sometimes used to refer to a "logical" access path also, but this latter term really has no precise definition.

actual operand   An argument. *Contrast* formal operand.

ad hoc polymorphism   *See* overloading.

additive identity   *See* Laws of Algebra.

additive inverse   *See* Laws of Algebra.

ADT   Abstract data type.

aggregate   (*Noun*) An aggregate value, q.v.

aggregate operator   A read-only operator that derives a single value, typically but not necessarily a scalar value, from some aggregate value. The aggregate value in question is either a set or a bag of individual values (all of the same type in each case), typically but not necessarily the set or bag of values of some specified attribute of some specified relation, and typically but not necessarily a set or bag of scalar values specifically.

    Examples: Let ST1, ST2, ST3, and ST4 be variables of declared type INTEGER. First of all, then, the following statement assigns to ST1 the sum of the status values for suppliers in London:

```
ST1 := SUM ( S WHERE CITY = 'London' , STATUS ) ;
```

The SUM invocation here has two arguments, denoted by a relational expression (q.v.) and an attribute reference (q.v.), respectively. With reference to the definition given above, (a) the first of these arguments is the "specified relation" (in the example, it's the relation that's the current value of the expression S WHERE CITY = 'London'), and (b) the second is the "specified attribute" (in the example, it's attribute STATUS). Given the sample values shown in Fig. 1, therefore, the aggregate value over which the sum is computed is the bag {20,20} of STATUS values in the relation that's the current value of the expression S WHERE CITY = 'London', and the SUM invocation in the example thus returns the value 40.

    In contrast to the previous example, the following statement assigns to ST2 the value 20, not 40, because the aggregate value over which the sum is computed in this case is the singleton set of STATUS values {20} (since it's obtained from the projection on {STATUS} of the relation that's the current value of the expression S WHERE CITY = 'London'):

```
ST2 := SUM ( ( S WHERE CITY = 'London' ) { STATUS } , STATUS ) ;
```

Typical aggregate operators include COUNT, SUM, AVG, MAX, and MIN. For SUM and AVG, the aggregate argument must consist of values of some numeric type; for MAX and MIN, it must consist of values of some ordered type. *Note:* COUNT is slightly special—it simply returns the cardinality of its aggregate argument and thus neither needs nor permits a second argument. Also, **Tutorial D** in particular allows the expression denoting the second argument (and the immediately preceding comma) to be omitted anyway—i.e., even if the aggregate operator is something other than COUNT—if the first argument is a relation of degree one (i.e., a unary relation), in which case the second argument expression is understood by default to be an attribute reference denoting the sole attribute of that unary relation. The foregoing assignment to ST2 could thus be abbreviated as follows:

```
ST2 := SUM ( ( S WHERE CITY = 'London' ) { STATUS } ) ;
```

By way of another example, consider the following assignment:

```
ST3 := SUM ( S WHERE CITY = 'London' , 2 * STATUS ) ;
```

This statement assigns to ST3 twice the sum of the status values for suppliers in London. As this example suggests, the expression denoting the second argument isn't necessarily limited to being a simple attribute reference but in fact can be arbitrarily complex. Nor does it necessarily have to contain any attribute references, though in practice it usually will (*see* **open expression**).

Note: Despite the foregoing, we can in fact assume without loss of generality that the expression denoting the second argument—when there is a second argument—is indeed a simple attribute reference after all, thanks to the availability of the EXTEND operator, q.v. For example, the SUM invocation in the assignment above to ST3 is logically equivalent to the following:

```
SUM ( ( EXTEND S WHERE CITY = 'London' : { X := 2 * STATUS } ) , X )
```

Simpler ("*n*-adic") versions of the aggregate operators are also available, in which the aggregate value argument (a set or bag of individual values) is represented by a simple commalist of argument expressions. For example, the following assignment makes use of the *n*-adic version of SUM (note the use of braces rather than parentheses to enclose the argument expression commalist):

```
ST4 := SUM { X , Y , Z } ;
```

The result in this case is the sum of the current values of variables X, Y, and Z, whatever they might happen to be.

Additional aggregate operators supported by **Tutorial D** include (a) AND, OR, XOR, and EQUIV, q.v. (for aggregates consisting of values of type BOOLEAN) and (b) UNION,

XUNION, D_UNION, JOIN, and INTERSECT, q.v. (for aggregates consisting of values of some relation type).

Note: Let *AggOp* be an aggregate operator other than COUNT, and let *agg* be the aggregate value over which some given invocation of *AggOp* is to be evaluated. If *agg* is of cardinality one, the result of the invocation in question is the single value contained in *agg*. If *agg* is of cardinality zero (i.e., if *agg* is empty), and if all three of the following are true—

a. The invocation in question is essentially just shorthand for repeated invocation of some dyadic operator *Op*

b. An identity value, q.v., exists for *Op*

c. The semantics of *AggOp* don't demand that the result of an invocation be a value actually appearing in *agg*

—then

d. The result of the invocation in question is the applicable identity value.

For example, suppose the operator SUM is invoked on an aggregate value consisting of a set or bag of values of type INTEGER. Since (a) SUM is essentially just shorthand for repeated invocation of the scalar operator "+", and (b) an identity value—viz., 0—exists for "+" on integers, the result if the aggregate value is empty is the integer 0. By contrast, the AVG, MAX, and MIN of an empty set or bag are undefined, because (a) for AVG, no appropriate identity value exists and (b) for MAX and MIN, the result is supposed to be a value actually appearing in the aggregate argument, and no such value exists (but see further discussion below).

As for COUNT, the foregoing remarks can be interpreted to apply to that operator as well by noting that any given COUNT invocation is logically equivalent to, and indeed defined to be shorthand for, a certain SUM invocation. For example, the COUNT invocation

```
COUNT ( S WHERE CITY = 'London' )
```

is logically equivalent to the following SUM invocation:

```
SUM ( S WHERE CITY = 'London' , 1 )
```

To return to MAX and MIN for a moment: Actually there's an argument that says the MAX and MIN of an empty aggregate shouldn't be undefined after all. For definiteness, consider MAX specifically. Let MAX2 be a dyadic operator that returns the larger of its two arguments (in other words, MAX2{$x1,x2$} returns $x1$ if $x1 \geq x2$ and $x2$ otherwise). Then (a) any given MAX invocation is essentially just shorthand for repeated invocation of MAX2, and (b) MAX2 clearly has an identity value, viz., "negative infinity" (meaning the minimum value of the pertinent type); so we might reasonably define MAX to return that identity value if its aggregate argument is empty. Likewise, we might reasonably define MIN to return "positive infinity" (the maximum value of the pertinent type) if its aggregate argument is empty. Perhaps the best approach in practice would be to provide both versions of MAX—they are, after all, different operators—and let the user decide. We might even provide a third version, one that takes an additional argument x, where x is supplied by the user and is the value to be returned if the aggregate argument is empty.

Incidentally, it's worth noting that (contrary to popular opinion, perhaps) SQL doesn't support aggregate operators at all. It does support the notion of a summary, q.v., but aggregate operator invocations and summaries aren't the same thing—there's a logical difference (q.v.) between them, as explained under **summary**.

aggregate type   In general, a nonscalar type for which the user visible components are usually required all to be of the same type. For example, array and relation types might be regarded as aggregate types, but tuple types usually wouldn't be.

aggregate value   Either a set or a bag of individual values (all of the same type in each case)—typically but not necessarily the set or bag of values of some specified attribute of some specified relation, and typically but not necessarily a set or bag of scalar values specifically. *See* aggregate operator.

ALGEBRA   *See* **A**.

algebra   1. Generically, a formal system consisting of (a) a set of elements and (b) a set of read-only operators that apply to those elements, such that those elements and operators together satisfy certain laws and properties (almost certainly closure, probably commutativity and associativity, and so on); also known as an *algebraic structure* or an *abstract algebra*. The word algebra itself derives from Arabic *al-jebr*, meaning a resetting (of something broken) or a combination. *Note:* The foregoing definition is admittedly not very precise, but the term just doesn't seem to have a very precise definition, not even in mathematics. Note in particular that not all algebras abide by The Laws of Algebra, q.v.!—for example, matrix algebra does not. *See also* **boolean algebra**. 2. Relational algebra specifically, q.v. (if the context demands).

algebra of sets   *See* boolean algebra (second definition).

alias   Strongly deprecated term sometimes used in SQL contexts to mean either a tuple calculus range variable, q.v., or the name of such a variable. The term *table alias* (also deprecated) is also sometimes used with the same meaning. *See also* **correlation name**.

ALL   Keyword sometimes used as an alternative spelling for the aggregate operator AND (*see* aggregate operator).

ALL BUT   *See* projection.

all key   Relvar *R* is "all key" if and only if the entire heading of *R* is a key (in which case it's the only key, necessarily). Equivalently, *R* is all key if and only if no proper subset of the heading is a key. Note that if *R* is all key, then it certainly has no nonkey attributes (q.v.), but the converse is false—a relvar can have no nonkey attributes and yet not be all key.

ALPHA   A proposal, due to Codd, for a concrete relational language based on tuple calculus; also known as Data Sublanguage ALPHA. ALPHA as such was never implemented, but its ideas were influential on the design of several languages that were, including QBE, QUEL, and (to a much lesser extent) SQL.

alternate key   Loosely, a key that isn't a primary key, q.v. More precisely, let relvar *R* have keys *K1*, *K2*, ..., *Kn* (and no others), and let some *Ki* $(1 \leq i \leq n)$ be chosen as the primary key for, or of, *R*; then each *Kj* $(1 \leq j \leq n, j \neq i)$ is an alternate key for, or of, *R*. The term isn't much used.

AND   1. A connective, q.v. (*see* conjunction). 2. An aggregate operator, q.v. *Note:* AND as conventionally understood is a logical operator (and this observation applies to both of the foregoing definitions); however, the algebra **A**, q.v., includes an operator it calls AND that—by definition—is a relational operator (in fact, it's just natural join).

antecedent   *See* implication.

antijoin   Term sometimes used as a synonym for semidifference, q.v. The term is deprecated, slightly, because the operator is really "anti" semijoin, q.v., not "anti" join as such.

antisymmetry   *See* partial ordering. Note that antisymmetry and asymmetry aren't the same thing—the former is as defined under **partial ordering**, the latter just means lack of symmetry.

ANY   Keyword sometimes used as an alternative spelling for the aggregate operator OR (*see* aggregate operator).

appearance   (*Of a value*) An occurrence or "instance" of a value in some context. Observe that there's a logical difference between a value as such (*see* value) and an appearance of that value in some context—for example, as the current value of some variable or as an attribute value within the current value of some tuplevar or relvar. Of course, every appearance of a value has an implementation that consists of some internal or physical representation, q.v., of the value in question (and distinct appearances of the same value might have distinct physical representations). Thus, there's also a logical difference between an appearance of a value, on the one hand, and the physical representation of that appearance, on the other; there might even be a logical difference between the physical representations used for distinct appearances of the same value. All of that being said, however, it's usual to abbreviate *physical representation of an appearance of a value* to just *appearance of a value*, or (more often) to just *value*, so long as there's no risk of ambiguity. Note, however, that *appearance of a value* is a model concept, whereas *physical representation of an appearance* is an implementation concept—users certainly might need to know whether (for example) two variables contain appearances of the same value, but they don't need to know whether those two appearances use the same physical representation.

Example: Let N1 and N2 be variables of declared type INTEGER. After the following assignments, then, N1 and N2 both contain an appearance of the integer value 3. The corresponding physical representations might or might not be the same (for example, N1 might use a base two representation and N2 a base ten representation), but either way it's of no concern to the user.

```
N1 := 3 ;
N2 := 3 ;
```

application relvar   *See* relvar.

argument   (*Without inheritance*) The actual operand that replaces—i.e., is substituted for—some parameter of some operator when the operator in question is invoked. That argument must be of the same type as the parameter it replaces. Note that there's a logical difference between an argument per se and the expression that denotes it (i.e., the argument expression, q.v.). To be specific, the argument per se is either a value or a variable; if the pertinent parameter is subject to update, then the argument is—in fact, must be—a variable specifically, denoted by some variable reference, otherwise it's a value and can be denoted by an arbitrarily complex expression (possibly just a variable reference). *Contrast* parameter.

Examples: Let operator DOUBLE be defined as follows:

```
OPERATOR DOUBLE ( X INTEGER ) RETURNS INTEGER ;
   RETURN ( 2 * X ) ;
END OPERATOR ;
```

X here is a parameter, of declared type INTEGER. Let N be a variable of declared type INTEGER. Then, e.g., DOUBLE (N+1) is an invocation of DOUBLE, and the value of the expression N+1 at the time of that invocation is an argument—in fact, the sole argument—to that invocation. What's more, that invocation is itself an expression, and it can appear wherever an integer literal can appear (because, thanks to the RETURNS clause, q.v., operator DOUBLE returns a value of type INTEGER when it's invoked).

Now suppose by contrast that DOUBLE is defined to be an update operator instead of a read-only one, as follows (observe that the RETURNS clause has been replaced by an UPDATES clause and the RETURN statement has been replaced by an assignment):

```
OPERATOR DOUBLE ( X INTEGER ) UPDATES { X } ;
   X := 2 * X ;
END OPERATOR ;
```

Now the parameter X is subject to update, and any argument corresponding to X must be a variable specifically. What's more, the only way DOUBLE can now be invoked is by means of an explicit CALL statement (or equivalent), as here:

```
CALL DOUBLE ( N ) ;
```

In this example, the variable N—not the value of that variable, observe—is the argument to the invocation. Moreover, note carefully that DOUBLE (N) here isn't an expression, and it can't appear "wherever an integer literal can appear." Note too that, e.g.,

```
CALL DOUBLE ( N + 1 ) ;
```

would be a syntax error, because N+1 isn't a variable reference.

argument expression   An expression denoting an argument (q.v.) to some operator invocation.

arity   Degree, q.v. The term isn't much used, except in formal or academic contexts.

Armstrong's axioms / Armstrong's inference rules   (*For FDs*) Let *X*, *Y*, and *Z* denote sets of attributes; also, let *XZ* denote the set theory union of *X* and *Z*, and similarly for *YZ*, etc. Then Armstrong's axioms (also known as Armstrong's inference rules) are as follows:

a   If $X \supseteq Y$, then $X \to Y$ (the reflexivity rule).

b.   If $X \to Y$, then $XZ \to YZ$ (the augmentation rule).

c.   If $X \to Y$ and $Y \to Z$, then $X \to Z$ (the transitivity rule).

These rules are both sound and complete (*see* **soundness; completeness**).

Examples: The FD $X \to Y$ is implied by the FD $X \to YZ$. To be specific, it can be derived from this latter FD using Armstrong's axioms, thus: (a) $X \to YZ$ (given); (b) $YZ \to Y$ by reflexivity; hence (c) $X \to Y$ by transitivity.

By way of a second example, given the FDs $X \to Y$ and $Z \to W$, it can be shown using Armstrong's axioms that the FD $XV \to YW$ (where *V* is the set theory difference $Z - Y$ between *Z* and *Y*, in that order) is implied by those given FDs. (This example, which is due to Darwen, can be regarded as another inference rule. It has the interesting property that the augmentation and transitivity rules, as well as several other rules not discussed here, are all special cases.)

arrow   *See* functional dependency.

arrow out of   An FD of the form $A \rightarrow B$ is sometimes referred to, informally, as "an arrow out of A" (or, even more informally, as an arrow out of the attribute(s) constituting A—especially if A is of degree one).

assignment   (*Without inheritance*) An operator, denoted ":=" in **Tutorial D**, that assigns a value (the source, denoted by an expression) to a variable (the target, denoted by a variable reference); also, the operation performed when that operator is invoked. The source and target must be of the same type, and the operation overall is required to abide by (a) *The Assignment Principle*, q.v. (always), as well as (b) **The Golden Rule**, q.v. (if applicable). *Note:* Every update operator invocation is logically equivalent to some assignment—possibly a multiple assignment, q.v.—in the second of the senses just defined. *See also* multiple assignment; relational assignment; tuple assignment.

Assignment Principle   After assignment of value v to variable V, the comparison $v = V$ is required to evaluate to TRUE.

associative addressing   Addressing by value instead of position. All addressing is associative in the relational model, implying among other things that pointers, q.v., are outlawed (and hence implying further that no database relvar can have an attribute of any pointer type).

associativity   Let Op be a dyadic operator, and assume for definiteness that it's expressed in infix style. Then Op is associative if and only if, for all x, y, and z, $x \; Op \; (y \; Op \; z) = (x \; Op \; y) \; Op \; z$.

> *Examples:* In ordinary arithmetic, addition ("+") is associative, because

$$x + (y + z) = (x + y) + z$$

for all numbers x, y, and z. Likewise, "||" (string concatenation) is associative, because

$$x \; || \; (y \; || \; z) = (x \; || \; y) \; || \; z$$

for all strings x, y, and z. In the same kind of way, UNION and JOIN are associative in relational algebra (by contrast, MINUS is not). Likewise, OR and AND are associative in logic (by contrast, IMPLIES is not). *Note:* Each of the associative operators mentioned in these examples except for "||" is also commutative, q.v. Another example of an operator that's associative but not commutative is the (conventionally unnamed) dyadic connective in logic that simply returns the value of its first argument. *See also* left associativity; right associativity.

atomic predicate   A simple predicate, q.v.

atomic projection   *See* atomic relvar; FD preservation.

atomic proposition   A simple proposition, q.v.

atomic relvar   A relvar that can't be nonloss decomposed into independent projections. *Note:* The term *independent projection* is being used here in a specific technical sense (*see* FD preservation). Note too that the term *atomic relvar* is deprecated, somewhat, because it's likely to be confused with the term *irreducible relvar* (*see* irreducible, second definition). While it's true that irreducible relvars are certainly atomic, the converse is false—a relvar can be atomic without being irreducible (see the example below). The concept is seldom needed, anyway; thus, it's probably best just to spell out the meaning as and when necessary.

    Example: Suppose relvar SP is subject to a constraint to the effect that part P1 (only) is always supplied in a quantity in the range 1-100, part P2 (only) is always supplied in a quantity in the range 101-200, and so on; then the FD $\{QTY\} \rightarrow \{PNO\}$ holds in that relvar. (This particular constraint isn't satisfied by the sample values in Fig. 1, of course. Indeed, the example overall is highly contrived; however, it suffices for the purpose at hand.) This revised version of SP can be nonloss decomposed into its projections on $\{SNO,QTY\}$ and $\{QTY,PNO\}$ (and it can't be nonloss decomposed in any other way, other than trivially); in fact, the relvar isn't in BCNF, q.v., because $\{QTY\}$ isn't a superkey (it is, however, in 3NF, q.v., and in fact in EKNF, q.v., also). Those two projections—i.e., on $\{SNO,QTY\}$ and $\{QTY,PNO\}$—are atomic. They're also in BCNF (the keys are $\{SNO,QTY\}$ and $\{QTY\}$, respectively). However, they aren't independent, because the FD $\{SNO,PNO\} \rightarrow \{QTY\}$, which holds in SP, isn't preserved in the decomposition. Relvar SP, revised as above, is thus atomic (*see* FD preservation) but not irreducible. Note that it follows from this example that the objectives of (a) decomposing into BCNF projections and (b) decomposing into independent projections, though both generally desirable, can sometimes be in conflict.

atomic statement   (*Programming languages*) Syntactically, a statement that contains no other statements nested inside itself (*contrast* compound statement); semantically, a statement that's guaranteed either to execute in its entirety or to have no effect (other than returning a status code or equivalent, perhaps). All syntactically atomic statements are semantically atomic in the relational model, except possibly if the statement in question represents an invocation of a user defined operator, q.v. (The converse is false, incidentally; an important counterexample is provided by multiple assignment, q.v., which is semantically atomic but not syntactically so.) *Note:* A statement might execute in its entirety and yet have no lasting effect, owing to the fact that its execution will necessarily be part of some transaction (q.v) and that transaction might subsequently be rolled back.

atomic type   Somewhat deprecated term for a scalar type, q.v.

atomic value   Old fashioned and somewhat deprecated term for a scalar value, q.v.

attribute   Very loosely, a column; more precisely, an <attribute name, type name> pair, though it's common to ignore the type name in informal contexts. (Ignoring the type name in this way is acceptable when the heading, q.v., of which the attribute in question is a component is known, because the relational model requires attribute names within any given heading to be unique, and the attribute names thus effectively imply the corresponding type names.)

Examples: In the suppliers-and-parts database, (a) the pair <SNAME,NAME> is an attribute of relvar S, and (b) the pair <SNO,SNO> is an attribute—in fact, a "common attribute," q.v.—of both relvar S and relvar SP. We might also say, more simply but less formally, just that (a) SNAME is an attribute of relvar S and (b) SNO is an attribute—a "common attribute"—of both relvar S and relvar SP. Attributes SNAME and SNO are of declared types NAME and SNO, respectively.

Caveat: The foregoing is the relational meaning of the term *attribute*. Be aware, however, that some systems, including SQL systems in particular (also certain OO systems), use the term with a meaning or meanings rather different from that ascribed to it here.

attribute assignment   An assignment in which the target is specified syntactically by means of an attribute reference, q.v. Attribute assignments are permitted in **Tutorial D** only in the context of an invocation of EXTEND, SUMMARIZE, or UPDATE.

Example: Consider the following UPDATE statement:

```
UPDATE S WHERE SNO = SNO('S1') : { STATUS := 10 , CITY := 'Rome' } ;
```

This UPDATE statement contains two attribute assignments, viz., STATUS := 10 and CITY := 'Rome'.

attribute constraint   A specification, conceptually part of a relvar constraint, q.v., to the effect that a given attribute of a given relvar is of a given type.

Example: Attribute SNAME of relvar S is declared to be of type NAME—i.e., it's constrained to contain values of type NAME only. Any operation (necessarily an update operation) that attempts to assign a value to relvar S in which some tuple contains a value for attribute SNAME that's not of type NAME will fail (and moreover will do so, ideally, at compile time).

attribute extractor   An operator for extracting the value of a specified attribute from a specified tuple (*attribute value extractor* would be a more accurate term).

Example: Let *t* denote the supplier tuple shown in Fig. 1 for supplier S1. Then the following **Tutorial D** expression extracts the status value 20 (an integer) from that tuple:

```
STATUS FROM t
```

STATUS here is an attribute reference, q.v. *Note:* SQL uses dot qualification, q.v., for such purposes (as well as for other purposes, beyond the scope of this dictionary). Here's the SQL analog of the foregoing **Tutorial D** example (though here, of course, *t* must be understood as denoting an SQL row, not a tuple):

```
t.STATUS
```

attribute level redundancy   *See* redundancy.

attribute reference   Syntactically, an attribute name (possibly dot qualified, though never so in **Tutorial D**). An attribute reference denotes either an attribute as such or the value of the attribute in question (frequently, though not invariably, within some specific tuple in each case), as the context demands. Note in particular that such a reference certainly denotes an attribute as such if it's used to specify the target for some attribute assignment within some EXTEND, SUMMARIZE, or UPDATE invocation.

Examples: Consider the following UPDATE statement:

```
UPDATE P WHERE CITY = 'London' :
       { WEIGHT := 2 * WEIGHT , CITY := 'Oslo' } ;
```

This statement contains two attribute assignments (q.v.) and four attribute references, viz., CITY (twice) and WEIGHT (also twice). Imagine the overall UPDATE being executed by processing the tuples of relvar P one by one in some sequence, and let *t* be the tuple currently being processed. Within the overall statement, then, (a) the first appearance of CITY and the second appearance of WEIGHT currently denote the CITY value and the WEIGHT value, respectively, within *t*; (b) the first appearance of WEIGHT and the second appearance of CITY currently denote the WEIGHT attribute as such and the CITY attribute as such, respectively, within *t*. See the example under UPDATE for further explanation.

attribute reference FROM   **Tutorial D** syntax for an attribute extractor, q.v.

attribute renaming   *See* renaming.

attribute type   *See* attribute. *Note:* Attributes can be of essentially any type whatsoever, except that (a) no attribute can be of a type that's defined, directly or indirectly, in terms of the type of the tuple or relation of which it's a part (*see* recursively defined type); (b) no database relvar can have an attribute of any pointer type (*see* pointer).

attribute value   *See* tuple value.

attribute value extractor   *See* attribute extractor.

audit trail   A special file or database, possibly but not necessarily integrated with the recovery log (q.v.), in which the system keeps track of database operations performed by users, with a view to assisting in the detection of actual or attempted security breaches, among other things. Further details are beyond the scope of this dictionary (but see the discussion of **logged time** in Part III).

augmentation   *See* Armstrong's axioms.

automatic action   An action carried out by the DBMS on the user's behalf without having been explicitly requested by the user in question. Compensatory actions, q.v., are an important special case.

automatic definition   (*Without inheritance*) Defining a scalar type T automatically causes certain associated operators to be defined as well. The operators in question are assignment (":="), equality ("="), and at least one selector, q.v., and at least one set of THE_ operators, q.v. *Note:* If operator Op is automatically defined in this way as an operator associated with type T, code to implement Op might or might not be automatically defined as well. In particular, for ":=" and "=" it probably will be, whereas for selectors and THE_ operators it might not. If it isn't, however, then whatever agency (either the system or some user) is responsible for defining type T must also define that code—in effect, as part of the process of defining T. Note too that operators analogous to the ones that are the subject of this entry are "automatically defined" for tuple and relation types as well, even though such types are generated (*see* **type generator**) instead of being explicitly defined.

automatic optimization   *See* optimization.

axiom   Something assumed to be true, available for use in deriving further truths (i.e., theorems, q.v.; *see also* **proof**). An axiom is a special case of a theorem. In a database, the tuples in the base relations can be regarded as axioms, because they represent propositions that are assumed to be true (*see Closed World Assumption*). *Note:* In a formal system, it's usually desirable that the axioms all be independent of one another, meaning none of them is derivable from the rest. For precisely analogous reasons, it's usually desirable in a database that there be no redundancy, q.v. (or at least no uncontrolled redundancy, q.v.).

   Example: The tuple <S1,Smith,20,London> in the base relation that's the current value of base relvar S represents the presumably true proposition *Supplier S1 is under contract, is named Smith, has status 20, and is located in city London*. This proposition thus serves as an axiom with respect to (the current value of) the suppliers-and-parts database.

axiom of choice   An axiom of set theory to the effect that, given a set S of nonempty, pairwise disjoint sets $s1, s2, ..., sn$, there exists a set of n elements $x1, x2, ..., xn$ such that each xi is an element of si ($i = 1, 2, ..., n$). The axiom implies among other things that, given some set s, it must be possible to choose an arbitrary element *x* from that set (*see* ZO). *Note:* The axiom of choice is obviously and intuitively valid (and noncontroversial) so long as the sets *s1*, *s2*, ..., *sn*, and *S* are all finite, but can be (and has been) questioned otherwise.

axiom of extension   An axiom of set theory, to the effect that two sets are equal, and hence are in fact the same set, if and only if they contain the same elements.

bag   Very informally, "a set that permits duplicates"; more precisely, a collection of objects, called elements, in which the same element can appear any number of times. An example is the collection {*x,y,y,y,z,z*}, which can alternatively be written as, e.g., {*y,y,x,z,y,z*}, since bags, like sets, have no ordering to their elements. The number of times a given element appears in a given bag is the multiplicity (of that element with respect to that bag). *Note:* As the foregoing text indicates, a bag is usually represented on paper by a commalist of items denoting the elements that constitute the bag in question, that whole commalist then being enclosed in braces.
Tutorial D in particular uses braces to enclose the commalist of argument expressions in certain *n*-adic operator invocations when the argument expression commalist in question denotes a bag of arguments (as well as when it denotes a set). For example, the **Tutorial D** expression SUM {1,2,2} denotes an invocation of the *n*-adic version of the aggregate operator SUM (*see* **aggregate operator**), and it returns 5, not 3.

    The set theory operations of inclusion, union, intersection, difference, exclusive union (also known as symmetric difference), and product—but not complement—can all be generalized to apply to bags, as follows. First, inclusion. Let *b1* and *b2* be bags, and let element *x* appear exactly *n1* times in *b1* and exactly *n2* times in *b2* ($n1 \geq 0$, $n2 \geq 0$). Then bag *b1* includes bag *b2* ("$b1 \supseteq b2$") if and only if $n1 \geq n2$ for all such elements *x*; further, *b2* is included in *b1* ("$b2 \subseteq b1$") if and only if *b1* includes *b2*, and *b1* is equal to *b2* ("*b1* = *b2*") if and only if each of *b1* and *b2* includes the other. *Note:* All of the terms associated with set inclusion (subset, proper subset, and so on) have analogs in connection with bag inclusion (subbag, proper subbag, and so on).

    Now let *Op* be union, intersection, difference, or exclusive union, and let *b* be the bag obtained by applying *Op* to bags *b1* and *b2* (in that order, in the case of difference), where as before element *x* appears exactly *n1* times in *b1* and exactly *n2* times in *b2* ($n1 \geq 0$, $n2 \geq 0$). Then element *x* appears exactly *n* times in *b*, where *n* is:

- MAX{*n1,n2*} if *Op* is union

- MIN{*n1,n2*} if *Op* is intersection

- MAX{*n1–n2*,0} if *Op* is difference

- ABS(*n1–n2*) if *Op* is exclusive union

In no case does *b* contain any other elements.

Again let elements *x1* and *x2* appear exactly *n1* times in *b1* and exactly *n2* times in *b2*, respectively (*n1* ≥ 0, *n2* ≥ 0), and let *b* be the product of *b1* and *b2*, in that order. Then the ordered pair <*x1*,*x2*> appears exactly *n1*n2* times as an element of *b*, and *b* contains no other elements.

Finally, there are two further operations, union plus and intersection star (also known by a variety of other names), that have no counterpart in set theory. Let *b* be the bag obtained by applying one of these operations to bags *b1* and *b2*, where once again element *x* appears exactly *n1* times in *b1* and exactly *n2* times in *b2* (*n1* ≥ 0, *n2* ≥ 0). Then *x* appears exactly *n* times as an element of *b*, where *n* is:

- *n1+n2* if *Op* is union plus

- *n1*n2* if *Op* is intersection star

(and *b* contains no other elements).

Examples: Let *b1* and *b2* be the bags {*w,w,x,x,y*} and {*x,y,y,y,z,z*}, respectively. Then the following expressions yield the indicated results:

- *b1* UNION *b2*   =   {w,w,x,x,y,y,y,z,z}

- *b1* INTERSECT *b2*   =   {x,y}

- *b1* MINUS *b2*   =   {w,w,x}

- *b2* MINUS *b1*   =   {y,y,z,z}

- *b1* XUNION *b2*   =   {w,w,x,y,y,z,z}

- *b1* TIMES *b2*   =   {<w,x>,<w,x>,<x,x>,<x,x>,<y,x>,
                            <w,y>,<w,y>,<x,y>,<x,y>,<y,y>,
                            <w,y>,<w,y>,<x,y>,<x,y>,<y,y>,
                            <w,y>,<w,y>,<x,y>,<x,y>,<y,y>,
                            <w,z>,<w,z>,<x,z>,<x,z>,<y,z>,
                            <w,z>,<w,z>,<x,z>,<x,z>,<y,z>}

- *b1* UNION+ *b2*   =   {w,w,x,x,x,y,y,y,y,z,z}

- *b1* INTERSECT* *b2* =   {x,x,y,y,y}

A note on SQL: SQL tables in general contain bags (not sets) of rows, and SQL supports certain bag operations on such tables. To be specific, it supports bag intersection and bag difference, through its operators INTERSECT ALL and EXCEPT ALL, respectively. It also supports union plus, through its operator UNION ALL. It doesn't support bag exclusive union, intersection star, or (oddly enough) true bag union. As for bag product, SQL's regular product operator—which is supported in a variety of syntactic styles, including, for example, the CROSS version of SQL's explicit JOIN operator—in fact represents an extended or expanded form of bag product, much as TIMES in **Tutorial D** represents an extended or expanded form of the set theory product operator. *See* cartesian product.

bag inclusion   *See* bag.

bag membership   (*Of an element*) The property of appearing in some given bag; the operation of testing for that property. Like set membership, q.v., bag membership is usually denoted by the symbol "∈" (sometimes pronounced *epsilon*, because it's a variant form of the lowercase Greek letter epsilon—i.e., "ε"—which is the first letter of the Greek word meaning "is"); thus, the boolean expression $x \in b$—which is logically equivalent to the expression $\{x\} \subseteq b$—returns TRUE if and only if element x does in fact appear at least once in bag b. *Note:* The expression $x \in b$ is logically equivalent to the expression $b \ni x$, where the symbol "∋" denotes containment (the inverse of membership, in effect).

bag operator   *See* bag.

bang bang   A relational operator, denoted in **Tutorial D** by the symbol "!!". *See* image relation for further explanation.

base relation   The value of a given base relvar at a given time. *Contrast* derived relation.
   Examples: The relations that are the values of relvars S, P, and SP at some given time.

base relvar   A relvar not defined in terms of others (*contrast* derived relvar.). *Note:* It's a popular misconception that base relvars are physically stored, in the sense that they correspond directly to physically stored files and their tuples and attributes correspond directly to records and fields within those files (*see* direct image). But the relational model deliberately has nothing to say about physical storage; in particular, it categorically doesn't say that base relvars, as such, are physically stored—not in the foregoing sense and not in any other sense, either. The only requirement is that there must be some defined mapping between whatever is physically stored and what's perceived by the user (i.e., base relvars or derived relvars or a mixture of both).
   Examples: Relvars S, P, and SP in the suppliers-and-parts database.

base table   SQL analog of either a base relation or a base relvar, as the context demands. *See also* table.

base type   (*Without inheritance*) Synonym for primitive type, q.v.

BCNF   Boyce/Codd normal form.

behavior   Term sometimes used (especially in OO contexts) to refer to the operators that apply to values and variables of some given type.

bi-implication   Logical equivalence.

BI-IMPLIES   Same as EQUIV.

bijection / bijective mapping   Terms used interchangeably to mean a mapping, or function, from set *s1* to set *s2* such that each element of *s2* is the image of exactly one element of *s1*; equivalently, a mapping that is both an injection and a surjection (in other words, a one to one correspondence, in the strict sense of that term, from *s1* to *s2*). Also known as a bijective or "one to one onto" mapping. Note that if a given mapping is bijective, then it has an inverse mapping that's bijective as well.
   Examples: The mapping from integers *x* to their successors *x*+1 is a bijection from the set of all integers to itself. So is the inverse mapping from integers *x* to their predecessors *x*−1.

binary   (*Of a heading, key, tuple, relation, etc.*) Of degree two. *Contrast* dyadic.

binding   1. In logic, quantifying a free variable, thereby converting it into to a bound variable. 2. (*Without inheritance*) In the programming context, the term *binding* has a variety of meanings—a name might be bound to a variable at compile time; a variable might be bound to a storage location at run time; a variable might be bound to a type at assignment time; and so on.

body   A set of tuples all of the same type—especially, the set of tuples appearing in a given relation, or in a given relvar at a given time. Every subset of a body is itself a body.
   Examples: The set of tuples appearing in relvar S at some given time; any subset of that set (including the empty subset in particular).

BOOLEAN   A scalar data type (the only one required by the relational model, and thus, in a relational DBMS, necessarily a system defined type), containing just two values: two truth values, to be precise, denoted in **Tutorial D** by the literals TRUE and FALSE, respectively.

boolean algebra   1. (*Simple case*) The truth values TRUE and FALSE, together with the logical operators NOT, OR, and AND, q.v. 2. (*General case*) Let *s* be a set; let "≤" be a partial ordering, q.v., on *s*; and let a monadic operator "¬" ("complement") and distinct dyadic operators "+" ("addition") and "*" ("multiplication") be defined on *s*, such that (a) "¬" satisfies the closure and involution laws; (b) "+" and "*" satisfy the closure, commutative, associative, distributive, idempotence, and absorption laws (meaning, in the case of the distributive law in particular, that each of "+" and "*" distributes over the other); and (c) "¬", "+", and "*" together satisfy De

Morgan's Laws, q.v. Let *s* also contain two elements 0 and 1 such that (a) 0 is the identity for "+"; (b) 1 is the identity for "*"; and (c) for all elements *x* in *s*, $0 \leq x \leq 1$. Then the combination of *s* and the operators "≤", "¬", "+", and "*" is a boolean algebra. *Note:* Although they're usually referred to in this context as addition and multiplication, respectively, it must be clearly understood that "+" and "*" aren't necessarily the operators referred to by those names in conventional arithmetic.

   Example (second definition only): Let *s* be an arbitrary set; let *P(s)* be the power set (q.v.) of *s*; and let "≤", "¬", "+", and "*" denote set inclusion, set complement, set union, and set intersection, respectively ("set complement" here meaning the relative complement, q.v., with respect to the set *s*). Then the combination of that power set *P(s)*—not the set *s*, observe—and the operators "≤", "¬", "+", and "*" as just defined is a boolean algebra, in which the empty set and the set *s* itself serve as the required additive identity and multiplicative identity, respectively. In other words, the familiar algebra of sets is in fact a boolean algebra.

boolean expression   A logical expression, q.v.

boolean operator   A logical operator, q.v. (especially one of the connectives, q.v.).

boolean value   A value of type BOOLEAN, q.v.; in other words, a truth value (either TRUE or FALSE, in 2VL).

bound variable   Within a predicate, q.v., a variable—more precisely, an occurrence of a reference to some variable—that either (a) appears within the scope of a quantifier that explicitly specifies that variable or (b) is that explicit specification itself. (The term *variable* is used here in the sense of logic, not in the programming language sense.) *Contrast* **free variable**.

   Examples: Let the symbols *x* and *y* denote integers. Then the following expressions are both predicates, and *x* appears as a bound variable, twice, in each of them:

```
EXISTS x ( x > 3 )
EXISTS x ( x > 3 ) AND y < 7
```

The first of these predicates is in fact a proposition, q.v., and its meaning is: *There exists an integer x such that x is greater than three* (a proposition that evaluates to TRUE, as it happens). By contrast, the second predicate is not a proposition, because it involves a free variable (namely, *y*) as well as two bound ones; thus, it has no truth value. *Note:* Instantiating that second predicate—i.e., substituting an argument value for the free variable, or parameter, *y*—will convert it into a proposition, and that proposition will have a truth value, of course. For example, substituting the argument value 2 will yield the true proposition EXISTS *x* (*x* > 3) AND 2 < 7. However (to repeat), the predicate as such has no truth value.

   Turning to a database example, the following is a query ("Get suppliers who supply at least one part") on the suppliers-and-parts database, expressed in tuple calculus, q.v.:

```
{ S } WHERE EXISTS SP ( SP.SNO = S.SNO )
```

The boolean expression following the keyword WHERE here is a predicate, and the references to SP in that predicate are bound (by contrast, the reference to S is free). Note, however, that in this particular example the symbols S and SP denote not only variables in the sense of logic but also variables in the conventional programming language sense—but that's because we've indulged in a certain sleight of hand, as it were. Here's an expanded version of the same example that should help clarify matters:

```
SX  RANGES OVER { S } ;
SPX RANGES OVER { SP } ;

{ SX } WHERE EXISTS SPX ( SPX.SNO = SX.SNO )
```

Here SX and SPX have been explicitly declared as range variables (q.v.)—in other words, they're variables in the sense of logic—ranging over (the current values of) relvars S and SP, respectively. Now it's the references to SPX that are bound and the reference to SX that's free (in the predicate following the keyword WHERE in both cases). In effect, what happened in the first version of the example was that we were appealing to a syntax rule that allowed a relvar name to be used to denote an implicitly defined range variable that ranges over (the current value of) the relvar with the same name. Note that SQL includes a syntax rule of exactly this kind.

Note: Let R be a range variable reference that occurs prior to the WHERE clause—i.e., in the proto tuple, q.v.—within some tuple calculus expression. If R also occurs in the predicate in that WHERE clause (which it usually but not invariably will), then it must be free, not bound, in that predicate. Observe that these remarks apply in particular to the references to the range variable SX in the example shown above.

Boyce/Codd normal form   "The" normal form with respect to functional dependencies (FDs). Relvar R is in Boyce/Codd normal form (BCNF) if and only if every FD that holds in R is implied by some superkey of R—equivalently, if and only if for every nontrivial FD $X \rightarrow Y$ that holds in R, X is a superkey for R. Every BCNF relvar is in 3NF (and in fact in EKNF, q.v.). *Note:* Although being in BCNF clearly doesn't preclude being in the next higher normal form (4NF) as well, the term *BCNF* is often used loosely to refer to a relvar that's in BCNF and not in 4NF.

Example: With the normal forms it's often more instructive to show a counterexample rather than an example per se. Suppose, therefore, that relvar SP has an additional attribute SNAME, representing the name of the applicable supplier; suppose also that supplier names are necessarily unique (i.e., no two suppliers ever have the same name at the same time). Then this revised version of SP has two keys, {SNO,PNO} and {SNAME,PNO}, and every subset of the heading—{QTY} in particular—is (of course) functionally dependent on both of them. However, the FDs {SNO} $\rightarrow$ {SNAME} and {SNAME} $\rightarrow$ {SNO} also hold in this relvar;

these FDs are certainly not trivial, nor are they "arrows out of superkeys," and so this version of relvar SP isn't in BCNF (though it is in 3NF, and in fact in EKNF, q.v.).

brute force join   A rather unsophisticated join implementation technique, involving an exhaustive comparison of each tuple from the first operand relation with each tuple from the second.   Sometimes known as a nested loops join; this terminology is deprecated, however, since all join implementation techniques involve nested loops of some kind.

built in   System defined. *Contrast* user defined.

business rule   A declaration of some kind, usually expressed in natural language, that's supposed to capture some aspect of what the data in the database means or how it's constrained. There's no consensus on any more precise definition of the term, but most if not all writers would probably agree (a) that relvar predicates, q.v., are an important special case and (b) that business rules other than relvar predicates map formally to integrity constraints, q.v.

   Examples: Consider the suppliers-and-parts database. The predicate for suppliers is *Supplier SNO is under contract, is named SNAME, has status STATUS, and is located in city CITY* (see the example under relvar predicate for further discussion). Along with this predicate, there'll be rules that specify what type of information is denoted by the associated parameters— for example, a rule to the effect that the STATUS parameter ("status values") denotes values expressed in integers. Then there'll be rules that constrain the values those parameters can take for a given supplier considered in isolation—for example, a rule that says status values must lie in the range 1 to 100, inclusive. There'll also be rules that constrain the set of suppliers taken as a whole, independent of other "entities" that might also be represented in the database—for example, a rule to the effect that supplier numbers must be unique. Finally, there'll be rules that constrain suppliers considered in combination with certain other entities—for example, a rule to the effect that every shipment must involve some known supplier, or a rule to the effect that no supplier with status less than 20 can supply part P6.

   Note: The set of all business rules that apply in some given context—for example, the set of rules that apply to a given database, or to a given enterprise in its entirety—is sometimes referred to as the conceptual schema (for the context in question). However, this latter term resembles the term *business rule* itself in that it too has no universally agreed precise definition.

———— ◆ ◆ ◆ ◆ ◆ ————

calculus 1. Generically, a system of formal computation (the Latin word *calculus* means a pebble, perhaps used in counting or some other form of reckoning). 2. Relational calculus specifically, q.v. (if the context demands).

candidate key   Loosely, a unique identifier. More precisely, let K be a subset of the heading of relvar R; then K is a candidate key (key for short) for, or of, R if and only if (a) no possible value for *R* contains two distinct tuples with the same value for *K* (the uniqueness property), while (b) the same can't be said for any proper subset of *K* (the irreducibility property). Note that every relvar, base or derived, does have at least one key. Note too that, by definition, keys are sets of attributes (and key values are therefore tuples); however, if the set of attributes constituting some key *K* contains just one attribute *A*, then it's common, though strictly incorrect, to speak informally of that attribute *A* per se as being that key. Note further that if *K* is a key for relvar *R*, then the functional dependency $K \rightarrow X$ necessarily holds in *R* for all subsets *X* of the heading of *R*. Note finally that the qualifier *candidate* is a hangover from earlier times when more of a distinction was made between primary and alternate keys and a generic term was required to cover both. It could be dropped without serious loss, and usually is. *See also* alternate key; key constraint; primary key. *Contrast* subkey; superkey.

Examples: In the suppliers-and-parts database, {SNO}, {PNO}, and {SNO,PNO} are the sole keys for relvars S, P, and SP, respectively. Note that {SNAME} isn't a key for S, because SNAME values aren't necessarily unique (even though the sample values shown in Fig. 1 do happen to be unique). Note too that, e.g., {SNO,CITY} isn't a key for S either, because although its values are necessarily unique, it isn't irreducible—we could remove the CITY attribute, and what would be left would still have the uniqueness property. (Irreducibility is desirable because, among other things, the system would be enforcing the wrong integrity constraint without it. In the case at hand, for example, it wouldn't be enforcing the constraint that supplier numbers are "globally" unique, but merely the weaker constraint that they're unique within each city.)

canonical form   Given a set *s1*, together with a stated notion of equivalence among the elements of that set, subset *s2* of *s1* is a set of canonical forms for *s1* if and only if every element *x1* of *s1* is equivalent to just one element *x2* of *s2* under that notion of equivalence (and that element *x2* is said to be the canonical form for the element *x1*). The set *s2* taken as a whole is also sometimes said to be the canonical form for the set *s1* as such. Various "interesting" properties that apply to *s1* also apply to *s2*; thus, we can study just the "small" set *s2*, not the "large" set *s1*, in order to prove a variety of interesting theorems or results. *Note:* It would be usual to require also that every element of *s2* be equivalent (under the stated notion of equivalence) to at least one element of *s1*. Note also that the set of all elements *x1* of *s1* that are equivalent to some specific element *x2* of *s2* in fact constitutes an equivalence class, q.v.

Example: Let *s1* be the set of nonnegative integers {0,1,2,...} and let two such integers be equivalent if and only if they leave the same remainder on division by five. Then we can define *s2* to be the set {0,1,2,3,4}. (Note in particular that *s2* here is finite while *s1* is infinite.) As for an "interesting" theorem that applies in this example, let *x1*, *y1*, and *z1* be any three elements of *s1*, and let their canonical forms in *s2* be *x2*, *y2*, and *z2*, respectively; then the product *y1* * *z1* is equivalent to *x1* if and only if the product *y2* * *z2* is equivalent to *x2*.

cardinality   The number of elements in a bag or (especially) set; hence, of a relation, the number of tuples in the body of that relation. Also used (a) of a relvar, to mean the cardinality of the relation that's the value of that relvar at a given time; (b) of an attribute of a relation or relvar, to mean the cardinality of the set of distinct values of that attribute appearing in the body of that relation or relvar (at a given time, in the case of a relvar). Of course, the cardinality of attribute *A* of relation *r* is the same as the cardinality of the projection *r*{*A*} of that relation on that attribute; definition (b) here is thus strictly redundant.

Examples: In Fig. 1, (a) the cardinality of the relation that's the current value of relvar SP is twelve (and the cardinality of relvar SP is thus currently twelve also); (b) the cardinality of attribute SNO in that relation is four (and the cardinality of that attribute in relvar SP is thus currently four also).

Note: Since types are sets (*see* **type**), types in particular have a cardinality: viz., the number of distinct values of the type in question. For example, the cardinality of type SNO is a count of all possible supplier numbers.

cardinality constraint 1. A constraint on the cardinality of a given relvar (a special case of a relvar constraint, q.v.); for example, a constraint to the effect that there can never be more than ten suppliers at any one time. 2. Let *r* be a relationship (q.v.) from set *s1* to set *s2*, and let *x1* and *x2* be typical elements of *s1* and *s2*, respectively. In E/R modeling (q.v.) and similar design schemes, then, the following are all cardinality constraints that can be specified for each of *s1* and *s2*: 1, 0..1, 0..*m*, 1..*m*. (Other notations are also used.) For definiteness, assume the constraint in question has been specified for set *s2*; then that constraint indicates how many *x2*'s correspond to any given *x1* in relationship *r*. The various specifications have the following meanings: 1 means there must be exactly one such *x2*; 0..1 means there must be at most one such *x2*; 0..*m* means there can be any number of such *x2*'s, from zero to some unspecified upper bound *m*; and 1..*m* means there can be any number of such *x2*'s, from one to some unspecified upper bound *m*. *Note:* The terms *optional participation* and *mandatory participation* are sometimes used to refer to the case where the lower bound is 0 and the case where it's 1, respectively; however, there's no universal agreement on what these terms mean, and they're probably best avoided.

cartesian join Same as cartesian product.

cartesian product 1. (*Dyadic case*) Let relations *r1* and *r2* have no attribute names in common. Then (and only then) the expression *r1* TIMES *r2* denotes the cartesian product of *r1* and *r2*, and it returns the relation with heading the set theory union of the headings of *r1* and *r2* and body the set of all tuples *t* such that *t* is the set theory union of a tuple from *r1* and a tuple from *r2*. 2. (*N-adic case*) Let relations *r1*, *r2*, ..., *rn* ($n \geq 0$) be such that no two of them have any attribute names in common. Then (and only then) the expression TIMES {*r1,r2,...,rn*} denotes the cartesian product of *r1*, *r2*, ..., *rn*, and it returns the relation with heading the set theory union of the headings of *r1*, *r2*, ..., *rn* and body the set of all tuples *t* such that *t* is the set theory union of a tuple from *r1*, a tuple from *r2*, ..., and a tuple from *rn*. *Note:* The relational cartesian product operator differs in several respects from the mathematical or set theory operator of the same name, q.v., and is sometimes explicitly said to be an expanded, or extended, cartesian product for that reason. *See also* **tuple product**.

Example: The expression S{SNO} TIMES P{PNO} denotes the cartesian product of the projections on {SNO} and {PNO}, respectively, of the relations that are the current values of relvars S and P, respectively. That product is a relation of type RELATION {SNO SNO, PNO PNO}. Moreover, if the current values of relvars S and P are *s* and *p*, respectively, the body of that relation contains (a) all possible tuples of the form <*sno,pno*> such that the tuple <*sno*> appears in *s* and the tuple <*pno*> appears in *p* and (b) no other tuples. (Given the values in Fig. 1, the result has cardinality 30.)

Note: TIMES is actually a special case of JOIN, as the following alternative definitions make explicit: 1. (*Dyadic case*) If and only if *r1* and *r2* have no attribute names in common, the expression *r1* TIMES *r2* denotes the cartesian product of *r1* and *r2*, and it reduces to *r1* JOIN *r2*. In the foregoing example, therefore, the expression S{SNO} TIMES P{PNO} is logically equivalent to the expression S{SNO} JOIN P{PNO}. 2. (*N-adic case*) If and only if no two of *r1, r2, ..., rn* (*n* ≥ 0) have any attribute names in common, the expression TIMES {*r1,r2,...,rn*} denotes the cartesian product of *r1, r2, ..., rn*, and it reduces to JOIN {*r1,r2,...,rn*}. In the foregoing dyadic example, therefore, the expression S{SNO} TIMES P{PNO}—which could alternatively have been written TIMES {S{SNO}, P{PNO}}—is logically equivalent to the expression JOIN {S{SNO}, P{PNO}}.

cartesian product (bag theory)   *See* bag.

cartesian product (set theory)   The cartesian product of two sets *s1* and *s2*, *s1* × *s2*, is the set of all ordered pairs of elements <*x1,x2*> such that the first element of the pair, *x1*, is an element of *s1* and the second element of the pair, *x2*, is an element of *s2*. *Note:* This definition can obviously be extended to apply to any number of sets (and is so, tacitly, in the mathematical definition of a relation, q.v.).

cascading   Performing an update of the same general kind as, but in addition to, some explicitly requested update; hence, a compensatory action, q.v. (but an important special case). Cascading a delete operation is a typical example. Note, however, that such cascading should occur, if and when logically required, regardless of the concrete syntactic form in which the original update request is expressed. For example, an update expressed as a pure relational assignment (using ":="), q.v., should nevertheless cause a cascade delete to be performed— assuming a pertinent cascade DELETE rule has been defined in the first place, of course.

CAST   Shorthand for CAST_AS_*T* for some *T*.

CAST_AS_*T*   Let *T* be a scalar type. Then CAST_AS_*T* is an operator for mapping values of some scalar type *T'* to corresponding values of type *T* (i.e., for performing what's loosely called type conversion—specifically, conversion from type *T'* to type *T*). *Note:* Type *T* here is said to be the target type. *See also* **coercion**.

Example: Let variables N and C be of declared types INTEGER and CHAR, respectively. Then CAST_AS_CHAR (N) casts or "converts" the current value of N to character string form, and CAST_AS_INTEGER (C) casts or "converts" the current value of C to integer form. (In the latter case, of course, the operation will fail if the current value in question isn't a character string representation of some integer.)

Observe that the argument to CAST_AS_*T* will typically be allowed to be of different types on different invocations; in other words, the operator will typically be overloaded (*see* **overloading**). Observe also that the number of CAST operators actually needed in any given situation can sometimes be reduced by good type design. For example, consider temperatures. A good design will involve a single TEMPERATURE type, together with operators (namely, selectors and THE_ operators) to expose a Celsius representation, a Fahrenheit representation, and so on (*see* **types vs. units**). A bad design would involve different types—CELSIUS, FAHRENHEIT, and so on—together with a set of CAST operators to convert between them.

catalog Within a given database, a set of database relvars that describe the database in question. *Note:* The catalog includes descriptions of the catalog relvars themselves; in other words, the catalog is self-describing. It's sometimes said to contain metadata, q.v. Catalog relvars are usually updated not by explicit assignment operations but rather by more user friendly data definition operators, q.v. (which are nevertheless essentially just shorthand for certain relational assignments—often multiple assignments, q.v.).

catalog relvar A special kind of database relvar, q.v. (probably but not necessarily a base relvar), forming part of the database catalog. *See* **catalog**.

Cautious Design Principle *See Principle of Cautious Design.*

cell Term sometimes used to refer to a row and column intersection in a table; not to be confused with the content of the cell in question. *Note:* The concept of "cells" makes sense in connection with the idea that a table is a picture of a relation (*see* **table**) but not in connection with the idea that a table *is* such a relation, which is why this definition is framed in terms of tables and not relations. It's true that we might think, very informally, of some relation in terms of "tuple and attribute intersections," but we can't sensibly regard those intersections as being somehow distinct from their content. (Take the content away from a relation and nothing remains; as Lewis Carroll might have remarked, a relation without its content would be like a grin without a cat.)

chase *See* chase algorithm.

chase algorithm An algorithm for determining whether some specified dependency (q.v.) *d* is a logical consequence of some specified set of dependencies *D*. In outline (and speaking somewhat loosely), the algorithm works by defining a relation *r* containing sample tuples conforming to the premises (q.v.) of *d* and repeatedly applying the dependencies of *D* to *r* (possibly adding further tuples to *r* in the process). Then:

■ If *d* is an equality generating dependency (q.v.) and this process causes the pertinent equality condition to be satisfied, then *d* is a logical consequence of *D*.

■ If *d* is a tuple generating dependency (q.v.) and this process causes the pertinent conclusion tuple(s) to be generated, then *d* is a logical consequence of *D*.

■ Otherwise *r* is a relation that satisfies the dependencies of *D* but doesn't satisfy *d*; *r* thus serves as a counterexample to show that *d* isn't a logical consequence of *D*.

Examples: Here are a couple of very simple examples of the chase in action. First, consider a heading consisting of attributes *A*, *B*, and *C* (and no others). Let *AB* denote the set {*A*,*B*}, and similarly for *AC*. Let *J* and *F* be the JD ✿{*AB*,*AC*} and the FD *A* → *B*, respectively. Here then is a proof that *J* is a logical consequence of *F*:

1. *J* says "If <*a1*,*b1*,*c1*> and <*a1*,*b2*,*c2*> appear, then <*a1*,*b1*,*c2*> and <*a1*,*b2*,*c1*> appear." So these two tuples—call them *t1* and *t2*, respectively—represent the premises of *J*:

    ```
    t1  :   a1  b1  c1
    t2  :   a1  b2  c2
    ```

2. If these tuples appear, then we have *b1* = *b2*, thanks to *F*, and so the tuples

    ```
    t3  :   a1  b1  c2
    t4  :   a1  b2  c1
    ```

    "also" appear ("also" in quotation marks because *t3* and *t4* are basically just *t1* and *t2* in disguise, as it were, shown in reverse order). But "if *t1* and *t2* appear, then *t3* and *t4* appear" is exactly what *J* says; i.e., *t3* and *t4* are the conclusion of *J*, given *t1* and *t2* as premises. So *J* is a logical consequence of *F*. *Note:* This result is basically Heath's Theorem, q.v.

By way of a second example, again let *J* and *F* be the JD ✿{*AB*,*AC*} and the FD *A* → *B*, respectively. Here then is a proof that *F* doesn't follow from *J* (i.e., the converse of Heath's Theorem is false):

1. *F* says "If *<a1,b1,c1>* and *<a1,b1,c2>* appear, then *b1* = *b2*." So these two tuples *t1* and *t2* represent the premises of *F*:

```
t1  :  a1  b1  c1
t2  :  a1  b2  c2
```

2. If these tuples appear, then the following tuples also appear, thanks to *J*:

```
t3  :  a1  b1  c2
t4  :  a1  b2  c1
```

Observe now that tuples *t1-t4* taken together satisfy *J* without requiring that *b1* = *b2*. They thus constitute (the body of) a relation that satisfies *J* but not *F*. So *F* isn't a logical consequence of *J*.

child / child table Deprecated, because inappropriate, terms sometimes used in SQL contexts to mean (the SQL analog of) a referencing relvar, q.v.

class 1. (*Mathematics*) Term usually used just as a synonym for set. However, it's also used to refer to certain collections—specifically, collections in which the elements are themselves sets—that aren't regarded as legitimate sets for some reason. For example, the (infinite) collection *C* of all sets is regarded by some mathematicians as a class but not a set. (One argument against regarding *C* as a set is that the cardinality of the power set, q.v., of any given set *s* is always greater than that of *s*; thus, if *s* is in fact *C*, the collection of all sets, then there's apparently at least one collection of sets that's of greater cardinality than *s*, which is a contradiction.) *See also* **equivalence class.** 2. (*OO*) Term used to mean, variously, (a) a type; (b) the implementation or physical representation of some type; (c) a type and one of its implementations in combination; (d) the set of all values of some type currently in use; and possibly (e) other things besides.

closed expression *See* open expression.

closed WFF A WFF, q.v., that denotes a proposition. *Contrast* open WFF.

Closed World Assumption Loosely, the assumption that everything stated or implied by the database is true and everything else is false. More precisely, let relvar *R* have predicate *P* (*see* relvar predicate). Then *The Closed World Assumption* (CWA) says (a) if tuple *t* appears in *R* at time *T*, then the instantiation of *P* corresponding to *t* is assumed to be true at time *T*; conversely, (b) if tuple *t* has the same heading as *R* but doesn't appear in *R* at time *T*, then the instantiation of *P* corresponding to *t* is assumed to be false at time *T*. Loosely speaking, in other words, tuple *t* appears in relvar *R* at a given time if and only if it satisfies the predicate for *R* at that time. What's more, it follows that if proposition *p* is represented by a tuple that appears in some relation that can be derived from the relations that are the values of the database relvars at time

T—see derived relation—then proposition *p* is true at time *T* (which is why the phrase "or implied" appears in the original loose characterization). *Contrast* **Open World Assumption.** *Caveat:* Be aware that very different interpretations of the term "closed world" can be found in the general computing literature—even in the database literature specifically, sometimes.

   Examples: The tuple <S1,P1,300> currently appears in relvar SP; we can therefore assume that it's currently the case that supplier S1 supplies part P1 in quantity 300. By contrast, the tuple <S5,P6,250> doesn't currently appear in that relvar, though presumably it could; we can therefore assume that it's currently not the case that supplier S5 supplies part P6 in quantity 250.

   As for an example of implied information, the tuple <S3> currently appears in the projection of relvar SP on {SNO}; we can therefore assume that it's currently the case that supplier S3 supplies some part in some quantity. By contrast, the tuple <S5> doesn't currently appear in that projection, though presumably it could; we can therefore assume that it's currently not the case that supplier S5 supplies any part in any quantity.

   Note: It follows from the CWA that if relvars *R1* and *R2* have predicates *P1* and *P2*, respectively, and if *P1* and *P2* are both currently satisfied by the same tuple *t*, then *t* must currently appear in both *R1* and *R2*. As a rule of thumb, it's a good idea to design the database in such a way as to ensure that *P1* and *P2* are specific enough to preclude such a situation (so long as *R1* and *R2* are both base relvars, at any rate).

closure   1. (*Of algebras in general*) See **Laws of Algebra.** 2. (*Of relational algebra in particular*) The property that the result of every relational algebra operation is a relation. 3. (*Of a set of FDs*) The set of all FDs implied by the given set (*see* **Armstrong's axioms**). 4. (*Of a set of attributes*) Loosely, the set of all attributes functionally dependent on those in the given set. More precisely, let *H* be a heading, let *F* be a set of FDs with respect to *H*, and let *Z* be a subset of *H*. Then the closure Z^+ of *Z* under *F* is the maximal subset *C* of *H* such that the FD $Z \rightarrow C$ is implied by the FDs in *F* (again *see* **Armstrong's axioms**).

closure, transitive   *See* transitive closure.

CNF   Conjunctive normal form.

Codd, E. F.   The inventor of the relational model. See especially the papers (a) "Derivability, Redundancy, and Consistency of Relations Stored in Large Data Banks," IBM Research Report RJ599, August 19th, 1969 (Codd's very first publication on the relational model); (b) "A Relational Model of Data for Large Shared Data Banks," *CACM 13*, No. 6, June 1970 (a revised and extended version of that first paper); and (c) "Relational Completeness of Data Base Sublanguages," in Randall Rustin (ed.), *Data Base Systems: Courant Computer Science Symposia 6*, Prentice-Hall (1972). The last of these papers in particular contains formal definitions of a relational calculus (actually a tuple calculus, q.v.) and a relational algebra ("Codd's relational algebra," q.v.), as well as of Codd's reduction algorithm, q.v. *Note:* The 1969 paper was republished in *ACM SIGMOD Record 38*, No. 1 (March 2009); the 1970 paper was republished in *Milestones of Research—Selected Papers 1958-1982 (CACM 25th Anniversary Issue)*, *CACM 26*, No. 1 (January 1983) and elsewhere. The 1972 paper has never been republished in hard copy form but can be found on the web.

Codd's reduction algorithm   An algorithm for reducing a given tuple calculus expression to a logically equivalent expression of Codd's relational algebra. Among other things, the algorithm relies on the fact that—speaking a trifle loosely (*see* division)—the operators project and divide are algebraic counterparts to the existential quantifier and the universal quantifier, respectively, of tuple calculus. Note that the existence of such an algorithm suffices to show that Codd's algebra is relationally complete, q.v.

Codd's relational algebra   Codd's first few papers all included definitions of certain operators of an algebraic nature, but the exact set of operations defined varied somewhat from one paper to the next, and so did the precise definitions. As a consequence, it's a little difficult to say exactly what's meant by the term "Codd's relational algebra." But most writers would agree that it does at least include the following operators in some shape or form: cartesian product, union, intersection, difference, restriction, projection, natural and theta join, and division. Note that extension and aggregate operators are definitely not included. Nor are relational comparisons of any kind.

codomain   *See* function.

coercion   Implicit type conversion (usually best avoided). Note that implicit conversion will be possible only when explicit conversion is also possible (unless the types involved are both system defined; a badly designed language might conceivably support coercion, but not explicit conversion, between such types). *Note:* Elsewhere—e.g., in its definitions of the various relational operations—this dictionary assumes for simplicity that coercions aren't supported.

collection   (*Of an attribute, type, value, or variable; noun used as an adjective; not much used in the relational context*) A special case of nonscalar, q.v., in which the user visible component parts are usually required all to be of the same type. For example, array and relation types might be regarded as collection types, but tuple types usually wouldn't be. The term is also used as a noun, in which case it serves as an abbreviation for any or all of *collection type* or *collection value* or *collection variable*, as the context demands. *See also* aggregate.

collection type   Same as aggregate type. *See* collection.

column   1. Term used variously to refer to the SQL analog of (a) an attribute of some relation or relvar, or (b) the bag or set of values of some attribute of some relation or relvar, or (c) the type of some attribute of some relation or relvar, or sometimes even (d) an attribute of some tuple or tuplevar or (e) the value of some attribute of some tuple or tuplevar or (f) the type of some attribute of some tuple or tuplevar (as the context demands). 2. More generally, a picture of an attribute (on paper, for example). *See also* cell; row; table.

common attribute An attribute that's common to two or more relations and/or relvars and/or tuples and/or tuplevars.

 Examples: In the suppliers-and-parts database, (a) <SNO,SNO> is a common attribute for relvars S and SP; (b) <PNO,PNO> is a common attribute for relvars SP and P; and (c) <CITY,CHAR> is a common attribute for relvars S and P. We might also say, more simply but less formally, just that (a) SNO is a common attribute for S and SP, (b) PNO is a common attribute for SP and P, and (c) CITY is a common attribute for S and P.

commutative group *See* group (mathematics).

commutativity Let *Op* be a dyadic operator, and assume for definiteness that it's expressed in infix style. Then *Op* is commutative if and only if, for all *x* and *y*, *x Op y* = *y Op x*.

 Examples: In ordinary arithmetic, addition ("+") is commutative, because

$$x + y = y + x$$

for all *x* and *y*. By contrast, subtraction ("−") is not commutative. In the same kind of way, UNION and JOIN are commutative in relational algebra while MINUS is not. Likewise, OR and AND are commutative in logic while IMPLIES is not. *Note:* It so happens that all of the commutative operators just mentioned are also associative, q.v. By contrast, the logical operators NAND and NOR, q.v., are examples of operators that are commutative but not associative. So too is COMPOSE, q.v.

comparison A boolean expression of the form (*exp1*) *theta* (*exp2*), where *exp1* and *exp2* are expressions of the same type *T* and *theta* is any comparison operator that makes sense for values of type *T* (certainly "=" or "≠", perhaps "<" and ">" also, and so on). *Note:* The parentheses enclosing *exp1* and *exp2* in the comparison might not be needed in practice.

compensating action / compensatory action Terms used interchangeably to mean an update performed automatically in addition to some explicitly requested update, with the aim of avoiding some integrity violation that might otherwise occur. Cascading a delete operation in order to avoid a referential integrity violation is a typical example; so too is the update performed on some underlying base relvar in response to some requested view update. Note that such compensatory actions should be performed, if and when logically required, regardless of the concrete syntactic form in which the original update request is expressed. For example, an INSERT operation expressed as a pure relational assignment (using ":="), q.v., should nevertheless cause the compensatory action for that INSERT to be performed—assuming, of course, that such an action has been defined in the first place.

Note: Compensatory actions should be specified declaratively, and users should generally be aware of them (that is, users should generally know when their update requests are shorthand for some more extensive set of actions), for otherwise they might perceive an apparent violation of *The Assignment Principle*, q.v. Note too, however, that—at least with regard to the compensatory actions needed in connection with view updating—the system should in fact be able to work out for itself what compensatory actions are needed, implying that the required declarative specifications can and should be provided by the system. *See also* controlled redundancy; multiple assignment. *Contrast* triggered procedure.

complement   Let relation *r* have heading *H* and body *B*. Then the complement of *r* is the relation with heading *H* and body consisting of all tuples with heading *H* not appearing in *B*.

complement (set theory)   The complement—also known as the absolute complement—of a set *s* is the set of all elements not appearing in *s*. *Note:* The difference *s1* – *s2* between sets *s1* and *s2*, in that order, is sometimes referred to as the relative complement of *s2* with respect to *s1* (*see* difference); thus, the absolute complement of *s* is in fact the relative complement of *s* with respect to the universal set, q.v. *See also* boolean algebra (second definition).

complementarity   1. (*Logic*) The disjunction of a predicate and its negation is a tautology, q.v.; the conjunction of a predicate and its negation is a contradiction, q.v. 2. (*Set theory*) The union of a set and its complement is the universal set, q.v.; the intersection of a set and its complement is the empty set, q.v.

Example (first definition only): The following identities are just a representation of the foregoing logic laws in symbolic form, but they might be a little easier to understand than the prose versions:

```
p OR  ( NOT p )  ≡  TRUE

p AND ( NOT p )  ≡  FALSE
```

completeness   (*Of a formal system; not to be confused with computational, relational, or truth functional completeness, q.v.*) A formal system is complete if and only if, given a set *s* of sentences of the system, all sentences implied by those in *s* can be derived using the rules of inference of that system (i.e., all tautologies are theorems). *See also* soundness.

component   1. (*Of a JD*) *See* join dependency. 2. (*Of a possrep*) *See* possrep. 3. (*Of a tuple*) *See* tuple component.

COMPOSE   *See* composition.

composite attribute / compound attribute Deprecated terms used interchangeably to mean a combination of two or more attributes. The terms are deprecated in part because a "composite" or "compound" attribute isn't actually an attribute at all.

composite key / compound key Terms used interchangeably to mean a key consisting of two or more attributes. *Contrast* simple key.
   Example: In the suppliers-and-parts database, SP is the only relvar with a composite key (namely, {SNO,PNO}).

composite predicate / compound predicate Terms used interchangeably to mean a predicate that involves at least one connective. *Contrast* simple predicate.

composite proposition / compound proposition Terms used interchangeably to mean a proposition that involves at least one connective. *Contrast* simple proposition.

composite statement / compound statement (*Programming languages*) Terms used interchangeably to mean a statement that contains other statements syntactically nested inside itself. *Contrast* atomic statement.
   Examples: Conventional IF, DO, WHILE, and CASE statements; BEGIN – END statement blocks; multiple assignment statements (q.v.); and many others.

composition   1. (*Dyadic case*) Let relations $r1$ and $r2$ be joinable, q.v., and let their common attributes be called $A1$, $A2$, ..., Am ($m \geq 0$). Then (and only then) the expression $r1$ COMPOSE $r2$ denotes the composition of $r1$ and $r2$, and it returns the relation denoted by the expression ($r1$ JOIN $r2$) {ALL BUT $A1$, $A2$, ..., Am}. *See also* tuple composition. *Note:* Dyadic COMPOSE is unusual, in a sense, in that it's commutative but not associative. 2. (*N-adic case*) Let relations $r1$, $r2$, ..., rn ($n \geq 0$) be n-way joinable, q.v., and let the attributes common to at least two of those relations be called $A1$, $A2$, ..., Am ($m \geq 0$). Then (and only then) the expression COMPOSE {$r1,r2,...,rn$} denotes the composition of $r1$, $r2$, ..., rn, and it returns the relation denoted by the expression (JOIN {$r1,r2,...,rn$}) {ALL BUT $A1$, $A2$, ..., Am}. *Caveat:* This definition is motivated by a desire to preserve commutativity (of a kind)—more precisely, to preserve the property that the value of the expression COMPOSE {$r1,r2,...,rn$} is independent of the order in which relations $r1$, $r2$, ..., rn are specified. It also has the property that the expression COMPOSE {$r1,r2$} is logically equivalent to the expression $r1$ COMPOSE $r2$ (i.e., the n-adic version degenerates to its dyadic counterpart in the special case where $n = 2$). On the other hand, the operator isn't associative; in other words, the expressions COMPOSE {$r1$,COMPOSE {$r2,r3$}}, COMPOSE {COMPOSE {$r1,r2$},$r3$}, and COMPOSE {$r1,r2,r3$} aren't logically equivalent. Thus, n-adic COMPOSE as here defined isn't just shorthand for repeated dyadic COMPOSE; rather, it's a logically distinct operator. Contrast the situation with, e.g., n-adic JOIN, which *is* shorthand for repeated dyadic JOIN.

Example: The expression S{SNO,CITY} COMPOSE P{PNO,CITY} denotes the composition of the projections on {SNO,CITY} and {PNO,CITY}, respectively, of the relations that are the current values of relvars S and P, respectively. That composition is a relation of type RELATION {SNO SNO, PNO PNO}. Moreover, if the current values of relvars S and P are *s* and *p*, respectively, the body of that relation consists of all tuples of the form *<sno,pno>* such that *sno* is a supplier number appearing in *s*, *pno* is a part number appearing in *p*, and supplier *sno* and part *pno* are located in the same city.

computable function   A function that can be computed by a Turing machine in a finite number of steps).

computational completeness   A language is computationally complete if and only if it supports the computation of all computable functions.
Examples: C++; PL/I; SQL; **Tutorial D**; and many others. Codd's relational algebra, q.v., is an example of a language that's not computationally complete (basically because it includes no support for either EXTEND, q.v., or aggregate operators, q.v.).

conceptual design   Synonym for conceptual modeling; in other words, the process, or the result of the process, of producing a conceptual schema, q.v. Note, however, that the boundaries between conceptual design and logical design are far from being hard and fast, and might not exist at all in some cases.

conceptual modeling   Term sometimes used as a synonym for the process of conceptual design, q.v. *See also* semantic modeling.

conceptual schema   *See* business rule.

conclusion   In logic, that which a proof proves or an attempted proof attempts to prove. See in particular equality generating dependency; tuple generating dependency.

conditional expression   A logical expression, q.v.

conditional operator   A logical operator, q.v. (especially one of the connectives, q.v.).

conjunct   A predicate that's ANDed with zero or more others.

conjunction   1. (*Dyadic case*) If and only if p and q are predicates, their conjunction (p) AND (q) is a predicate also. Let (ip) AND (iq) be an invocation of that predicate, where ip and iq are invocations of p and q, respectively. Then that invocation (ip) AND (iq) evaluates to TRUE if and only if ip and iq both evaluate to TRUE. *Note:* The parentheses enclosing p and q in the predicate, and ip and iq in the invocation, might not be needed in practice. 2. (*N-adic case*) Let *p1, p2, ..., pn* (*n* ≥ 0) be predicates; then (and only then) the conjunction AND {*p1,p2,...,pn*} is defined to be shorthand for the expression (*p1*) AND (*p2*) AND ... AND (*pn*). (Note that this expression evaluates to TRUE if *n* = 0, because TRUE is the identity with respect to AND.) *See also* universal quantifier.

conjunctive normal form A predicate is in conjunctive normal form, CNF, if and only if it's of the form (*p1*) AND (*p2*) AND ... AND (*pn*), where none of the conjuncts (*p1*), (*p2*), ..., (*pn*) involves any ANDs—more precisely, where each of *p1, p2, ..., pn* is a disjunction of literals (*see* literal, second definition). *Note:* The parentheses enclosing the individual predicates *p1, p2, ...,* *pn* might not be needed in practice.

connection trap A term used by some writers to refer to an alleged flaw in the relational model. By way of illustration, consider the expression (S JOIN P) {SNO,PNO}. This expression denotes a relation, *r* say, that—given the sample values in Fig. 1—happens to contain the tuple <S2,P5>, because supplier S2 and part P5 are both located in the same city, Paris. Now, from the fact that this tuple appears in *r*, it obviously can't be inferred (at least, not validly) that supplier S2 supplies part P5—the predicate for *r* is *Supplier SNO and part PNO are located in the same city*, not *Supplier SNO supplies part PNO* (speaking a trifle loosely). However, it's claimed by certain writers that users will nevertheless make that invalid inference, and hence that the relational model is flawed because it lets users fall into that trap. But it should be clear from the example that the flaw lies not with the model but with a failure on the part of those users—or those writers, perhaps—to understand the semantics of join properly. (Indeed, the flaw, such as it is, really has nothing to do with the relational model as such. Instead, it has to do with the intrinsic nature of data.) *Note:* As the example suggests, the term *connection trap* is typically regarded as an issue that arises in connection with join specifically (indeed, some writers even refer to it as *the join trap* for that reason); however, similar issues can clearly arise in connection with other operations also.

connective A read-only monadic or dyadic logical operator. There are exactly 20 connectives in two-valued logic, four monadic and 16 dyadic (corresponding directly to the four possible monadic and 16 possible dyadic truth tables). The connectives most frequently encountered in practice are NOT (negation), OR (disjunction), AND (conjunction), IMPLIES (implication), and EQUIV (equivalence); others include NAND, NOR, and XOR, q.v. *Note:* A variety of other symbols and keywords, some but not all of which are mentioned in this dictionary, are also used to denote these connectives. *See also* *n*VL; truth functional completeness; two-valued logic; three-valued logic.

Here for the record are truth tables for the connectives of two-valued logic. First the monadic ones:

Monadic operators:

T	T
F	T

T	T
F	F

NOT	
T	F
F	T

T	F
F	F

And here are the dyadic ones (using, for typographic reasons, IF for IMPLIES and IFF for EQUIV):

	T	F		IF	T	F		NAND	T	F			T	F
T	T	T		T	T	F		T	F	T		T	F	F
F	T	T		F	T	T		F	T	T		F	T	T

OR	T	F			T	F		XOR	T	F			T	F
T	T	T		T	T	F		T	F	T		T	F	F
F	T	F		F	T	F		F	T	F		F	T	F

	T	F		IFF	T	F			T	F		NOR	T	F
T	T	T		T	T	F		T	F	T		T	F	F
F	F	T		F	F	T		F	F	T		F	F	T

	T	F		AND	T	F			T	F			T	F
T	T	T		T	T	F		T	F	T		T	F	F
F	F	F		F	F	F		F	F	F		F	F	F

consequent　*See* implication.

consistency　Loosely, a synonym for integrity, q.v.; sometimes used more specifically to refer to the state of a database that conforms to just those declared integrity constraints that have to do with controlled redundancy, q.v. Note, however, that there's an important distinction to be drawn between what might be called formal consistency and informal consistency. To elaborate:

- (*Formal consistency*) Formally speaking, a database is in a state of consistency if and only if it conforms to all declared integrity constraints—and the term *consistency*, unqualified, is usually taken to mean consistency in this formal (or logical) sense, unless the context demands otherwise. *Note:* It follows from this definition that a database is formally inconsistent if and only if there's some declared constraint it should satisfy but doesn't. Equivalently, a database is formally inconsistent if and only if it's self-contradictory— meaning that it asserts, either explicitly or implicitly, that some proposition *p* and its negation NOT(*p*) are both true. The relational model requires databases to be consistent in this formal sense at all times (where "at all times" effectively means at statement boundaries or, loosely, "at semicolons"). Consistency in this sense is necessary but not sufficient for correctness, q.v. *See also* **atomic statement; controlled redundancy; integrity.**

■   (*Informal consistency, also known as "eventual" consistency*) Consistency in the foregoing formal sense isn't necessarily the same thing as consistency as conventionally understood in the real world (meaning consistency as understood outside the realm of databases in particular). For example, suppose there are two items *A* and *B* in the database that, in the real world, are supposed to have the same value (they might both be the selling price for some given commodity, stored twice in the database to improve availability). If *A* and *B* in fact have different values at some given time, we might certainly say, informally, that there's an inconsistency in the database at that time. But that "inconsistency" is an inconsistency as far as the system is concerned if and only if the system has been told that *A* and *B* are supposed to be equal—i.e., if and only if "*A* = *B*" has been declared as a formal constraint. If it hasn't, then (a) the fact that *A* and *B* are unequal at some time doesn't in itself constitute a consistency violation as far as the system is concerned, and (b) importantly, the system will nowhere rely on an assumption that *A* and *B* are equal. Thus, if all we want is for *A* and *B* to be equal "eventually"—i.e., if we're content for that requirement to be handled outside the database system by some application program—then all we have to do as far as the system is concerned is omit any declaration of "*A* = *B*" as a formal constraint.

Examples (formal consistency): Suppose there's an integrity constraint on the suppliers-and-parts database to the effect that part weights must be positive. However, suppose the database were to show some part as having a negative weight (not possible, of course, if the DBMS is enforcing constraints properly). Then the database would be inconsistent (and a fortiori incorrect).

By way of a second example, suppose there's an integrity constraint in effect that says that every part must be supplied by at least one supplier (i.e., the projections P{PNO} and SP{PNO} must be equal). However, suppose the database were to show part P7 as represented in relvar P but not in relvar SP (not possible, of course, if the DBMS is enforcing constraints properly). Again, then, the database would be inconsistent (and a fortiori incorrect).

consistent   1. (*Logic*) A set of predicates is consistent if and only if there exists at least one set of arguments that can be substituted for the parameters of those predicates in such a way that every resulting proposition evaluates to TRUE. 2. (*Database*) *See* **consistency**. Note, however, that consistency in the database sense is really nothing more than a special case of consistency in the sense of logic, where the predicates involved are simply the predicates that apply to the particular database in question.

Examples (logical consistency): Let the symbols x, y, and z denote integers. Then the predicates $x > y$ and $y > z$ form a consistent set, while the predicates $x > y$, $y > z$, and $z > x$ do not.

constant   1. (*Logic*) *See* **individual constant**. 2. (*Programming languages*) A value, especially one that's given a name that's not just a simple literal representation of the value as such; not to be confused with a literal, q.v.

Examples (second definition only): See relation constant.

constant reference (*Programming languages*) Syntactically, the name of a named constant (q.v.), used to denote the corresponding value. It can be regarded as an invocation of a read-only operator—and hence as an expression, q.v.—where the read-only operator in question is essentially "Return [the value of] the specified constant." Like all expressions, therefore, it can appear wherever a literal of the appropriate type can appear.

CONSTRAINT (*Without inheritance*) A **Tutorial D** keyword, used in connection with the definition of type constraints (q.v.) for scalar types. (It's also used in connection with database constraints, q.v.) Let *T* be such a type. Then the definition of type *T* must include at least one POSSREP specification (q.v.), and that POSSREP specification must include exactly one CONSTRAINT specification (either explicitly or implicitly; CONSTRAINT TRUE is assumed if nothing is specified explicitly).

Example: Let ELLIPSE be a scalar type. Then the corresponding type definition might look like this (irrelevant details omitted):

```
TYPE ELLIPSE
     POSSREP { A LENGTH , B LENGTH , CTR POINT
                              CONSTRAINT A ≥ B } } ;
```

In other words, ellipses are such that they can possibly be represented by two lengths *a* and *b* and a point *ctr*, where *a* is the length of the ellipse's major semiaxis, *b* is the length of its minor semiaxis, *ctr* is its center, and $a \geq b$ (see the introduction to Part II of the dictionary for further discussion). *Note:* The user defined types LENGTH and POINT have already been defined (at least, let's assume so for the sake of the example). Also, the constraint B > 0 ought by rights to be specified as well but has been omitted to keep the example simple.

Now let *e* be a scalar value. Then *e* is of type ELLIPSE if and only if the following constraint—call it *ETC*—is satisfied: The value *e* can possibly be represented by a length *a*, a length *b*, and a point *ctr*, such that $a \geq b$. *ETC* here is the type constraint for type ELLIPSE. Note, therefore, that the CONSTRAINT specification as such doesn't define the type constraint in its entirety, though it's often referred to informally as if it did.

constraint An integrity constraint, q.v. Usually understood to mean a database constraint specifically (i.e., not a type constraint), unless the context demands otherwise.

constraint inference The process of determining the constraints that hold in a given derived relvar or are satisfied by a given derived relation.

constructor function Term used in OO contexts for the operator that creates a new "instance" of a given object type (*see* instance, first definition; *see also* mutable object).

containment   Generally, the relationship between a container and the things it contains; in particular, the relationship between a bag or set and its elements. The containment relationship is the inverse of the membership relationship, q.v. Containment is sometimes denoted by the symbol "∋"; thus, the boolean expression $X \ni x$ —which is logically equivalent to both of the expressions $x \in X$ and $X \supseteq \{x\}$—returns TRUE if and only if X does in fact contain x. *Contrast* inclusion.

Examples: A relation contains a heading and a body; a heading contains attributes; a body contains tuples; a tuple contains tuple components; a tuple component contains an attribute value; and so on.

contradiction   A predicate whose every possible invocation is guaranteed to yield FALSE, regardless of what arguments are substituted for its parameters. *Note:* A contradiction in logic isn't quite the same thing as a contradiction in ordinary discourse. Loosely, we might say a contradiction in ordinary discourse is something that implies that some proposition *p* and its negation NOT(*p*) are both true; in logic, by contrast, it's anything that's "always false." Thus, propositions of the form *p* AND NOT(*p*) are certainly contradictions in the logical sense, but so are propositions of the form, e.g., *p* AND FALSE, and so is the proposition consisting of just the literal FALSE itself. *Contrast* **tautology**.

Examples: Let *p1* be the predicate (actually a proposition) 2+2 = 5; let *p2* be the predicate $x > x$, where *x* denotes an arbitrary integer; and let *p3* be the predicate (*p*) AND (NOT(*p*)), where *p* denotes an arbitrary predicate. Then *p1*, *p2*, and *p3* are all contradictions. Note that a contradiction isn't necessarily a proposition, even though (like some propositions) it does unequivocally evaluate to FALSE. For example, $x > x$ isn't a proposition; rather, it's a predicate with exactly one parameter.

contrapositive   The implicational predicates IF (*p*) THEN (*q*) and IF (NOT(*q*)) THEN (NOT (*p*)) are contrapositives of each other. Any given implication and its contrapositive are logically equivalent.

Example: Consider the predicates—actually propositions—*If it's raining, then the streets are getting wet* and *If the streets aren't getting wet, then it isn't raining.* Each of these is the contrapositive of the other, and, clearly, each is logically equivalent to the other.

controlled redundancy   Redundancy, q.v., is controlled if (a) it does exist (and the user is aware of it) but (b) it's guaranteed never to lead to any formal inconsistencies in the database. Uncontrolled redundancy, q.v., can be a problem, but controlled redundancy shouldn't be. As a general rule, databases shouldn't involve any uncontrolled redundancy.

Example: Suppose there's a business rule to the effect that all suppliers in the same city must have the same status. Of course, the sample value shown for relvar S in Fig. 1 doesn't satisfy this rule; however, it would do so if we changed the status for supplier S2 from 10 to 30, so let's suppose, just for the sake of the example, that this change has in fact been made. Then the fact that the status associated with Paris is 30 appears twice, and so there's some redundancy.

(By contrast, if the status for supplier S2 were left at 10 instead of being changed to 30, then the database would be formally inconsistent, and hence incorrect.) So to say that the database involves some redundancy is to say that some specific business rule is supposed to hold, and hence that some specific integrity constraint is supposed to apply (though the converse is false, of course—not all integrity constraints have to do with controlling redundancy as such). For example, the "same status" constraint might be stated thus:

```
CONSTRAINT CRX COUNT ( S { CITY } ) = COUNT ( S { CITY , STATUS } ) ;
```

Stating this constraint explicitly serves to inform the user that the redundancy exists; enforcing it serves to ensure that it won't lead to any formal inconsistencies, thereby guaranteeing that the redundancy in question is controlled. *Note:* Of course, enforcing such constraints should be done by the DBMS, not by the user. In some cases, it might even be possible for the DBMS to "propagate updates" appropriately in order to keep the data formally consistent (*see* **compensatory action**).

correct *See* **correctness**.

correctness (*Of a database*) The property of truly reflecting the state of affairs that exists in the real world (see the example under **relvar predicate** for further discussion). *Contrast* **consistency**.

correlation name SQL term denoting (the SQL analog of) either a tuple calculus range variable, q.v., or the name of such a variable, as the context demands.

COUNT 1. Loosely, a synonym for cardinality, q.v. 2. An aggregate operator, q.v.

cover (*Of a set of FDs*) If *s1* and *s2* are sets of FDs, then *s2* is a cover for *s1* if and only if every FD implied by *s1* is implied by those in *s2* (*see* **Armstrong's axioms**). *Note:* Some writers use the term *cover* in a stronger sense, to mean a set of FDs that's equivalent to some given set (*see* **equivalence**).

cross join / cross product Terms sometimes used to mean cartesian product, q.v.

CWA *The Closed World Assumption.*

cyclic ordering Let *s* be a set. Loosely speaking, then, a cyclic ordering on *s* is like a linear ordering (q.v.) on *s*, except that it wraps around in such a way that what would otherwise be the first element is considered the immediate successor of what would otherwise be the last element. An example is provided by the hours of the day (0, 1, 2, ..., 23), where the the available values can be thought of as being arranged around the circumference of a clockface and every value thus has both a successor and a predecessor. Note that "<" and ">" both degenerate to "≠" in a cyclic ordering.

-------- ♦ ♦ ♦ ♦ ♦ --------

D   Generic name (note the boldface) used to refer to any language that conforms to the principles laid down by *The Third Manifesto*. *Contrast* **Tutorial D**.

D_INSERT   *See* disjoint INSERT.

D_UNION   *See* disjoint union.

data   (*Plural noun treated as singular*) An encoded representation of some set of propositions, assumed by convention to be true ones.

data definition operator   An operator that either defines some database object, such as a base relvar or a view or a snapshot or a constraint, or deletes ("drops") or updates such a definition; in other words, an operator that updates the catalog. *Note:* Dropping a definition effectively causes the corresponding object to be dropped as well, of course (at least as far as the user is concerned), and is usually described in such terms. For example, **Tutorial D** provides an operator called for psychological reasons DROP CONSTRAINT (not "drop constraint definition").
    Examples: See the definitions of relvars S, P, and SP. Other examples could be an operation to add an attribute to one of those relvars, or an operation to define a constraint on those relvars, or an operation to delete any of these definitions. *Note:* Strictly speaking, the first of the foregoing examples—"adding an attribute" to some relvar, say relvar S—has the effect of dropping the original relvar with that name and introducing a new one with the same name but an extended heading, at the same time preserving, somehow, the current information content of, and the constraints that apply to, the original relvar. Details of how this effect might be achieved are beyond the scope of this dictionary.

data independence   The ability to change either the physical or the logical design of a database without having to make corresponding changes in the way the database is perceived by users (thereby protecting investment in, among other things, existing user training and existing applications). The terms *physical data independence* and *logical data independence* refer to the two cases. Both involve having two sets of definitions and mappings between them, such that (a) if the physical design changes, physical data independence is preserved by changing the mapping between the physical design and the logical design, and (b) if the logical design changes, logical data independence is preserved by defining a mapping between the old logical design and the new one (or, equivalently, by changing the mapping between the logical design and the physical design). *Note:* If the logical design changes, the new logical design will consist of views of relvars in the old logical design—at least conceptually, if not in actual fact. Thus, logical data independence in particular implies the need to be able to update views, q.v.

data manipulation operator   Loosely, an operator that isn't a data definition operator. However, the distinction isn't hard and fast; in fact, it's quite difficult to find an operator that doesn't, in the last analysis, "manipulate" data of some kind (unless it's a read-only operator, possibly; some writers might claim that update operators are the only ones that actually "manipulate" data). The term is really a hangover from prerelational systems, where it arguably made a little more sense than it does now; in relational contexts, it's probably better avoided.

data model   1. An abstract, self-contained, logical definition of the data structures, data operators, and so forth, that together make up the abstract machine with which users interact (*contrast* implementation). 2. A model of the persistent data of some particular enterprise (in other words, a conceptual or logical database design).

   Examples: For the first definition, the most obvious example is of course the relational model itself. As for the second definition, any conceptual or logical database design will suffice as an example.

   Note: There's a nice analogy that can help explain the difference between the two definitions, as follows: A data model in the first sense is like a programming language, whose constructs can be used to solve many specific problems but in and of themselves have no direct connection with any such specific problem; a data model in the second sense is like a specific program written in that language—it uses the facilities provided by the model, in the first sense of that term, to solve some specific problem. Note also that we can usefully characterize the distinction between a data model in that first sense and an implementation (q.v.) of that model by saying the model is what the user has to know, while the implementation is what the user doesn't have to know.

data modeling   Term sometimes used—with reference to the second meaning of the term *data model* specifically, q.v., though never very precisely defined—to describe either the conceptual or the logical design process. *See* conceptual design; logical design.

data sublanguage   A language that provides database support for one or more host languages, q.v., in which its statements can be embedded or from which they can be invoked.

   Example: SQL is an obvious case in point; application programs that access an SQL database are usually written in some host language but invoke certain SQL operations, either in "embedded" form or via some kind of call level interface, to obtain the necessary database functionality.

Data Sublanguage ALPHA   *See* ALPHA.

data type   Same as type.

database   Strictly, a database value, q.v.; more commonly used, in this dictionary in particular, to refer to what would more accurately be called a database variable, q.v. *Note:* We assume throughout this dictionary that databases are relational, barring explicit statements to the contrary. Be aware, however, that the term *database* is used in nonrelational contexts to mean a variety of other things—for example, a collection of data as physically stored. It's also used, all too frequently, to mean a DBMS, but this particular usage is strongly deprecated. (If we call the DBMS a database, what do we call the database?)

database assignment   An operation that assigns a database value to a database variable; in other words, any operation that updates the database. For further explanation, *see* **database variable; multiple assignment.**

database catalog   *See* catalog.

database constraint   1. (*"A" database constraint*) Formally, any constraint that isn't a type constraint; informally, any constraint that refers to two or more distinct relvars (also, and better, known as a multirelvar constraint, q.v.). *Note:* These definitions aren't meant to be equivalent in any sense—they refer to two distinct concepts. 2. (*"The" database constraint*) The logical AND of all constraints, other than type constraints, that apply to a given database (*the* database constraint—sometimes called the *total* database constraint, for emphasis—for the database in question). *Note:* It follows from this second definition that one constraint that applies to every database is the degenerate ("default") constraint TRUE. *See also* **relvar constraint.**

Examples: First, the key and foreign key constraints specified in the definition of the suppliers-and-parts database are all database constraints. Second, here are some more database constraints that might also apply to that database:

```
CONSTRAINT C1 IS_EMPTY ( S WHERE STATUS < 1 OR STATUS > 100 ) ;
/* status values must be in the range 1 to 100 inclusive */

CONSTRAINT C2 IS_EMPTY ( P WHERE CITY = 'London'
                         AND   COLOR ≠ COLOR('Red') ) ;
/* parts in London must be red */

CONSTRAINT C3 IS_EMPTY
       ( ( S JOIN SP ) WHERE STATUS < 20 AND PNO = PNO('P6') ) ;
/* no supplier with status less than 20 can supply part P6 */
```

Here for interest is an alternative formulation of constraint C1 that makes use of the AND aggregate operator, q.v.:

```
CONSTRAINT C1 AND ( S , STATUS ≥ 1 AND STATUS ≤ 100 ) ;
/* status values must be in the range 1 to 100 inclusive */
```

This same style could also be used with constraints C2 and C3, of course.

Finally, suppose for the sake of the example that the specified key and foreign key constraints, together with constraints C1-C3 above, are the only database constraints that apply to the suppliers-and-parts database. Then the logical AND of all of them is "the" (total) database constraint for that database.

database design   *See* logical database design; physical database design. *Note:* The unqualified term *database design*, or sometimes even just *design*, is usually taken to mean logical database design specifically, unless the context demands otherwise. *See also* conceptual design.

database management system   The software system (abbreviated DBMS, plural DBMSs) that manages, and in particular handles all access to, some database or collection of databases. *Note:* A relational DBMS in particular can be thought of, or even defined, as an implementation of the relational model. *Contrast* database.

database programming language   A programming language that includes fully integrated ("native") database support. *Contrast* data sublanguage; host language.

Examples: **Tutorial D** might be regarded as a fully fledged database programming language, except that it currently includes no exception handling and no I/O support. A similar remark applies to SQL; SQL is widely thought of as just a data sublanguage, q.v., but with the introduction in the 1992 version of the standard ("SQL:1992") of such features as local variables, exception handling, IF, CASE, WHILE, CALL, RETURN, and assignment (SET) statements, it too became a fully fledged database programming language (except that, like **Tutorial D,** it currently includes no I/O facilities).

database relation   The value of a given database relvar at a given time.

Database Relativity Principle   *See Principle of Database Relativity.*

database relvar   *See* relvar.

database statistics   Metadata, typically kept in the catalog, that (among other things) might be helpful to the optimizer, q.v.

Examples: Relvar and attribute cardinalities; minimum, maximum, and average attribute values; attribute value frequencies; index selectivities; and so on.

database value   Either the actual (i.e., current) or some possible "state" for some database; in other words, a collection of relations, those relations being actual or possible values for the applicable relvars. Abstractly, therefore, a database value can be thought of as a collection of propositions (assumed by convention to be true ones), those propositions being represented by the tuples in the applicable relations. *Contrast* **database variable**.

Example: The relations (i.e., relation values) shown in Fig. 1 constitute the "state" of the suppliers-and-parts database that happens to be current at this time. But if we were to look at that database at some different time, we would probably see a different state. In other words, the database is really a variable—a database variable, to be precise, meaning a variable whose values are database values (*see* **database variable**). Moreover, the tuples in the relations that are the values of relvars S, P, and SP at any given time represent propositions—propositions that are assumed to be true at that time—so, as the foregoing definition indicates, the database at the time in question can be thought of, a trifle loosely, as a collection of true propositions.

database variable Loosely, a container for relvars; more accurately, a variable whose value at any given time is a database value. Strictly speaking, there's a logical difference, analogous to that between relation values and relation variables, between database values and database variables; thus, what we usually call a database is really a variable (typically a rather large one), and updating that database has the effect of replacing one value of that variable by another such value, where the values in question are database values and the variable in question is a database variable. More precisely still, a database is really a tuple variable, with one attribute (relation valued) for each relvar in the database in question. Note, therefore, that a database isn't really a set of relation variables, despite the fact that we usually think of it that way; rather, the relvars within any given database are really pseudovariables, q.v. All of that being said, however, we bow to traditional usage in this dictionary (most of the time, at any rate) and use the term *database* to refer to both database values and database variables, relying on context to make clear which is intended. *See also* **database**; **database value**.

Examples: For an example of a database value, see Fig. 1. As for the matter of a database really being a tuple variable, the suppliers-and-parts database in particular can be thought of as a tuple variable (SPDB, say) of the following tuple type:

```
TUPLE { S   RELATION { SNO SNO , SNAME NAME ,
                                  STATUS INTEGER , CITY CHAR } ,
        P   RELATION { PNO PNO , PNAME NAME , COLOR COLOR ,
                                  WEIGHT WEIGHT , CITY CHAR } ,
        SP RELATION { SNO SNO , PNO PNO , QTY QTY } }
```

It follows that, e.g., the following relational update on tuplevar SPDB—

```
DELETE SP WHERE QTY < QTY(150) ;
```

—is really shorthand for the following tuple update:

```
UPDATE SPDB : { SP := SP WHERE NOT ( QTY < QTY(150) ) } ;
```

And this statement in turn is shorthand for the following tuple assignment:

```
SPDB := TUPLE { S    ( S   FROM SPDB ) ,
                P    ( P   FROM SPDB ) ,
                SP ( ( SP FROM SPDB ) WHERE NOT ( QTY < QTY(150) ) ) } ;
```

As previously indicated, therefore, the names S, P, and SP really denote pseudovariables, q.v. Note, however, that if we're to be able to write explicit database assignments as in the foregoing example, then databases—or database variables, rather—like SPDB will certainly have to have user visible names, which in **Tutorial D** they don't (at least, not as the language is currently defined). Thus, database assignments in **Tutorial D** have to be expressed in the form of relational assignments (in general, multiple assignments) to the relvar(s) within the database in question. For further explanation, see multiple assignment.

Incidentally, assuming the name SPDB is indeed user visible, then **Tutorial D** would certainly allow the foregoing tuple assignment to be written in the form of an explicit tuple UPDATE statement as shown above, thus—

```
UPDATE SPDB : { SP := SP WHERE NOT ( QTY < QTY(150) ) } ;
```

—or even as follows:

```
UPDATE SPDB : { DELETE SP WHERE QTY < QTY(150) } ;
```

Finally, note that a database isn't just a set of relvars—rather, it's a set of relvars that are subject to a certain constraint (viz., the pertinent total database constraint). And it seems reasonable to require the database to be *fully connected* (and hence to form a coherent whole); in other words, it seems reasonable to require the total database constraint to be such that every relvar in the database is logically connected to every other (not necessarily directly, of course). The following definition is intended as an aid in formalizing this requirement. Let *DB* be a set of relvars, and let *TC* be the logical AND of all constraints that mention any relvar in *DB*. Assume without loss of generality that *TC* is in conjunctive normal form. Now let *A* and *B* be distinct relvars in *DB*. Then *A* and *B* are logically connected if and only if there exist relvars *R1*, *R2*, ..., *Rn* in *DB* ($n > 0$, *A* and *R1* not necessarily distinct, *Rn* and *B* not necessarily distinct) such that there's at least one conjunct in *TC* that mentions both *A* and *R1*, at least one that mentions both *R1* and *R2*, ..., and at least one that mentions both *Rn* and *B*. *Note:* It should be clear that if a given database isn't fully connected in the foregoing sense, then the relvars it contains can be partitioned into two or more disjoint sets, each of which *is* fully connected.

DBMS   Database Management System; plural DBMSs.

dbvar   A database variable, q.v. The term isn't much used, though perhaps it should be.

DCO   Domain check override, q.v.

De Morgan's Laws   1. (*Logic*) The negation of the disjunction of predicates *p* and *q* is logically equivalent to the conjunction of the negations of *p* and *q*; the negation of the conjunction of predicates *p* and *q* is logically equivalent to the disjunction of the negations of *p* and *q*.   2. (*Set theory*) The complement of the union of sets *s1* and *s2* is equal to the intersection of the complements of *s1* and *s2*; the complement of the intersection of sets *s1* and *s2* is equal to the union of the complements of *s1* and *s2*.

    Example (first definition only):   The following identities are just a representation of the foregoing logic laws in symbolic form, but they might be a little easier to understand than the prose versions:

```
NOT ( ( p ) OR ( q ) )   ≡   ( NOT ( p ) ) AND ( NOT ( q ) )

NOT ( ( p ) AND ( q ) )  ≡   ( NOT ( p ) ) OR  ( NOT ( q ) )
```

decidability   (*Of a formal system*) A formal system is decidable if and only if, given an arbitrary sentence *s*, it can be determined mechanically whether *s* is a sentence of the system.

    Examples: Propositional calculus is decidable; predicate calculus is not.

declared   Term often used as a synonym for *defined* or *specified*.

declared possrep   *See* possible representation. *Note:*   The unqualified term *possrep* is used almost invariably to refer to a declared possrep specifically.

declared type   (*Without inheritance*) Type. *Note:*   The following more specific definitions are logically correct but reduce, in the absence of support for inheritance, merely to saying that—as already indicated—the declared type of some item *x* is just the type of *x*, as this latter term is usually understood.   1. (*Of a constant, variable, attribute, or parameter*) The type specified when the constant, variable, attribute, or parameter in question is declared.   2. (*Of a read-only operator*) The type of the result, specified when the operator in question is declared (*see* RETURNS).   3. (*Of an expression*) The type of the outermost operator involved in the expression in question; in other words, the type of the operator whose execution is last in sequence (logically speaking, at any rate) in evaluating the expression in question.

    Examples:

■ First, the declared type of the literal 5 is INTEGER.

■ Second, let variables E and R be defined as follows:

```
VAR E ELLIPSE ;

VAR R RECTANGLE ;
```

Then the declared types of these variables are (the presumably user defined types) ELLIPSE and RECTANGLE, respectively.

■ Next, let ER be the relation type

```
RELATION { E ELLIPSE , R RECTANGLE }
```

Then the declared type of attribute R within relation type ER is RECTANGLE.

■ Finally, let the specification signature (q.v.) for operator MOVE be:

```
MOVE ( ELLIPSE , RECTANGLE ) RETURNS ELLIPSE
```

Then the declared type of that operator is ELLIPSE, and the declared types of the first and second parameter to that operator are ELLIPSE and RECTANGLE, respectively.

Note: Declared types are always known at compile time. Also, note in particular that x can have an empty declared type—*see* **empty type**—only if x is an attribute of some tuple type or some relation type.

decomposition Nonloss decomposition, q.v. (unless the context demands otherwise).

deductive axiom Term occasionally used to mean a rule of inference.

DEE Shorthand for TABLE_DEE.

default value Let A be an attribute of relvar R. Barring explicit rules to the contrary, then, a default value (default for short) can optionally be declared for A; that value, a say, will then be used as the value for attribute A in any tuple for which no value is specified explicitly when the tuple in question is entered into relvar R.

Example: Suppose attribute STATUS of relvar S has default value 10. Then the following INSERT might be valid, syntactically speaking:

```
INSERT S RELATION { TUPLE { SNO   SNO('S6') ,
                            SNAME NAME('Lopez') ,
                            CITY  'Madrid' } } ;
```

The relation that's actually inserted will look like this:

```
RELATION { TUPLE { SNO    SNO('S6') ,
                   SNAME  NAME('Lopez') ,
                   STATUS 10 ,
                   CITY   'Madrid' } }
```

Note: **Tutorial D** has no support for default values at the time of writing, and the foregoing INSERT on relvar S would thus currently not be valid in **Tutorial D**.

deferred checking Checking a database integrity constraint at some time (typically commit time) later than the time when an update is performed that might cause it to be violated. The relational model rejects such checking as logically flawed. *Contrast* immediate checking.

deferred constraint A database integrity constraint for which the checking is deferred (*see* deferred checking). The relational model rejects such constraints as logically flawed. *Contrast* immediate constraint.

degree The number n ($n \geq 0$) of attributes in a given heading, key, tuple, relation (etc.). *See also* arity.

Examples: The degrees of relvars S, P, and SP are four, five, and three, respectively; the degrees of the corresponding keys (one per relvar) are one, one, and two, respectively.

DELETE Loosely, an operator—shorthand for a certain relational assignment—that deletes specified tuples from a specified relvar. The syntax is:

```
DELETE R rx
```

Here R is a relvar reference (syntactically, just a relvar name) and rx is a relational expression (denoting some relation r of the same type as R), and the effect is to delete the tuples of r from R. In other words, the DELETE invocation just shown is shorthand for the following explicit assignment:

```
R := R MINUS rx
```

It follows that an attempt via DELETE to delete a tuple that's not present in the first place is not considered an error (*contrast* included DELETE).

Examples: The statement

```
DELETE SP RELATION
          { TUPLE { SNO SNO('S3') , PNO PNO('P2') , QTY QTY(200) } ,
            TUPLE { SNO SNO('S1') , PNO PNO('P1') , QTY QTY(400) } } ;
```

is shorthand for the following explicit assignment statement:

```
SP := SP MINUS RELATION
          { TUPLE { SNO SNO('S3') , PNO PNO('P2') , QTY QTY(200) } ,
            TUPLE { SNO SNO('S1') , PNO PNO('P1') , QTY QTY(400) } } ;
```

Given the sample values shown in Fig. 1, however, this assignment will delete just one tuple, not two (speaking a trifle loosely), because the tuple <S1,P1,400> doesn't currently appear in relvar SP.

By way of another example, the statement

```
DELETE S WHERE CITY = 'London' ;
```

is shorthand for the following relational assignment statement:

```
S := S MINUS ( S WHERE CITY = 'London' ) ;
```

Note: Strictly speaking, this second example is shorthand for a DELETE statement of the same form as the first example that might look like this:

```
DELETE S S WHERE CITY = 'London' ;
```

It's clear, however, that if as in this example the expression denoting the set of tuples to be deleted from relvar *R* takes the form *R* WHERE *bx* (where WHERE TRUE is assumed if no WHERE clause is specified explicitly), then (a) there's no point in mentioning *R* twice in concrete syntax, and (b) the question of attempting to delete tuples not present in the first place simply doesn't arise. Indeed, this common special case can be defined more simply as shorthand for the following:

```
R := R WHERE NOT ( bx )
```

For example, the second DELETE statement shown above is shorthand for:

```
S := S WHERE NOT ( CITY = 'London' ) ;
```

DELETE anomaly   Same as deletion anomaly.

DELETE rule   A rule specifying the action to be taken by the DBMS automatically—typically but not necessarily a compensatory action, q.v.—to ensure that DELETE operations on a given relvar don't violate any associated multivariable constraint, q.v. Foreign key DELETE rules (e.g., cascade) are an important special case. Note, however, that such automatic actions should occur, if and when logically required, regardless of the concrete syntactic form in which the original DELETE request is expressed. For example, a DELETE request expressed as a pure relational assignment (using ":="), q.v., should nevertheless cause the action specified by the pertinent DELETE rule to be performed— assuming, of course, that such a rule has been defined in the first place.

delete set   *See* relational assignment.

deletion anomaly   Term originally used (though never very precisely defined) to refer to the fact that DELETE operations on a relvar that's subject to FD redundancy, q.v., can sometimes "delete too much." E.g., suppose for the sake of the example that relvar S is subject to the FD {CITY} → {STATUS}. Of course, the sample value shown for that relvar in Fig. 1 doesn't satisfy this FD; however, it would do so if we changed the status for supplier S2 from 10 to 30, so let's suppose, just for the sake of the example, that this change has in fact been made (though actually it has no effect on the specific anomaly to be discussed). Here then is a deletion anomaly: If we delete the tuple for supplier S5 (the only supplier in Athens), we lose the fact that the status for Athens is 30. *Note:* A relvar that's in BCNF, q.v., is guaranteed to be free of deletion anomalies in this "FD redundancy" sense.

The term *deletion anomaly* is also used in connection with relvars that are subject to JD redundancy, q.v.; in this case, however, the concept is more precisely defined. To be specific, let the JD *J* hold in relvar *R*; then *R* suffers from a deletion anomaly with respect to *J* if and only if there exists a relation *r* containing a tuple *t* such that (a) *r* satisfies *J* and (b) the relation *r'* whose body is obtained from that of *r* by removing *t* violates *J*. *Note:* A relvar that's in ETNF, q.v., is guaranteed to be free of deletion anomalies in this "JD redundancy" sense.

Finally, this latter definition can be generalized, as follows: Relvar *R* suffers from a deletion anomaly if and only if (a) there exists a single-relvar constraint *C* on *R* and (b) there exists a relation *r* containing a tuple *t* such that *r* satisfies *C* and the relation *r'* whose body is obtained from that of *r* by removing *t* violates *C*. *Note:* A relvar that's in DK/NF, q.v., is guaranteed to be free of deletion anomalies in this generalized sense.

denormalization   Replacing a set of relvars *R1*, *R2*, ..., *Rn* by their join *R*, such that (a) for all *i* (*i* = 1, 2, ..., *n*) the projection of *R* on the attributes of *Ri* at any given time is guaranteed to be equal to *Ri* at the time in question, and usually also such that (b) *R* is at a lower level of normalization than at least one of *R1*, *R2*, ..., *Rn*. Denormalization is generally done for performance reasons; however, it typically has the effect of increasing redundancy, q.v., thereby increasing (a) the amount of integrity checking that has to be done, by the user or the system or both (thereby, incidentally, undermining the performance advantage that was the justification for doing the denormalization in the first place), or (b) the likelihood that certain update anomalies, q.v., will occur, or (c) both. It can also increase the complexity of certain queries. *Contrast* **unnormalized.** *Note:* Denormalization, at least to a level below ETNF, q.v., is always contraindicated from a logical point of view. Sometimes it can't reasonably be avoided, however, given the level of technology found in today's commercial products.

Example: A denormalization that might be applied to the suppliers-and-parts database would be to replace relvars S and SP by their join (SSP, say). Relvars S and SP could then be derived by projecting relvar SSP on the attributes of S and the attributes of SP, respectively. Note that S and SP are both in 5NF (in fact, SP is in 6NF), while SSP isn't even in 2NF. Note too, however, that such a denormalization would be valid only if S and SP are both true projections of SSP—in other words, if and only if every supplier number appearing in relvar S at any given time also appears in relvar SP at that same time (and vice versa, of course)—which isn't guaranteed to be the case (and indeed isn't the case, given the sample values in Fig. 1).

dependant / dependent   Terms used interchangeably to mean the set of attributes on the right side of an FD or MVD. *Contrast* **determinant**.

    Example: In the FD {SNO,PNO} → {QTY}, which holds in relvar SP, {QTY} is the dependant and {SNO,PNO} is the determinant.

dependence / dependency   Terms used generically and interchangeably to mean an integrity constraint, typically but not necessarily an EQD or IND or JD or MVD or (especially) FD specifically. *See also* **generalized dependency**.

dependency preservation   FD preservation, q.v.; occasionally, analogous preservation of some other kind of dependency.

dependency theory   A body of theory, built on top of—i.e., relying on certain features of—the relational model and having to do with the formal properties of FDs, MVDs, and JDs among other things, that can be used to help with the process of logical database design (though not limited to that purpose alone).

dereferencing   *See* **referencing**.

derived relation   Loosely, a relation defined in terms of others. More precisely, let *s* be a set of relations. Then relation *r* is derived (or, perhaps more accurately, derivable) from the relations in *s* if and only if it doesn't itself appear in *s* but can be obtained by means of some relational expression from those that do. *Contrast* **base relation**. *Note:* The phrase "those that do" here is meant to be understood as referring to those relations that appear in *s* and those relations *only*. The reason is that *any* relation *x* can be "derived from the relations in *s*" by means of (e.g.) an expression of the form *r*{ } JOIN *exp*, where (a) *r* denotes some nonempty relation in *s* and (b) *exp* is a relation literal whose value is precisely the desired relation *x*. In other words, the introduction of relation literals into such derivation expressions isn't allowed.

    Example: Consider the expression S JOIN SP. If the current values of relvars S and SP are *s* and *sp*, respectively, this expression defines the derived relation that is the join of *s* and *sp*.

derived relvar   A relvar defined in terms of others by means of some relational expression; more specifically, a view or snapshot, q.v. (the only kinds of derived relvars supported at the time of writing). *Contrast* **base relvar**.

    Examples: See **snapshot; view**.

descriptor   Metadata that describes, e.g., a relvar or an attribute or a constraint.

design dilemma   *See* relvar vs. type.

designator   A name, possibly complex, used in a predicate to designate some specific object (as opposed to a parameter, which doesn't designate a specific object but instead stands for an arbitrary value of the pertinent type). For example, in the predicate *The cardinality of relvar S is n*, the phrase "relvar S" is a designator, designating the relation that's the current value of the suppliers relvar (by contrast, *n* is a parameter). Similarly, in the predicates—actually propositions—*Earth has a moon* and *Earth has a satellite*, "a moon" and "a satellite" are both designators (designating the same object, as it happens).

determinant   The set of attributes on the left side of an FD or MVD. *Contrast* dependant.
   Example: See **dependant.**

difference   (*Without inheritance*) Let relations *r1* and *r2* be of the same type *T*. Then (and only then) the expression *r1* MINUS *r2* denotes the difference between *r1* and *r2* (in that order), and it returns the relation of type *T* with body the set of all tuples *t* such that *t* appears in *r1* and not in *r2*. *Note:* The relational difference operator differs in certain respects from the mathematical or set theory operator of the same name, q.v.; in fact, it's a special case of semidifference, q.v.
   Example: The expression S{CITY} MINUS P{CITY} denotes the difference between (a) the relation that's the projection on {CITY} of the current value of relvar S and (b) the relation that's the projection on {CITY} of the current value of relvar P (in that order). That difference is a relation *r* of type RELATION {CITY CHAR}. Moreover, if the current values of relvars S and P are *s* and *p*, respectively, then the body of that relation *r* consists of all tuples of the form <*c*> that appear in *s*{CITY} and not *p*{CITY}—meaning *c* is a current supplier city that isn't also a current part city. Note that the expression S{CITY} MINUS P{CITY} is logically equivalent to the expression S{CITY} NOT MATCHING P{CITY}—or to either of the simpler expressions S{CITY} NOT MATCHING P and (S NOT MATCHING P) {CITY}, come to that. (NOT MATCHING is **Tutorial D** syntax for the semidifference operator, q.v.)

difference (bag theory)   *See* bag.

difference (set theory)   The difference between two sets *s1* and *s2* (in that order), *s1* − *s2*, is the set of all elements *x* such that *x* is an element of *s1* and not an element of *s2*. *Note:* The difference *s1* − *s2* is also known as the relative complement (q.v.) of *s2* with respect to *s1*.

direct image   A somewhat unsophisticated style of implementation, found in most if not all of today's mainstream database products, in which what's physically stored is effectively just a direct image of what the user logically sees. In other words (and simplifying slightly), relvars are stored as physical files, and tuples and attributes are stored as records and fields within those files. *Contrast* TransRelational™ Model.

direct proof   *See* proof.

direct reasoning   *See modus ponens.*

directed relationship   A relationship (in the sense of the third definition of that term, q.v.) from one set to another.

discernibility   Distinguishability. *See* indiscernibility; *see also Principle of Identity of Indiscernibles.*

discriminant   *See* discriminated union (set theory).

discriminated union (set theory)   Let $s1 = \{a1,a2,...,am\}$ and $s2 = \{b1,b2,...,bn\}$ be sets. Define sets $s1'$ and $s2'$ as follows:

```
s1' = {<a1,1>,<a2,1>,...,<am,1>}
s2' = {<b1,2>,<b2,2>,...,<bn,2>}
```

Observe that (a) $s1'$ and $s2'$ are sets of ordered pairs, one such pair for each element of $s1$ or $s2$, as applicable; (b) the first element of each such pair is an element from $s1$ or $s2$, as applicable; and (c) the second element of each such pair (the discriminant) is either *1* or *2*, indicating which of $s1$ and $s2$ that first element is taken from.   Then the discriminated union of $s1$ and $s2$ is the set theory union—the disjoint union, in fact—of $s1'$ and $s2'$.

Note: The foregoing definition is essentially the one given in the literature.   However, it suffers from the weakness—surely unintended, and certainly undesirable—that the operator thus defined won't be commutative, unless there's some systematic way of assigning discriminants that guarantees that $s1$ and $s2$ are assigned discriminants *1* and *2*, respectively, and not the other way around.   Be that as it may, note too that the operator as here defined is dyadic; however, it would clearly be possible to define an *n*-adic version if desired.

Caveat: Be aware that discriminated union is sometimes referred to in the literature, rather unfortunately, as disjoint union.   That is (to spell the point out), the discriminated union of $s1$ and $s2$ is sometimes referred to in the literature as the disjoint union of $s1$ and $s2$ as such, instead of as the disjoint union of $s1'$ and $s2'$.

disjoint   1. (*Of bags or sets*) Having no elements in common. 2. (*Of relations all of the same type*) Having no tuples in common. 3. (*Of types*) Having no value in common. *Note:* Distinct types are always disjoint, except possibly if inheritance is supported (see Part II of this dictionary). *Contrast* overlapping.

disjoint INSERT   Loosely, an operator, D_INSERT (shorthand for a certain relational assignment), that inserts specified tuples into a specified relvar, just so long as the tuples in question don't already appear in that relvar. The syntax is:

```
D_INSERT R rx
```

Here *R* is a relvar reference (syntactically, just a relvar name) and *rx* is a relational expression (denoting some relation *r* of the same type as *R*), and the effect is to insert the tuples of *r* into *R*, just so long as none of those tuples is already present in *R*. In other words, the D_INSERT invocation just shown is shorthand for the following explicit assignment:

```
R := R D_UNION rx
```

It follows that an attempt via D_INSERT to insert a tuple that's already present is an error (*contrast* INSERT).
   Example: The statement

```
D_INSERT SP RELATION
             { TUPLE { SNO SNO('S3') , PNO PNO('P1') , QTY QTY(150) } ,
               TUPLE { SNO SNO('S4') , PNO PNO('P5') , QTY QTY(400) } } ;
```

is shorthand for the following relational assignment statement:

```
SP := SP D_UNION RELATION
             { TUPLE { SNO SNO('S3') , PNO PNO('P1') , QTY QTY(150) } ,
               TUPLE { SNO SNO('S4') , PNO PNO('P5') , QTY QTY(400) } } ;
```

Given the sample values shown in Fig. 1, this assignment will fail—more precisely, the implicit D_UNION invocation will fail—and no updating will be done, because the tuple <S4,P5,400> already appears in relvar SP.

disjoint union   A variant on the relational union operator, q.v., in which the operand relations are required to be disjoint, q.v. In other words, if (a) relations *r1* and *r2* are of the same type *T*, and (b) they have no tuples in common, then (and only then) the expression *r1* D_UNION *r2* denotes the disjoint union of *r1* and *r2*, and it reduces to *r1* UNION *r2*. *Note:* An *n*-adic version of this operator could also be defined (and is so, in **Tutorial D**). Note too that a version of the operator could be defined to apply to sets in general as well as to relations in particular; in fact, elsewhere in this dictionary, such an operator is indeed assumed to exist. Note finally that disjoint union can also be used as an aggregate operator, q.v. *Contrast* discriminated union.
   Example: Consider the expression S{CITY} D_UNION P{CITY}. If the current values of relvars S and P are as shown in Fig. 1, this expression will raise a run-time error, because some supplier cities are also part cities. If such were not the case, however, the expression would then be logically equivalent to S{CITY} UNION P{CITY}.

disjunct   A predicate that's ORed with zero or more others.

disjunction   1. (*Dyadic case*) If and only if p and q are predicates, their disjunction (p) OR (q) is a predicate also. Let (ip) OR (iq) be an invocation of that predicate, where ip and iq are invocations of p and q, respectively. Then that invocation (ip) OR (iq) evaluates to TRUE if and only if at least one of ip and iq evaluates to TRUE. *Note:* The parentheses enclosing p and q in the predicate, and ip and iq in the invocation, might not be needed in practice. 2. (*N-adic case*) Let $p1, p2, ..., pn$ ($n \geq 0$) be predicates; then (and only then) the disjunction OR $\{p1,p2,...,pn\}$ is defined to be shorthand for the expression $(p1)$ OR $(p2)$ OR ... OR (pn). (Note that this expression evaluates to FALSE if $n = 0$, because FALSE is the identity with respect to OR.) *See also* **existential quantifier**.

disjunctive normal form   A predicate is in disjunctive normal form, DNF, if and only if it's of the form $(p1)$ OR $(p2)$ OR ... OR (pn), where none of the disjuncts $(p1)$, $(p2)$, ..., (pn) involves any ORs—more precisely, where each of $p1, p2, ..., pn$ is a conjunction of literals (*see* **literal**, second definition).

DISTINCT   *See* SELECT expression.

distinct type (SQL)   *See* **user defined type (SQL)**.

distributivity   1. (*Monadic over dyadic*) Let operators $Op1$ and $Op2$ be monadic and dyadic, respectively, and assume for definiteness that they're expressed in prefix and infix style, respectively. Then $Op1$ distributes over $Op2$ if and only if, for all x and y, $Op1(x\ Op2\ y) = (Op1(x))\ Op2\ (Op1(y))$. 2. (*Dyadic over dyadic*) Let operators $Op1$ and $Op2$ both be dyadic, and assume for definiteness that they're expressed in infix style. Then $Op1$ distributes over $Op2$ if and only if, for all x, y, and z, $x\ Op1\ (y\ Op2\ z) = (x\ Op1\ y)\ Op2\ (x\ Op1\ z)$.

   Examples: 1. (*Monadic over dyadic*) In ordinary arithmetic, nonnegative square root ("$\sqrt{\ }$") distributes over multiplication ("*"), because

$$\sqrt{\ } (x * y) = (\sqrt{\ } x) * (\sqrt{\ } y)$$

for all x and y. (By contrast, "$\sqrt{\ }$" does not distribute over "+".) In the same kind of way, restriction distributes over UNION, INTERSECT, and MINUS in relational algebra. 2. (*Dyadic over dyadic*) In ordinary arithmetic, multiplication ("*") distributes over addition ("+"), because

$$x * (y + z) = (x * y) + (x * z)$$

for all x, y, and z. (By contrast, "+" does not distribute over "*".) In the same kind of way, each of UNION and INTERSECT distributes over the other in relational algebra. Likewise, each of OR and AND distributes over the other in logic.

DIVIDEBY *See* Great Divide; Small Divide; *see also* division.

division Over the years several logically distinct relational division operators (i.e., operators that "divide" one relation by another) have been defined—so many, in fact, that it's probably better not to use the term at all, or at least to state explicitly in any given context which particular operator is intended. Two such operators are defined in this dictionary, the Great Divide and the Small Divide, q.v. *Note:* **Tutorial D** does currently support both of these operators, but they're in the process of being dropped, since (as is shown under **Great Divide** and **Small Divide**) their functionality can be obtained by a variety of other, and psychologically preferable, means.

DK/NF Domain-key normal form.

DNF Disjunctive normal form.

domain Type. *Note:* Earlier relational writings favored the term *domain*; more recent ones favor the term *type* instead.

domain (mathematics) *See* function; relation (mathematics).

domain calculus A form of relational calculus in which the range variables range over domains (i.e., types) instead of relations and thus denote values from those domains. *Note:* Domain calculus and tuple calculus, q.v., are expressively equivalent, because for every expression of the former there's a logically equivalent expression of the latter and vice versa. In fact, they're both relationally complete, q.v.

Example: Here's a domain calculus formulation of the query "Get supplier names for suppliers who supply at least one part" (*see* **tuple calculus** for a tuple calculus analog):

```
NX RANGES OVER { NAME } ;
SX RANGES OVER { SNO } ;
PX RANGES OVER { PNO } ;

{ NX } WHERE EXISTS SX ( EXISTS PX ( S { SNO SX , SNAME NX } AND
                                     SP { SNO SX , PNO PX } ) )
```

In stilted English: "Get names NX where there exist a supplier number SX and a part number PX such that a tuple with supplier number SX and supplier name NX appears in relvar S and a tuple with the same supplier number SX and part number PX appears in relvar SP." As you can see, this particular example is somewhat clumsier than its tuple calculus counterpart (*see* **tuple calculus**), but there are cases where the reverse is true.

domain check override An ad hoc and logically flawed—and therefore deprecated— mechanism for performing comparisons between values of different types. (It's flawed because it's based on a confusion over the logical difference between types and representations.)

domain constraint *See* domain-key normal form.

domain-key normal form The "ultimate" normal form, in the following special (and limited) sense: Relvar *R* is in domain-key normal form (DK/NF) if and only if *every single-relvar constraint* that holds in *R* is implied by the domain and key constraints that hold in *R*, where (a) the phrase "every single-relvar constraint" includes but isn't limited to FDs and JDs, q.v., in particular, and (b) a "domain constraint" in this context is a constraint to the effect that values of a given attribute are taken from some prescribed set of values—for example, a constraint on relvar S to the effect that STATUS values must be in the range 1-100 inclusive. Every DK/NF relvar is in 5NF, though not necessarily in 6NF. *Note:* A relvar in DK/NF is guaranteed to be free of insertion and deletion anomalies as defined elsewhere in this dictionary; however, the concept is mainly of academic interest, because relvars can easily be fully normalized—i.e., in 5NF or even 6NF—and still not be in DK/NF. In other words, DK/NF isn't always achievable. What's more, the question "Exactly when can it be achieved?" has still not been answered.

    Example: As noted under **Boyce/Codd normal form**, with the normal forms it's often more instructive to show a counterexample rather than an example per se. Suppose, therefore, that shipments are subject to a constraint to the effect that odd numbered parts can be supplied only by odd numbered suppliers and even numbered parts only by even numbered suppliers. (This example is very contrived, of course, but it suffices for the purpose at hand.) Then that constraint is clearly not implied by the domain and key constraints that hold in relvar SP, and so the relvar isn't in DK/NF; yet it's certainly in 6NF.

domain of discourse Same as universe of discourse.

domain relational calculus Domain calculus, q.v.

dot qualification In tuple calculus and languages based on it, a dot qualified name is an expression of the form *R.A*, where *R* is the name of a range variable and *A* is the name of an attribute of the relation *r* over which *R* ranges. Such an expression serves as an attribute reference, q.v.; it denotes the value of attribute *A* (or possibly attribute *A* as such) within the particular tuple of *r* to which *R* currently refers. Dot qualification is used for disambiguation purposes in tuple calculus—also in SQL—but not in domain calculus or relational algebra (these latter use attribute (re)naming and/or name scoping to achieve an equivalent effect). *Note:* Since it's directly based on relational algebra, **Tutorial D** in particular has no dot qualification.

    Example: The following tuple calculus formulation of the query "Get suppliers who supply at least one part" makes use of two dot qualified names, SPX.SNO and SX.SNO:

```
SX  RANGES OVER { S } ;
SPX RANGES OVER { SP } ;

{ SX } WHERE EXISTS SPX ( SPX.SNO = SX.SNO )
```

Here for comparison is a relational algebra (**Tutorial D**) formulation of the same query:

```
S MATCHING SP
```

The "matching" here is done on the basis of attribute SNO (since that attribute is the only one common to relvars S and SP). *See* semijoin.

double arrow   *See* multivalued dependency.

double arrow out of   An MVD of the form $A \rightarrow\rightarrow B$ is sometimes referred to, informally, as "a double arrow out of A" (or, even more informally, as a double arrow out of the attributes constituting A—especially if A is of degree one).

double bang   Same as bang bang.

double negation   (*Logic*) Same as involution.

double underlining   A convention used in pictures like Fig. 1 for indicating or highlighting primary key attributes. To elaborate, there are two cases to consider: (a) The relation depicted is a sample value for some relvar R (this case is illustrated by Fig. 1); (b) the relation depicted is a sample value for some relational expression rx, where rx is something other than a simple relvar reference (i.e., just the pertinent relvar name, syntactically speaking). In the first case, double underlining simply indicates that a primary key PK has been declared for R and the pertinent attribute is part of PK. In the second case, rx can be thought of as the defining expression for some temporary relvar R (equivalently, it can be thought of as a view defining expression and R as the corresponding view); then double underlining indicates that a primary key PK could in principle be declared for R and the pertinent attribute is part of PK.

DRC   Domain relational calculus.

drop   *See* data definition operator.

dual   1. (*Logic*) The duals of AND, OR, TRUE, and FALSE are OR, AND, FALSE, and TRUE, respectively (NOT is its own dual). More generally, let *exp* be a logical expression involving no connectives other than NOT, AND, and OR, and let *exp'* be obtained from *exp* by replacing every occurrence of AND, OR, TRUE, and FALSE by its dual; then *exp* and *exp'* are duals of each other. *Note:* Since every logical expression is logically equivalent to one involving no connectives other than NOT, AND, and OR, it follows that every logical expression has a dual. Note too that logical expressions *exp1* and *exp2* are logically equivalent if and only if their duals *exp1'* and *exp2'* are logically equivalent. 2. (*Set theory*) The duals of intersection, union, the universal set, and the empty set are union, intersection, the empty set, and the universal set, respectively (complement is its own dual). More generally, let *exp* be a set theory expression involving no operators other than complement, intersection, and union, and let *exp'* be obtained from *exp* by replacing every occurrence of intersection, union, the universal set, and the empty set by its dual; then *exp* and *exp'* are duals of each other. *Note:* Since every set theory expression is logically equivalent to one involving no operators other than complement, intersection, and union, it follows that every set theory expression has a dual. Note too that set theory expressions *exp1* and *exp2* are logically equivalent if and only if their duals *exp1'* and *exp2'* are logically equivalent. *See also Duality Principle.*

dual mode principle   The principle that any relational operation that can be invoked interactively can also be invoked from an application program and vice versa.

Duality Principle   1. (*Logic*) Let *exp* be a tautology of the form $p \equiv q$, and let *exp'* be obtained from *exp* by replacing every appearance of AND, OR, TRUE, and FALSE by its dual, q.v.; then *exp'* is a tautology. 2. (*Set theory*) Let *exp* be a theorem of the form $p = q$, and let *exp'* be obtained from *exp* by replacing every appearance of intersection, union, the universal set, and the empty set by its dual, q.v.; then *exp'* is a theorem.

Examples: Each of De Morgan's Laws (q.v.) is a tautology, and each is the dual of the other.

DUM   Shorthand for TABLE_DUM.

duplicate   Let *a* and *a'* be appearances (q.v.) in some context of values *v* and *v'*, respectively. Then *a* and *a'* are duplicates of each other if and only if *v* and *v'* are equal (in other words, if and only if *v* and *v'* are the very same value). *Note:* It should be clear from this definition that the well known dictum to the effect that no relation ever contains duplicate tuples really means no relation ever contains duplicate *appearances* of the *same* tuple—though we stay with the less precise formulation elsewhere in this dictionary (for the most part, at any rate), for reasons of familiarity. Observe that since (a) relations never contain duplicate tuples and (b) every relational operation yields a relation, the DBMS is required to eliminate redundant duplicate tuples—meaning, more precisely, redundant appearances of the same tuple—from the result of any such operation, if such duplicates would otherwise appear (i.e., as artifacts of the algorithm used to implement the operation in question).

Examples (duplicate elimination): Given the sample values shown in Fig. 1, the projection on {CITY} of the current value of relvar S has cardinality three, not five; similarly, the union of (a) the projection on {CITY} of the current value of relvar S and (b) the projection on {CITY} of the current value of relvar P has cardinality four, not eleven. (Note that projection and union are the only relational operators defined in this part of the dictionary for which duplicate elimination is a consideration.)

duplicate elimination   Term used ubiquitously to mean what would more accurately be called duplication elimination. *See* duplicate.

dyadic   Of an operator, having exactly two operands; of a predicate, being defined in terms of exactly two parameters. *Contrast* binary.

———— ♦ ♦ ♦ ♦ ♦ ————

E/R   Entity/relationship.

E/R diagram   *See* entity/relationship diagram.

E/R model   *See* entity/relationship model.

E/R modeling   *See* entity/relationship modeling.

E-relation / E-relvar   *See* RM/T.

EKNF   Elementary key normal form.

element   *See* bag; set.

elementary key   Let K be a subset of the heading of relvar R. Then K is an elementary key for, or of, relvar R if and only if (a) it's a key for R and (b) there exists some subset A of the heading of R such that the FD $K \rightarrow A$ is nontrivial and irreducible. *See* elementary key normal form.
    Examples: 1. Suppose relvar SP has, instead of the usual QTY attribute, an attribute CITY, representing the city of the applicable supplier. The sole key of this revised version of SP is still {SNO,PNO}; however, it's not an elementary key, because the only nontrivial FD that holds with that key as determinant is {SNO,PNO} $\rightarrow$ {CITY}, which isn't irreducible (because the FD {SNO} $\rightarrow$ {CITY} also holds). 2. Suppose now that relvar SP has an attribute CITY (supplier city) as well as—not instead of—the usual QTY attribute. The sole key is still {SNO,PNO}. Now, however, that key is elementary, because the FD {SNO,PNO} $\rightarrow$ {QTY}, which certainly holds, is both nontrivial and irreducible.

elementary key normal form   Relvar R is in elementary key normal form (EKNF) if and only if, for every nontrivial FD $X \rightarrow Y$ that holds in R, (a) X is a superkey or (b) Y is a subkey of some elementary key (q.v.). Every EKNF relvar is in 3NF.
    Example: As noted under Boyce/Codd normal form, with the normal forms it's often more instructive to show a counterexample rather than an example per se. Suppose, therefore, that relvar SP has, instead of the usual QTY attribute, an attribute SNAME, representing the name of the applicable supplier; suppose also that supplier names are necessarily unique (i.e., no two

distinct suppliers ever have the same name at the same time). Then this revised version of SP has two keys, {SNO,PNO} and {SNAME,PNO}. However, these keys aren't elementary keys, because the only nontrivial FDs that hold with one of these keys as determinant are {SNO,PNO} → {SNAME} and {SNAME,PNO} → {SNO}, and these FDs are both reducible (in both cases PNO can be dropped from the determinant without loss). So the relvar is subject to two nontrivial FDs, {SNO} → {SNAME} and {SNAME} → {SNO}, in which the determinant isn't a superkey and the dependant isn't a subkey of an elementary key. So this version of relvar SP isn't in EKNF (though it is in 3NF).

embedded dependency   A dependency that's satisfied by some projection of some relation but not by the relation itself, or—more important—a dependency that holds in some projection of some relvar but not in the relvar itself. *Note:* If *F* is an FD that holds in some projection of relvar *R*, then *F* certainly holds in *R* itself; thus, embedded dependencies aren't FDs, by definition.

   Example: Consider relvar CTXD, with attributes C (course), T (teacher), X (textbook), and D (days) and predicate *Teacher T spends D days with textbook X on course C*. Let the sole key for that relvar be {C,T,X}. Assume also that for a given course, the set of teachers and the set of textbooks are quite independent of each other. Then CTXD is in 6NF—it can't be nonloss decomposed at all, other than trivially—but its projection on {C,T,X} is subject to the embedded multivalued dependencies {C} →→ {T} and {C} →→ {X}.

empty   (*Of a bag or set*) Having no elements.

empty bag   The bag with no elements (note that there's exactly one such); written { } or $\varnothing$. *Note:* Of course, the empty bag and the empty set, q.v., are logically indistinguishable—though if B and S are variables of some bag type and some set type, respectively, they won't "compare equal" even if their values are the empty bag and the empty set, respectively. (In fact, of course, such a comparison wouldn't even be syntactically legal, precisely because the comparands are of different types.)

empty database   1. A database containing only empty relvars. 2. A database containing no relvars at all. (Of course, the second definition here is just a special case—but an important special case—of the first.)

empty foreign key   A foreign key of degree zero. Note that the corresponding target key will necessarily be of degree zero also (*see* **empty key**), and the pertinent referential constraint—from relvar *R2* to relvar *R1*, say—will therefore be satisfied if and only if either *R1* is nonempty or *R2* is empty or both. *Note:* Either or both of *R1* and *R2* here might in fact be "hypothetical views," in the sense of that term explained under, e.g., **foreign key constraint**.

empty heading   The heading of degree zero (note that there's exactly one such).

empty key A key of degree zero. Note that a relvar with an empty key can't have any other keys apart from the empty one, thanks to the key irreducibility requirement, q.v. Note too that such a relvar can't contain more than one tuple, thanks to the key uniqueness requirement, q.v. Declaring relvar *R* to have an empty key is thus a convenient way of stating a cardinality constraint, q.v., to the effect that *R* must never contain more than one tuple.

empty possrep A possrep with no components. If type *T* has an empty possrep, then (a) *T* can't have any possreps apart from that empty one; (b) the associated set of THE_ operators is also empty, a fortiori; (c) *T* has exactly one value, *v* say; (d) *T* has exactly one associated—and necessarily niladic—selector operator, *S* say; and (e) the sole legal invocation of *S*, viz., *S* ( ), returns that value *v*.

empty range *See* existential quantifier; UNIQUE; universal quantifier.

empty relation Slightly imprecise term used to refer to a relation with an empty body. Given a relation type *T*, there's exactly one empty relation of that type: viz., the relation of type *T* that contains no tuples at all. Note that two relations can both be empty and yet not equal; to be specific, they'll be equal if and only if they're of the same type. *Contrast* universal relation.
    Example: Suppose relvars S and P are both currently empty; that is, their current values *s* and *p* are both empty relations. Then *s* and *p* aren't equal, even though their bodies are equal, precisely because they're of different types (equivalently, because their headings aren't equal).

empty relvar A relvar whose current value is an empty relation.

empty restriction A restriction of a given relation *r* that contains no tuples (i.e., is equal to *r* WHERE FALSE); especially, a restriction of the form *r* WHERE *c*, where *c* is a contradiction, q.v. *Note:* The term is also used of a relvar.
    Examples: Given the sample values in Fig. 1, the expressions S WHERE STATUS = 25 and S WHERE STATUS ≠ STATUS both denote empty restrictions (the second necessarily so, because STATUS ≠ STATUS is a contradiction).

empty set The set with no elements (note that there's exactly one such); written { } or ∅. The empty set is a subset of every set. All theorems, properties, definitions, etc., that apply to sets in general apply to the empty set in particular; for example, relation headings and bodies are both defined to be sets (of attributes and tuples, respectively), and so each is allowed to be the empty set in particular. *See* nullology.

empty tuple The tuple of degree zero (note that there's exactly one such).

empty type (*Without inheritance*) A type with no values. This concept is of crucial importance if type inheritance is supported—see Part II of this dictionary—but perhaps not otherwise.

encapsulated Scalar—though it's not always obvious from the literature (especially the OO literature) that *scalar* is indeed what the term means. For example, here's a typical definition (it's taken from James Martin and James J. Odell, *Object-Oriented Methods: A Foundation*, Prentice-Hall, 1998):

> [Encapsulation is a] protective encasement that permits access to an object's data only via specifically assigned operations. With encapsulation, an object's interface is stated in terms of its permissible operations. All other implementation details about the object are hidden from the user. This is why the term encapsulation is often used interchangeably with *information hiding*.

And here's another (this one is from Douglas K. Barry, *The Object Database Handbook: How to Select, Implement, and Use Object-Oriented Databases*, Wiley Publishing, 1996):

> [Encapsulation is] the separation of the external aspects of an object from the object's internal implementation.

As you can see, the emphasis in both of these definitions is on what the conventional database literature would call data independence, q.v. (physical data independence, to be specific). But such data independence is intrinsic to the very notion of scalar data, so it's not clear why there's so much emphasis—at least in some circles—on the concept of encapsulation as such.

Note: The term *encapsulated* is also used, especially in OO contexts, to refer to the physical bundling, or packaging together, of code and data (or operator definitions and data representation definitions, to be a little more precise about the matter). But to use the term in this way is to mix model and implementation considerations; the user shouldn't care, and shouldn't need to care, whether code and data are physically bundled together or not.

entity A thing. *Note:* It's frequently suggested that there should be a one to one correspondence between "entities of interest" and tuples in base relvars. The suggestion is hard to sustain, however, given that the term *entities of interest* has no precise definition. (Of course, the same is true of the term *entity* itself, come to that.)

entity integrity A rule, articulated in certain of Codd's writings, to the effect that attributes of primary keys in base relvars don't allow nulls. However, since (a) relvars, base or otherwise, don't necessarily have to have primary keys at all (*see* primary key) and (b) rules that apply to base relvars but not to other kinds are more than a little suspect anyway (because they violate *The Principle of Interchangeability*, q.v.), the entity integrity rule could be, and in fact has been, dropped without serious loss. We mention it here mainly for historical reasons. In any case, it refers to a concept, null, that is totally incompatible with the relational model; it would thus require major revision anyway before any suggestion that it be kept could be seriously entertained.

entity modeling   *See* semantic modeling.

entity/relationship diagram   A picture intended to explicate the logical or conceptual design of a given database at a level of abstraction in which many details—in particular, details of the underlying types and almost all integrity constraints—are omitted. (The most important constraints not omitted are, typically, key and foreign key constraints.) Such pictures can be helpful in connection with the design process, but they're certainly not, as some people seem to think, a total solution to the design problem.

entity/relationship model   A set of conventions for drawing entity/relationship diagrams, q.v. *Note:* Actually, there's no consensus on exactly what the entity/relationship model consists of—different writers define it in different ways. Thus, the term is best thought of as referring to a family of similar but distinct schemes.

entity/relationship modeling   Using some form of entity/relationship model, q.v., as a tool to assist in the database design process.

enumerated type   A type whose definition specifies the legal values of the type by simply enumerating or listing them.
   Example: Here's a **Tutorial D** definition for a type called WEEKDAY (irrelevant details omitted):

```
TYPE WEEKDAY POSSREP
   { WD CHAR CONSTRAINT WD ∈
      { 'Sun' , 'Mon' , 'Tue' , 'Wed' , 'Thu' , 'Fri' , 'Sat' } } ;
```

EQ   Same as EQUIV.

EQD   Equality dependency.

equality   (*Without inheritance*) A truth valued or logical operator ("="). Two values are equal if and only if they're the very same value; that is, the comparison $v1 = v2$ (where $v1$ and $v2$ are values) evaluates to TRUE if and only if $v1$ and $v2$ are in fact the very same value. For example, the integer 3 is equal to the integer 3 and not the integer 4 or any other integer (and not to anything else either, for that matter). Note that it follows from this definition that if $v1 = v2$ evaluates to TRUE, then $v1$ and $v2$ must be of the same type T. It also follows that if (a) there exists an operator Op (other than "=" itself) with a parameter P such that (b) two successful invocations of Op—invocations that are identical in all respects except that the argument corresponding to P is the value $v1$ in one invocation and the value $v2$ in the other—are distinguishable in their effect, then (c) *v1* = *v2* must evaluate to FALSE. *Note:* The equality operator (which is defined for every type, necessarily) is also known, especially in logic contexts, as *identity*. *See also* bag membership; duplicate; equivalence; identity; overloading; set membership; relation equality; tuple equality; and elsewhere.

equality dependency An expression of the form *rx* = *ry*, where *rx* and *ry* are relational expressions of the same type; it can be read as "The relations denoted by *rx* and *ry* are equal" (in other words, they're one and the same relation). An important special case is as follows: Let *R1* and *R2* be relvars, not necessarily distinct. Let *X1* and *X2* be subsets of the heading of *R1* and the heading of *R2*, respectively, such that there exists a possibly empty set of attribute renamings on *R1* that maps *X1* into *X1'*, say, where *X1'* and *X2* contain exactly the same attributes (in other words, *X1'* and *X2* are in fact one and the same). Further, let *R1* and *R2* be subject to the constraint that, at all times, (a) every tuple *t1* in *R1* has an *X1'* value that's the *X2* value for at least one tuple *t2* in *R2* at the time in question, and (b) every tuple *t2* in *R2* has an *X2* value that's the *X1'* value for at least one tuple *t1* in *R1* at the time in question. Then that constraint is an equality dependency (EQD for short)—very loosely, an EQD "on" *R1* and *R2*. *Note:* EQDs shouldn't be confused with equality generating dependencies, q.v.; in fact, they're a special case of inclusion dependencies, q.v.

Example: Suppose the suppliers-and-parts database is subject to a constraint to the effect that every part must be supplied by at least one supplier:

```
CONSTRAINT EQDX P { PNO } = SP { PNO } ;
/* every part must be supplied */
```

This constraint is an EQD "on" relvars P and SP (and it's satisfied by the sample values shown in Fig. 1).

Note: The comparands in an EQD can be specified by means of arbitrarily complex expressions. As a consequence, all possible database constraints (in the more formal sense of that term, q.v.) can in fact be expressed as equality dependencies! To elaborate, let *C* be such a constraint; let *s* be a set of tuples (all of the same type) that together violate *C*; let *r* be the relation whose body is *s*; and let *rx* be a relational expression denoting *r*. Then *r* must be empty, and *C* must thus conceptually be of the form IS_EMPTY (*rx*). But IS_EMPTY (*rx*) is logically equivalent to each of the following expressions—

```
rx { } = TABLE_DUM

rx = rx WHERE FALSE
```

—and each of these expressions is an EQD. (The subexpression *rx*{ } in the first of these equivalent expressions denotes the projection of relation *r* on the empty set of attributes. Such a projection evaluates, necessarily, either to TABLE_DEE, if *r* is nonempty, or to TABLE_DUM otherwise.)

equality generating dependency   An expression of the form *{t1,t2,...,tn} / a = b*; it can be read as "If tuples *t1, t2, ..., tn* appear (in some given relvar at some given time), then *a* and *b* must be equal." Tuples *t1, t2, ..., tn* are the premises of the dependency and *a = b* is the conclusion. Observe that FDs in particular are equality generating dependencies—not the only possible kind, but the only kind considered in this dictionary—because they take the basic form "If certain tuples appear (in some given relvar at some given time), then certain attributes within those tuples must have equal values." *Note:* Equality generating dependencies should not be confused with equality dependencies, q.v. *Contrast* **tuple generating dependency**.

equijoin   A theta join, q.v., in which theta is "=".
    Example: The following expression represents the equijoin of suppliers and parts on cities:

```
( ( S RENAME { CITY AS SC } )
        TIMES
            ( P RENAME { CITY AS PC } ) ) WHERE SC = PC
```

Observe the need to rename at least one of the two CITY attributes before we can apply the operator TIMES, q.v. (the example renames them both, for symmetry).
    Note: The result of an equijoin necessarily has two attributes—SC and PC, in the example—whose values are equal in every tuple. If one of those two attributes is projected away and the other then renamed back to CITY, the result is the natural join (q.v.) of suppliers and parts (so natural join can be defined in terms of cartesian product, restriction, projection, and renaming).

EQUIV   1. A connective, q.v. 2. An aggregate operator, q.v. *Note:* In practice, the equivalence connective is often represented by the symbol "≡". For further explanation, *see* **equivalence** (sixth and seventh definitions). *Contrast* **XOR**.

equivalence   1. (*General*) Let *x* and *y* be elements of some set, and let that set be partitioned into a set of equivalence classes, q.v. Then *x* and *y* are equivalent (in symbols, $x \equiv y$) if and only if they're members of the same equivalence class. 2. (*Logical*) *See* **logical equivalence**. 3. (*Truth functional*) *See* **truth functional equivalence**. 4. (*Information*) *See* **information equivalence**. 5. (*Sets of FDs*) Two sets of FDs are equivalent if and only if each is a cover for the other. *Note:* Any given set of FDs always has at least one equivalent set that's irreducible. *See* **irreducible**, fourth definition. 6. (*Connective, dyadic case*) If and only if *p* and *q* are predicates, the equivalence (*p*) EQUIV (*q*) is a predicate also. Let (*ip*) EQUIV (*iq*) be an invocation of that predicate, where *ip* and *iq* are invocations of *p* and *q*, respectively. Then that invocation (*ip*) EQUIV (*iq*) evaluates to TRUE if and only if *ip* and *iq* both evaluate to TRUE or both evaluate to FALSE. In other words, (*p*) EQUIV (*q*) is equivalent to ((*p*) IMPLIES (*q*)) AND ((*q*) IMPLIES (*p*)). It's also equivalent to NOT ((*p*) XOR (*q*)). *Note:* The parentheses enclosing *p* and *q* in the predicate, and *ip* and *iq* in the invocation, might not be needed in practice. For further discussion, see **truth functional equivalence**; *contrast* **logical equivalence**.

7. (*Connective, n-adic case*) Let *p1, p2, ..., pn* (*n* ≥ 0) be predicates. Then (and only then) the equivalence EQUIV {*p1,p2,...,pn*} is a predicate also; and if *ip1, ip2, ..., ipn* are invocations of *p1, p2, ..., pn*, respectively, then the invocation EQUIV {*ip1,ip2,...,ipn*} returns TRUE if and only if exactly *m* of the invocations *ip1, ip2, ..., ipn* return FALSE, where *m* is even. *Caveat:* This definition is motivated by a desire to preserve associativity; to be specific, it has the property that the expressions EQUIV {*p1*,EQUIV {*p2,p3*}}, EQUIV {EQUIV {*p1,p2*},*p3*}, and EQUIV {*p1,p2,p3*} are all truth functionally equivalent. On the other hand, it also has the property that EQUIV {*p1,p2,p3*} and NOT (XOR {*p1,p2,p3*}), as this latter expression is defined in this dictionary, are *not* truth functionally equivalent. It would be possible to come up with a different and possibly more intuitive definition, according to which the invocation EQUIV {*ip1,ip2,...,ipn*} returns TRUE if and only if all *n* of the invocations *ip1, ip2, ..., ipn* return the same truth value. However, the two definitions are themselves clearly not equivalent (!); in other words, they define two logically distinct operators (though they both reduce to the simple dyadic case if *n* = 2, as is surely to be desired).

equivalence class A subset *s'* of some given set *s* with the property that the elements of *s'* are (a) all equivalent to one another, under some stated definition of equivalence, and (b) not equivalent to any other element of *s*, under that same definition of equivalence. (Note the relevance of this concept to the relational grouping operation, q.v.; *see also* image relation.) Observe that (a) equivalence classes are pairwise disjoint, and (b) together, they partition the values in the given set *s*. For a more formal definition, *see* equivalence relation. *See also* canonical form.

   Examples: 1. Let *s* be the set of all positive integers, and define positive integers *x* and *y* to be equivalent if and only if they have the same number of digits in conventional decimal notation (no leading zeros). Then the subset of *s* containing all one-digit integers is an equivalence class under this definition of equivalence; so too are the subsets consisting of all two-digit integers, all three-digit integers, and so on. 2. Consider the set of parts currently represented by relvar P. Define two such parts to be equivalent if and only if they're of the same color. Then the set of all red parts currently represented in P is an equivalence class under this definition of equivalence; so too is the set of all blue parts, and so is the set of all yellow parts, and so on. 3. Consider the set of tuples in the current value of relvar SP. Define two such tuples to be equivalent if and only if they contain the same SNO value. Then the set of all such tuples for supplier number S1 is an equivalence class under this definition of equivalence; so too is the set of all such tuples for supplier S2, and so is the set of all such tuples for supplier S3, and so on.

equivalence relation Let *r* be a binary relation. Then *r* is an equivalence relation if and only if it's reflexive (q.v.), symmetric (q.v.), and transitive (q.v.). Further, let *x* be a value such that the tuple <*x,y*> appears in *r* for some *y*. Given that value *x*, then, the set of all such corresponding values *y* is an equivalence class with respect to *r*—namely, that specific equivalence class that corresponds to the given value *x* (*see* equivalence class). Observe that if *ry* is the set of all *y* values appearing in *r*, then every value in *ry* appears in exactly one equivalence class with respect to *r*—in other words, as noted under **equivalence class**, equivalence classes are pairwise disjoint, and together they partition the pertinent set of values.

essential tuple   Tuple *t* is essential in relation *r* if and only if it's not redundant in *r*. *Contrast* redundant tuple.

essential tuple normal form   Relvar *R* is in essential tuple normal form (ETNF) if and only if every relation *r* that's a legitimate value for *R* is such that every tuple is essential in *r*—equivalently, if and only if (a) *R* is in BCNF and (b) for every JD *J* that holds in *R*, at least one component of *J* is a superkey for *R*. Every ETNF relvar is in 4NF. Also, it's easy to see that if relvar *R* is in BCNF and has at least one simple key (q.v.), then it's in ETNF.

    Example: As noted under **Boyce/Codd normal form**, with the normal forms it's often more instructive to show a counterexample rather than an example per se. Consider, therefore, relvar SPJ, with attributes SNO (supplier number), PNO (part number), and JNO (project number), and predicate *Supplier SNO supplies part PNO to project JNO.* Let that relvar be all key (i.e., let no proper subset of the heading be a key). Let the relvar also be subject to the constraint that if (a) supplier *sno* supplies part *pno* and (b) part *pno* is supplied to project *jno* and (c) project *jno* is supplied by supplier *sno*, then (d) supplier *sno* supplies part *pno* to project *jno*. Then SPJ is equal to the join of its projections on {SNO,PNO}, {PNO,JNO}, and {JNO,SNO}—in other words, the join dependency

```
     ✪  { { SNO , PNO } , { PNO , JNO } , { JNO , SNO  } }
```

holds in SPJ—and so that relvar can be nonloss decomposed into those three projections. Since no component of that JD is a superkey (the sole superkey being the entire heading), relvar SPJ isn't in ETNF, though it is in 4NF.

    Note: The ETNF definition refers to "every JD that holds in *R*." In checking whether some relvar *R* is in fact in ETNF, however, it's easy to see that it's sufficient just to check those JDs that have been explicitly declared for *R*. In fact, it's sufficient just to check those JDs that have been explicitly declared for *R* and are irreducible (*see* irreducible JD).

essentiality   Let *DM* be a data model in the first sense of that term, q.v., and let *DS* be a data structure supported by *DM*. Let *dm* be a data model in the second sense of that term, constructed in accordance with the features provided by *DM*, and let *dm* include an occurrence *ds* of *DS*. Let *db* be a database conforming to *dm*. If removal from *db* of the data corresponding to *ds* would cause a loss of information from *db*, then *ds* is essential in *dm* (and, loosely, *DS* is essential in *DM*).

    Examples: 1. Consider a hierarchic analog of the suppliers-and-parts database, in which (a) suppliers are represented by records with fields SNO, SNAME, STATUS, and CITY, (b) shipments are represented by records with fields SNO, PNO, and QTY, and (c) there's a hierarchic "link" connecting each supplier record to the corresponding shipment records. (The "link" can be thought of as a pointer chain that starts at the pertinent supplier record, runs through all of the corresponding shipment records in some order, and finally connects back to the supplier record in question.) Then that link is inessential—there's no information that can be obtained from the database using it that can't alternatively be obtained without it. 2. Suppose the foregoing hierarchic design is modified in such a way as to remove the SNO field from the shipment records, while leaving everything else unchanged. Then the link is now essential (for without it, there's no way to tell which shipments correspond to which suppliers).

Note: Hierarchic and other nonrelational systems provide numerous different ways of representing data, any or all of which can be used "essentially"—links and pointers, record ordering, repeating groups, and so forth. By contrast, relational systems provide just one way (viz., relations themselves), and so relations themselves are the sole essential information carrier in relational systems. Now, if data model *DM* provides *n* distinct ways, essential or inessential, of representing information, then it's axiomatic that *DM* must also support *n* distinct sets of operators. However, there's nothing useful that can be done if *n* > 1 that can't be done if *n* = 1 (and *n* = 1 is the minimum, of course). And for the relational model, we do have *n* = 1; that is, the relational model supports just one data structure, the relation itself, and that data structure is clearly essential, since if it were removed that model would be incapable of representing anything at all. However, since the relational model is in fact capable of representing absolutely any data whatsoever, any data model that supports relations in some shape or form as well as some additional data structure *DS* must be such that either relations are inessential or *DS* is. But if relations are inessential, then *DS* must be effectively equivalent to relations anyway!—in which case it could be argued that it's really *DS* that's inessential, not relations. What's more, a data model that doesn't "support relations in some shape or form" is unlikely in the extreme; even SQL could be said to support relations if various SQL idiosyncrasies—nulls, anonymous columns, duplicate rows, etc.—are avoided. Thus, for example, pointers (object IDs), bags, lists, and arrays could all be removed from the so called object model without any loss of representational power. Indeed, the fact that they're not removed is prima facie evidence that "the object model" fails to distinguish properly between model and implementation issues.

ETNF Essential tuple normal form.

eventual consistency *See* consistency.

EVERY Keyword sometimes used as an alternative spelling for the aggregate operator AND (*see* aggregate operator).

example value (*Without inheritance*) Let *T* be a scalar type other than *omega* (see Part II of this dictionary). Then *The Third Manifesto* requires an example value of type *T* to be specified when *T* is defined, in order to ensure that *T* is nonempty. In the case of user defined types, **Tutorial D** uses the keyword INIT for this purpose, as here:

```
TYPE WEEKDAY ... INIT ( WEEKDAY('Sun') ) ;
```

Use of the keyword INIT here reflects an assumption that, in practice, otherwise uninitialized variables of type *T* will almost certainly be initialized to the example value defined for type *T*.

   Note: In type definitions elsewhere in this dictionary, example values would mostly just be a distraction and are therefore usually omitted.

EXCEPT   SQL analog of MINUS.

exclusive OR   1. (*Dyadic case*) If and only if *p* and *q* are predicates, their "exclusive OR" (*p*) XOR (*q*) is a predicate also. Let (*ip*) XOR (*iq*) be an invocation of that predicate, where *ip* and *iq* are invocations of *p* and *q*, respectively. Then that invocation (*ip*) XOR (*iq*) evaluates to TRUE if and only if exactly one of *ip* and *iq* evaluates to TRUE. In other words, (*p*) XOR (*q*) is equivalent to NOT((*p*) EQUIV (*q*)). *Note:* The parentheses enclosing *p* and *q* in the predicate, and *ip* and *iq* in the invocation, might not be needed in practice. 2. (*N-adic case*) Let *p1*, *p2*, ..., *pn* ($n \geq 0$) be predicates. Then (and only then) the "exclusive OR" XOR {*p1,p2,...,pn*} is a predicate also; and if *ip1*, *ip2*, ..., *ipn* are invocations of *p1*, *p2*, ..., *pn*, respectively, then the invocation XOR {*ip1,ip2,...,ipn*} returns TRUE if and only if exactly *m* of the invocations *ip1*, *ip2*, ..., *ipn* return TRUE, where *m* is odd. *Caveat:* This definition is motivated by a desire to preserve associativity; to be specific, it has the property that the expressions XOR {*p1*,XOR {*p2,p3*}}, XOR {XOR {*p1,p2*},*p3*}, and XOR {*p1,p2,p3*} are all truth functionally equivalent. On the other hand, it also has the property that XOR {*p1,p2,p3*} and NOT (EQUIV {*p1,p2,p3*}), as this latter expression is defined in this dictionary, are *not* truth functionally equivalent. It would be possible to come up with a different and possibly more intuitive definition, according to which the invocation XOR {*ip1,ip2,...,ipn*} returns TRUE if and only if exactly one of the invocations *ip1*, *ip2*, ..., *ipn* returns TRUE. However, the two definitions are themselves clearly not equivalent; in other words, they define two logically distinct operators (though they both reduce to the simple dyadic case if $n = 2$, as is surely to be desired).

exclusive union   1. (*Dyadic case*) Let relations *r1* and *r2* be of the same type *T*. Then (and only then) the expression *r1* XUNION *r2* denotes the exclusive union of *r1* and *r2*, and it returns the relation of type *T* with body the set of all tuples *t* such that *t* appears in exactly one of *r1* and *r2*. 2. (*N-adic case*) Let relations *r1*, *r2*, ..., *rn* ($n \geq 0$) all be of the same type *T*. Then (and only then) the expression XUNION {*r1,r2,...,rn*} denotes the exclusive union of *r1*, *r2*, ..., *rn*, and it returns the relation of type *T* with body the set of all tuples *t* such that *t* appears in exactly *m* of *r1*, *r2*, ..., *rn*, where *m* is odd (and possibly different for different tuples *t*). *Note:* If $n = 0$, (a) some syntactic mechanism, not shown here, is needed to specify the pertinent type *T* and (b) the result is the empty relation, q.v., of that type. Note too (a) that exclusive union (which is also known as symmetric difference) is to exclusive OR as union is to inclusive OR, and (b) that the relational exclusive union operator differs in certain respects from the mathematical or set theory operator of the same name, q.v. Note finally that exclusive union can also be used as an aggregate operator, q.v.

Example: The expression S{CITY} XUNION P{CITY} denotes the exclusive union of the projections on {CITY} of the relations that are the current values of relvars S and P. That exclusive union is a relation *r* of type RELATION {CITY CHAR}. Moreover, if the current values of relvars S and P are *s* and *p*, respectively, the body of that relation *r* consists of all tuples of the form <*c*> that appear in either *s*{CITY} or *p*{CITY} but not both—meaning *c* is either a current supplier city that's not a current part city or vice versa. Note that the expression S{CITY} XUNION P{CITY} is logically equivalent to the expression (S{CITY} MINUS P{CITY}) UNION (P{CITY} MINUS S{CITY}).

exclusive union (bag theory) *See* bag.

exclusive union (set theory) The set of all elements appearing in either but not both of two given sets. *Note:* The foregoing definition could be extended to apply to any number of sets, thus: The exclusive union of sets *s1*, *s2*, ..., *sn* ($n \geq 0$) is the set of all values *v* such that *v* appears in exactly *m* of *s1*, *s2*, ..., *sn*, where *m* is odd (and possibly different for different values *v*).

existential quantifier Let *p(x)* be a predicate with a parameter *x*; then EXISTS *x* (*p(x)*) is a predicate, and it means "There exists at least one argument value *v* that can be substituted for the parameter *x* such that *p(v)* evaluates to TRUE." In this example, EXISTS *x* is an existential quantifier, and *x* is an existentially quantified bound variable, q.v. *Note:* Some writers refer to EXISTS by itself as the quantifier; the literature is not consistent on this point. More important, note that if *v1*, *v2*, ..., *vn* are all of the possible argument values in the foregoing example, then EXISTS *x* (*p(x)*) is defined to be shorthand for OR {(*p(v1)*), (*p(v2)*),...,(*p(vn)*)} (*see* disjunction, second definition). Observe in particular that this expression evaluates to FALSE if *n* = 0 (i.e., if the bound variable *x* has an empty range), because FALSE is the identity with respect to OR. Observe further that the expression EXISTS *x* (*p(x)*) is logically equivalent to the expression NOT (FORALL *x* (NOT (*p(x)*))). *See also* EXISTS; UNIQUE; *contrast* universal quantifier.
    Examples: See bound variable; domain calculus; free variable; tuple calculus; and elsewhere.

EXISTS *See* existential quantifier. *Note:* In the literature (but not in this dictionary), EXISTS is often represented by a backward E, thus: ∃. The keyword is also sometimes used as an alternative spelling for the aggregate operator OR (*see* aggregate operator). For example, the aggregate operator invocation OR (S,STATUS > 10), which means "At least one supplier has status greater than 10," might alternatively, and intuitively very reasonably, be written thus: EXISTS (S, STATUS > 10).

expanded cartesian product *See* cartesian product.

explicit dependency   A dependency—e.g., an FD or JD, or some more general constraint—that's explicitly declared for some relvar, and is thereby required to hold in that relvar. *Contrast* implicit dependency.

explicit dynamic variable   *See* instance.

expressible database   *See Principle of Database Relativity.*

expressible relation   Any relation that, given a particular set of relations, either is contained in that set or can be derived from those that are (*see* derived relation).

expressible relvar   Any relvar that, given a particular set of relvars, either is contained in that set or can be derived from those that are (*see* derived relvar).

expression   (*Without inheritance*) In a programming language, a read-only operator invocation; a construct that denotes a value; in effect, a rule for computing, or determining, the value in question. Every expression is of some type—namely, the type of the value it denotes. Literals (q.v.), constant references (q.v), and variable references (q.v.) are all considered to be read-only operator invocations and thus all constitute legal expressions. *See also* closed expression; open expression; *contrast* statement.
  Examples: X+Y is an expression; in fact, it's an invocation of the operator "+", and it denotes the value that's the sum of the current values of the variables X and Y. By contrast,

```
Z := X + Y ;
```

is a statement; it assigns the value denoted by the expression X+Y appearing on the right side to the variable Z referenced on the left side. *Note:* In both of the foregoing examples, X and Y are variable references and thus themselves constitute (sub)expressions in turn.

expression transformation   Transforming a given expression into another expression that's logically equivalent to the given expression and thus denotes the same value. The process applies to relational expressions in particular, where it's sometimes called "query rewrite." Query rewrite is typically done for performance reasons; it can be done either by the user or—much more important—by the system (*see* optimizer). *Note:* The term *query rewrite* is also used in certain commercial products with a somewhat more limited meaning. *Caveat lector.*
  Example: The relational expression (*r1* WHERE *bx1*) JOIN (*r2* WHERE *bx2*), where *r1* and *r2* are relations and *bx1* and *bx2* are restriction conditions, q.v., is logically equivalent to the relational expression (*r1* JOIN *r2*) WHERE (*bx1*) AND (*bx2*); therefore, either of these relational expressions can be transformed into the other. Transforming the second into the first is likely to be advantageous from a performance standpoint, because the first means doing the restrictions before the join; thus, it's likely that the input relations to the join will be smaller and the output

will be smaller too. In fact, this transformation could make the difference between keeping the result of the join in main memory and having to spill it out to secondary storage.

expressive completeness A database design is expressively complete if and only if it's capable of representing all facts about the real world that need to be represented.

Example: Consider the suppliers-and-parts database. That database is expressively complete (or let's agree so for the sake of the example, at least). Now suppose we were to replace relvars S and SP by their join (SSP, say). Then the resulting design wouldn't be expressively complete, because it would be incapable of representing information concerning suppliers (such as supplier S5 in Fig. 1) who currently supply no parts.

EXTEND *See* extension.

extended cartesian product *See* cartesian product.

Extensible Markup Language *See* XML.

extension 1. (*Relational algebra, first form*) Let relation *r* not have an attribute called *A*. Then (and only then) the expression EXTEND *r* : {*A* := *exp*} denotes an extension of *r*, and it returns the relation with heading the heading of *r* extended with attribute *A* and body the set of all tuples *t* such that *t* is a tuple of *r* extended with a value for *A* that's computed by evaluating the expression *exp* on that tuple of *r*. *See also* **tuple extension; WITH.** 2. (*Relational algebra, second form*) Let relation *r* have an attribute called *A*. Then (and only then) the expression EXTEND *r* : {*A* := *exp*} denotes an extension of *r*, and it returns the relation with heading the same as that of *r* and body the set of all tuples *t* such that *t* is derived from a tuple of *r* by replacing the value of *A* by a value that's computed by evaluating the expression *exp* on that tuple of *r*. Again, *see also* **tuple extension; WITH.** 3. (*Predicate*) Let *p* be a predicate; then the extension of *p* consists of all full instantiations of *p* (i.e., all propositions that can be derived from *p* by full instantiation) that evaluate to TRUE. 4. (*Relation*) Following on from the previous definition, let *r* be a relation. Then the heading of *r* can be regarded as representing a predicate (*see* **relation predicate**), and the body of *r* can be regarded as representing the extension of that predicate. Hence, the term *extension* is also sometimes used to refer to the body of a relation. *Contrast* **intension.** 5. (*Set theory*) *See* **axiom of extension.**

Examples: By way of an example of the first definition, consider the following expression, which denotes an extension of the relation that's the current value of relvar P:

```
EXTEND P : { GMWT := WEIGHT * 454 }
```

That extension is a relation just like the current value of relvar P, except that it has an additional attribute GMWT ("gram weight"), whose value in any given tuple is 454 times the WEIGHT value in that same tuple. The text enclosed in braces here represents an attribute assignment, q.v. Note that relvar P per se remains unaltered in the database—EXTEND isn't like ALTER TABLE in SQL, it's just a read-only operator (like restrict, for example) that takes a certain relation as input and returns a relation as output. Note too that WEIGHT * 454 in this example is an open expression, q.v.—it relies on context for its meaning.

Here's another example of the first definition:

```
EXTEND S { SNO } : { CT := COUNT ( !!SP ) }
```

The subexpression !!SP here is an image relation reference, and the expression overall denotes a certain summarization, q.v. For further explanation, see **image relation**.

Here now is an example of the second definition:

```
EXTEND P : { WEIGHT := 2 * WEIGHT }
```

This expression denotes a relation just like the current value of relvar P, except that all WEIGHT values are doubled; in fact, this EXTEND invocation is an example of a "what if" operation, q.v. Again relvar P remains unchanged in the database, and again the subexpression 2 * WEIGHT (within the attribute assignment in braces) is an open expression.

Note: **Tutorial D** additionally supports a form of EXTEND that allows two or more individual attribute assignments to be carried out in parallel ("multiple EXTEND"). Here's an example:

```
EXTEND P : { GMWT := WEIGHT * 454 ,
             WEIGHT := 2 * WEIGHT ,
             NC := 'Oslo' }
```

This example illustrates both of the relational algebra meanings of the term *extension*.

Note finally that the second form of EXTEND can be defined in terms of the first. For example, the expression

```
EXTEND P : { WEIGHT := 2 * WEIGHT }
```

can be regarded as shorthand for an expression of the following form:

```
( ( EXTEND P : { temp := 2 * WEIGHT } ) { ALL BUT WEIGHT } )
                                            RENAME { temp AS WEIGHT }
```

external predicate The relvar predicate for a given relvar. *Contrast* **internal predicate**. *Note:* Since this latter term is deprecated, the term *external predicate* is deprecated (somewhat) as well.

———— ♦ ♦ ♦ ♦ ♦ ————

factorial   Let *n* be a nonnegative integer. Then the factorial of *n*, written *n*! (which is read as either "*n* factorial" or "factorial *n*" and is often pronounced "*n* bang") is defined to be the product $n * (n-1) * ... * 2 * 1$. *Note:* If $n = 0$, then *n*! is 1 (unity).

Fagin's Theorem   Let *X*, *Y*, and *Z* be subsets of the heading *H* of relvar *R*, such that the set theory union of *X*, *Y*, and *Z* is equal to *H*. Let *XY* denote the set theory union of *X* and *Y*, and similarly for *XZ*. Then *R* is equal to the join of its projections on *XY* and *XZ* (and so can be nonloss decomposed into those projections) if and only if it's subject to the MVDs $X \to\to Y$ and $X \to\to Z$. *Note:* This theorem—which can be regarded as a stronger form of Heath's Theorem, q.v.—is one of many due to Fagin. Like Heath's Theorem, it can be used as a guide in the process of normalization, q.v.

FALSE   *See* BOOLEAN.

FD   Functional dependency.

FD implied by a key   *See* FD implied by a superkey.

FD implied by a superkey   Let relvar *R* have heading *H* and let $X \to Y$ be an FD, *F* say, with respect to *H*. Then *F* is implied by a superkey of *R* if and only if every relation *r* that satisfies *R*'s superkey constraints also satisfies *F*—equivalently, if and only if *F* is trivial or *X* is a superkey for *R* or both. *See* Boyce/Codd normal form. *Note:* The term *superkey* could be replaced by the term *key* throughout the foregoing definition without making any substantive difference.

FD preservation   Decomposing a relvar *R* into its projections *R1*, *R2*, ..., *Rn* in such a way that FDs are preserved—that is, every FD that holds in *R* is implied (in accordance with Armstrong's axioms, q.v.) by those that hold in *R1*, *R2*, ..., *Rn*. *R1*, *R2*, ..., *Rn* here are said to be independent projections. *Note:* Projections that aren't independent are said to be, not dependent, but interdependent. *See also* atomic relvar; Rissanen's Theorem.

Example: Suppose relvar S is subject to the additional FD {CITY} $\to$ {STATUS}. (Of course, the sample value shown for that relvar in Fig. 1 doesn't satisfy this FD; however, it would do so if we changed the status for supplier S2 from 10 to 30, so let's suppose for the sake of the example that this change has in fact been made.) Then replacing S by its projections on {SNO,SNAME,CITY} and {CITY,STATUS} preserves FDs, because every FD that holds in S either holds in one of those projections or is implied by those that do (i.e., the projections in question are independent, q.v.). By contrast, suppose S is replaced by its projections on {SNO,SNAME,CITY} and {SNO,STATUS} instead. Now the FD {CITY} $\to$ {STATUS}, which holds in S, isn't implied by the FDs that hold in those projections (even though the decomposition is nonloss). One practical consequence of this state of affairs is that updates to either of the two projections must now at least be monitored (either by the DBMS or—more likely in practice, given the level of technology found in current products—by some user) to ensure that the FD {CITY} → {STATUS} continues to hold in S, the join of those two projections; for example, consider what's involved if supplier S1 moves from London to Paris. In other words, the projections aren't independent in this decomposition but are, rather, interdependent. Given the state of today's commercial products, therefore, it's generally preferable to perform decomposition in such a way as to preserve FDs—i.e., to decompose into independent projections—whenever possible. *Note:* Unfortunately, however, the objectives of (a) decomposing into BCNF projections and (b) decomposing into independent projections, though both generally desirable, can sometimes be in conflict. See **atomic relvar**.

FD redundancy   Relvar *R* is subject to FD redundancy if and only if it's not in BCNF.

field   Term sometimes used to mean a column, in any of the possible senses of that term. All such uses are deprecated, however; the term is better reserved for an operating system or even physical level construct.

field (mathematics)   An algebra, q.v., for which the operators "+" and "*" have all of the properties—commutativity, associativity, etc.—that addition and multiplication of real numbers have; equivalently, a formal system that obeys all of The Laws of Algebra, q.v.

fifth normal form   "The" normal form with respect to JDs (*but see* **essential tuple normal form; redundancy free normal form; sixth normal form; superkey normal form**). Relvar *R* is in fifth normal form, 5NF, if and only if every JD that holds in *R* is implied by the superkeys of *R* (*see* **JD implied by superkeys**, where further explanation of the intuition behind this definition can be found). Every 5NF relvar is in 4NF (and in fact in SKNF, q.v.). Also, it can be shown that if relvar *R* is in 3NF and has no composite key (q.v.), then it's in 5NF. *Note:* Although being in 5NF clearly doesn't preclude being in 6NF as well, the term *5NF* is often used loosely to refer to a relvar that's in 5NF and not in 6NF.

    Example: As noted under **Boyce/Codd normal form**, with the normal forms it's often more instructive to show a counterexample rather than an example per se. Consider, therefore, a relvar *R* with attributes *A*, *B*, and *C* (and no others); let {*A,B*}, {*B,C*}, and {*C,A*} each be a key of *R*; and let the JD ⌂{{*A,B*},{*B,C*},{*C,A*}}—call it *J*—hold in *R*. Then it can be shown that (a) no additional dependencies are implied by *J* and those keys, other than trivial ones; (b) *J* is irreducible with respect to *R*. However, *J* isn't implied by the superkeys of *R* (again, *see* **JD implied by superkeys**), and so *R* isn't in 5NF. (On the other hand, since each component of *J* is a superkey for *R*, *R is* in SKNF, but—as indicated above—SKNF is strictly weaker than 5NF.) *Note:* If you'd prefer a slightly more concrete example, take *A*, *B*, and *C* to be "favorite color," "favorite food," and "favorite composer," respectively, and let the predicate be *Some person has favorite color A, favorite food B, and favorite composer C*. Further, let there be integrity constraints in effect that require (a) no two distinct persons to have more than one favorite in common and (b) no three distinct persons to be such that, for each favorite, two of those three have it in common.

file   Term sometimes used to mean a table, in any of the possible senses of that term, or even a relation or relvar. All such uses are deprecated, however; the term is better reserved for an operating system or even physical level construct.

FIRST   *See* ordinal type.

First Great Blunder   Equating types and either relations or relvars. *See* type; *see also* Second Great Blunder.

first normal form   Normalized. All relvars are in first normal form, 1NF, by definition; in other words, the terms *1NF* and *normalized*, applied to a relvar, mean the same thing (*see* normalized for further explanation). It follows that a "table," in the context of a language like SQL, can be considered to be in 1NF if and only if it's a direct and faithful representation of some relvar, where the phrase *direct and faithful* means among other things that every row and column intersection (i.e., every cell, q.v.) in that table contains exactly one value, nothing more and nothing less, and that value is a value of the applicable type. (The value in question can be arbitrarily complex—it can even be a table—but, to repeat, there must be exactly one such, and it must be of the applicable type.) In particular, therefore, a table isn't in first normal form if it contains any nulls, since nulls aren't values. It's also not in first normal form if it contains any repeating groups, q.v. This latter fact accounts for the usual informal characterization of first normal form as meaning just *no repeating groups*. *Note:* Although being in 1NF clearly doesn't preclude being in 2NF as well, the term *1NF* is often used loosely to refer to a relvar that's in 1NF only and not in any higher normal form. For an example of such a relvar, see second normal form.

first order logic   A form of predicate logic in which the sets over which variables range aren't allowed to contain predicates (*variables* here meaning variables in the sense of logic, not programming language variables). *Contrast* second order logic. *Note:* Propositional logic, q.v., might be regarded as a "zeroth order" logic, because it has no variables at all (and its variables thus don't range over anything at all).

flat relation   The idea that "relations are flat" is a popular misconception (and the term "flat relation" is strongly deprecated for that reason). *See* *n*-dimensional; *see also* table.

FORALL   *See* universal quantifier. *Note:* In the literature (but not in this dictionary), FORALL is often represented by an upside down A, thus: ∀. The keyword is also sometimes used as an alternative spelling for the aggregate operator AND (*see* aggregate operator). For example, the aggregate operator invocation AND (S,STATUS > 10), which means "Every supplier has status greater than 10," might alternatively, and intuitively very reasonably, be written thus: FORALL (S, STATUS > 10).

foreign key   Let *R1* and *R2* be relvars, not necessarily distinct, and let *K* be a key for *R1*. Let *FK* be a subset of the heading of *R2* such that there exists a possibly empty set of attribute renamings on *R1* that maps *K* into *K'*, say, where *K'* and *FK* contain exactly the same attributes (in other words, *K'* and *FK* are in fact one and the same). Further, let *R1* and *R2* be subject to the constraint that, at all times, every tuple *t2* in *R2* has an *FK* value that's the *K'* value for some necessarily unique tuple *t1* in *R1* at the time in question. Then *FK* is a foreign key, the associated constraint is a foreign key constraint, q.v. (or referential constraint, q.v.), and *R2* and *R1* are the referencing relvar and the corresponding referenced relvar (or target relvar), respectively, for that constraint. Also, *K*—not *K'*—is referred to, sometimes, as the referenced key or target key. *Note:* A referential constraint is a special case of an inclusion dependency, q.v. Also, note that the referencing, referenced, and target terminology carries over to tuples in the obvious way; that is, tuples *t2* and *t1* from the foregoing discussion are a referencing tuple and the corresponding referenced or target tuple, respectively.

    Examples: In relvar SP, {SNO} and {PNO} are foreign keys corresponding to the keys {SNO} and {PNO} in relvars S and P, respectively (see the definitions of these relvars in the introduction to this dictionary). By way of another example, here's one where some attribute renaming is required:

```
VAR EMP BASE RELATION
   { ENO ENO , ... , MNO ENO , ... }
     KEY { ENO }
     FOREIGN KEY { MNO }
           REFERENCES ( EMP { ENO } RENAME { ENO AS MNO } ) ;
```

Attribute MNO here denotes the employee number of the manager of the employee identified by ENO (the referencing relvar and the referenced relvar in this example are one and the same; in other words, we're dealing here with a referential cycle, q.v., of length one). Thus, for example, the EMP tuple for employee E3 might contain an MNO value of E2, which constitutes a reference to the EMP tuple for employee E2. *Note:* The parentheses in the last line of the example are logically unnecessary—they're included purely for clarity.

    Observe that there's no requirement that the key in the referenced relvar that corresponds to a given foreign key be a primary key specifically. Nor is there a requirement that the referencing relvar and the referenced relvar be base relvars specifically; for example, there might be a foreign key constraint from a base relvar to a view, or from a view to a base relvar, or from one view to another. In fact (speaking a little loosely), **Tutorial D** allows foreign key constraints to be specified between arbitrary relational expressions. *See* foreign key constraint for further discussion.

foreign key constraint   A referential constraint (*see* foreign key); hence, a special case of an inclusion dependency, q.v. *Note:* **Tutorial D** allows foreign key constraints to be specified not just for relvars as such (base or otherwise), but in fact for arbitrary relational expressions. For example, the specification

```
CONSTRAINT FKX ( S JOIN P ) FOREIGN KEY { SNO , PNO } REFERENCES SP ;
```

represents the following constraint: *If supplier sno and part pno are in the same city, then supplier sno must supply part pno.* In other words, this CONSTRAINT statement can be understood as saying that if a view were to be defined with S JOIN P as its defining expression, then the attribute combination {SNO,PNO} in that hypothetical view would be a foreign key referencing the key {SNO,PNO} in relvar SP.

Analogously, **Tutorial D** also allows the target for a given foreign key constraint to be specified by means of an arbitrary relational expression. For example, if it were part of the definition of relvar SP, the following specification—

```
FOREIGN KEY { SNO , PNO } REFERENCES ( S JOIN P )
```

— would represent the constraint *If supplier sno supplies part pno, then supplier sno and part pno must be in the same city.* In other words, this FOREIGN KEY specification can be understood as saying that if a view were to be defined with S JOIN P as its defining expression, then the attribute combination {SNO,PNO} would be a key for that hypothetical view, and the attribute combination {SNO,PNO} in relvar SP would be a foreign key referencing that key of that hypothetical view.

foreign key rule A rule specifying the action to be taken automatically—typically but not necessarily a compensatory action, q.v.—to ensure that updates affecting the foreign key in question don't violate the associated foreign key constraint. Typical examples are CASCADE (which is in fact a compensatory action) and NO CASCADE (which isn't).

Example: Suppose NO CASCADE is specified in connection with DELETE operations on relvar S and the foreign key constraint from relvar SP to that relvar. Then an attempt to delete a supplier with existing shipments without deleting those shipments as well (which would necessarily have to be done by means of an appropriate multiple assignment operation, q.v.) will fail.

formal Having to do with form rather than content—though the term also carries connotations of precision, and its opposite, informal, is often used as if it were a synonym for intuitive.

Example: Consider the expression—actually an FD—{SNO} $\rightarrow$ {CITY}. This FD can be regarded as a purely formal expression, of a kind that can be reasoned about and manipulated in accordance with certain formal laws (viz., Armstrong's axioms, q.v., and/or laws derived therefrom). Those manipulations can be done without paying any attention whatsoever to what those formal expressions might mean (i.e., how they might be interpreted in the real world). Of course, those formal expressions can certainly be given such an interpretation; for example, the FD {SNO} $\rightarrow$ {CITY} is interpreted to mean that whenever certain tuples have the same SNO value, they also have the same CITY value. But the advantage (or part of the advantage, at any rate) of being able to deal with such expressions in a purely formal manner, without paying any attention to their meaning, is that we can mechanize the process—that is, we can get the machine to do the work.

formal operand   A parameter, q.v. *Contrast* actual operand.

formal system   A logical system, q.v.

four-valued logic   *See* *n*VL.

formula   Same as well formed formula.

fourth normal form   "The" normal form with respect to multivalued dependencies (MVDs). Relvar R is in fourth normal form, 4NF, if and only if every MVD that holds in R is implied by some superkey of R—equivalently, if and only if for every nontrivial MVD $X \rightarrow\rightarrow Y$ that holds in R, X is a superkey for R (in which case the MVD $X \rightarrow\rightarrow Y$ effectively degenerates to the FD $X \rightarrow Y$). Every 4NF relvar is in BCNF. *Note:* Although being in 4NF clearly doesn't preclude being in some higher normal form as well, the term *4NF* is often used loosely to refer to a relvar that's in 4NF and not in any higher normal form. In any case, fourth normal form as such is no longer very important (BCNF, 5NF—or perhaps ETNF—and 6NF being the normal forms of most practical significance); we mention it here mainly for historical reasons.

   Example: As noted under **Boyce/Codd normal form**, with the normal forms it's often more instructive to show a counterexample rather than an example per se. Consider, therefore, relvar CTX, with attributes C (course), T (teacher), and X (textbook), and predicate *Course C can be taught by teacher T and uses textbook X.* Let that relvar be all key (i.e., let no proper subset of the heading be a key). Assume also that for a given course, the set of teachers and the set of textbooks are quite independent of each other. Then CTX is equal to the join of its projections on {C,T} and {C,X}—in other words, CTX is subject to the MVDs {C} $\rightarrow\rightarrow$ {T} and {C} $\rightarrow\rightarrow$ {X}—and so it can be nonloss decomposed into those two projections. Since those MVDs are certainly neither trivial nor implied by the sole superkey (namely, the entire CTX heading), relvar CTX isn't in 4NF, though it is in BCNF.

   Note: The predicate for relvar CTX in the foregoing example might alternatively be stated thus: *Course C can be taught by teacher T and course C uses textbook X.* This alternative formulation makes the possibility of decomposition obvious; it also makes the redundancies obvious (the redundancies, that is, that are eliminated by that decomposition).

free variable   Within a predicate, q.v., a variable—more precisely, an occurrence of a reference to some variable—that isn't bound; in other words, a parameter. (The term *variable* is used here in the sense of logic, not in the programming language sense.) *Contrast* **bound variable**.

Examples: Let the symbols *x* and *y* denote integers. Then the following expressions are both predicates, and *x* appears as a free variable in both of them:

```
x < 7

EXISTS y ( y > 3 ) AND x < 7
```

The first of these examples is self-explanatory. The second is a little more complicated, because it involves a quantified subexpression (in which *y* appears, twice, as a bound variable) as well as the free variable *x*.

Turning to a database example, the following is a query ("Get suppliers who supply at least one part") on the suppliers-and-parts database, expressed in tuple calculus:

```
{ S } WHERE EXISTS SP ( SP.SNO = S.SNO )
```

The boolean expression following the keyword WHERE here is a predicate, and the reference to S in that predicate is free (by contrast, the references to SP are bound). Note, however, that in this particular example the symbols S and SP denote not only variables in the sense of logic but also variables in the conventional programming language sense—but that's because we've indulged in a certain sleight of hand, as it were. Here's an expanded version of the same example that should help clarify matters:

```
SX  RANGES OVER { S } ;
SPX RANGES OVER { SP } ;

{ SX } WHERE EXISTS SPX ( SPX.SNO = SX.SNO )
```

Here SX and SPX have been explicitly declared to be range variables (q.v.)—in other words, they're variables in the sense of logic—ranging over (the current values of) relvars S and SP, respectively. Now it's the reference to SX that's free and the references to SPX that are bound (in the predicate following the keyword WHERE in both cases). In effect, what happened in the first version of the example was that we were appealing to a syntax rule that allowed a relvar name to be used to denote an implicitly defined range variable that ranges over (the current value of) the relvar with the same name. Note that SQL includes a syntax rule of exactly this kind.

Note: Let *R* be a range variable reference that occurs prior to the WHERE clause—i.e., within the proto tuple, q.v.—in some tuple calculus expression. If *R* also occurs in the predicate in that WHERE clause (which it usually but not invariably will), then it must be free, not bound, in that predicate. Observe that these remarks apply in particular to the references to the range variable SX in the example shown above.

friendship   An ad hoc and thus somewhat deprecated OO mechanism that allows the code that implements some operator for values and/or variables of some type *T1* to have access—access, that is, that it wouldn't otherwise have—to the physical representation of values and/or variables of some other type *T2*. The operator in question is "associated with" type *T1* but is "a friend of" type *T2*.

full FD   Old fashioned and somewhat deprecated (because slightly inappropriate) term for an irreducible FD.

full instantiation   *See* instantiation.

fully connected   (*Of a database*) *See* database variable.

fully dependent   Old fashioned and somewhat deprecated (because slightly inappropriate) term for irreducibly dependent.

fully normalized   A slightly fuzzy term whose meaning varies somewhat, depending on context. Loosely, however, we can say a database is fully normalized if and only if every relvar it contains is in at least 5NF (i.e., if and only if every such relvar is fully normalized in turn). Note, however, that the concept of normalization as such really applies to relvars, not databases.

fully redundant   Tuple *t* is fully redundant in relation *r* if and only if it's forced to appear in *r* by virtue of the fact that certain other tuples *t1*, *t2*, …, *tn*, all distinct from *t*, also appear in *r* (*see* tuple forcing JD). Note that a tuple can be fully redundant without being partly redundant (*see* partly redundant). Note too that a relvar can contain a fully redundant tuple only if that relvar isn't in ETNF, q.v; thus, normalizing to (at least) ETNF is guaranteed to eliminate the possibility of fully redundant tuples.

function   1. (*Mathematics*) Given two sets, not necessarily distinct, a rule—also known as a map or mapping—pairing each element of the first set (the domain) with exactly one element of the second set (the codomain); equivalently, the set of ordered pairs <*x,y*> that constitutes that pairing. The unique element *y* of the codomain corresponding to element *x* of the domain is the image of *x* under the specified function, and the set of all such images is the range of that function. Note that the range is a subset (in general, a proper subset) of the codomain, and the function can be regarded as a directed relationship—in fact, a many to one correspondence, q.v., in the strict sense of that term—from the domain to the range. Note too that a function is a special case of a binary relation. *See also* partial function; total function. 2. (*Programming languages*) A read-only operator (sometimes more specifically one denoted by an identifier such as PLUS instead of a special symbol such as "+"). Note, however, that the programming language construct denoted by this term is precisely a function in the mathematical sense; thus, there's really just one concept here, not two. Note also that nothing in the definition requires the domain and codomain to be sets of scalars; thus, a read-only operator could be defined in terms of, say, three parameters, in which case the domain would consist of a set of triples. A similar remark applies to the codomain.

Example: Let f be the rule that maps nonnegative integers x to their squares x^2. Then f is a function with (a) domain and codomain both the set of all nonnegative integers and (b) range that subset of the codomain consisting only of perfect squares. Observe in particular that—to spell the point out—f here, like all functions, has the property that the output value (i.e., the image) for any given input value is well defined and unique. *Contrast* possibly nondeterministic; ZO.

functional dependency   Let H be a heading; then a functional dependency (FD) with respect to H is an expression of the form $X \to Y$, where X (the determinant) and Y (the dependant) are both subsets of H. (The qualifying phrase "with respect to H" can be omitted if H is understood.) The expression $X \to Y$ is read as "Y is functionally dependent on X," or "X functionally determines Y," or, more simply, just "X arrow Y."

Let relation r have heading H, and let $X \to Y$ be an FD, F say, with respect to H. If all pairs of tuples $t1$ and $t2$ of r are such that whenever (a) the projections of $t1$ and $t2$ on X are equal then (b) the projections of $t1$ and $t2$ on Y are also equal, then (c) r satisfies F; otherwise r violates F. (Note the appeal in this definition to the operation of tuple projection, q.v.) Now let relvar R have heading H. Then R is subject to the FD F—equivalently, the FD F holds in R—if and only if every relation r that can ever be assigned to R satisfies that FD F. The FDs that hold in relvar R are the FDs of R, and they serve as constraints (q.v.) on R.

Note that FDs are defined with respect to some heading, not with respect to some relation or some relvar. Note too that from a formal point of view, an FD is just an expression: an expression that, when interpreted with respect to some specific relation, becomes a proposition that, by definition, evaluates to either TRUE or FALSE. Now, it's common informally to define $X \to Y$ to be an FD only if it actually holds in the pertinent relvar—but that definition leaves no way of saying a given FD fails to hold in some relvar, because, by that definition, an FD that fails to hold isn't an FD in the first place.

Example: Suppose for the sake of the example that relvar SP has an additional attribute CITY, representing the city of the applicable supplier. Then that revised version of SP is subject to the FD {SNO} $\to$ {CITY}. (Note in particular in this example that the determinant isn't a key of the relvar concerned. By definition, every relvar R is always subject to all possible FDs of the form $K \to X$, where K is a key—or, more generally, a superkey—for R and X is an arbitrary subset of the heading of R. In other words, there are always "arrows out of superkeys," and it's "arrows not out of superkeys" that are the interesting ones, in a sense.)

Note finally that X and Y in the FD $X \to Y$ are, specifically, sets of attributes; informally, however, it's common (though strictly incorrect) to speak of the attributes in X as if Y were functionally dependent on those attributes per se, instead of on the set X that contains those attributes. Likewise, it's common (though strictly incorrect) to speak of the attributes in Y as if those attributes per se, instead of the set Y that contains those attributes, were functionally dependent on X. *Note:* The foregoing remarks apply with especial force to the common special case in which either X or Y is a singleton set.

functionally dependent   *See* functional dependency.

functionally determines *See* functional dependency.

further normalization A slightly more accurate, or more descriptive, term for what is more conventionally referred to simply as normalization, q.v.

———— ♦ ♦ ♦ ♦ ♦ ————

generalized dependency Somewhat inappropriate term used to refer to a specific kind of constraint—viz., a constraint that's either an equality generating dependency, q.v., or a tuple generating dependency, q.v.

generated type *See* type generator.

generic constraint A constraint that's automatically enforced in connection with every type that can be produced by invocation of some given type generator, q.v. For example, given an array type generator, there might be a generic constraint to the effect that no array of any type that can be produced by invocation of that generator can have a dimension for which the lower bound is greater than the upper bound.

generic operator An operator that's available in connection with every type that can be produced by invocation of some given type generator, q.v. For example, the operators of the relational algebra are generic: They're available for relations of every type that can be produced by invocation of the relation type generator—in other words, for relations of all possible types, and hence for all possible relations.

generic polymorphism The kind of polymorphism exhibited by a generic operator, q.v.

generic type Term sometimes used as a synonym for type generator. The term is inappropriate because a type generator isn't a type.

GET_ operator An OO operator (an "observer," q.v.) that retrieves the value of a specified property—typically represented by an instance variable, q.v.—of a specified object. It might be thought of, very loosely, as the OO counterpart to a THE_ operator, except that THE_ operators are defined in terms of possrep components, not "object properties." *Contrast* SET_ operator.

Golden Rule The rule—its name is set in all boldface because of its fundamental importance—that no database is ever allowed to violate its own total database constraint. It follows that no relvar is ever allowed to violate its own total relvar constraint either, a fortiori. *Note:* This latter, weaker requirement is often referred to as **The Golden Rule** as well, though strictly speaking it's merely a logical consequence of **The Golden Rule** proper.

Great Blunder A somewhat contentious term that has been used in connection with certain egregious violations of fundamental relational principles. *See* First Great Blunder; Second Great Blunder.

Great Divide One of the many relational division operators that have been defined over the years (*see* division). Let relations $r1$, $r2$, $r3$, and $r4$ be such that (a) $r1$ and $r3$ are joinable, q.v., and so are $r3$ and $r4$, and so are $r4$ and $r2$; (b) the common attributes of $r1$ and $r3$ are called $A1$, $A2$, ..., Am ($m \geq 0$); (c) the common attributes of $r3$ and $r4$ are called $B1$, $B2$, ..., Bn ($n \geq 0$); (d) the common attributes of $r4$ and $r2$ are called $C1$, $C2$, ..., Cp ($p \geq 0$); and finally (e) no Ai has the same name as any Bj, and no Bj has the same name as any Ck ($1 \leq i \leq m$, $1 \leq j \leq n$, $1 \leq k \leq p$). Then (and only then) the expression $r1$ DIVIDEBY $r2$ PER ($r3,r4$)—where $r1$ is the dividend, $r2$ is the divisor, and $r3$ and $r4$ are the "mediators"—denotes the division of $r1$ by $r2$ according to $r3$ and $r4$, and it returns the relation denoted by the expression ($r1$ JOIN $r2$) NOT MATCHING (($r1\{A1,A2,...,Am\}$ JOIN $r4\{B1,B2,...,Bn,C1,C2,...,Cp\}$) NOT MATCHING $r3$). In other words, relation r has heading the set theory union of the headings of $r1$ and $r2$ and body defined as follows: Tuple t appears in that body if and only if it appears in $r1$ JOIN $r2$ and a tuple $<a1,a2,..,am,b1,b2,...,bn>$, with $a1$ equal to the $A1$ value in t, $a2$ equal to the $A2$ value in t, ..., and am equal to the Am value in t appears in $r3\{A1,A2,...,Am,B1,B2,...,Bn\}$ for all tuples $<b1,b2,...,bn,c1,c2,...,cp>$ appearing in $r4\{B1,B2,...,Bn,C1,C2,...,Cp\}$ with $c1$ equal to the $C1$ value in t, $c2$ equal to the $C2$ value in t, ..., and cp equal to the Cp value in t. *Contrast* Small Divide.

Examples: Suppose we're given a revised version of the suppliers-and-parts database, a version that's both extended and simplified compared to our usual running example and looks like this:

```
S    { SNO }
SP   { SNO , PNO }
PJ   { PNO , JNO }
J    { JNO }
```

Relvar J here represents projects (JNO stands for project number), and relvar PJ indicates which parts are used in which projects. Then the expression S DIVIDEBY J PER (SP,PJ) yields a relation with heading {SNO,JNO} and body consisting of all possible tuples of the form $<sno,jno>$—where *sno* is an SNO value currently appearing in relvar S, *jno* is a JNO value currently appearing in relvar J, and supplier *sno* supplies all parts used in project *jno*—and no other tuples. The expression is logically equivalent to this one:

```
( S JOIN J ) NOT MATCHING ( ( S JOIN PJ ) NOT MATCHING SP )
```

An equivalent tuple calculus formulation is:

```
SX   RANGES OVER { S } ;
SPX  RANGES OVER { SP } ;
PJX  RANGES OVER { PJ } ;
JX   RANGES OVER { J } ;

{ SX , JX } WHERE FORALL PJX ( EXISTS SPX ( SX.SNO = SPX.SNO AND
                                            SPX.PNO = PJX.PNO AND
                                            PJX.JNO = JX.JNO ) )
```

An equivalent **Tutorial D** formulation is:

```
( S JOIN J ) WHERE !!PJ ⊆ !!SP
```

(The expressions !!PJ and !!SP here are image relation references, q.v.)

Incidentally, observe what happens if the operands to the foregoing division are switched around, thus: J DIVIDEBY S PER (PJ,SP). This expression yields a relation with heading {JNO,SNO} and body consisting of all possible tuples of the form *<jno,sno>*—where *jno* is a JNO value currently appearing in relvar J, *sno* is an SNO value currently appearing in relvar S, and project *jno* uses all parts supplied by supplier *sno*—and no other tuples. An equivalent tuple calculus formulation (using the same range variables as before) is:

```
{ JX , SX } WHERE FORALL SPX ( EXISTS PJX ( JX.JSNO = PJX.JNO AND
                                            PJX.PNO = SPX.PNO AND
                                            SPX.SNO = SX.SNO ) )
```

(The only difference is in the quantifiers.) An equivalent **Tutorial D** formulation is:

```
( J JOIN S ) WHERE !!SP ⊆ !!PJ
```

greater-than join   A theta join, q.v., in which theta is ">".

GROUP   *See* grouping.

group   Term sometimes used in connection with the grouping operator, q.v. Let *r* be a relation, let *X* be a subset of the heading of *r*, and let the projection of *r* on *X* have cardinality *n* ($n \geq 0$). Then *r* can be partitioned into exactly *n* groups, where each such group *g* is a restriction of *r* (and hence a relation) with the property that (a) every tuple in *g* has the same value for *X*—i.e., for all pairs of tuples *t1* and *t2* in *g*, the (tuple) projections on *X* of *t1* and *t2* are equal—and (b) no tuple of *r* not in *g* has that same value for *X*. (In fact, each such group *g* is an equivalence class, q.v.)

Example: See the example under **grouping**.

group (mathematics)   A formal system that obeys all of The Laws of Algebra, q.v., except that (a) multiplication ("*") isn't necessarily defined and (b) addition ("+") isn't necessarily commutative (if it is, then the group is a commutative or abelian group, otherwise it's a noncommutative or nonabelian group).

grouping Let relation *r* have attributes called *A1, A2, ..., Am, B1, B2, ..., Bn* (and no others), and let *BR* be an attribute name that's distinct from that of every attribute *Ai* ($1 \leq i \leq m$). Then (and only then) the expression *r* GROUP {*B1,B2,...,Bn*} AS *BR* denotes the grouping of *r* on {*B1,B2,...,Bn*}, and it returns the relation denoted by the expression EXTEND *r* {*A1,A2,...,Am*} : {*BR* := !!*r*}. *Note:* The subexpression !!*r* here is an image relation reference, q.v.

Example: The following expression denotes a grouping of the relation that's the current value of relvar SP:

```
SP GROUP { PNO , QTY } AS PQ_REL
```

That grouping is a relation *spq* of type RELATION {SNO SNO, PQ_REL RELATION {PNO PNO, QTY QTY}}. Relation *spq* contains one tuple for each distinct SNO value currently appearing in relvar SP, and no other tuples. Given the sample values in Fig. 1, for example, the *spq* tuple for supplier S2 has SNO value S2 and PQ_REL value a relation whose body contains just the tuples <P1,300> and <P2,400>. (Attribute PQ_REL here is a relation valued attribute, q.v.)

Note: Given a relation *r* and some grouping of *r*, there's always an inverse ungrouping that will yield *r* again; however, the converse isn't necessarily so (*see* ungrouping).

———— ♦♦♦♦♦ ————

hand optimization *See* optimization.

hash A specific kind of physical access path; hence, an implementation construct.

hash join A join implementation technique.

heading A set of attributes, in which (by definition) each attribute is a pair of the form <*A,T*>, where *A* is an attribute name and *T* is the name of the type of attribute *A*; especially, the set of attributes for a given relation or given relvar. Every subset of a heading is itself a heading. Within any given heading, (a) distinct attributes are allowed to have the same type name but not the same attribute name; (b) the number of attributes is the degree (of the heading in question). *Note:* Given that it's common to refer to an attribute, informally, by its attribute name alone, it's also common to regard a heading, informally, as a set of attribute names alone.

Examples: The heading of relvar S is

```
{ <SNO , SNO> , <SNAME , NAME> , <STATUS , INTEGER> , <CITY , CHAR> }
```

The following (corresponding to a certain projection of relvar S) is also a heading:

```
{ <CITY , CHAR> , <SNAME , NAME> }
```

These two headings might be represented less formally thus:

```
{ SNO , SNAME , STATUS , CITY }

{ CITY , SNAME }
```

In **Tutorial D** they could be represented as follows:

```
{ SNO SNO , SNAME NAME , STATUS INTEGER , CITY CHAR }

{ CITY CHAR , SNAME NAME }
```

(In other words, **Tutorial D** uses spaces instead of commas or other separators to separate attribute names from their corresponding type names.)

Heath's Theorem   Let X, Y, and Z be subsets of the heading H of relvar R, such that the set theory union of X, Y, and Z is equal to H. Let XY denote the set theory union of X and Y, and similarly for XZ. Finally, let R be subject to the FD $X \to Y$. Then R is equal to the join of its projections on XY and XZ (and so can be nonloss decomposed into those projections). This theorem is often used as a guide in the process of normalization, q.v. Note that the converse of the theorem is false; that is, just because R is equal to the join of its projections on XY and XZ, it doesn't follow that R is subject to the FD $X \to Y$. However, if we replace the FD $X \to Y$ by the MVD $X \to\to Y$ throughout, then the resulting statement is true in both directions; that is, R is equal to the join of its projections on XY and XZ if *and only if* it's subject to the MVD $X \to\to Y$. *See* Fagin's Theorem; multivalued dependency; *see also* Heath's Theorem (extended version). *Note:* Heath's Theorem was originally formulated in terms of relations, not relvars; however, the reason for this state of affairs (at least in part) was simply that the term *relvar* wasn't in use at the time when Heath proved his theorem, back in 1971.

    Example: Relvar S is subject to the FD {SNO} $\to$ {SNAME,CITY}, and so it's equal to the join of its projections on {SNO,SNAME,CITY} and {SNO,STATUS}.

Heath's Theorem (extended version)   Let X, Y, and Z be subsets of the heading H of relvar R, such that the set theory union of X, Y, and Z is equal to H. Let XY denote the set theory union of X and Y, and similarly for XZ. If R is subject to the FD $X \to Y$, then (a) R is equal to the join of its projections on XY and XZ and (b) XZ is a superkey for R; conversely, if (a) R is equal to the join of its projections on XY and XZ and (b) XZ is a superkey for R, then R is subject to the FD $X \to Y$.

    Example: Relvar S is subject to the FD {SNO} $\to$ {SNAME,CITY}, and so (a) it's equal to the join of its projections on {SNO,SNAME,CITY} and {SNO,STATUS} and (b) {SNO,STATUS} is a superkey for S; conversely, (a) relvar S is equal to the join of its projections on {SNO,SNAME,CITY} and {SNO,STATUS} and (b) {SNO,STATUS} is a superkey for S, and so the FD {SNO} → {SNAME,CITY} holds in S.

hold   Constraint *C* holds for variable *V*—equivalently, variable *V* is subject to constraint *C*—if and only if every value *v* that can ever be assigned to *V* satisfies *C*. *Contrast* **satisfy** (first meaning).

horizontal decomposition   Informal term for decomposition into restrictions (*see also* **orthogonal decomposition**). Be aware, however, that the term is given an additional, or extended, meaning in the temporal data context—see Part III of this dictionary—and possibly in other contexts also.
    Note: The physical database design technique known informally as "sharding" consists essentially of (a) performing horizontal decomposition as just defined on each of a set of hierarchically related base relvars based on values of a common attribute, that attribute being a key attribute for the relvar at the root of the hierarchy; (b) grouping together those restrictions with common values for that key attribute into a "shard"; and then (c) physically storing "direct images" (q.v.) of distinct shards at distinct sites. In the case of the suppliers-and-parts database, for example, tuples of relvars S and SP having SNO value either S1 or S2 might constitute one such shard and tuples of those same two relvars having SNO value S3, S4, or S5 might constitute another.

host language   A programming language that relies on some data sublanguage, q.v., for its database support. *Contrast* **database programming language**.

—— ◆◆◆◆◆ ——

I_DELETE   *See* **included DELETE**.

I_MINUS   *See* **included difference**.

idempotence   1. (*Monadic*) Let *Op* be a monadic operator, and assume for definiteness that *Op* is expressed in prefix style. Then *Op* is idempotent if and only if, for all *x*, $Op(Op(x)) = Op(x)$. 2. (*Dyadic*) Let *Op* be a dyadic operator, and assume for definiteness that *Op* is expressed in infix style. Then *Op* is idempotent if and only if, for all *x*, $x\ Op\ x = x$. *Note:* Mathematics textbooks typically define idempotence as a concept that applies to just one of these two cases. However, some define it for the monadic case only and others for the dyadic case only. But both cases clearly make sense; hence the foregoing definition.
    Examples: 1. (*Monadic case*) Let *x* be a real number, and define the monadic operator CEIL(*x*) to return the least integer greater than or equal to *x*. Then CEIL is idempotent, because $CEIL(CEIL(x)) = CEIL(x)$ for all *x*. (By contrast, the monadic operator HALF—"return half

of"—is certainly not idempotent.) 2. (*Dyadic case*) In logic, the dyadic operators OR and AND are both idempotent, because

```
x OR x = x
```

and

```
x AND x = x
```

for all *x* (by contrast, the dyadic operator XOR is not idempotent). *Note:* It follows as a direct consequence that UNION and JOIN, respectively, are idempotent (and XUNION is not) in relational algebra.

identity 1. (*General*) That which distinguishes a given entity from all others. 2. (*Operator*) Equality. 3. (*Logic*) Equality; also, a tautology of the form $(p) \equiv (q)$ (the parentheses enclosing *p* and *q* here might not be needed in practice). 4. (*Comparison*) A boolean expression of the form $(exp1) = (exp2)$, where *exp1* and *exp2* are expressions of the same type, that's guaranteed to evaluate to TRUE regardless of the values of any variables involved. The parentheses enclosing *exp1* and *exp2* in the comparison might not be needed in practice. 5. (*Identity value*) Let *Op* be a commutative dyadic operator, and assume for definiteness that *Op* is expressed in infix style. If there exists a value *i* such that *i Op v* and *v Op i* are both equal to *v* for all possible values *v*, then *i* is the identity, or identity value, with respect to *Op* (*see* **Laws of Algebra**; *see also* **left identity**; **right identity**). *Note:* Identity values are also known variously as identity elements; neutral elements; unit elements; or sometimes just as units.

Examples (fifth definition only): The dyadic operators "+", "*", OR, AND, EQUIV, XOR, and JOIN have identity values 0, 1, FALSE, TRUE, TRUE, FALSE, and TABLE_DEE, respectively. Note the last of these in particular; it means, to spell the point out, that *r* JOIN TABLE_DEE = TABLE_DEE JOIN *r* = *r* for all possible relations *r*. It also means that, just as the sum of no integers is zero (*see* **aggregate operator**), so the join—and hence, as a special case, the cartesian product—of no relations is TABLE_DEE (*see* **natural join**).

Continuing with the examples, the dyadic set theory union, exclusive union, and intersection operators have identity values the empty set, the empty set, and the universal set, respectively. As for the relational counterparts to these set theory operators, there's one such identity value, in effect, for each possible relation type; thus, if the type in question is *T*, the identity value for both union and exclusive union is the empty relation of type *T*, and the identity value for intersection is the universal relation of type *T*.

identity projection The projection of a relation on all of its attributes. Let relation *r* have attributes called *A1, A2, ..., An* (and no others). Then the expression *r*{*A1,A2,...,An*} denotes the identity projection of *r*, and it returns *r* itself. *Note:* The term is also used of a relvar; for example, the expression SP{SNO,QTY,PNO} denotes the identity projection of relvar SP (and its value at any given time is the identity projection of the relation that's the value of relvar SP at the time in question). *See also* nonloss decomposition.

identity restriction   A restriction of a relation *r* that's equal to *r* itself (i.e., is equal to *r* WHERE TRUE); especially, a restriction of the form *r* WHERE *t*, where *t* is a tautology, q.v. *Note:* The term is also used of a relvar (see the examples immediately following).

   Examples: Given the sample values in Fig. 1, the expressions S WHERE STATUS ≠ 25 and S WHERE STATUS = STATUS both denote identity restrictions (the second necessarily so, because STATUS = STATUS is a tautology).

identity value   *See* identity.

IF AND ONLY IF   Same as EQUIV.

IF ... THEN ...   Same as IMPLIES (more precisely, IF (*p*) THEN (*q*) is the same as, or is equivalent to, (*p*) IMPLIES (*q*)).

IFF   Short for "if and only if"; hence, same as EQUIV.

image   *See* function.

image relation   In **Tutorial D**, the value (a relation) denoted by an image relation reference, where an image relation reference is an open expression, q.v., of the form !!*r* (where *r* in turn is a relational expression). Such an expression can appear in a WHERE clause or in the expression denoting the source for an attribute assignment within an EXTEND, SUMMARIZE, or UPDATE invocation (in each case, wherever a relational expression can appear). For definiteness, suppose the expression !!*r2* appears in the boolean expression component *bx* of the relational expression *r1* WHERE *bx* (other uses of image relation references are defined analogously). Relations *r1* and *r2* here must be joinable, q.v. Let their common attributes be called *A1, A2, ..., An* ($n \geq 0$). In this context, then, the expression !!*r2* is logically equivalent to the expression ((*r2*) MATCHING RELATION {TUPLE {*A1 A1, A2 A2, ..., An An*}}) {ALL BUT *A1,A2,...,An*}. In this latter expression, (a) the subexpression TUPLE {*A1 A1, A2 A2, ..., An An*} is a tuple selector invocation; (b) each pair within that tuple selector invocation is of the form *Ai Ai* (*i* = 1, 2, ..., *n*), where the first *Ai* is an attribute name and the second is an attribute reference, being a reference to the attribute of that name within *r1*; (c) that attribute reference *Ai* denotes the value of attribute *Ai* within "the current tuple" of *r1*; (d) "the current tuple" of *r1* is the tuple of *r1* that's currently being processed. For further explanation, see the example below.

   Note: In mathematics the expression "*n*!" (*n* factorial) is often pronounced "*n* bang" (*see* factorial); hence the symbol "!!" might reasonably be pronounced "bang bang" or "double bang." Alternatively, the expression "!!*r*" might be pronounced "image in *r* [of the current tuple]."

   Example: The expression

```
S WHERE ( !!SP ) { PNO } = P { PNO }
```

yields a relation with heading the same as that of relvar S and body consisting of all possible tuples *<sno,sn,st,sc>* from the current value of relvar S such that supplier *sno* supplies all parts mentioned in the current vaue of relvar P. (Given the sample values of Fig. 1, the result contains just the tuple for supplier S1.) The expression overall is logically equivalent to this one:

```
S WHERE ( ( SP MATCHING RELATION { TUPLE { SNO SNO } } )
                  { ALL BUT SNO } ) { PNO } = P { PNO }
```

To elaborate: Let *s* and *sp* be the current values of relvars S and SP, respectively. For a given tuple *t* in *s*, then, the expression—actually a relation selector invocation—RELATION {TUPLE {SNO SNO}} evaluates to a relation with just one attribute, SNO, and just one tuple, and that tuple contains just the SNO value from *t*. So the corresponding image relation within SP—i.e., the one corresponding to tuple *t*, denoted by the expression !!SP—contains just those tuples of SP that match that tuple *t*, projected on {PNO,QTY} (equivalently, projected on {ALL BUT SNO}). The projection (!!SP){PNO} thus evaluates to a relation *ps*, say, with just one attribute, PNO, giving part numbers for all parts supplied by the supplier corresponding to tuple *t*. For that supplier, the boolean expression (!!SP){PNO} = P{PNO} then tests the corresponding relation *ps* to see if it's equal to the projection of the current value of P on {PNO}. That test will give TRUE if and only if the supplier corresponding to tuple *t* currently supplies all parts currently mentioned in P.

Here now is an example of the use of an image relation with EXTEND:

```
EXTEND S { SNO } : { CT := COUNT ( !!SP ) }
```

This expression denotes a certain summarization (q.v.); it yields a relation of type RELATION {SNO SNO, CT INTEGER}, containing one tuple for each distinct SNO value currently appearing in relvar S, and no other tuples. Each such tuple contains one such supplier number, together with a count of the number of times the supplier number in question currently appears in relvar SP (the expression !!SP is, again, shorthand for the expression (SP MATCHING RELATION {TUPLE {SNO SNO}}) {ALL BUT SNO}). Given the sample values in Fig. 1, for example, the tuple for supplier S2 in the result has SNO value S2 and CT value two, and the tuple for supplier S5 has SNO value S5 and CT value zero.

image relation reference　An open relational expression of the form !!*r*, where *r* in turn is a relational expression (and the symbol "!!" is usually pronounced "bang bang" or "double bang"). Since it's an open expression, an image relation reference can appear only in certain limited contexts. *See* **image relation**.

immediate checking Checking a database constraint whenever an update is performed that might cause it to be violated. All database constraint checking is immediate in the relational model. *Contrast* deferred checking.

immediate constraint A database constraint for which the checking is immediate (*see* immediate checking). All database constraints are immediate in the relational model. *Contrast* deferred constraint.

immutable object OO term for a value (*contrast* mutable object).

impedance mismatch Term sometimes used, especially in OO contexts, to refer to—among quite a number of other things—the problems that can arise if the types used inside the database differ from those available outside.

implementation A physical realization on a physical computer system of the abstract machine that constitutes some given data model (in the first sense of that term, q.v.). In the interest of physical data independence, the model and its implementation should be kept rigidly apart; that is, the model should have nothing whatsoever to say about any aspect of implementation.

implementation defined Term used, in the SQL standard in particular, to refer to a feature whose specifics can vary from one implementation to another but do at least have to be defined for any individual implementation. In other words, the implementation is free to decide how it will implement the feature in question, but the result of that decision does have to be documented. An SQL example is the maximum length of a character string.

implementation dependent Term used, in the SQL standard in particular, to refer to a feature whose specifics can vary from one implementation to another and don't even have to be defined for any individual implementation. In other words, the term effectively means "undefined"; the implementation is free to decide how it will implement the feature in question, and the result of that decision doesn't even have to be documented (it might vary from release to release, or possibly more frequently still). An SQL example is the full effect of an ORDER BY clause, if the specifications in that clause fail to specify a total ordering, q.v.

implication If and only if p and q are predicates, the implication (p) IMPLIES (q) is a predicate also. Let (ip) IMPLIES (iq) be an invocation of that predicate, where ip and iq are invocations of p and q, respectively. Then that invocation (ip) IMPLIES (iq) evaluates to TRUE if and only if ip evaluates to FALSE or iq evaluates to TRUE or both. (In other words, (p) IMPLIES (q) is logically equivalent to $(NOT(p))$ OR (q).) *Note:* In the predicate (p) IMPLIES (q), p and q are the antecedent and the consequent, respectively; likewise, in the invocation (ip) IMPLIES (iq), ip and iq are the antecedent and the consequent, respectively. The parentheses enclosing p and q in the predicate, and ip and iq in the invocation, might not be needed in practice.

Examples: For people with no training in formal logic, implication can be notoriously difficult to come to grips with. Consider, e.g., the proposition

```
( 2 + 2 = 4 ) IMPLIES ( the sun is a star )
```

or, in more user friendly terms,

```
IF ( 2 + 2 = 4 ) THEN ( the sun is a star )
```

This proposition evaluates to TRUE, because the antecedent and the consequent are both true; yet whether the sun is a star clearly has nothing to do with whether 2+2 = 4, so what does the implication really "mean"? The following observations might help. Of the 16 available dyadic connectives (*see* **connective**), some but not all are given common names such as AND and OR. But those names are really nothing more than a mnemonic device—they don't have any intrinsic meaning, they're chosen simply because the connectives so named have behavior that's similar to (not necessarily the same as) that of their natural language counterparts. In particular, the connective called IMPLIES has, of those 16 connectives, behavior that most closely resembles that of implication as usually understood in natural language. But nobody would or should claim that the two are the same thing. In fact, of course, the connectives are defined purely formally—that is, they're defined purely in terms of the truth values, not the meanings, of their arguments (viz., the antecedent and consequent, in the case of IMPLIES)—whereas the same obviously can't be said of their natural language counterparts.

By way of another example, the proposition

```
IF ( 2 + 2 = 5 ) THEN ( Elvis lives )
```

also—perhaps even more counterintuitively—evaluates to TRUE, because the antecedent is false; yet whether Elvis is alive clearly has nothing to do with whether 2+2 = 5. Again, part of the justification (for the fact that the implication evaluates to TRUE, that is) is just that IMPLIES is formally defined. In this case, however, there's another argument that might be a little more satisfying in the database context specifically. Suppose the suppliers-and-parts database is subject to the constraint that all red parts must be stored in London (constraint C2 from the examples under **database constraint**). Formally, that constraint is a logical implication:

```
IF ( COLOR = COLOR('Red') ) THEN ( CITY = 'London' )
```

Obviously we don't want this constraint to be violated by a part that isn't red. It follows that we want the expression overall—which, as previously stated, is a logical implication—to evaluate to TRUE if the antecedent evaluates to FALSE.

implicit dependency   A dependency—e.g., an FD or JD, or some more general constraint—that isn't explicitly declared for some relvar but is implied by those that are (and therefore holds in that relvar, implicitly). *Contrast* explicit dependency.

implied by FDs   Given a set *s* of FDs, a given FD is implied by *s* if and only if it's a logical consequence of the FDs in *s* according to Armstrong's axioms, q.v.

implied by key(s)   Same as implied by superkey(s).

implied by superkey(s)   *See* FD implied by a superkey; JD implied by superkeys; MVD implied by a superkey.

IMPLIES   A connective, q.v. (*see* implication).

improper inclusion   Set *s1* improperly includes set *s2*, and set *s2* is improperly included in set *s1*, if and only if *s1* and *s2* are the same set.

improper subkey   A subkey that's not a proper subkey; in other words, a key.

improper subset   Set *s2* is an improper subset of set *s1* if and only if *s2* and *s1* are the same set.

improper superkey   A superkey that's not a proper superkey; in other words, a key.

improper superset   Set *s1* is an improper superset of set *s2* if and only if *s1* and *s2* are the same set.

included DELETE   Loosely, an operator, I_DELETE (shorthand for a certain relational assignment), that deletes specified tuples from a specified relvar, just so long as the tuples in question do currently appear in that relvar. The syntax is:

```
I_DELETE R rx
```

Here *R* is a relvar reference (syntactically, just a relvar name) and *rx* is a relational expression (denoting some relation *r* of the same type as *R*), and the effect is to delete the tuples of *r* from *R*, just so long as those tuples do currently appear in *R*. In other words, the DELETE invocation just shown is shorthand for the following explicit assignment:

```
R := R I_MINUS rx
```

It follows that an attempt via I_DELETE to delete a tuple that's not present in the first place is an error (*contrast* DELETE).

Example: The statement

```
I_DELETE SP RELATION
          { TUPLE { SNO SNO('S3') , PNO PNO('P2') , QTY QTY(200) } ,
            TUPLE { SNO SNO('S1') , PNO PNO('P1') , QTY QTY(400) } } ;
```

is shorthand for the following relational assignment statement:

```
SP := SP I_MINUS RELATION
          { TUPLE { SNO SNO('S3') , PNO PNO('P2') , QTY QTY(200) } ,
            TUPLE { SNO SNO('S1') , PNO PNO('P1') , QTY QTY(400) } } ;
```

Given the sample values shown in Fig. 1, this assignment will fail—more precisely, the implicit I_MINUS invocation will fail—and no updating will be done, because the tuple <S1,P1,400> doesn't currently appear in relvar SP.

included difference   A variant on the relational difference operator, q.v., for which the second operand relation is required to be included in the first, meaning that every tuple appearing in the second relation also appears in the first. In other words, if (a) relations *r1* and *r2* are of the same type *T*, and (b) no tuple appears in *r2* and not in *r1*, then (and only then) the expression *r1* I_MINUS *r2* denotes the included difference between *r1* and *r2* (in that order), and it reduces to *r1* MINUS *r2*. *Note:* A version of this operator could also be defined to apply to sets in general as well as relations in particular.

   Example: Consider the expression S{CITY} I_MINUS P{CITY}. If the current values of relvars S and P are as shown in Fig. 1, this expression will raise a run-time error, because not every part city is also a supplier city. If such were not the case, however, the expression would then be logically equivalent to S{CITY} MINUS P{CITY}.

included MINUS   *See* included difference.

inclusion   *See* bag; relational inclusion; set inclusion.

inclusion dependency   An expression of the form *rx* ⊆ *ry*, where *rx* and *ry* are relational expressions of the same type; it can be read as "The relation denoted by *rx* must be included in the relation denoted by *ry*." Note that foreign key constraints (q.v.) and equality dependencies (q.v.) are both special cases.

   Example: Suppose the suppliers-and-parts database is subject to a constraint to the effect that no part can be stored in a city unless there's at least one supplier in that city:

```
CONSTRAINT INDX P { CITY } ⊆ S { CITY } ;
/* every part city must also be a supplier city */
```

This constraint is an inclusion dependency (IND for short). Note, however, that it's not satisfied by the sample values shown in Fig. 1.

Note: Actually, constraint INDX here is an example of an important special case of INDs in general. That special case can be defined as follows. Let *R1* and *R2* be relvars, not necessarily distinct. Let *X1* and *X2* be a subset of the heading of *R1* and a subset of the heading of *R2*, respectively, such that there exists a possibly empty set of attribute renamings on *R1* that maps *X1* into *X1'*, say, where *X1'* and *X2* contain exactly the same attributes (in other words, *X1'* and *X2* are in fact one and the same). Further, let *R1* and *R2* be subject to the constraint that, at all times, every tuple *t2* in *R2* has an *X2* value that's the *X1'* value for at least one tuple *t1* in *R1* at the time in question. Then that constraint is an IND "on" *R1* and *R2*, and *R2* and *R1* are the source relvar and corresponding target relvar, respectively, for that IND.

inclusive OR   Term sometimes used as a synonym for OR, used primarily to distinguish it from exclusive OR, q.v.

inclusive union   Term sometimes used as a synonym for union, used primarily to distinguish it from exclusive union, q.v.

Incoherent Principle   *See Principle of Incoherence.*

inconsistency   *See* consistency.

inconsistent   Not consistent, q.v.

IND   Inclusion dependency.

independent projection   *See* FD preservation.

index   A specific kind of physical access path; hence, an implementation construct.

indirect proof   *See* proof.

indirect reasoning   *See modus tollens.*

indiscernibility   Lack of discernibility; not to be confused with interchangeability. *See Principle of Identity of Indiscernibles; Principle of Interchangeability.*

individual constant   (*Logic*) A symbol denoting a value (in effect, a literal in the programming language sense, q.v.); loosely, a value. Intuitively, we might say the individual constants available in a given formal system are what that system is "about." For example, we might say that ordinary arithmetic is "about" the individual constants 0, 1, 2, etc.

inference rule   A rule for deriving a conclusion (i.e., a theorem) from a set of premises (i.e., other theorems, possibly axioms). The derivation process is known as inference. *See also* Armstrong's axioms; constraint inference; key inference; logical system; relation type inference; tuple type inference; type inference.

inferential equivalence   Same as logical equivalence.

information equivalence   Let *DB1* be a set of relvars and let *TC1* be the logical AND of all constraints that apply to the relvars in *DB1*, and let *DB2* and *TC2* be defined analogously. Then *DB1* and *DB2* are information equivalent if and only if *TC1* and *TC2* are such that the set of propositions represented (explicitly or implicitly) by *DB1* and the set of propositions represented (explicitly or implicitly) by *DB2* are one and the same—i.e., every proposition represented by *DB1* is represented by *DB2* and vice versa.

   Example: Let *DB1* and *DB2* be, respectively, the set of relvars consisting of just the suppliers relvar S considered in isolation and the set of relvars consisting of relvars LS and NLS considered together, where at any given time relvar LS is equal to that restriction of S where the city is London and relvar NLS is equal to that restriction of S where the city is something other than London. Then it's intuitively obvious that *DB1* and *DB2* are information equivalent.

   Now let *DB1* and *DB2* be information equivalent sets of relvars, and let the current values of *DB1* and *DB2* be *db1* and *db2*, respectively. Then:

■ Those values *db1* and *db* can be said to be information equivalent in turn (certainly it's true that every proposition represented by *db1* is represented by *db2* and vice versa). In other words, the notion of information equivalence can be extended to apply to sets of relations as well as to sets of relvars.

■ If *db1* and *db2* are information equivalent, then there must exist mappings that transform *db1* into *db2* and *db2* into *db1*, respectively, where the mappings in question can be expressed in terms of operations of the relational algebra. Conversely, if such mappings exist, then *db1* and *db2* are information equivalent. Note moreover that to say that *DB1* and *DB2* per se are information equivalent is to say that (a) such mappings exist for all possible pairs of current values *db1* and *db2* of *DB1* and *DB2*, respectively, and hence that (b) such a mapping also exists, in effect, between *DB1* and *DB2* as such.

■ For every query *Q1* on *db1*, there must exist a query *Q2* on *db2* that yields the same result.

■ Let *U1* be an update on *DB1* that yields a "new" value *db1'* of *DB1*; then there must exist an update *U2* on *DB2* that yields a "new" value *db2'* of *DB2*, such that *db1'* and *db2'* are information equivalent. Note in particular that this observation applies to the important special case in which *DB1* consists of base relvars only and *DB2* consists only of views of the relvars in *DB1*.

■ Conversely, let *db1* and *db2* (and hence *DB1* and *DB2*, a fortiori) not be information equivalent. Then (a) there must exist a query on *db1* with no counterpart on *db2* (or vice versa), and (b) there must exist an update on *DB1* with no counterpart on *DB2* (or vice versa). Again note in particular that these observation apply to the important special case in which *DB1* consists of base relvars only and *DB2* consists only of views of the relvars in *DB1*.

Finally, note that the definition of what it means for two sets of relvars to be information equivalent relies on an understanding of what it means for two propositions to be "the same"—or (perhaps better) what it means for two propositions to be information equivalent in turn. This state of affairs is the motivation for the following definition (which, be it noted, is tailored somewhat to the specific purpose at hand):

■ Two propositions are information equivalent if and only if the predicates of which they are instantiations (a) are logically equivalent, q.v., and (b) reference the same relvars.

Information Principle The principle that the only kind of variable allowed in a relational database is the relation variable—i.e., the relvar—specifically. Equivalently, a relational database contains relvars, and nothing but relvars. Yet another equivalent formulation is: At any given time, the entire information content of the database is represented in one and only one way: namely, as relations (*see* **essentiality**). *Note:* It has to be said that this principle isn't very well named. It might more accurately be called *The Principle of Uniform Representation*, or even *The Principle of Uniformity of Representation*, since the crucial point about it is that it implies that all information in a relational database is represented in the same way: namely, as relations.

inheritance Type inheritance (see Part II of this dictionary), unless the context demands otherwise.

INIT *See* **example value**.

initialization Assigning an initial value to a variable—typically but not necessarily at the time the variable in question is defined—before any reference to that variable (i.e., within some expression) needs to be evaluated in order to provide a value to be used for some purpose. *Note:* *The Third Manifesto* requires all variables, relational or otherwise, to be initialized at the time they're defined (*see* **variable**); in fact, in the case of base relvars in particular, it requires them to be initialized either (a) to a value specified explicitly as part of the operation that defines that relvar or (b) to the empty relation of the pertinent type, if no such explicit value is specified.

injection / injective mapping   Terms used interchangeably to mean a mapping, or function, from set *s1* to set *s2* such that each element of *s2* is the image of at most one element of *s1*. Also known as a nonloss, injective, or "one to one into" mapping (though *one to one* here isn't being used in its strict sense, q.v.).

Example: The mapping from nonnegative integers *x* to their squares x^2 is an injection from the set of all nonnegative integers to (or into) itself.

inner join   Same as join. The qualification *inner* is used when it's necessary to distinguish the join in question from its outer counterpart. Outer join in turn—at least as usually understood— has to do with nulls and three-valued logic and is therefore deliberately not discussed further in this dictionary (though in fact it would be possible to define a slightly more "respectable" form of outer join that didn't involve nulls at all).

INSERT   Loosely, an operator—shorthand for a certain relational assignment—that inserts specified tuples into a specified relvar. The syntax is:

```
INSERT R rx
```

Here *R* is a relvar reference (syntactically, just a relvar name) and *rx* is a relational expression (denoting some relation *r* of the same type as *R*), and the effect is to insert the tuples of *r* into *R*. In other words, the INSERT invocation just shown is shorthand for the following explicit assignment:

```
R := R UNION rx
```

It follows that an attempt via INSERT to insert a tuple that's already present is not considered an error (*contrast* **disjoint INSERT**).

Example: The statement

```
INSERT SP RELATION
            { TUPLE { SNO SNO('S3') , PNO PNO('P1') , QTY QTY(150) } ,
              TUPLE { SNO SNO('S4') , PNO PNO('P5') , QTY QTY(400) } } ;
```

is shorthand for the following relational assignment statement:

```
SP := SP UNION RELATION
            { TUPLE { SNO SNO('S3') , PNO PNO('P1') , QTY QTY(150) } ,
              TUPLE { SNO SNO('S4') , PNO PNO('P5') , QTY QTY(400) } } ;
```

Given the sample values shown in Fig. 1, however, this assignment will insert just one tuple, not two (speaking a trifle loosely), because the tuple <S4,P5,400> already appears in relvar SP.

INSERT anomaly   Same as insertion anomaly.

INSERT rule A rule specifying the action to be taken automatically—typically but not necessarily a compensatory action, q.v.—to ensure that INSERT operations on a given relvar don't violate any associated multivariable constraint, q.v. Note, however, that such automatic actions should occur, if and when logically required, regardless of the concrete syntactic form in which the original INSERT request is expressed. For example, an INSERT request expressed as a pure relational assignment (using ":="), q.v., should nevertheless cause the action specified by the pertinent INSERT rule to be performed—assuming, of course, that such a rule has been defined in the first place.

insert set *See* relational assignment.

insertion anomaly Term originally used (though never very precisely defined) to refer to the fact that certain information can't even be represented in a relvar that's subject to FD redundancy, q.v. E.g., suppose for the sake of the example that relvar S is subject to the FD $\{CITY\} \rightarrow \{STATUS\}$. Of course, the sample value shown for that relvar in Fig. 1 doesn't satisfy this FD; however, it would do so if we changed the status for supplier S2 from 10 to 30, so let's suppose for the sake of the example that this change has in fact been made (though actually it has no effect on the specific anomaly to be discussed). Here then is an insertion anomaly: We can't insert a tuple to say the status for Rome is 10 until we have a supplier in Rome (in other words, the design violates the goal of expressive completeness, q.v.). *Note:* A relvar that's in BCNF, q.v., is guaranteed to be free of insertion anomalies in this "FD redundancy" sense.

    The term *insertion anomaly* is also used in connection with relvars that are subject to JD redundancy, q.v.; in this case, however, the concept is more precisely defined. To be specific, let the JD J hold in relvar R; then R suffers from an insertion anomaly with respect to J if and only if there exist a relation r and a tuple t, each with the same heading as R, such that (a) r satisfies J, and (b) the relation r' whose body is obtained from that of r by adding t satisfies R's key constraints but violates J. *Note:* A relvar that's in ETNF (q.v.) is guaranteed to be free of insertion anomalies in this "JD redundancy" sense.

    Finally, this latter definition can be generalized, as follows: Relvar R suffers from an insertion anomaly if and only if (a) there exists a single-relvar constraint C on R and (b) there exist a relation r and a tuple t, each with the same heading as R, such that r satisfies C and the relation r' whose body is obtained from that of r by adding t satisfies R's key constraints but violates C. *Note:* A relvar that's in DK/NF, q.v., is guaranteed to be free of insertion anomalies in this generalized sense.

instance 1. Term sometimes used, especially in OO contexts, as a synonym for occurrence or appearance of a value, q.v.—or possibly of a variable (?). *Note:* The latter possibility arises because at least some objects in at least some OO systems are really what are known in more conventional programming systems (perhaps not very appropriately) as "explicit dynamic variables." The storage for such objects is allocated at run time by explicit program action (*see* constructor function). As a consequence, (a) there can be any number of "instances" of such objects in existence simultaneously at run time; (b) those "instances" have (and can have) no distinguishing name in the conventional sense; and therefore (c) those "instances" can be referenced only by their address or object ID, q.v. (which is essentially why OO systems require support for object IDs in the first place). *See* **mutable object** for further explanation. 2. An instance of a relation schema (q.v.) is any relation that conforms to the schema in question; in other words, it's just a value (a relation) of the type represented by that schema. This usage is deprecated, however, if only because the term *instance* has also been used on occasion—most inappropriately!—to refer to an individual tuple within some relation.

instance variable   The physical representation, q.v., of an object in OO contexts is usually assumed to consist of a set of named instance variables (also known among other things as state variables, attributes, or members), whose values at any given time together represent the overall value of the object in question at that time. Ideally, such instance variables should be visible only to implementation code (i.e., the code that implements the operators that apply to the object in question); in particular, they should be invisible to users. In practice, however, various compromises are typically made in this connection. To be more specific, instance variables are typically divided into two categories: public ones, which are visible to users (as well as, of course, to implementation code of all kinds), and private ones, which are visible only to implementation code that applies to objects of the type of the object in question (*but see* friendship).

   Examples: Let BEGIN and END be public instance variables, both of type POINT, for type LINE_SEG ("line segments"); then the system will typically allow the user to write expressions of the form (e.g.) LS.BEGIN and LS.END to "get" the BEGIN and END points for a given line segment LS.

   Of course, the problem with public instance variables is that they effectively expose physical representations. (Note that, by definition, access to such variables must be via some special syntax—typically dot qualification, as the previous paragraph suggests—for otherwise there's no point in distinguishing between public and private variables in the first place. See further discussion below.) So if the physical representation changes—say to the combination of MIDPOINT, LENGTH, and SLOPE, in the case of line segments—then any program that includes expressions such as LS.BEGIN and LS.END will now fail. In other words, physical data independence is lost.

   But public instance variables are logically unnecessary anyway. Suppose operators GET_BEGIN, GET_END, GET_MIDPOINT, GET_LENGTH, and GET_SLOPE are defined for line segments (*see* **GET_ operator**). Then the user can "get" the begin point, the end point, the midpoint, and so on, for line segment LS by means of appropriate operator invocations: GET_BEGIN (LS), GET_END (LS), GET_MIDPOINT (LS), and so on. And now it makes no difference what the physical representation of line segments is—just so long as the various GET_ operators are implemented appropriately, and reimplemented appropriately if that physical representation changes. In other words, physical data independence is preserved.

instantiation   1. Loosely, an invocation of a predicate, q.v., in which (by definition) each parameter is replaced by some argument. The result of such instantiation is a proposition, q.v. *Note:* Actually, the logical notion of instantiation is more general than the familiar programming language notion of operator invocation. To be specific, we can instantiate an *n*-place predicate by substituting arguments for just *m* of its parameters ($m \leq n$), thereby obtaining a *k*-place predicate, where $k = n - m$. If $m = n$, the instantiation is said to be full (and the term *instantiation*, unqualified, is usually taken to mean full instantiation specifically, unless the context demands otherwise); otherwise it's said to be partial. 2. In OO contexts, the term *instantiation* is sometimes used to refer to the creation of a new mutable object. *See* constructor function.

integrity   A database is in a state of integrity if and only if it satisfies all defined integrity constraints. Of course, a properly implemented DBMS can't possibly allow the database ever to violate any defined integrity constraint, and so databases really ought to be in a state of integrity at all times (this is one possible formulation of **The Golden Rule**, q.v.). Note, however, that—in the relational model, at least—"at all times" effectively means at statement boundaries (or, loosely, "at semicolons"), not merely at transaction boundaries. In other words, all integrity checking is immediate in the relational model. *See also* consistency.

integrity constraint   A named boolean expression, or something equivalent to such an expression, that's required to be satisfied—i.e., to evaluate to TRUE—at all times, where "at all times" effectively means at statement boundaries (or, loosely, "at semicolons"), not merely at transaction boundaries. There are two basic kinds, database constraints and type constraints, q.v. (*but see* attribute constraint; relvar constraint; tuple constraint); however, the term is usually taken to mean a database constraint specifically, unless the context demands otherwise. The DBMS will reject any attempt to perform an update that would otherwise cause some integrity constraint to be violated (i.e., to evaluate to FALSE). *Note:* Type constraints effectively constrain selector invocations (*see* selector). By contrast, database constraints effectively constrain database update operations—and since database update operations apply, by definition, to relvars specifically (i.e., not to relations as such), it follows that such constraints can be thought of as applying to relvars specifically too (i.e., anything constrained by a database integrity constraint must be a relvar, not a relation, by definition).

intelligent key   A single-attribute key whose values, in addition to their main purpose of serving as unique identifiers (typically for certain real world "entities," q.v.), carry some kind of encoded information embedded within themselves. *Contrast* surrogate key.
  Example: Let parts purchased from domestic suppliers be assigned part numbers in the range 0-499 and parts purchased elsewhere be assigned part numbers in the range 500-999. Now assume the 501st different kind of part is purchased from a domestic supplier. Clearly, the part numbering scheme will now have to be revised, and any application that previously relied on the

fact that parts purchased domestically have numbers less than 500 will now fail. As this example suggests, intelligent keys should be used with caution. (It's tempting to suggest, therefore, that "intelligent keys" might better be referred to as "*un*intelligent keys.") *Note:* Actually, similar remarks apply to the encoding of information within values of *any* attribute, not just "entity identifying" attributes specifically, but "entity identifying" attributes do seem to be particularly prone to this kind of abuse.

intended interpretation   For a given relvar, the informal, user understood meaning; in other words, the relvar predicate, q.v. Also referred to as interpretation, unqualified. *Contrast* relvar constraint (second definition).

intension   For a given relation or relvar, the intended interpretation, or sometimes the heading. Note the spelling! *Contrast* extension (fourth definition).

Interchangeability Principle   (*Of base and virtual relvars*) The principle that there should be no arbitrary and unnecessary distinctions between base and virtual relvars; i.e., virtual relvars should "look and feel" just like base ones so far as users are concerned. *See also* information equivalence; view updating.

interdependent projections   *See* FD preservation.

interface   (*Without inheritance*) A shared boundary between two systems. Often used more specifically to refer to the specification signature, q.v., for some operator; sometimes also used, especially in OO contexts, to refer to the complete set of operators supported by values and variables of some particular type. (As indicated, this latter use of the term occurs in connection with OO systems in particular. Note, however, that some OO systems also use it to mean something else entirely. See Part II of this dictionary.)

internal predicate   The total relvar constraint for a given relvar. The term is deprecated because it's at least arguably misleading (since relvar constraints are in fact not general predicates but, more specifically, propositions).

interpretation   Same as intended interpretation.

INTERSECT   *See* intersection.

intersection   (*Without inheritance*) 1. (*Dyadic case*) Let relations $r1$ and $r2$ be of the same type T. Then (and only then) the expression $r1$ INTERSECT $r2$ denotes the intersection of $r1$ and $r2$, and it returns the relation of type T with body the set of all tuples t such that t appears in each of $r1$ and $r2$. 2. (*N-adic case*) Let relations $r1, r2, ..., rn$ ($n \geq 0$) all be of the same type T. Then (and only then) the expression INTERSECT $\{r1,r2,...,rn\}$ denotes the intersection of $r1, r2, ...,$

rn, and it returns the relation of type *T* with body the set of all tuples *t* such that *t* appears in each of *r1*, *r2*, ..., *rn*. *Note:* If *n* = 0, (a) some syntactic mechanism, not shown here, is needed to specify the pertinent type *T* and (b) the result is the universal relation, q.v., of that type. Note too that the relational intersection operator differs in certain respects from the mathematical or set theory operator of the same name, q.v.; in fact, it's a special case of join, q.v. Note finally that INTERSECT can also be used as an aggregate operator, q.v.

Example: The expression S{CITY} INTERSECT P{CITY} denotes the intersection of (a) the relation that's the projection on {CITY} of the current value of relvar S and (b) the relation that's the projection on {CITY} of the current value of relvar P. That intersection is a relation *r* of type RELATION {CITY CHAR}. Moreover, if the current values of relvars S and P are *s* and *p*, respectively, then the body of that relation *r* consists of all tuples of the form <*c*> that appear in both *s*{CITY} and *p*{CITY}—meaning *c* is a current supplier city that's also a current part city. Note that the expression S{CITY} INTERSECT P{CITY} is logically equivalent to the expression S{CITY} JOIN P{CITY}.

intersection (bag theory)   *See* bag.

intersection (set theory)   The intersection of two sets *s1* and *s2*, *s1* ∩ *s2* (where the symbol "∩" can conveniently be pronounced "cap"), is the set of all elements *x* such that *x* is an element of *s1* and an element of *s2*. *Note:* This definition can obviously be extended to apply to any number of sets.

intersection star   *See* bag.

into   (*Of a function; preposition used as an adjective*) Having range equal to some proper subset of the codomain (*contrast* onto). *See* injection.

inverse   *See* Laws of Algebra.
Examples: 1. In ordinary arithmetic, the identities for "+" and "*" are 0 and 1, respectively (*see* identity). As a consequence, (a) for "+", the inverse of *x* is −*x*; (b) for "*", the inverse of *x* is 1/*x* (unless *x* is 0, the only number that has no multiplicative inverse). 2. In two-valued logic, the identities for OR and AND are FALSE and TRUE, respectively (again, *see* identity). As a consequence, (a) for OR, FALSE is its own inverse but TRUE has no inverse (there's no truth value *v* such that TRUE OR *v* yields FALSE); (b) for AND, TRUE is its own inverse but FALSE has no inverse (there's no truth value *v* such that FALSE AND *v* yields TRUE). 3. Also in two-valued logic, the identities for EQUIV and XOR are TRUE and FALSE, respectively (again, *see* identity). As a consequence, for both operators, each of TRUE and FALSE is its own inverse. (To spell out the details: TRUE EQUIV TRUE and FALSE EQUIV FALSE both yield TRUE, while TRUE XOR TRUE and FALSE XOR FALSE both yield FALSE.)

invocation 1. (*Operator*) *See* read-only operator; update operator. 2. (*Predicate*) *See* instantiation.

invocation signature *See* RETURNS.

involution 1. (*Logic*) If *v* is a truth value, then the negation of the negation of *v* is equal to *v*. (It follows that, in logic, adjacent NOTs "cancel out"—that is, the predicate NOT(NOT(*p*)) can be simplified to just (*p*).) 2. (*Set theory*) If *s* is a set, then the complement of the complement of *s* is equal to *s*.

irrational number A real number (q.v.) that can't be expressed as the ratio of two integers. Examples include π and $\sqrt{2}$. Irrational numbers have the property that, in decimal notation, the fractional part of such a number consists of an infinite, nonrepeating sequence of decimal digits (e.g., $\pi = 3.14159...$, $\sqrt{2} = 1.41421...$). *Contrast* rational number.

irreducible 1. (*Of a key*) *See* candidate key. 2. (*Of a relvar*) Sixth normal form. 3. (*Of an FD*) *See* irreducible FD. 4. (*Of a set of FDs*) *See* irreducible cover. 5. (*Of a JD*) *See* irreducible JD. 6. (*Of an MVD*) *See* irreducible MVD.

irreducible cover Let *s1* and *s2* be sets of FDs. Then *s2* is an irreducible cover for *s1* if and only if it's a cover for *s1* (q.v.) and, for every FD in *s2*, (a) the dependant consists of a single attribute; (b) no attribute can be discarded from the determinant without losing the property that *s2* is a cover for *s1*; and (c) the FD can't be discarded from *s2* without losing the property that *s2* is a cover for *s1*.

irreducible FD The FD $X \rightarrow Y$ is irreducible with respect to relvar *R* (or just irreducible, if *R* is understood) if and only if it holds in *R* and $X' \rightarrow Y$ doesn't hold in *R* for any proper subset X' of *X*.

    Examples: Of the FDs {SNO} $\rightarrow$ {CITY} and {SNO,STATUS} $\rightarrow$ {CITY}, both of which hold in relvar S, the first is irreducible and the second isn't. Likewise, of the FDs {SNO,PNO} $\rightarrow$ {QTY} and {SNO,PNO,QTY} $\rightarrow$ {QTY}, both of which hold in relvar SP, the first is irreducible and the second isn't.

irreducible JD Let $\Leftrightarrow${*X1,X2,...,Xn*} be a JD, *J* say, that holds in relvar *R*, and let there be no proper subset {*Y1,Y2,...,Ym*} of {*X1,X2,...,Xn*} such that the JD $\Leftrightarrow${*Y1,Y2,...,Ym*} also holds in *R*; then *J* is irreducible with respect to *R* (or just irreducible, if *R* is understood). *Note:* If some component *Xi* is irrelevant (q.v.) in *J*, then *J* is certainly reducible with respect to every relvar in which it holds; however, *J* can still be reducible with respect to some relvar even if all components are relevant (see the examples immediately following).

    Examples: The following JD, which holds in relvar S, is reducible, because the {CITY,STATUS} component can be dropped without significant loss:

⟂ { { SNO , SNAME , STATUS } , { SNO , CITY } , { CITY , STATUS } }

By contrast, the following JD—i.e., the JD that results when the {CITY,STATUS} component is dropped from the JD just shown—(a) still holds in relvar S but (b) is irreducible:

⟂ { { SNO , SNAME , STATUS } , { SNO , CITY } }

irreducible MVD Since—to speak a trifle loosely—(a) an MVD is basically just a JD with exactly two components and (b) a JD is reducible if and only if one or more of its components can be dropped without loss, (c) the notion of reducibility doesn't seem to make much sense in connection with MVDs, and hence (d) the notion of irreducibility doesn't seem to make much sense either.

irreducibly dependent (*Of a dependant in an FD*) Let X and Y be subsets of the heading of some relvar R. Then Y is irreducibly dependent on X with respect to R if and only if the FD $X \rightarrow Y$ is irreducible with respect to R.

    Examples: In relvar S, {STATUS} is irreducibly dependent on {SNO}; it's also dependent on {SNO,CITY}, but not irreducibly so. Similarly, in relvar SP, {QTY} is irreducibly dependent on {SNO,PNO}; it's also dependent on {SNO,PNO,QTY}, but not irreducibly so.

irreducibly equivalent (*Of sets of FDs*) Let $s1$ and $s2$ be sets of FDs. Then $s1$ and $s2$ are irreducibly equivalent if and only if each is an irreducible cover for the other.

irrelevant component (*Of a JD*) Let ⟂{$X1,X2,..., Xn$} be a JD, J say; then Xi is irrelevant in J if and only if (a) there exists some Xj in J such that Xi is a proper subset of Xj or (b) there exists some Xj in J ($i > j$) such that $Xi = Xj$. *Note:* If we assume (as we normally do in practice) that the commalist of components $X1$, $X2$, ..., Xn of J contains no duplicates, we can drop part (b) of this definition. *See also* **irreducible JD**.

IS_EMPTY A **Tutorial D** operator that returns TRUE or FALSE according as its argument relation is empty or not.

    Examples: See the examples under **database constraint** and elsewhere.

IS_NOT_EMPTY A **Tutorial D** operator that returns FALSE or TRUE according as its argument relation is empty or not. In other words, the expression IS_NOT_EMPTY(*rx*), where *rx* is a relational expression, is logically equivalent to the expression NOT (IS_EMPTY(*rx*)). *Note:* SQL supports the IS_NOT_EMPTY operator fairly directly, but it calls it EXISTS.

isomorphism Let X and Y be sets, not necessarily distinct, and let f be a bijective mapping from X to Y. Let OpX be an operator that takes elements of X as its operands and returns an element of X as its result. Then the mapping f is an isomorphism if and only if, for all such operators *OpX*, there exists an analogous operator *OpY* that takes elements of *Y* as its operands and returns an element of *Y* as its result such that, whenever (a) *OpX* applied to *x1, x2, ..., xn* returns *x*, then (b) *OpY* applied to *y1, y2, ..., yn* returns *y*, where (c) *y1, y2, ..., yn*, and *y* are the images of *x1, x2, ..., xn*, and *x*, respectively, under *f*. In other words, an isomorphism is a bijective mapping that preserves the algebraic structure of the domain *X* in the codomain *Y*. *Note:* If the bijective mapping *f* is an isomorphism, its inverse is an isomorphism also.

   Example: Let *X* be the set {EVEN,ODD}—the names are meant to be suggestive—and let operators "+" and "*" be defined as follows:

+	EVEN	ODD
EVEN	EVEN	ODD
ODD	ODD	EVEN

*	EVEN	ODD
EVEN	EVEN	EVEN
ODD	EVEN	ODD

   Now let *Y* be the set {TRUE,FALSE} and let *f* be a bijection from *X* to *Y* that maps EVEN and ODD to TRUE and FALSE, respectively. Further, let the logical operators EQUIV and OR correspond to "+" and "*", respectively. Then *f* is an isomorphism from *X*, with its operators "+" and "*", to *Y* with its operators EQUIV and OR.

———— ♦ ♦ ♦ ♦ ♦ ————

JD   Join dependency.

JD implied by keys   *See* JD implied by superkeys.

JD implied by superkeys   Let relvar *R* have heading *H* and let ✡{*X1,X2,...,Xn*} be a JD, *J* say, with respect to *H*. Then *J* is implied by the superkeys of *R* if and only if every relation *r* that satisfies *R*'s superkey constraints also satisfies *J*—equivalently, if and only if the following membership algorithm succeeds. Let *S* be the set {*X1,X2,...,Xn*}. If two distinct members of *S* both include the same superkey of *R*, replace them in *S* by their union, and repeat this process until no further such replacements are possible. Then the algorithm succeeds (and *J* is therefore implied by superkeys of *R*) if and only if *S* now contains *H* as a member. *See* **fifth normal form**. *Note:* The term *superkey* could be replaced by the term *key* throughout the foregoing definition without making any substantive difference. Note too that the membership algorithm succeeds trivially if *J* itself is trivial.

   Examples: Let relvar R have attributes A, B, C, D, E, and F (and no others); let AB denote the set of attributes {A,B}, and similarly for other attribute name combinations (also, let single attribute names denote the corresponding singleton sets—e.g., let A denote the set {A}); finally, let R have keys A, B, and CD (and no others). Then the following are all JDs that are implied by the superkeys of R (and they all hold in R, necessarily):

✿ { AB , ACDE , BF }

✿ { ABC , ACD , BEF , EF }

✿ { AB , AC , ADEF }

Observe in the second of these examples that the component EF is irrelevant, q.v., and could thus be dropped from the JD without significant loss.

Here by contrast are some JDs that aren't implied by the superkeys of R:

✿ { ABC , CDEF }

✿ { ABD , ACDE , DF }

Note that the first of these two JDs necessarily fails to hold in relvar R, because C isn't a key. The second might or might not hold. If it does, then R isn't in 5NF; conversely, if R is in 5NF, then that JD can't possibly hold.

Note: It's worth elaborating on the intuition behind the foregoing. Using notation as in the formal definition, and using J to denote the JD ✿$\{X1,X2,...,Xn\}$, the basic idea is as follows. Let the current value of relvar R be relation r, and for some i and j ($i \neq j$) let ri and rj be the projections of r on Xi and Xj, respectively. If Xi and Xj both include the same superkey of R, then the join rk of ri and rj—whose heading Xk will be the set theory union of Xi and Xj—will be strictly one to one, and so ri and rj can be replaced by rk without loss of information. (At the same time, Xi and Xj can be replaced in J by Xk.) Since the original version of J was implied by the superkeys of R, performing such replacements repeatedly will, by definition, eventually yield a relation (a) that's equal to the original relation r (because no information will be lost at any step in the process), and in particular (b) will therefore have a heading equal to the entire heading H of r.

The foregoing argument shows that every relation satisfies every JD that's implied by the pertinent superkeys, and this fact is appealed to in the definition of 5NF (q.v.): Essentially, a relation conforms to the requirements for 5NF if and only if it fails to satisfy any additional JDs, over and above those implied by the pertinent superkeys. Note, however, that the concept of 5NF applies to relvars, while the foregoing intuitive explanation is expressed in terms of relations, not relvars.

JD redundancy   Relvar R is subject to JD redundancy if and only if some tuple forcing JD (q.v.) holds in R.

JOIN   *See* natural join.

join   Natural join, q.v. (unless the context demands otherwise).

join dependency   Let *H* be a heading; then a join dependency (JD) with respect to *H* is an expression of the form ✪{*X1,X2,...,Xn*}, such that the set theory union of *X1*, *X2*, ..., *Xn* is equal to *H*. (The qualifying phrase "with respect to *H*" can be omitted if *H* is understood.) The expression overall can be read as "star *X1*, *X2*, ..., *Xn*." *Note:* The concept of join dependency is a generalization of the concept of multivalued dependency (MVD); that is, every MVD is a JD, but some JDs aren't MVDs. (To be specific, an MVD is a JD with exactly two components, thus: ✪{*X1,X2*}.) Informally, however, it's common to use the term *JD* to mean a JD that isn't an MVD.

Note: Different writers use different symbols to denote a JD; in this dictionary we use a special kind of star ("✪"), but the "bow tie" symbol "⋈" is more often encountered in recent research literature (*see* **natural join**).

Let relation *r* have heading *H* and let ✪{*X1,X2,...,Xn*} be a JD, *J* say, with respect to *H*. If *r* is equal to the join of its projections on *X1*, *X2*, ..., *Xn*, then *r* satisfies *J*; otherwise *r* violates *J*. Now let relvar *R* have heading *H*. Then *R* is subject to the JD *J*—equivalently, the JD *J* holds in *R*—if and only if every relation *r* that can ever be assigned to *R* satisfies that JD *J*. The JDs that hold in relvar *R* are the JDs of *R*, and they serve as constraints (q.v.) on *R*.

Note that JDs are defined with respect to some heading, not with respect to some relation or some relvar. Note too that from a formal point of view, a JD is just an expression: an expression that, when interpreted with respect to some specific relation, becomes a proposition that, by definition, evaluates to either TRUE or FALSE. Now, it's common informally to define ✪{*X1,X2,...,Xn*} to be a JD only if it actually holds in the pertinent relvar—but that definition leaves no way of saying a given JD fails to hold in some relvar, because, by that definition, a JD that fails to hold isn't a JD in the first place. Note finally that it's immediate from the definition that relvar *R* can be nonloss decomposed into its projections on *X1*, *X2*, ..., and *Xn* if and only if the JD ✪{*X1,X2,...,Xn*} holds in *R*.

Examples: The suppliers relvar S is subject to the JD

```
✪ { { SNO , SNAME } , { SNO , STATUS } , { SNO , CITY } }
```

because every relation that's a legal value for S is equal to the join of its projections on {SNO,SNAME}, {SNO,STATUS}, and {SNO,CITY}; thus, relvar S could be nonloss decomposed into those three projections. Of course, there's no requirement that this decomposition actually be performed—whether it should or not depends on whether there's any advantage to be gained by doing so.

By way of a second example, observe that, thanks to Heath's Theorem (q.v.), if a certain FD holds in a given relvar, then a certain JD holds in that relvar as well. (In other words, every FD implies some JD.) For example, the FD {SNO} → {STATUS} holds in relvar S, and hence the following JD holds as well:

```
✪ { { SNO , STATUS } , { SNO , SNAME , CITY } }
```

So too do both of these JDs, incidentally:

⚭ { { SNO , STATUS } , { SNO , STATUS } , { SNO , SNAME , CITY } }

⚭ { { SNO , STATUS } , { STATUS } , { SNO , SNAME , CITY } }

In each of these latter JDs, however, one of the components can obviously be dropped; in other words, these JDs aren't irreducible, q.v.

join trap   *See* connection trap.

joinable   (*Without inheritance*) 1. (*Dyadic case*) Relations *r1* and *r2* are joinable if and only if attributes with the same name are of the same type—equivalently, if and only if the set theory union of their headings is a legal heading. Note that dyadic joinability isn't transitive (q.v.); that is, just because (a) *r1* and *r2* are joinable and (b) *r2* and *r3* are joinable, it doesn't necessarily follow that (c) *r1* and *r3* are joinable. 2. (*N-adic case*) Relations *r1, r2, ..., rn* ($n \geq 0$) are joinable—sometimes *n*-way joinable, for emphasis—if and only if for all *i* and *j*, relations *ri* and *rj* are joinable ($1 \leq i \leq n$, $1 \leq j \leq n$).

    Examples: Let relation *r1* have attributes called A and B (and no others), let relation *r2* have attributes called B and C (and no others), and let relation *r3* have attributes called C and A (and no others). Further, let attribute B in *r1* and attribute B in *r2* be of the same type—in other words, let them be, formally, the very same attribute—and likewise for attribute C in *r2* and attribute C in *r3*; but let attribute A in *r1* and attribute A in *r3* be of different types. Then *r1* and *r2* are joinable, and so are *r2* and *r3*, but *r1* and *r3* aren't. (It follows that *r1, r2,* and *r3* aren't 3-way joinable.)

———— ◆◆◆◆◆ ————

KCNF   Key complete normal form.

KEY   *See* key constraint.

key   A candidate key, q.v. (unless the context demands otherwise).

key attribute   An attribute of a given relvar that's part of at least one key of that relvar. *See also* primary key attribute; subkey.

key complete normal form   Same as redundancy free normal form.

key constraint   A constraint to the effect that a given subset of the heading of a given relvar is a key (more precisely, a candidate key) for that relvar. In **Tutorial D**, such a constraint is defined by means of a KEY specification within the pertinent relvar definition (e.g., see the definitions for relvars S, P, and SP in the introduction to this dictionary). Note, however, that while the system certainly can and will enforce the uniqueness constraint implied by such a specification—*see* **candidate key**—it can't in general enforce the corresponding irreducibility constraint as well; in other words, specifying KEY{*K*} as part of the definition of relvar *R* means that {*K*} is certainly a superkey, q.v., but not necessarily a key as such, for relvar *R*.

Example: Suppose we were to specify KEY{SNO,CITY} instead of KEY{SNO} in the definition of relvar S. Then the system obviously wouldn't be able to enforce the constraint that supplier numbers as such, as opposed to supplier-number / city combinations, are unique. (On the other hand, if we were to specify both KEY{SNO,CITY} and KEY{SNO}, the system should at least be able to recognize that {SNO,CITY} is a proper superset of {SNO} and so reject the specification KEY{SNO,CITY}.)

Note: **Tutorial D** allows key constraints to be specified not just for relvars as such, but in fact for arbitrary relational expressions. For example, the statement

```
CONSTRAINT KX ( S JOIN SP ) KEY { PNO , CITY } ;
```

defines a constraint corresponding to the following business rule: *If suppliers sx and sy (sx ≠ sy) supply the same part, then they must be in different cities.* In other words, this CONSTRAINT statement can be understood as saying that if a view were to be defined with S JOIN SP as its defining expression, then the attribute combination {PNO,CITY} would be a key for that hypothetical view.

key inference   The process of determining the key constraints that hold in a given derived relvar or are satisfied by a given derived relation. Key inference is a special case of constraint inference, q.v.

———— ◆◆◆◆◆ ————

LAST   *See* ordinal type.

Laws of Algebra   Let *A* be a formal system consisting of a set *s* of elements *x*, *y*, *z*, ..., together with two distinct dyadic operators "+" and "*" (usually called addition and multiplication, respectively, though they aren't necessarily the operators known by those names in conventional arithmetic). Then *A* is certainly an algebra if it abides by the following laws:

- *Closure laws:* The set *s* is closed under both "+" and "*"; that is, for all *x* and *y* in *s*, each of the expressions *x*+*y* and *x**y yields an element of *s*.

- *Commutative laws:* For all *x* and *y* in *s*, *x*+*y* = *y*+*x* and *x**y = *y**x.

- *Associative laws:* For all *x*, *y*, and *z* in *s*, *x*+(*y*+*z*) = (*x*+*y*)+*z* and *x**(*y**z) = (*x**y)*z.

■ *Identity laws:* There exist elements 0 and 1 in *s* such that for all *x* in *s*, $0+x = x+0 = x$ and $1*x = x*1 = x$. Those elements 0 and 1 are the additive identity and the multiplicative identity, respectively.

■ *Inverse laws:* For all *x* in *s*, there exist elements $-x$ and (unless $x = 0$) $1/x$ in *s* such that $x+(-x) = 0$ and $x*(1/x) = 1$. Those elements $-x$ and $1/x$ are the additive inverse and the multiplicative inverse, respectively (of *x* in each case). *Note:* The expressions $x+(-y)$ and $x*(1/y)$ are usually abbreviated $x-y$ and x/y, respectively.

■ *Distributive law* (of "*" over "+"): For all *x*, *y*, and *z* in *s*, $x*(y+z) = (x*y)+(x*z)$.

However, not all algebras abide by all of these laws. In the algebra of sets, for example, the "+" and "*" operators are union and intersection, respectively, and the corresponding identities are the empty set and the universal set, respectively; however, the inverse laws don't hold (i.e., given an arbitrary set *s1*, in general there's no set *s2* such that the union of *s1* and *s2* is the empty set or the intersection of *s1* and *s2* is the universal set). Relational algebra likewise fails to obey the inverse laws, a fortiori.

left associativity Let *Op* be a dyadic operator, and assume for definiteness that *Op* is expressed in infix style. Then *Op* is left associative if and only if, for all *x*, *y*, and *z*, *x Op y Op z* can be correctly evaluated left to right (i.e., as (*x Op y*) *Op z*); similarly, it's right associative if and only if, for all *x*, *y*, and *z*, it can be correctly evaluated right to left (i.e., as *x Op* (*y Op z*)). *Note:* In mathematics and logic, left and right associativity both reduce to just associativity, q.v., as normally understood. However, such is not necessarily the case in computing. For example, let *x*, *y*, and *z* be floating point numbers and let *Op* be "+". In the computing context, then, it might well be the case that $(x+y)+z$ and $x+(y+z)$ produce different results; it might even be the case that one of these expressions raises an exception (e.g., overflow) and the other doesn't.

left identity Let *Op* be a dyadic operator, and assume for definiteness that it's expressed in infix style. If there exists a value *i* such that *i Op v* is equal to *v* for all possible values *v*, then *i* is the left identity, or left identity value, with respect to *Op*. *See also* identity (fifth definition); right identity.

Examples: Every identity, q.v., is necessarily a left identity in particular (and also a right identity, q.v., of course). As for an example of a left identity that's not a right identity, let the operator "\" be defined in such a way that the invocation *m\n* returns the result of dividing the integer *m* into the integer *n*; then, since $1\backslash v$ is equal to *v* for all numbers *v* whereas $v\backslash 1$ is not, 1 is a left identity but not a right identity with respect to "\".

left irreducible FD Same as irreducible FD. (The qualifier "left" derives from the fact that it's the left side—i.e., the determinant—that can't be reduced in an irreducible FD.)

less-than join   A theta join, q.v., in which theta is "<".

lexical   (*Of a language, sentence, etc.*) Pertaining to individual words and other basic symbols (punctuation, etc.). *Contrast* semantic; syntactic.

linear ordering   Same as total ordering. *Contrast* cyclic ordering.

literal   1. (*Logic*) A simple proposition, q.v., or its negation; a simple predicate, q.v., or its negation. Note that, by definition, a literal in this sense is in both conjunctive normal form, q.v., and disjunctive normal form, q.v. 2. (*Programming languages*) Loosely, a self-defining symbol; a symbol that denotes a value that can be determined at compile time. More precisely, a literal is a symbol that denotes a value that's fixed and determined by the symbol in question (and the type of that value is therefore also fixed and determined by the symbol in question). Every value of every type, tuple and relation types included, is—in fact, must be—denotable by means of some literal. *Note:* A literal in the programming language sense is a special case of a selector invocation (*see* selector); to be precise, a literal is a selector invocation if and only if all of the argument expressions in that selector invocation are literals in turn. Note too that there's a logical difference between a literal as such and the value it denotes (*see* constant, second definition). Be aware, however, that some systems, including certain OO systems in particular, do use the term *literal* to mean a value as such. *Caveat lector.*
    Examples (second definition only):

```
4              /* a literal of type INTEGER                           */

'ABC'          /* a literal of type CHAR                              */

FALSE          /* a literal of type BOOLEAN                           */

SNO('S1')      /* a literal of type SNO                               */

TUPLE { SNO SNO('S1') , PNO PNO('P1') , QTY QTY(300) }
               /* a literal of type TUPLE {SNO SNO, PNO PNO, QTY QTY}) */

RELATION { TUPLE { SNO SNO('S1') , PNO PNO('P1') , QTY QTY(300) } ,
         { TUPLE { SNO SNO('S5') , PNO PNO('P6') , QTY QTY(100) } }
               /* a literal of type RELATION {SNO SNO, PNO PNO, QTY QTY}*/
```

log   A record in persistent storage of all of the updates that have been made to the database since some prescribed time (possibly the time when the system was first installed), showing for each update in question (a) the value of the updated object before and after that update was done, (b) the time when that update was done, (c) the user and transaction responsible for that update, and (d) almost certainly other things besides. The log is used as a basis (a) for undoing updates if some transaction fails to reach a successful conclusion, and also (b) for redoing updates if a system failure causes the updates in question to be lost. *See also* audit trail.

logic The science or scientific study of the methods and principles used in valid reasoning.

logic system / logical system / system of logic Terms used interchangeably to mean, loosely, a system consisting of axioms and inference rules, together with a set of theorems that can be derived from the former by means of the latter. More precisely, a logic system consists of (a) a set of symbols (connectives, punctuation symbols, variable names, "individual constants," etc.); (b) a set of grammatical rules for forming "sentences" of the system; (c) a set of given sentences (the axioms); and (d) a set of rules for inferring "new" sentences from "old" ones. *See also* connective; individual constant; inference rule; truth functional completeness; and elsewhere.

Examples: Propositional logic and predicate logic are both systems of logic, in which the legal sentences are propositions and predicates, respectively. The relational model is another example, in which the legal "sentences" are relational algebra or relational calculus expressions.

logic variable A variable that can appear either bound or free in expressions of predicate logic (*see* bound variable; free variable); not to be confused with a logical variable, q.v. *See also* range variable.

logical access path *See* access path.

logical data independence *See* data independence.

logical database design The process, or the result of the process, of deciding what relvars some database should contain, what attributes they should have, and what constraints they should be subject to. Ideally, the goal of the logical design process is to produce a design that's independent of all considerations having to do either with physical implementation or with specific applications—the latter objective being desirable for the very good reason that it's generally not the case that all uses to which the database will be put are known at design time. Overall, the logical design process can be summed up as one of (a) pinning down the relvar predicates and other business rules (q.v.) as carefully as possible, albeit necessarily somewhat informally, and then (b) mapping those informal predicates and rules to specific relvars and formal constraints—preferably in such a way as to ensure the result involves no uncontrolled redundancy, q.v.

logical design Same as logical database design (if the context demands).

logical difference A difference that's logical, not (e.g.) merely psychological, in nature. The term derives from a maxim of Wittgenstein's: *All logical differences are big differences.* The relevance of this maxim for database systems in particular, and in fact for computing systems in general, can be explained as follows: The relational model is a formal system (just as a DBMS is, or an operating system, or indeed any computer program). Formal systems are what computers are—or can be made to be—good at. And since the basis of any formal system is logic, it follows that in such contexts differences that are logical in nature are very important ones, and we need to pay careful attention to them. In those same contexts, by contrast, differences that aren't logical in nature are comparatively unimportant; in programming languages, for example, semantic differences are very significant, while mere syntactic differences are much less so.

Example: In **Tutorial D,** there's a syntactic difference, but no semantic or logical difference, between the expressions S{SNO} MINUS SP{SNO} and S{SNO} NOT MATCHING SP. *Note:* Many further illustrations of, and references to, the notion of logical difference can be found elsewhere in this dictionary.

logical equivalence   Two expressions are logically equivalent if and only if each is derivable from the other in accordance with the rules of the particular system of logic in effect. In conventional 2VL, for example, the expressions NOT$((p)$ AND $(q))$ and (NOT (p)) OR (NOT (q)) are logically equivalent. (This equivalence—which is in fact one of De Morgan's Laws, q.v.—can easily be shown by means of truth tables, q.v.) And in the relational algebra, the expressions A INTERSECT B and A MINUS (A MINUS B) are logically equivalent, and so are the expressions A and A INTERSECT (A UNION B). Observe in particular in this latter example that one of the expressions mentions a variable, B, that the other one doesn't. *Contrast* information equivalence; truth functional equivalence.

logical expression   An expression denoting a truth value.

logical implication   Implication, q.v.

logical operator   An operator that takes values or variables or both of type BOOLEAN as operands and either returns a value, or updates a variable, of type BOOLEAN. The connectives are an important special case.

logical variable   (*Programming languages*) A variable of type BOOLEAN. The term is probably best avoided because of possible confusion with the term *logic variable,* q.v.

lossless decomposition   Nonloss decomposition, q.v.

lossless join   Nonloss join, q.v. The term is probably best avoided, just as the term *nonloss join* (q.v.) is, and for essentially the same reasons.

lossy decomposition   A decomposition that isn't nonloss.

Example: The decomposition of relvar S into its projections on {SNO,SNAME} and {SNAME,STATUS,CITY} is lossy because it isn't guaranteed that, at all times, S is equal to the join of those projections.

lossy join   A join that isn't a nonloss join, q.v., in either sense of that term. The term is probably best avoided, just as the term *nonloss join* (q.v.) is, and for essentially similar reasons.

——— ♦♦♦♦♦ ———

managed redundancy   Same as controlled redundancy.

mandatory participation   *See* cardinality constraint.

manual optimization   *See* optimization.

many to many correspondence   Strictly, a rule pairing two sets *s1* and *s2* (not necessarily distinct) such that each element of *s1* corresponds to at least one element of *s2* and each element of *s2* corresponds to at least one element of *s1*; equivalently, that pairing itself. Often used loosely, however, to mean a pairing such that either (a) each element of *s1* corresponds to any number of elements of *s2* (possibly none at all) and each element of *s2* corresponds to at least one element of *s1*, or (b) each element of *s1* corresponds to at least one element of *s2* and each element of *s2* corresponds to any number of elements of *s1* (possibly none at all), or (c) each element of *s1* corresponds to any number of elements of *s2* (possibly none at all) and each element of *s2* corresponds to any number of elements of *s1* (possibly none at all). The term is probably best avoided unless the intended meaning is clear.

Example (strict sense only): Let *s* be the set of all positive integers. Consider the pairing of positive integers *x* and *y* defined as follows: Positive integers *x* and *y* are paired if and only if they have the same number of digits in conventional decimal notation (no leading zeros). Then that pairing is a many to many correspondence from *s* to itself.

many to many join   Let relations *r1* and *r2* be joinable, q.v. Then the join of *r1* and *r2* is said— somewhat loosely—to be many to many if and only if the pairing of tuples from *r1* and *r2* under the join is a many to many correspondence, q.v., in any of the senses of this latter term. *Note:* The foregoing definition is expressed in terms of relations, but the phrase *many to many join* is often applied to relvars instead of relations.

Example: The join of suppliers and parts, S JOIN P, would typically be said to be many to many, even though there might be some tuples in S that join to no tuple in P and vice versa.

many to one correspondence   Strictly, a rule pairing two sets *s1* and *s2* (not necessarily distinct) such that each element of *s1* corresponds to exactly one element of *s2* and each element of *s2* corresponds to at least one element of *s1* (in other words, a surjection, q.v.); equivalently, that pairing itself. Often used loosely, however, to mean a pairing such that (a) each element of *s1* corresponds to at most one element of *s2* and each element of *s2* corresponds to at least one element of *s1*, or (b) each element of *s1* corresponds to exactly one element of *s2* and each element of *s2* corresponds to any number of elements of *s1* (possibly none at all), or (c) each element of *s1* corresponds to at most one element of *s2* and each element of *s2* corresponds to any number of elements of *s1* (possibly none at all). The term is probably best avoided unless the intended meaning is clear.

 Example (strict sense only): Let *s1* and *s2* be the set of all integers and the set of all nonnegative integers, respectively. Then the pairing of integers *x* with their absolute values ABS(*x*) is a many to one correspondence from *s1* to *s2*.

many to one join Let relations *r1* and *r2* be joinable, q.v. Then the join of *r1* and *r2* is said—somewhat loosely—to be many to one if and only if the pairing of tuples from *r1* and *r2* under the join is a many to one correspondence, q.v., in any of the senses of this latter term. *Note:* The foregoing definition is expressed in terms of relations, but the phrase *many to one join* is often applied to relvars instead of relations.

 Example: The join of shipments and suppliers, SP JOIN S, would typically be said to be many to one from SP to S, even though there might be some tuples in S that join to no tuple in SP.

many-valued logic Same as *n*VL, q.v., for some *n* > 2.

map / mapping Terms used interchangeably to mean a function, q.v. Often used—in this dictionary in particular, on occasion—to mean a function that's a bijection (q.v.) specifically, together with its inverse.

mark *See* null.

MATCHING **Tutorial D** keyword denoting semijoin, q.v.

material equivalence Logical equivalence, q.v.

material implication Logical implication, q.v.

materialization 1. A technique for evaluating relational expressions in which intermediate result relations are produced in their entirety before being passed on as input to another operation. *Contrast* pipelining. 2. View materialization, q.v.

materialized view Deprecated term for a snapshot. Note the difference between (a) materialization as a technique for implementing read-only operations on views (*see* view materialization) and (b) a "materialized view"—i.e., a snapshot—as such. The former is an implementation technique and should have no logical consequences for the user at all (i.e., users shouldn't need to know whether a given read-only operation on a given view is implemented by materialization). By contrast, the latter is an issue that certainly does concern the user; i.e., the user certainly does need to know whether a given relvar is a snapshot, because whether it is or not affects the semantics of the relvar in question (as well as dictating whether update operations are allowed on that relvar). The problem is, however, that—as the definition indicates— snapshots have come to be known, at least in some circles, not as snapshots at all but as materialized views. But snapshots aren't views; views are virtual and snapshots aren't, and *materialized view* is a contradiction in terms, at least as far as the relational model is concerned. Worse yet, the unqualified term *view* is now often taken to mean a materialized view specifically, and we're thus in danger of no longer having a good term for a view in the original sense. This dictionary does use *view* in its original sense, but be warned that the term doesn't always have that meaning elsewhere. *Caveat lector.*

MAX   (*Aggregate operator, dyadic version*) Let *v1* and *v2* be values of the same ordered type. Then the expression MAX{*v1,v2*} returns *v1* if *v1* > *v2* is true and *v2* otherwise. In other words, MAX{*v1,v2*} is shorthand for:

```
IF v1 > v2 THEN v1 ELSE v2 END IF
```

Note: This operator is really just that special case of the *n*-adic version of MAX (*see* **aggregate operator**) in which the commalist of argument expressions contains exactly two such expressions (equivalently, it's the MAX2 operator also defined under **aggregate operator**). The definition is included here primarily because it's appealed to elsewhere in this dictionary (in Part III in particular).

meaning   (*Of a relvar*) *See* **intended interpretation; intension; relvar constraint** (second definition); **relvar predicate.**

mediator   *See* **Great Divide; Small Divide.**

member   An element of a bag or (especially) set. *Note:* The term is also used in OO systems to mean an instance variable (q.v.), but this usage is best avoided because of possible conflict with the mathematical sense of the term.

membership   *See* **bag membership; set membership;** *contrast* **containment.**

membership algorithm   *See* **JD implied by superkeys.**

merge join   A join implementation technique.

message   Term used in OO contexts to mean an operator invocation. However, messages are usually considered as being "sent" to a specific object: viz., the object that's the argument that corresponds, in the invocation in question, to the "distinguished parameter"—see Part II of this dictionary—to the operator in question (hence the message terminology). *See* **selfish method** (also in Part II of this dictionary).

metadata   Data about data. *See* **catalog**; *see also* **database statistics**.

method   Term used in OO contexts to mean either an operator per se, which is a model concept, or an implementation version of some operator, which is an implementation concept (see Part II of this dictionary). Unfortunately it's not uncommon to find the term used with both meanings in the same text, or even in the same sentence. For example: "The attributes [*i.e., the instance variables, q.v.*] associated with an object are private, and only an object's methods may examine or update these data; the methods are public" (from R. G. G. Cattell, *Object Data Management: Object-Oriented and Extended Relational Database Systems*, revised edition, Addison-Wesley, 1994).

MIN   (*Aggregate operator, dyadic version*) Let *v1* and *v2* be values of the same ordered type. Then the expression MIN {*v1,v2*} returns *v1* if *v1* < *v2* is true and *v2* otherwise. In other words, MIN {*v1,v2*} is shorthand for:

```
IF v1 < v2 THEN v1 ELSE v2 END IF
```

Note: This operator is really just that special case of the *n*-adic version of MIN (*see* **aggregate operator**) in which the commalist of argument expressions contains exactly two such expressions. The definition is included here primarily because it's appealed to elsewhere in this dictionary (in Part III in particular).

minimality   (*Of a key or FD, and possibly other things besides*) Old fashioned and somewhat deprecated (because inaccurate) term for irreducibility.

MINUS   *See* **difference**.

missing information   Term often used to refer to information that's either currently unknown or not applicable. *Note:* To describe information that's currently unknown as missing is possibly reasonable; for example, if some person has failed to provide their date of birth (e.g., in filling out some form), it's reasonable to say the date of birth for that person is missing. However, to describe information that's not applicable as missing isn't reasonable at all (and the usage is therefore deprecated). For example, if some person doesn't have an email address, the email address for that person isn't missing—rather, it simply doesn't exist.

model   In the database world, either a data model in general (in either sense of that term) or the relational model specifically, as the context demands. *Note:* Actually, the term *model* has been given a great number of additional meanings as well, both in the computing literature as such and also in the literature of logic and related disciplines—more meanings, in fact, than it can reasonably be expected to bear. Such additional meanings are deliberately ignored here.

modification anomaly   Term originally used (though never very precisely defined) to refer to the fact that UPDATE operations on a relvar that's subject to FD redundancy, q.v., can lead to inconsistency. *Note:* A relvar that's in BCNF, q.v., is guaranteed to be free of modification anomalies in this "FD redundancy" sense.

Example: Suppose relvar SP is subject to the FD {CITY} → {STATUS}, meaning that whenever two tuples agree on CITY, they must also agree on STATUS. (Of course, the sample value shown for that relvar in Fig. 1 doesn't satisfy this FD; however, it would do so if we changed the status for supplier S2 from 10 to 30, so let's suppose for the sake of the example that this change has in fact been made.) Then it's possible—though only if a less than perfect job is being done on defining and enforcing integrity constraints—that after an UPDATE, two tuples might agree on CITY and not on STATUS.

Note: In general, of course, redundancy of any kind—at least if it's uncontrolled, q.v.— can always lead to inconsistency, because redundancy means, loosely, that some piece of information is represented twice, and so there's always the possibility that the two representations don't agree: namely, when one has been updated and the other hasn't. (Of course, these remarks do tacitly assume that the kind of consistency under discussion is merely what this dictionary elsewhere—*see* **consistency**—calls informal or "eventual" consistency. Formal consistency can be violated only if, to say it again, a less than perfect job is being done on integrity constraint definition and enforcement.)

modus ponens   Loosely, proof by affirmation; more precisely, a rule of inference to the effect that if we know that (*p*) IMPLIES (*q*) is true and we also know that *p* is true, we can infer that *q* must be true. Also known as direct reasoning.

modus tollens   Loosely, proof by denial; more precisely, a rule of inference to the effect that if we know that (*p*) IMPLIES (*q*) is true but we also know that *q* is false, we can infer that *p* must be false. Also known as indirect reasoning. *Note:* In the database context, *modus tollens* is relevant to the process of integrity constraint checking. In effect, when some given update is requested, the proposed new database value is checked against all applicable constraints; if the proposition expressed by some such constraint evaluates to FALSE, the new database value must also represent falsehood—in other words, it must be incorrect (*see* **correctness**)—and so the update must be rejected.

monadic   Of an operator, having exactly one operand; of a predicate, being defined in terms of exactly one parameter. *Contrast* **unary**.

multidependent   *See* **multivalued dependency**.

multidetermines   *See* multivalued dependency.

multiple assignment   An operation that allows several individual assignments all to be performed in parallel (in effect, simultaneously). In the important special case in which the target(s) for some or all of the individual assignments are database relvars, no database constraint checking is done until all of those individual assignments have been executed in their entirety. Note that multiple assignments, relational or otherwise, are involved implicitly in a variety of other operations—for example, updating some join or union view, or updating some relvar in such a way as to cause a cascade delete or other compensatory action (q.v.) to be performed.

Example: The following "double DELETE" is, logically, a multiple assignment operation:

```
DELETE S  WHERE SNO = SNO('S1') ,
DELETE SP WHERE SNO = SNO('S1') ;
```

Note the comma separator after the first DELETE, which indicates syntactically that the end of the overall statement hasn't yet been reached. Here's the corresponding expanded form, using explicit assignment:

```
S  := S  WHERE NOT ( SNO = SNO('S1') ) ,
SP := SP WHERE NOT ( SNO = SNO('S1') ) ;
```

In general, the semantics of multiple assignment are as follows: First, all of the source expressions in the individual assignments are evaluated; then all of those individual assignments are executed in parallel. *Note:* This explanation requires some slight refinement in the case where two or more of the individual assignments specify the same target (see below). Ignoring that refinement for the moment, however, we can say that since the source expressions are all evaluated before any of the individual assignments are done, none of those individual assignments can depend on the result of any other (and so "executing them in parallel" is really just a manner of speaking). In the example, the effect on the database would be exactly the same if the two individual DELETEs were specified in reverse order.

Observe now that a multiple assignment in which the target variables are all relvars in the same database is actually just a syntactic device that allows us to formulate what is logically a database assignment (q.v.) as a collection of individual relational assignments. (And a "single" relational assignment—i.e., a "multiple" relational assignment consisting of just one individual assignment, to one individual database relvar—is just a special case, of course.) In other words, database relvars aren't really variables, as such, at all; instead, they're pseudovariables, q.v., and they act as a convenient fiction that gives the illusion that the database can be updated in a piecemeal fashion, individual relvar by individual relvar.

As for repeated targets: If two or more of the individual assignments involved in a given multiple assignment specify the same target variable, then those particular individual assignments are effectively executed in sequence as written (thereby effectively reducing to a single assignment to that target variable). For example, the double assignment

```
S := S MINUS ( S WHERE SNO = SNO('S1') ) ,
S := S MINUS ( S WHERE SNO = SNO('S2') ) ;
```

is logically equivalent to the following single assignment:

```
S := WITH ( S := S MINUS ( S WHERE SNO = SNO('S1') ) ) :
                 S MINUS ( S WHERE SNO = SNO('S2') ) ;
```

An important special case of the foregoing arises in connection with assignment via two or more THE_ pseudovariables to the same target variable. For example, the multiple assignment

```
THE_A ( E ) := LENGTH ( 5.0 ) ,
THE_B ( E ) := LENGTH ( 4.0 ) ;
```

(where E is a variable of declared type ELLIPSE—see the example under CONSTRAINT) is semantically equivalent to the following single assignment:

```
E :=
WITH ( E := ELLIPSE ( LENGTH ( 5.0 ) , THE_B ( E ) , THE_CTR ( E ) ) ) :
            ELLIPSE ( THE_A ( E ) , LENGTH ( 4.0 ) , THE_CTR ( E ) ) ;
```

Note: Actually the foregoing explanation—i.e., of multiple assignments of the form illustrated by this particular example—is still slightly oversimplified, inasmuch as special precautions need to be taken in order to ensure that selector invocations in the WITH specification don't cause any type constraints to be violated. Further details are byond the scope of this dictionary.

multiple EXTEND   *See* extension; tuple extension.

multiple RENAME   *See* renaming; tuple renaming.

multiple SUMMARIZE   *See* summarization.

multiplicative identity   *See* Laws of Algebra.

multiplicative inverse   *See* Laws of Algebra.

multiplicity   Strictly, the state of being manifold; loosely, a large number. In bag theory, however, the term is given a rather special meaning (*see* **bag**).

multirelvar constraint   Term sometimes used for a database constraint that references two or more distinct relvars. *Contrast* multivariable constraint; single-relvar constraint. *Note:* Actually the difference between single-relvar and multirelvar constraints is more a matter of pragma than logic, thanks to *The Principle of Interchangeability* among other things. For example, the constraint on suppliers to the effect that supplier numbers are unique is a single-relvar constraint if all suppliers are represented in a single relvar as in Fig. 1, but would become a multirelvar constraint if that relvar were decomposed "horizontally" into a set of restrictions (one for each supplier city, say).

Examples: The foreign key constraints from relvar SP to relvars S and P are multirelvar constraints; so is constraint C3 from the examples under **database constraint**.

multiset   Same as bag.

multituple constraint   Term occasionally used for a relvar or database constraint that isn't a single-tuple constraint, q.v.

Examples: Constraint C3 from the examples under **database constraint** might be regarded as a multituple constraint; so might the key constraints for relvars S, P, and SP.

multivalued attribute   Extremely inappropriate term—because, by definition, a "multivalued attribute" isn't an attribute at all—sometimes used to mean a repeating field or repeating group, q.v.

multivalued dependency   A join dependency, q.v., with exactly two components (but typically expressed, not in conventional JD notation, but rather in a notation specific to multivalued dependencies as such). To elaborate: Let H be a heading; then a multivalued dependency (MVD) with respect to H is an expression of the form $X \rightarrow\rightarrow Y$, where X (the determinant) and Y (the dependant) are both subsets of H. (The qualifying phrase "with respect to H" can be omitted if H is understood.) The expression $X \rightarrow\rightarrow Y$ is read as "Y is multidependent on X," or "X multidetermines Y," or, more simply, just "X double arrow Y."

Let relation r have heading H; let X, Y, and Z be such their set theory union is equal to H; and let M be the MVD $X \rightarrow\rightarrow Y$. If r satisfies the JD $\Leftcirclearrowright\{\{X,Y\},\{X,Z\}\}$, then r satisfies M; otherwise r violates M. Now let relvar R have heading H. Then R is subject to the MVD M—equivalently, the MVD M holds in R—if and only if every relation r that can ever be assigned to R satisfies that MVD M. The MVDs that hold in relvar R are the MVDs of R, and they serve as constraints (q.v.) on R.

Note that it follows from the previous paragraph that the expression $X \rightarrow\rightarrow Y$—or, a little more precisely, the expression $X \rightarrow\rightarrow Y \mid Z$ (see below)—is indeed, as claimed above, logically equivalent to a certain JD with exactly two components: viz., the JD $\Leftcirclearrowright\{\{X,Y\},\{X,Z\}\}$. Note too that MVDs are defined with respect to some heading, not with respect to some relation or some relvar. Note also that from a formal point of view, an MVD is just an expression: an expression that, when interpreted with respect to some specific relation, becomes a proposition that, by definition, evaluates to either TRUE or FALSE. Now, it's common informally to define $X \rightarrow\rightarrow Y$ to be an MVD only if it actually holds in the pertinent relvar—but that definition leaves no way of saying a given MVD fails to hold in some relvar because, by that definition, an MVD that fails to hold isn't an MVD in the first place.

Example: As in the example under fourth normal form, let relvar CTX have attributes C (course), T (teacher), and X (textbook), and predicate *Course C can be taught by teacher T and uses textbook X.* Let that relvar be all key (i.e., let no proper subset of the heading be a key). Assume also that for a given course, the set of teachers and the set of texts are quite independent of each other. Then the MVDs {C} $\rightarrow\rightarrow$ {T} and {C} $\rightarrow\rightarrow$ {X} hold in that relvar (equivalently, the JD ✪{{C,T},{C,X}} holds in that relvar).

Note that X and Y in the MVD $X \rightarrow\rightarrow Y$ are, specifically, sets of attributes. Informally, however, it's common (though strictly incorrect) to speak of the attributes in X as if Y were multidependent on those attributes per se, instead of on the set X that contains those attributes. Likewise, it's common (though strictly incorrect) to speak of the attributes in Y as if those attributes per se, instead of the set Y that contains those attributes, were multidependent on X. (The foregoing remarks apply with especial force to the common special case in which either X or Y is a singleton set.) Note too that, given X, Y, and Z as defined above, relvar R is subject to the MVD $X \rightarrow\rightarrow Y$ if and only if it's subject to the MVD $X \rightarrow\rightarrow Z$ (MVDs always come in pairs in this way); for this reason, it's usual to write them as a "one liner," thus: $X \rightarrow\rightarrow Y | Z$. Note finally that it follows from the definition that if R is subject to the MVDs $X \rightarrow\rightarrow Y | Z$, then if it contains the tuples <*x,y1,z1*> and <*x,y2,z2*>, it also contains the tuple <*x,y1,z2*> (and hence, as can immediately be seen by interchanging the given tuples, the tuple <*x,y2,z1*> as well).

multivariable constraint   Term sometimes used to mean a database constraint that involves at least two distinct range variables if expressed in tuple calculus form. *Contrast* multirelvar constraint; single-variable constraint.

Examples: Constraint C3 from the examples under **database constraint** is both a multirelvar constraint and a multivariable constraint. Note that a multirelvar constraint is necessarily a multivariable constraint as well; however, the converse is false, because the two or more range variables involved in a given multivariable constraint might all range over (the current value of) the same relvar. Key constraints are a case in point; by definition, such a constraint applies to a single relvar, but it's also a multivariable constraint, necessarily. For example, here's a relational calculus formulation of the key constraint for relvar S:

```
CONSTRAINT CSK FORALL SX ( UNIQUE SY ( SX.SNO = SY.SNO ) ) ;
```

(*See* FORALL; UNIQUE. The range variables SX and SY here are both defined to range over the relation that's the value of relvar S at the time the constraint is checked.)

mutable object   OO term for a variable (*contrast* immutable object). Note, however, that (a) the unqualified term *variable* is typically used in OO contexts to mean not an object at all but, rather, either a local variable or an instance variable, q.v. (meaning in both cases, typically but not necessarily, one that holds an object ID, q.v.); (b) the term *mutable object* is very frequently abbreviated in OO contexts to just *object*, unqualified. (In fact, some OO languages and systems actually define the term *object* to mean a mutable object specifically, and use some quite different term—typically *literal*, q.v.—to refer to an immutable object.)

Example: As suggested under **instance**, an illuminating analogy can be drawn between mutable objects as such and the "explicit dynamic variables" supported by certain conventional programming languages (PL/I's based variables are a case in point). Like mutable objects of a given class, there can be any number of explicit dynamic variables of a given type, the storage for which is allocated at run time by explicit program action. Furthermore, those variables, again like mutable objects, are unnamed and must therefore be addressed via pointers. For example, consider the following PL/I code fragment:

```
DECLARE 1 ABOBJ BASED ,
         2 A INTEGER ,
         2 B FLOAT ;

DECLARE P POINTER ;

ALLOCATE ABOBJ SET ( P ) ;

P -> ABOBJ.A = 3 ;
```

Now observe the parallels between this PL/I code and conventional OO code:

- The declaration of the based variable ABOBJ is akin to creating a new object class. Any number of individual objects (or variables) of that class can now be created in turn.

- Individual objects (or variables) of that class have two "public instance variables" A and B, of types INTEGER and FLOAT, respectively. *Note:* In the OO context, A and B would probably contain pointers (i.e., "object IDs," in effect) rather than numbers.

- P is a program variable whose values are pointers (i.e., "object IDs," in effect).

- The ALLOCATE statement is akin to an OO constructor function invocation (q.v.): It creates a new object (or variable) of class ABOBJ, allocating storage for that object, and setting P to point to it. Observe that this new object has no distinguishing name apart from its address—which is precisely why object IDs are necessary, in the OO world.

- The assignment statement "mutates" the object that P points to by assigning the value three to its A instance variable.

And so on.

mutation Term sometimes used (especially in OO contexts) to mean updating.

mutator   Term sometimes used (especially in OO contexts) to mean an update operator. To quote Stanley B. Zdonik and David Maier, "Fundamentals of Object-Oriented Databases," in *Readings in Object-Oriented Database Systems* (Zdonik and Maier, eds.; Morgan Kaufmann, 1990): "[If] *m* is ... a mutator, it must be possible to observe its effect on some object." *Contrast* observer. *Note:* SQL's use of the term is unorthodox, in that its mutators are read-only.

MVD   Multivalued dependency.

MVD implied by a key   *See* MVD implied by a superkey.

MVD implied by a superkey   Let relvar R have heading H and let $X \rightarrow\rightarrow Y$ be an MVD, M say, with respect to H. Then M is implied by a superkey of R if and only if every relation r that satisfies R's superkey constraints also satisfies M—equivalently, if and only if either M is trivial or X is a superkey for R or both. (Actually, if X is a superkey for R, then the MVD $X \rightarrow\rightarrow Y$ effectively degenerates to the FD $X \rightarrow Y$.) *See* fourth normal form. *Note:* The term *superkey* could be replaced by the term *key* throughout the foregoing definition without making any substantive difference.

───────── ◆ ◆ ◆ ◆ ◆ ─────────

n-adic   Of an operator, having exactly n operands ($n \geq 0$); of a predicate, being defined in terms of exactly n parameters ($n \geq 0$). *Contrast n-ary. Note:* Many operators that are conventionally regarded as dyadic can readily be—and often are, in this dictionary—extended to n-adic versions for arbitrary nonnegative n. Such extended versions are certainly legitimate so long as the dyadic operator in question is associative (q.v.) and commutative (q.v.) and has an identity value (q.v.). Examples of such operators include (a) the logical operators AND, EQUIV, OR, and XOR, and (b) the relational operators union and join and their variants (disjoint union, cartesian product, etc.). Note that some of these operators are idempotent, q.v., and some not. Note too that even if a given dyadic operator isn't associative, it might still be possible to define an n-adic counterpart to it, but that counterpart will necessarily be a logically different operator (though it might, and ideally should, reduce to the dyadic case if $n = 2$). For an example and further discussion, *see* composition; see also the discussion of alternative definitions for n-adic versions of EQUIV (under equivalence) and XOR (under exclusive OR).

n-adic aggregate operator   *See* aggregate operator.

n-ary   (*Of a heading, key, tuple, relation, etc.*) Of degree n ($n \geq 0$). *Contrast n-adic.*

n-dimensional   (*Of a relation or relvar*) Of degree n ($n \geq 0$). Observe, therefore, that relations and relvars are not, as many people seem to think, "flat" or two-dimensional (unless they happen to be binary, of course); rather, a relation or relvar of degree n is n-dimensional, in the sense that its tuples represent points in a certain *n*-dimensional space. One consequence of this state of affairs is that, contrary to popular opinion, relations are perfectly capable of representing "multidimensional data" and thereby supporting "online analytical processing" (OLAP).

   Example: Each tuple in the suppliers relvar S represents a certain 4-point—a point, that is, in a certain four-dimensional space (where the dimensions in question are, of course, supplier number, name, status, and city, represented by the four attributes of the relvar)—and the relvar overall can thus be said to be four-dimensional.

***n*-place**   (*Of a predicate*) Same as *n*-adic ($n \geq 0$).

***n*-tuple**   A tuple of degree *n* ($n \geq 0$). Hence the special case terms *0-tuple, 1-tuple, 2-tuple, 3-tuple*, etc. *Note:* The familiar relational term *tuple* itself is simply an abbreviation of the term *n-tuple*.

***n*-way joinable**   *See* joinable.

named constant   A value that can be referenced by means of a name that's not just a simple literal representation of the value in question. A named constant differs from a variable in two obvious ways—first, it can never serve as the target for an assignment operation; second, every reference to the name in question always denotes the same value. *See* **constant**; *contrast* variable.

naming of types   *See* type naming.

Naming Principle   The principle that everything we need to talk about needs to have a name (including *The Naming Principle* itself, of course!). It's very difficult to talk about things that have no name, and yet examples where *The Naming Principle* is violated abound. For example, the SQL standard defines a construct it calls an exception handler. But such handlers have no name in SQL, and so the standard's explanation of them begins by saying, in effect, "Let *H* be a handler"; in other words, it introduces a name for the otherwise anonymous construct. Other examples of constructs that at least potentially have no name include (a) columns in SQL tables, (b) databases in **Tutorial D**, and (c) objects, methods, and parameters in OO systems.

NAND   In logic, a dyadic connective (also known as the Sheffer stroke and usually written as a vertical bar, "|", though this symbol is used for many other purposes as well); if and only if *p* and *q* are predicates, then (*p*)|(*q*) is a predicate also. Let (*ip*)|(*iq*) be an invocation of that predicate, where *ip* and *iq* are invocations of *p* and *q*, respectively. Then that invocation (*ip*)|(*iq*) evaluates to FALSE if and only if *ip* and *iq* both evaluate to TRUE. (In other words, (*p*)|(*q*) is equivalent to NOT ((*p*) AND (*q*)).) *Note:* The parentheses enclosing *p* and *q* in the predicate, and *ip* and *iq* in the invocation, might not be needed in practice. Also, NAND as just defined is a logical operator; however, the algebra **A**, q.v., includes an operator called NAND that—by definition—is an algebraic operator instead (it's basically "complement of join").

native key Same as natural key.

natural join (*Without inheritance*) 1. (*Dyadic case*) Let relations *r1* and *r2* be joinable, q.v. Then (and only then) the expression *r1* JOIN *r2* denotes the natural join of *r1* and *r2*, and it returns the relation with heading the set theory union of the headings of *r1* and *r2* and body the set of all tuples *t* such that *t* is the set theory union of a tuple from *r1* and a tuple from *r2*. 2. (*N-adic case*) Let relations *r1, r2, ..., rn* ($n \geq 0$) be *n*-way joinable, q.v. Then (and only then) the expression JOIN {*r1,r2,...,rn*} denotes the natural join of *r1, r2, ..., rn*, and it returns a relation *r* defined as follows: If $n = 0$, *r* is TABLE_DEE; if $n = 1$, *r* is *r1*; otherwise, choose any two distinct relations from the set *r1, r2, ..., rn* and replace them by their (dyadic) natural join, and repeat this process until the set consists of just one relation *r*, which is the final result.

    Note: Although there are various kinds of join (or so it might be argued, at any rate), natural join is far and away the most important kind, which is why this dictionary uses the unqualified term *join* and the keyword JOIN to refer to the natural join specifically. (By contrast, in the research literature—at least, the recent research literature—natural join is often represented not by a keyword at all but by the "bow tie" symbol ⋈.)

    Examples: The expression S JOIN SP—which could equally well be written JOIN {S,SP}—denotes the natural join of the relations that are the current values of relvars S and SP. That join is a relation of type RELATION {SNO SNO, SNAME NAME, STATUS INTEGER, CITY CHAR, PNO PNO, QTY QTY}. Moreover, if the current values of relvars S and SP are *s* and *sp*, respectively, the body of that relation consists of all tuples of the form <*sno,sn,t,c,pno,q,*> such that the tuple <*sno,sn,t,c*> appears in *s* and the tuple <*sno,pno,q*> appears in *sp*.

    By way of another example, the expression S JOIN SP JOIN P—which could equally well be written JOIN {S,SP,P}—denotes the natural join of the relations that are the current values of relvars S, SP, and P (note that S, SP, and P are indeed 3-way joinable, as required). That join is a relation of type RELATION {SNO SNO, SNAME NAME, STATUS INTEGER, CITY CHAR, PNO PNO, QTY QTY, PNAME NAME, COLOR COLOR, WEIGHT WEIGHT}. Moreover, if the current values of relvars S, SP, and P are *s*, *sp*, and *p*, respectively, the body of that relation consists of all tuples of the form <*sno,sn,t,c,pno,q,pn,l,w*> such that the tuple <*sno,sn,t,c*> appears in *s*, the tuple <*sno,pno,q*> appears in *sp*, and the tuple <*pno,pn,l,w,c*> appears in *p*.

natural key Term sometimes used to refer to a key that's not a surrogate key, q.v.

natural numbers The positive integers 1, 2, 3, etc. *Note:* Some writers additionally consider zero to be a natural number; the literature is not consistent on this point, but the majority of writers, and indeed common usage, do exclude the zero case.

negation   If and only if *p* is a predicate, its negation NOT (*p*) is a predicate also. Let NOT (*ip*) be an invocation of that predicate, where *ip* is an invocation of *p*. Then that invocation NOT (*ip*) evaluates to TRUE if and only if *ip* evaluates to FALSE. *Note:* The parentheses enclosing *p* in the predicate, and *ip* in the invocation, might not be needed in practice.

negation as failure   A concept closely related to *The Closed World Assumption,* q.v.; it means, loosely, that if a given tuple has the same heading as the result of a given query and hence could appear in that result (at least in principle) but doesn't, then the proposition represented by that tuple is false.

negative   Strictly less than zero. *Note:* The expression −0 is legal, of course, but it doesn't denote a negative value; rather, it denotes the nonnegative value 0.

negative remainder   Let $p = n*q + r$, where *p*, *q*, *r*, and *n* are integers, *q* is nonzero, *r* is nonnegative, and $r < q$. Then the negative remainder after dividing *p* by *q* is $r - q$ (unless *r* is zero, in which case no negative remainder exists).

   Example: Let $p = -17$ and $q = 7$. Then the nonnegative remainder *r* (q.v.) after dividing *p* by *q* is 4, and so the negative remainder is −3. Observe that $-17 = (-2)*7 + (-3)$.

nested loops join   *See* brute force join.

nested relation   *See* relation valued attribute.

nesting and unnesting   For relations, *see* grouping and ungrouping, respectively; for tuples, *see* wrapping and unwrapping, respectively

NEXT   *See* ordinal type.

NF²   NF squared; short for NFNF ("non first normal form"). An NF² relvar is, loosely, a relvar with at least one relation valued attribute. The term is very strongly deprecated, however, because it's based on a flawed understanding of the concept of first normal form (note that all relvars are in 1NF—very likely in some higher normal form as well—even if they do have relation valued attributes). Also, the NF² concept is usually taken to include certain extensions to the conventional relational operators, extensions that aren't just shorthand and are therefore not included (nor are they needed) in the relational model. For example, some writers have proposed an extended form of dyadic union that (a) recursively and/or repeatedly ungroups both operands until they involve no relation valued attributes at all, either directly or indirectly, then (b) performs a regular union on those ungrouped operands, and then (c) recursively and/or repeatedly (re)groups the result again. And it's that recursion and/or repetition that makes the operator an "extended" one; that is, while any specific extended union invocation is shorthand for some specific combination of regular relational ungroup and union and (re)group operator invocations, nothing analogous applies to the extended union operator in general.

niladic   Of an operator, having no operands; of a predicate, being defined in terms of no parameters. *Contrast* **nullary**. *Note:* An operator might appear to be niladic syntactically and yet not be limited to having the same effect on every invocation, owing to its use of what might be called hidden operands, such as the current reading of the system clock. Indeed, such operators—which are, of course, not truly niladic anyway—are the normal case.

   Example: Many languages provide an operator of the form RANDOM ( ) for generating random (or, rather, pseudorandom) numbers. Such operators effectively have a hidden operand—e.g., the random number returned on the previous invocation, or perhaps the current reading of the system clock.

noncommutative group   *See* **group (mathematics)**.

nongenerated type   A type not produced by invocation of any type generator, q.v. Note that nongenerated types are always scalar (by contrast, generated types might be scalar or nonscalar). For examples, *see* **system defined type; user defined type**.

nonkey attribute   An attribute of a given relvar that isn't part of any key of that relvar.

nonloss decomposition   Replacing a relvar R by certain of its projections $R1, R2, ..., Rn$, such that (a) the join of $R1, R2, ..., Rn$ is guaranteed to be equal to R, and usually also such that (b) each of $R1, R2, ..., Rn$ is needed in order to provide that guarantee (i.e., none of those projections is redundant in the join), and usually also such that (c) at least one of $R1, R2, ..., Rn$ is at a higher level of normalization than R is. In other words, nonloss decomposition is essentially just normalization, q.v., as this latter term is usually understood. (It would be possible to define the concept more generally to encompass more than just conventional normalization, but this dictionary doesn't do so.) Note, incidentally, that one "nonloss decomposition" that's always available for any given relvar R is to "replace" R by its identity projection, q.v.

   Example: A nonloss decomposition that might be applied to the suppliers-and-parts database would involve the replacement of relvar S by its projections on {SNO,SNAME} and {SNO,STATUS,CITY}. Relvar S could then be reconstructed by joining those two projections back together again.

nonloss join   1. The join of relations $r1$ and $r2$ is nonloss with respect to $r1$ if and only if $(r1$ MATCHING $r2) = r1$; nonloss with respect to $r2$ if and only if $(r2$ MATCHING $r1) = r2$; and nonloss unconditionally (or simply nonloss, unqualified, for short) if and only if it's nonloss with respect to both $r1$ and $r2$. 2. Let X and Y be subsets of the heading H of relation r, such that the set theory union of X and Y is equal to H. Then the join of $r\{X\}$ and $r\{Y\}$ is nonloss with respect to r if and only if it's equal to r. *Note:* These two meanings are related and easily confused, but they're not the same, and the term is probably best avoided for that reason. (Observe in particular in the second case that the join of $r\{X\}$ and $r\{Y\}$ is certainly nonloss in the first sense with respect to each of $r\{X\}$ and $r\{Y\}$.) Be that as it may, the concepts apply to, and are used in connection with, relvars as well as relations.

nonnegative   Greater than or equal to zero. *Contrast* positive.

nonnegative remainder   Let $p = n*q + r$, where p, q, r, and n are integers, q is nonzero, r is nonnegative, and $r < q$. Then r is the nonnegative remainder after dividing p by q.
    Example: Let $p = -17$ and $q = 7$. Then the nonnegative remainder after dividing p by q is 4, because $-17 = (-3)*7 + 4$.

nonscalar   Not scalar; i.e., having user visible component parts. The most important nonscalar constructs in the relational model are tuples and (especially) relations themselves, where the "user visible component parts" are, of course, the pertinent attributes (and arguably the pertinent tuples as well, in the case of a relation). For further discussion, *see* scalar.

nonscalar type   *See* type.

nontrivial   (*Of an EQD, FD, IND, JD, or MVD*) Not trivial. *See* trivial EQD; trivial FD; trivial IND; trivial JD; trivial MVD. *See also* trivial decomposition.

NOR   In logic, a dyadic connective (also known as the Peirce arrow and usually written as a down arrow, "↓"); if and only if p and q are predicates, then $(p)\!\downarrow\!(q)$ is a predicate also. Let $(ip)\!\downarrow\!(iq)$ be an invocation of that predicate, where ip and iq are invocations of p and q, respectively. Then that invocation $(ip)\!\downarrow\!(iq)$ evaluates to TRUE if and only if ip and iq both evaluate to FALSE. (In other words, $(p)\!\downarrow\!(q)$ is equivalent to NOT $((p)$ OR $(q))$.) *Note:* The parentheses enclosing p and q in the predicate, and ip and iq in the invocation, might not be needed in practice. Also, NOR as just defined is a logical operator; however, the algebra **A**, q.v., includes an operator called NOR that—by definition—is an algebraic operator instead (it's basically "complement of union," though "union" here refers not to the relational operator of that name but to a generalized form of that operator).

normal form   1. (*General*) Canonical form, q.v. 2. (*Of a relvar*) *See* first normal form; second normal form; etc. The most important relational normal forms are BCNF and 5NF—or perhaps ETNF—and 6NF; the others are mainly of historical interest. *See also* normal form hierarchy. *Note:* Other normal forms mentioned in this dictionary—viz., CNF (q.v.), DNF (q.v.), and PNF (q.v.)—have nothing to do with relvars per se.

normal form hierarchy   Term sometimes used to refer to the sequence, or progression, 1NF – 2NF – 3NF – EKNF – BCNF – 4NF – ETNF – RFNF – SKNF – 5NF – 6NF. Note that 6NF implies 5NF, but the reverse implication does *not* hold; that is, if a given relvar is in 6NF, then it's certainly in 5NF, but a relvar can be in 5NF without being in 6NF. Similarly, 5NF implies SKNF; SKNF implies RFNF; RFNF implies ETNF; ETNF implies 4NF; 4NF implies BCNF; BCNF implies EKNF; EKNF implies 3NF; 3NF implies 2NF; 2NF implies 1NF; and in none of these cases does the reverse implication hold. *Note:* It's also true that DK/NF (q.v.) implies 5NF, while the reverse implication does not hold; however, DK/NF doesn't imply 6NF, nor does 6NF imply DK/NF, which is why DK/NF fails to appear in the normal form hierarchy as here defined.

normalization Replacing a relvar *R* by certain of its projections *R1, R2, ..., Rn*, such that (a) the join of *R1, R2, ..., Rn* is guaranteed to be equal to *R*, and usually also such that (b) each of *R1, R2, ..., Rn* is needed in order to provide that guarantee (i.e., none of those projections is redundant in the join), and usually also such that (c) at least one of *R1, R2, ..., Rn* is at a higher level of normalization than *R* is (*see* **nonloss decomposition**). Observe, therefore, that projection is the decomposition operator, and join the recomposition operator, with respect to the normalization process (as this latter term is usually understood). The usual objective of normalization is to reduce redundancy, q.v., and thereby to eliminate certain update anomalies, q.v., that might otherwise occur (but see the note following the example below).

Example: Suppose relvar S is subject to the additional FD {CITY} $\rightarrow$ {STATUS}; i.e., the status for a given supplier is a function of that supplier's location. (Of course, the sample value shown for that relvar in Fig. 1 doesn't satisfy this FD; however, it would do so if we changed the status for supplier S2 from 10 to 30, so let's suppose for the sake of the example that this change has in fact been made.) Then relvar S involves some redundancy, because it states *n* times, for any city it mentions, that the city in question has a given status (where *n* is always greater than zero and generally greater than one). Replacing S by its projections on {SNO,SNAME,CITY} and {CITY,STATUS} will eliminate that redundancy.

Note: Following on from the foregoing example, suppose we want to be able to record the status for some city even if there are currently no suppliers located in that city. Then the design consisting of just relvar S is simply wrong (because it isn't capable of representing such a city at all), and the design consisting of the "projections" of S on {SNO,SNAME,CITY} and {CITY,STATUS} is better (because it is so capable). Note, however, that the "projection" on {CITY,STATUS} here isn't truly a projection of relvar S (hence the quotation marks), precisely because it might contain a tuple that has no counterpart in relvar S (and such a tuple is obviously not derived from any tuple in S). In such a situation, therefore, replacing S by its "projections" on {SNO,SNAME,CITY} and {CITY,STATUS} might be described—indeed, it usually is—as a process of normalization, but it really isn't: not according to the foregoing definition, at any rate. Note in particular that the aim of such a "normalization" isn't so much to reduce redundancy as it is to replace a logically incorrect design by a correct one.

One final point on the foregoing example: If indeed we do want to be able to record the status for some city even if there are currently no suppliers located in that city, then the formal reason why the design consisting of just relvar S is wrong is that it's not expressively complete. *See* expressive completeness for another example and further discussion.

normalization principles   A set of principles used to guide the practical process of normalization. The principles in question are as follows: (a) A relvar not in ETNF should be decomposed into a set of projections that are in ETNF (and possibly some higher normal form, such as 5NF or 6NF); (b) the original relvar should be reconstructable by joining those projections back together again; (c) the decomposition process should preserve dependencies; (d) every projection should be needed in the reconstruction process.

normalized   That property of relations, and hence of relvars, according to which every tuple in the relation or relvar in question contains exactly one value, of the appropriate type, for each of its attributes. (Actually, a "tuple" that didn't contain exactly one value of the appropriate type for each of its attributes wouldn't be a tuple in the first place. It follows that a "relation" that contained such a "tuple" wouldn't be a relation, and a "relvar" whose value was such a "relation" wouldn't be a relvar, either. In other words, it's immediate from the definition of what a tuple is that all relations, and hence all relvars, are normalized in the foregoing sense.) *Contrast* unnormalized. *Note:* Relvars in particular are equivalently said to be in first normal form, 1NF (q.v.); i.e., a normalized relvar is just a relvar that's in 1NF, which is to say it's just a relvar. However, the term *normalized* is frequently, though inaccurately, used to refer to some normal form higher than just first (typically at least BCNF).

normalized relvar   A relvar. (Relvars are always normalized by definition, in the sense that they're in at least first normal form. *See* normalized.)

NOT   A connective, q.v. (*see* negation). *Note:* As just indicated, NOT as conventionally understood is a logical operator; however, the algebra **A,** q.v., includes an operator it calls NOT that—by definition—is an algebraic operator (in fact, it's basically "complement").

NOT MATCHING   **Tutorial D** keywords denoting semidifference, q.v.

null   A construct, used in SQL in particular, for representing "missing information"—or, rather, for representing the fact that some piece of information is unavailable for some reason (*see* missing information). *Note:* By definition, nulls aren't values (they're sometimes said to be *marks*); it follows that a "type" that "contains a null" isn't a type, a "tuple" that "contains a null" isn't a tuple, a "relation" that "contains a null" isn't a relation, and a "relvar" that "contains a null" isn't a relvar. It further follows that the concept of nulls as usually understood does serious violence to the relational model, and this dictionary therefore has very little further to say regarding that concept or matters related to it.

null set   Deprecated term sometimes used (most unfortunately!) to mean the empty set.

nullary   (*Of a heading, key, tuple, relation, etc.*) Of degree zero. The term is probably best avoided because of the potential confusion with null, q.v. *Contrast* niladic.

nullary foreign key   An empty foreign key; i.e., a foreign key of degree zero.

nullary heading   The empty heading; i.e., the heading of degree zero.

nullary key   An empty key; i.e., a key of degree zero.

nullary projection   1. (*Of a relation*) The projection of a given relation r on no attributes (i.e., $r\{\ \}$); the result is TABLE_DUM if r is empty and TABLE_DEE otherwise. 2. (*Of a tuple*) The projection of a given tuple t on no attributes (i.e., $t\{\ \}$); the result is always the empty tuple.

nullary relation   A relation of degree zero. There are exactly two such, TABLE_DEE and TABLE_DUM, q.v.

nullary tuple   The empty tuple; i.e., the tuple of degree zero.

nullology   The study of the empty set. The term has nothing to do with null, q.v.
   Examples: Sets as such crop up all over the relational world, and in every case nullology requires us to consider what the implications might be if the set in question happens to be empty. Note that all of the following are sets of one kind or another, and they can all legitimately be empty in a relational context: a body; a heading; a tuple; a key or foreign key; the dependant or determinant in an FD or MVD; a component in a JD; a type; and various other things besides.

nVL   A logic with n "truth values"; in other words, n-valued logic for some $n \ge 2$. *See also* truth functional completeness. *Note:* If $n = 2$, those "truth values" really are truth values in the conventional sense of that term, and we can drop the quotation marks. In general, however, the number of monadic connectives for nVL is n^2 and the number of dyadic connectives is n to the power n^2. Thus, 2VL has 4 monadic connectives and 16 dyadic connectives; 3VL has 27 monadic connectives and 19,683 dyadic connectives; 4VL has 256 monadic connectives and 4,294,967,296 dyadic connectives; and so on.

———— ♦ ♦ ♦ ♦ ♦ ————

O/R   Object/relational.

object   A thing.

object class   *See* class (second definition).

object ID   A unique identifier for an object, distinct from the object as such but usable (and used) as a reference to the object in question; in other words, an address or pointer. *Note:* There's a logical difference between object IDs and keys in the relational model; to be specific, the former really are just pointers (or, at best, a tiny abstraction of the pointer concept), which keys in the relational model most certainly aren't. See "Object Identifiers vs. Relational Keys," in C. J. Date, *Relational Database Writings 1994-1997* (Addison-Wesley, 1998) for further discussion.

object modeling   *See* semantic modeling.

object oriented / object orientation   Leaning toward things.

object/relational database   A relational database (*see* object/relational DBMS).

object/relational DBMS   A relational DBMS. *Note:* In practice, the major distinction between DBMSs that provide "object/relational" functionality and those that provide only "relational" functionality (at least from the user's perspective) is simply that the former allow users to define their own types. But a true relational DBMS does so too, and a DBMS that doesn't provide such functionality thus can't reasonably claim to be fully relational, even if it supports other aspects of the relational model. The fact is, the term "object/relational" is little more than a marketing label, dreamed up to conceal the fact that early so called "relational" products weren't very relational at all (not that most modern ones are either, at least at the time of writing).

observer   Term sometimes used (especially in OO contexts) to mean a read-only operator. To quote Stanley B. Zdonik and David Maier, "Fundamentals of Object-Oriented Databases," in *Readings in Object-Oriented Database Systems* (Zdonik and Maier, eds.; Morgan Kaufmann, 1990): "We call the operations that report on an object's state *observers* or *reporters*." *Contrast* mutator.

one to many correspondence   Strictly, a rule pairing two sets *s1* and *s2* (not necessarily distinct) such that each element of *s1* corresponds to at least one element of *s2* and each element of *s2* corresponds to exactly one element of *s1*; equivalently, that pairing itself. Often used loosely, however, to mean a pairing such that either (a) each element of *s1* corresponds to any number of elements of *s2* (possibly none at all) and each element of *s2* corresponds to exactly one element of *s1*, or (b) each element of *s1* corresponds to at least one element of *s2* and each element of *s2* corresponds to at most one element of *s1*, or (c) each element of *s1* corresponds to any number of elements of *s2* (possibly none at all) and each element of *s2* corresponds to at most one element of *s1*. The term is probably best avoided unless the intended meaning is clear.

Example (strict sense only): Let *s1* and *s2* be the set of all nonnegative numbers and the set of all numbers, respectively. Then the pairing of nonnegative numbers *x* with their positive and negative square roots $\pm\sqrt{x}$ is a one to many correspondence from *s1* to *s2*.

one to many join Let relations *r1* and *r2* be joinable, q.v. Then the join of *r1* and *r2* is said—somewhat loosely—to be one to many if and only if the pairing of tuples from *r1* and *r2* under the join is a one to many correspondence, q.v., in any of the senses of this latter term. *Note:* The foregoing definition is expressed in terms of relations, but the phrase *one to many join* is often applied to relvars instead of relations.

Example: The join of suppliers and shipments, S JOIN SP, would typically be said to be one to many from S to SP, even though there might be some tuples in S that join to no tuple in SP.

one to one correspondence Strictly, a rule pairing two sets *s1* and *s2* (not necessarily distinct) such that each element of *s1* corresponds to exactly one element of *s2* and each element of *s2* corresponds to exactly one element of *s1* (in other words, a bijection, q.v.); equivalently, that pairing itself. Often used loosely, however, to mean a pairing such that (a) each element of *s1* corresponds to at most one element of *s2* and each element of *s2* corresponds to exactly one element of *s1*, or (b) each element of *s1* corresponds to exactly one element of *s2* and each element of *s2* corresponds to at most one element of *s1*, or (c) each element of *s1* corresponds to at most one element of *s2* and each element of *s2* corresponds to at most one element of *s1*. The term is probably best avoided unless the intended meaning is clear.

Example (strict sense only): Let *s* be the set of all integers. Then the pairing of elements *x* with their successors *x*+1 is a one to one correspondence from *s* to itself; so too is the pairing of elements *x* with their predecessors *x*−1.

one to one join Let relations *r1* and *r2* be joinable, q.v. Then the join of *r1* and *r2* is said—somewhat loosely—to be one to one if and only if the pairing of tuples from *r1* and *r2* under the join is a one to one correspondence, q.v., in any of the senses of this latter term. *Note:* The foregoing definition is expressed in terms of relations, but the phrase *one to one join* is often applied to relvars instead of relations.

Example: Let *R1* and *R2* be, respectively, the projection of the suppliers relvar S on {SNO,STATUS} and the projection of that same relvar on {SNO,CITY}. Then the join of *R1* and *R2* would typically be said to be one to one (and in fact is so in the strictest sense, given that every supplier has exactly one status and exactly one city).

onto (*Of a function; preposition used as an adjective*) Having range equal to the codomain (*contrast* into). *See* bijection; surjection.

OO Object oriented or object orientation, as the context demands.

open expression Expressions in general are of two kinds, open and closed. A closed expression is one that isn't open, and it can appear wherever expressions in general are allowed. By contrast, an open expression is one that can appear only in certain limited contexts, because it contains references—typically but not necessarily attribute references, in the relational context— whose meaning depends on the context in question. (Image relation references, q.v., are an important special case of open expressions in general.) Simplifying slightly, an open expression can appear in a relational context (a) as the boolean expression in a WHERE clause; (b) as the expression denoting the source for an attribute assignment in an EXTEND, SUMMARIZE, or UPDATE invocation; or (c) as the expression whose values are to be aggregated within an aggregate operator invocation. *Note:* The unqualified term *expression* is usually taken to mean a closed expression specifically, unless the context demands otherwise. Also, it's sometimes convenient to regard a closed expression as a degenerate special case of an open expression.

    Example: Consider the following expression:

```
S WHERE STATUS > 10
```

This expression overall is closed, but it contains an open subexpression: namely, the boolean expression STATUS > 10. That subexpression is open because it contains an attribute reference (viz., STATUS), and can therefore be evaluated only in contexts in which that attribute reference has a well defined meaning. (In the example, that attribute reference effectively denotes the STATUS value from each tuple in turn within the current value of relvar S.)

open WFF   A WFF, q.v., that isn't closed; i.e., a WFF that denotes a predicate that isn't a proposition.

Open World Assumption   Loosely, the assumption—strongly contraindicated, because it appears to lead directly to a need to support three-valued logic, q.v.—that everything stated or implied by the database is true and everything else is unknown (i.e., it might be true and it might not). More precisely, let relvar R have predicate P (*see* **relvar predicate**). Then *The Open World Assumption* (OWA) says (a) if tuple t appears in R at time T, then the instantiation p of P corresponding to t is assumed to be true at time T; conversely, (b) if tuple t has the same heading as R but doesn't appear in R at time T, then the instantiation p of P corresponding to t is not assumed to be true at time T (to repeat, it might be true and it might not). Loosely speaking, in other words, tuple t appears in relvar R at a given time only if—not if and only if—it satisfies the predicate for R at that time. However, it does at least follow that if proposition p corresponds to a tuple that appears in some relation that can be derived from the relations that are the values of the database relvars at time T—*see* **derived relation**—then proposition p is true at time T (which is why the phrase "or implied" appears in the original loose characterization). *Contrast Closed World Assumption.* *Caveat:* Be aware that very different interpretations of the term "open world" can be found in the general computing literature—even in the database literature specifically, sometimes.

operand   Something on which an operation is performed. *See also* argument; parameter.

operation   An operator; sometimes, the process performed when an operator is invoked.

operator   Either a read-only operator or an update operator. *Note:* The term is often used, more specifically but a trifle loosely, to mean a read-only operator in particular. It's also often used even more specifically to mean a read-only operator that's denoted by some special symbol such as "+" instead of by an identifier such as PLUS, in which case other read-only operators (i.e., those denoted by identifiers) are typically referred to as functions. However, this latter usage is misleading, and hence deprecated, because all read-only operators are functions, strictly speaking. (At least, they should be! SQL, however, supports numerous read-only operators— including its well known SELECT operator in particular—that are explicitly defined in certain circumstances to be "possibly nondeterministic," q.v., meaning their results given certain specific inputs aren't fully predictable. *See also* ZO.)

operator invocation   Given an operator *Op*, an expression (if *Op* is read-only) or statement (otherwise) that causes that operator *Op* to be invoked; also used, though mostly not so in this dictionary, to refer to the process performed when that expression is evaluated or that statement is executed. Note that there's a logical difference between an operator as such and an invocation of that operator. *See also* argument; instantiation.

operator overloading   *See* overloading.

operator overriding   *See* overriding.

operator signature   Same as signature, q.v., in any of the senses of that term. See Part II of this dictionary for further discussion.

optimization   In the relational context, the process of converting a relational expression—in effect, a query or an update or a constraint, loosely speaking—into the "best possible" executable code, where "best possible" basically means *best performing*. The term represents somewhat of an overclaim, however, since it can rarely be guaranteed that the executable code produced is truly optimal in any very precise sense. *Note:* The term *optimization*, unqualified, is best reserved for "automatic" optimization—i.e., optimization done by the DBMS (*see* optimizer). Unfortunately, however, it has become increasingly common in recent years to find it applied to what might better be called hand or manual optimization, or in other words optimization—or would-be optimization—that's carried out by some user instead of the system (i.e., by choosing, or attempting to choose, the "best" way to formulate some query or other database request in concrete syntax). *Caveat lector. See also* database statistics; expression transformation; semantic optimization.

optimizer   The DBMS component responsible for optimization, q.v.

optional participation   *See* cardinality constraint.

OR   1. A connective, q.v. (*see* disjunction).   2. An aggregate operator, q.v. *Note:* OR as conventionally understood is a logical operator (and this observation applies to both of the foregoing definitions); however, the algebra **A**, q.v., includes an operator it calls OR that—by definition—is an algebraic operator (in fact, it's a generalized form of union). Note also that OR is sometimes known explicitly as inclusive OR, in order to distinguish it from exclusive OR, q.v.

ORDER BY   *See* ordering.

ordered *n*-tuple   Loosely, a combination, denoted $<x1,x2,...,xn>$, of exactly n elements $x1$, $x2$, ..., xn ($n \geq 0$) such that xi is the ith element of the ordered n-tuple in question ($1 \leq i \leq n$). More precisely, the ordered n-tuple $<x1,x2,...,xn>$ is recursively defined in terms of the concept of an ordered pair (q.v.) as follows: If $n = 0$, the corresponding ordered n-tuple, written $<>$, is empty (and is unique); if $n = 1$, the corresponding ordered n-tuple is the 1-tuple $<x1>$; if $n = 2$, the corresponding ordered n-tuple is the ordered pair $<x1,x2>$; if $n > 2$, the corresponding ordered n-tuple is the ordered pair $<<x1,x2,...,xm>,xn>$, where $m = n - 1$. Note that an ordered n-tuple is not a tuple in the relational model sense—tuples in the relational model have no ordering to their components (which is why tuples in the relational model have a heading, which ordered n-tuples typically don't). Of course, the concept of ordering is irrelevant anyway if $n \leq 1$.

ordered pair   A combination, usually denoted $<x,y>$ (though other notations are also used), of exactly two elements x and y such that x is the first element of the pair and y the second. The ordered pairs $<x1,y1>$ and $<x2,y2>$ are equal if and only if $x1 = x2$ and $y1 = y2$ (thus $<x,y> \neq <y,x>$, in general). Formally, the ordered pair $<x,y>$ is defined to be shorthand for the set $\{\{x\},\{x,y\}\}$; observe that one of the elements in this set determines the elements that constitute the ordered pair and the other determines which of those elements comes first.

   Note: The foregoing definition might be thought to break down in the case where the elements x and y are equal, since the expression $\{\{x\},\{x,y\}\}$ then reduces to just $\{\{x\}\}$. However, such is not the case—or at least it can be argued, somewhat tortuously, not to be the case. The argument in question goes like this. Let p be an ordered pair and let P be the set p is defined to be shorthand for. Then (a) the value x is defined to be the first element of p if and only if, for all sets s in P, x is an element of s, and (b) the value y is defined to be the second element of p if and only if y is an element of some set s in P and for all sets $s1$ and $s2$ in P, if $s1 \neq s2$, then either y is not an element of $s1$ or y is not an element of $s2$.

ordered set   Strictly speaking, a contradiction in terms, since sets are unordered by definition. However, the term is often used informally to refer to the combination of a given set and a total ordering (q.v.) imposed on the elements of that set.

ordered tuple   Same as ordered *n*-tuple.

ordered type   A type for which a total ordering (q.v.) is defined. Let *T* be such a type and let *v1* and *v2* be values of that type. With respect to that ordering, then, exactly one of the following comparisons will return TRUE and the other two will return FALSE:

    v1 < v2   v1 = v2   v1 > v2

Contrast ordinal type.
   Examples: Type INTEGER is an obvious example of an ordered type; however, that type is in fact an ordinal type, q.v., and is thus something of a special case. For an example of a type that's ordered but not ordinal, see the examples under **ordinal type**. For an example of a type that's not ordered at all (i.e., one that's not ordered and hence definitely not ordinal either, a fortiori), consider the case of a user defined type POINT, representing geometric points in two-dimensional space. Type POINT wouldn't be an ordered type, because the notion of one point being somehow less than another makes no sense. *Note:* It's worth mentioning in passing that even if a type isn't ordered at all, it might still be possible to impose an artificial ordering on it for implementation purposes, based perhaps on the internal (i.e., physical) representation for values of the type in question as patterns of bits.

ordering   In the relational world, the process, or the result of the process, of imposing a left to right sequence on the attributes, and more particularly a top to bottom sequence on the tuples, of a relation, so that the data in the relation in question can be transferred out of the relational context and into an environment that relies on such sequences—for example, an environment in which results are displayed visually. Operators that request such sequencing, or ordering, are of major pragmatic importance, but they aren't relational operators as such because their result isn't a relation. In particular, therefore, it makes no sense to allow such operators to appear within a relational expression (unless, perhaps, they're treated in that context merely as operators that just return their input). *Note:* A convenient way to think of such operators informally is as ones that convert a relation into a table (given that, unlike relations as such, tables—i.e., tabular pictures of relations—do have a left to right ordering to their columns and a top to bottom ordering to their rows).
   Example: The SQL operators that provide the foregoing functionality are SELECT (for left to right column sequence) and ORDER BY (for top to bottom row sequence). In the case of ORDER BY, every column mentioned must be of some ordered type. Incidentally, it's worth pointing out in passing that ORDER BY isn't a function—meaning, more specifically, that the result of a given ORDER BY invocation is indeterminate, in general (consider, e.g., the effect of ORDER BY CITY on the relation that's the current value of relvar S as shown in Fig. 1). By contrast, the operators of the relational algebra are indeed all functions (*but see* ZO). The same can't always be said of the SQL analogs of those operators, incidentally, owing to the fact that certain SQL expressions are explicitly defined to be "possibly nondeterministic," q.v.

Note: Actually ORDER BY is unusual in another respect also. To be specific, it produces a sequence of tuples as its result, and yet the operators "<" and ">" are explicitly not defined for tuples (*see* tuple comparison).

ordering (mathematics)   *See* partial ordering; total ordering.

ordinal type   An ordered type (q.v.), *T*, for which the following operators are available:
(a) niladic FIRST and LAST operators, which return the first and last value, respectively, of type *T* with respect to the applicable total ordering; (b) monadic NEXT and PRIOR operators, which, given a value *v* of type *T*, return the value of type *T* immediately succeeding *v* and the value of type *T* immediately preceding *v*, respectively, again with respect to the applicable total ordering. *Note:* In practice, these four operators will generally (if not universally) need a qualifier to be included in their name in order to specify the pertinent type *T*, thus: FIRST_*T*, LAST_*T*, NEXT_*T*, PRIOR_*T*. See Part III of this dictionary for further discussion.
   Examples: Type INTEGER is an obvious example of an ordinal type—the NEXT and PRIOR operators are basically just "add one" and "subtract one," respectively, and the FIRST and LAST operators are operators that return the minimum and maximum integers, respectively. By contrast, let *T* be the type "rational numbers" (type RATIONAL, in **Tutorial D**). Then *T* is an ordered type but not an ordinal one—because if *p/q* is a rational number, then (in mathematics at least, if not in computer arithmetic) no rational number can be said to be the "next" one, immediately following *p/q*.

orthogonal   At right angles; independent.

orthogonal decomposition   A decomposition of some given relvar into restrictions, such that the restrictions in question abide by *The Principle of Orthogonal Design*, q.v. *See also* horizontal decomposition.
   Examples: Suppose we were to replace relvar P by two relvars LP and HP, LP containing tuples for parts with weight less than or equal to 17.0 and HP containing tuples for parts with weight greater than 17.0; then that decomposition would be orthogonal. By contrast, suppose relvar HP were defined to contain tuples for parts with weight greater than *or equal to* 17.0; then the decomposition wouldn't be orthogonal, because tuples for parts with weight equal to 17.0 would logically belong in, and should therefore appear in, both LP and HP.

Orthogonal Design Principle   *See* Principle of Orthogonal Design.

orthogonality   The property of being orthogonal, q.v. Sometimes used to refer specifically, albeit loosely, to *The Principle of Orthogonal Design*, q.v. Also used as a principle of good programming language design ("if features *A* and *B* should logically be unrelated, make sure they stay unrelated").

overlapping 1. (*Of bags or sets*) Either having at least one element in common or all being empty. Note, therefore, that empty bags or sets are considered as overlapping, as well as being disjoint. Of course, if they're empty, they're really all the same bag or set anyway. 2. (*Of relations all of the same type*) Either having at least one tuple in common or all being empty. Note, therefore, that empty relations of the same type overlap, as well as being disjoint. Of course, if they're empty, they're really all the same relation anyway. 3. (*Of scalar types*) Either having at least one value in common or all being empty. Of course, if they're empty, they're really all the same type anyway. 4. (*Of tuple types*) See Part II of this dictionary. 5. (*Of relation types*) Again, see Part II of this dictionary.

Note: Distinct types never overlap, except possibly if inheritance is supported (once again, see Part II of this dictionary). *Contrast* **disjoint**.

overloading (*Without inheritance*) Using the same name for two or more different operators. Notice, therefore, that it's really the name, not some operator as such, that's overloaded; despite this fact, however, overloading polymorphism—overloading for short—is often referred to more specifically as operator overloading. The operators in question must have different specification signatures (q.v.) but should preferably have similar semantics. *Contrast* **overriding**. *Note:* Overloading is also referred to more specifically as overloading polymorphism. It's also known as ad hoc polymorphism.

Examples: UNION is overloaded, because it—i.e., the operator name—is used to denote both relational union and tuple union, as well as a certain aggregate operator (and in SQL it's also used to denote the "union plus" operator, q.v., though oddly enough not (a) the true bag union operator per se—which SQL doesn't support at all—and not (b) SQL's approximation to the UNION aggregate operator, which SQL does support but calls FUSION). Likewise, "=" is overloaded, because it applies to values of every type (i.e., there's an "=" operator for integers, another for supplier numbers, another for relations of type RELATION {SNO SNO, PNO PNO, QTY QTY}, and so on). Similar remarks apply to ":=" also.

Note: The definition above suggests that the operators in question "should preferably have similar semantics." An example of where this recommendation is flouted is provided by those languages—C++ is a case in point—that use the symbol "+" to denote string concatenation as well as numeric addition. Precisely because they're used to the fact that numeric addition is commutative, users of such languages might be tempted to fall into the trap of thinking string concatenation is commutative too, which of course it isn't.

overloading polymorphism *See* **overloading**.

overriding (*Without inheritance*) Replacing an operator by another with the same specification signature, q.v., but different semantics. (It has nothing to do with domain check override, q.v.) *Contrast* **overloading**.

Example: Suppose there exists an operator called LOG (possibly built in) that returns natural logarithms. Then it might be possible to override that operator by one that returns logarithms to base ten instead.

OWA   *The Open World Assumption.*

———— ♦ ♦ ♦ ♦ ♦ ————

P-relation / P-relvar   *See* RM/T.

pair   Either a set of cardinality two or, more usually, an ordered pair (q.v.), as the context demands.

parameter   A formal operand in terms of which some operator is defined, to be replaced by some argument when the operator in question is invoked. Simplifying slightly (*see* polymorphism), every parameter is declared to be of some type, and any argument corresponding to a given parameter is required to be of the same type as that parameter. *Contrast* argument.

parameterized type   Term sometimes used as a synonym for type generator. The term is inappropriate because a type generator isn't a type.

parent / parent table   Deprecated, because inappropriate, terms sometimes used in SQL contexts to mean (the SQL analog of) a referenced relvar, q.v.

partial function   Let f be a function with domain d and let $dd \supseteq d$; then f can be regarded as a partial function with domain dd. Loosely speaking, in other words, a partial function is a function, q.v., except that there can exist elements of the "domain"—"domain" in quotes because it isn't actually the domain as defined under **function** elsewhere in this dictionary—that have no image in the codomain. *Contrast* total function.
    Example: Let s be the set of real numbers. Then "reciprocal of" is a partial function with "domain" and codomain both s (it's partial because there's one element of the "domain," namely 0, that has no reciprocal).

partial instantiation   *See* instantiation.

partial ordering   Let s be a set. Then a partial ordering on s is a dyadic truth valued operator, usually denoted "$\leq$", such that for all x, y, and z in s, (a) $x \leq y$ or $y \leq x$ or both, or possibly neither; (b) $x \leq x$ (reflexivity); (c) if $x \leq y$ and $y \leq z$, then $x \leq z$ (transitivity); and (d) if $x \leq y$ and $y \leq x$, then $x = y$ (antisymmetry). *Contrast* total ordering.
    Example: Let s be an arbitrary set, let $P(s)$ be the power set (q.v.) of s, and let "$\leq$" denote the set inclusion operator (more usually written "$\subseteq$"). Then "$\leq$" is a partial ordering on $P(s)$.

Moreover, it's a partial ordering that isn't a total ordering (except for the degenerate cases in which the cardinality of *s* is either zero or one). For example, let *s*, *x*, and *y* be the sets {1,2,3}, {1,2}, and {2,3}, respectively. Then *x* and *y*, which are distinct elements of *P*(*s*), are such that $x \leq y$ and $y \leq x$ are both false.

partition   *See* partitioning.

partitioning   Let *s* be a set. Then a partitioning of *s* is a set of subsets ("partitions") of *s* such that every element of *s* is an element of exactly one such subset. Note that (a) partitions are pairwise disjoint; (b) their union (necessarily a disjoint union) is equal to *s*. Note too that if *s* is empty, then it has exactly one partitioning, consisting of an empty set of partitions. *See also* equivalence class.

partly redundant   Tuple *t* is partly redundant in relation *r* if and only if it has a projection *t*{*X*} that's forced, by virtue of the fact that *r* satisfies some FD, to be equal to the projection *t'*{*X*} of some distinct tuple *t'* in *r*. Note that *t* and *t'* are interchangeable in this definition; that is, if *t* is partly redundant because *t'* exists, then *t'* is partly redundant because *t* exists. Note too that a relvar can contain a partly redundant tuple only if it—i.e., the relvar—isn't in BCNF, q.v.; thus, normalizing to (at least) BCNF is guaranteed to eliminate the possibility of partly redundant tuples. Note finally that a tuple can be partly redundant without being fully redundant (*see* fully redundant).

Peirce arrow   *See* NOR.

persistence   That property according to which data, once entered into the database, remains there ("persists") until it's removed—possibly in accordance with some compensatory action, q.v.—in response to some explicit user request. Data in database relvars is persistent in this sense (and in a relational database, nothing else is).

physical access path   An implementation construct, intended to improve the speed of access to data as physically stored. Typical examples include hashes, indexes, and pointer chains. *Note:* By definition, there aren't any physical access paths in the relational model, since that model is concerned only with the logical level of the system. In other words, all access to data as far as the relational model is concerned is via associative addressing, q.v.

physical data independence   *See* data independence.

physical database design   The process, or the result of the process, of deciding, given some logical database design, how that logical design should map to whatever physical constructs (including physical access paths in particular) the target DBMS happens to support. Note, therefore, that the physical design should be derived from the logical design and not the other way around; ideally, in fact, it should be derived automatically.

physical design   Same as physical database design (if the context demands).

physical representation   Internal representation of data in physical storage. Physical representations are an implementation concern, not a model concern, and thus are—or should be—of no interest to the user. *Contrast* possible representation; *see also* appearance.

picture   (*Of a relation, attribute, or tuple*) *See* table, column, and row, respectively; *see also* cell. *Note:* Of course, there's a logical difference between a picture as such and the thing that picture depicts; in the case of relations, attributes, and tuples, however, that difference seems not to be very well understood, at least if today's DBMS products are anything to go by. This failing is unfortunate, given that the pictures in question often suggest things that aren't true. For example, pictures of relations as tables (as in Fig. 1) strongly suggest that relations have a top to bottom ordering to their tuples and a left to right ordering to their attributes, neither of which is the case. *See also* flat relation.

pipelining   A technique for evaluating relational expressions in which tuples of intermediate result relations are produced and passed on as input to another operation one at a time instead of en bloc. *Contrast* materialization (first definition).

PJ/NF   Projection-join normal form, q.v.

placeholder   A free variable (i.e., a parameter).

PNF   Prenex normal form.

pointer   An implementation construct. As is well known, pointers are excluded from the relational model. In fact, mixing pointers and relations—that is, allowing a relation (or would-be relation) in the database to have an attribute whose values are supposed to be pointers to tuples somewhere else in the database—has been described as The Second Great Blunder. (For the first, *see* First Great Blunder; *see also* referencing.) Indeed, such mixing clearly violates *The Information Principle*, q.v., among other things (see further discussion below). And yet such a state of affairs is explicitly supported by several SQL products, and is in fact required by the SQL standard (*see* REF type)—strong prima facie evidence that SQL and the relational model are very far from being the same thing.

Note: Some writers reserve the term *pointer* to mean, specifically, one whose value is some kind of physical address, and use the term *reference* (or some such term) for other kinds of pointers. This distinction might be useful in certain contexts but is irrelevant to the relational model—although of course it's true that the relational model does make use of the term *reference* in another sense, in connection with foreign keys. But there are numerous logical differences between foreign key values and pointers, of which the most fundamental is that foreign key values identify tuples, which are values, whereas pointer values are addresses and therefore, by definition, identify variables. Indeed, it's precisely this fact—the fact, that is, that pointers point specifically to variables—that justifies the claim made above to the effect that allowing database relations to contain pointers that "point to tuples somewhere else in the database" leads directly to a violation of *The Information Principle*. For further explanation, see "Don't Mix Pointers and Relations!" and "Don't Mix Pointers and Relations—*Please!*" (both in C. J. Date, *Relational Database Writings 1994-1997*, Addison-Wesley, 1998).

polymorphic operator   *See* polymorphism.

polymorphic type   Term sometimes used as a synonym for type generator. The term is inappropriate on at least two counts, because (a) a type generator isn't a type and (b) generic polymorphism (which is the kind of polymorphism associated with type generators) isn't the only kind of polymorphism.

polymorphism   Loosely, the idea that an operator might permit its arguments to be of different types on different invocations. *See* generic polymorphism; inclusion polymorphism (in Part II of this dictionary); overloading polymorphism.

positive   Strictly greater than zero. *Contrast* nonnegative.

possible representation   Let T be a scalar type, and let v be an appearance, q.v., of some value of type T. By definition, v has exactly one physical representation and one or more possible representations (at least one, because there's obviously always one that's the same as the physical representation). If T is user defined, then at least one possible representation ("possrep" for short) for values of type T must be explicitly declared; if T is system defined, one or more possreps for values of type T can optionally be declared. Each possrep consists of zero or more components, where each such component consists in turn of a name and a corresponding declared type. *Note:* Elsewhere in this dictionary, the unqualified term *possible representation*, or the abbreviated form *possrep*, refers to a declared possrep specifically, unless the context demands otherwise. Note too that unlike physical representations, possreps are explicitly (if slightly indirectly) exposed to the user, via an associated selector, q.v., and associated set of THE_ operators, q.v. Also, possreps are always named; by default, however, the possrep name is the same as that of the corresponding type, and almost all of the examples elsewhere in this dictionary make use of this default option. Note finally that there's no requirement, or even suggestion, that any declared possrep be the same as any underlying physical representation; however, there's certainly a requirement that if *PR1* and *PR2* are distinct possreps for the same type T, then every value representable via *PR1* must be representable via *PR2* and vice versa. *See also* selector; THE_ operator.

Examples: Here in outline is a **Tutorial D** definition for the user defined type QTY ("quantities"):

```
TYPE QTY POSSREP QPR ( Q INTEGER ) ;
```

Observe in particular that the sole possrep here is called QPR ("QTY possible representation"). But specifying an explicit possrep name is optional. Here's another possible definition for type QTY:

```
TYPE QTY POSSREP ( Q INTEGER ) ;
```

This definition is shorthand for the following:

```
TYPE QTY POSSREP QTY ( Q INTEGER ) ;
```

By way of an example where specifying more than one possrep makes obvious sense, consider a user defined type POINT, representing geometric points in two-dimensional space:

```
TYPE POINT
    POSSREP CARTESIAN { X RATIONAL , Y RATIONAL ... }
    POSSREP POLAR { RHO RATIONAL , THETA RATIONAL ... } ;
```

Type POINT has two distinct possreps, CARTESIAN and POLAR, reflecting the fact that points in two-dimensional space can indeed possibly be represented by either cartesian or polar coordinates.

possibly nondeterministic An SQL term, deriving from the fact that SQL's support for the equality operator "=" is seriously defective. To be more specific, SQL allows certain comparisons of the form $v1 = v2$ to return TRUE even if $v1$ and $v2$ aren't the same value, or even of the same type (this isn't the only defect in SQL's support for "=", but it's certainly one of the most egregious). As a direct consequence, certain SQL expressions are explicitly defined to be "possibly nondeterministic," meaning their results aren't fully predictable. Such expressions are explicitly prohibited from appearing in integrity constraints. Oddly enough, however, they *are* allowed to appear in queries and updates, where they can surely do just as much harm (?).

Example: Suppose the CITY values for suppliers S2 and S3 are given as 'Paris' and 'Paris ', respectively (note the trailing blank in the S3 value here, and note the logical difference between the two values; for example, if CHAR_LENGTH is a scalar operator with the intuitively obvious semantics, then CHAR_LENGTH applied to 'Paris' returns the value 5, while CHAR_LENGTH applied to 'Paris ' returns the value 6). Then the result of the SQL expression SELECT DISTINCT CITY FROM S will include either 'Paris' or 'Paris ' or both, but which of these three possibilities applies in any given situation is, in general, undefined.

POSSREP The **Tutorial D** construct that defines a possible representation, q.v.

Example: See the examples under **possible representation** and elsewhere.

possrep Shorthand for possible representation.

possrep component *See* possible representation; selector; THE_ operator.

power set The set of all subsets of a given set. If the given set *s* has cardinality *n*, the corresponding power set $P(s)$ has cardinality 2^n (this count includes both the empty set and the set that's identical to the original set, both of which are indeed subsets of the original set). Note, therefore, that the cardinality of $P(s)$ is always strictly greater than that of *s*. (In particular, $2^0 = 1$; thus, if *s* is the empty set { }, which has cardinality zero, the corresponding power set $P(s)$ is the set {{ }}, which has cardinality one.)

precision (*Of a numeric type*) The maximum number of significant digits in a value of the type in question. For example, consider the SQL type NUMERIC(5,2). Values of that type are decimal numbers with precision five and scale factor (q.v.) two. In other words, values of that type are precisely the following:

$$-999.99 \ , \ -999.98 \ , \ \dots \ , \ -000.01 \ , \ 000.00 \ , \ 000.01 \ , \ \dots \ , \ 999.99$$

In general, the precision for a given numeric type specifies the total number of digits, and the scale factor specifies the position of the assumed radix point, in the string of digits denoting any given value of the type in question. Observe that the precision and scale factor between them serve as an a priori constraint on values of the type; in effect, they constitute the applicable type constraint.

  Note: Actually there's some confusion in the literature over the term *precision*. To be specific, some writers and some languages use it to mean either the scale, q.v., or the scale factor, q.v. (at least as these latter terms are defined in this dictionary). *Caveat lector*.

predicate Loosely, a truth valued function. Given an arbitrary predicate, invoking, or instantiating, that predicate—i.e., substituting arguments for the parameters of that predicate— yields a proposition, which by definition evaluates unequivocally to either TRUE or FALSE. Thus, another way of thinking about a predicate is as a parameterized or generalized proposition. And if and only if the set of parameters is empty, the predicate degenerates to a proposition per se; in other words, all propositions are predicates, but "most" predicates aren't propositions. *Note:* Strictly speaking, if *P* is a truth valued function, the corresponding predicate isn't really *P* as such—rather, it's the meaning of *P*, or in other words what *P* denotes. Consider the following examples (both of which are deliberately written in a kind of functional style): *is_a_star*(*x*) and *est_une_étoile*(*x*). Clearly there are two different functions here, even though, equally clearly, they both denote the same predicate. However, it's usual to ignore this distinction—the distinction, that is, between the truth valued function as such and what that function denotes—in informal contexts (and indeed in more formal contexts as well, sometimes). *See also* proposition; relvar predicate.

Examples: 1. *X* is a star. 2. Neptune is a star. (This particular example is actually a proposition, of course—a false one, as it happens.) 3. Politician *p* is corrupt. 4. Supplier SNO is under contract, is named SNAME, has status STATUS, and is located in city CITY. 5. Supplier SNO supplies part PNO in some quantity (or, in more stilted English, *There exists a quantity QTY such that* supplier SNO supplies part PNO in quantity QTY). Note that this example is a 2-place predicate, not a 3-place one (QTY here isn't a parameter but a bound variable, q.v., thanks to the quantifier *There exists a quantity QTY such that*).

predicate calculus A sound and complete formal system having to do with predicates and connectives and the inferences that can be made using such predicates and connectives. *Note:* The principal difference between predicate calculus and propositional calculus, q.v.—the former of which subsumes the latter—is that predicates, unlike propositions, are allowed to contain logic variables (both free and bound), which makes predicate calculus more expressively powerful and hence more widely applicable.

predicate constant Same as predicate.

predicate expression An expression denoting a predicate; i.e., an expression involving predicate constants, predicate variables, connectives, and parentheses. *Note:* Few logic texts if any actually use this term; in fact, logic texts in general don't seem to have a term for the construct at all other than *predicate* itself (not even those that use *propositional form,* q.v., for a propositional expression, which might be expected to use the surely obvious *predicate form* for a predicate expression).

Examples: If *p* and *q* are predicate variables, then *p*, *q*, the conjunction (*p*) AND (*q*), the disjunction (*p*) OR (*q*), and the negation NOT(*p*) are all predicate expressions.

predicate form *See* predicate expression.

predicate logic Same as predicate calculus.

predicate variable A variable whose value is a predicate. *Note:* Some writers use this term to mean a free variable, but this usage is deprecated; surely a predicate variable should be to a predicate just what an integer variable is to an integer, or a relation variable is to a relation (etc.).

premise / premiss In logic, something assumed to be true for the purposes of a proof or attempted proof. See in particular equality generating dependency; tuple generating dependency.

prenex normal form   Loosely speaking, a predicate is in prenex normal form, PNF, if and only if the quantifiers all appear at the beginning. More precisely, a predicate is in PNF if and only if (a) it's quantifier free or (b) it's of the form $Q x (p)$, where $Q x$ is a quantifier and p in turn is in PNF. Thus, a PNF predicate takes the form

```
Q1 x1 ( Q2 x2 ( ... ( Qn xn ( q ) ) ... ) )
```

where (a) $n \geq 0$; (b) each of $Q1, Q2, ..., Qn$ is, typically, either EXISTS or FORALL; and (c) the predicate q—which is sometimes called the matrix—is quantifier free.

Example: Consider the following tuple calculus query ("Get suppliers who supply at least one red part"):

```
SX  RANGES OVER { S } ;
SPX RANGES OVER { SP } ;
PX  RANGES OVER { P } ;

{ SX } WHERE EXISTS PX ( PX.COLOR = COLOR('Red') AND
                   EXISTS SPX ( SPX.SNO = SX.SNO AND
                                SPX.PNO = PX.PNO ) )
```

The predicate in the WHERE clause here is not in prenex normal form. Here, however, is a logically equivalent formulation of the query in which the predicate *is* in prenex normal form:

```
{ SX } WHERE EXISTS PX ( EXISTS SPX ( PX.COLOR = COLOR('Red') AND
                     SPX.SNO  = SX.SNO AND
                     SPX.PNO  = PX.PNO ) )
```

Prenex normal form is no more logically correct than any other, but with a little practice it does tend to become the easiest to write. Note, however, that it isn't always achievable. For example, here's another query on the suppliers-and-parts database ("Get suppliers who either are located in Athens or supply at least one part or both"):

```
{ SX } WHERE SX.CITY = 'Athens' OR EXISTS SPX ( SPX.SNO = SX.SNO )
```

The predicate in the WHERE clause here is not in prenex normal form, nor does it have a prenex normal form equivalent.

preserving dependencies   *See* FD preservation.

primary domain   Let R be a base relvar; let R have a primary key K; let K be simple (*see* simple key); and let K be defined on domain (i.e., type) D. Then, and only then, D is a primary domain. *Note:* Since (a) it clearly violates *The Principle of Interchangeability* and (b) it relies on a concept, primary key, that's hard to justify from a logical point of view (*see* primary key), the primary domain concept is rather strongly deprecated. In any case, the term—perhaps fortunately—isn't much used; we mention it here mainly for historical reasons.

Examples: Assume the declared keys for the suppliers-and-parts database are in fact primary keys. Then the sole primary domains with respect to that database are the domains (types) SNO and PNO.

primary key A candidate key that has been singled out for special treatment (certainly special syntactic treatment, possibly special semantic treatment also) for some reason. While a given relvar can have any number n of candidate keys ($n > 0$), it can have at most one primary key. For a given relvar, however, whether some candidate key is to be chosen as primary, and if so which one, are essentially psychological issues, beyond the purview of the relational model as such. *Note:* The relational model as originally formulated did in fact insist that base relvars, at least, should always have a primary key. It also insisted that foreign keys reference primary keys specifically (partly because it also insisted that foreign keys reference base relvars specifically, as well as being attached to base relvars specifically). However, there were never any good logical reasons for these rules, and in any case rules that apply to base relvars but not to other kinds are more than a little suspect anyway (because they violate *The Principle of Interchangeability*); thus, the primary key notion could be dropped without serious loss. We mention it here mainly for historical reasons. **Tutorial D** in particular makes no distinction between primary keys and alternate keys (q.v.), referring to them all just as keys.

primary key attribute An attribute of a given relvar that participates in the primary key (if any) for that relvar. *Contrast* key attribute.

prime attribute Old fashioned and somewhat deprecated term for a key attribute (not necessarily a primary key attribute).

primitive operator Loosely, an operator not defined in terms of others. More precisely, let s be a set of operators. Let Op be an operator in s that can be defined in terms of other operators in s; remove Op from s, and repeat this step until it can't be repeated any more. What remains is a set of operators that are primitive with respect to s. Note that the set of primitive operators with respect to a given set s is not necessarily unique.

Examples: 1. For relational algebra, a primitive set of operators (a) will definitely include projection, (b) will probably include join (*but see* **A**), but (c) will probably not include semijoin (because semijoin can be defined in terms of projection and join). 2. For the relational operators supported by **Tutorial D** (not counting relational inclusion), the following set of operators is primitive: {UNION, NOT MATCHING, JOIN, restriction, projection, EXTEND}. 3. For two-valued logic, any of the following sets of operators can be taken as primitive: {NOT,OR}; {NOT,AND}; {NOR}; {NAND}.

primitive type Term sometimes used to mean a system defined type—necessarily scalar—with no declared possrep (the term *primitive* derives from the fact that all of the types available in any given context are ultimately defined in terms of such types). Typical examples include INTEGER and BOOLEAN. (Of course, type BOOLEAN in particular is required by the prescriptions of the relational model.)

Principle of Cautious Design A guiding principle in the design of formal systems (including databases, DBMSs, database languages, and many other such systems). It can be stated thus: Given a design choice between options *A* and *B*, where *A* is upward compatible with *B* and the full consequences of going with *B* aren't yet known, the cautious decision is to go with *A*. Going with *A* permits subsequent "opening up" of the design to *B* if such opening up becomes desirable. By contrast, going with *B* prohibits subsequent "closing down" of the design to *A*, even if such closing down turns out to be desirable (i.e., if it becomes clear that *B* was a bad choice in the first place).

    Example: The designers of SQL had a choice between prohibiting duplicate rows (*Option A*) and permitting them (*Option B*). The cautious decision would have been to prohibit them (*Option A*); they could then have been supported in the future, if a clear need for such support were ever demonstrated. Unfortunately, the designers chose to permit them (*Option B*). Of course, this decision turned out to be a very bad one, but now there's no compatible way for SQL to go back to *Option A*. *Note:* As this example suggests, *The Principle of Cautious Design* can help avoid situations in which the language (or the DBMS, or the database, or whatever else it is that's being designed) provides certain options that users have to be explicitly told not to exercise.

Principle of Database Relativity Consider a database ("the real database") in which all of the relvars are base ones. In general, a typical user will interact not with that real database as such, but rather with what might be called an "expressible" database that consists of some mixture of base relvars and views. Now, we can assume that none of the relvars in that expressible database can be derived from the rest, because such a relvar could be dropped without loss of information. From the user's point of view, therefore, the relvars in that expressible database are effectively all base relvars. And likewise for the database itself—i.e., the choice of which database is the "real" one is arbitrary too, just so long as the choices are all information equivalent, q.v. Which is essentially what *The Principle of Database Relativity* says: Any given body of data can, in general, be represented by means of several distinct but information equivalent database designs. *See also* information equivalence; *Interchangeability Principle*.

Principle of Identity of Indiscernibles The principle that if there's no way whatsoever of distinguishing between two objects, then there aren't two objects but only one. Or equivalently: Every object has its own unique identity. *Note:* In the relational model, such unique identities are represented in the same way as everything else—namely, by means of attribute values (*see Information Principle*)—and numerous benefits accrue from this fact. Note too that there's a logical difference between indiscernibility and interchangeability—two objects might be distinguishable but interchangeable (think of two pennies, for example); in other words, the concepts of interchangeability and indiscernibility are themselves not interchangeable. (Confusion over this particular logical difference might help explain why some people seem to think SQL's support for duplicate rows is a good idea.) Note finally that the term *object* here is intended to be generic—it's not being used in its special OO sense.

Principle of Incoherence   A principle, sometimes invoked in defense of an attempt (successful or otherwise) at criticizing some technical proposal or position, to the effect that it's hard to criticize something coherently if what's being criticized is itself not very coherent in the first place—a state of affairs that goes some way toward explaining why such criticisms can often be longer (sometimes much longer) than what's being criticized. Occasionally referred to, a little unkindly, as *The Incoherent Principle.*

Example: Here's a piece of text that, because it's so badly written, is hard to criticize coherently (it's quoted verbatim from the SQL reference manual for a certain well known mainstream SQL product):

> A *table check constraint* is a rule that specifies the values allowed in one or more columns of every row of a table. They are optional and can be defined using the SQL statements CREATE TABLE and ALTER TABLE. The specification of table check constraints is a restricted form of a search condition. One of the restrictions is that a column name in a table check constraint on table *T* must identify a column of *T* ... The check-condition "IS NOT NULL" can be specified, however it is recommended that nullability be enforced directly using the NOT NULL attribute of a column. For example, CHECK (salary + bonus > 30000) is accepted if salary is set to NULL, because CHECK constraints must be either satisfied or unknown and in this case salary is unknown. However, CHECK (salary IS NOT NULL) would be considered false and a violation of the constraint if salary is set to NULL.

Principle of Interchangeability   *See Interchangeability Principle.*

Principle of Orthogonal Design   Loosely, the principle that no two relvars in a given database should have overlapping meanings. More precisely, let *R1* and *R2* be relvars (not necessarily distinct), and let the JD ✿{*X1,X2,...,Xn*} be irreducible with respect to *R1*. Let there exist some *Xi* ($1 \leq i \leq n$) and some possibly empty set of attribute renamings on the projection, *R1X* say, of *R1* on *Xi* that maps *R1X* into *R1Y*, say, where *R1Y* has the same heading as some subset *Y* (distinct from *Xi*, if *R1* and *R2* are one and the same) of the heading of *R2*. Further, let the projection of *R2* on *Y* be *R2Y*. Then *The Principle of Orthogonal Design* is violated by *R1* and *R2* if and only if there exist restriction conditions *c1* and *c2*, nether of which is a contradiction (q.v.), such that the equality dependency (*R1X* WHERE *c1*) = (*R2Y* WHERE *c2*) holds.

Examples: See the examples under **orthogonal decomposition**. *Note:* The equality dependency that holds in the second of those examples is:

```
( LP WHERE WEIGHT = WEIGHT(17.0) ) = ( HP WHERE WEIGHT = WEIGHT(17.0) )
```

Principle of Uniform Representation *See Information Principle.*

Principle of Uniformity of Representation *See Information Principle.*

principles of normalization *See normalization principles.*

PRIOR *See ordinal type.*

private instance variable *See instance variable.*

privileged operator An operator whose implementation code has access at run time to the physical representation of its argument(s), or indeed to the physical representation of anything at all. *Note:* As a matter of good practice, the only privileged operators should be selectors and THE_ operators (also IS_*T* operators, defined in Part II of this dictionary).

product Cartesian product, q.v. (unless the context demands otherwise).

product (bag theory) *See bag.*

product (set theory) *See cartesian product (set theory).*

projection Let relation *r* have attributes called *A1, A2, ..., An* (and possibly others). Then (and only then) the expression *r{A1,A2,...,An}* denotes the projection of *r* on {*A1, A2, ..., An*}, and it returns the relation with heading {*A1,A2,...,An*} and body consisting of all tuples *t* such that there exists a tuple in *r* that has the same value for attributes *A1, A2, ..., An* as *t* does. *See also* **tuple projection.**
    Example: The expression S{STATUS,CITY} denotes a projection of the relation that's the current value of relvar S. That projection is a relation of type RELATION {STATUS INTEGER, CITY CHAR}, containing all possible tuples of the form <*st,sc*> (and no other tuples) such that there exists some supplier number *sno* and some name *sn* such that the tuple <*sno,sn,st,sc*> appears in the current value of relvar S. Given the sample values shown in Fig. 1, the result has cardinality four. *Note:* For psychological reasons, **Tutorial D** allows projections to be expressed in terms of the attributes to be removed instead of those to be retained; thus, for example, the projection S{STATUS,CITY} can alternatively, but equivalently, be expressed as S{ALL BUT SNO, SNAME}. Analogous remarks apply to several other **Tutorial D** constructs also—KEY, GROUP, WRAP, and so on (wherever ALL BUT makes sense, in fact).

projection-join normal form The original name for fifth normal form, 5NF. The name derives from the fact that 5NF is "the" normal form with respect to projection and join, as those operators are classically understood (*but see* **essential tuple normal form; sixth normal form**).

pronunciation (SQL)   *See* SQL.

pronunciation (tuple)   *See* tuple.

proof   (*Logic*) In general, a sequence of sentences in some logical system that together establish some sentence as a logical consequence of certain given sentences; if the given sentences are true, then the consequential sentence is also true. A direct proof is such a sequence in which each sentence either (a) is an axiom or (b) is a previously proved theorem or (c) can be deduced from previous sentences in the sequence by means of the rules of inference of the system; the final sentence is a theorem. An axiom is a theorem with a single-sentence direct proof. An indirect proof, also known as a *reductio ad absurdum* proof (q.v.), is a sequence of sentences that together establish some sentence as a theorem by adopting its negation as a premise and then showing that such adoption leads to a contradiction.

propagating updates   *See* controlled redundancy.

proper inclusion   Set *s1* properly includes set *s2* ("*s1* ⊃ *s2*") if and only if it is a proper superset of *s2*; set *s2* is properly included in set *s1* ("*s2* ⊂ *s1*") if and only if it is a proper subset of *s1*.

proper subkey   A subkey that isn't a key (i.e., a proper subset of a key).

proper subset   Set *s2* is a proper subset of set *s1* ("*s2* ⊂ *s1*") if and only if it is a subset of *s1* and *s1* and *s2* are distinct.

proper superkey   A superkey that isn't a key (i.e., a superkey that doesn't have the irreducibility property); loosely, a proper superset of a key.

proper superset   Set *s1* is a proper superset of set *s2* ("*s1* ⊃ *s2*") if and only if it is a superset of *s2* and *s1* and *s2* are distinct.

property   A thing belonging to another thing. *Note:* It's frequently suggested that there should be a one to one correspondence between the properties of a given entity type and the attributes in some base relvar. The suggestion is hard to sustain, however, given that the term *properties of a given entity type* has no precise definition. (Of course, the same is true of the term *entity type*. In fact, it's true of the term *property* as well, come to that.)

proposition   A 0-place predicate; a predicate with no parameters (i.e., no free variables); a declarative statement (in the sense of logic, not the programming language sense); hence, something that evaluates unequivocally to either TRUE or FALSE. *Note:* Strictly speaking, if *P* is a declarative statement, the corresponding proposition isn't really *P* as such—rather, it's the assertion made by *P*. For example, consider the statements *The sun is a star* and *Le soleil est une étoile*. Clearly there are two different statements here. Equally clearly, however, they both denote the same proposition. Be aware, therefore, that it's usual to ignore the foregoing distinction—i.e., between the statement as such and what that statement denotes—in informal contexts (and indeed in more formal contexts as well, sometimes).

Examples: 1. The sun is a star. 2. Neptune is a star. 3. All politicians are corrupt. 4. Supplier S1 is under contract, is named Smith, has status 20, and is located in city Paris. 5. There exists a city CITY such that there exists a supplier number SNO such that the supplier with supplier number SNO is located in city CITY. Notice that there are two variables, SNO and CITY, in this example (variables in the sense of logic, that is, not variables in the programming language sense); however, the variables in question are bound, not free, and the example overall still evaluates unequivocally to either TRUE or FALSE (i.e., it's either the case or not the case that at least one supplier is located in at least one city). 6. Let *p* be an arbitrary predicate. If every parameter of *p* is either subjected to quantification or replaced by some argument (not both!), then what results is a proposition. For example, given the predicate *The supplier with supplier number SNO is under contract, is named SNAME, has status STATUS, and is located in city CITY*, the statement *There exists a city CITY such that there exists a supplier number SNO such that the supplier with supplier number SNO is under contract, is named Smith, has status 20, and is located in city CITY* is a proposition. 7. By way of a counterexample, the expression *x* > 0 OR TRUE is not a proposition (because it involves a parameter, *x*), even though it does evaluate unequivocally to TRUE. In other words, although propositions always evaluate unequivocally to either TRUE or FALSE, not everything that evaluates unequivocally to either TRUE or FALSE is a proposition. *Note:* A useful though not infallible informal test for checking whether some statement *S* is a proposition is the following: *P* is a proposition if and only if "Is it the case that *P*?" is a well formed question in natural language.

propositional calculus   A sound, complete, and decidable formal system having to do with propositions and connectives and the inferences that can be made using such propositions and connectives. *Contrast* predicate calculus.

propositional constant   Same as proposition.

propositional expression   An expression denoting a proposition; i.e., an expression involving propositional constants, propositional variables, connectives, and parentheses. *Note:* Logic texts don't use this term much, typically preferring the term *propositional form*, q.v. (if they use any term for the concept at all, that is).

Examples: If *p* and *q* are propositional variables, then *p*, *q*, the conjunction (*p*) AND (*q*), the disjunction (*p*) OR (*q*), and the negation NOT(*p*) are all propositional expressions.

propositional form   *See* propositional expression.

propositional function   Same as predicate.

propositional logic   Same as propositional calculus.

propositional variable   A variable whose value is a proposition and thus effectively denotes either TRUE or FALSE. *Note:* Some writers use the term to mean a free variable, but this usage is deprecated; surely a propositional variable should be to a proposition just what an integer variable is to an integer, or a relation variable is to a relation (etc.).

proto tuple   Loosely, the portion of a relational calculus expression that precedes the WHERE clause. The term is shorthand for "prototype tuple"; it's useful but nonstandard.
   Example: Here's a tuple calculus formulation of the query "Get supplier number and city for suppliers who supply at least one part":

```
SX   RANGES OVER { S } ;
SPX RANGES OVER { SP } ;

{ SX.SNO , SX.CITY } WHERE EXISTS SPX ( SPX.SNO = SX.SNO )
```

In this example, the proto tuple is {SX.SNO,SX.CITY}. *Note:* A proto tuple consisting of just a range variable reference *R* enclosed in braces is shorthand for one of the form

```
{ R.A1 , R.A2 , ..., R.An }
```

where *A1, A2, ..., An* are all of the attributes of the relation *r* over which *R* ranges, in some arbitrary order. For example, given range variable definitions as above, the proto tuple {SX} is shorthand for the proto tuple {SX.SNO,SX.SNAME,SX.STATUS,SX.CITY}.

pseudovariable   *See* pseudovariable reference.

pseudovariable reference   The use of an operational expression instead of a simple variable reference to denote the target for some assignment (":=") or other update operation (in particular, *see* THE_ pseudovariable). *Note:* It's convenient for definitional purposes to regard pseudovariable references as if they were regular variable references (and this dictionary does so); in other words, pseudovariables are variables, loosely speaking.
   Examples: Let CS be a variable of declared type CHAR, with current value the string 'Middle', and consider the following assignment statement:

```
SUBSTR ( CS , 2 , 1 ) := 'u' ;
```

SUBSTR here is the substring operator, and the effect of the assignment is to "zap" the second character position within CS, replacing the 'i' by a 'u' (after the update, therefore, the current value of CS is the string 'Muddle'). The expression on the left side of the assignment symbol ":=" is a pseudovariable reference.

For a second example, let LS be a view, defined as the restriction of relvar S to just suppliers in London, and consider the following DELETE statement:

```
DELETE LS WHERE STATUS > 15 ;
```

Logically speaking, this DELETE is equivalent to the following:

```
DELETE ( S WHERE CITY = 'London' ) WHERE STATUS > 15 ;
```

In this expanded form (which isn't, nor is it meant to be, valid **Tutorial D** syntax), the target of the DELETE is specified as an operational expression, or in other words a pseudovariable reference. As the example suggests, therefore, updating a view is logically equivalent to updating a certain pseudovariable (thus, views are pseudovariables, loosely speaking). Here's the expanded form (again not valid **Tutorial D** syntax):

```
( S WHERE CITY = 'London' ) :=
        ( S WHERE CITY = 'London' ) WHERE NOT ( STATUS > 15 ) ;
```

And this latter simplifies in turn to the following (which *is* valid **Tutorial D** syntax):

```
S := S WHERE NOT ( CITY = 'London' AND STATUS > 15 ) ;
```

For a third example, showing that even updating a base relvar is in fact logically equivalent to updating a certain pseudovariable (and hence that base relvars too are really pseudovariables, logically speaking), see the examples under **database variable**.

public instance variable   *See* instance variable.

———— ♦ ♦ ♦ ♦ ♦ ————

QBE   A relational language based on domain calculus. (Actually QBE incorporates aspects of both domain and tuple calculus, but the emphasis is on the former.) The name is an abbreviation for Query-By-Example. Unlike QUEL (q.v.), **Tutorial D**, and most other relational or would-be relational languages, QBE is explicitly designed for use with a display screen interface. To be more specific, it's based on the idea of making entries in blank tables on the screen.

Example: A QBE formulation of the query "Get supplier names for suppliers who supply at least one part supplied by supplier S2" might look like this:

S	SNO	SNAME		SP	SNO	PNO
	_SX	P._NX			_SX	_PX
					_S2	_PX

To elaborate: The user here has asked the system to display two blank tables on the screen, one for suppliers and one for shipments, and has made entries in them as shown. Entries beginning with a leading underscore are "example elements" (in other words, domain calculus range variables); "S2" is a literal. (For simplicity, we ignore here the fact that supplier numbers are supposed to be of a user defined type, called SNO.) Thus, the user is asking the system to "print" or "present" ("P.") supplier names _NX such that, if the supplier with supplier number _SX has that name_NX, then that supplier _SX supplies some part _PX, and that part _PX in turn is supplied by supplier S2. Note the implicit existential quantifications involved in this example. Here for comparison purposes is the same query expressed in pure domain calculus:

```
NX RANGES OVER { NAME } ;
SX RANGES OVER { SNO } ;
PX RANGES OVER { PNO } ;

{ NX } WHERE EXISTS SX ( EXISTS PX ( S { SNO SX , SNAME NX } AND
                                     SP { SNO SX , PNO PX } ) AND
                                     SP { SNO 'S2' , PNO PX } )
```

quantification   Applying a quantifier (q.v.) to a free variable, thereby converting that free variable into a bound variable (*see* **binding**), and hence converting the predicate containing that free variable into a different predicate, logically distinct from the original. If the original predicate has n free variables and we quantify just m of them ($m \leq n$), we obtain a k-place predicate, where $k = n-m$. *Note:* If $m = n$ (i.e., if every free variable in the original predicate is quantified in this way), what results is a proposition.

quantifier   *See* **existential quantifier; universal quantifier**. *Note:* Other quantifiers are possible—for example, "there exists exactly one of" (*see* **UNIQUE**); "for all but one of"; "there exists an odd number of"; and so on—but EXISTS and FORALL are far and away the ones most frequently encountered in practice.

   Note: As explained under **existential quantifier** and **universal quantifier**, each of EXISTS and FORALL can be defined in terms of the other. It follows that either one could be dropped without any loss of functionality. But it's desirable for psychological reasons to support both, because some problems are "more naturally" formulated in terms of EXISTS and others are "more naturally" formulated in terms of FORALL. Note, however, that SQL doesn't really support either of these two quantifiers! It does support an operator it calls EXISTS, but that operator is indeed an operator and not a quantifier. In fact, it's essentially the operator that **Tutorial D** calls IS_NOT_EMPTY, q.v.

QUEL   A relational language, based on tuple calculus, that was at one time a serious competitor to SQL.

Example: Here's a QUEL formulation of the query "Get supplier numbers for suppliers who supply at least one London part" (note the implicit existential quantification on shipments in particular):

```
RETRIEVE S.SNO
WHERE     S.SNO = SP.SNO
AND       SP.PNO = P.PNO
AND       P.CITY = "London"
```

Here for comparison purposes is the same query expressed in pure tuple calculus:

```
SX  RANGES OVER { S } ;
SPX RANGES OVER { SP } ;
PX  RANGES OVER { P } ;

{ SX.SNO } WHERE EXISTS SPX ( EXISTS PX
                            ( SX.SNO = SPX.SNO AND
                            SPX.PNO = PX.PNO AND
                            PX.CITY - 'London' ) )
```

query   A retrieval request (i.e., a relational expression, or a statement that asks for the evaluation of such an expression). Sometimes used, loosely, to refer to update requests also; also used to refer to the informal natural language counterpart to some retrieval or update request.

Query-By-Example   *See* QBE.

query decomposition   A divide and conquer technique for evaluating relational expressions by recursively dividing them into subexpressions.

query rewrite   *See* expression transformation.

quota query   A query that imposes a desired limit, or quota, on the cardinality of the result.
   Example: Here's a possible, though perhaps a little tricky, formulation of the quota query "Get the three heaviest parts" (the quota here is three):

```
WITH ( q  := 3    /* quota */ ,
       t1 := P RENAME { WEIGHT AS WT } ,
       t2 := EXTEND P : { N1 := COUNT ( t1 WHERE WT > WEIGHT ) } ,
       t3 := t2 WHERE N1 < q ) :
t3 { ALL BUT N1 }
```

Note: Using the RANK shorthand, q.v., we could express this query more succinctly thus:

```
WITH ( q := 3 ) :
     ( ( RANK P BY ( DESC WEIGHT AS N2 ) ) WHERE N2 ≤ q ) { ALL BUT N2 }
```

Explanation: Given the sample value for relvar P shown in Fig. 1, the RANK invocation returns a relation looking like this—

PNO	PNAME	COLOR	WEIGHT	CITY	N2
P6	Cog	Red	19.0	London	1
P2	Bolt	Green	17.0	Paris	2
P3	Screw	Blue	17.0	Oslo	2
P4	Screw	Red	14.0	London	4
P1	Nut	Red	12.0	London	6
P5	Cam	Blue	12.0	Paris	6

—and the overall result thus looks like this:

PNO	PNAME	COLOR	WEIGHT	CITY
P6	Cog	Red	19.0	London
P2	Bolt	Green	17.0	Paris
P3	Screw	Blue	17.0	Oslo

Note that the cardinality of the result of a given quota query might not be exactly equal to the specified quota; in fact, it might be either less than or greater than that specified quota, depending on the query itself, and depending also on the current values of whatever relvars are involved in that query.

———— ♦♦♦♦♦ ————

R-table Term used in Codd's later writings to mean either a relation or a relvar or both, as the context demanded. The "R-" prefix was intended to stress the point that certain properties commonly associated with tables as such (in particular, top to bottom row ordering and left to right column ordering) didn't apply. However, the term is deprecated because it fails to make the crucial distinction between values and variables.

range 1. *See* function. 2. *See* range variable.

range variable Relational calculus analog of a logic variable; in other words, a variable that "ranges over" some specified set of values—either the set of tuples in some relation (in tuple calculus) or the set of values of some type (in domain calculus)—and can appear either bound or free in relational calculus expressions.
Examples: See the examples under **domain calculus**, **tuple calculus**, and elsewhere.

RANK *See* ranking.

ranking   Let relation *r* not have an attribute called *A*. Then (and only then) the expression RANK *r* BY (*item*, ..., *item* AS *A*) denotes a ranking of *r*. Within that overall expression, each *item* consists of the keyword ASC (ascending) or DESC (descending) followed by an (open) expression *exp*—typically but not necessarily just an attribute reference identifying an attribute of *r*—and the left to right sequence of such items specifies major to minor ordering in the usual way, in accordance with values of the specified expressions *exp* within the specified items. The overall expression returns a relation identical to *r* except that it has an additional attribute *A* whose value in any given tuple of that result shows that tuple's ranking position with respect to the specified ordering.

Example: See the example under **quota query**.

RATIONAL   In **Tutorial D**, a system defined type whose values are rational numbers (more precisely, rational numbers "of the first kind"). *See* **rational number**.

rational number   A number that can be expressed as the ratio of two integers *p* and *q* ($q \neq 0$)— e.g., 3/8, 593/370, −4/3. Such numbers fall into two categories: (a) those whose fractional part can be expressed in decimal notation by means of a finite sequence of digits followed by an infinite sequence of zeros, which can be ignored without loss (e.g., 3/8 = 0.375000...), and (b) those whose fractional part can be expressed in decimal notation by means of a possibly empty finite sequence of digits followed by another finite sequence of digits, the first of which is nonzero, that infinitely repeats (e.g., 593/370 = 1.60270270...). *Note:* It follows that rational numbers of the second kind can't be precisely represented on a finite computer system—at least, not using conventional decimal notation. (In fact, of course, the same is true of "most" rational numbers of the first kind as well.) *Contrast* **irrational number; real number**.

read operator   Same as read-only operator.

read-only operator   Generally, a function; i.e., an operator that, when invoked, updates nothing (except possibly variables local to the implementation of the operator in question) but returns a value, of a type declared when the operator in question is defined (*see* **specification signature**). A read-only operator invocation thus denotes a value; i.e., it's an expression—in fact, *expression* and *read-only operator invocation* are just two different terms for the very same concept—and it can therefore appear wherever a literal of the appropriate type is allowed. In particular, it can be nested inside other expressions.

Example: See the first example under **argument**.

Note: As mentioned elsewhere in this dictionary, certain read-only operators in SQL in particular are explicitly defined to be "possibly nondeterministic," q.v., meaning they're not functions at all, technically speaking. In truth, they really are functions; however, they're ones that are deliberately underspecified and thus don't behave like functions from the user's point of view. *See also* ZO.

real database *See Principle of Database Relativity.*

real number Either a rational or an irrational number. The set of all real numbers forms a continuum called the real number line, q.v.

real number line An infinitely long straight line on which the real numbers are plotted according to their distance in a positive or negative direction from an arbitrarily chosen origin point (corresponding to the real number zero). Every point on the line corresponds to a unique real number and vice versa.

real relation The value of a given real relvar at a given time.

real relvar A base relvar or a snapshot (*contrast* virtual relvar).

record Term sometimes used to mean a row, in any of the possible senses of that term. All such uses are deprecated, however; the term is better reserved for an operating system or even physical level construct.

recovery log Same as log.

recursive query A relational expression, which by definition can be thought of as the invocation of some relation valued operator *Op*, whose evaluation involves further invocations of that same operator *Op*.
  Example: Here's a recursive definition of an operator that computes the transitive closure, q.v., of a binary relation with attributes PA and PB, both of type PNO (the code isn't very efficient, but it can obviously be improved in a variety of ways):

```
OPERATOR TRANCLO ( PAB RELATION { PA PNO , PB PNO } )
               RETURNS RELATION { PA PNO , PB PNO } ;
   RETURN ( WITH ( temp := PAB UNION ( ( PAB RENAME { PB AS PC } )
                              COMPOSE ( PAB RENAME { PA AS PC } ) ) ) :
              IF temp = PAB THEN temp ELSE TRANCLO ( temp ) END IF ) ;
END OPERATOR ;
```

  Now the invocation TRANCLO (*rx*), where *rx* is a relational expression denoting a relation of the appropriate type, can be thought of as a "recursive query," because its evaluation involves further invocations of TRANCLO itself (in general).

recursive relationship A relationship (in the sense of the third definition of that term, q.v.) in which the two sets participating are one and the same. The term isn't particularly apt, since there's no recursion, as such, involved (though such relationships do often give rise to recursive processing of some kind).

Example: The well known bill of materials application involves a relationship between parts and their components. That relationship is "recursive" because components are parts in turn and can have further components of their own.

recursive type Shorthand for recursively defined type.

recursively defined type (*Without inheritance*) A type defined in terms of itself. Let T be a scalar type, and let $S(1)$, $S(2)$, ... be a sequence of sets defined as follows:

$S(1) = \{\, t : t$ is the declared type of some scalar component,
  or of some attribute of some tuple valued or relation valued component,
  of some possrep for $T \,\}$

$S(i) = \{\, t : t$ is the declared type of some scalar component,
  or of some attribute of some tuple valued or relation valued component,
  of some possrep for some type in $S(i-1) \,\}$
    $(i > 1)$

If there exists some n $(n > 0)$ such that T is a member of $S(n)$, then T is recursively defined.
  As for tuple and relation types: Let H be a heading, and let $S(1)$, $S(2)$, ... be a sequence of sets defined as follows:

$S(1) = \{\, t : t$ is the declared type of some attribute in $H \,\}$

$S(i) = \{\, t : t$ is the declared type of some component of some possrep for some scalar type,
  or of some attribute of some tuple or relation type, in $S(i-1) \,\}$
    $(i > 1)$

If there exists some n $(n > 0)$ such that TUPLE H or RELATION H is a member of $S(n)$, then the heading H is recursively defined (and any tuple or relation type with heading H is therefore recursively defined as well).
  The relational model currently prohibits recursively defined types.

reductio ad absurdum "Reduction to absurdity"; a method of proof, q.v., that establishes something as true by showing that assuming its negation leads to a contradiction. Also known as indirect proof.

redundancy In general, something displays redundancy if and only if it "says the same thing twice." With respect to databases in particular, however, it seems to be quite difficult to pin this notion down completely precisely. The following definition must therefore be regarded as somewhat tentative at this time: Let *DB* be a database variable (equivalently, a database design); let *db* be a database value that conforms to *DB* (i.e., let *db* consist of a collection of relation values, one for each relvar mentioned in *DB*); and let p be a proposition not involving any existential quantification. If *db* contains two or more distinct representations of *p* (either implicitly or implicitly), then *db* contains, and *DB* permits, redundancy. Note, however, that this definition says only that *if* (not if and only if) a certain condition holds, *then* there's redundancy; it would be nice if that *if* could be strengthened to *if and only if*, but it's not yet clear whether it can be (further research is needed). Note carefully too that a database can display redundancy by the foregoing definition even if it fully conforms to *The Principle of Orthogonal Design* and all normalization principles. For a detailed discussion of such matters, with numerous examples, see the book *Database Design and Relational Theory: Normal Forms and All That Jazz*, by C. J. Date (O'Reilly Media Inc., 2012).

Here are some further relevant considerations:

1. A relvar is subject to redundancy that can be eliminated by taking projections if and only if it's not in ETNF, q.v. To put the point another way, a relvar allows redundant tuples (q.v.) if and only if it's not in ETNF. *Note:* In fact, BCNF is sufficient to prohibit partly redundant tuples, q.v.; however, ETNF is necessary to prohibit fully redundant tuples, q.v.

2. *(Attribute level redundancy):* The following has been proposed as a definition of what it might mean for redundancy to exist at the level of the appearance, or occurrence, of some individual value of some individual attribute: Let relation *r* be a value of relvar *R*; let *t* be a tuple in *r*; and let *v* be an attribute value occurring within *t*. Then that occurrence of that value *v* within *t* is redundant in *r*, and *R* is subject to redundancy, if and only if replacing that occurrence of *v* by an occurrence of some value *v'* (*v'* ≠ *v*), while leaving everything else unchanged, leads to some dependency of *R* being violated. Note very carefully, however, that the term *dependency* in this definition refers only to dependencies that are FDs or JDs specifically—even embedded JDs are excluded. Be that as it may, a relvar is subject to this kind of redundancy if and only if it's not in RFNF (q.v.).

    Example (attribute level redundancy): Suppose the FD {CITY} → {STATUS} holds in our usual suppliers relvar S. Of course, the sample value shown for that relvar in Fig. 1 doesn't satisfy this FD; however, it would do so if we changed the status for supplier S2 from 10 to 30, so let's suppose for the sake of the example that this change has in fact been made. Suppose also that (as in Fig. 1) the tuple for supplier S1 in that relvar has city London and status 20, and the tuple for supplier S4 also has city London. Then this latter tuple must also have status 20, for otherwise the FD {CITY} → {STATUS} would be violated. In a sense, therefore, the occurrence of that status value 20 in the tuple for supplier S4 is redundant, because there's nothing else it could possibly be—it's a logical consequence of, and is fully determined by, the values appearing elsewhere in the relation that's the current value of the relvar at the time in question. *Note:* The notion of partly redundant tuples—*see* **partly redundant**—is motivated by such considerations, in part.

    Caveat: This dictionary is of course primarily concerned with the relational or logical level of the system—i.e., with the database as perceived by the user. Now, there will almost certainly be redundancy at the internal level of the system (i.e., redundancy in the data as physically stored: between an index and the data it indexes, for example). But such physical redundancy exists purely for performance, data recovery, and other such pragmatic reasons—it has no effect (or should have no effect) on the data as seen by the user. Thus, the term *redundancy* must be understood throughout this dictionary as referring to what might more accurately be called *logical* redundancy, meaning redundancy in the data as perceived by the user (barring explicit statements to the contrary, of course).

redundancy free normal form   Relvar R is in redundancy free normal form (RFNF) if and only if it's not subject to redundancy at the level of the appearance, or occurrence, of some individual value of some individual attribute of the relvar in question (*see* **redundancy**)—equivalently, if and only if (a) R is in BCNF and (b) for every JD J that holds in R, the union of those components of J that are superkeys for R is equal to the heading of R. Every RFNF relvar is in ETNF. *Note:* RFNF is logically equivalent to KCNF, q.v.

   Example: As noted under **Boyce/Codd normal form**, with the normal forms it's often more instructive to show a counterexample rather than an example per se. Consider, therefore, relvar SPJ, with attributes SNO (supplier number), PNO (part number), and JNO (project number), and predicate *Supplier SNO supplies part PNO to project JNO.* Let the sole key for that relvar be {SNO,PNO}. Also, let the relvar be subject to the constraint that if (a) supplier *sno* supplies part *pno* and (b) part *pno* is supplied to project *jno* and (c) project *jno* is supplied by supplier *sno*, then (d) supplier *sno* supplies part *pno* to project *jno*. Then SPJ is equal to the join of its projections on {SNO,PNO}, {PNO,JNO}, and {JNO,SNO}—i.e., the JD

   ☼ { { SNO , PNO } , { PNO , JNO } , { JNO , SNO } }

holds in SPJ—and so that relvar can be nonloss decomposed into those three projections. However, since the only component of that JD that's a superkey is {SNO,PNO}, relvar SPJ isn't in RFNF, though it is in ETNF.

redundant tuple   Tuple t is redundant in relation r if and only if it's either partly redundant, q.v., or fully redundant, q.v., in r. *Contrast* **essential tuple**; *see also* **essential tuple normal form**.

REF type (SQL)   In SQL, defining a structured type (q.v.) causes automatic definition of an associated REF type. If T is the structured type in question, the corresponding REF type is denoted REF(T), and its values are "references"—i.e., pointers—to rows in some "typed table" (see Part II of this dictionary) that's defined to be "of" type T. Thus, REF is really a type generator, and values of a REF type are SQL's analog of object IDs; in other words, they're pointers. Further details are beyond the scope of this dictionary.

reference   *See* **referencing**.

reference (SQL)   Term used in SQL to mean (among several other things) a value of some REF type, q.v.

referenced key   *See* foreign key.

referenced relvar   *See* foreign key.

referenced tuple   *See* foreign key.

referencing   The relational meaning of this term is as described under foreign key; it should not be confused with the operator of the same name, found in systems that support pointers (and perhaps more aptly called "address of"), that, given a variable *V*, returns a pointer to *V*. Note that this latter operator is rather unusual, inasmuch as (a) it's certainly read-only and yet (b) as with an update operator, its argument—its sole argument, that is—must be a variable specifically.

   Note: Systems that support pointers usually support an operator called *dereferencing* as well, which, given a pointer *p*, returns the variable *V* that *p* points to; equivalently, given an address *p*, the operator returns the variable at that address *p*. (This operator is unusual too, in that, in general, it returns a variable instead of a value. However, the use of the term found in SQL in particular is unorthodox, in that SQL's dereferencing operator—which exists in two distinct forms, incidentally—returns a value, not a variable: namely, the value of whatever it is that its pointer argument points to. What's more, SQL doesn't support a corresponding referencing operator at all!)

referencing relvar   *See* foreign key.

referencing tuple   *See* foreign key.

referential action   The action specification portion of a foreign key rule (e.g., "cascade," in a cascade DELETE rule); also used to refer to the specified action as such.

referential constraint   *See* foreign key.

referential cycle   A referential path, q.v., from some relvar *R* to itself. Database designs involving such cycles are best avoided because they lead to a need for multiple assignment, which today's DBMS products don't support. (At least, they don't support it in the form tacitly being considered here—the form, that is, in which the individual assignments involved in the multiple assignment in question are, specifically, explicit assignments to database relvars.)

referential integrity   Loosely, the rule that no referencing tuple is allowed to exist if the corresponding referenced tuple doesn't also exist. More precisely, let *FK* be some foreign key in some referencing relvar *R2*; let *K* be the corresponding key in the corresponding referenced relvar *R1*; and let *K'* be derived from *K* in the manner explained under **foreign key**. Then the referential integrity rule requires there never to be a time at which there exists an *FK* value in *R2* that isn't the *K'* value for some (necessarily unique) tuple in *R1*. *Note:* Either or both of *R1* and *R2* in the foregoing definition might in fact be "hypothetical views," in the sense of that term explained under, e.g., **foreign key constraint**. *See also* **foreign key; foreign key rule**.

referential path   Let relvars *Rz, Ry, Rx, ..., Rb, Ra* be such that there exists a referential constraint from *Rz* to *Ry*, a referential constraint from *Ry* to *Rx*, ..., and a referential constraint from *Rb* to *Ra*. Then the chain of such constraints from *Rz* to *Ra* constitutes a referential path from *Rz* to *Ra* (and the number of constraints in the chain is the length of the path). *Note:* Any or all of *Rz, Ry, Rx, ..., Rb, Ra* in the foregoing definition might in fact be a "hypothetical view," in the sense of that term explained under, e.g., **foreign key constraint**.

reflexivity   1. (*Of a dyadic logical operator*) The dyadic logical operator *Op*, which we assume for definiteness is expressed in infix style, is reflexive if and only if, for all *x*, *x Op x* is true. 2. (*Of a binary relation*) The binary relation *r* is reflexive if and only if, for all *x*, the tuple <*x,x*> appears in *r*. 3. (*Of FDs*) *See* **Armstrong's axioms**. *Note:* The first two of these definitions are slightly oversimplified, in that they deliberately fail to specify the range of possible values for *x*.
   Examples (first definition only): The logical operators EQUIV and IMPLIES; the partial ordering operator "≤"; the equality operator "=".

refresh   *See* **snapshot**.

RELATION   In **Tutorial D**, the name of the type generator for relation types. Also used in **Tutorial D** to denote a relation selector.
   Examples: For examples showing the RELATION type generator, see the examples under **relation type**. Here by contrast is an example of a relation selector invocation:

```
RELATION { TUPLE { SNO    SNO('S1') ,
                   SNAME  NAME('Smith') ,
                   STATUS 20 ,
                   CITY   'London' } ,
           TUPLE { SNO    SNO('S5') ,
                   SNAME  NAME('Adams') ,
                   STATUS 30 ,
                   CITY   'Athens' } }
```

relation   A relation value, q.v. *Note:* The term is also commonly used to refer to a relation variable, of course, but that usage is strongly deprecated as the source of much confusion.

relation (mathematics)   Given sets *s1, s2, ..., sn*, not necessarily distinct, *r* is a relation on those sets if and only if it's a set of *n*-tuples each of which has its first element from *s1*, its second element from *s2*, and so on. (In other words, *r* is a subset of the cartesian product *s1* × *s2* × ... × *sn*.) Set *si* is the *i*th domain of *r* (*i* = 1, 2, ..., *n*).

Note: There are several important logical differences between a relation in mathematics and its relational model counterpart. Here are some of them:

- Mathematical relations have a left to right ordering to their attributes.

- Actually, mathematical relations have, at best, only a very rudimentary concept of attributes anyway. Certainly their attributes aren't named, other than by their ordinal position.

- As a consequence, mathematical relations don't really have a heading (nor, a fortiori, a type) in the relational model sense.

- Mathematical relations are usually either binary or, just occasionally, unary. By contrast, relations in the relational model are of degree *n*, where *n* can be any nonnegative integer (possibly even zero).

- Relational operators such as JOIN, EXTEND, and the rest were first defined in the context of the relational model specifically; the mathematical theory of relations includes few such operators.

And so on (the foregoing isn't an exhaustive list).

relation assignment   Same as relational assignment.

relation comparison   Same as relational comparison.

relation constant   A relation, especially one that's named; not to be confused with a relation literal, q.v.

Examples: TABLE_DEE and TABLE_DUM. *Note:* These two relation constants are probably built in (assuming they're supported at all, that is, which in today's products they're probably not). Here by contrast is one that's user defined:

```
CONST STATES_OF_THE_USA
      RELATION { TUPLE { STATE NAME('Alabama') } ,
                 TUPLE { STATE NAME('Alaska' ) } ,
                 .............
                 TUPLE { STATE NAME('Wyoming') } } ;
```

relation equality   (*Without inheritance*) Equality of relations; relations *r1* and *r2* are equal— i.e., the relational comparison *r1* = *r2* evaluates to TRUE—if and only if *r1* and *r2* are the very same relation, meaning they have the same heading and the same body (i.e., their headings are equal and their bodies are equal too).

relation expression Same as relational expression.

relation level *See* set level.

relation literal A literal that denotes a relation; not to be confused with a relation constant, q.v.
Examples: See the examples under literal.

relation inclusion Same as relational inclusion.

relation predicate Let *r* be a relation. Then the relation predicate for *r* is the predicate that represents the user understood meaning of *r* in some particular context. If *r* is of degree *n*, that predicate will be *n*-adic (it will have a parameter for each attribute of *r*). In accordance with *The Closed World Assumption*, moreover, the body of *r* will contain all and only those tuples that correspond to invocations (instantiations) of that predicate that evaluate to TRUE.
Examples: 1. Let *r* be the projection of the current value of relvar S on {SNO,CITY}. Then the predicate for *r* is *There exists a name sn and a status st such that supplier SNO is under contract, is named sn, has status st, and is located in city CITY.* Note that this predicate is dyadic, as is to be expected for a binary relation. 2. Consider the relations *r1* and *r2*, where *r1* is the projection of the current value of relvar S on {CITY} and *r2* is the projection of the current value of relvar P on {CITY}. Then it's certainly possible for *r1* and *r2* to be equal; nevertheless, they have different predicates, corresponding to their two different contexts (loosely speaking, the predicates are *There exists a supplier located in city CITY* and *There exists a part stored in city CITY*, respectively).

relation schema / relation scheme Terms much used in the research literature, though very little in commercial practice, to mean a relation heading or (especially) relvar heading—or sometimes such a heading in combination with a relvar name and/or with certain dependencies (e.g., FDs), q.v.

relation selector Let *T* be a relation type; then the corresponding selector is an operator that allows a relation of type *T* to be selected, or specified, by supplying a set of tuple values. More precisely, let *T* be a relation type, and let the corresponding heading be *H*; then there's exactly one selector, *S* say, for that type *T*, and *S* is such that (a) the sole argument to any given invocation of *S* is a set of tuples all with heading *H*; (b) every relation of type *T* is producible by means of some invocation of *S* in which those tuples are all represented by tuple literals; and (c) every successful invocation of *S* produces a relation of type *T*. *See also* selector.

Examples: See the examples under **selector** and elsewhere. Of course, those examples illustrate, not incidentally, the syntax used for relation selectors in **Tutorial D** specifically; other syntactic styles might be possible, but they must be logically equivalent to the **Tutorial D** style.

relation type   Let *H* be a heading; then (and only then) RELATION *H* denotes a relation type—in fact, the sole relation type—with the same degree and attributes as *H*. *Note:* The following lightly edited extract from *The Third Manifesto* elaborates on the foregoing relation type naming convention:

> When we say "the name of [a certain relation type] shall be RELATION *H*," we do not mean to prescribe specific syntax. The *Manifesto* does not prescribe syntax. Rather, what we mean is that the type in question shall have a name that does both of the following, no more and no less: First, it shall specify that the type is indeed a relation type; second, it shall specify the pertinent heading. Syntax of the form "RELATION *H*" satisfies these requirements, and we therefore use it as a convenient shorthand; however, all appearances of that syntax throughout this *Manifesto* are to be interpreted in the light of these remarks.

Examples: Consider the **Tutorial D** definition for relvar S:

```
VAR S BASE
    RELATION { SNO SNO , SNAME NAME , STATUS INTEGER , CITY CHAR }
    KEY { SNO } ;
```

The second line of this definition constitutes an invocation of the RELATION type generator and thereby specifies the declared type of the variable being defined. To be specific, the keyword RELATION shows it's a relation type, while the rest of the line—a commalist, enclosed in braces, of <attribute name, type name> pairs—defines the pertinent heading. The declared type of relvar S is thus exactly the result of the specified invocation:

```
RELATION { SNO SNO , SNAME NAME , STATUS INTEGER , CITY CHAR }
```

By way of a second example, the following (corresponding to a certain projection of relvar S) also denotes a certain relation type:

```
RELATION { CITY CHAR , SNAME NAME }
```

Note that **Tutorial D** provides nothing analogous to a TYPE statement, q.v., for defining relation types. Instead, such types can be defined only by invoking the relation type generator, q.v., as illustrated in the foregoing examples.

relation type generator   *See* RELATION; *see also* type generator.

relation type inference   The process of determining the type of the value denoted by a given relational expression. Note that this process is completely specified by the rules defining the types of the results of the various relational operators, q.v.

relation value   Very loosely, a table (value). More precisely, let *H* be a heading, let *B* be a body consisting of tuples with heading *H*, and let *r* be the pair *<H,B>*. Then (and only then) *r* is a relation value (relation for short), with heading *H* and body *B*, and the same degree and attributes as *H* and the same cardinality as *B*. *See also* relation predicate; *contrast* relation variable. *Note:* It follows from this definition that a relation doesn't really contain tuples (it contains a body, and that body in turn contains tuples), but it's usual to talk as if relations contained tuples directly, for simplicity. Note too that relations in the relational model differ in several important respects from the mathematical construct of the same name. In particular, relations in mathematics typically don't have named attributes; instead, their attributes are identified by ordinal position, left to right. For other differences, *see* relation (mathematics).

relation valued attribute   An attribute whose type is some relation type. Values of such an attribute are relations of the specified type (sometimes called nested relations, since they're "nested" inside tuples—typically but not necessarily tuples within the relation that's the current value of some relvar, or tuples within the relation that's the result of some query). *Note:* If some relvar has a relation valued attribute, that fact in and of itself doesn't constitute a violation of any particular level of normalization (not even first); however, such attributes are usually contraindicated in base relvars in particular, because they necessarily imply some structural asymmetry in the database and thereby give rise to asymmetry (and hence complexity) in queries, constraints, and updates as well. *See also* grouping; ungrouping.
  Example: See the example under grouping.

relation variable   Very loosely, a table (variable); more precisely, a variable whose type is some relation type. Let relation variable *R* be of declared type *T*; then *R* has the same heading (and therefore the same attributes and degree) as type *T* does. Let the value of *R* at some given time be *r*; then *R* has the same body and cardinality at that time as *r* does. Note that a relation variable is *not* the same thing as a set of tuple variables (not even a set of tuple variables all of the same type). *See also* relvar predicate; variable; *contrast* relation value.

relational algebra   An open ended collection of read-only operators on relations, each of which takes one or more relations as operands and produces a relation as a result. Exactly which operators are included is somewhat arbitrary, but the collection overall is required to be at least as powerful as relational calculus, meaning that for every relational calculus expression there exists some logically equivalent expression in relational algebra (in other words, the algebra is required to be relationally complete, q.v.). Also, the operators are generic, in the sense that they apply to all possible relations, loosely speaking. *See also* Codd's relational algebra.

Note: If we want relational algebra to be regarded as an algebra in the same sense that the algebra of sets, q.v., is so regarded—which presumably we do—then we ought really to require, in addition to the operators that produce a relation as a result, support for the relational inclusion operator (q.v.), which produces a truth value, not a relation, as a result. Note also that relational assignment (q.v.) is also a relational operator, but it isn't a relational algebra operator as such because it isn't read-only.

relational assignment (*Without inheritance*) An operation that assigns a relation value of type *T* to a relation variable of that same type *T*. The relational operations INSERT, D_INSERT, DELETE, I_DELETE, and UPDATE are all special cases; in fact, every invocation of one of these operators is logically equivalent to some specific invocation of the explicit relational assignment operation (":=") as such. Fundamentally, therefore, relational assignment is the only relational update operator logically required. Conversely, however, any given relational assignment is logically equivalent to a certain DELETE / INSERT combination (more precisely, a certain I_DELETE / D_INSERT combination). To be specific, the relational assignment

```
R := rx
```

(where *R* is a relvar reference and *rx* is a relational expression of the same type as *R*) is logically equivalent to an explicit relational assignment of the form

```
R := ( r MINUS d ) UNION i
```

where:

- *r* is the "old" value of *R*

- *d* is the set of tuples to be deleted from *R* (the "delete set")

- *i* is the set of tuples to be inserted into *R* (the "insert set")

- *d* is a subset of *r*

- *i* and *r* are disjoint

- *d* and *i* are disjoint a fortiori

- *d* and *i* are unique

In other words, the original assignment *R* := *rx* is logically equivalent to the following multiple assignment—in fact, a multiple assignment (q.v.) in which the individual assignments both involve the same target, q.v.:

```
DELETE R d , INSERT R i
```

Thus, any given relational assignment to relvar *R* can always be thought of as a combination of a delete operation on *R* and an insert operation on *R*. In fact, given that (a) *d* is a subset of *r* and (b) *i* and *r* are disjoint, the original assignment is logically equivalent to either of the following:

```
I_DELETE R d , D_INSERT R i

D_INSERT R i , I_DELETE R d
```

If *d* is empty, the assignment is effectively a pure insert operation; if *i* is empty, it's effectively a pure delete operation.

relational calculus An applied form of predicate calculus, tailored to operating on relations, with the property that every relational calculus expression is logically equivalent to some relational algebra expression. *Note:* The converse is true, too—i.e., every relational algebra expression is logically equivalent to some relational calculus expression. In other words, the algebra and the calculus can be regarded as functionally equivalent, and hence interchangeable. In fact, they're both relationally complete, q.v. (It's interesting to note, incidentally, that the first version of relational calculus to be defined—see E. F. Codd, "Relational Completeness of Data Base Sublanguages," in Randall J. Rustin, ed., *Data Base Systems, Courant Computer Science Symposia Series 6*, Prentice-Hall, 1972—was in fact not as expressive as the relational algebra as defined in that same paper, because it failed to support any calculus counterpart to the algebraic union operator.)
    Examples: See the examples under **domain calculus** and **tuple calculus**.

relational comparison (*Without inheritance*) A boolean expression of the form (*rx1*) *theta* (*rx2*), where *rx1* and *rx2* are relational expressions of the same type *T* and *theta* is any comparison operator that makes sense for relations ("=", "≠", "⊆", etc.). *Note:* The parentheses enclosing *rx1* and *rx2* in the comparison might not be needed in practice. Note too that all possible relational comparisons can be defined in terms of the relational inclusion operator "⊆", q.v. Fundamentally, therefore, relational inclusion is the only relational comparison operator logically required.

relational completeness A basic measure of the expressive power of a language. Essentially, a language is relationally complete if and only if it's at least as expressive as relational calculus, meaning that any relation definable by some relational calculus expression is also definable by some expression of the language in question.
    Examples: Relational algebra is relationally complete, because for every relational calculus expression there exists some logically equivalent expression in relational algebra. (In fact, as noted under **relational calculus**, the converse is true as well; that is, for every relational

algebra expression there exists some logically equivalent expression in relational calculus, at least with the algebra and calculus as usually defined.) For example, the relational calculus expression

```
{ SX.SNAME } WHERE EXISTS SPX ( SPX.SNO = SX.SNO )
```

(where SX and SPX are range variables, q.v., that range over the current values of S and SP, respectively) is logically equivalent to this relational algebra expression:

```
( S MATCHING SP ) { SNAME }
```

It follows that in order to prove some given language *L* is relationally complete, it suffices to prove that every relational algebra expression is logically equivalent to some expression in *L*—which is often easier than proving that every relational calculus expression is logically equivalent to some expression in *L*. SQL, for example, can be shown to be "almost" relationally complete in this way ("almost" because SQL fails to support TABLE_DEE and TABLE_DUM, q.v.). *Note:* Actually SQL is also "more than" relationally complete, in a sense, in that its expressions permit the definition of many objects that aren't relations at all. As this example should be sufficient to suggest, being more than relationally complete isn't necessarily a good thing.

relational database A database that abides by *The Information Principle*. We assume throughout this dictionary that all databases are relational, barring explicit statements to the contrary. *Note:* SQL databases must be regarded as only approximately relational at best, since SQL involves so many departures from *The Information Principle* (including but not limited to the departures identified under **table**, q.v.).

relational DBMS A DBMS that manages relational databases (and relational databases only); equivalently, a DBMS that implements the relational model. *Note:* SQL DBMSs must be regarded as only approximately relational at best, since SQL involves so many departures from the relational model (including but not limited to the departures identified under **table**, q.v.).

relational expression An expression denoting a relation. Relation selector invocations (and hence relation literals), relcon and relvar references, and relational algebra operator invocations are all special cases.

relational inclusion Let relations *r1* and *r2* be of the same type. Then *r1* includes *r2* ("*r1* $\supseteq$ *r2*") if and only if its body is a superset of that of *r2*, and *r2* is included in *r1* ("*r2* $\subseteq$ *r1*") if and only if its body is a subset of that of *r1*. Relation *r1* is equal to relation *r2* ("*r1* = *r2*") if and only if each includes the other. Observe that every relation is included in itself, also that every relation both (a) includes the empty relation of the applicable type and (b) is included in the universal relation of the applicable type. Observe also that the term *relational inclusion* is usually taken, a trifle arbitrarily, to refer to the operator "$\subseteq$" specifically, not the operator "$\supseteq$".

relational model A data model, in the first sense of that term, q.v.; the formal theory or foundation on which relational databases in particular and relational technology in general are based. The relational model is often loosely characterized as having three aspects: a structural aspect, which has to do with relations per se; an integrity aspect, which has to do with keys and foreign keys; and a manipulative aspect, which has to do with operators such as join. A more precise characterization is as follows. The relational model consists of the following five components: (a) an open ended collection of types, including in particular the scalar type BOOLEAN; (b) a relation type generator and an intended interpretation for relations of types generated thereby; (c) facilities for defining relation variables of such generated relation types; (d) a relational assignment operator; and (e) a relationally complete, q.v., but otherwise open ended collection of generic read-only operators (i.e., relational algebra or relational calculus or something logically equivalent) for deriving relations from relations. Note part (e) in particular; it's a far too common error to regard the relational model as consisting of structure only and to overlook the operators, and yet (as Codd once said) structure without operators is rather like anatomy without physiology. Note too that those operators aren't just meant for writing queries, as many seem to think; rather, they're for writing expressions, expressions that serve many different purposes, including query but not limited to query alone. One particularly important purpose is the formulation of constraints (though in this case the relational expression will be just a subexpression of some boolean expression, frequently though not invariably an invocation of IS_EMPTY, q.v.). Note too that, in the interest of physical data independence, q.v., the relational model is deliberately silent on everything to do with performance (including physical storage representations in particular). *See also* **essentiality**.

Caveat: The term *relational model* is often used in the commercial world to mean a data model in the second sense of that term, when the data model in question is specifically a relational one. This second meaning is somewhat deprecated, however, because of the potential confusion with the first (and vastly more important) meaning as defined above.

relational operator An operator that takes relations or relvars or both as operands and either returns a relation or updates a relvar.

relationally complete *See* relational completeness.

relationship 1. A term used briefly in Codd's earliest papers (but quickly discarded) to mean what we would now call either a relation or a relvar, as the context demands. It was used to distinguish relations in the relational model sense (which don't have a left to right ordering to their attributes) from their mathematical counterparts, q.v. (which do). 2. In E/R modeling, "an association among entities" (this extremely imprecise definition is taken from Chen's original E/R paper, "The Entity-Relationship Model—Toward a Unified View of Data," *ACM TODS 1*, No. 1, March 1976). 3. More generally, given two sets (not necessarily distinct), a rule pairing elements of the first set with elements of the second set; equivalently, that pairing itself. *Note:*

This last definition can easily be extended to three, four, ..., or any number of given sets. By way of illustration, consider the relationship involving suppliers, parts, and projects mentioned in the example under **essential tuple normal form** and elsewhere.

relative complement   *See* complement (set theory).

relcon   A relation constant, q.v.

relcon reference   Syntactically, a relcon name, used to denote the value of that relcon. *See also* constant reference.

relvar   A relation variable, q.v. *Note:* For simplicity, we assume in this dictionary that all relvars are part of some database ("database relvars"). However, there's no good reason why relvars that are local to some application ("application relvars") shouldn't be supported as well.

relvar constraint   1. (*"A" relvar constraint*) Formally, any constraint that refers to the relvar in question, as well as possibly others; informally, a single-relvar constraint, q.v. *Note:* These definitions aren't meant to be equivalent in any sense—they refer to two distinct concepts. 2. (*"The" relvar constraint*) The logical AND of all constraints, apart from type constraints, that refer to a given relvar (*the* relvar constraint—sometimes called the *total* relvar constraint, for emphasis—for the relvar in question); in other words, the formal, system understood "meaning" for the relvar in question (*contrast* **relvar predicate**). Note that it follows from this definition that one constraint that applies to every relvar is the degenerate ("default") constraint TRUE. (In fact, of course, every relvar is necessarily subject to at least one key constraint, anyway.) Note too that all relvar constraints, in either sense, are also database constraints, q.v.

Examples: First, the key constraint specified in the definition of relvar S is a relvar constraint on that relvar (and the same would be true for all FDs, MVDs, and JDs—in particular, ones not implied by the keys—that apply to that relvar, if any such had been specified). Second, the foreign key constraint from SP to S is a relvar constraint for both relvar S and relvar SP. Third, here are a couple more relvar constraints (repeated from the examples under **database constraint**) that might apply to relvar S:

```
CONSTRAINT C1 IS_EMPTY ( S WHERE STATUS < 1 OR STATUS > 100 ) ;
/* status values must be in the range 1 to 100 inclusive */

CONSTRAINT C3 IS_EMPTY
     ( ( S JOIN SP ) WHERE STATUS < 20 AND PNO = PNO('P6') ) ;
/* no supplier with status less than 20 can supply part P6 */
```

(Constraint C3 is also a relvar constraint for relvar SP.)

Finally, suppose for the sake of the example that the foregoing constraints (the key constraint on relvar S, the foreign key constraint from relvar SP to relvar S, and constraints C1 and C3 above) are the only ones that apply to relvar S. Then the logical AND of all of them is "the" (total) relvar constraint for that relvar.

relvar predicate Let *R* be a relvar. Then the relvar predicate for *R* is the predicate that represents the user understood meaning of *R*. If *R* is of degree *n*, that predicate will be *n*-adic (it will have a parameter for each attribute of *R*). In accordance with *The Closed World Assumption*, moreover, at any given time the body of *R* will contain all and only those tuples that correspond to invocations (instantiations) of that predicate that evaluate to TRUE at that time. *Contrast* **relvar constraint** (second definition); this latter is a formal construct, but relvar predicates are necessarily somewhat informal. *Note:* Relvar predicates are sometimes called business rules, q.v.—though most writers take this latter term to include a variety of other constructs in addition to relvar predicates as such, including in particular the informal counterparts to various integrity constraints. (Conversely, some writers regard such additional constructs as part of the relvar predicates. There's no consensus on such matters.)

     Example: The relvar predicate for relvar S is *Supplier SNO is under contract, is named SNAME, has status STATUS, and is located in city CITY*. At least, this predicate is the one assumed (and indeed stated) elsewhere in this dictionary to be the one for relvar S. However, it would really be more accurate to say the predicate is, rather, *We know that*—or (perhaps better) *We believe that—supplier SNO is under contract, is named SNAME, has status STATUS, and is located in city CITY*. The point is, there can't be any guarantee that the database truly reflects the state of affairs that exists in the real world (*see* **correctness**); all it can do is reflect what users tell it, and what users tell it in turn will reflect their beliefs about the real world, not necessarily the real world per se. Note in particular, therefore, that if a certain tuple—say the tuple <S6,Lopez,30,Madrid>—currently fails to appear in relvar S, the accurate interpretation isn't *It's not the case that supplier S6 is under contract, is named Lopez, has status 30, and is located in city Madrid*; rather, it's *It's not the case that we know that*—or, more colloquially and more simply, *We don't know whether—supplier S6 is under contract, is named Lopez, has status 30, and is located in city Madrid*. Of course, it's customary to ignore such considerations in informal contexts, but perhaps it ought not to be. For further discussion, see Appendix C ("A Relational Approach to Missing Information") in C. J. Date, *SQL and Relational Theory: How to Write Accurate SQL Code* (3rd edition, O'Reilly Media Inc., 2015).

relvar reference Syntactically, a relvar name, used to denote either the relvar as such or the value of that relvar, as the context demands.

relvar vs. type The logical difference between these two concepts is discussed under First Great Blunder. But the question is sometimes asked: When should a given "entity type" be represented as a relvar and when as a type? A detailed discussion of this issue can be found in the *Manifesto* book, but here are some relevant observations:

■ If *T* is a type, there's no way to insert new values into or delete existing values from *T*. By contrast, if *R* is a relvar, it's certainly possible to insert new tuples into or delete existing tuples from *R*. To take a concrete example, if the given entity type is "employees," representing them as a type would mean there would be no way to hire and fire them.

■ Tuples in a relvar correspond to propositions and thus assert certain facts—e.g., the fact that "Supplier S1 is under contract, is named Smith, has status 20, and is located in London." By contrast, values of some type don't in and of themselves assert anything at all (e.g., what does the integer 3 assert?). For example, if suppliers are represented as a type, with type name S, the following might be a corresponding selector invocation:

```
S ( SNO('S1') , NAME('Smith') , 20 , CITY 'London' )
```

But this selector invocation constitutes, in effect, nothing more than a certain rather heavy duty noun—something like "an S1-numbered, Smith-named, status-20, London-located supplier." To repeat, it doesn't assert any facts, as such, at all.

REMOVE   An operator of the algebra **A,** q.v., equivalent to "project on all attributes but one" (i.e., the **A** expression *r* REMOVE *A*, where *r* is a relation and *A* is an attribute of *r*, is equivalent to the **Tutorial D** expression *r*{ALL BUT *A*}).

RENAME   *See* renaming.

renaming   Let relation *r* have an attribute called *A* and no attribute called *B*. Then (and only then) the expression *r* RENAME {*A* AS *B*} denotes an attribute renaming on *r*, and it returns the relation with heading identical to that of *r* except that attribute *A* in that heading is renamed *B*, and body identical to that of *r* except that all references to *A* in that body—more precisely, in tuples in that body—are replaced by references to *B*. *See also* tuple renaming.
   Example: The expression

```
P RENAME { WEIGHT AS WT }
```

returns a relation identical to the current value of relvar P, except that attribute WEIGHT is renamed WT. Note that relvar P per se remains unaltered in the database—RENAME is not like ALTER TABLE in SQL, it's just a read-only operator (like restrict, for example) that takes a certain relation as input and returns another as output.
   Note: **Tutorial D** additionally supports a form of RENAME that allows two or more separate renamings to be carried out in parallel ("multiple RENAME"). Here's an example:

```
P RENAME { WEIGHT AS WT , COLOR AS COL }
```

Note in particular that this feature simplifies the process of interchanging attribute names. For example, the multiple renaming

```
r RENAME { A AS B , B AS A }
```

is equivalent to, and can be thought of as shorthand for, an expression of the form

```
( ( r RENAME { B AS C } ) RENAME { A AS B } ) RENAME { C AS A }
```

for some arbitrary attribute name *C* that's distinct from *A* and *B* but is otherwise unspecified.

repeating field   *See* repeating group.

repeating group   Let some table have a column *C* of type *T*. Then *C* is a repeating group column if and only if the values appearing within *C* aren't values of type *T* but are, rather, collections (i.e., sets or bags or sequences or arrays or ...) of values of type *T*. Repeating groups are outlawed in the relational model (which is why this definition is phrased in terms of tables and columns instead of relations and attributes); in fact, a "relation" with a repeating group "attribute" is a contradiction in terms. *Note:* Technically, the foregoing definition might be considered as defining a repeating field rather than a repeating group. A repeating group would then be a repeating field in which the pertinent "field" is actually a combination of two or more columns, considered as a unit. For example, a row in an employee table might contain the employee number and a repeating group of job history information, giving, for each job held by the employee in question, the job title, start date, and end date. However, the distinction in question—i.e., between repeating fields and repeating groups—is unimportant for present purposes. In any case, there's a great deal of confusion in the literature over the precise meaning of either term; the foregoing definitions are offered in an attempt to clarify the situation, but there's much more that could be said. In particular, note carefully that—contrary to popular opinion, perhaps—a relation valued attribute, q.v., is quite definitely *not* a "repeating group column" by the foregoing definition, and any or all suggestions to the contrary should be firmly resisted. (In particular, relation valued attributes are permitted by the relational model, while repeating groups aren't.)

reporter   *See* observer.

representation   Either a physical representation (q.v.) or a possible representation (q.v.), as the context demands.

restriction   Let *r* be a relation and let *bx* be a restriction condition, q.v., on *r* (implying in particular that every attribute reference in *bx* identifies some attribute of *r*). Then (and only then) the expression *r* WHERE *bx* denotes the restriction of *r* according to *bx*, and it returns the relation with heading the same as that of *r* and body consisting of all tuples of *r* for which *bx* evaluates to TRUE.

Example: The following expression denotes a restriction of the relation that's the current value of relvar P:

```
P WHERE WEIGHT < WEIGHT(17.5)
```

Note: Restriction is often referred to as selection, but this term is deprecated, slightly, because of the potential confusion with either selector operations or the SELECT operation of SQL or both. Regarding selector operations, *see* **selector**. As for the SELECT operation of SQL—meaning, more specifically, just the SELECT portion of an SQL SELECT expression, q.v.—that operation can be loosely characterized as a combination of summarize, extend, rename, and "project" operations ("project" in quotes because SELECT doesn't eliminate duplicates, in general, unless explicitly requested to do so via DISTINCT). Note in particular, therefore, that "selection" in the sense of restriction is explicitly *not* one of the operations performed by the SELECT portion of an SQL SELECT expression (!).

restriction condition   Let *r* be a relation; then a restriction condition on *r* is a boolean expression—typically an open expression, q.v.—in which all attribute references are references to attributes of *r* and there are no relvar references. *See* **restriction**.

Note: WHERE clauses in real languages typically permit boolean expressions that are more general than simple restriction conditions on the pertinent relation. (Certainly this is the case for both SQL and **Tutorial D.**) Strictly speaking, in fact, a restriction condition isn't even supposed to contain any connectives; rather, it's supposed to consist, at its most complex, of a simple comparison, q.v. In practice, however, the following identities let real languages support the connectives in WHERE clauses after all:

```
r WHERE ( ( p ) AND ( q ) )   ≡   ( r WHERE p ) INTERSECT ( r WHERE q )

r WHERE ( ( p ) OR ( q ) )    ≡   ( r WHERE p ) UNION ( r WHERE q )

r WHERE ( NOT ( p ) )         ≡   r MINUS ( r WHERE p )
```

Examples: For an example of a WHERE clause in which the boolean expression is just a simple restriction condition on the pertinent relation, see **restriction**. Here by contrast is an example in which the boolean expression is more general:

```
S WHERE P { PNO } =
          ( ( SP RENAME { SNO AS ZNO } ) WHERE ZNO = SNO ) { PNO }
```

The boolean expression in the (outer) WHERE clause here isn't just a simple restriction condition on the relation that's the current value of relvar S, because (a) it contains attribute references that don't identify attributes of that relation, and (b) it also contains two relvar references. However, the expression overall can be seen as shorthand for something like the following:

```
WITH ( temp := EXTEND S : { X := P { PNO } , Y := !!SP { PNO } } ) :
      temp WHERE X = Y
```

In this expanded formulation, X and Y are attributes—in fact, relation valued attributes, q.v.—of *temp*, and the predicate in the WHERE clause in the second line is indeed a restriction condition as formally defined. *Note:* The expression !!SP in the first line is an image relation reference, q.v.

RETURN   Let *Op* be a read-only operator, and let the implementation code for *Op* be written in **Tutorial D**; then that code must contain at least one **Tutorial D** RETURN statement. The purpose of that statement is (a) to terminate execution of an invocation of *Op* and (b) to specify the value (the "return value") to be returned to the invoker by the invocation in question. *Note:* The foregoing remarks also apply if *Op* is an update operator, except that (a) there won't be any return value—so the RETURN statement will consist simply of the keyword RETURN followed by a semicolon—and (b) that RETURN statement need not be specified explicitly, because such a statement will implicitly be placed in the code anyway, immediately prior to the END OPERATOR specification.

Examples: The code fragments shown below constitute two versions, a read-only version and an update version, of an operator called MOVE that moves a specified ellipse such that it becomes centered on the center of a specified rectangle. (CTR is a read-only operator that returns the center of its rectangle argument.) Note the RETURN statement in the first version and the absence of such a statement from the second.

```
OPERATOR MOVE ( E ELLIPSE , R RECTANGLE ) RETURNS ELLIPSE ;
   RETURN ELLIPSE ( THE_A ( E ) , THE_B ( E ) , CTR ( R ) ) ;
END OPERATOR ;

OPERATOR MOVE ( E ELLIPSE , R RECTANGLE ) UPDATES { E } ;
   THE_CTR ( E ) := CTR ( R ) ;
END OPERATOR ;
```

RETURNS   (*Without inheritance*) Let *Op* be an operator; then *Op* has an invocation signature, consisting essentially of the specification signature, q.v., minus the operator name. In **Tutorial D**, therefore, the invocation signature consists of the combination of (a) the declared types (in order) of the parameters to *Op*, and either (b) the declared type—defined via the RETURNS clause—of the result, if any, of executing *Op* or (c) an indication of those parameters to *Op*, if any, that are subject to update. (In case (c), the RETURNS clause is replaced by an UPDATES clause. *See* UPDATES.)

Example: The invocation signature for the first version of the MOVE operator as defined in the examples under RETURN is:

```
( ELLIPSE , RECTANGLE ) RETURNS ELLIPSE
```

reversible decomposition   Replacing a relvar *R* by a set of relvars *R1, R2, ..., Rn* in such a way that it's guaranteed that *R* can be derived from *R1, R2, ..., Rn*. Nonloss decomposition, q.v., is an important special case.

rewrite rule   An identity, q.v., in the sense of the fourth definition of that term. As the name suggests, a rewrite rule of the form $x \equiv y$ allows any expression that contains an occurrence of *x* to be rewritten, without changing the meaning, as an expression that contains an occurrence of *y* (parenthesized if necessary) in its place but is otherwise unchanged. *See* expression transformation; query rewrite; substitution.

RFNF   Redundancy free normal form.

right associativity   *See* left associativity.

right identity   Let *Op* be a dyadic operator, and assume for definiteness that it's expressed in infix style. If there exists a value *i* such that *v Op i* is equal to *v* for all possible values *v*, then *i* is the right identity, or right identity value, with respect to *Op*. *See also* identity (fifth definition); left identity.
  Examples: Every identity, q.v., is necessarily a right identity in particular (and also a left identity, of course). As for an example of a right identity that's not also a left identity, let *Op* be the regular arithmetic subtraction operator; then, since *v*−0 is equal to *v* for all numbers *v* whereas 0−*v* is not, 0 is a right identity but not a left identity with respect to that operator.

ring (mathematics)   A formal system that obeys all of The Laws of Algebra, q.v., except that the commutative, identity, and inverse laws don't necessarily apply to multiplication ("*"). *Note:* Every ring is a commutative group, q.v., with respect to addition ("+").

Rissanen's Theorem   Let relvar *R*, with heading *H*, have projections *R1* and *R2*, with headings *H1* and *H2*, respectively; further, let *H1* and *H2* both be proper subsets of *H*, and let their union be equal to *H*; then *R1* and *R2* are independent projections (q.v.) if and only if (a) their common attributes constitute a superkey for at least one of them and (b) every FD that holds in *R* is a logical consequence (in accordance with Armstrong's axioms, q.v.) of those that hold in at least one of them.

RM/T   An extended form of the relational model, due to Codd, with the explicit goal of capturing more of the meaning of the data than the relational model per se is capable of. The name *RM/T* is an abbreviation for Relational Model / Tasmania (so called because Codd first described it at a conference in Tasmania). RM/T includes a variety of "semantic" constructs (e.g., E- and P-relations, which are meant to represent entities and properties, respectively, together with operators for operating on such relations). RM/T as such has never been implemented in a commercial product (in fact it couldn't be, since Codd's only paper on the topic—"Extending the Database Relational Model to Capture More Meaning," *ACM TODS 4*, No. 4—fails to specify it adequately), but its ideas can be useful as an aid in conventional database design. *Note:* E- and P-relations are better referred to as E- and P-relvars, but the term *relvar* wasn't in widespread use in 1979, when Codd first defined RM/T.

RM/V1 *See* RM/V2.

RM/V2 Codd spent much of the late 1980s revising and extending his original relational model, which he referred to as "the Relational Model Version 1" or RM/V1, to produce "the Relational Model Version 2" or RM/V2. However, definitions in the present dictionary are (as noted in the introduction) intended to conform to the relational model as defined by *The Third Manifesto*; as a consequence, therefore, they don't always agree with Codd's RM/V1 or (especially) RM/V2 definitions. For details of these latter, see Codd's book *The Relational Model for Database Management Version 2* (Addison-Wesley, 1990).

row 1. SQL analog of either a tuple value or a tuple variable, as the context demands. 2. More generally, a picture of a tuple (on paper, for example). *See also* cell; column; table.

row ID An implementation construct (typically though not necessarily some kind of pointer, q.v.); sometimes rather inappropriately called a tuple ID. *Note:* In some commercial products, row IDs are exposed to the user—usually, and unfortunately, in such a way as to violate either *The Information Principle* or *The Principle of Interchangeability* or both. Also, don't confuse row IDs with surrogates, q.v. Here are some differences between the two constructs:

- First, row IDs identify rows, while surrogates identify entities (note the logical difference here).

- Second, row IDs have performance connotations, but surrogates don't.

- Third, row IDs are usually (though not always, as already indicated) hidden from the user, but surrogates mustn't be, because of *The Information Principle*.

In a nutshell: Surrogates are a model concept; row IDs are an implementation concept.

row subquery *See* subquery.

rule of inference *See* inference rule.

RVA Relation valued attribute.

———— ♦ ♦ ♦ ♦ ♦ ————

safe expression   A relational expression that would be guaranteed to evaluate to a finite result even if the underlying domains (types) were infinite. In practice, various rules are imposed to ensure that unsafe expressions can never occur. An example of an unsafe expression, if it were permitted, would be one denoting the set of all tuples with heading the same as that of relvar S that don't currently appear in that relvar (in other words, a request for the complement of the relation that's the current value of relvar S). *Note:* As should be obvious, it's generally desirable for various pragmatic reasons to prohibit unsafe expressions even if all domains are in fact finite (as of course they are in real systems).

satisfy   1. (*Integrity constraint*) Let *C* be a constraint that refers to variables *V1*, *V2*, ..., *Vn* (*n* ≥ 0) and no others. Then values *v1*, *v2*, ..., *vn* (in that order) satisfy *C* if and only if evaluating *C* with *V1* equal to *v1*, *V2* equal to *v2*, ..., and *Vn* equal to *vn* yields TRUE. *Note:* An analogous definition applies to business rules also, q.v. *Contrast* **hold; violate.** 2. (*Predicate*) Let *P* be a predicate, with parameters *P1*, *P2*, ..., *Pn* (*n* ≥ 0) and no others. Then values *v1*, *v2*, ..., *vn* (in that order) satisfy *P* if and only if substituting *v1* for *P1*, *v2* for *P2*, ..., and *vn* for *Pn* produces a proposition that evaluates to TRUE.

scalar   1. (*Of a type, attribute, value, or variable*) Having no user visible component parts. The term is often used as a noun as an abbreviation for *scalar value* specifically. *See also* **encapsulated.** 2. (*Of a read-only operator*) Returning a scalar result. Note that in order to have a type at all—i.e., to be considered either scalar or nonscalar—an operator must be read-only; update operators return nothing, and the concept of scalar vs. nonscalar thus doesn't apply. *Note:* Support for the scalar type BOOLEAN is required by the relational model, and support for scalar values and scalar attributes—at least ones of that particular type—is therefore required also. Scalar variables aren't required by the relational model, but they'll almost be certainly needed in the external environment; for example, such a variable will certainly be needed to serve as the target for retrieval of the value of some scalar attribute from some tuple of some relation. An analogous remark applies to scalar operators also. Note too that there's no such thing as "absolute scalarness" (or "absolute atomicity," as it's sometimes called)—the concept is necessarily somewhat relative, and indeed somewhat informal to boot. For example, a phone number might be perceived equally well as an "atomic" (i.e., scalar) value or as a tuple value consisting of country code, area code, and local number (and a database design involving phone numbers ought to be capable of supporting both perceptions). Consider also the case of TABLE_DUM, which is clearly a relation and yet (like a scalar, but unlike all other relations) has no user visible component parts. Note finally that because the term is indeed informal, the relational model nowhere depends on the scalar vs. nonscalar distinction in any formal sense.

scalar attribute   *See* **scalar.**

scalar operator   *See* scalar.

scalar selector   *See* selector.

scalar subquery   *See* subquery.

scalar type   A type having no user visible component parts (*contrast* possible representation; tuple type; relation type). *See* type for further discussion.

scalar value   *See* scalar; value.

scalar variable   *See* scalar; variable.

scale   (*Of a numeric type*) Loosely, the size of the increment from one value of the type to the next, where "next" means next in sequence according to the natural ordering for the type in question. For example, consider the SQL type NUMERIC(5,2). Values of that type are decimal numbers with precision (q.v.) five and scale factor (q.v.) two, whence the scale as such is 0.01, or in other words one hundredth. Thus, values of that type are precisely the following:

```
-999.99 , -999.98 , ... , -000.01 , 000.00 , 000.01 , ... , 999.99
```

See precision and scale factor for further discussion.

By way of another example, let EVEN_INTEGER be a user defined type with the intuitively obvious semantics. The scale for that type is two.

Note: Actually there's some confusion in the literature over the term *scale*. To be specific, some writers and some languages use it to mean the scale factor (at least as that term is defined in this dictionary); others use it to refer to the distinction between fixed and floating point; and still others use it as a synonym for base or radix. Finally, note that (a) the term can also sensibly be used (and indeed is used) of certain nonnumeric types, such as dates and times; (b) scales are usually assumed to be linear but don't have to be (e.g., consider the well known example of the Richter Scale, where the scale is logarithmic to base ten). *Caveat lector*.

scale factor   (*Of a numeric type; for reasons of simplicity, however, the following explanation is couched in terms of decimal types only*) Consider the SQL type NUMERIC(p,q). Values of that type are decimal numbers with precision (q.v.) p and scale factor q. The scale factor specifies the position of the assumed decimal point in the string of digits denoting any given value of the type in question, as follows: A nonnegative scale factor q means the decimal point is assumed to be q decimal places to the left of the rightmost decimal digit of such a string of digits; a negative scale factor $-q$ means the decimal point is assumed to be q decimal places to the right of the rightmost decimal digit of such a string of digits. In other words, if v is a value of type NUMERIC(p,q), then v can be thought of in terms of a p-digit integer, n say; however, that p-digit integer n must be interpreted as denoting the value $v = n * (10^{-q})$. The multiplier 10^{-q} is the scale defined by the scale factor q (e.g., for NUMERIC(5,2), the scale is 0.01, or in other words one hundredth). Observe that, by definition, every value of the type is evenly divisible by the scale (i.e., dividing the value in question by the scale always leaves a zero remainder). *See* precision and scale for further discussion.

schema / scheme   1. Terms sometimes used to mean either the logical design of a database or the collection of data definitions that represents that design. (The term *schema*, at least, is also frequently used in the context of conceptual design, q.v. *See* conceptual schema.) 2. Shorthand for a relation schema (or relation scheme) specifically, q.v., if the context demands.

Second Great Blunder   Mixing pointers and relations (*see* pointer). Note that committing The First Great Blunder, q.v., seems to lead inevitably to committing the second as well; however, it's possible to commit the second without committing the first (witness SQL).

second normal form   Relvar R is in second normal form, 2NF, if and only if every nonkey attribute A of R is such that the set $\{A\}$ is irreducibly dependent on every key of R—equivalently, if and only if, for every nontrivial FD $X \rightarrow Y$ that holds in R, (a) X is a superkey or (b) Y is a subkey or (c) X isn't a subkey. Every 2NF relvar is in 1NF (as indeed every relvar is, of course). *Note:* Although being in 2NF clearly doesn't preclude being in the next higher normal form (3NF) as well, the term *2NF* is often used loosely to refer to a relvar that's in 2NF and not in 3NF. Also, second normal form as such is no longer very important (BCNF, 5NF—or perhaps ETNF—and 6NF being the normal forms of most practical significance); we mention it here mainly for historical reasons.

Example: As noted under Boyce/Codd normal form, with the normal forms it's often more instructive to show a counterexample rather than an example per se. Suppose for the sake of the example, therefore, that relvar SP has an additional attribute CITY, representing the city of the applicable supplier. This revised version of SP is subject to the FD $\{SNO\} \rightarrow \{CITY\}$ and is therefore not in 2NF (because CITY is a nonkey attribute, yet $\{CITY\}$ isn't irreducibly dependent on the key $\{SNO,PNO\}$; equivalently, because $\{SNO\}$ isn't a superkey, *is* a subkey, and $\{CITY\}$ isn't a subkey).

second order logic   A form of predicate logic in which the sets over which logic variables range are allowed to be sets of predicates. *Contrast* first order logic.

Example: Consider the well known principle of mathematical induction, limited here for simplicity to its application to monadic predicates p whose sole parameter i is of type nonnegative integer. That principle can be stated in somewhat stilted English as follows: For all such predicates p, if (a) $p(0)$ is true and if also (b) for all i ($i \geq 0$), if $p(i)$ is true then $p(i+1)$ is true, then (c) $p(n)$ is true for all n ($n \geq 0$). In symbols:

```
FORALL p ( ( p(0) AND FORALL i ( p(i) IMPLIES p(i+1) ) )
                                        IMPLIES FORALL n ( p(n) ) )
```

In this example the variables i and n range over nonnegative integers, but the variable p ranges over predicates—specifically, monadic predicates whose sole parameter is of type nonnegative integer—and is thus a predicate variable, q.v. The expression overall is thus second order.

SELECT expression In SQL, the vast majority of table expressions—i.e., expressions that denote a table—involve, in sequence as written, a SELECT clause (with an optional DISTINCT specification), a FROM clause, an optional WHERE clause, an optional GROUP BY clause, and an optional HAVING clause. Such expressions are known generically, and loosely, as SELECT – FROM – WHERE – GROUP BY – HAVING expressions, or more simply as SELECT – FROM – WHERE expressions, or more simply still as just SELECT expressions. Unfortunately, it's impossible in a dictionary of this nature to give a complete and accurate definition of this SQL construct, owing in part to the complicated interdependencies that exist among the various clauses. For example, the syntax and the semantics of the SELECT clause both depend on whether or not there's an accompanying GROUP BY clause, among other things. However, the following (extremely loose!) conceptual algorithm gives a rough idea of the overall semantics:

■ (*FROM*) Form the cartesian product of the tables specified in the FROM clause.

■ (*WHERE*) Discard rows from that product that fail to satisfy the boolean expression in the WHERE clause.

■ (*GROUP BY*) Partition the remaining rows into groups in accordance with values of the columns specified in the GROUP BY clause.

■ (*HAVING*) Discard groups from that partitioning that fail to satisfy the boolean expression in the HAVING clause.

■ (*SELECT*) From each remaining group, derive a row by applying whatever combination of summarize, extend, rename, and "project" operations is specified by the SELECT and GROUP BY clauses taken in combination.

■ (*DISTINCT*) Discard redundant duplicate rows from the result of the previous step.

Observe in particular that the clauses aren't evaluated in the sequence in which they're written (which is in fact the sequence in which they *must* be written).

Here are some additional factors that would need to be taken into account in any more precise explanation:

■ The fact that the various clauses can all contain subqueries, q.v.

- The fact that certain subqueries can be "correlated"

- The fact that certain correlated subqueries can be "lateral"

- The fact that certain fundamental operations, including equality ("=") in particular, aren't fully defined (in some cases, in fact, they're explicitly defined to be what the SQL standard calls "possibly nondeterministic," q.v., meaning their results aren't fully predictable)

- The fact that there are numerous differences between SQL tables and their relational counterparts (*see* **table** for a partial list of such differences)

Further explanation of such matters is beyond the scope of this dictionary.

   Note: Let *exp1* and *exp2* be SELECT expressions. Then SQL permits various unions, intersections, and differences to be formulated in terms of *exp1* and *exp2*. Again, however, the details are beyond the scope of this dictionary.

selection (relational algebra)   *See* restriction.

selector   An operator—read-only by definition—for selecting, or specifying, an arbitrary value of a given type; not to be confused with either relational restriction (which is, perhaps rather unfortunately, sometimes called selection), q.v., or the SELECT operation of SQL. (For a loose characterization of this latter, *see* **SELECT expression**.) Note that, by definition, the type in question must be nonempty. Every such type, tuple and relation types included, has at least one associated selector (see below for further details). Let *T* be such a type, and let *S* be a selector for type *T*. Then (a) every value of type *T* is producible by means of some invocation of *S* in which the argument expressions are all literals, and (b) every successful invocation of *S* produces a value of type *T*. To be more specific:

- If *T* is a user defined scalar type, definition of a possrep *PR* for *T* causes automatic definition of a corresponding selector operator (with the same name as *PR*, in **Tutorial D**), which allows a value of type *T* to be selected by supplying a value for each component of *PR*.

- If *T* is a system defined scalar type, one or more possreps might or might not be defined for it. If one is defined (*PR*, say), then it behaves exactly as if *T* were user defined and *PR* were a corresponding possrep. If no possrep is defined, then at least one selector operator for type *T* must be provided by the system. In this latter case, however, invocations of such a selector will probably be limited to being simple literals (see further discussion of literals below).

■ If *T* is a tuple type, the (unique) corresponding selector operator allows a tuple of type *T* to be selected by supplying a value for each attribute of *T*.

■ If *T* is a relation type, the (unique) corresponding selector operator allows a relation of type *T* to be selected by specifying a set of tuple expressions, each denoting one tuple of the relation in question. In other words, a relation selector invocation effectively just enumerates the relevant tuples.

Note: If *S* is a selector for type *T*, then *T* is said to be the target type for *S*. Note further that, ultimately, the only way any expression can ever yield a value of type *T* is via invocation of some selector for that type *T*. In fact, the selector notion is essentially a generalization of the familiar concept of a literal (as noted under literal, all literals are selector invocations, but some selector invocations aren't literals; to be specific, a selector invocation is a literal if and only if all of its argument expressions are literals in turn).

Examples: First some scalar examples. *User defined types:* The expressions SNO('S3') and SNO('S5') are selector invocations for type SNO; the expression PNO('P1') and PNO('P2') are selector invocations for type PNO; and the expressions QTY(150) and QTY(500) are selector invocations for type QTY. *System defined types:* The expressions 'S3', 'P1', and 150 are selector invocations for types CHAR, CHAR, and INTEGER, respectively (assumed for the sake of the example to be system defined types).

Here now are a couple of selector invocations for tuple type TUPLE {SNO SNO, PNO PNO, QTY QTY}:

```
TUPLE { SNO SNO('S3') , PNO PNO('P1') , QTY QTY(150) }
TUPLE { SNO SNO('S5') , PNO PNO('P2') , QTY QTY(500) }
```

And here's a selector invocation for relation type RELATION {SNO SNO, PNO PNO, QTY QTY}:

```
RELATION
    { TUPLE { SNO SNO('S3') , PNO PNO('P1') , QTY QTY(150) ,
      TUPLE { SNO SNO('S5') , PNO PNO('P2') , QTY QTY(500) } }
```

Note: All of the foregoing examples are actually literals, since their argument expressions are all literals in turn. Here by contrast are some selector invocations that aren't literals. Let X, Y, and Z be variables of declared types CHAR, CHAR, and INTEGER, respectively. Then (a) the expressions SNO(X), PNO(Y), and QTY(Z) are selector invocations for types SNO, PNO, and QTY, respectively; (b) the expression TUPLE {SNO SNO(X), PNO PNO(Y), QTY QTY(Z)} is a selector invocation for tuple type TUPLE {SNO SNO, PNO PNO, QTY QTY}; and (c) the expression RELATION {*ts*}, where *ts* is the tuple selector invocation just shown, is a selector invocation for relation type RELATION {SNO SNO, PNO PNO, QTY QTY}.

self-referencing relvar   A relvar *R* with a foreign key that references some key of *R* itself (hence giving rise to a referential cycle, q.v., of length one). Database designs involving such relvars are best avoided if possible; in fact, as noted under **referential cycle**, designs involving referential cycles of any length are best avoided if possible.

semantic   (*Of a language, sentence, etc.*) Pertaining to meaning. *Contrast* lexical; syntactic.

semantic modeling   A rather vague term, never very precisely defined, having to do with the representation of meaning within a database design. Other terms used in the same or a related sense include *conceptual modeling*; *data modeling*; *entity modeling*; *entity/relationship modeling*; and *object modeling. See also* RM/T.

semantic optimization   Using database integrity constraints as a basis for transforming relational expressions, usually with the aim of improving performance. *See* expression transformation; optimizer.
  Example: Consider the query

```
P WHERE CITY = 'London' AND COLOR = COLOR('Red')
```

Suppose relvar P is subject to the constraint that all parts in London must be red. Then the query can clearly be transformed—possibly "manually" by the user, preferably automatically by the optimizer, q.v.—into the following simpler one:

```
P WHERE CITY = 'London'
```

Moreover, if the original query had requested blue parts instead of red ones, the optimizer might be able to determine that the result is empty without actually having to execute the query at all.

semantic override   Same as domain check override.

semantic transformation   The kind of expression transformation performed in connection with semantic optimization, q.v.

semantics   (*Plural noun treated as singular*) Meaning; pertaining to meaning. *Note:* Semantics is often confused with syntax (especially in nontechnical contexts, where for some reason the term is frequently used with pejorative intent). But when we say something, semantics is what we mean, while syntax is merely how we say it. Semantics is more important than syntax, at least from a logical or conceptual point of view.

semidifference   Let relations *r1* and *r2* be joinable, q.v. Then (and only then) the expression *r1* NOT MATCHING *r2* denotes the semidifference between *r1* and *r2* (in that order), and it returns the relation denoted by the expression *r1* MINUS (*r1* MATCHING *r2*).

Examples: The expression

```
S NOT MATCHING SP
```

represents the query "Get suppliers who supply no parts at all," and the expression

```
S { CITY } NOT MATCHING P { CITY }
```

represents the query "Get supplier cities that aren't also part cities." *Note:* As this latter example indicates, *r1* NOT MATCHING *r2* degenerates to *r1* MINUS *r2* when *r1* and *r2* are of the same type. In other words, as noted under **difference**, regular relational difference is actually just a special case of semidifference.

SEMIJOIN Same as (but in **Tutorial D** superseded by) MATCHING.

semijoin Let relations *r1* and *r2* be joinable, q.v., and let *r1* have attributes called *A1*, *A2*, ..., *An* (and no others). Then (and only then) the expression *r1* MATCHING *r2* denotes the semijoin of *r1* with *r2* (in that order), and it returns the relation denoted by the expression (*r1* JOIN *r2*) {*A1,A2, ...,An*}. Note that *r1* MATCHING *r2* and *r2* MATCHING *r1* aren't equivalent, in general (i.e., MATCHING is noncommutative).
  Example: The expression

```
S MATCHING SP
```

represents the query "Get suppliers who supply at least one part."

SEMIMINUS Same as (but in **Tutorial D** superseded by) NOT MATCHING.

sentence (*Logic*) A statement (*see* **logical system**).

SEQUEL An acronym for "Structured English Query Language" (the original name for SQL).

set A collection of objects, called elements, with the property that given an arbitrary object *x*, it can be determined whether or not *x* appears in the collection (*see* **set membership**). An example is the collection {*a,b,c*}, which can equivalently be written as, e.g., {*b,a,c*}, since sets have no ordering to their elements (nor do they contain any duplicate elements). Every subset or superset of a set is itself a set. *See also* **class** (first definition). *Note:* There's a logical difference— actually a difference in type—between an element *x* and the singleton set {*x*} that contains just that element *x*. Thus, a database language needs to provide both (a) an operator for extracting the single tuple from a relation of cardinality one and (b) an operator for extracting the single attribute value from a tuple of degree one (*see* **tuple extractor** and **attribute extractor**, respectively). Note too that the inverse functionality—in effect, building up a tuple from specified attribute values and building up a relation from specified tuple values—is provided by the appropriate tuple and relation selectors, respectively (*see* **tuple selector**; **relation selector**).

SET_ operator   An OO operator (a "mutator," q.v.) that assigns a specified value to a specified property—typically represented by an instance variable, q.v.—of a specified object. It might be thought of, very loosely, as the OO counterpart to a THE_ pseudovariable, except that (a) THE_ pseudovariables are defined in terms of possrep components, not "object properties," and (b) THE_ operator invocations can be nested, whereas the same might not be true of SET_ operator invocations. *Contrast* **GET_ operator.**

set algebra   *See* **boolean algebra** (second definition).

set function   Strictly, a function (i.e., a read-only operator) that takes sets as input and produces a set as output. Unfortunately, the term is mainly used in practice to refer to an aggregate operator (q.v.) or a summary (q.v.) or both; such usage is doubly deprecated, because in both cases (a) the input is typically not a set but a bag and (b) the output is typically not a set but a scalar. *Note:* SQL in particular uses the term to refer to a summary (but not to an aggregate operator, because—as noted under **aggregate operator**—SQL doesn't support aggregate operators, as such, at all).

set inclusion   Set *s1* includes set *s2* ("*s1* $\supseteq$ *s2*") if and only if it is a superset of *s2*; set *s2* is included in set *s1* ("*s2* $\subseteq$ *s1*") if and only if it is a subset of *s1*. Set *s1* is equal to set *s2* ("*s1* = *s2*") if and only if each includes the other. Observe that every set is included in itself, also that every set includes the empty set. Observe also that the term *set inclusion* is usually taken, a trifle arbitrarily, to refer to the operator "$\subseteq$" specifically, not the operator "$\supseteq$". *Note:* The term *containment* is sometimes used as a synonym for inclusion in the present sense, but this usage is generally deprecated—better to say of a set that it *contains* its elements (*see* **containment**) but *includes* its subsets.

set level   The operators of the relational model are all set level, in the sense that they take entire relations or relvars or both as operands and either produce entire relations as results or update entire relvars. (*Relation level* would be a better term.) One important implication of this state of affairs, for update operators in particular, is that applicable compensatory actions must not be done until all of the explicitly requested updating has been done; another is that database integrity checking must not be done until all of the updating has been done (including applicable compensatory actions, if any). *Contrast* **tuple level.**

set membership   (*Of an element*) The property of appearing in some given set; the operation of testing for that property. Set membership is usually denoted by the symbol "$\in$" (sometimes pronounced *epsilon*, because it's a variant form of the lowercase Greek letter epsilon—i.e., "ε"— which is the first letter of the Greek word meaning "is"); thus, the boolean expression $x \in s$—

which is logically equivalent to the expression $\{x\} \subseteq s$—returns TRUE if and only if element x does in fact appear in set s. *Note:* The expression $x \in s$ is logically equivalent to the expression $s \ni x$, where the symbol "$\ni$" denotes containment (the inverse of membership, in effect).

set operator *See* boolean algebra (second definition); *see also* difference (set theory), intersection (set theory), set function, and so on; not to be confused with either SET_ operators (q.v.) or the SET operator of SQL, which is basically just assignment (e.g., SET A = B is SQL syntax for the assignment A := B).

set theory A branch of mathematics, closely related to logic, that deals with the nature of sets. Among other things, it formalizes the concept of a set in terms of certain axioms, such as the axiom of extension, q.v.

sharding A physical database design technique (*see* horizontal decomposition).

Sheffer stroke *See* NAND.

SI prefixes Part of the International System of Units, the standard for scientific measurements of all kinds (SI is an abbreviation for *Système Internationale d'Unités*). The following table lists SI prefixes and their abbreviations and meanings:

yotta	Y	10 to the power 24	yocto	z	10 to the power −24
zetta	Z	10 to the power 21	zepto	z	10 to the power −21
exa	E	10 to the power 18	atto	a	10 to the power −18
peta	P	10 to the power 15	femto	f	10 to the power −15
tera	T	10 to the power 12	pico	p	10 to the power −12
giga	G	10 to the power 9	nano	n	10 to the power −9
mega	M	10 to the power 6	micro	μ	10 to the power −6
kilo	k	10 to the power 3	milli	m	10 to the power −3
hecto	h	10 to the power 2	centi	c	10 to the power −2
deca	da	10 to the power 1	deci	d	10 to the power −1

Note: In the computing world, the prefixes yotta through kilo are used a little differently. To be specific, they're usually interpreted in terms of powers of 2, not 10, as indicated here:

yotta	Y	2 to the power 80
zetta	Z	2 to the power 70
exa	E	2 to the power 60
peta	P	2 to the power 50
tera	T	2 to the power 40
giga	G	2 to the power 30
mega	M	2 to the power 20
kilo	K	2 to the power 10

For example, one kilobyte (1KB—the prefix *kilo* is usually abbreviated K, not k, in the computing world) is 1,024 bytes, not 1,000 bytes. Note in particular that a gigabyte is a billion bytes, roughly speaking (the abbreviation BB is sometimes used instead of GB; similarly, the abbreviation XB is sometimes used instead of EB). Note also that—contrary to popular belief—the prefix *giga* is properly pronounced with a soft initial *g* (as in *gigantic*).

signature   *See* invocation signature; specification signature.

simple attribute   An attribute, q.v. *Contrast* composite attribute.

simple key   A key that's not composite.

simple predicate   A predicate that involves no connectives. *Contrast* compound predicate.

simple proposition   A proposition that involves no connectives. *Contrast* compound proposition.

single arrow   Same as arrow (*see* functional dependency). *Contrast* double arrow.

single assignment   *See* multiple assignment.

single-relvar constraint   Term sometimes used to mean a database constraint that mentions exactly one relvar. *Contrast* multirelvar constraint; single-variable constraint. *Note:* As noted under multirelvar constraint, the difference between single- and multirelvar constraints is more a matter of pragma than logic, thanks to *The Principle of Interchangeability* (q.v.) among other things.
  Examples: The key constraints for relvars S, SP, and P; also constraints C1 and C2 from the examples under database constraint.

single-tuple constraint   Same as tuple constraint.

single-variable constraint   Term sometimes used to mean a database constraint that involves exactly one range variable if expressed in tuple calculus form. *Contrast* multivariable constraint; single-relvar constraint.
  Examples: Constraints C1 and C2 from the examples under database constraint are single-relvar constraints that are also single-variable constraints. By contrast, the key constraints for relvars S, SP, and P are single-relvar constraints but not single-variable constraints, because it takes two range variables to express the fact that (e.g.) values of {SNO} within relvar S are unique.

singleton set   A set of cardinality one.

sixth normal form Relvar R is in sixth normal form, 6NF, if and only if it can't be nonloss decomposed at all, other than trivially—i.e., if and only if the only JDs to which it's subject are trivial ones. Equivalently, relvar R is in 6NF if and only if it's in 5NF, is of degree n, and has no key of degree less than $n-1$. Observe, therefore, that (a) 6NF is the ultimate normal form with respect to normalization as conventionally understood; (b) every 6NF relvar is in 5NF; (c) 6NF relvars are irreducible, q.v. *Note:* Part III of this dictionary gives an extended definition of this particular normal form.

    Examples: 1. Relvar SP is in 6NF, since it can't be nonloss decomposed at all other than trivially. (In other words, SP is irreducible. Observe that it's certainly in 5NF; it's of degree three; and it has no key of degree less than two.) By contrast, relvars S and P aren't in 6NF, because they can each be nonloss decomposed, nontrivially, into two or more projections (in several different ways, in fact). 2. Let relvar PLUS have attributes A, B, and C, all of declared type INTEGER, and let the corresponding relvar predicate be

```
A + B = C
```

Then relvar PLUS has three distinct keys: {A,B}, {B,C}, and {C,A}. But PLUS is in 6NF, since it's certainly in 5NF, it's of degree three, and it has no key of degree less than two.

SKNF Superkey normal form.

skolem constant By definition, the expression EXISTS x ($p(x)$) is logically equivalent to the expression $p(v)$ for some unknown value v; that is, the original expression effectively asserts that some such value v exists, even if we don't know what it is. That value v is a skolem constant. *See also* skolem function.

skolem function By definition, the expression FORALL y (EXISTS x ($q(y,x)$)) is logically equivalent to the expression FORALL y ($q(y,f(y))$) for some unknown function f of the universally quantified variable y; that is, the original expression effectively asserts that some such function f exists, even if we don't know what it is. That function f is a skolem function. Together, skolem constants, q.v., and skolem functions (which are named for the logician T. A. Skolem) provide a basis for systematically eliminating existential quantifiers from an arbitrary logical expression, thereby making that expression more amenable to subsequent formal manipulation. Further details are beyond the scope of this dictionary.

Small Divide One of the many relational division operators that have been defined over the years (*see* division). Let relations $r1$, $r2$, and $r3$ be such that (a) $r1$ and $r3$ are joinable, q.v., and so are $r3$ and $r2$; (b) the common attributes of $r1$ and $r3$ are called $A1, A2, ..., Am$ ($m \geq 0$); (c) the common attributes of $r3$ and $r2$ are called $B1, B2, ..., Bn$ ($n \geq 0$); and finally (d) no Ai has the same name as any Bj ($1 \leq i \leq m$, $1 \leq j \leq n$). Then (and only then) the expression $r1$ DIVIDEBY *r2* PER (*r3*)—where *r1* is the dividend, *r2* is the divisor, and *r3* is the "mediator"—denotes the division of *r1* by *r2* according to *r3*, and it returns the relation *r* denoted by the expression *r1* NOT MATCHING ((*r1*{*A1,A2,...,Am*} JOIN *r2*{*B1,B2,...,Bn*}) NOT MATCHING *r3*). In other words, relation *r* has heading the same as that of *r1* and body defined as follows: Tuple *t* appears in that body if and only if it appears in *r1* and a tuple <*a1,a2,..,am,b1,b2,...,bn*>, with *a1* equal to the *A1* value in *t*, *a2* equal to the *A2* value in *t*, ..., and *am* equal to the *Am* value in *t* appears in *r3*{*A1,A2,...,Am,B1,B2,...,Bn*} for all tuples <*b1,b2,...,bn*> appearing in *r2*{*B1,B2,...,Bn*}. *Contrast* Great Divide.

  Example: The expression S DIVIDEBY P PER (SP) yields a relation with heading the same as that of relvar S and body consisting of all possible tuples <*sno,sn,st,sc*> from relvar S such that supplier *sno* supplies all parts mentioned in relvar P. (Given the sample values of Fig. 1, the result contains just the tuple for supplier S1.) The expression is logically equivalent to this one:

```
S NOT MATCHING ( ( S { SNO } JOIN P { PNO } ) NOT MATCHING SP )
```

An equivalent tuple calculus formulation is:

```
SX   RANGES OVER { S } ;
SPX  RANGES OVER { SP } ;
PX   RANGES OVER { P } ;

{ SX } WHERE
       FORALL PX ( EXISTS SPX ( SPX.SNO = SX.SNO AND SPX.PNO = PX.PNO ) )
```

An equivalent **Tutorial D** formulation is:

```
S WHERE ( !!SP ) { PNO } = P { PNO }
```

(The expression !!SP here is an image relation reference, q.v.)

snapshot A derived relvar that's real, not virtual (*contrast* view). The value of a given snapshot at a given time is the result of evaluating a certain relational expression—the snapshot defining expression, specified when the snapshot itself is defined—at some time prior to the time in question: to be precise, at the most recent "refresh time" (see the explanation immediately following). The snapshot is "refreshed" (i.e., the snapshot defining expression is reevaluated and the result assigned as the new current value of the snapshot) on explicit user request or, more usually, when some prescribed event occurs, such as the passing of a certain interval of time. *Note:* The snapshot defining expression must mention at least one relvar, for otherwise the snapshot wouldn't be a variable as such. However, the only kind of update permitted on that variable is the periodic refreshing already described; in other words, snapshots are "almost" read-only.

Example: The following statement is a hypothetical **Tutorial D** definition for a snapshot called LSS (it's hypothetical because **Tutorial D** doesn't actually support snapshots at the time of writing):

```
VAR LSS SNAPSHOT ( S WHERE CITY = 'London' )
        REFRESH EVERY DAY ;
```

The relation that's the value of snapshot LSS at any given time is equal to the value of the snapshot defining expression S WHERE CITY = 'London' as it was at most 24 hours prior to the time in question.

SNF   Same as SKNF.

SOME   Keyword sometimes used as an alternative spelling for the aggregate operator OR (*see* aggregate operator).

sort/merge join   A join implementation technique.

sorted logic   A form of logic—nothing to do with sorting in the usual computing sense—in which the values or "individual constants," q.v., that are the subject of the logic are divided up into "sorts," or in other words types. *Note:* Most logic texts pay little or no attention to the notion of types; instead, they deal with unsorted logic, which effectively means they assume that everything is of the same type (often referred to as the universe, or domain, of discourse).

soundness   (*Of a formal system*) A formal system is sound if and only if, given a set *s* of sentences of the system, no sentence not implied by those in *s* can be derived using the rules of inference of that system (i.e., all theorems are tautologies). *See also* completeness.

source   (*Assignment*) *See* assignment.

source relvar   For the general meaning, *see* inclusion dependency. In the foreign key context in particular, the term is sometimes used as a synonym for a referencing relvar, q.v.

source tuple   Term sometimes used in the foreign key context as a synonym for a referencing tuple, q.v.

specification signature   (*Without inheritance*) Let *Op* be an operator; then *Op* has a specification signature, denoting that operator as perceived by the user. The specification signature consists of the combination of (a) the operator name *Op*, (b) the declared types of the parameters to *Op*, and either (c) the declared type of the result, if any, of executing *Op* or (d) an indication of those parameters to *Op*, if any, that are subject to update. *See also* invocation signature.

Examples:

1. Consider the read-only version of the operator DOUBLE from the examples under **argument**. The specification signature for that operator is:

```
DOUBLE ( INTEGER ) RETURNS INTEGER
```

2. For the read-only version of the operator MOVE (see the first example under **RETURN**), the specification signature is:

```
MOVE ( ELLIPSE , RECTANGLE ) RETURNS ELLIPSE
```

3. For the update version of the operator MOVE (see the second example under **RETURN**), the specification signature is the same as in the previous case, except that the specification RETURNS ELLIPSE is replaced by an indication of the fact that the first parameter is subject to update.

Caveat: Some writers give definitions of the term (specification signature, that is) that differ slightly from the one just given; for example, it's sometimes taken to include parameter names. In fact, most writers fail to distinguish explicitly between specification and invocation signatures (q.v.) anyway, referring to them both as just signatures. (The distinction is important if inheritance is supported but not perhaps otherwise; nevertheless, use of the unqualified term *signature* is probably best avoided unless there's no risk of ambiguity.) Note finally that if two operators are distinct but have the same name—*see* **overloading**—their specification signatures must differ in either the number or the declared types of their parameters or both (possibly in the declared types of their results as well, if any).

SQL   The best known attempt (unfortunately a seriously flawed one) to realize the abstract ideas of the relational model in concrete syntactic form. The name SQL—the official pronunciation, and the one adhered to in this dictionary, is "ess cue ell," though the pronunciation "sequel" is often heard (*see* **SEQUEL**)—was originally an abbreviation for *Structured Query Language*. In its standard incarnation, however, the name is just a name and isn't an abbreviation for anything at all. *Note:* The version of the standard current at the time of writing is SQL:2011 (so called because it was ratified in 2011), and all remarks concerning SQL in this dictionary are intended to apply to that version specifically (*see* **SQL standard**). However, every SQL product supports its own SQL dialect, and the remarks in question might thus not apply to all products.

SQL standard   The "official" definition of SQL. The full reference is as follows:

International Organization for Standardization (ISO), *Database Language SQL*, Document ISO/IEC 9075:2011 (2011)

As this citation indicates, the standard is indeed an international or "ISO" standard, not just (as many seem to think) an American or "ANSI" standard (ANSI being an abbreviation for the American National Standards Institute). *Note:* The SQL standard has been through several versions, or editions, over the years. The first two appeared in 1986 and 1989 and were known as SQL/86 and SQL/89, respectively. The version current at the time of writing is SQL:2011; the previous version was SQL:2003, the one before that was SQL:1999, and the one before that was SQL:1992.

star join A join implementation technique, primarily intended for use in connection with star schemas, q.v.

star schema A database design, or the collection of data definitions representing such a design, intended primarily to support so called online analytical processing (OLAP). *Note:* In principle, there's no reason why a star schema should be distinguishable in any way from a conventional and properly normalized relational design. In practice, however, star schemas typically (and deliberately) violate numerous relational design principles, including the principles of normalization in particular. Such violations are deemed necessary, or at least desirable, in order to overcome certain deficiencies in existing SQL product implementations, but they're to be deplored nevertheless. (Of course, the same goes for the products in question.) Further details are beyond the scope of this dictionary.

state (*Of a variable*) Slightly deprecated (because logically unnecessary) term used to refer to the actual—i.e., current—or some possible value of the variable in question; frequently used to refer to the current or some possible value of a database variable in particular, q.v.

state constraint A database constraint, q.v., that isn't a transition constraint, q.v.

state variable *See* instance variable.

statement 1. (*Logic*) A proposition (or, perhaps more precisely, the representation of a proposition in some concrete syntactic form). 2. (*Programming languages*) A construct that causes some action to occur, such as defining or updating a variable or changing the flow of control. *Contrast* expression. *Note:* Throughout this dictionary, the term *statement* should be understood in the programming language sense, unless the context demands otherwise.

    Examples (second definition only): See the examples under DELETE, INSERT, and elsewhere. Note that (as in many other languages) statements in **Tutorial D** terminate in a semicolon.

stored procedure A subroutine, possibly parameterized; in other words, the implementation code for some operator. *Note:* Like the term *encapsulated,* q.v., the term *stored procedure* has unfortunately come to mean something in practice that mixes model and implementation considerations. From the point of view of the model, a stored procedure is basically, as just stated, nothing more than an operator (or the implementation code for such an operator, rather). In practice, however, stored procedures have a number of properties that make them much more important than they would be if they were just operators as such (although the first two of the following properties will probably apply to operators in general, at least if the operators in question are system defined). First, they're compiled separately and can be shared by distinct applications. Second, their compiled code is, typically, physically stored at the site at which the data itself is physically stored, with obvious performance benefits. Third, they're often used to provide shared functionality that ought to be provided by the DBMS but isn't (integrity checking is a good example here, given the state of today's SQL implementations). *See also* triggered procedure.

strong typing   A programming language is strongly typed if and only if every expression of the language is of a known type and type errors are always detected (preferably though not necessarily at compile time). The relational model explicitly requires strong typing for relational expressions.

structured type (SQL)   *See* user defined type (SQL).

subexpression   An expression nested inside another such.

subject to   Variable V is subject to constraint C—equivalently, constraint C holds for variable V—if and only if every value v that can ever be assigned to V satisfies C.

subject to update   Let Op be an update operator that, when invoked, updates the argument corresponding to parameter P. Then parameter P is said to be subject to update (and any argument corresponding to P must be a variable specifically). *See* UPDATES.
   Example: See the second example under RETURN.

subkey   Loosely, a subset of a key. More precisely, let X be a subset of the heading of relvar R; then X is a subkey for, or of, R if and only if there exists some key K for R such that $K \supseteq X$.
   Examples: The subkeys for relvar SP are {SNO,PNO}, {SNO}, {PNO}, and { }. Note that the empty set { } is necessarily a subkey for all possible relvars R.

subquery   If a relational expression is regarded as a "query"—slightly deprecated usage—then a relational expression nested inside another such is a "subquery."
   Note: The term *subquery* is given a rather more specific meaning in SQL, where it refers to an expression that denotes a table—usually but not invariably a SELECT expression specifically, q.v.—enclosed in parentheses. Note, however, that not all parenthesized expressions in SQL that denote an SQL table are subqueries in the SQL sense. Note too that the

SQL notion of a subquery is considerably more complex than the foregoing definition might suggest. In particular, if *t* is the table denoted by SQL subquery *sq*, then (a) if table *t* contains just one row *r*, then *sq* can be used in certain contexts as if it denoted *r* as such (in which case *sq* is acting as a "row subquery"); (b) if table *t* contains just one row *r* and just one column *C*, and therefore contains just a single value *v*, then *sq* can be used in certain contexts as if it denoted *v* as such (in which case *sq* is acting as a "scalar subquery," despite the fact that the value *v* isn't limited to being a scalar value specifically); and (c) if *sq* is neither a row subquery nor a scalar subquery, then it's a "table subquery." There's a lot more that could be said here, too, but further details are beyond the scope of this dictionary.

subrelation   Let relations *r1* and *r2* be such that *r2* is derived from *r1* by eliminating a subset of the attributes (via projection) or eliminating a subset of the tuples (via restriction) or both. Then relation *r2* is a subrelation of relation *r1*. The term isn't much used.

subschema / subscheme   Terms occasionally used to mean either (a) the (possibly restructured) logical design of some subset of a given database as it's perceived by some given user or (b) the collection of data definitions representing such a design.

subset   Set *s2* is a subset of set *s1* ("*s2* ⊆ *s1*") if and only if every element of *s2* is also an element of *s1*. Observe that every set is a subset of both itself and the universal set, also that the empty set is a subset of every set. *Contrast* **proper subset**.

substitution   1. (*Logic*) Let *x* be an expression containing an occurrence of *y* as a subexpression; let *y'* be logically equivalent to *y*; and let *x'* be the expression obtained by substituting *y'* (parenthesized if necessary) for the occurrence of *y* in question in *x*. Then *x* and *x'* are logically equivalent. 2. (*View implementation*) A technique for implementing operations on views, according to which references to view *V* are effectively replaced by the view defining expression for *V* (*contrast* **view materialization**). 3. (*Operator invocation*) Replacing a parameter by an argument. Note that this last definition applies to predicate instantiation (q.v.) in particular.
    Examples: 1. (*Logic*) See the example under **expression transformation**. 2. (*View implementation*) See the second example under **pseudovariable reference**. 3. (*Operator invocation*) See the examples under **argument**.

subtuple   A subset of a tuple; hence, a tuple.

summarization   Let relations *r1* and *r2* be such that the heading of *r2* is some subset of that of *r1*. Let *r2* have attributes called *A1*, *A2*, ..., *An* and no others (in particular, no attribute called *B*). Then (and only then) the expression SUMMARIZE *r1* PER (*r2*) : {*B* := *exp*} denotes a summarization of *r1* according to *r2*, and it returns the relation with heading {*A1,A2,...,An,B*} and body the set of all tuples *t* such that *t* is a tuple of *r2*, extended with a value *b* for attribute *B*.

That value *b* is computed by evaluating the expression *exp* over all tuples of *r1* that have the same value for attributes *A1*, *A2*, ..., *An* as *t* does. *Note:* The construct referred to as *exp* here will typically be an open expression, q.v.; in particular, it can, and in practice usually will, include at least one summary, q.v. *See also* WITH.

    Examples: The following expression denotes a certain summarization of the current value of relvar SP "per" the current value of relvar S:

```
SUMMARIZE SP PER ( S { SNO } ) : { CT := COUNT ( ) }
```

COUNT( ) here is an example of a summary, q.v. Observe that it's the PER relation, not the SUMMARIZE relation, that drives the operation—the result contains one tuple for each tuple in the PER relation, not one tuple for each tuple in the SUMMARIZE relation. Thus, the expression overall is logically equivalent to the following (arguably much clearer!) EXTEND invocation:

```
EXTEND S { SNO } : { CT := COUNT ( !!SP ) }
```

Note in particular that the COUNT summary in the SUMMARIZE invocation has been replaced by an invocation of the COUNT aggregate operator in this revised (i.e., EXTEND) version; note also that the argument expression in that aggregate operator invocation is an image relation reference, q.v. In both cases (i.e., regardless of whether the SUMMARIZE or the EXTEND formulation is used), the result is a relation of type RELATION {SNO SNO, CT INTEGER}, containing one tuple for each distinct SNO value currently appearing in relvar S (and no other tuples). Each such tuple contains the pertinent supplier number and a count of the number of times that supplier number currently appears in relvar SP. Given the sample values in Fig. 1, for example, the tuple for supplier S2 in the result has SNO value S2 and CT value two, and the tuple for supplier S5 has SNO value S5 and CT value zero.

    By way of a second example, consider this expression:

```
SUMMARIZE SP PER ( SP { SNO } ) : { CT := COUNT ( ) }
```

The only difference between this example and the previous one is that the PER operand is specified as SP{SNO} instead of S{SNO}. The expression thus yields a relation of type RELATION {SNO SNO, CT INTEGER} as before, but with one tuple for each distinct SNO value currently appearing in relvar SP instead of relvar S. Given the sample values in Fig. 1, for example, the result contains no tuple for supplier S5. The expression overall is logically equivalent to the following EXTEND invocation:

```
EXTEND SP { SNO } : { CT := COUNT ( !!SP ) }
```

Note: Because the PER relation in the SUMMARIZE version of this second example actually is a projection of the SUMMARIZE relation (instead of merely having the same heading as such a projection), the expression overall can be simplified, slightly, to

```
SUMMARIZE SP BY { SNO } : { CT := COUNT ( ) }
```

The simplification consists in replacing the PER specification by a BY specification. More generally, the expression SUMMARIZE *r1* BY {*Ax,Ay,...,Az*} : {*B := exp*} is logically equivalent to, and is defined to be shorthand for, the expression SUMMARIZE *r1* PER (*r1*{*Ax,Ay,...,Az*}) : {*B := exp*}; in other words, the specification BY {*Ax,Ay,...,Az*} is shorthand for the specification PER (*r1*{*Ax,Ay,...,Az*}).

Tutorial D also allows the PER and BY specifications both to be omitted, in which case PER (TABLE_DEE) is assumed by default. Thus, the expression

```
SUMMARIZE SP : { CT := COUNT ( ) }
```

evaluates to a relation with heading {CT INTEGER} and body consisting of just one tuple, containing (given our usual sample values) just the value 12. Here's an EXTEND equivalent:

```
EXTEND TABLE_DEE : { CT := COUNT ( SP ) }
```

Incidentally, it's worth pointing out that any summarization involving COUNT is logically equivalent to one involving SUM instead. For example, the first SUMMARIZE example shown above is logically equivalent to the following:

```
SUMMARIZE SP PER ( S { SNO } ) : { CT := SUM ( 1 ) }
```

EXTEND equivalent:

```
EXTEND S { SNO } : { CT := SUM ( !!SP , 1 ) }
```

Here's another example ("For each supplier, get the sum of *distinct* shipment quantities"):

```
SUMMARIZE SP { SNO , QTY } PER ( S { SNO } ) : { SDQ := SUM ( QTY ) }
```

EXTEND equivalent:

```
EXTEND S { SNO } : { SDQ := SUM ( ( !!SP ) { QTY } ) }
```

Here for interest is an SQL analog of this last example (note the need for a DISTINCT specification within the SQL SUM invocation, also the need to use SQL's COALESCE operator in order to prevent the overall result from showing the sum for supplier S5 as null):

```
SELECT SNO , ( SELECT COALESCE ( SUM ( DISTINCT QTY ) , 0 )
               FROM    SP
               WHERE   SP.SNO = S.SNO ) AS SDQ
FROM    S
```

Note the use of a scalar subquery in the SELECT clause here (*see* subquery).

Note: **Tutorial D** additionally supports a form of SUMMARIZE that allows two or more summarizations to be performed in parallel ("multiple SUMMARIZE"). Here's an example:

```
SUMMARIZE SP BY { SNO } : { SQ := SUM ( QTY ) , AQ := AVG ( QTY ) }
```

EXTEND equivalent (a "multiple EXTEND"):

```
EXTEND SP : { SQ := SUM ( !!SP , QTY ) , AQ := AVG ( !!SP , QTY ) }
```

Alternatively (note the WITH specification within the braces here):

```
EXTEND SP : { WITH ( temp := !!SP ) :
              SQ := SUM ( temp , QTY ) , AQ := AVG ( temp , QTY ) }
```

Note finally that (as the foregoing examples should be sufficient to suggest) any given SUMMARIZE invocation, multiple or otherwise, is always—in fact, is defined to be—logically equivalent to a certain EXTEND invocation. Partly for this reason, the SUMMARIZE operator per se is in the process of being dropped from **Tutorial D**. (The current version of the language does still support it, but the main reason it does so is for compatibility with earlier versions.)

SUMMARIZE   *See* summarization.

summary   A construct that can appear within an attribute assignment within a SUMMARIZE invocation wherever a literal of the appropriate type is allowed. Note that summaries aren't aggregate operator invocations, though they might look rather like them (and indeed every aggregate operator does have a summary counterpart). An aggregate operator invocation is an expression (open or closed as the case may be). A summary, by contrast, is merely an operand to SUMMARIZE (speaking a trifle loosely); it has no meaning outside the context of SUMMARIZE, and in fact can't appear outside that context. *See* summarization for further explanation.

superkey   Loosely, a superset of a key; it has the uniqueness property of keys, but not necessarily the irreducibility property. More precisely, let X be a subset of the heading of relvar R; then X is a superkey for, or of, R if and only if no possible value for R contains two distinct tuples with the same value for X.

Examples: Relvar S has exactly eight superkeys (why?), of which {SNO} and {SNO,CITY} are two. Note that the heading of any given relvar R is necessarily a superkey for

R. Note too that if *SK* is a superkey for relvar *R*, then the FD $SK \rightarrow X$ necessarily holds for all subsets *X* of the heading of *R*.

superkey constraint   A constraint to the effect that a given subset of the heading of a given relvar is a superkey for that relvar. In **Tutorial D,** such a constraint is defined by means of a KEY specification within the pertinent relvar definition (*see* **key constraint**).

superkey normal form   Relvar *R* is in superkey normal form (SKNF) if and only if every component of every irreducible JD that holds in *R* is a superkey for *R*. Every SKNF relvar is in RFNF.

    Example: As noted under **Boyce/Codd normal form,** with the normal forms it's often more instructive to show a counterexample rather than an example per se. Consider, therefore, relvar SPJ, with attributes SNO (supplier number), PNO (part number), and JNO (project number), and predicate *Supplier SNO supplies part PNO to project JNO.* Let that relvar have just two keys, {SNO,PNO} and {PNO,JNO}. Also, let the relvar be subject to the constraint that if (a) supplier *sno* supplies part *pno* and (b) part *pno* is supplied to project *jno* and (c) project *jno* is supplied by supplier *sno*, then (d) supplier *sno* supplies part *pno* to project *jno*. Then SPJ is equal to the join of its projections on {SNO,PNO}, {PNO,JNO}, and {JNO,SNO}—in other words, the JD

        ✩ { { SNO , PNO } , { PNO , JNO } , { JNO , SNO } }

holds in SPJ—and so that relvar can be nonloss decomposed into those three projections. However, since that JD has a component that's not a superkey, relvar SPJ isn't in SKNF, though it is in RFNF.

superset   Set *s1* is a superset of set *s2* ("$s1 \supseteq s2$") if and only if every element of *s2* is also an element of *s1*. Observe that every set is a superset of both itself and the empty set, also that the universal set is a superset of every set. *Contrast* **proper superset.**

surjection / surjective mapping   Terms used interchangeably to mean a mapping, or function, from set *s1* to set *s2* such that each element of *s2* is the image of at least one element of *s1* (in other words, a many to one correspondence, in the strict sense of that term). Also known as a surjective or "many to one onto" mapping.

    Example: Let *s1* and *s2* be the set of all integers and the set of all nonnegative integers, respectively. Then the mapping from integers *x* to their absolute values ABS(*x*) is a surjection from *s1* to (or onto) *s2*.

surrogate   Abbreviation for surrogate key or surrogate key value, as the context demands.

surrogate key   A single-attribute (i.e., simple) key with the property that its values serve solely as surrogates—hence the name—for the entities they're supposed to stand for. In other words, those surrogate key values serve merely to represent the fact that the corresponding entities exist, and they carry absolutely no additional information or meaning. *Contrast* composite key; intelligent key; natural key; row ID.

symmetric difference   Same as exclusive union.

symmetry   1. (*Of a dyadic logical operator*) Commutativity. 2. (*Of a binary relation*) The binary relation r is symmetric if and only if, for all x and y, if the tuple $<x,y>$ appears in r, then so does the tuple $<y,x>$.

   Examples (first definition only): The logical operator EQUIV (or "≡"); the equality operator "=".

synonym   1. (*Of an operator*) An alternative name for an operator. For example, the operator that returns the angle at vertex B of a triangle ABC might reasonably be referred to equally well as either ABC or CBA. Similarly, the operator that returns the length of the side connecting vertices A and B might reasonably be referred to equally well as either AB or BA. 2. (*Of a type*) *See* type naming.

syntactic   (*Of a language, sentence, etc.*) Pertaining to grammatical structure. Contrast lexical; semantic.

syntactic substitution   A language design principle, according to which new operators are defined purely in terms of ones that already exist in the language in question (thus, invocations of such a new operator are effectively just shorthand for something that can already be expressed, possibly more longwindedly). Advantages of such an approach to language design include teachability, understandability, raising the level of abstraction, and the possibility of improved performance.

   Examples: In **Tutorial D**, the operators MATCHING, q.v., and COMPOSE, q.v., are both defined in terms of join and projection (and nothing else).

syntax   *See* semantics.

system defined   *See* user defined.

system defined type   A type defined by the system; i.e., one that's built in. *Contrast* user defined type. *Note:* The system vs. user defined types distinction applies only to nongenerated types, not to types produced via invocation of some type generator. It follows that system defined types are always scalar, by definition.

   Examples: Of the scalar types used in the suppliers-and-parts database, types CHAR (the set of all character strings) and INTEGER (the set of all integers) are system defined (or, at least, so we assume for the purposes of this dictionary). *See also* BOOLEAN.

system of logic *See* logic system.

table 1. SQL analog of either a relation or a relvar, as the context demands. Here are some of the major differences between tables in SQL and their relational counterparts: (a) SQL tables can contain duplicate rows; (b) SQL tables can contain nulls; (c) SQL tables have a left to right ordering to their columns; (d) SQL tables can have two or more columns with the same name; (e) SQL tables can have what are, in effect, columns with no name at all; (f) SQL tables—even ones in the database—can contain pointers; (g) SQL tables have no types. 2. More generally, a picture of a relation (on paper, for example). *See also* cell; column; row. *Note:* A confusion between relations and such tabular pictures probably accounts for the popular misconception that relations are "flat" or two-dimensional (*see* flat relation). While it's obviously true that those pictures are two-dimensional, relations in general aren't; rather, a relation of degree n is n-dimensional (q.v.), in the sense that its tuples correspond to points in some n-dimensional space (one dimension for each attribute of the relation in question).

table alias *See* alias.

TABLE_DEE and TABLE_DUM Two relation constants, preferably built in. TABLE_DEE is the unique relation with no attributes and exactly one tuple (necessarily the empty tuple); TABLE_DUM is the unique relation with no attributes and no tuples at all. They can be interpreted as TRUE (or *yes*) and FALSE (or *no*), respectively. (More precisely, the relation predicate for TABLE_DEE is any 0-place predicate that evaluates to TRUE, and the relation predicate for TABLE_DUM is any 0-place predicate that evaluates to FALSE.) *Note:* The names are perhaps not very well chosen, since TABLE_DEE and TABLE_DUM are precisely the two relations for which the popular understanding of a relation as a table most obviously breaks down.

table subquery *See* subquery.

tables and views / tables or views Phrases frequently appearing in SQL contexts that strongly suggest that views are somehow different from tables. But the whole point about views is that, in SQL terms, they *are* tables—just as, in mathematics, the whole point about a set that's (e.g.) the union or intersection of two sets is that it is itself a set. In other words, views are supposed to "look and feel" just like base tables to the user (*The Principle of Interchangeability*, q.v., translated into SQL terms).

target (*Assignment*) *See* assignment.

target key   *See* foreign key.

target relvar   1. (*IND*) For the general meaning, *see* inclusion dependency. In the foreign key context in particular, the term is sometimes used as a synonym for referenced relvar, q.v.
2. (*Assignment*) The relvar being updated in a relational assignment operation.

target tuple   Term sometimes used in the foreign key context as a synonym for referenced tuple, q.v.

target type   (*Without inheritance*) 1. Let *S* be a selector for type *T*; then the target type for an invocation of *S* is *T*. 2. In the CAST invocation CAST_AS_*T* (...), the target type is *T*.

tautology   A predicate whose every possible invocation is guaranteed to yield TRUE, regardless of what arguments are substituted for its parameters. *Contrast* contradiction.
   Examples: Let *p1* be the predicate (actually a proposition) 2+2 = 4; let *p2* be the predicate *x* = *x*, where *x* denotes an arbitrary integer; and let *p3* be the predicate (*p*) OR (NOT(*p*)), where *p* denotes an arbitrary predicate. Then *p1*, *p2*, and *p3* are all tautologies. Note that a tautology isn't necessarily a proposition, even though (like some propositions) it does unequivocally evaluate to TRUE. For example, *x* = *x* isn't a proposition; rather, it's a monadic predicate (i.e., a predicate with exactly one parameter, viz., *x*).

TCLOSE   *See* transitive closure.

THE_ operator   Let *T* be a scalar type. Then definition of a possrep *PR* for *T* causes automatic definition of a set of operators of the form THE_*A*, THE_*B*, ..., THE_*C* (**Tutorial D** syntax), where *A*, *B*, ..., *C* are the names of the components of *PR*. Let *v* be a value of type *T*, and let *PR*(*v*) denote the possible representation corresponding to *PR* for that value *v*. Then invoking THE_*X* on *v* (*X* = *A*, *B*, ..., *C*) returns the value of the *X* component of *PR*(*v*).
   Examples: Let type POINT have two distinct possreps called CARTESIAN and POLAR, respectively, with the obvious semantics:

```
POSSREP CARTESIAN { X RATIONAL , Y RATIONAL }
POSSREP POLAR { R RATIONAL , THETA RATIONAL }
```

Then the following are valid THE_ operator invocations for type POINT:

```
THE_X ( P )
/* denotes the X coordinate of the point in */
/* P, where P is a variable of type POINT   */

THE_R ( P )
/* denotes the R coordinate of the point in P */
```

```
THE_Y ( exp )
/* denotes the Y coordinate of the point denoted  */
/* by the expression exp (which is of type POINT) */
```

THE_ operator invocations can also be used as pseudovariable references (loosely, "THE_ pseudovariables"). For example:

```
THE_X ( P ) := Z ;
```

This example is shorthand for the following expanded version:

```
P := CARTESIAN ( Z , THE_Y ( P ) ) ;
```

THE_ operator invocations and THE_ pseudovariable references can both be nested. For example, let type LINESEG ("line segments") be defined as follows (irrelevant details omitted):

```
TYPE LINESEG POSSREP { BEGIN POINT , END POINT } ;
```

Also, let LS be a variable of declared type LINESEG. Then the assignment

```
Z  :=  THE_X ( THE_BEGIN ( LS ) ) ;
```

"gets" the X coordinate of the begin point of LS, and the assignment

```
THE_X ( THE_BEGIN ( LS ) )  :=  Z ;
```

"sets" the X coordinate of the begin point of LS. Here for interest is the expanded form of this latter assignment:

```
LS  :=  LINESEG ( CARTESIAN ( Z , THE_Y ( THE_BEGIN ( LS ) ) ) ,
                  THE_END ( LS ) ) ;
```

THE_ pseudovariable *See* THE_ operator.

theorem Something that follows from given axioms according to given rules of inference (and is therefore true if the axioms are true and the inference rules valid). In the database context, tuples in derived relations can be regarded as theorems, because they represent propositions derived from the ones represented by tuples in the base relations. Theorems include axioms, q.v., as a degenerate special case. *See* proof.

Example: Given the sample values of Fig. 1, the relation denoted by the expression (S JOIN P) {SNO,PNO} contains the tuple <S1,P1> among others. That tuple can be regarded as a theorem; it represents the (true) proposition *Supplier S1 and part P1 are in the same city*, a "true fact" that can be inferred from the axioms represented by the pertinent tuples in the pertinent base relations.

theta join   A relational operator whose invocation is logically equivalent to an expression of the form (*r1* TIMES *r2*) WHERE *A1 theta A2*, where (a) *A1* and *A2* denote attributes (of the same type *T*) of *r1* and *r2*, respectively, and (b) *theta* is any comparison operator that makes sense for values of type *T* (e.g., "=", ">", etc.). Note that *r1* and *r2* can't have any attribute names in common, for otherwise the subexpression *r1* TIMES *r2* will be undefined. In particular, therefore, the attribute names *A1* and *A2* must obviously be different.

Example: The following expression represents the greater-than join (i.e., theta here is ">") of suppliers and parts, in that order, on cities (note the renamings):

```
( ( S RENAME { CITY AS SC } )
        TIMES
            ( P RENAME { CITY AS PC } ) ) WHERE SC > PC
```

We assume here that CHAR—the declared type of attribute CITY—is an ordered type (">" on CHAR values presumably means "greater in alphabetic ordering"). Note that we could replace TIMES by JOIN in the foregoing expression without changing the meaning. Also, replacing ">" by "<" would yield a less-than join, while replacing it by "=" would yield an equijoin.

Note: Theta join was defined in one of Codd's early papers as part of what is now known as Codd's relational algebra, q.v. As a consequence, it has rather unfortunately received more attention than it really deserves. For one thing, the operator is, as the definition makes clear, nothing more than shorthand for a certain combination of more primitive operations (and a rather unimportant combination at that). More significant, the idea that many different kinds of join can be defined makes it look as if join as such—meaning natural join specifically—is just one of a family of similar operators; however, the fact is that join as such is a truly important operator (one of the most fundamental operators of all, in fact). Use of the term *theta join* is thus deprecated, slightly.

Third Manifesto   A formal proposal for the future of data and database management systems. Like Codd's original papers, the *Manifesto* can be seen as an abstract blueprint for the design of a DBMS and the language interface to such a DBMS. See the introduction to this dictionary for further explanation.

third normal form   Relvar *R* is in third normal form, 3NF, if and only if, for every nontrivial FD $X \rightarrow Y$ that holds in *R*, (a) *X* is a superkey or (b) *Y* is a subkey. Every 3NF relvar is in 2NF. *Note:* Many of the "definitions" of 3NF in the literature are actually definitions of BCNF, q.v.; *caveat lector.* Also, although being in 3NF clearly doesn't preclude being in some higher normal form as well, the term *3NF* is often used loosely to refer to a relvar that's in 3NF and not in (e.g.) BCNF. In any case, third normal form as such is no longer very important (BCNF, 5NF—or perhaps ETNF—and 6NF being the normal forms of most practical significance); we mention it here mainly for historical reasons.

Example: As noted under **Boyce/Codd normal form**, with the normal forms it's often more instructive to show a counterexample rather than an example per se. Suppose, therefore, that relvar S is subject to the additional FD {CITY} → {STATUS}; i.e., the status for a given supplier is a function of that supplier's location. (Of course, the sample value shown for that relvar in Fig. 1 doesn't satisfy this FD; however, it would do so if we changed the status for supplier S2 from 10 to 30, so let's suppose for the sake of the example that this change has in fact been made.) Since {CITY} isn't a superkey and {STATUS} isn't a subkey, this version of relvar S isn't in 3NF (though it is in 2NF).

third truth value   *See* three-valued logic.

three-valued logic   A logic in which there's a "third truth value" (usually called UNKNOWN) in addition to the conventional TRUE and FALSE; abbreviated 3VL. Note that tautologies in two-valued logic (2VL), q.v., aren't necessarily tautologies in 3VL; likewise, contradictions in 2VL aren't necessarily contradictions in 3VL. (By way of a simple example, let *bx* be a boolean expression, and consider the expression *bx* OR NOT (*bx*), which is certainly a tautology in 2VL but not in 3VL.) As a result, theorems that hold in 2VL don't necessarily hold in 3VL, and expression transformations that are valid in 2VL aren't necessarily valid in 3VL.

 Note: As is well known, SQL's support for nulls, q.v., is based on a three-valued logic (by contrast, the relational model is based on two-valued logic). However, that SQL support is logically flawed. For example, SQL treats UNKNOWN and null as identical, even though there's a clear logical difference (q.v.) between the two—UNKNOWN is a value, while null isn't a value at all but a "mark." (This is just one of many logical errors in SQL's 3VL support. Perhaps a more serious one is that the 3VL in question isn't even fully defined! For example, the SQL standard nowhere defines the semantics of implication. Nor does it consider the question of whether SQL's 3VL is truth functionally complete—that is, does SQL support all 27 monadic and 19,683 dyadic connectives of 3VL?)

time-varying relation   Term used in Codd's early papers to mean what we now call a relvar; the term is deprecated because relations are values and thus simply don't "vary over time," by definition (*see* value).

TIMES   *See* cartesian product.

total database constraint   *See* database constraint.

total function   A partial function, q.v., in which every element *x* in the domain has an image *y* in the codomain; in other words, a function.

total ordering   A special case of partial ordering, q.v. Let *s* be a set. Then a total ordering on *s* is a partial ordering, usually denoted "≤", with the property that for all pairs of elements *x* and *y* of *s*, either *x* ≤ *y* or *y* ≤ *x* (or both, if and only if *x* and *y* are in fact the same element of *s*). *Note:* Given that the "=" operator and the NOT connective are both always available, it follows that all of the usual comparison operators "=", "≠", "<", "≤", ">", and "≥" are available for all pairs of values in such a set *s*. Note also that the unqualified term *ordering* is usually taken to mean a total ordering specifically, unless the context demands otherwise. *Contrast* cyclic ordering.

   Examples: See the examples under ordered type and ordinal type.

total relvar constraint   *See* relvar constraint.

transaction   A unit of recovery and concurrency; loosely, a unit of work. Transactions are all or nothing, in the sense that they either execute in their entirety or have no effect (other than returning a status code or equivalent, perhaps). *Note:* Transactions are often said to be a unit of integrity (or consistency) also. Since the relational model requires all integrity checking to be immediate, however, the unit of integrity as far as the relational model is concerned is the statement, not the transaction. *See* atomic statement; immediate checking.

transition   The change in value of some variable (especially a database variable, q.v.) caused by a single updating statement. *Contrast* state.

transition constraint   A database constraint, q.v., that limits the transitions a given database can validly make, as a consequence of a single updating statement, from one state to another. *Contrast* state constraint.

   Example ("No supplier's status must ever decrease"):

```
CONSTRAINT TRC1 IS_EMPTY (
    ( ( S  { SNO , STATUS } ) JOIN
    ( ( S' { SNO , STATUS } RENAME { STATUS AS STATUS' } ) )
    WHERE STATUS < STATUS' ) ;
```

This formulation relies on a convention to the effect that a primed relvar name such as S′ refers to the value of the corresponding relvar as it was prior to the update under consideration.

   Note: It's worth pointing out that most if not all transition constraints can easily be subverted by performing two or more separate updates in sequence. Stating such constraints declaratively can be helpful in avoiding mistakes, therefore, but it provides little by way of protection against deliberate malicious action.

transitive closure   Let *r* be a binary relation with attributes *A* and *B*, both of type *T*. Then (and only then) the expression TCLOSE (*r*) denotes the transitive closure of *r*, and it returns a relation r^+ defined as follows: The tuple <*a,b*> appears in r^+ if and only if it appears in *r* or there exists a value *c* of type *T* such that the tuple <*a,c*> appears in *r* and the tuple <*c,b*> appears in r^+. (Observe that this is a recursive definition; observe too that r^+ is indeed a transitive relation, as the name "transitive closure" suggests. *See* transitivity, second definition.) As the following pseudocode algorithm indicates, computing TCLOSE (*r*) conceptually involves repeated formation of the union of an intermediate result (computed on the previous iteration) and a new partial result (computed on the current iteration), until that union ceases to grow—in other words, until it reaches a fixed point or "fixpoint."

```
r⁺ := r ;
do until r⁺ ceases to grow ;
    r⁺ := WITH ( t1 := r⁺ RENAME { B AS C } ,
                 t2 := r  RENAME { A AS C } ) :
                 r⁺ UNION ( t1 COMPOSE t2 ) ;
end do ;
```

See also recursive query.

transitive FD   The FDs $X \to Y$ and $Y \to Z$ together imply the transitive FD $X \to Z$ (*see* Armstrong's axioms); thus, if relvar R is subject to the FDs $X \to Y$ and $Y \to Z$, it's also subject to the transitive FD $X \to Z$.

transitivity   1. (*Of a dyadic logical operator*) The dyadic logical operator *Op*, which we assume for definiteness is expressed in infix style, is transitive if and only if, for all x, y, and z, if x *Op* y and y *Op* z are both true, then so is x *Op* z. 2. (*Of a binary relation*) The binary relation r is transitive if and only if, for all x, y, and z, if the tuples <x,y> and <y,z> both appear in r, then so does the tuple <x,z>. 3. (*Of FDs*) *See* Armstrong's axioms.
  Examples (first definition only): The logical operator IMPLIES; the partial ordering operator "$\leq$". By way of a counterexample, consider the operator "father of"—"x father of y" and "y father of z" most certainly do not together imply "x father of z" (in fact, they imply "x not father of z," loosely speaking).

TransRelational™ Model   A proprietary DBMS implementation technology, not based on conventional direct image techniques. A brief introduction to this technology can be found in Appendix A of the book *An Introduction to Database Systems*, by C. J. Date (8th edition, Addison-Wesley, 2004). A much more extensive description can be found in the book *Go Faster! The TransRelational™ Approach to DBMS Implementation*, by C. J. Date (Ventus Publishing, 2002, 2011; free download available at *bookboon.com*).

TRC   Tuple relational calculus.

trigger   *See* triggered procedure.

triggered procedure   Strictly, an action (the "triggered action") to be performed if a specified event (the "triggering event") occurs, though the term is often used loosely to refer to the triggered action and the triggering event taken in combination. (Moreover, that combination is often known more simply just as a trigger.) A triggered procedure can be thought of as a stored procedure, q.v., except that stored procedures must be explicitly invoked, whereas a triggered procedure is invoked automatically whenever the triggering event occurs. Apart from this difference, however, triggered procedures have many of the same properties, and are used for many of the same purposes, as stored procedures. No triggered procedures are prescribed by the relational model, but they aren't necessarily proscribed either—though they would be if they were to violate either *The Assignment Principle* (q.v.) or the set level nature of the relational model, both of which in practice they're quite likely to do.

Note: Triggered procedures, or triggers, shouldn't be confused with compensatory actions, q.v., though they might be used to simulate such actions if the system provides no direct support for them. Here are some of the differences between the two concepts:

- Details of the operation, and possibly even the existence, of triggers are typically concealed from the user. Such is not the case with compensatory actions.

- There's no notion with triggers that the system should be able to determine for itself what actions are to be performed (indeed, if it could, then triggers wouldn't be necessary in the first place). With compensatory actions, by contrast, the system should be able (at least in some cases) to work out for itself just what actions are required.

- Triggers can and usually do involve procedural code; in fact, as already noted, triggers can and often do violate the set level nature of the relational model.

trivial decomposition   A nonloss decomposition, q.v., that's performed on the basis of some trivial FD, JD, or MVD, q.v.

Examples: 1. Consider the suppliers relvar S. Let X, Y, and Z denote the sets of attributes {SNO,SNAME}, { } (the empty set), and {SNO,SNAME,STATUS,CITY}, respectively; then X, Y, and Z satisfy the requirements of Heath's Theorem—in particular, the FD $X \to Y$ holds—and S can thus be nonloss decomposed into its projections on XY and XZ (i.e., on {SNO,SNAME} and {SNO,SNAME,STATUS,CITY}, respectively). However, $X \to Y$ here is a trivial FD, and the decomposition is trivial in turn. (Moreover, the projection on {SNO,SNAME} can now be discarded, since it clearly isn't needed in the associated reconstruction process.)

2. Any relvar can be trivially decomposed into just its identity projection. To elaborate briefly: Let relvar R have heading H; then the trivial FD $H \to \{ \}$ certainly holds in R, and so R can be nonloss decomposed into its projection on the entire heading H—i.e., the identity projection—and its projection on no attributes at all. (And this latter projection can now be discarded without loss.)

trivial dependency   A dependency d that's necessarily satisfied by every relation whose heading H is such that d is defined with respect to H; in other words, a dependency that can't possibly be violated. From a logical point of view, such a dependency is implied by the empty set of constraints, and hence by every superset of that set also. In particular, therefore, we can certainly, and usefully (albeit perhaps a trifle counterintuitively), say that such trivial dependencies are implied by the pertinent keys or superkeys, and hence that such dependencies don't cause the relvar in question to violate any of the usual normal forms. *See* trivial EQD; trivial FD; trivial IND; trivial JD; trivial MVD.

Example: The FD {CITY} → {CITY}, which holds in relvar S, is trivial—it can't possibly be violated—and is therefore implied by the sole key {SNO} of that relvar. (In fact that same FD holds in relvar P as well, of course, as indeed it does in every possible relvar with a CITY attribute.)

trivial EQD   An EQD that can't possibly be violated. The EQD $r1\{X\} = r2\{X\}$ is trivial if and only if one of $r1$ and $r2$ is a projection of the other (so long as the projection in question preserves all of the attributes of X, of course).

trivial FD   An FD that can't possibly be violated. The FD $X \rightarrow Y$ is trivial if and only if $X \supseteq Y$.

trivial IND   An IND that can't possibly be violated. The IND $r1\{X\} \subseteq r2\{X\}$ is trivial if and only if one of $r1$ and $r2$ is a projection of the other (a projection that preserves all of the attributes of X, of course), in which case the IND is in fact an EQD.

trivial JD   A JD that can't possibly be violated. The JD $\Leftcirclearrowleft \{X1,X2,...,Xn\}$ is trivial if and only if at least one of $X1$, $X2$, ..., Xn is equal to the pertinent heading.

trivial MVD   An MVD that can't possibly be violated. The MVD $X \rightarrow\rightarrow Y$ is trivial if and only if either $X \supseteq Y$ or the set theory union of X and Y is equal to the pertinent heading. Observe that, given the pair of MVDs $X \rightarrow\rightarrow Y \mid Z$, the MVD $X \rightarrow\rightarrow Y$ is trivial if and only if the MVD $X \rightarrow\rightarrow Z$ is trivial as well.

TRUE   *See* BOOLEAN.

truth functional completeness   A logical system is truth functionally complete if and only if it supports, directly or indirectly, all possible connectives—meaning, more specifically, that all possible connectives either (a) are supported explicitly or (b) can be expressed in terms of the ones that are supported explicitly (*see* **primitive operator**). Truth functional completeness is an extremely important property; a logical system without it would be like a system of arithmetic that had no support for certain operations, say the operation of addition. (And a database language based on such an incomplete logic would be one in which certain queries couldn't be formulated; moreover, it might not even be clear, give such a language, which queries could be formulated and which ones couldn't.) *See also* *n*VL.

truth functional equivalence   Two logical expressions are truth functionally equivalent if and only if they evaluate to the same truth value. For example, the propositions "Earth has two moons" and "Venus has two moons" are truth functionally equivalent, since they both evaluate to FALSE. Note that logical equivalence (q.v.) implies truth functional equivalence, but the latter doesn't imply the former. Note too that the connective EQUIV, q.v., denotes truth functional equivalence specifically.

truth table   Let x be a propositional expression. Then the possible truth values of x can be defined by means of a truth table that shows, for each possible combination of truth values for the propositional variables mentioned in x, the truth value of the overall expression.

Example: Let x be the expression $(p$ AND $q)$ OR r, where p, q, and r are propositional variables. Then, using T and F to represent TRUE and FALSE, respectively, the possible truth values of x are defined by the following self-explanatory truth table:

p	q	r	p AND q	$(p$ AND $q)$ OR r
T	T	T	T	T
T	T	F	T	T
T	F	T	F	T
T	F	F	F	F
F	T	T	F	T
F	T	F	F	F
F	F	T	F	T
F	F	F	F	F

By way of another example, the logical equivalence of the expressions NOT$((p)$ AND $(q))$ and (NOT $(p))$ OR (NOT $(q))$—*see* **De Morgan's Laws**—can readily be demonstrated by showing that the final columns of the respective truth tables are identical.

truth value   In two-valued logic (2VL), either TRUE or FALSE; in other words, a boolean value. *Note:* Many-valued logics, q.v., support additional "truth values" over and above the conventional TRUE and FALSE. For example, three-valued logic (3VL) supports one such additional value, usually called UNKNOWN.

truth value of   In logic, an operator (in symbols, "/.../") that, given a logical expression, returns the truth value of that expression. For example, let the symbols x and y denote integers. Then the expression $/x > y/$ returns TRUE if the integer denoted by x is greater than that denoted by y and FALSE otherwise. Note that /TRUE/ and /FALSE/ return TRUE and FALSE, respectively. Note too that the logical expression p EQUIV q (or $p \equiv q$) means the same as $/p/ = /q/$; for example, the expression (Neptune is a planet) EQUIV (Mars has exactly two moons) means the same as the expression /(Neptune is a planet)/ = /(Mars has exactly two moons)/. Similarly, the logical expression p XOR q means the same as $/p/ \neq /q/$. Note further that, in the computing literature at any rate, authors often write $p = q$ when what they really mean is $/p/ = /q/$ (or $p \equiv q$); *caveat lector*.

truth valued expression   A logical expression, q.v.

truth valued operator   A read-only logical operator, q.v. (especially one of the connectives, q.v.).

TUPLE   In **Tutorial D,** the name of the type generator for tuple types. Also used in **Tutorial D** to denote a tuple selector.
    Examples: For examples showing the TUPLE type generator, see the examples under tuple type. Here by contrast is an example of a tuple selector invocation:

```
TUPLE { SNO SNO('S1') , SNAME NAME('Smith') , STATUS 20 , CITY 'London' }
```

tuple   A tuple value, q.v. The term is short for *n*-tuple, q.v., and is usually pronounced to rhyme with "couple."

tuple (mathematics)   Given sets $s1, s2, ..., sn$, not necessarily distinct, t is an n-tuple (tuple for short) on those sets if and only if it's an ordered collection of elements, the first of which is from $s1$, the second from $s2$, and so on. Set si is the ith domain of t ($i = 1, 2, ..., n$). *Note:* There are several important logical differences between a tuple in mathematics and its relational model counterpart. *See* relation (mathematics); tuple value.

tuple assignment   (*Without inheritance*) An operation that assigns a tuple value of type T to a tuple variable of that same type T. *See* assignment.

tuple calculus   A form of relational calculus in which the range variables range over relations and thus denote tuples from those relations. Tuple calculus and domain calculus, q.v., are logically equivalent, because for every expression of the former there's a logically equivalent expression of the latter and vice versa (in fact, they're both relationally complete, q.v.).
    Example: Here's a tuple calculus formulation of the query "Get supplier names for suppliers who supply at least one part" (*see* **domain calculus** for a domain calculus analog):

```
SX  RANGES OVER { S } ;
SPX RANGES OVER { SP } ;

{ SX.SNAME } WHERE EXISTS SPX ( SPX.SNO = SX.SNO )
```

In stilted English: "Get names of suppliers SX where there exists a shipment SPX with the same supplier number as SX."

tuple comparison   (*Without inheritance*) A boolean expression of the form (*tx1*) *theta* (*tx2*), where *tx1* and *tx2* are tuple expressions of the same type T and *theta* is any comparison operator that makes sense for tuples ("=", "≠", "⊆", etc., but definitely not "<" and ">"; tuples are sets and "<" and ">" are therefore explicitly not defined for tuples). *Note:* The parentheses enclosing *tx1* and *tx2* in the comparison might not be needed in practice.

tuple component   An <attribute, attribute value> pair appearing in the tuple in question. Note that attributes in turn are defined to be <attribute name, type name> pairs, whence it follows that tuple components are of the form <<attribute name, type name>, attribute value>. However, other formalisms are possible; in particular, it would be possible to define a tuple component as an <attribute name, type name, attribute value> triple instead of an <attribute, attribute value> pair. (As a matter of fact, *The Third Manifesto* does exactly this.) Of course, the two definitions are clearly isomorphic.

   Examples: The pairs <<SNO,SNO>,S1> and <<SNAME,NAME>,Smith> are both components of the supplier tuple for supplier S1 in Fig. 1. *Note:* In **Tutorial D**, tuple components are specified more simply as <attribute name, attribute value> pairs (not meant to be actual **Tutorial D** syntax). This simplified form is acceptable because the relational model requires attribute names to be unique within the pertinent heading, and those names thus effectively imply the corresponding type names.

tuple composition   Let tuples *t1* and *t2* be such that attributes with the same name are of the same type and have the same value, and let their common attributes be called *A1, A2, ..., An* ($n \geq 0$). Then (and only then) the expression *t1* COMPOSE *t2* denotes the tuple composition of *t1* and *t2*, and it returns the tuple denoted by the expression (*t1* UNION *t2*){ALL BUT *A1, A2, ..., An*}. *Note:* The operator as defined here is dyadic, but it would clearly be possible to define an *n*-adic version if desired (*see* **composition**).

tuple constant   A tuple, especially one that's named; not to be confused with a tuple literal, q.v.

tuple constant reference   Syntactically, a tuple constant name, used to denote the value of that tuple constant. *See also* **constant reference**.

tuple constraint   Slightly deprecated term sometimes used to refer to a relvar constraint of the form IS_EMPTY (*R* WHERE *bx*), where *R* is a relvar and *bx* is a restriction condition, q.v., on *R* (and can therefore be evaluated for an individual tuple, proposed for entry into *R*, by examining just that tuple in isolation). Note that a tuple constraint is indeed a constraint on a relvar and not on a tuplevar. (There aren't any tuplevars in a relational database; a fortiori, therefore, there aren't any "tuplevar constraints" either. *See* **Information Principle**.) *Contrast* **multituple constraint**.

   Example: Constraints C1 and C2 from the examples under **database constraint** are both tuple constraints; constraint C3 is not.

tuple difference   *See* **tuple union**.

tuple equality   (*Without inheritance*) Equality of tuples; tuples *t1* and *t2* are equal—i.e., the tuple comparison *t1* = *t2* evaluates to TRUE—if and only if *t1* and *t2* are the very same tuple (implying among other things that *t1* and *t2* must certainly be of the same type). More specifically, let tuples *t1* and *t2* be of the same type, and let their attributes be called *A1*, *A2*, ..., *An*. Then *t1* and *t2* are equal if and only if, for all *i* (*i* = 1, 2, ..., *n*), the value *v1* of *Ai* in *t1* is equal to the value *v2* of *Ai* in *t2*. *Note:* The importance of this concept can hardly be overstated, since so much in the relational model depends on it. For example, keys, foreign keys, and most if not all of the operators of relational algebra are defined in terms of it. Note in particular too that all 0-tuples are equal to one another, since in fact there's only one such tuple.

tuple exclusive union   *See* tuple union.

tuple expression   An expression denoting a tuple. Tuple selector invocations (and hence tuple literals), tuplecon and tuplevar references, and read-only tuple operator invocations are all special cases.

tuple extension   1. (*First form*) Let tuple *t* not have an attribute called *A*. Then (and only then) the expression EXTEND *t* : {*A* := *exp*} returns a tuple identical to *t* except that it has an additional attribute called *A*, with a value that's computed by evaluating the expression *exp* on *t*. 2. (*Second form*) Let tuple *t* have an attribute called *A*. Then (and only then) the expression EXTEND *t* : {*A* := *exp*} returns a tuple identical to *t* except that the value for attribute *A* is replaced by a value that's computed by evaluating the expression *exp* on *t*.
Examples: By way of an example to illustrate the first definition, let *t* be some tuple in the current value of relvar P, and consider the following expression:

```
EXTEND t : { GMWT := WEIGHT * 454 }
```

This expression yields a tuple just like *t*, except that it has an additional attribute GMWT ("gram weight") whose value is 454 times the WEIGHT value in that same tuple. Note that WEIGHT * 454 in this example is an open expression—it relies on context for its meaning.
Here now is an example to illustrate the second definition:

```
EXTEND t : { WEIGHT := 2 * WEIGHT }
```

This expression yields a tuple just like *t*, except that the WEIGHT value is doubled (note that the subexpression 2 * WEIGHT is an open expression).
Note: **Tutorial D** additionally supports a form of tuple EXTEND that allows two or more attribute assignments to be carried out in parallel ("multiple tuple EXTEND"). Here's an example:

```
EXTEND t : { GMWT := WEIGHT * 454 ,
             WEIGHT := 2 * WEIGHT ,
             NC := 'Oslo' }
```

This example illustrates both meanings of the term *tuple extension*.

Note finally that the second form of tuple EXTEND can be defined in terms of the first. For example, the expression

```
EXTEND t : { WEIGHT := 2 * WEIGHT }
```

can be regarded as shorthand for an expression of the following form:

```
( ( EXTEND t : { temp := 2 * WEIGHT } ) { ALL BUT WEIGHT } )
                                     RENAME { temp AS WEIGHT }
```

tuple extractor   An operator for extracting the single tuple from a specified relation of cardinality one.

Example: The following expression extracts the supplier tuple for supplier S1 from the current value of relvar S:

```
TUPLE FROM ( S WHERE SNO = SNO('S1') )
```

A run-time error will occur if the TUPLE FROM argument doesn't have cardinality exactly one.

Note: SQL has no explicit counterpart to **Tutorial D**'s TUPLE FROM; instead, it relies on certain coercions to perform the analogous function. For example, consider the following SQL expression:

```
SELECT SNO
FROM   S
WHERE  ( CITY , STATUS ) =
       ( SELECT CITY , STATUS
         FROM   S
         WHERE  SNO = SNO('S1') )
```

Overall, this expression returns supplier numbers for suppliers with the same city and status as supplier S1. Note that it contains a subquery ("SELECT CITY, STATUS ..."). By definition, that subquery evaluates to a table; however, the table in question contains just one row—it's what SQL calls a "row subquery," q.v.—and, precisely because it appears in the context of a "row comparison," that table is then coerced to the single row it contains. For further discussion, refer to the book *SQL and Relational Theory: How to Write Accurate SQL Code*, by C. J. Date (3rd edition, O'Reilly Media Inc., 2015).

tuple forcing JD   Let J be a JD that holds in relvar R. Then J is tuple forcing with respect to R if and only if it requires that if certain tuples $t1, t2, ..., tn$ appear in R at some given time, then some other tuple t, distinct from each of $t1, t2, ..., tn$, is forced to appear in R as well at that time. *Note:* Not all JDs are tuple forcing (though they're all tuple generating, q.v.; that is, all tuple forcing JDs are tuple generating JDs, but the converse is not the case). In fact, a JD is tuple forcing (with respect to the pertinent relvar R) if and only if it's (a) nontrivial, (b) not implied by any FD of R, and (c) not implied by the keys of R.

TUPLE FROM   **Tutorial D** syntax for a tuple extractor, q.v.

tuple generating dependency   An expression of the form {*t1,t2,...,tn*} / *t*; it can be read as "If tuples *t1*, *t2*, ..., *tn* appear (in some given relvar at some given time), then tuple *t* must appear (in that same relvar at that same time)." Tuples *t1*, *t2*, ..., *tn* are the premises of the dependency and tuple *t* is the conclusion. *Note:* JDs in particular are tuple generating dependencies (not the only possible kind, but the only kind considered in this dictionary). *See also* **tuple forcing JD**.

tuple ID   *See* row ID.

tuple intersection   *See* tuple union.

tuple join   *See* tuple union. Note that this dictionary frequently appeals, informally, to the notion of "joining tuples"—see, for example, the example under **many to one join**.

tuple level   An operator is tuple level if it takes individual tuples or tuplevars or both as operands and either produces a tuple as a result or updates a tuple variable. There are no tuple level operators in the relational model as such (except as noted under **database variable**), but such operators are likely to be needed in the external environment in order to support, e.g., extraction of some tuple from some relation. (By contrast, SQL in particular does support certain tuple level operations—specifically, DELETE and UPDATE operations via some cursor, or in other words so called "positioned" deletes and updates—that aren't just part of the external environment but are supposed to affect the database directly. The operators in question thus constitute a serious departure from the relational model.) *Note:* The foregoing is not to say that, e.g., an operator that "updates an individual tuple" couldn't be defined in a relational language like **Tutorial D**, but (a) invoking such an operator would have to be understood, logically, as asking for a set of tuples to be updated where the set in question simply happens to have cardinality one, and (b) such an invocation will necessarily fail if certain multivariable constraints, q.v., happen to be in effect.

tuple literal   A literal that denotes a tuple.
   Examples: See the examples under literal.

tuple operator   An operator that takes either tuples or tuplevars or both as operands and either returns a tuple or updates a tuplevar (*see* **tuple level**).

tuple product   *See* tuple union.

tuple projection   Let tuple *t* have attributes called *A1*, *A2*, ..., *An* (and possibly others). Then the expression *t*{*A1,A2,...,An*} denotes the projection of *t* on {*A1*, *A2*, ..., *An*}, and it returns the tuple obtained by removing from *t* all components other than those corresponding to attributes *A1, A2, ..., An.*

Example: Let *t* be some tuple in relvar S. Then the expression *t*{STATUS,CITY} yields a tuple of type TUPLE {STATUS INTEGER, CITY CHAR}, containing just the STATUS and CITY components from that tuple *t*.

tuple relational calculus   Tuple calculus, q.v.

tuple renaming   Let tuple *t* have an attribute called *A* and no attribute called *B*. Then (and only then) the expression *t* RENAME {*A* AS *B*} denotes an attribute renaming on *t*, and it returns the tuple that's identical to *t* except that attribute *A* in that tuple is renamed *B*.

Example: Let *t* be some tuple from relvar P. Then the expression

```
t RENAME { WEIGHT AS WT }
```

yields a tuple just like *t*, except that attribute WEIGHT is renamed WT.

Note: **Tutorial D** additionally supports a form of tuple RENAME that allows two or more separate tuple renamings to be carried out in parallel ("multiple tuple RENAME"). *See* renaming for further explanation.

tuple selector   Let *T* be a tuple type; then the corresponding selector is an operator that allows a tuple of type *T* to be selected by supplying a value for each attribute of *T*. More precisely, let *T* be a tuple type, and let the corresponding heading be *H*; then there's exactly one selector, *S* say, for that type *T*, and *S* is such that (a) the sole argument to any given invocation of *S* is a set of values, one such value for each attribute in *H*; (b) every tuple of type *T* is producible by means of some invocation of *S* in which those attribute values are all represented by literals; and (c) every successful invocation of *S* produces a tuple of type *T*.

Examples: See the examples under **selector** and elsewhere. Of course, those examples illustrate, not incidentally, the syntax used for tuple selectors in **Tutorial D** specifically; other syntactic styles might be possible, but they must be logically equivalent to the **Tutorial D** style.

tuple symmetric difference   *See* tuple union.

tuple type   Let *H* be a heading; then (and only then) TUPLE *H* denotes a tuple type—in fact, the sole tuple type—with the same degree and same attributes as *H*. *Note:* The following lightly edited extract from *The Third Manifesto* elaborates on the foregoing tuple type naming convention:

> When we say "the name of [a certain tuple type] shall be TUPLE *H*," we do not mean to prescribe specific syntax. The *Manifesto* does not prescribe syntax. Rather, what we mean is that the type in question shall have a name that does both of the following, no more and no less: First, it shall specify that the type is indeed a tuple type; second, it shall specify the pertinent heading. Syntax of

the form "TUPLE *H*" satisfies these requirements, and we therefore use it as a convenient shorthand; however, all appearances of that syntax throughout this *Manifesto* are to be interpreted in the light of these remarks.

Examples: Consider the following **Tutorial D** definition for a tuplevar called TS:

```
VAR TS TUPLE { SNO SNO , SNAME NAME , STATUS INTEGER , CITY CHAR } ;
```

This definition includes an invocation of the TUPLE type generator (syntactically, everything from the keyword TUPLE to the closing brace following the keyword CHAR, inclusive), which specifies the type of the variable being defined. To be specific, the keyword TUPLE shows it's a tuple type, while the commalist, enclosed in braces, of <attribute name, type name> pairs defines the pertinent heading. Thus, the type of the tuple variable, or tuplevar, TS is exactly as follows (the result of the specified invocation):

```
TUPLE { SNO SNO , SNAME NAME , STATUS INTEGER , CITY CHAR }
```

By way of a second example, the following (corresponding to a certain projection of tuplevar TS) also denotes a certain tuple type:

```
TUPLE { CITY CHAR , SNAME NAME }
```

Note that **Tutorial D** provides nothing analogous to a TYPE statement, q.v., for defining tuple types. Instead, such types can be defined only by invoking the tuple type generator, q.v., as illustrated in the foregoing examples.

tuple type generator   *See* TUPLE; *see also* type generator.

tuple type inference   The process of determining the type of the value denoted by a given tuple expression. Note that this process is completely specified by the rules defining the types of the results of the various tuple operators, q.v.

tuple union   Let tuples *t1* and *t2* be such that attributes with the same name are of the same type and have the same value. Then (and only then) the expression *t1* UNION *t2* denotes the union of *t1* and *t2*, and it returns the tuple that's the set theory union of *t1* and *t2*. (This operation could obviously be generalized to apply to any number of tuples.) *Note:* Tuple union might reasonably be called tuple join; analogously, the special case in which the given tuples *t1* and *t2* have no attribute names in common might reasonably be called tuple product. Also, it would clearly be possible to define tuple intersection, difference, and exclusive union (or symmetric difference) operators if desired.

Example: Let *t1* and *t2* be a tuple from the current value of relvar S and relvar SP, respectively, and let *t1* and *t2* have the same SNO component (and hence the same SNO value in particular). Then the expression *t1* UNION *t2* yields a tuple of type TUPLE {SNO SNO, SNAME NAME, STATUS INTEGER, CITY CHAR, PNO PNO, QTY QTY}, with components as in *t1* or *t2* or both, as applicable.

tuple unwrapping   Let tuple *t* have attributes called *A1, A2, ..., Am*, and *BT* (and no others), and let attribute *BT* be tuple valued and have attributes called *B1, B2, ..., Bn* (and no others); further, let no *Ai* have the same name as any *Bj* ($1 \leq i \leq m$, $1 \leq j \leq n$). Then (and only then) the expression *t* UNWRAP *BT* denotes the unwrapping of *t* on *BT*, and it returns the tuple denoted by the expression (EXTEND *t* : {*B1* := *B1* FROM *BT*, *B2* := *B2* FROM *BT*, ..., *Bn* := *Bn* FROM *BT*}){ALL BUT *BT*}.

  Example: Let *t* be a tuple from the current value of relvar SP, and let *tw* be the tuple resulting from the expression

```
t WRAP { PNO , QTY } AS PQ_TUP
```

(*see* **tuple wrapping**). Then the expression

```
tw UNWRAP PQ_TUP
```

yields *t*.

tuple value   Very loosely, a row (value). More precisely, let *H* be a heading, and let *t* be a set of pairs <<*A,T*>,*v*>, called components (q.v.), obtained from *H* by attaching to each attribute <*A,T*> in *H* some value *v* of type *T*, called the attribute value in *t* for attribute *A*. Then (and only then) *t* is a tuple value (tuple for short) with heading *H* and the same degree and attributes as *H*. Every subset of a tuple value is itself a tuple value. *Note:* Other formalisms are possible; in particular, it would be possible to define a tuple as a set of <attribute name, type name, attribute value> triples instead of <attribute, attribute value> pairs (as a matter of fact, *The Third Manifesto* does exactly this). Of course, the two definitions are clearly isomorphic. Either way, tuples as defined in the relational model differ in certain important respects from the mathematical construct of the same name. In particular, tuples in mathematics typically don't have named attributes; instead, their attributes are identified by ordinal position, left to right. *See* **tuple (mathematics)**.

tuple valued attribute   An attribute whose type is some tuple type. Values of such an attribute are tuples of the specified type. *Note:* If a relvar has a tuple valued attribute, that fact in and of itself doesn't constitute a violation of any particular level of normalization (not even first); however, such attributes are usually contraindicated in database design, at least in base relvars, because they necessarily imply some structural asymmetry and thereby give rise to asymmetry (and hence complexity) in queries, constraints, and updates as well. *See also* **tuple unwrapping**; **tuple wrapping**.

  Examples: See the examples under **wrapping** and **tuple wrapping**.

tuple variable   Very loosely, a row (variable); more precisely, a variable whose type is some tuple type. Let tuple variable *V* be of type *T*; then *V* has the same heading (and therefore attributes) and degree as type *T* does. *Note:* Tuple variables aren't required by the relational model as such (except as noted under **database variable**), but they're likely to be needed in the external environment (e.g., such a variable will be needed to serve as the target for retrieval of some tuple from some relation). *See also* **variable** and (for a discussion of the fact that a database is really a tuple variable) **database variable**.

tuple wrapping   Let tuple *t* have attributes called *A1, A2, ..., Am, B1, B2, ..., Bn* (and no others), and let *BT* be an attribute name that's distinct from that of every attribute *Ai* ($1 \leq i \leq m$). Then (and only then) the expression *t* WRAP {*B1,B2,...,Bn*} AS *BT* denotes the wrapping of *t* on {*B1,B2,...,Bn*}, and it returns the tuple denoted by the expression (EXTEND *t* : {*BT* := TUPLE {*B1 B1,B2 B2,...,Bn Bn*}}) {*A1,A2,...,Am,BT*}.

    Example: Let *t* be the tuple for supplier S1 and part P1 from the current value of relvar SP. Then the expression

```
t WRAP { PNO , QTY } AS PQ_TUP
```

yields a tuple *tw* of type TUPLE {SNO SNO, PQ_TUP TUPLE {PNO PNO, QTY QTY}}, with SNO value S1 and PQ_TUP value a tuple with PNO value P1 and QTY value 300. (Attribute PQ_TUP here is an example of a tuple valued attribute.)

tuplecon   A tuple constant, q.v.

tuplevar   A tuple variable, q.v.

tuplevar reference   Syntactically, a tuplevar name, used to denote either the tuplevar as such or the value of that tuplevar, as the context demands.

Tutorial D   A particular **D**, q.v., designed primarily to serve as a teaching vehicle (see the introduction to this dictionary). Note that the name **Tutorial D**, like the name **D**, is always set in boldface.

TVA   Tuple valued attribute.

two-valued logic   Conventional propositional or predicate logic, in which there are just two truth values, TRUE and FALSE; abbreviated 2VL. The relational model is based on 2VL.

TYPE   The **Tutorial D** operator for defining (user defined) scalar types. For example, here's a sample type definition for a user defined scalar type called POINT (irrelevant details omitted):

```
TYPE POINT ...
     POSSREP CARTESIAN { X RATIONAL , Y RATIONAL
                      CONSTRAINT ( X↑2 + Y↑2 ) ≤ 10000 } ;
```

Type POINT denotes geometric points in two-dimensional space. Points have a possible representation called CARTESIAN, with components X and Y (both of declared type RATIONAL); also, they're subject to a constraint—imposed somewhat arbitrarily, and purely for the sake of the example—that says, in effect, that the only points we're interested in are those that lie on or inside a circle with center the origin and radius of length 100 (the symbol "↑" denotes exponentiation). *See* CONSTRAINT for further explanation.

Note: As explained under **possible representation**, possible representations ("possreps") are always named; by default, however, the possrep name is the same as that of the corresponding type. Here, for example, is a slightly simpler version of the foregoing definition for type POINT:

```
TYPE POINT ...
     POSSREP { X RATIONAL , Y RATIONAL
             CONSTRAINT ( X↑2 + Y↑2 ) ≤ 10000 } ;
```

Now the possrep is called POINT instead of CARTESIAN. Most of the examples involving user defined types elsewhere in this dictionary make use of this default option.

As for tuple and relation types, there aren't any explicit "define tuple type" or "define relation type" operators in **Tutorial D**. Rather, the availability of a given scalar type tacitly implies the availability of an unbounded number of tuple and relation types with names of the form TUPLE *H* or RELATION *H* (as applicable)—where (a) TUPLE and RELATION are type generators, q.v.; (b) *H* is a heading, consisting of a possibly empty commalist of attributes enclosed in braces; and (c) each attribute in turn consists of an attribute name followed by a type name. (This definition is recursive, of course.) Such a tuple or relation type can be specified as the type for (e.g.) some variable by simply specifying the appropriate type name as part of the definition of the variable in question. Here are some examples of such types:

```
TUPLE { E ELLIPSE , R RECTANGLE }

RELATION { E ELLIPSE , AB TUPLE { A ELLIPSE , B RECTANGLE } }

TUPLE { E ELLIPSE , AB RELATION { A RECTANGLE , B ELLIPSE } }

RELATION { E ELLIPSE , AB RELATION { A RECTANGLE , B ELLIPSE } }
```

And so on.

type   A named (and in practice finite) set of values; not to be confused with the internal or physical representation of the values in question, which is an implementation issue. Every value, every variable, every attribute, every read-only operator, every parameter, and every expression is of some type. Types can be either scalar or nonscalar (in particular, they can be tuple or relation types); as a consequence, attributes of relations in particular can also be either scalar or nonscalar. Types can also be either system defined (i.e., built in) or user defined. They can also be generated (*see* **type generator**). *See also* **domain**; **type naming**. *Note:* A type isn't a value, nor is it a variable; in particular, relation values and relation variables aren't types. Equating types and either relation values or relation variables—positions that have been advocated in the literature—has been referred to as The First Great Blunder, q.v. (For the second, *see* **pointer**; **Second Great Blunder**.)

  Example: Here's a sample type definition (basically as shown in the example under TYPE):

```
TYPE POINT ... { ... CONSTRAINT ( X↑2 + Y↑2 ) ≤ 10000 } ;
```

POINT here is a user defined type, denoting geometric points in two-dimensional space. It's subject to a type constraint—imposed somewhat arbitrarily, and purely for the sake of the example—that says, in effect, that the only points of interest are those that lie on or inside a circle with center the origin and radius of length 100. (The symbols X and Y denote the cartesian coordinates of the point in question, and the symbol "↑" denotes exponentiation.)

type checking   (*Without inheritance*) Checking that the types of the arguments to a given operator invocation conform to the type requirements as defined in the applicable invocation signature, q.v. Note that all type checking can be done at compile time, in the absence of support for inheritance.

  Example: Let MOVE be an operator with invocation signature as follows:

```
( ELLIPSE , RECTANGLE ) RETURNS ELLIPSE
```

Also, let variables E and R be of declared types ELLIPSE and RECTANGLE, respectively. Then the first of the following MOVE invocations will raise a type error (q.v.) but the second won't:

```
MOVE ( R , E )
MOVE ( E , R )
```

type constraint   A definition of the set of values that make up a given type. The type constraint for type *T* is checked, in effect, whenever some selector is invoked for that type *T*; in other words, a type constraint error occurs if and only if some selector is invoked with arguments that violate the applicable type constraint. *See also* **CONSTRAINT**; *contrast* **type error**.

  Examples: For scalar types, see the examples under CONSTRAINT; TYPE; and elsewhere. For tuple and relation types, no type constraints are defined explicitly (at least as far as *The Third Manifesto* is concerned); rather, the constraints in question are defined implicitly by the constraints that apply to the scalar types in terms of which the tuple or relation type in question is (ultimately) defined. For example, the type constraint for type RELATION {E ELLIPSE,

R RECTANGLE} is simply a constraint to the effect that (a) attribute E is subject to the type constraint that applies to type ELLIPSE and (b) attribute R is subject to the type constraint that applies to type RECTANGLE.

Incidentally, it's worth noting that the only type constraints that apply to user defined types in SQL—*see* **user defined type (SQL)**—are those that follow from the underlying physical representation. For example, suppose type SHOE_SIZE (with the obvious interpretation) is defined to have an INTEGER physical representation. Then the only constraint on shoe sizes is that they must be representable as an integer; thus, e.g., –5000 is apparently a valid shoe size (!).

type constraint error *See* type constraint.

type constructor Term used in SQL and certain other languages to mean a type generator.

type conversion *See* CAST_AS_*T*.

type definition *See* TYPE.

type error (*Without inheritance*) The error that occurs if type checking fails (i.e., if some operator is invoked with an argument of some type not equal to the declared type of the corresponding parameter). Such errors should be detectable at compile time, in the absence of support for inheritance.

type generator An operator that's invoked at compile time instead of run time and returns a type instead of a value. For example, conventional programming languages typically support an array type generator, which lets users specify an unlimited number and variety of individual array types. In the relational model, the tuple and (especially) relation type generators are the important ones; they allow users to specify an unlimited number and variety of individual tuple and relation types. *See* relation type; tuple type.

Examples: Consider the suppliers relvar definition:

```
VAR S BASE RELATION
  { SNO SNO , SNAME NAME , STATUS INTEGER , CITY CHAR }
    KEY { SNO } ;
```

This definition includes an invocation of the RELATION type generator (syntactically, everything from the keyword RELATION to the closing brace following the keyword CHAR, inclusive). That invocation returns a specific relation type—namely, the type

```
RELATION { SNO SNO , SNAME NAME , STATUS INTEGER , CITY CHAR }
```

So this type is in fact a generated type—as indeed are all relation types, and all tuple types also, at least as far as this dictionary, and indeed **Tutorial D** and *The Third Manifesto*, are concerned.

Observe that nongenerated types are always scalar. Generated types are typically nonscalar, but don't have to be. An example of a scalar generated type is the SQL type CHAR(25); CHAR here is a type generator—not, as commonly supposed, a type as such—and the length specification 25 is the argument to a specific invocation of that generator. Analogous remarks apply to the SQL type NUMERIC(5,2).

type inference   The process of determining the type of the value denoted by a given expression. Note that this process is completely specified by the rules defining the types of the results of the various operations involved in the expression in question. (In fact, of course, the type of the value denoted by expression *exp* is, precisely, the type of the result of the outermost operation involved in *exp*.)

type inheritance   An organizing principle according to which one type can be defined as a subtype of one or more other types, called supertypes (of the type in question). If T' is a subtype of supertype T, then all values of type T' are also values of type T, and read-only operators and type constraints that apply to values of type T therefore also apply to (i.e., "are inherited by") values of type T'. However, values of type T' will have read-only operators and type constraints of their own that don't apply to values that are only of type T and not of type T'. See Part II of this dictionary for further explanation.

type naming   *The Third Manifesto* requires every type to have exactly one name and distinct types to have distinct names. In the case of tuple and relation types, however, there might well be more than one way of writing the corresponding name on paper. For example, the following all represent the same relation type name in **Tutorial D**:

```
RELATION { SNO SNO , CITY CHAR }

RELATION { CITY CHAR , SNO SNO }

RELATION { SNO SNO , CITY CHAR , SNO SNO }
```

Note: Although it's true that every type has just one unique name, for psychological reasons **Tutorial D** does allow types to have one or more synonyms. For example, CHAR, INT, and BOOL are system defined synonyms for CHARACTER, INTEGER, and BOOLEAN, respectively, in **Tutorial D**. Thus, e.g., a given variable can be defined to have type either INTEGER or INT, and the definitions in question are regarded as equivalent. As for tuple and relation types, that same synonym mechanism allows the keywords TUPLE and RELATION to be abbreviated to TUP and REL, respectively.

type schema   (*Without inheritance*) Term sometimes used to refer to a collection of type definitions. For example, the collection of type definitions for all of the user defined types (SNO, PNO, NAME, COLOR, WEIGHT, QTY) involved in the suppliers-and-parts database could be regarded as a type schema.

type vs. relvar   *See* relvar vs. type.

types vs. units   Some types are such that values of the type in question have to be understood as being expressed in terms of certain units in order to be fully understood. For example, consider type LENGTH. A sample value of that type might be 24, with inches understood; or, equivalently, 2, with feet understood; or 60.96, with centimeters understood; and so on. One approach to this issue would be to design a single LENGTH type with different possreps corresponding to different units of measure: an inches possrep, a feet possrep, a centimeters possrep, and so on. For further discussion of this approach, see the *Manifesto* book; *see also* CAST_AS_*T*.

———— ♦♦♦♦♦ ————

UDT   User defined type.

unary   (*Of a heading, key, tuple, relation, etc.*) Of degree one. *Contrast* monadic.

uncontrolled redundancy   Redundancy, q.v., that has the potential to lead to inconsistency. Database designs should preferably not permit such redundancy. *Contrast* controlled redundancy; *see also* consistency.

UNGROUP   *See* ungrouping.

ungrouping   Let relation *r* have attributes called *A1*, *A2*, ..., *Am*, and *BR* (and no others), and let attribute *BR* be relation valued and have attributes called *B1*, *B2*, ..., *Bn* (and no others); further, let no *Ai* have the same name as any *Bj* ($1 \leq i \leq m$, $1 \leq j \leq n$). Then (and only then) the expression *r* UNGROUP *BR* denotes the ungrouping of *r* on *BR*, and it returns the relation denoted by the expression UNION (EXTEND *r* : { *temp* := (!!*r*){ALL BUT *BR*} TIMES *BR*}, *temp*)—an invocation of the UNION aggregate operator, q.v. *Note:* The subexpression !!*r* here is an image relation reference, q.v.
    Example: Let *spq* be the relation resulting from the expression

```
SP GROUP { PNO , QTY } AS PQ_REL
```

(*see* grouping). Then the expression

```
spq UNGROUP PQ_REL
```

denotes an ungrouping of *spq*. That ungrouping is a relation of type RELATION {SNO SNO, PNO PNO, QTY QTY}; and if *spq* is obtained from the relation *sp* shown as the value of relvar SP in Fig. 1, then the result of ungrouping *spq* is just *sp*. Suppose, however, that *spq* additionally contains a tuple, say for supplier S5, in which the PQ_REL value is an empty relation; then the result of the foregoing UNGROUP won't contain a tuple for supplier S5 (in fact, the result will still be, exactly, that same relation *sp*). In general, therefore, ungrouping a relation *r* and then grouping it again in what might look like an inverse way isn't guaranteed to take us back to *r* (*contrast* grouping).

uniform representation / uniformity of representation   *See Information Principle.*

UNION   *See* union.

union   (*Without inheritance*) 1. (*Dyadic case*) Let relations *r1* and *r2* be of the same type *T*. Then (and only then) the expression *r1* UNION *r2* denotes the union of *r1* and *r2*, and it returns the relation of type *T* with body the set of all tuples *t* such that *t* appears in at least one of *r1* and *r2*. 2. (*N-adic case*) Let relations *r1*, *r2*, ..., *rn* ($n \geq 0$) all be of the same type *T*. Then (and only then) the expression UNION {*r1,r2,...,rn*} denotes the union of *r1*, *r2*, ..., *rn*, and it returns the relation of type *T* with body the set of all tuples *t* such that *t* appears in at least one of *r1*, *r2*, ..., *rn*. *Note:* If $n = 0$, (a) some syntactic mechanism, not shown here, is needed to specify the pertinent type *T* and (b) the result is the empty relation of that type. Note too that the relational union operator differs in certain respects from the mathematical or set theory operator of the same name, q.v.; also, union is sometimes known explicitly as inclusive union in order to distinguish it from exclusive union, q.v. (but the term *union*, unqualified, is always taken to mean inclusive union specifically, unless the context demands otherwise). Note finally that UNION can also be used as an aggregate operator, q.v. *See also* disjoint union; tuple union.
　　Example: The expression S{CITY} UNION P{CITY} denotes the union of (a) the relation that's the projection on {CITY} of the current value of relvar S and (b) the relation that's the projection on {CITY} of the current value of relvar P. That union is a relation *r* of type RELATION {CITY CHAR}. Moreover, if the current values of relvars S and P are *s* and *p*, respectively, then the body of that relation *r* consists of all tuples of the form <*c*> that appear in *s*{CITY} or *p*{CITY} or both—meaning *c* is a current supplier city or a current part city or both.

union (bag theory)   *See* bag.

union (set theory)   The union of two sets *s1* and *s2*, *s1* ∪ *s2* (where the symbol "∪" can conveniently be pronounced "cup"), is the set of all elements *x* such that *x* is an element of *s1* or an element of *s2*. *Note:* This definition can obviously be extended to apply to any number of sets.

union compatible   (*Of relations*) Of the same type. The term is deprecated for many reasons, of which inappropriateness is one.

union plus   *See* bag.

UNIQUE   Keyword sometimes used to denote the quantifier "there exists exactly one of." In other words, let $p(x)$ be a predicate with a parameter x; then UNIQUE x $(p(x))$ is a predicate, and it means "There exists exactly one argument value v that can be substituted for the parameter x such that $p(v)$ is true."

Example: Here's a tuple calculus formulation of the foreign key constraint "Every shipment has exactly one corresponding supplier":

```
SX  RANGES OVER { S } ;
SPX RANGES OVER { SP } ;

CONSTRAINT SP_REFERENCES_S
          FORALL SPX ( UNIQUE SX ( SX.SNO = SPX.SNO ) ) ;
```

Note: The expression UNIQUE x $(p(x))$ is logically equivalent to the expression EXISTS x $(p(x)$ AND NOT EXISTS y $(y \neq x$ AND $p(y)))$. Observe that this expression evaluates to FALSE if the bound variable x has an empty range.

unique index   An index—hence, an implementation construct—on (the stored analog of) some relvar on the basis of some superkey for that relvar; not to be confused with a superkey per se, even though the index might be used to implement the associated superkey constraint. *Note:* In practice, the superkey in question is usually (or is usually intended to be) a key as such, not a proper superkey.

uniqueness   *See* candidate key; superkey.

units   *See* types vs. units.

universal quantifier   Let $p(x)$ be a predicate with a parameter x; then FORALL x $(p(x))$ is a predicate, and it means "For all argument values v that can be substituted for the parameter x, $p(v)$ is true." In this example, FORALL x is a universal quantifier, and x is a universally quantified bound variable, q.v. *Note:* Some writers refer to FORALL by itself as the quantifier; the literature is not consistent on this point. More important, note that if $v1$, $v2$, ..., vn are all of the possible argument values in the foregoing example, then FORALL x $(p(x))$ is equivalent to AND $\{(p(v1)), (p(v2)),...,(p(vn))\}$ (*see* conjunction, second definition). Observe in particular that this expression evaluates to TRUE if $n = 0$ (i.e., if the bound variable x has an empty range), because TRUE is the identity with respect to AND. Observe further that the expression FORALL x $(p(x))$ is logically equivalent to the expression NOT (EXISTS x (NOT $(p(x))))$. *See also* FORALL; *contrast* existential quantifier.

Example: Here's a tuple calculus query that makes use of the universal quantifier as well as the existential quantifier ("Get suppliers who supply all parts"):

```
SX   RANGES OVER { S } ;
SPX  RANGES OVER { SP } ;
PX   RANGES OVER { P } ;

{ SX } WHERE FORALL PX ( EXISTS SPX ( SPX.SNO = SX.SNO AND
                                      SPX.PNO = PX.PNO ) )
```

The expression in the last two lines here can be read as "Suppliers SX where for all parts PX there exists a shipment SPX with the same supplier number as SX and the same part number as PX."

universal relation   Given a heading *H*, the relation with heading *H* that contains all possible tuples with heading *H*. Note, therefore, that there's exactly one universal relation for each relation type, and every relation of a given type is a subrelation (q.v.) of the pertinent universal relation. *Contrast* empty relation. *Caveat:* The term *universal relation* is often used in the database literature (e.g., in discussions of normalization) to refer to what would more appropriately be called a universal relvar, q.v.

universal relvar   Very loosely, the join of all relvars in a given set of relvars; slightly less loosely, a hypothetical relvar whose heading is the set theory union of the headings of all of the relvars in a given set. The normalization procedure, q.v., if viewed in isolation (i.e., ignoring other possible aids to database design), tacitly assumes it's possible to define an initial universal relvar—unfortunately more usually referred to in the literature not as a universal relvar as such but rather as a universal relation—that has all of the attributes relevant to the database under consideration, and then shows how that relvar can and/or should be replaced by successively "smaller" (i.e., lower degree) projections until a "good" design is reached. Incidentally, note the implications for attribute naming that underlie the foregoing assumption. To be specific, it implies that (e.g.) the supplier number attributes in relvars S and SP will both have the same name instead of being called, say, SNO in one relvar and SNUM in the other. This attribute naming discipline is strongly recommended anyway, because it has the effect among other things of simplifying the formulation—both formal and informal—of queries, constraints, and so on (as indeed should be clear from a careful study of the definitions in this dictionary of the various relational operators).

universal set   The universe of discourse, q.v.; the set that contains all of the elements of interest in some given context. Every set is a subset of the universal set.

universe of discourse   *See* sorted logic.

UNKNOWN   *See* three-valued logic.

unnesting   *See* nesting and unnesting.

unnormalized   Not normalized (i.e., not in first normal form, q.v.); not to be confused with denormalized (*see* **denormalization**). *Note:* By definition, relations and relvars are never unnormalized. However, certain data structures—in particular, tables with repeating groups, q.v.—might "look something like" relations or relvars and yet not be normalized (and thus in fact not corresponding directly to relations or relvars, as such, after all).

unsorted logic   *See* sorted logic.

UNWRAP   *See* unwrapping.

unwrapping   Let relation *r* have attributes called *A1, A2, ..., Am*, and *BT* (and no others), and let attribute *BT* be tuple valued and have attributes called *B1, B2, ..., Bn* (and no others); further, let no *Ai* have the same name as any *Bj* ($1 \leq i \leq m$, $1 \leq j \leq n$). Then (and only then) the expression *r* UNWRAP *BT* denotes the unwrapping of *r* on *BT*, and it returns the relation denoted by the expression (EXTEND *r* : {*B1* := *B1* FROM *BT*, *B2* := *B2* FROM *BT*, ..., *Bn* := *Bn* FROM *BT*}){ALL BUT *BT*}. *See also* **tuple unwrapping**.
 Example: Let *spw* be the relation resulting from the expression

```
SP WRAP { PNO , QTY } AS PQ_REL
```

(*see* **wrapping**). Then the following expression denotes an unwrapping of *spw*:

```
spw UNWRAP PQ_REL
```

That unwrapping is a relation of type RELATION {SNO SNO, PNO PNO, QTY QTY}. If *spw* is obtained by wrapping the relation *sp* shown as the value of relvar SP in Fig. 1, then the result of unwrapping *spw* is just *sp*.

UPDATE   Very loosely, an operator that updates a given set of attributes in a given set of tuples in a given relvar; slightly less loosely, an operator that replaces a given set of tuples in a given relvar by another such set. It's shorthand for a certain relational assignment. The syntax is:

```
UPDATE R [ WHERE bx ] : { attribute assignment commalist }
```

Here *R* is a relvar reference (syntactically, just a relvar name), *bx* is a boolean expression, the target for the attribute assignments are attributes of relvar *R*, and the invocation just shown is shorthand for the following explicit assignment:

```
R := ( R WHERE NOT ( bx ) )
     UNION
     ( EXTEND ( R WHERE bx ) : { attribute assignment commalist } )
```

See also WITH.

Example: The UPDATE statement

```
UPDATE P WHERE CITY = 'London' :
       { WEIGHT := 2 * WEIGHT , CITY := 'Oslo' } ;
```

is shorthand for the following relational assignment statement:

```
P := ( P WHERE NOT ( CITY = 'London' ) )
       UNION
     ( EXTEND ( P WHERE CITY = 'London' ) :
               { WEIGHT := 2 * WEIGHT , CITY := 'Oslo' } ) ;
```

In this example, we might say, loosely, that attributes WEIGHT and CITY are being updated in the tuples for London parts; we might also say, still loosely but a little less so, that the tuples for London parts are being replaced; but what's really happening is that a certain relation value is being assigned to a certain relation variable.

Note: In **Tutorial D** in particular, the UPDATE operator can be used to update scalar and tuple variables as well as relation variables per se (in other words, UPDATE is overloaded).

UPDATE anomaly   Same as modification anomaly.

UPDATE rule   A rule specifying the action to be taken automatically—typically but not necessarily a compensatory action, q.v.—to ensure that UPDATE operations on a given relvar don't violate any associated multivariable constraint, q.v. *Note:* The relational model rejects UPDATE rules as logically flawed (since, unlike DELETE and INSERT rules, q.v., they're apparently driven by syntax, not semantics). *Contrast* DELETE rule; INSERT rule.

update   An assignment, especially a relational assignment; more especially still, a relational INSERT, D_INSERT, DELETE, I_DELETE, or UPDATE operation, q.v.

update anomaly   A deletion anomaly (q.v.), insertion anomaly (q.v.), or modification anomaly (q.v.).

update operator   An operator that, when invoked, returns no value but updates a variable (usually an argument) that's not local to the implementation of the operator in question. An update operator invocation doesn't denote a value—loosely speaking, it's a statement (typically a CALL statement of some kind), not an expression—and thus it can't appear where an expression is required. In particular, it can't be nested inside an expression. Every update operator invocation is logically equivalent to some assignment (possibly a multiple assignment, q.v.).

Example: See the second example under RETURN.

update propagation   *See* controlled redundancy.

UPDATES Let *Op* be an update operator; then *Op* has a set of parameters that are subject to update, q.v., each of which must be identified as such as part of the definition of *Op*. In **Tutorial D**, this function is performed by means of the UPDATES clause. *Contrast* RETURNS.
  Example: See the second example under RETURN.

user Either an end user (knowledgeable or otherwise concerning database matters) or an application programmer or both, as the context demands.

user defined Defined by some agency other than the system; i.e., not system defined (not built in). User defined operators and user defined types provide obvious examples. *Note:* The term "user defined" is sanctioned by usage but really isn't very good. Consider the case of a user defined type *T*, for example. To the user who merely makes use of that type—as opposed to the user who actually defines it—type *T* behaves in all major respects just like a system defined type (indeed, that's the whole point). In other words, what's being sought here is not so much a distinction between users and the system as it is a distinction between different roles played by different users (possibly even by the same user) in different contexts.

user defined type *See* type; user defined. *Contrast* system defined type. *Note:* The system vs. user defined types distinction applies only to nongenerated types, not to types produced via invocation of some type generator.
  Examples: Of the scalar types used in the suppliers-and-parts database, SNO, PNO, NAME, COLOR, WEIGHT, and QTY are all user defined.

user defined type (SQL) SQL divides user defined types into two kinds, "distinct types" and "structured types." In essence:

- A distinct type *D*—note that the term *distinct* is being used here in a highly specialized sense—(a) is defined in terms of just one underlying type *T*, which is explicitly visible to the user, must be system defined, must be scalar, and is in fact the physical (not just some possible) representation for values of type *D*; (b) has no type constraint, except for the obvious constraint that values of type *D* must be representable as values of type *T*; (c) inherits comparison and assignment operators, but no other operators, from type *T*; (d) effectively does have selector and THE_ operators, though terminology and syntax both differ from their counterparts as defined in this dictionary; and (e) can't have proper subtypes.

- A structured type *S*—note that the term *structured* is being used here in a highly specialized sense—(a) is defined in terms of a construct somewhat akin to a possrep, except that the "possrep" in question is really the physical (not just some possible) representation for values of type *S*; (b) has no type constraint, except for the obvious constraint that values of type *S* must be representable in terms of that specified physical representation; (c) has no comparison operators (not even "=") other than ones explicitly defined by means of a special and separate CREATE ORDERING operator [*sic*]; (d) effectively does have assignment, selector, and THE_ operators, though terminology and syntax both differ from their counterparts as defined in this dictionary; and (e) can have proper subtypes.

Further details, of both distinct and structured types, are exceedingly complex and are beyond the scope of this dictionary, except for occasional passing references here and there.

value An "individual constant," q.v. (for example, the individual constant denoted by the integer literal 3). Values can be of arbitrary complexity; in particular, they can be either scalar or nonscalar (note in particular that tuples and relations are both values). Values have no location in time or space; however, they can be represented in memory by means of some encoding, and those representations do have location in time and space—indeed, distinct occurrences of the same value can appear at any number of distinct locations in time and space, meaning, loosely, that the same value can occur as the current value of any number of distinct variables, and/or as any number of attribute values within the current value of any number of distinct tuplevars and/or relvars, at the same time or different times (*see* **appearance**). Note that, by definition, a value can't be updated; for if it could, then after such an update it would no longer be that value. Note too that every value is of some type—in fact, of exactly one type (and types are thus disjoint), except possibly if type inheritance is supported. Note finally that a value isn't a type, nor is it a variable. *Contrast* **literal**.

value set Term sometimes used in E/R contexts to mean a type—almost certainly a scalar type specifically, though the literature isn't really clear on this point.

VAR The **Tutorial D** operator for defining variables (relation variables in particular).
Examples: See the introduction to this dictionary and elsewhere.

variable 1. (*Logic*) *See* **logic variable**. 2. (*Programming languages*) A holder for a representation of a value, q.v. Unlike values, variables (a) do have location in time and space and (b) can be updated (that is, the current value of the variable can be replaced by another value). Indeed, to be a variable is to be updatable, and to be updatable is to be a variable; equivalently, to be a variable is to be assignable to, and to be assignable to is to be a variable. Every variable is declared to be of some type. Note that a variable isn't a type, nor is it a value. Note too that the language **D**, q.v., requires variables always to have a value; in particular, therefore, it requires the operation of defining variable *V* to have the effect, among other things, of initializing *V* to some value—typically but not necessarily a value explicitly specified as part of that defining operation (*but see* **example value**).

variable reference   1. (*Logic*) *See* bound variable; free variable. 2. (*Programming languages*) Syntactically, a variable name, used to denote either the variable as such or the value of that variable, as the context demands. Note that such a reference definitely denotes the variable as such if it's used to specify a target for some update operation (in particular, if it appears on the left side of an assignment). If on the other hand it denotes the value of the variable, then it can be regarded as an invocation of a read-only operator—and hence as an expression, q.v.—where the read-only operator in question is essentially "Return the current value of the specified variable." Like all expressions, therefore, it can appear wherever a literal of the appropriate type can appear. *See also* pseudovariable reference.

vertical decomposition   Informal term for decomposition into projections.

view   A derived relvar that's virtual, not real (*contrast* snapshot). The value of a given view at a given time is the result of evaluating a certain relational expression—the view defining expression, specified when the view itself is defined—at the time in question. *Note:* The view defining expression must mention at least one relvar, for otherwise the view wouldn't be, specifically, a variable as such. Note too that the view must be updatable for the same reason.
   Example: The following statement defines a view called LS:

```
VAR LS VIRTUAL ( S WHERE CITY = 'London' ) ;
```

The relation that's the value of view LS at any given time is equal to the value of the view defining expression S WHERE CITY = 'London' at that time.

view materialization   A somewhat unsophisticated technique for implementing operations on views, according to which (a) the relational expression that defines the view is evaluated at the time the operation on the view is invoked, (b) a relation is thereby materialized, and (c) the operation in question is then executed against the relation so materialized. Observe that operations on views can always be implemented using this technique (albeit perhaps not very efficiently) if the operation in question is a read-only operation but not if it's an update operation. *Contrast* substitution (second definition). *See also* materialized view.

view updating   Either the theory or the process of updating views, as the context demands. View updating is still a somewhat controversial topic, but there are those who believe that— contrary to popular opinion, perhaps—all views are at least theoretically updatable. The details are beyond the scope of this dictionary, except to note that (a) a view update can fail on an integrity violation, of course, just as a base relvar update can, and (b) an argument can be made that view updates that are regarded by some writers as "impossible" aren't intrinsically impossible after all but instead fail on just such a violation. Moreover, if a system does support views but doesn't support view updating correctly (or at all!), then such a state of affairs would constitute the clearest possible violation of *The Principle of Interchangeability*. For a detailed discussion of such matters, with numerous examples, see the book *View Updating and Relational Theory: Solving the View Update Problem*, by C. J. Date (O'Reilly Media Inc., 2013).

violate   Let *C* be a constraint that refers to variables *V1, V2, ..., Vn* ($n \geq 0$) and no others. Then values *v1, v2, ..., vn* (in that order) violate *C* if and only if evaluating *C* with *V1* equal to *v1*, *V2* equal to *v2*, ..., and *Vn* equal to *vn* yields FALSE. *Note:* An analogous definition applies to business rules also, q.v. *Contrast* **satisfy**.

virtual relation   The value of a given virtual relvar at a given time.

virtual relvar   A view, q.v. (*contrast* real relvar).

void   Empty (e.g., the empty set is sometimes referred to as the void set). Not to be confused with null, q.v.

———— ♦ ♦ ♦ ♦ ♦ ————

well formed formula   In logic, a formal expression denoting a predicate.

WFF   A well formed formula. The abbreviation is variously pronounced "weff" or "wiff" or "woof." *See also* closed WFF; open WFF.

what if   A read-only relational operator that returns the relation that would result if certain changes were made to a specified relation (ignoring the fact that such changes couldn't in fact be made, because a relation is a value). *Note:* **Tutorial D** uses the EXTEND operator to provide this functionality—*see* extension, second definition. (The keyword EXTEND is perhaps not the best in the circumstances, but it's hard to find a word that catches the overall sense better and yet is equally succinct.) *See also* WITH.
    Example: The expression

```
EXTEND ( S WHERE CITY = 'Paris' ) :
            { STATUS := 2 * STATUS , CITY := 'Nice' }
```

denotes a relation containing exactly one tuple *t* for each tuple *s* in the current value of relvar S for which the city is Paris—except that, in that tuple *t*, the status is double that in tuple *s* and the city is Nice, not Paris.

WHERE clause   A syntactic construct of the form WHERE *bx* (where *bx* is a boolean expression, typically an open one) that appears ubiquitously in SQL, **Tutorial D**, and many other languages. *See* DELETE; restriction; restriction condition; SELECT expression; UPDATE; and elsewhere.

WITH A syntactic device, supported by **Tutorial D** in particular, for introducing names for the results of subexpressions. The introduced names are then available for subsequent use (but only within the overall expression or statement of which the WITH specification forms a part) to denote those results.

Examples: 1. The following is a **Tutorial D** formulation of the query "Get pairs of supplier numbers, *Sx* and *Sy* say, such that suppliers *Sx* and *Sy* each supply exactly the same set of parts":

```
WITH ( tx := ( S RENAME { SNO AS SX } ) { SX } ,
       ty := ( S RENAME { SNO AS SY } ) { SY } ) :
     ( tx JOIN ty ) WHERE ( SP WHERE SNO = SX ) { PNO } =
                          ( SP WHERE SNO = SY ) { PNO }
```

Note the relational comparison in the WHERE clause here. 2. **Tutorial D** also allows a WITH specification to appear inside the braces, preceding the commalist of attribute assignments, in an EXTEND, SUMMARIZE, or UPDATE invocation. The following example is repeated from the discussion in the entry for **summarization**:

```
EXTEND SP : { WITH ( temp := !!SP ) :
              SQ := SUM ( temp , QTY ) , AQ := AVG ( temp , QTY ) }
```

Note: SQL also supports a WITH construct, with semantics similar but not identical to those of the **Tutorial D** construct—and, it has to be said, with much less practical utility, owing to the fact that SQL's support for any given relational operator is, in general, quite hard to disentangle from its support for other such operators. (Simplifying slightly, the problem is that, in SQL, the subexpressions whose results can be named via WITH can't be anything less than an entire SELECT expression, q.v.)

WRAP *See* **wrapping**.

wrapping Let relation *r* have attributes called *A1, A2, ..., Am, B1, B2, ..., Bn* (and no others), and let *BT* be an attribute name that's distinct from that of every attribute *Ai* ($1 \leq i \leq m$). Then (and only then) the expression *r* WRAP *{B1,B2,...,Bn}* AS *BT* denotes the wrapping of *r* on *{B1,B2,...,Bn}*, and it returns the relation denoted by the expression (EXTEND *r* : *{BT* := TUPLE *{B1 B1,B2 B2,...,Bn Bn}}*) *{A1,A2,...,Am,BT}*. *See also* **tuple wrapping**.

Example: The following expression denotes a wrapping of the relation that's the current value of relvar SP:

```
SP WRAP { PNO , QTY } AS PQ_TUP
```

That wrapping is a relation *spw* of type RELATION {SNO SNO, PQ_TUP TUPLE {PNO PNO, QTY QTY}}; it contains one tuple for each tuple currently appearing in relvar SP, and no other tuples. Given the sample values in Fig. 1, for example, the *spw* tuple for supplier S1 and part P1 has SNO value S1 and PQ_TUP value a tuple with PNO value P1 and QTY value 300. (Attribute PQ_TUP here is an example of a tuple valued attribute.)

write operator   Same as update operator.

———— ♦♦♦♦♦ ————

XMINUS   If exclusive union (q.v.) is referred to as symmetric difference (q.v.), then XMINUS might be psychologically preferable to XUNION (q.v.) as the corresponding keyword.

XML   Extensible Markup Language. *Note:* From a database point of view, XML—or "XML document," rather—is best regarded as just another data type, albeit one of considerable pragmatic importance at the time of writing. Values of that type are XML documents. Among other things, therefore, relations should be allowed to have attributes of that type, and tuples in such relations should thus be allowed to contain attribute values that are XML documents.

XOR   1. A connective, q.v. (*see* exclusive OR). 2. An aggregate operator, q.v. *Contrast* EQUIV.

XUNION   *See* exclusive union.

———— ♦♦♦♦♦ ————

ZO   A **Tutorial D** operator that, given a relation r, returns a relation with heading the same as that of r and body either (a) empty if r is empty or (b) consisting of precisely one tuple otherwise, that tuple being some arbitrary tuple from the body of r. The name ZO is shorthand for "zero or one"; it derives from the fact that the cardinality of the result is either zero or one. *See also* axiom of choice.

    Example: Here is a possible formulation of a constraint to the effect that the cardinality of some given relvar R must never exceed two:

```
CONSTRAINT ZOX WITH ( X := R MINUS ZO ( R ) ) :
               IS_EMPTY ( X MINUS ZO ( X ) ) ;
```

Of course, the same constraint can be more readily expressed thus:

```
CONSTRAINT ZOX COUNT ( R ) ≤ 2 ;
```

However, this formulation relies, as the former did not, on the availability of the aggregate operator COUNT.

———— ♦♦♦♦♦ ————

Part II

Inheritance

Several of the entries appearing in this part of the dictionary consist essentially of expansions of, or elaborations on, entries marked "Without inheritance" in Part I. Such entries are marked "With inheritance" accordingly.

Examples in what follows are based for the most part on either the simple type hierarchy shown in Fig. 2 or the slightly more general type graph shown in Fig. 3. Note that Fig. 2 involves single inheritance only and Fig. 3 involves multiple inheritance.

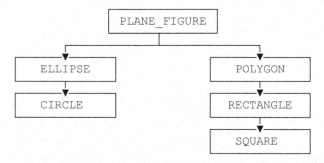

Fig. 2: Sample type hierarchy (single inheritance, q.v.)

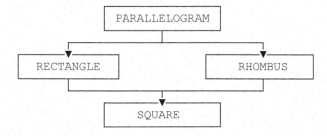

Fig. 3: Sample type graph (multiple inheritance, q.v.)

The Type Hierarchy of Fig. 2

Fig. 2 is based on a collection of more or less self-explanatory geometric types—ELLIPSE, POLYGON, SQUARE, and so on.[1] What it shows is that, e.g., type CIRCLE is a subtype of supertype ELLIPSE, which means that all circles are ellipses but the converse is false (some ellipses aren't circles). As a consequence, all properties that apply to ellipses in general apply to—i.e., are inherited by—circles in particular, but the converse is false (circles have properties of their own that don't apply to ellipses in general). *Note:* "Properties" here means, primarily, *read-only operators* and *type constraints*; in other words, read-only operators and type constraints that apply to ellipses in general apply to circles in particular (because circles are ellipses), but read-only operators and type constraints that are specific to circles don't apply to mere ellipses (meaning ellipses that don't happen to be circles).

Here now in outline are the type definitions for types ELLIPSE and CIRCLE (other types omitted for space reasons):

```
TYPE ELLIPSE
     IS { PLANE_FIGURE
           POSSREP { A LENGTH , B LENGTH , CTR POINT
                     CONSTRAINT A ≥ B } } ;

TYPE CIRCLE
     IS { ELLIPSE
           CONSTRAINT THE_A ( ELLIPSE ) = THE_B ( ELLIPSE )
           POSSREP { R   = THE_A   ( ELLIPSE ) ,
                     CTR = THE_CTR ( ELLIPSE ) } } ;
```

Explanation:

- The definition for type ELLIPSE contains an IS specification indicating that every ellipse is a plane figure (in other words, type ELLIPSE is a subtype of type PLANE_FIGURE; hence, properties that apply to plane figures in general apply to ellipses in particular, because ellipses are plane figures). That IS specification also contains a POSSREP specification indicating that ellipses can possibly be represented by two lengths A and B and a point CTR (where, for a given ellipse *e*, A and B denote the lengths of *e*'s major and minor semiaxis, respectively, and CTR denotes the point that's *e*'s center).[2] *Note:* As in Part I of this dictionary, (a) I'm assuming the user defined types LENGTH and POINT have already been defined, and (b) to keep the example simple, I've omitted the constraint B > 0 that ought by rights to be specified as well.

---

[1] Note, however, that (e.g.) values of type ELLIPSE are really ellipses *at some specific location in two-dimensional space*; in other words, ellipses that occupy different positions in space but are otherwise identical are assumed for the sake of the example to be distinct (and similarly for rectangles, circles, etc.). Analogous remarks apply to Figs. 3-5 as well.

[2] For the sake of the example, ellipses are assumed always to have their major axis horizontal and their minor axis vertical, so that A, B, and CTR are indeed sufficient to serve as a possrep.

■ Likewise, the IS specification for type CIRCLE indicates that every circle "is a" ellipse (i.e., type CIRCLE is a subtype of type ELLIPSE). However, it also constrains the ellipse in question to have semiaxes of equal length. That CONSTRAINT specification is then followed by a POSSREP specification indicating (a) that circles can possibly be represented by a length R and a point CTR (where, for a given circle c, R denotes the length of c's radius and CTR denotes the point that's c's center), and indicating also (b) how that CIRCLE possrep is derived from the ELLIPSE possrep. Note the use of the supertype name ELLIPSE, within both the constraint and the derived possrep definition, to denote a specific ellipse—namely, the specific ellipse that the circle under consideration happens to be.

■ Any possrep for ellipses is necessarily, albeit implicitly, a possrep for circles as well, because circles are ellipses. (Of course, the converse is false—a possrep for circles isn't necessarily a possrep for ellipses.) Thus, possreps in particular might be regarded as further "properties" that are inherited by subtypes from supertypes. For technical reasons, however (*see* **possrep inheritance**), such an inherited possrep isn't considered to be a *declared* one in the sense in which this latter term is defined in Part I of this dictionary.

The Type Graph of Fig. 3

Turning now to the subtype / supertype relationships illustrated in Fig. 3, the following observations should suffice to show that those relationships make good intuitive sense:

■ Every parallelogram has a "long" diagonal of length ld and a "short" one of length sd, where $ld \geq sd$.

■ Every parallelogram also has two "long" sides of length ls and two "short" ones of length ss, where $ls \geq ss$.

■ A rectangle is a parallelogram for which $ld = sd$. Unlike parallelograms in general, every rectangle has a unique circumscribed circle (i.e., a circle that passes through each of that rectangle's four vertices); hence, every rectangle has a property that's unique to those parallelograms that happen to be rectangles—viz., that circumscribed circle.

■ A rhombus is a parallelogram for which $ls = ss$. Unlike parallelograms in general, every rhombus has a unique inscribed circle (i.e., a circle that touches each of that rhombus's four sides); hence, every rhombus has a property that's unique to those parallelograms that happen to be rhombi—viz., that inscribed circle.

■ A square is a parallelogram that is both a rectangle and a rhombus. Unlike rectangles and rhombi in general, every square has a unique associated annulus that's defined by the difference between the corresponding circumscribed and inscribed circles; hence, every square has a property that's unique to those parallelograms that happen to be both rectangles and rhombi—viz., that annulus. Moreover, every square has both (a) a unique side length, which rectangles in general don't have, and (b) a unique diagonal length, which rhombi in general don't have.

Here now are some possible type definitions. First, type PARALLELOGRAM:

```
TYPE PARALLELOGRAM
     POSSREP { A POINT , B POINT , C POINT , D POINT
               CONSTRAINT DISTINCT ( A , B , C , D )
                          AND NOT ( COLLINEAR ( A , B , C ) )
                          AND NOT ( COLLINEAR ( B , C , D ) )
                          AND NOT ( COLLINEAR ( C , D , A ) )
                          AND NOT ( COLLINEAR ( D , A , B ) )
                          AND DIST ( A , B ) = DIST ( C , D )
                          AND DIST ( B , C ) = DIST ( D , A ) } ;
```

Explanation:

■ Many different possreps could have been specified here; for simplicity, I show just one, consisting of the four vertices A, B, C, D. What's more, I'll use that same possrep for each of the other three types, again for simplicity.

■ DISTINCT returns TRUE if and only if its POINT arguments are all distinct. COLLINEAR returns TRUE if and only if its three POINT arguments lie on a straight line. DIST returns the distance between its two POINT arguments as a value of type LENGTH.

Next, types RECTANGLE and RHOMBUS (operators LD, SD, LS, and SS return the length of the long diagonal, short diagonal, long side, and short side, respectively, of a given parallelogram):

```
TYPE RECTANGLE
     IS { PARALLELOGRAM
          CONSTRAINT LD ( PARALLELOGRAM ) = SD ( PARALLELOGRAM )
          POSSREP { A = THE_A ( PARALLELOGRAM ) ,
                    B = THE_B ( PARALLELOGRAM ) ,
                    C = THE_C ( PARALLELOGRAM ) ,
                    D = THE_D ( PARALLELOGRAM ) } } ;

TYPE RHOMBUS
     IS { PARALLELOGRAM
          CONSTRAINT LS ( PARALLELOGRAM ) = SS ( PARALLELOGRAM )
          POSSREP { A = THE_A ( PARALLELOGRAM ) ,
                    B = THE_B ( PARALLELOGRAM ) ,
                    C = THE_C ( PARALLELOGRAM ) ,
                    D = THE_D ( PARALLELOGRAM ) } } ;
```

Finally, type SQUARE:

```
TYPE SQUARE
     IS { RECTANGLE , RHOMBUS
          POSSREP { A = THE_A ( RECTANGLE ) ,
                    B = THE_B ( RECTANGLE ) ,
                    C = THE_C ( RECTANGLE ) ,
                    D = THE_D ( RECTANGLE ) } } ;
```

Explanation:

■ The IS specification here states that a given value is of type SQUARE if and only if it's both of type RECTANGLE and of type RHOMBUS. No additional CONSTRAINT specification is needed, or indeed permitted.

■ The POSSREP specification defines a possrep for type SQUARE in terms of the possrep for type RECTANGLE. However, it could equally well have defined that possrep in terms of the possrep for type RHOMBUS instead—it would have made no difference.

An Extended Example

Certain of the entries in this part of the dictionary make use of the extended example shown in Fig. 4.

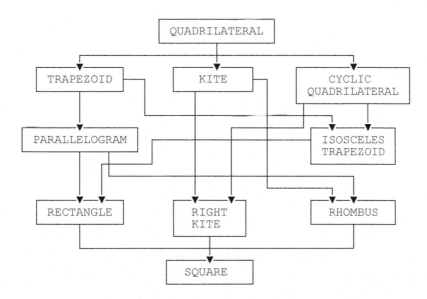

Fig. 4: An extended example

Explanation:

■ A trapezoid is a quadrilateral with at least one pair of opposite sides parallel. *Caveat:* Be aware that a quadrilateral with at least one pair of opposite sides parallel is called a trapezoid in the U.S. and a trapezium in the U.K., while a quadrilateral with possibly no parallel sides at all is called a trapezium in the U.S. and a trapezoid in the U.K.

■ A kite is a quadrilateral with mirror symmetry about a diagonal, such that no interior angle is greater than 180°. (If this latter condition isn't satisfied, the figure isn't a kite, it's a dart.) If ABCD is a kite (or a dart) that's symmetric about diagonal AC, then AB = AD and CB = CD.

■ A cyclic quadrilateral is a quadrilateral whose vertices lie on a circle. A quadrilateral is cyclic if and only if its opposite angles add up to 180°.

■ An isosceles trapezoid is a trapezoid with mirror symmetry about the line that connects the midpoints of its parallel sides. If ABCD is an isosceles trapezoid with AB parallel to CD, then (a) BC = AD and (b) the interior angles at A and B are equal, as are the interior angles at C and D.

■ A right kite is a kite in which the angles subtended by the diagonal of symmetry are right angles. If ABCD is a kite that is symmetric about diagonal AC, then the angles at B and D are right angles.

Tuple and Relation Inheritance

Consider the following set of tuple types:

```
TUPLE { E ELLIPSE , R RECTANGLE }    /* "tuple type ER" */
TUPLE { E CIRCLE  , R RECTANGLE }    /* "tuple type CR" */
TUPLE { E ELLIPSE , R SQUARE    }    /* "tuple type ES" */
TUPLE { E CIRCLE  , R SQUARE    }    /* "tuple type CS" */
```

Note the informal names for these types ("tuple type ER," etc.), as indicated in the comments. Now, observing with reference to Fig. 2 that CIRCLE is a subtype of ELLIPSE and SQUARE is a subtype of RECTANGLE, it should be clear that every tuple of type CS is also a tuple of type CR and a tuple of type ES, and further that every tuple of either type CR or type ES is also a tuple of type ER. Thus, it should be clear that type CS is a subtype of both type CR and type ES, and further that types CR and ES are both subtypes of type ER. In other words, tuple subtype / supertype relationships hold as indicated in the type graph of Fig. 5.

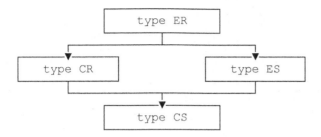

Fig. 5: Sample type graph (tuple or relation types)

The foregoing remarks apply to relation types also, mutatis mutandis. That is, given relation types as follows—

```
RELATION { E ELLIPSE , R RECTANGLE }    /* "relation type ER" */
RELATION { E CIRCLE  , R RECTANGLE }    /* "relation type CR" */
RELATION { E ELLIPSE , R SQUARE    }    /* "relation type ES" */
RELATION { E CIRCLE  , R SQUARE    }    /* "relation type CS" */
```

—it should be clear that relation type CS is a subtype of both relation types CR and ES, and further that relation types CR and ES are both subtypes of relation type ER. Thus, Fig. 5 can serve to depict these relation subtype / supertype relationships as well.

Possreps Revisited

With reference to Fig. 3 again, I said I'd give just one possrep for type PARALLELOGRAM, consisting of the four vertices A, B, C, D. Actually that possrep as specified is probably incomplete in at least one respect. To be specific, the very same parallelogram can clearly be specified by giving its vertices in any of several different orders; in some circumstances this state of affairs might not matter, but in general it will. In general, therefore, we'd need a way of pinning down the precise order in which the vertices are to be specified. For example, we might want to say they're specified in terms of increasing distance from the origin (but even then we'd still need a way of breaking ties). Further details are beyond the scope of this dictionary.

A Note on Tutorial D

The current version of **Tutorial D** (as defined in the book *Database Explorations: Essays on The Third Manifesto and Related Topics*, by C. J. Date and Hugh Darwen, Trafford, 2010) has no support for inheritance. However, Chapter 21 of that same book contains some proposals for extending the language to incorporate such support, and the name "**Tutorial D**" in this part of the dictionary should be understood as referring to a version of the language that has been extended in accordance with the proposals of that chapter.

———— ♦♦♦♦♦ ————

abstract type   (*With inheritance*) Term sometimes used to refer to a union type, q.v. (and a type that's not a union type is then sometimes called a concrete type accordingly). But the term *union type* better captures the essence of what such a type involves, and has a longer pedigree to boot; the term *abstract type* is thus not really appropriate for the concept at hand—especially since, as noted in Part I of this dictionary, it's also used with other meanings anyway—and its use in this context is therefore deprecated.

alpha   The maximal scalar type. Type *alpha* (a) contains all scalar values, (b) has no immediate supertype, and (c) is an immediate supertype for every scalar root type (with respect to the set of available types, q.v., in the case of (a) and (c)). Note that, by definition, type *alpha* is system defined; unique; primarily conceptual in nature; a dummy type, q.v. (and in fact a union type, q.v., except as noted below); and not a root type, q.v. Note further that the type constraint for *alpha* is simply TRUE; the expression IS_*alpha* (*exp*), where *exp* is any scalar expression, always evaluates to TRUE; and the expression TREAT_AS_*alpha* (*exp*), where *exp* is any scalar expression, always succeeds. *See also* **T_alpha**.

    Note: Consider the extreme, and pathological, case in which the set of available types contains just one regular type (necessarily type BOOLEAN). Then that type would itself be both the sole root type (q.v.) and the sole leaf type (q.v.), and it would satisfy property (a), though not property (b) or property (c). Moreover, in this case type *alpha* would be indistinguishable from type BOOLEAN and would thereby violate various other prescriptions of the *Manifesto* model, albeit only in minor ways. Apart from this pathological exception, however, no scalar type other than type *alpha* possesses or can possess any of properties (a), (b), and (c).

ancestor type   Term occasionally used to mean a proper supertype.

argument   (*With inheritance*) An actual operand that replaces—i.e., is substituted for—some parameter of some operator when the operator in question is invoked. Let *Op* be the operator in question, let *P* be a parameter to *Op*, let *T* be the declared type of *P*, and let *A* be the argument that replaces *P* in some invocation of *Op*. Also, for simplicity let *Op* not be a generic operator (see Part I of this dictionary). Then:

- ■ If *P* isn't subject to update, then *A* is a value, not a variable (though of course it might be denoted by some variable reference), and its most specific type can be any nonempty subtype of *T*. *See* **Principle of Value Substitutability**; **Principle of Read-Only Operator Inheritance**; signature.

- ■ By contrast, if *P* is subject to update, then *A* is a variable, not a value, and its most specific type can be either *T* or possibly (depending on circumstances) some proper but nonempty subtype of *T. See Principle of Variable Substitutability, Principle of Update Operator Inheritance*; signature.

Examples: Here's the definition of an operator called MOVE that, loosely speaking, moves a specified ellipse such that it becomes centered on the center of a specified rectangle (CTR here is a read-only operator that returns the center of its rectangle argument):

```
OPERATOR MOVE ( E ELLIPSE , R RECTANGLE ) RETURNS ELLIPSE ;
   RETURN ELLIPSE ( THE_A ( E ) , THE_B ( E ) , CTR ( R ) ) ;
END OPERATOR ;
```

This operator is read-only (neither of its parameters is subject to update). In an invocation, therefore, the argument that's substituted for the first parameter can be a value of any nonempty subtype of type ELLIPSE, and the argument that's substituted for the second parameter can be a value of any nonempty subtype of type RECTANGLE.

Here now by contrast is MOVE as an update operator:

```
OPERATOR MOVE ( E ELLIPSE , R RECTANGLE ) UPDATES { E } ;
   THE_CTR ( E ) := CTR ( R ) ;
END OPERATOR ;
```

With this revised definition, the argument that's substituted for the second parameter in an invocation can still be a value of any nonempty subtype of type RECTANGLE. However, the first parameter is now subject to update, so the argument that's substituted for that parameter must be a variable specifically, and that variable will be updated as a result of the invocation in question. Hence, the declared type of that variable must be such that assignment to THE_CTR of that variable makes sense. So that declared type can be ELLIPSE (of course), and it can also be CIRCLE. But suppose type CIRCLE has a proper subtype O_CIRCLE (where an "O-circle" is a circle with center the origin):

```
TYPE O_CIRCLE
     IS { CIRCLE
          CONSTRAINT THE_CTR ( CIRCLE ) = POINT ( 0.0 , 0.0 )
          POSSREP { R = THE_R ( CIRCLE ) } } ;
```

Then the argument that's substituted for the first MOVE parameter can't be of type O_CIRCLE, because the center of an O-circle is always the origin and can't be changed (see the CONSTRAINT specification in the foregoing definition). As far as the first parameter is concerned (i.e., the one that's subject to update), therefore, the update form of MOVE is defined for type ELLIPSE, is inherited by type CIRCLE, but isn't inherited by type O_CIRCLE. (It can't be inherited by any proper subtype of type O_CIRCLE, either, a fortiori. *See Principle of Update Operator Inheritance.*)

argument contravariance   A deprecated concept much discussed in the OO literature. The concept is hard to explain—*see Principle of Incoherence* in Part I of this dictionary—because it seems to be based on (a) a confusion between model and implementation, (b) a confusion between arguments and parameters, and quite possibly (c) a flawed definition of the subtype concept as well. (Regarding points (b) and (c) here, see the further remarks near the end of the present entry.) Be that as it may, consider *The Principle of Value Substitutability*, q.v. That principle requires that if (a) *Op* is an operator, (b) *P* is a parameter to *Op*, (c) *P* isn't subject to update, and (d) *T* is the declared type of *P*, then (e) the declared type *T'* of the argument expression—and therefore the most specific type of the argument as such—corresponding to *P* in any given invocation of *Op* must be some nonempty subtype of *T* (not necessarily a proper subtype, of course). Unfortunately, some systems not only fail to abide by this requirement but, in effect, claim their failure as a feature! Here's an example. Consider a read-only operator called MOVE—a variant on the operator with that same name discussed elsewhere in this part of the dictionary, as well as in Part I—which returns a result just like its first argument (an ellipse) except that it's centered on the center of its second (a square). Thus, the specification signature (q.v.) for this operator looks like this:

```
MOVE ( ELLIPSE , SQUARE ) RETURNS ELLIPSE
```

(The type names ELLIPSE and SQUARE within the parentheses here specify the declared type of the first and second parameter, respectively; the type name ELLIPSE following the keyword RETURNS specifies the declared type of the result.)

Now suppose distinct implementation versions (q.v.) of this operator—call them CMOVE and EMOVE—are provided for the case where the first argument is a circle and the case where it's "just an ellipse" (i.e., an ellipse that's not a circle), respectively, and consider what happens if MOVE is invoked with first argument a circle. At run time, then, thanks to the binding process (q.v.), the system will invoke CMOVE, not EMOVE. Since the second argument to that invocation is of type SQUARE (necessarily so), it follows that the declared type of the second parameter to CMOVE could have been some proper supertype of SQUARE, say RECTANGLE, and the type checking, at both compile time and run time, would still work. And this property—the property, that is, that if (a) *Op* is an operator with a parameter that (according to the pertinent specification signature) is of declared type *T*, and (b) *Op* is invoked with an argument corresponding to that parameter that's of some proper subtype of *T*, then (c) the declared type of some other parameter to the pertinent implementation version might be allowed to be some proper supertype of the type specified in the pertinent specification signature—is the "argument contravariance" property.

However, the notion of (in effect) allowing an operator to be invoked with an argument of type some proper supertype of the corresponding parameter declared type, as given by the pertinent specification signature, is surely more than a little suspect. In the case at hand, surely it would be better to define MOVE as having a specification signature that looks like this (note the revised declared type of the second parameter):

```
MOVE ( ELLIPSE , RECTANGLE ) RETURNS ELLIPSE
```

Now the user knows, because of value substitutability, q.v., that the arguments to any given MOVE invocation can be of any nonempty subtypes of ELLIPSE and RECTANGLE, respectively. In particular, of course, they can be of most specific types ELLIPSE and RECTANGLE as such, because every type is a subtype of itself. By contrast, the "argument covariance" property seems to be saying—in the example at hand, and now going back to the original specification signature—that MOVE can be invoked (a) with arguments of most specific types ELLIPSE and SQUARE, respectively, and (b) with arguments of most specific types CIRCLE and RECTANGLE, respectively (and therefore (c) with arguments of most specific types CIRCLE and SQUARE, respectively), but not (d) with arguments of most specific types ELLIPSE and RECTANGLE, respectively! As already noted, this state of affairs violates value substitutability—it could be argued that it violates orthogonality too—and is therefore strongly deprecated. In fact, there would be no need to introduce the argument contravariance concept at all if only value substitutability were taken seriously. ("Taking value substitutability seriously" here boils down merely to saying that every argument value should be allowed to have most specific type the same as the declared type of the corresponding parameter, as given by the pertinent specification signature. Indeed, not to allow such a state of affairs is surely perverse in the extreme.)

Note: In strong contradistinction to the foregoing, the property of result covariance, q.v., which is often spoken of in the same breath with argument contravariance, is both desirable and logically necessary.

A few further observations:

■ The term *argument contravariance* is presumably meant to reflect the fact that the type of one argument "contravaries" with that of another. But in a sense it's parameters that "contravary," not arguments, so at the very least the term ought really to be parameter contravariance (?).

■ There seems to be a tacit assumption underlying the terminology to the effect that there are exactly two parameters. In the case of MOVE (original version), there are indeed two parameters, which do seem to "contravary" (or so it might be argued, at least); but what if there had been three?

■ The "flawed definition" of the subtype concept mentioned earlier in this entry (at least, the relevant part of that definition) looks like this:

A type T' is a subtype of a type T if ... for each method M of T there is a corresponding method M' of T' such that ... the ith argument type of M is a subtype of the ith argument type of M' (*rule of contravariance in arguments*).

This definition—which is paraphrased just slightly from Elisa Bertino and Lorenzo Martino, *Object-Oriented Database Systems: Concepts and Architectures* (Addison-Wesley, 1993)—is flawed because it's circular: It defines the concept of some type being a subtype of another in terms of the concept of some type being a subtype of another. Note too the apparent confusion over arguments and parameters.

■ Here for interest is another definition from the OO literature (it's from Stanley B. Zdonik and David Maier, "Introduction to Object-Oriented Fundamentals," in *Readings in Object-Oriented Database Systems* (Zdonik and Maier, eds.; Morgan Kaufmann, 1990):

[The] important contravariance rule ... If function signatures are viewed as types for functions, then a function type **G** can be viewed as a subtype of a function type **F** if and only if the inputs to **F** are subtypes of the inputs to **G** and the result type of **G** is a subtype of the result type of **F**.

(Incidentally, note the sloppy phrasing here; to be specific, inputs aren't types, they have types.) Whether this definition is consistent with the explanations given previously is left as an exercise for the reader.

assignment (*With inheritance*) Let X and x be a variable and a value, respectively, such that the most specific type $MST(x)$ of x is some subtype of the declared type $DT(X)$ of X. Then (and only then) x can be assigned to X; the assignment has the effect of setting $v(X)$ equal to x and $MST(X)$ equal to $MST(x)$. *Note:* In order for the assignment to be syntactically valid, the declared type $DT(exp)$ of the expression *exp* used to denote the value x must be some subtype of the declared type $DT(X)$ of the variable X (this condition is implied by the fact that $MST(x)$ is required to be some subtype of $DT(X)$, and is a compile time check).

Examples: With reference to Fig. 2, let variables E and C be of declared types ELLIPSE and CIRCLE, respectively, and consider the following assignment:

```
E := C ;
```

In this example, compile time type checking succeeds ($DT(C)$ is a subtype of $DT(E)$), and at run time $v(E)$ and $MST(E)$ are set equal to $v(C)$ and $MST(C)$, respectively.

Now consider this assignment:

```
C := E ;
```

This example raises a compile time type error, because $DT(E)$ isn't a subtype of $DT(C)$. By contrast, if the expression E in this example were replaced by the expression TREAT_AS_CIRCLE (E), thus—

```
C := TREAT_AS_CIRCLE ( E ) ;
```

—then compile time type checking would succeed; however, this TREAT expression will raise a run time type error if *MST*(E) isn't some subtype of CIRCLE at run time. *See* TREAT; *see also* relation assignment; tuple assignment.

automatic definition *(With inheritance)* Defining a scalar type *T* automatically causes the following associated operators to be defined as well: (a) assignment (":="); (b) equality ("="); (c) IS_*T*, q.v.; (d) TREAT_AS_*T*, q.v.; and—so long as *T* is a regular type, q.v.—(e) at least one selector and at least one set of THE_ operators. *Note:* Operators analogous to the ones that are the subject of this entry are defined automatically for tuple and relation types as well, even though such types are generated instead of being explicitly defined. With regard to parts (c) and (d) of the definition in particular, *see* IS_SAME_TYPE_AS; TREAT_AS_SAME_TYPE_AS.

available types In any given situation there will be some specific set—necessarily nonempty, and effectively unbounded, though obviously finite—of types available for use. That set provides the context for certain of the concepts defined elsewhere in this dictionary. Obvious examples of such concepts are root type, q.v., and leaf type, q.v.; in other words, those concepts are relative, not absolute. For example, suppose *T* is a leaf type. Clearly, then, *T* will cease to be a leaf type if some new immediate subtype of *T* is introduced as an additional "available type."

Example: Given the type hierarchy of Fig. 2, the available types are (a) PLANE_FIGURE, ELLIPSE, CIRCLE, POLYGON, RECTANGLE, and SQUARE; (b) the types in terms of which the possreps for those types are defined; (c) the types in terms of which the possreps for the types included under (b), such as LENGTH and POINT, are defined (and so on, recursively, all the way down to and including the pertinent primitive types—see Part I of this dictionary); (d) the maximal scalar type *alpha*, q.v., and the minimal scalar type *omega*, q.v.; and (e) tuple and relation types that can be generated using any or all of these available types.

——— ♦♦♦♦♦ ———

base type *(With inheritance) See* extends relationship.

behavioral inheritance Somewhat deprecated term, used in OO contexts in particular, to refer to the fact that if type *T'* is a subtype of type *T*, then objects of type *T'* inherit the "behavior" of objects of type *T* (*see* behavior in Part I of this dictionary)—meaning in particular that if operator *Op* applies to objects of type *T*, it also applies to objects of type *T'*. *Contrast* structural inheritance. *Caveat:* Whether "objects" in the foregoing definition is intended to include variables as well as values is unclear (the answer might vary from system to system, and probably does). Likewise, whether "operator *Op*" is allowed to be an update operator and not just a read-only operator is also unclear (again the answer might vary from system to system, and probably does).

Note: The *Manifesto* inheritance model might be said (very loosely) to support behavioral inheritance, so long as (a) "objects" is indeed interpreted as including both values and variables and (b) "behavior" is interpreted in turn as including type constraints as well as operators. However, the "behavioral inheritance" in question applies to values and read-only operators unconditionally but to variables and update operators only where it makes sense. *See Principle of Value Substitutability; Principle of Variable Substitutability.*

binding   (*With inheritance*) The process of determining which implementation version of a given operator is to be executed in response to a given invocation of the operator in question. See the discussion under **implementation version** for examples and further explanation. Note that, as that discussion makes clear, binding—at least in the sense here defined—is an implementation concern, not a model concern (*but see* **changing semantics**). However, the *Manifesto* model does require that all arguments to the operator invocation in question participate equally in the binding process; in other words, it doesn't support the concept of selfish methods, q.v., nor the concept of a distinguished parameter, q.v., nor the concept of "messages," all of which it regards as both unnecessary and undesirable. *See also* **compile time binding; run time binding.**

———— ◆◆◆◆◆ ————

changing most specific type   (*Of a variable*) *See* **assignment; generalization; specialization.**

changing semantics   (*Of an operator*) *See* **implementation version.**

child type   Term occasionally used to mean an immediate subtype.

circular noncircle   A contradiction in terms, typical of the logical absurdities that can and do occur if S by C, q.v., and G by C, q.v., aren't supported, and used as a convenient shorthand to refer to such absurdities in general. To spell out the details of this particular solecism: Consider the type hierarchy of Fig. 2; however, let's agree for simplicity to ignore all of the types in that figure apart from types ELLIPSE and CIRCLE. Then a circular noncircle is something the system thinks isn't a circle but actually is—i.e., it's a value whose most specific type as far as the system is concerned is ELLIPSE and yet has equal semiaxis lengths, and thus logically ought to have most specific type CIRCLE. *Note:* Circular noncircles and suchlike solecisms can't occur in the *Manifesto* model. *See also* **noncircular circle.**

class hierarchy   *See* **type hierarchy.**

classification   Systems and languages (especially OO systems and languages) that use the term *class* to mean a type—see Part I of this dictionary—sometimes also use the term *classification* to refer to the process, or the result of the process, of determining the type(s) possessed by some object.

code reuse 1. (*Of implementation versions*) Loosely, using the type *T* implementation version of some operator *Op* to operate without change on values or variables of some proper subtype *T'* of *T*. *See* **implementation version**. 2. (*Of application programs*) Using an application program that operates on values or variables of type *T* to operate without change on values or variables of some proper subtype *T'* of *T*. Note that the amount of such application program reuse achievable in practice is likely to be quite limited if G by C, q.v., isn't supported. *See Principle of Update Operator Inheritance*. 3. (*Via delegation*) *See* **delegation**.

coercion vs. substitutability It's sometimes argued that permitting coercions (see Part I of this dictionary) can undermine the goal of value substitutability, q.v. Essentially, that argument goes something like this. Suppose for the sake of discussion that type INTEGER (integers) is defined to be a subtype of type RATIONAL (rational numbers). Then:

■ By definition, every integer is a rational number.

■ Therefore, any code that works for rational numbers should also work for integers, even if type INTEGER hadn't been defined when the code in question was written (*see* **code reuse**). *Note:* Let's agree throughout this discussion that the code in question concerns itself with rational number (or integer) values only, and not with rational number (or integer) variables. The reason is that value substitutability works unconditionally but variable substitutability works only conditionally, and it's better not to get sidetracked into issues that are secondary to the main point of the discussion. *See Principle of Value Substitutability, Principle of Variable Substitutability*.

■ In other words, it should be possible to invoke such code and pass it an integer instead of a rational number and have it still work.

■ Thus, wherever a rational number is expected, it should be possible to substitute an integer.

■ However, value substitutability also requires that even if an integer is substituted for a rational number in this way, it remains an integer and retains an integer's specific properties—e.g., the property of having a successor. (Note that, in mathematics at least if not in computer science, rational numbers don't have successors; that is, if *r* is a rational number, there's no such thing as "the next" rational number after *r*.)

■ But if passing an integer when a rational number is expected were to cause that integer to be coerced to type RATIONAL, then that integer would become "just a rational number" (thus ceasing to be an integer as such) and would thereby lose its specific properties.

■ Therefore—it's claimed—coercions undermine value substitutability.

But the foregoing argument is incorrect. Suppose for a moment that INTEGER isn't defined to be a subtype of RATIONAL after all. Then:

■ The concept of value substitutability doesn't arise (i.e., integers can't be substituted for rationals).

■ Therefore the idea of converting integers to rationals seems useful.

■ Therefore it seems reasonable to assume that an operator to perform such conversions will have been defined.

■ Therefore no harm is done to value substitutability by invoking that conversion operator implicitly in, e.g., an INTEGER-to-RATIONAL comparison or an INTEGER-to-RATIONAL assignment. To be more specific, value substitutability isn't undermined because, as already noted, the concept simply doesn't apply.

Alternatively, suppose INTEGER *is* defined to be a subtype of RATIONAL. Then:

■ Integers can be substituted for rationals (i.e., value substitutability does apply).

■ Therefore there's no point in defining an operator to convert integers to rationals, because integers *are* rationals.

■ Therefore no such operator will be defined.

■ Therefore the question of invoking such an operator implicitly simply doesn't arise, and so (again) value substitutability isn't undermined.

In other words, coercions are likely to be useful precisely in those situations where substitutability doesn't apply. Of course, it's true that (as noted in Part I of this dictionary) prohibiting coercions in general is a good idea anyway, for a variety of reasons; however, undermining value substitutability isn't one of them.

One final point: Actually, the idea of defining type INTEGER to be a subtype of type RATIONAL is more than a little suspect, as is shown in Chapter 22 ("Numeric Data Types") of *Database Explorations: Essays on The Third Manifesto and Related Topics*, by C. J. Date and Hugh Darwen (Trafford, 2010). However, this state of affairs doesn't undermine the foregoing argument in any essential respect.

colored circle   A typical example of the kind of construct often but misleadingly used to illustrate inheritance ideas—"misleadingly," because the idea that type COLORED_CIRCLE ("colored circles") is a plausible example of a proper subtype of type CIRCLE ("just plain circles") might sound reasonable but isn't. Here are some reasons why not. Let type T' be a proper subtype of type T. Then:

■ There can't be more values of type T' than there are of type T (*see* **subtype**). But—on the assumption that two circles that differ in color but are otherwise identical are the same circle but different colored circles—there are clearly more colored circles than there are just plain circles.

■ If S is a selector for type T, then every value of type T—including values of type T' in particular—must be producible by means of some invocation of S. But no invocation of any selector for type CIRCLE can possibly produce a value of type COLORED_CIRCLE, because no such selector has a color parameter.

■ Every possrep for type T is a possrep for type T' also, at least implicitly. But no CIRCLE possrep is a possrep for type COLORED_CIRCLE, because no such possrep has a color component.

■ There's no way to obtain a colored circle from a circle via S by C, q.v.—i.e., there's no constraint that can be specified for type COLORED_CIRCLE that, if satisfied by some value of type CIRCLE, means the circle in question is really a colored circle (because, to say it again, no CIRCLE possrep has a color component, and any such constraint would necessarily have to be expressed in terms of some such possrep).

It follows that colored circles in particular aren't a special case of circles in general; rather, they're images (on a display screen, perhaps), whereas circles as such aren't images but abstract geometric figures. Thus, it seems reasonable to regard COLORED_CIRCLE not as a subtype of CIRCLE but rather as a completely separate type. Now, that separate type will almost certainly have a possrep in which one component is of type CIRCLE, perhaps as follows (irrelevant details omitted):

```
TYPE COLORED_CIRCLE POSSREP { CIR CIRCLE , COL COLOR } ;
```

To repeat, however, this type isn't a subtype of type CIRCLE; in fact, it's no more a subtype of type CIRCLE than it is a subtype of type COLOR. Another, albeit informal, way of saying the same thing is to say that every colored circle has a circle property but isn't a circle (just as it has a color property but isn't a color). In other words, the relationship between colored circles (i.e., images) and circles as such (i.e., abstract figures) is the HAS A relationship, q.v., not the IS A relationship, q.v., that characterizes subtyping as such. *See also* **extends relationship**.

Note: If (as in the example above) type COLORED_CIRCLE does indeed have a possrep *PR* in which one component is of type CIRCLE, then (e.g.) the operator—call it CTR—that returns the center of a given colored circle is basically just the THE_CTR operator that applies to the CIRCLE component CIR of *PR*. In other words, the example illustrates the notion of delegation, q.v.: The responsibility for implementing CTR for type COLORED_CIRCLE is delegated to the type, CIRCLE, of a certain component of a certain possrep for that type (where "that type" is type COLORED_CIRCLE, in the example under consideration). Indeed, it seems plausible to suggest in general that the IS A relationship—i.e., subtyping as such—leads to inclusion polymorphism, q.v., while the HAS A relationship leads to delegation, q.v.

common subtype   Let $T1, T2, ..., Tm$ ($m \geq 0$) be types from the same type lattice, q.v. Then type T' is a common subtype for types $T1, T2, ..., Tm$ if and only if, whenever a given value is of type T', it's also of each of types $T1, T2, ..., Tm$. (More formally, T' is a common subtype for $T1, T2, ..., Tm$ if and only if the following predicate—

```
FORALL v ( IF v ∈ T' THEN v ∈ INTERSECT { T1 , T2 , ..., Tm } )
```

—is satisfied by T'.) Note that T' must necessarily be from the same type lattice as $T1, T2, ..., Tm$. Note too that every such set of types $T1, T2, ..., Tm$ does have at least one common subtype, though it might be one of those specified types $T1, T2, ..., Tm$, or even the pertinent minimal type. Note finally that (a) if $m = 1$, then the set of types $T1, T2, ..., Tm$ reduces to just $T1$, and $T1$ itself is a common subtype for that set; (b) if $m = 0$, then the set of types $T1, T2, ..., Tm$ is empty, and every type in the pertinent type lattice, including both the pertinent maximal type and the pertinent minimal type in particular, is a common subtype for that set. *See also* least specific common subtype; most specific common subtype. *Contrast* common supertype.

    Examples: With reference to Fig. 4, (a) SQUARE is a common subtype for RECTANGLE, RIGHT KITE, and RHOMBUS; (b) SQUARE is also a common subtype for TRAPEZOID and CYCLIC QUADRILATERAL; (c) KITE is a common subtype for KITE and QUADRILATERAL; (d) *omega* is a common subtype for every subset of the set of types in the figure; and so on. *Note:* For examples involving tuple and relation types, *see* common subtype (tuple types) and common subtype (relation types), respectively.

common subtype (relation types)   Let $T1, T2, ..., Tm$ ($m \geq 0$) be relation types from the same type lattice, q.v.; by definition, then, those types all have the same attribute names, say $A1, A2, ..., An$ ($n \geq 0$). Let the type of attribute Aj ($j = 1, 2, ..., n$) within type Ti ($i = 1, 2, ..., m$) be Tij. Then type T' = RELATION $\{<A1,T01'>,<A2,T02'>,...,<An,T0n'>\}$ is a common subtype for types $T1, T2, ..., Tm$ if and only if, for all j ($j = 1, 2, ..., n$), type $T0j'$ is a common subtype for types $T1j, T2j, ..., Tmj$. *See also* common subtype; *contrast* common supertype (relation types).

    Examples: With reference to Fig. 5, (a) relation type CS is a common subtype for relation types CR and ES; (b) relation type CS is also a common subtype for relation types ES and ER; (c) relation type ES is also a common subtype for relation types ES and ER; (d) type RELATION {E *omega*, R *omega*}—which contains just one value, viz., an empty relation—is a common subtype for every subset of the set of relation types in the figure; and so on.

common subtype (tuple types)   Let $T1, T2, ..., Tm$ $(m \geq 0)$ be tuple types from the same type lattice, q.v.; by definition, then, those types all have the same attribute names, say $A1, A2, ..., An$ $(n \geq 0)$. Let the type of attribute Aj $(j = 1, 2, ..., n)$ within type Ti $(i = 1, 2, ..., m)$ be Tij. Then type $T' = $ TUPLE $\{<A1,T01'>,<A2,T02'>,...,<An,T0n'>\}$ is a common subtype for types $T1, T2,$ $..., Tm$ if and only if, for all j $(j = 1, 2, ..., n)$, type $T0j'$ is a common subtype for types $T1j, T2j, ...,$ Tmj. *See also* **common subtype;** *contrast* **common supertype (tuple types).**

Examples: With reference to Fig. 5, (a) tuple type CS is a common subtype for tuple types CR and ES; (b) tuple type CS is also a common subtype for tuple types ER and ES; (c) tuple type ES is also a common subtype for tuple types ES and ER; (d) type TUPLE {E *omega*, R *omega*}—which is an empty type—is a common subtype for every subset of the set of tuple types in the figure; and so on.

common supertype   Let $T1, T2, ..., Tm$ $(m \geq 0)$ be types from the same type lattice, q.v. Then type T is a common supertype for types $T1, T2, ..., Tm$ if and only if, whenever a given value is of any of types $T1, T2, ..., Tm$, it's also of type T. (More formally, T is a common supertype for $T1, T2, ..., Tm$ if and only if the following predicate—

```
FORALL v ( IF v ∈ UNION { T1 , T2 , ..., Tm } THEN v ∈ T )
```

—is satisfied by T.) Note that T must necessarily be from the same type lattice as $T1, T2, ..., Tm$. Note too that every such set of types $T1, T2, ..., Tm$ does have at least one common supertype, though it might be one of those specified types $T1, T2, ..., Tm$, or even the pertinent maximal type. Note finally that (a) if $m = 1$, then the set of types $T1, T2, ..., Tm$ reduces to just $T1$, and $T1$ itself is a common supertype for that set; (b) if $m = 0$, then the set of types $T1, T2, ..., Tm$ is empty, and every type in the pertinent type lattice, including the pertinent maximal type and the pertinent minimal type in particular, is a common supertype for that set. *See also* **least specific common supertype; most specific common supertype.** *Contrast* **common subtype.**

Examples: With reference to Fig. 4, (a) QUADRILATERAL is a common supertype for RECTANGLE, RIGHT KITE, and RHOMBUS; (b) KITE is a common supertype for RIGHT KITE and RHOMBUS; (c) KITE is a common supertype for KITE and RHOMBUS; (d) *alpha* is a common supertype for every subset of the set of types in the figure; and so on. *Note:* For examples involving tuple and relation types, *see* **common supertype (tuple types)** and **common supertype (relation types),** respectively.

common supertype (relation types)   Let $T1, T2, ..., Tm$ $(m \geq 0)$ be relation types from the same type lattice, q.v.; by definition, then, those types all have the same attribute names, say $A1,$ $A2, ..., An$ $(n \geq 0)$. Let the type of attribute Aj $(j = 1, 2, ..., n)$ within type Ti $(i = 1, 2, ..., m)$ be Tij. Then type $T = $ RELATION $\{<A1,T01>,<A2,T02>,...,<An,T0n>\}$ is a common supertype for types $T1, T2, ..., Tm$ if and only if, for all j $(j = 1, 2, ..., n)$, type $T0j$ is a common supertype for types $T1j, T2j, ..., Tmj$. *See also* **common supertype;** *contrast* **common subtype (relation types).**

Examples: With reference to Fig. 5, (a) relation type ER is a common supertype for relation types CR and ES; (b) relation type ER is also a common supertype for relation types ER and ES; (c) relation type CR is a common supertype for relation types CR and CS; (d) type RELATION {E *alpha*, R *alpha*} is a common supertype for every subset of the set of relation types in the figure; and so on.

common supertype (tuple types)   Let $T1, T2, ..., Tm$ $(m \geq 0)$ be tuple types from the same type lattice, q.v.; by definition, then, those types all have the same attribute names, say $A1, A2,$ $..., An$ $(n \geq 0)$. Let the type of attribute Aj $(j = 1, 2, ..., n)$ within type Ti $(i = 1, 2, ..., m)$ be Tij. Then type $T = $ TUPLE $\{<A1,T01>,<A2,T02>,...,<An,T0n>\}$ is a common supertype for types $T1,$ $T2, ..., Tm$ if and only if, for all j $(j = 1, 2, ..., n)$, type $T0j$ is a common supertype for types $T1j,$ $T2j, ..., Tmj$. *See also* **common supertype**; *contrast* **common subtype (tuple types)**.

Examples: With reference to Fig. 5, (a) tuple type ER is a common supertype for tuple types CR and ES; (b) tuple type ER is also a common supertype for tuple types ER and ES; (c) tuple type CR is a common supertype for tuple types CR and CS; (d) type TUPLE {E *alpha*, R *alpha*} is a common supertype for every subset of the set of tuple types in the figure; and so on.

compile time binding   As noted under binding, q.v., the term *binding* is used in the inheritance context to refer to the process of determining which implementation version of a given operator is to be executed in response to a given invocation of the operator in question. Such binding can be done at compile time or run time or both. Compile time binding in particular (at least as that term is understood in the *Manifesto* model) can be defined thus: Given an expression *exp* denoting an invocation of some operator *Op*, it's the process of finding, at compile time, the unique invocation signature for *Op*—*see* **signature**—for which the declared types of the parameters exactly match the declared types of the corresponding argument expressions in *exp*, thereby causing the unique corresponding implementation version, q.v., of *Op* to be invoked at run time (unless the compiler's decision is overridden at run time by run time binding, q.v.). *Note:* In principle, binding can always be done at compile time—run time binding is logically unnecessary (though it might lead to better performance). *See* **implementation version** for further discussion; *see also* **run time binding**.

compile time type checking   Checking at compile time that the types of the arguments to an invocation of some operator conform to that operator's parameter type requirements, as specified by that operator's specification signature. In other words, given an expression *exp* that denotes an invocation of some operator *Op*, compile time type checking is the process of ensuring at compile time that there exists a unique invocation signature for *Op*—*see* **signature**—for which the declared types of the parameters exactly match the declared types of the corresponding argument expressions in *exp*. *Contrast* **run time type checking**.

compile time type error   The error that occurs if compile time type checking (q.v.) fails.

concrete type Term sometimes used, especially in systems that use the term *abstract type* to mean a union type, to mean a type that's not a union type. In other words, a concrete type is a type with the property that there exists at least one value having the type in question as its most specific type. But since (as noted under **abstract type**) the foregoing use of the term *abstract type* is deprecated, the term *concrete type* is deprecated also, somewhat.

CONSTRAINT (*With inheritance*) A **Tutorial D** construct, used in connection with the definition of type constraints for regular—and hence necessarily scalar—types. (It's also used in connection with database constraints. See Part I of this dictionary.) There are two basic cases to consider. First, if T is a regular root type, then the explanation from Part I of this dictionary applies unchanged, because all scalar types are regular root types in the absence of support for inheritance. So consider the second case, where T is a regular proper subtype. Let T have precisely one immediate supertype. (What happens if T has two or more immediate supertypes is described under **IS**, q.v.) This case in turn divides into two subsidiary cases: one where the immediate supertype is a dummy type, and one where it's a regular type. For an example of the first of these possibilities, let PLANE_FIGURE be a dummy type and let ELLIPSE be an immediate subtype of that dummy type (see Fig. 2). Then the ELLIPSE type definition might look like this (irrelevant details omitted):

```
TYPE ELLIPSE
     IS { PLANE_FIGURE
          POSSREP { A LENGTH , B LENGTH , CTR POINT
                    CONSTRAINT A ≥ B } } ;
```

This case is very similar to the first (where T is a regular root type), except that the POSSREP specification and implicit or explicit CONSTRAINT specification—which is actually part of that POSSREP specification—are now part of the IS specification (*see* **IS**). The type constraint for type ELLIPSE here is exactly the same as it would have been if that type had been a regular root type.

Turning now to the case where the immediate supertype is a regular type instead of a dummy type, consider type CIRCLE, which has just one immediate supertype (ELLIPSE), which is indeed a regular type (again, see Fig. 2). The CIRCLE type definition might look like this (irrelevant details omitted):

```
TYPE CIRCLE
     IS { ELLIPSE
          CONSTRAINT THE_A ( ELLIPSE ) = THE_B ( ELLIPSE )
          POSSREP { R   = THE_A   ( ELLIPSE ) ,
                    CTR = THE_CTR ( ELLIPSE ) } } ;
```

Now the CONSTRAINT specification—which in cases like the one under discussion must be stated explicitly—is part of the IS specification, not the POSSREP specification (which is likewise part of the IS specification and now defines a derived possrep, q.v.). Let c be a scalar value. Then *c* is a value of type CIRCLE if and only if the following constraint—call it *CTC*—is satisfied: The value *c* is of type ELLIPSE, and so has a major semiaxis of length *a* and a minor semiaxis of length *b*, and *a* = *b*. *CTC* here is the type constraint for type ELLIPSE. Note, therefore, that (as in fact was pointed out under CONSTRAINT in Part I of this dictionary) the CONSTRAINT specification as such doesn't define the type constraint in its entirety, though it's often referred to informally as if it did.

constraint inheritance   Inheritance of type constraints. *See* type inheritance.

containment hierarchy   A term used in OO systems to refer (somewhat loosely) to an object that contains other objects or an object type that's defined to contain other object types. For example, a department object might contain a set of employee objects, and the relationship from departments to employees is thus indeed one of containment. Moreover, that relationship is hierarchic, in that the containing object can be regarded as superior, in a sense, to the contained objects (likewise, of course, the contained objects can be regarded as inferior, in a sense, to the containing object).

    Note: Actually there's some confusion, or even sleight of hand, here. Typically, the "containing" object doesn't really contain the "contained" objects; instead, it contains object IDs of—i.e., pointers to—those "contained" objects, and these latter objects might thus be "contained" in several distinct "containing" objects simultaneously. If such is indeed the case, the semantics are, of course, quite different. For example, does deleting the containing object cascade to delete the contained objects? The answer is probably yes if those contained objects truly are contained, no if not (because in the latter case it's likely that it'll just be the pointers that are deleted, not the "contained objects" as such).

contravariance   *See* argument contravariance.

covariance   *See* result covariance.

current most specific type   Same as most specific type (of a variable in particular).

current type   Abbreviation for current most specific type, q.v.

declared type   (*With inheritance*) 1. (*Of a constant, variable, attribute, or parameter*) The type specified when the constant, variable, attribute, or parameter in question is declared. 2. (*Of a read-only operator*) The type of the result, specified when the operator in question is declared. Note, however, that the concept of operator declared type, as such, isn't all that important in the inheritance context; what's more important is the related concept of the declared type of an invocation of the operator in question, which largely subsumes the former notion (*see* **signature**

for further explanation). 3. (*Of an expression*) Let *exp* be a read-only operator invocation (note that constant, variable, attribute, and parameter references can all be regarded as read-only operator invocations, as can literals also). Then the declared type of *exp* is the declared type of the pertinent invocation signature (again, *see* **signature** for further explanation). *Note:* If *exp* is in fact a constant, variable, attribute, or parameter reference or a literal, the declared type of the pertinent invocation signature is of course just the declared type of the constant, variable, attribute, parameter, or literal in question. *See also* **most specific type (relation types)**.

Note: Elsewhere in this part of the dictionary, the declared type of some construct X is denoted $DT(X)$. Note that $DT(X)$ can be empty only if X is an attribute of some tuple or relation type. (This latter point applies to attributes of minimal tuple and relation types, q.v., in particular. However, a tuple or relation type doesn't have to be a minimal type in order to have such an attribute.)

delegation A mechanism according to which the implementation of some operator Op is delegated to—i.e., defined in terms of—the analog of Op on some component(s) of some possrep(s) for the parameter(s) to Op. For example, suppose type LENGTH has a possrep consisting of a single component, say M, of type RATIONAL. Then the operator for adding two lengths can be implemented in terms of regular rational addition on the pertinent M values; in other words, the responsibility for implementing addition for type LENGTH can be delegated to the type, RATIONAL, of a certain component of one of its possreps, and some code reuse can thus be obtained. However, delegation has nothing to do with type inheritance as such, even though code reuse is indeed one of the objectives of type inheritance. *See* **colored circle; HAS A**. *Note:* The operator being implemented and the operator providing the implementation will very likely have the same name—for example, the name "+" might be used both for addition of rational numbers and for addition of lengths—in which case that name will be overloaded. *See* **overloading polymorphism** in Part I of this dictionary.

DELETE ONLY Let T' be a subtable of supertable T (*see* **subtables and supertables**). Then DELETE ONLY is an operator—not supported by SQL, incidentally, even though SQL does support subtables and supertables as such—that deletes a row from T' without simultaneously deleting the corresponding row from T.

Example: With reference to the example under **subtables and supertables**, it should be possible to use DELETE ONLY to delete a row from table PGMR without at the same time deleting the corresponding row from table EMP, to reflect the fact that some existing employee has ceased to be a programmer.

derived possrep Let T' be a regular type with at least one regular immediate supertype. Then each possrep specified for type T' is a derived possrep, explicitly derived in some way from—in fact, explicitly defined in terms of—some possrep for some regular immediate supertype of type T'. Note that there's a logical difference between a derived possrep and an inherited one (*see* **possrep inheritance**), as follows. First, to repeat, a derived possrep for type T' is explicitly declared for that type *T'*, and it's defined in terms of some possrep for some regular immediate supertype of that type *T'*. By contrast, an inherited possrep for type *T'* isn't explicitly declared for that type *T'*; rather, it's simply any possrep—derived, inherited, or otherwise—that applies to some regular immediate supertype of type *T'*, and hence applies to type *T'* as well a fortiori.

Example: With reference to Fig. 2, the sole possrep for type CIRCLE—a derived possrep, by definition—is defined as follows:

```
POSSREP { R   = THE_A   ( ELLIPSE ) ,
          CTR = THE_CTR ( ELLIPSE ) } } ;
```

In other words, circles can possibly be represented by a length *r* and a point *ctr*. The length *r* is identical to the *a* component of a certain possrep that applies to type ELLIPSE; likewise, the point *ctr* is identical to the *ctr* component of that same ELLIPSE possrep. Thus, the explicitly specified possrep shown for type CIRCLE is derived from, or defined in terms of, a certain possrep—actually the only one explicitly declared—for type ELLIPSE.

Incidentally, note that it's perfectly possible for some type *T'* to have a possrep *PR'* that differs markedly from any of the possreps declared for the pertinent immediate supertype *T*, even though as just explained *PR'* is necessarily derived from one of those possreps for *T*. For example, let *T* and *T'* be POLYGON and RECTANGLE, respectively. Then *T* might have a possrep *PR* consisting of a sequence of *n* points, representing the *n* vertices of the polygon in some specific order, while *T'* has a possrep *PR'* consisting of a pair of points, representing the center and the bottom left vertex of the rectangle. (The assumption here is that rectangles always have their long side horizontal and their short side vertical, so that the center and the bottom left vertex can indeed validly serve as a possrep.) Nevertheless, it's still the case—in fact, it must be the case—that if *PR* is a possrep for *T*, then every explicitly declared possrep *PR'* for *T'* is expressible in terms of, and thus derivable from, *PR*.

derived type   *See* extends relationship.

derived type graph   Not a graph of derived types (q.v.), but a type graph that's derived from another type graph. Let *TG* be a type graph, q.v.; then *TG* can be divided into a set of disjoint partitions—a nonempty set, unless *TG* itself is empty—such that (a) each partition in the set has exactly one root node and one or more leaf nodes, and (b) no type in any partition in the set overlaps any type in any other partition in the set. Then:

- Let *G* be a graph obtained from *TG* by removing zero or more partitions. Then *G* is a derived type graph—specifically, a type graph derived from *TG*. *Note:* It follows that *TG* itself and the empty graph can both be regarded as type graphs derived from *TG*.

- Let *G* be a type graph derived from *TG*; let *P* be a partition within *G*; and let *P* be in fact a type hierarchy, q.v. Then any graph obtained from *G* by replacing *P* by some type hierarchy derived from *P* (*see* **derived type hierarchy**) is a derived type graph—again, a type graph derived from *TG*.

derived type hierarchy   Not a hierarchy of derived types (q.v.), but a type hierarchy that's derived from another type hierarchy. Let *TH* be a type hierarchy, q.v. Then:

■ *TH* itself is considered to be a type hierarchy derived from *TH*.

■ Let *DH* be a graph obtained from *TH* by choosing the node corresponding to some type *T* and removing (a) all nodes not corresponding to some subtype *T'* of *T* and (b) all arcs emanating from those nodes. Then *DH* is a derived type hierarchy, with *T* as its root—specifically, a type hierarchy derived from *TH*.

■ Let *DH* be a type hierarchy derived from *TH*. Then any graph obtained from *DH* by removing the node corresponding to some type *T* is a derived type hierarchy, with the root of *DH* as its root (unless the node corresponding to the root of *DH* was the one deleted)—specifically, a type hierarchy derived from *TH*—provided that removal of a node is always accompanied by removal of (a) the arc, if any, entering into that node and (b) all corresponding immediate subtype nodes. *Note:* It follows that the empty graph can be regarded as a type hierarchy derived from *TH*.

By contrast, if (a) *TH* is a type hierarchy with root *T*, and if (b) type *T* is an immediate supertype of type *T'* and type *T'* is an immediate supertype of type *T''* (and if—let's assume for simplicity—type *T'* is an immediate supertype of no type other than type *T''*), and if (c) *XH* is the graph derived from *TH* by removing node *T'* and coalescing the arc connecting nodes *T* and *T'* and the arc connecting nodes *T'* and *T''* into a single arc connecting nodes *T* and *T''*, then (d) *XH* is not a derived type hierarchy (at least, not one that can be derived from *TH*), because it causes *T''* to lose some of its inheritance, as it were.

Examples: The following are all type hierarchies that can be derived from the type hierarchy of Fig. 2 (assuming in all cases that pertinent connecting arcs are retained):

■ The graph that's obtained by removing all nodes except POLYGON, RECTANGLE, and SQUARE

■ The graph that's obtained by removing all nodes except POLYGON and RECTANGLE

■ The graph that's obtained by removing just the CIRCLE and SQUARE nodes

■ The graph that's obtained by removing all nodes

(and so on). By contrast, the graph that's obtained by removing all nodes except POLYGON and SQUARE isn't a derived type hierarchy—at least, not one that can be derived from the type hierarchy of Fig. 2. *Note:* As a matter of interest, there are exactly 22 distinct type hierarchies that can be derived from the type hierarchy of Fig. 2.

descendant type   Term occasionally used to mean a proper subtype.

difference   (*With inheritance*) *See* dyadic relational operators.

direct subtype   SQL term for an immediate subtype.

direct supertype   SQL term for an immediate supertype.

disjoint types   Types *T1* and *T2* are disjoint if and only if no value is a value of both. Note that:

- If *T1* and *T2* are distinct scalar leaf types, they're certainly disjoint.

- If *T1* and *T2* are distinct scalar types, they're certainly disjoint if one is type *omega*.

- If *T1* and *T2* are distinct root types (scalar or otherwise), they're certainly disjoint.

- If *T1* and *T2* are from distinct type lattices, they're certainly disjoint.

- If *T1* and *T2* are distinct leaf types from the same tuple type lattice, they're certainly disjoint.

- If *T1* and *T2* are distinct types from the same relation type lattice, they're not disjoint, even if they're leaf types or if one is the pertinent minimal type.

Contrast overlapping types.
    Examples: 1. With reference to Fig. 2, scalar types ELLIPSE and RECTANGLE are disjoint; by contrast, with reference to Fig. 3, scalar types RECTANGLE and RHOMBUS overlap. 2. With reference to Fig. 5, tuple types CR and ES overlap, as do tuple types ER and CS (in this latter case, of course, one is a proper subtype of the other). 3. Let scalar type PARALLELOGRAM be a union type, with immediate subtypes RECTANGLE and NONRECTANGLE (with the intuitively obvious semantics), and consider relation types RELATION {P RECTANGLE} and RELATION {P NONRECTANGLE}. Then these relation types might be thought to be disjoint, but they're not. The reason is that the empty relation of type RELATION {P PARALLELOGRAM} is a value of both of them. In fact, that empty relation—whose most specific type is RELATION {P *omega*}, incidentally—is a value of every

type in the pertinent type lattice, including even the corresponding minimal type RELATION {P *omega*}.

disjointness assumption   A simplifying assumption, valid with single but not multiple inheritance, to the effect that types *T1* and *T2* are disjoint if and only if neither is a subtype of the other. Note, however, that single inheritance is possible in general only with scalar types (and even then only if type *omega* is ignored—but the fact that type *omega* is a subtype of every scalar type does not in and of itself violate the disjointness assumption).

   Examples: With reference to Fig. 2, let *T1* and *T2* be any nonempty subtype of ELLIPSE and any nonempty subtype of POLYGON, respectively; then neither of types *T1* and *T2* is a subtype of the other, and they're disjoint.

   Note: It follows directly from the disjointness assumption that (a) distinct root types are disjoint; (b) distinct leaf types are disjoint; and (c) every value has a unique most specific type. (In fact, if *v* is a value of most specific type *T*, then the set of types possessed by *v* is, precisely, the set of all supertypes of *T*.) Now, it should be obvious that these properties hold with single inheritance; as a matter of fact, however, they hold with multiple inheritance as well, even though the disjointness assumption doesn't. In particular, therefore, they hold for tuple and relation types as well as for scalar types, even though (to say it again) the disjointness assumption doesn't.

dispatching / despatching   Terms sometimes used, especially in OO contexts, as synonyms for binding, q.v. (especially run time binding, q.v.). Here's a (very loose!) definition from the OO literature: "[Dispatching is the] execution of methods based on polymorphism" (from Douglas K. Barry, *The Object Database Handbook: How to Select, Implement, and Use Object-Oriented Databases,* Wiley Publishing, 1996).

distinguished parameter   *See* selfish method.

***DT* (...)**   Declared type of. *See* model of a variable; model of an expression.

dummy type   A given type *T* is a dummy type if and only if (a) it's either *alpha* or *omega*, q.v., or (b) all three of the following are true:

1. *T* is a union type, q.v. (and hence a scalar type, necessarily).

2. *T* has no declared possrep (and hence no selector and no "automatic" THE_ operators).

3. *T* has no regular supertype.

(In fact type *alpha* satisfies the second and third of these conditions anyway, and usually the first as well; type *omega* satisfies the first of them—albeit vacuously—and the second, but not the third.) Note that, by definition, (a) dummy types are always scalar (but see the further remarks below regarding tuple and relation types); (b) a dummy type has no values that aren't values of some regular proper subtype of the dummy type in question (*see* **regular type**); and (c) if *T* is a dummy type other than type *omega*, all of *T*'s proper supertypes are dummy types also. Note too, however, that—to spell the point out explicitly—defining a variable to be of type *T* is perfectly legitimate even if *T* is a dummy type, though of course such a variable can never have a value whose most specific type is *T*.

Examples: Consider the following outline type definitions (based on a revised version of the type hierarchy of Fig. 2):

```
TYPE ELLIPSE UNION
     IS { PLANE_FIGURE } ;

TYPE CIRCLE
     IS { ELLIPSE
          POSSREP { R LENGTH , CTR POINT } } ;

TYPE NONCIRCLE
     IS { ELLIPSE
          POSSREP { A LENGTH , B LENGTH , CTR POINT
                    CONSTRAINT A > B } } ;
```

Explanation:

■ Type ELLIPSE as defined here is a dummy type: It has no possrep, and therefore no possrep constraint, no selector, and no "automatic" THE_ operators. (It might have some explicit THE_ operators, though. See further discussion below.)

■ No variable can ever have a value of most specific type ELLIPSE, even if its declared type is ELLIPSE.

■ Type CIRCLE has a selector and THE_ operators THE_R and THE_CTR; type NONCIRCLE has a selector and THE_ operators THE_A, THE_B, and THE_CTR. Note in particular that the operators THE_A and THE_B don't apply to type CIRCLE.

■ Specialization by constraint (q.v.) doesn't apply to types CIRCLE and NONCIRCLE—i.e., there's no formal way, given these definitions, that a circle or a noncircle can be derived from an ellipse—because type ELLIPSE has no possrep in terms of which the pertinent specialization constraints (q.v.) can be formulated.

■ Let AREA_OF ("return the area of") be an operator that applies to both circles and noncircles. No implementation code can be provided for that operator at the ELLIPSE level, because type ELLIPSE has no possrep—and (let's assume for the sake of the example, at least) no physical representation either—in terms of which that code can be formulated. However, an appropriate specification signature, at least, can be defined at that level (*see* **signature**). In **Tutorial D**, that signature might look like this (note the declared type AREA of the result):

```
AREA_OF ( ELLIPSE ) RETURNS AREA
```

Two implementation versions will now have to be provided, one for circles and one for noncircles, perhaps as follows (note the explicit VERSION specifications):

```
OPERATOR AREA_OF VERSION C_AREA ( C CIRCLE ) RETURNS AREA ;
    RETURN 3.14159 * ( THE_R ( C ) ↑ 2 ) ;
END OPERATOR ;

OPERATOR AREA_OF VERSION NC_AREA ( NC NONCIRCLE ) RETURNS AREA ;
    RETURN 3.14159 * ( THE_A ( NC ) * THE_B ( NC ) ) ;
END OPERATOR ;
```

■ The foregoing discussion of operator AREA_OF gives some idea of the purpose of dummy types: Union types in general (q.v.) provide a way of specifying operators that apply to values or variables of several different types, all of them proper subtypes of the union type in question—and the same is true of dummy types in particular; the difference is simply that for some union types, there might not exist a reasonable possrep, in which case the union type in question thus becomes a dummy type (see further discussion below).

Now, the foregoing example isn't very realistic, because we could easily make ELLIPSE a regular union type (i.e., one with a possrep) instead of a dummy type, and then we could define an implementation version of AREA_OF at the ELLIPSE level that would work for both circles and noncircles (see the first example under **implementation version**). But consider type PLANE_FIGURE. That type would almost certainly be a dummy type—it's hard to think of a sensible possrep that could work for an arbitrary plane figure!—and so it might well make sense to define just a specification signature for AREA_OF at the PLANE_FIGURE level and implementation versions at (say) the ELLIPSE and POLYGON levels. *Note:* Actually the foregoing remarks are slightly oversimplified. *See* **signature** for further discussion.

Despite the foregoing, let's stay with the example of ELLIPSE as a dummy type, for simplicity. Observe now that the operator THE_CTR applies to both values of type CIRCLE and values of type NONCIRCLE—i.e., values of every proper subtype of type ELLIPSE—and yet not to values of type ELLIPSE itself. But such a state of affairs is clearly absurd; to say that every ellipse is either a circle or a noncircle, and circles and noncircles both have a center but ellipses don't, is an affront to common sense. The anomaly is easily fixed, however—we define THE_CTR *explicitly* to be an operator that applies at the ELLIPSE level, as follows (note that implementation versions of that operator are certainly available for both circles and noncircles):

```
OPERATOR THE_CTR VERSION E_CTR ( E ELLIPSE ) RETURNS POINT ;
   RETURN ( CASE
                WHEN IS_CIRCLE ( E ) THEN
                    THE_CTR ( TREAT_AS_CIRCLE ( E ) )
                WHEN IS_NONCIRCLE ( E ) THEN
                    THE_CTR ( TREAT_AS_NONCIRCLE ( E ) )
            END CASE ) ;
END OPERATOR ;
```

Note: Actually there's no need to define the implementation code for this operator as shown—it would be sufficient to define just the appropriate specification signature at the ELLIPSE level:

```
THE_CTR ( ELLIPSE ) RETURNS POINT
```

Here's another moderately realistic example of an operator for which implementation code can be—and this time definitely should be—defined at a dummy type level:

```
OPERATOR DOUBLE_AREA_OF
   VERSION PF_DOUBLE_AREA ( PF PLANE_FIGURE ) RETURNS AREA ;
   RETURN 2 * AREA_OF ( PF ) ;
END OPERATOR ;
```

What about tuple and relation dummy types? For definiteness, let's focus on tuple types specifically. Now, tuple types, like dummy types, have no declared possreps; unlike dummy types, however, they do have selectors (except in the very special case where the tuple type in question is empty, which can happen if and only if one of the attributes of the tuple type in question is an empty type in turn). Partly for such reasons, the concept of a "dummy tuple type" doesn't really make much sense (and the same goes for the concept of a "union tuple type," come to that). However, we might informally regard a tuple type that has at least one attribute of a dummy type as a dummy tuple type, if we wanted to. For example, suppose once again that scalar type ELLIPSE is a dummy type, with immediate regular subtypes CIRCLE and NONCIRCLE, and consider the following tuple types:

- `TUPLE { E ELLIPSE }`

There aren't any values of this type that aren't values of some proper subtype of the type; thus, the type might implicitly be considered a union tuple type, and in fact a dummy tuple type to boot. Such notions seem to serve little practical purpose, however, which is why they're not formally defined in this dictionary.

- `TUPLE { E CIRCLE , X alpha }`

This one too might be considered a tuple dummy type, if it were thought useful to do so.

■ `TUPLE { E omega }`

This is an example of an empty tuple type. It too might be regarded as a dummy tuple type.

Remarks analogous to the foregoing apply to relation types also, except that relation types are never empty (not even if they have an attribute of some empty type).

Now getting back to scalar types specifically: We've seen that if *T* is a dummy type, it has no possrep—but the converse isn't true. To be specific, certain system defined types (e.g., type INTEGER, perhaps) are allowed not to have a possrep; however, such types certainly aren't dummy types, because (a) values do exist whose most specific type is the type in question and (b) the system is required to provide at least one corresponding selector operator for each such type (*see* **selector** in Part I of this dictionary).

One final point: Some systems use dummy types to provide a kind of type generator facility. For example, RELATION might be defined as a dummy type in such a system, and then every specific relation type would be a proper subtype of that RELATION type. The *Manifesto* model rejects such a scheme, however, for the following reasons (and possibly others):

■ First, we don't want type generator support to be conditional on support for type inheritance.

■ Second, we certainly don't want to have to define specific implementation versions of the usual relational operators—restrict, project, join, and so on—for every specific relation type.

■ Third, we don't believe in the kind of "relation type inheritance" such a scheme would provide (it doesn't give us the kind of substitutability we want).

dyadic relational operators   Let relational expressions *R1* and *R2* denote relations *r1* and *r2*, respectively, and let *Ai* and *Aj* be attributes of *r1* and *r2*, respectively. Note that *Ai* can be regarded as an attribute of *R1* per se and *Aj* can be regarded as an attribute of *R2* per se. Let the declared types of *Ai* and *Aj* within *R1* and *R2* be *DT1* and *DT2*, respectively. Finally, let attributes <*A1,DT1*> and <*A2,DT2*> be said to *correspond* if and only if their names *Ai* and *Aj* are the same, *A* say, and their declared types *DTi* and *DTj* have a common supertype (i.e., *DTi* and *DTj* belong to the same type lattice, q.v.). Then the expressions *R1* UNION *R2*, *R1* INTERSECT *R2*, and *R1* MINUS *R2* are each defined if and only if each attribute of *R1* corresponds in the foregoing sense to some attribute of *R2* and vice versa. Moreover, for each pair of corresponding attributes <*A,DT1*> in *R1* and <*A,DT2*> in *R2*—here we change our notation slightly—the declared type *DT(A)* of attribute *A* within each of these expressions is as follows:

■ (*Union*) The most specific common supertype *DT* of *DT1* and *DT2*. *Note:* In practice, the implementation might want to outlaw, or at least flag, any attempt to form such a union if

DT is the pertinent maximal type (because such a situation probably constitutes an error on the user's part).

■ (*Intersection*) The least specific common subtype *DT'*—the intersection type, in fact—of *DT1* and *DT2*. *Note:* In practice, the implementation might want to outlaw, or at least flag, any attempt to form such an intersection if *DT'* is the pertinent minimal type (again because such a situation probably constitutes an error on the user's part).

■ (*Difference*) *DT1*. *Note:* In practice, the implementation might want to outlaw, or at least flag, any attempt to form such a difference if the most specific common supertype *DT* of *DT1* and *DT2* is the pertinent maximal type and/or if their least specific common subtype *DT'* is the pertinent minimal type (once again because either of these situations probably constitutes an error on the user's part).

Note: The concept of corresponding attributes is introduced purely for the purposes of the the foregoing definitions, in order to allow the rules regarding declared types to be stated precisely. In fact, however, those rules can be stated without using the notion of corresponding attributes at all, as follows. First, *DT(R1)* and *DT(R2)* must have a common supertype in all three cases. Then the declared type of each of the three expressions is as follows:

■ (*Union*) The most specific common supertype of *DT(R1)* and *DT(R2)*.

■ (*Intersection*) The least specific common subtype—the intersection type, in fact—of *DT(R1)* and *DT(R2)*.

■ (*Difference*) *DT(R1)*.

As for join, the expression *R1* JOIN *R2* is defined if and only if *r1* and *r2* are joinable, q.v. If they are, then for each pair of corresponding attributes *<A,DT1>* in *R1* and *<A,DT2>* in *R2*, the declared type of the corresponding attribute within that expression is the least specific common subtype—the intersection type, in fact—of *DT1* and *DT2*. (As for attributes in *r1* that have no corresponding attribute in *r2* or vice versa, such attributes simply become attributes of the result in the usual way.) *Note:* Of course, join is basically a generalization of intersection, and the declared type of the result overall is thus just the least specific common subtype—the intersection type, in fact—of *DT(R1)* and *DT(R2)*.

Examples: With reference to Fig. 3, let relations *r1* and *r2* be as follows:

```
r1                                r2
┌─────────────────────┐           ┌──────────────────┐
│ P  : RECTANGLE      │           │ P  : RHOMBUS     │
├─────────────────────┤           ├──────────────────┤
│ px : rectangle      │           │ py : square      │
│ py : square         │           │ pz : rhombus     │
└─────────────────────┘           └──────────────────┘
```

(Most specific types are shown in lowercase italics.) Then *r1* UNION *r2*, *r1* INTERSECT *r2*, and *r1* MINUS *r2* are as shown below (*r1* JOIN *r2* is identical to *r1* INTERSECT *r2* in this example). Note the result attribute declared types in particular.

```
r1 UNION r2                  r1 INTERSECT r2        r1 MINUS r2
┌─────────────────────┐      ┌───────────────┐      ┌──────────────────┐
│ P  : PARALLELOGRAM  │      │ P  : SQUARE   │      │ P  : RECTANGLE   │
├─────────────────────┤      ├───────────────┤      ├──────────────────┤
│ px : rectangle      │      │ py : square   │      │ px : rectangle   │
│ py : square         │      └───────────────┘      └──────────────────┘
│ pz : rhombus        │
└─────────────────────┘
```

Finally, the rules for other dyadic relational operators—D_UNION, I_MINUS, XUNION, MATCHING, NOT MATCHING, and COMPOSE—can be derived straightforwardly from the rules presented above for union, intersection, difference, and join.

dynamic binding   Term sometimes used as a synonym for run time binding, q.v.

dynamic classification   Systems and languages (especially OO systems and languages) that use the term *class* to mean a type—see Part I of this dictionary—sometimes also use the term *dynamic classification* to refer to the process, or the result of the process, of determining at run time the type(s) possessed by some object.

dynamic dispatching / dynamic despatching   Term sometimes used (especially in OO systems and languages) as a synonym for run time binding, q.v.

dynamic type checking   Term sometimes used as a synonym for run time type checking, q.v.

early binding   Compile time binding, q.v.

empty set of types   The least specific common subtype and least specific common supertype for an empty set of types are both *T_alpha* (q.v.), the pertinent maximal type; likewise, the most specific common subtype and most specific common supertype for an empty set of types are both *T_omega* (q.v.), the pertinent minimal type. *Note:* To see that these definitions are reasonable, consider the following. Let *TL* be a type lattice, q.v., with maximal and minimal types *GT* and *LT*, respectively, and let $S = \{T1, T2, ..., Tm\}$ ($m \geq 0$) be a subset of the types in *TL*. If $m = 0$—i.e., if *S* is empty—then (a) by definition, every type in *TL* is a common subtype for *T1*, *T2*, ..., *Tm*, and so the corresponding least specific and most specific common subtype are *GT* and *LT*, respectively; likewise (b) again by definition, every type in *TL* is also a common supertype for *T1*, *T2*, ..., *Tm*, and so the corresponding least specific and most specific common supertype are also *GT* and *LT*, respectively.

empty type   (*With inheritance*) A scalar type is empty if and only if it's type *omega*, q.v. A tuple type is empty if and only if it has an attribute of some empty type. A relation type is never empty, even if it has an attribute of some empty type (because if *T* is a relation type, there always exists at least one relation of type *T*—viz., the empty relation of that type).

   Examples: Here are some examples of empty tuple types:

```
TUPLE { E omega }

TUPLE { E omega , R omega }

TUPLE { X CIRCLE , Y TUPLE { Z omega } }
```

   By contrast, the following tuple type isn't empty (instead, it contains exactly one value— viz., the 0-tuple):

```
TUPLE { }
```

(Incidentally, this type has just one valid corresponding selector invocation, which looks like this in **Tutorial D**: TUPLE { }.)
   The following relation type is also nonempty (as are all relation types), even though it has at least one attribute of an empty type:

```
RELATION { E omega , R RECTANGLE }
```

   Another interesting (necessarily nonempty) relation type is the one with an empty heading:

```
RELATION { }
```

This type contains exactly two values—namely, TABLE_DUM and TABLE_DEE, the only relations of degree zero.
   Note: An empty type is permitted to appear (a) as the declared type of some attribute of some tuple or relation type and (b) nowhere else. To be more specific:

■ *Scalar and tuple variables:* An attempt to define a scalar or tuple variable with an empty declared type will fail at run time (if not at compile time), because there's no initial value that can be assigned to that variable.

■ *Relation variables:* A relvar can't be defined with an empty declared type because there aren't any empty relation types.

■ *Possrep components:* An attempt to define a scalar type *T* with a possrep component of some empty declared type will fail at run time (if not at compile time) because there's no example value—see Part I of this dictionary—that can be specified for *T*.

■ *Read-only operators:* An attempt to define a read-only operator *Op*—or, more precisely, an attempt to define an invocation signature, q.v., for such an operator—with a result of some empty declared type is illegal. If the violation isn't caught at compile time, an invocation coresponding to that signature will certainly fail at run time.

■ *Expressions:* By definition, every expression denotes a value. It follows that no expression can be of an empty declared type.

■ *Parameters:* An attempt to define an operator *Op* with a parameter of some empty declared type is illegal. If the violation isn't caught at compile time, an invocation of *Op* will certainly fail at run time.

■ *Attributes:* Attributes of tuple and relation types are allowed to be of an empty declared type. However, if *T* is a tuple type with an attribute of declared type some empty type, then *T* can't be used as the declared type of anything other than some attribute of some other tuple or relation type. Note that no analogous remark applies to relation types.

equality   (*With inheritance*) Let *x* and *y* be values such that the most specific types *MST*(*x*) and *MST*(*y*) overlap. Then (and only then) *x* and *y* can be compared for equality; the comparison returns TRUE if and only if *x* is equal to *y* (in which case *MST*(*x*) is equal to *MST*(*y*) also). *Note:* In order for the comparison to be syntactically valid, the declared types *DT*(*expx*) and *DT*(*expy*) of the expressions *expx* and *expy* used to denote the values *x* and *y*, respectively, must overlap (this condition is implied by the fact that *MST*(*x*) and *MST*(*y*) are required to overlap, and is a compile time check).

Examples: With reference to Fig. 2, let variables EX, EY, C, and R be of declared types ELLIPSE, ELLIPSE, CIRCLE, and RECTANGLE, respectively. Of the following comparisons, then, the first two are syntactically valid and the third isn't:

```
EX = EY

EX = C

EX = R
```

The first two of these comparisons will certainly give FALSE if the most specific types of the comparands are different; they'll also give FALSE if the most specific types are the same but the current values are different; otherwise they'll give TRUE.

Now consider Fig. 3. Let variables S, RE, RH, and P be of declared types SQUARE, RECTANGLE, RHOMBUS, and PARALLELOGRAM, respectively. Then all of the following comparisons are syntactically valid:

```
P  = RH

RH = RE

RE = S

S  = P
```

In all cases, the comparison will give TRUE if and only if the current values of the comparands are the same (in which case the most specific types will be the same as well, necessarily).

example value 1. A value of scalar type *T* that's specified when *T* is defined, thereby ensuring that *T* is nonempty. 2. (*With inheritance*) A value of scalar type *T* and not *T′* (where *T′* is an immediate subtype of *T*) that's specified as part of the definition of *T′*, thereby ensuring that the set of values constituting *T′* is a proper subset of the set of values constituting *T*. Note that *T′* here can't be a root type (i.e., *T* is not type *alpha*).

Examples (second definition): 1. With reference to the type hierarchy of Fig. 2, the complete definition for type CIRCLE might look as follows:

```
TYPE CIRCLE
     IS { ELLIPSE
          CONSTRAINT THE_A ( ELLIPSE ) = THE_B ( ELLIPSE )
          POSSREP { R   = THE_A   ( ELLIPSE ) ,
                    CTR = THE_CTR ( ELLIPSE ) }
          NOT { ELLIPSE ( LENGTH ( 2.0 ) ,
                          LENGTH ( 1.0 ) ,
                          POINT ( 0.0 , 0.0 ) ) } } ;
```

The intent of the NOT specification here is to say that the specified ELLIPSE value is a value of type ELLIPSE that's not a value of type CIRCLE. (It might be nice to find a better keyword than NOT for this purpose.) 2. With reference to the type graph of Fig. 3, the complete definition for type SQUARE might look as follows:

```
TYPE SQUARE
     IS { RECTANGLE , RHOMBUS
          POSSREP { A = THE_A ( RECTANGLE ) ,
                    B = THE_B ( RECTANGLE ) ,
                    C = THE_C ( RECTANGLE ) ,
                    D = THE_D ( RECTANGLE ) }
          NOT { RECTANGLE ( POINT ( 0.0 , 0.0 ) ,
                            POINT ( 0.0 , 1.0 ) ,
                            POINT ( 2.0 , 1.0 ) ,
                            POINT ( 2.0 , 0.0 ) ) ,
                RHOMBUS   ( POINT ( 0.0 , 0.0 ) ,
                            POINT ( √3.0 , 1.0 ) ,
                            POINT ( √3.0 + 2 , 1.0 ) ,
                            POINT ( 2.0 , 0.0 ) ) } } ;
```

Note: In type definitions elsewhere in this dictionary, such NOT specifications would just be a distraction and are therefore omitted. In any case, they aren't currently supported in **Tutorial D**.

extends relationship   Let type T' inherit public instance variables (see Part I of this dictionary) from type T—i.e., let structural inheritance, q.v., apply to types T and T'—and let type T' have additional public instance variables of its own. Then type T' is said to extend type T (and types T and T' are said to be the base type and the derived type, respectively, for the "extends relationship" in question). To quote *The Object Data Standard: ODMG 3.0* (R. G. G. Cattell and Douglas K. Barry, eds., Morgan Kaufmann, 2000):

> The EXTENDS relationship is a single inheritance relationship between two classes whereby the subordinate class inherits all of the properties ... of the class that it extends.

(And elsewhere that same reference defines *properties* as "attributes of the object itself or relationships between the object and one or more other objects"—although elsewhere again it defines them as "state variables," and, as noted in Part I of this dictionary, state variables are usually understood to be merely instance variables by another name (?).) *See also* HAS A; structural inheritance; subtables and supertables.

Example: In an OO system, circles might have a CTR ("center") public instance variable, because all ellipses have such an instance variable; however, they might also have an R ("radius") public instance variable, which ellipses in general don't have. In this example, therefore, type CIRCLE might be said to extend type ELLIPSE.

Note: The foregoing example is actually not very realistic, because circles will presumably have A and B public instance variables as well—inherited from type ELLIPSE and corresponding to the major and minor semiaxis length, respectively—and for a given circle the values of A, B, and R will all be the same. A more realistic example in the OO context might involve "colored circles," which extend circles by adding a COLOR public instance variable (*see* colored circle.) Moreover, the "colored circles" example—in which CIRCLE is the base type and COLORED_CIRCLE the derived type—makes it very clear that the derivation process (i.e., the process by which a derived type, in an "extends relationship" context, is derived from the corresponding base type) is most certainly not specialization by constraint, q.v. More specifically, that derivation process doesn't occur automatically but is, rather, a matter of explicit definition—by fiat, as it were.

Since the type theory espoused by *The Third Manifesto* has no support for public instance variables, it has no support for the extends relationship a fortiori.

———— ◆ ◆ ◆ ◆ ◆ ————

four out of five rule   The three out of four "rule" (q.v.) asserts that at most three of the following four allegedly desirable features can be supported at the same time: (a) substitutability; (b) compile time type checking; (c) mutability; and (d) "specialization via constraints," q.v. By contrast, the four out of five rule asserts that all four of those features can be supported at the same time after all (at least insofar as is logically possible), just so long as objects in the OO sense—meaning object IDs in particular—aren't supported! In other words, the feature that can and should be dropped is objects as such, not one of the four features here alleged to be desirable. Detailed arguments in support of this position (which is the position adopted in the *Manifesto* model) can be found in the *Manifesto* book.

function resolution   Term sometimes used as a synonym for binding, q.v. (especially run time binding, q.v.).

———— ◆ ◆ ◆ ◆ ◆ ————

G by C   Generalization by constraint.

generalization   Let types T'', T', and T be such that T'' is a subtype of T' and T' is a subtype of T, and let v' be a value of most specific type T'. Also, let V be a variable of declared type T, and let the current most specific type $MST(V)$ of V be T''. Finally, let the value v' be assigned to V. Then the current most specific type of V is now T'; in other words, $MST(V)$ has been generalized from T'' to T'. (Of course, T'' and T' might be one and the same, and so might T' and T, but in general they won't be.) *Contrast* **generalization by constraint; specialization.**

Note: The foregoing definition explains how the *Manifesto* model works. In most systems, however, such generalization doesn't happen at all. For example, with reference to Fig. 2, let variable E be of declared type ELLIPSE, and consider the following sequence of events. First, a value of most specific type CIRCLE is assigned to E; the most specific type of E thus becomes CIRCLE (*see* **assignment**). Next, a value of most specific type ELLIPSE is assigned to E. In the *Manifesto* model, then, the most specific type of E now becomes ELLIPSE again (again, *see* **assignment**); in those other systems, by contrast, the most specific type of E remains unchanged—i.e., it's still CIRCLE—and so E now contains a "noncircular circle," q.v.

generalization by constraint   Let types T'', T', and T be such that T'' is a subtype of T' and T' is a subtype of T, and let v' be a value that satisfies the type constraint for type T' (and not for any proper subtype of T'). Also, let V be a variable of declared type T, and let the current most specific type $MST(V)$ of V be T''. Finally, let the value v' be assigned to V. Then the current most specific type of V is now T'; in other words, $MST(V)$ has been generalized from T'' to T'. (Of course, T'' and T' might in fact be one and the same, and so might T' and T, but in general they won't be.) Moreover, that generalization is said to be "by constraint" ("G by C"), because it occurs as a consequence of the fact that v' satisfies the type constraint for T' (and not for any proper subtype of T'). *Contrast* generalization; specialization by constraint.

   Example: See the examples under **generalization** and **specialization by constraint**. *Note:* All generalization in the *Manifesto* model is by constraint, because a value in that model is of a given type if and only if it satisfies the type constraint for that type. But in a system that permits such absurdities as circular noncircles (q.v.) and noncircular circles (q.v.), generalization—if it even happens at all—will almost certainly not be by constraint. *See* **specialization by constraint** for further discussion.

GLB   Greatest lower bound.

greatest lower bound   Let s be a set; let a partial ordering be defined on s; and let s' be a subset of s. Then x is a lower bound for s' if and only if $x \in s$ and x is less than or equal to every element of s' with respect to the specified ordering. Moreover, if there do exist any such x's, it's easy to show there must be a largest one, and that largest x is the greatest lower bound (GLB) for s' with respect to the specified ordering. (Note that the GLB for s' might or might not itself be contained within s'.) *See also* **lattice**.

   Examples: See the examples under **type lattice**.

———— ◆◆◆◆◆ ————

HAS A   Let types $T1$ and $T2$ be such that all of the properties (i.e., type constraints and read-only operators) that apply to type $T1$ apply to type $T2$ also. However, let some additional property P apply to $T2$, where P is such that it can't be derived in any way from the properties that apply to $T1$. Then (a) the IS A relationship, q.v., doesn't apply (i.e., $T2$ isn't a subtype of $T1$—at least, not according to the *Manifesto* model); (b) by contrast, the HAS A relationship does apply (a value of type $T2$ does "have a" property P). Note that IS A always implies inclusion polymorphism, q.v., whereas HAS A typically seems to imply delegation, q.v. *See also* **extends relationship; subtables and supertables**.

   Example: See the discussion under **colored circle**. *Caveat:* Unfortunately, the informal terms "IS A" and "HAS A" can be seriously misleading (not to say confusing). For example, consider employees and programmers. In natural language, we might very reasonably say that every programmer "is a" employee, suggesting rather strongly that what we have here is an example of "the IS A relationship." But it isn't; rather, programmers "have a" property, say language skill, that employees in general don't have—a property, what's more, that can't be derived in any way from the properties that employees in general do have. So the crucial issue here isn't the IS A relationship but, rather, the HAS A relationship; that is, it's not the case that a programmer "is a" employee—rather, it's the case that a programmer "has a" language skill. Contrast the situation with, e.g., ellipses and circles: Although we might say, informally, that a circle "has a" property (the radius length) that ellipses in general don't have, that property is really just a degenerate form of a property (a semiaxis length) that ellipses in general do have. By contrast, to say it again, a programmer's language skill doesn't correspond to *any* property of employees in general. Note in particular, therefore, that—as a direct consequence of the foregoing point—S by C doesn't apply: There's no constraint, expressible purely in terms of employee properties as such, that an employee can and must satisfy in order to be a programmer.

———— ♦♦♦♦♦ ————

immediate subtype   Type T'' is an immediate subtype of type T if and only if (a) it's a proper subtype of T and (b) there's no type T' that's both a proper supertype of T'' and a proper subtype of T. *See also* **immediate supertype**.

Examples: 1. With reference to Fig. 2, CIRCLE is an immediate subtype of ELLIPSE, and ELLIPSE is an immediate subtype of PLANE_FIGURE (CIRCLE is a subtype of PLANE_FIGURE too, but not an immediate one). 2. With reference to Fig. 3, SQUARE is an immediate subtype of RECTANGLE and RHOMBUS, each of which is an immediate subtype of PARALLELOGRAM. 3. With reference to Fig. 5, relation type CS is an immediate subtype of relation types CR and ES, each of which is an immediate subtype of relation type ER.

immediate supertype   Type T is an immediate supertype of type T'' if and only if (a) it's a proper supertype of T'' and (b) there's no type T' that's both a proper subtype of T and a proper supertype of T''. *See also* **immediate subtype**.

Examples: 1. With reference to Fig. 2, PLANE_FIGURE is an immediate supertype of ELLIPSE, and ELLIPSE is an immediate supertype of CIRCLE (PLANE_FIGURE is a supertype of CIRCLE too, but not an immediate one). 2. With reference to Fig. 3, PARALLELOGRAM is an immediate supertype of RECTANGLE and RHOMBUS, each of which is an immediate supertype of SQUARE. 3. With reference to Fig. 5, relation type ER is an immediate supertype of relation types CR and ES, each of which is an immediate supertype of relation type CS.

implementation version   Let scalar type T be a proper supertype of scalar type T', and let PR and PR' be possreps for T and T', respectively, such that $PR \neq PR'$. Further, let Op be a read-only operator that applies to values of type T and hence, by definition, to values of type T' also (read-only just to be definite; the discussion that follows pertains to update operators too, mutatis mutandis). Then it's at least possible for Op to have two distinct implementation versions, one implemented in terms of PR, which works for values of type T (and therefore, necessarily, for values of type T' also—*see* **possrep inheritance**), and the other in terms of PR', which works for values of type T' only. To illustrate:

- Let types T and T' be ELLIPSE and CIRCLE, respectively, and let AREA_OF be an operator that takes an ellipse as input and returns the corresponding area as output. For type ELLIPSE, the sole declared possrep consists of a, b, and the center (where a and b are the lengths of the semiaxes); for type CIRCLE, the sole declared possrep consists of r and the center (where r is the length of the radius). The area of an ellipse is πab. But if the ellipse happens to be a circle, the semiaxes degenerate to the radius, the formula degenerates to πr^2, and so the code that implements AREA_OF for ellipses in general will still work if the ellipse is in fact a circle.

- For a counterexample, let types T and T' be POLYGON and RECTANGLE, respectively, and assume now that the operator AREA_OF is defined for polygons. The algorithm (based on integral calculus) that computes the area of a general polygon will certainly work for a rectangle; for rectangles, however, a much more efficient algorithm—viz., multiply the height by the width—is available. At least for performance reasons, therefore, it might be desirable to have two implementation versions of the operator, thus (in outline only, but note the VERSION specifications in particular):

```
OPERATOR AREA_OF VERSION P_AREA ( P POLYGON ) RETURNS AREA ;
    RETURN ... ;
END OPERATOR ;

OPERATOR AREA_OF VERSION R_AREA ( R RECTANGLE ) RETURNS AREA ;
    RETURN ... ;
END OPERATOR ;
```

The net of the foregoing discussion is that what appears to be a single operator above the covers can have any number n ($n > 0$) of implementation versions—versions for short—under the covers. (We note in passing that each such version might be regarded as having its own *version signature*, but version signatures are purely an implementation concern, not part of the model as such.) Of course, it makes no difference to the user how many implementation versions exist; in the case of AREA_OF, for example, the user knows the operator works for, say, ellipses, and therefore it works for circles too, by definition, because circles are ellipses (*see* **inclusion polymorphism**).

So what are the consequences? Consider the following example. Suppose with reference to Fig. 2 that some program needs to display some diagram, made up of squares, circles, ellipses, etc. Without support for implementation versions, the code for this task will look something like this:

```
FOR EACH x ∈ DIAGRAM
    CASE ;
        WHEN IS_SQUARE ( x ) THEN DISPLAY_SQUARE ... ;
        WHEN IS_CIRCLE ( x ) THEN DISPLAY_CIRCLE ... ;
        WHEN ........................................ ;
    END CASE ;
```

With such support, by contrast, the code is much simpler:

```
FOR EACH x ∈ DIAGRAM DISPLAY ( x ) ;
```

Note: The argument expressions to the various DISPLAY operator invocations in the first version of this code are omitted in order to avoid distracting irrelevancies. For the record, however, in the case of DISPLAY_SQUARE that argument expression will probably take the form TREAT_AS_SQUARE (*x*) (*see* TREAT), and of course the other cases are analogous.

Explanation: DISPLAY in the second version of the code is a polymorphic operator, defined—let's assume for the sake of the example—for type PLANE_FIGURE (i.e., the sole parameter to that operator is of declared type PLANE_FIGURE). SQUARE, CIRCLE, etc., are all subtypes of that type, of course. Now, if it turns out to be desirable, for some given subtype, to define a specific version of that operator for values of the subtype in question, then that version will typically be defined when that subtype is defined. Then, at run time, when the system encounters the DISPLAY invocation with argument *x*, it will determine the implementation version that's appropriate to the type of *x*—i.e., *MST(x)*—and will invoke that version. (*See* run time binding. Note, however, that it's at least theoretically possible to do the binding at compile time. See further discussion of this possibility below.) Thus, inclusion polymorphism effectively leads to certain CASE expressions and CASE statements that would otherwise have had to appear in the user's source code being moved under the covers: in effect, being performed by the system on the user's behalf.

Observe now the implications of the foregoing for program maintenance. Suppose a new type TRIANGLE is defined (another subtype of PLANE_FIGURE, and in fact an immediate subtype of POLYGON) and a corresponding new implementation version of DISPLAY is defined as well. Without support for implementation versions, it would be necessary to examine every source program to see whether any CASE expression or statement needed to be modified to include the following:

```
WHEN IS_TRIANGLE ( x ) THEN DISPLAY_TRIANGLE ... ;
```

With such support, however, no such modifications will be needed.

Because of examples like the foregoing, inclusion polymorphism is sometimes characterized, a little colorfully, as meaning that "old code can invoke new code"; that is, a program *P* can effectively invoke some version of an operator *Op* that didn't exist—the version, that is—when *P* was written. Thus, we have, at least potentially, what's called code reuse, q.v.: The very same program *P* might be usable on data of a type that wasn't defined when *P* was written. (Certainly the code of program *P* is being reused here. The code that implements operator *Op* under the covers might or might not be; for example, the code that implements the AREA_OF operator for polygons might or might not be reused for rectangles, as previously discussed.)

Unfortunately, there's a fly in the ointment. To be specific, there can be no guarantee that the various implementation versions of a given operator all implement the same semantics. If they don't, then we don't have true inclusion polymorphism any more, we have overloading polymorphism instead; such a state of affairs constitutes a violation of the model (the *Manifesto* model, that is), and the consequences are unpredictable. Regrettably, however, the requirement that all versions of a given operator do implement the same semantics is unenforceable. What's more, some writers even claim, in effect, that the ability to change semantics is desirable! To quote *The Object Data Standard: ODMG 3.0* (R. G. G. Cattell and Douglas K. Barry, eds.; Morgan Kaufmann, 2000):

> For example, the Employee type might have an operation for calculate_paycheck. The Salaried_Employee and Hourly_Employee class implementations might each refine that behavior to reflect their specialized needs.

(*Refine that behavior* here means, precisely, changing the semantics. Note, however, that there does seem to be a tacit assumption in the example that the "subtypes" in question aren't true subtypes as such but rather are "derived types." *See* **extends relationship** for further explanation.)

To return to ellipses and circles for a moment, observe now that the ellipse AREA_OF code will definitely not work for circles if it's written in terms of a physical representation instead of a possible one, and the physical representations for types ELLIPSE and CIRCLE differ. The practice of implementing operators in terms of physical representations is thus clearly contraindicated. As a general rule, in fact, the only code that accesses physical representations at all should be the code that implements (a) selectors, (b) THE_ operators, and (c) IS_*T* operators (*see* **privileged operator** in Part I of this dictionary). Note that most if not all of this implementation code will probably be provided by the system anyway.

Finally (and just to spell the point out), again let scalar type *T* be a proper supertype of scalar type *T'*, and let *PR* and *PR'* be possreps for *T* and *T'*, respectively (*PR* ≠ *PR'*). Let *Op* be a read-only operator that applies to values of type *T* and hence, by definition, to values of type *T'* also. Finally, let *OpV* and *OpV'* be versions of *Op* that apply to values of type *T* and values of type *T'*, respectively, where *OpV* is implemented in terms of *PR* and *OpV'* is implemented in terms of *PR'*. By definition, then, *PR* is an "inherited possrep" (*see* **possrep inheritance**) for type *T'*. As previously indicated, then, *OpV* will always at least work—perhaps not as efficiently as *OpV'* does—for values of type *T'*; hence, compile time binding should always work too, and run time binding is logically unnecessary, though it might be desirable for performance reasons. Of course, this argument does assume (a) that implementation versions are written in terms of possreps, not physical representations, and (b) that distinct versions of the same operator do implement the same semantics.

inclusion polymorphism   By definition (*see* type inheritance), any read-only operator that applies to values of a given type T necessarily applies to values of every proper subtype T' of T. Such an operator is thus polymorphic, and the kind of polymorphism it exhibits is called inclusion polymorphism, on the grounds that the relationship between T and T' is that of set inclusion (because the set of values constituting type T is a superset—in general a proper superset—of the set of values constituting type T'). Note that this kind of polymorphism is a logical consequence of the very notion of type inheritance. *Contrast* **overloading.** *Note:* An update operator that applies to variables of type T might or might not apply to variables of some proper subtype T' of T (*see* **Principle of Variable Substitutability**). If it does, then it too is said to exhibit inclusion polymorphism.

   Example: With reference to Fig. 2, let AREA_OF ("return the area of") be an operator that applies to values of type RECTANGLE. Then AREA_OF also applies to values of type SQUARE, necessarily, because squares are rectangles. See also the examples under **argument.**

inherited possrep   *See* possrep inheritance.

INSERT ONLY   Let T' be a subtable of supertable T (*see* **subtables and supertables**). Then INSERT ONLY is an operator—not supported by SQL, incidentally, even though SQL does support subtables and supertables as such—that inserts a row into T' without simultaneously inserting a corresponding row into T.

   Example: With reference to the example under **subtables and supertables**, it should be possible to use INSERT ONLY to insert a row into table PGMR without at the same time inserting a corresponding row into table EMP, to reflect the fact that some existing employee has become a programmer.

instantiable type   Term sometimes used in OO contexts to mean a type that's not a union type. The name presumably derives from the fact that such a type has "instances," where the term "instances" presumably means—at least in this context—values whose most specific type is the type in question; it has nothing to do with instance variables, q.v., nor with instantiation in the sense of logic (see Part I of this dictionary). Note, however, that elsewhere in those same OO contexts that same term *instance* is certainly taken to include variables, etc., as well as values as such; in fact, it's often used a synonym for *object*. *Contrast* **noninstantiable type.**

interface   (*With inheritance*) Term used in some OO systems to mean a union type (possibly a dummy type). *Note:* Such systems typically refer to nonunion types simply as types, implying, tacitly, that union types ("interfaces") aren't considered to be types at all. This somewhat idiosyncratic use of both terms (i.e., *type* and *interface*) is deprecated accordingly.

intersection (*With inheritance*) *See* dyadic relational operators.

intersection subtype Same as intersection type.

intersection type Same as least specific common subtype. The term *intersection type* is perhaps to be preferred, at least in informal contexts, because it's intuitively easier to understand. (On the other hand, it does carry with it an implicit suggestion that *union type* might be just another term for most specific common supertype, which is incorrect. Why? Because if *T* is the most specific common supertype of types *T1*, *T2*, ..., *Tm*, then it might legitimately contain a value that's not a value of any of types *T1*, *T2*, ..., *Tm*—in which case it isn't the union, as such, of those types *T1*, *T2*, ..., *Tm*, but is, rather, a proper superset of that union. *See* **most specific common supertype**.)

invocation signature (*With inheritance*) *See* signature.

IS The **Tutorial D** construct that defines some (scalar) subtype / supertype relationship; more specifically, the construct that defines some scalar type *T'* to be an immediate subtype of another scalar type *T* (single inheritance) or an immediate subtype of two or more other scalar types *T1*, *T2*, ..., *Tm* (multiple inheritance). There are thus two basic cases to consider. The first case (single inheritance) subdivides into two further cases, one in which the immediate supertype is a dummy type and one in which it's a regular type. For example, with reference to Fig. 2, let PLANE_FIGURE be a dummy type; then the definitions for types ELLIPSE and CIRCLE illustrate both of these two "further cases." First, type ELLIPSE:

```
TYPE ELLIPSE
     IS { PLANE_FIGURE
          POSSREP { A LENGTH , B LENGTH , CTR POINT
                    CONSTRAINT A ≥ B } } ;
```

The IS specification here defines a value *e* to be of type ELLIPSE if and only if it conforms to the indicated POSSREP specification (including the constraint $a \geq b$). It also defines—by fiat, as it were—such values to be of type PLANE_FIGURE as well as type ELLIPSE (i.e., if *e* does conform to the indicated POSSREP specification, then IS_PLANE_FIGURE(*e*) evaluates to TRUE).

Now here's the definition for type CIRCLE (in outline):

```
TYPE CIRCLE
     IS { ELLIPSE
          CONSTRAINT THE_A ( ELLIPSE ) = THE_B ( ELLIPSE )
          POSSREP { ... } } ;
```

Here the IS specification defines both (a) a specialization constraint, q.v., which in turn defines a value *c* to be of type CIRCLE if and only if IS_ELLIPSE(*c*) and THE_A(*c*) = THE_B(*c*) both evaluate to TRUE, and (b) a derived possrep, q.v.—details omitted here for simplicity—for type CIRCLE in terms of (some possrep for) its sole immediate supertype ELLIPSE.

The other case (multiple inheritance), in which type T' has m immediate supertypes $T1$, $T2$, ..., Tm ($m > 1$), is straightforward: The IS specification simply names those supertypes and—if and only if T' is a regular type—defines at least one derived possrep, q.v., for that type T'. With reference to Fig. 3, for example, the definition for type SQUARE might look like this (in outline):

```
TYPE SQUARE
     IS { RECTANGLE , RHOMBUS
          POSSREP { ... } } ;
```

The specialization constraint here (q.v.) defines a value s to be of type SQUARE if and only if IS_RECTANGLE(s) and IS_RHOMBUS(s) both evaluate to TRUE. No additional CONSTRAINT specification is stated, or indeed permitted (because a rectangle is a square if and only if it's a rhombus, and a rhombus is a square if and only if it's a rectangle). The POSSREP specification—details again omitted for simplicity—defines a derived possrep for type SQUARE in terms of some possrep for one of its immediate supertypes (viz., either RECTANGLE or RHOMBUS, in the case at hand).

IS A The subtype / supertype relationship; i.e., the relationship between a subtype T' and any (usually proper) supertype T of T'. For example, every circle "is a" ellipse, and "is a" plane figure as well. As noted elsewhere in this dictionary, the IS A relationship leads directly to inclusion polymorphism, q.v., and value substitutability, q.v. *Contrast* HAS A.

IS_SAME_TYPE_AS *See* IS_T.

IS_T Let *exp* be a scalar expression, let T be a scalar type, and let $DT(exp)$ and T overlap (this is a compile time check). Then the "type testing" expression IS_T (*exp*)—or some logical equivalent to that expression—returns TRUE if and only if $v(exp)$ is of type T (equivalently, if and only if $MST(exp)$ is some subtype of T).

Tutorial D additionally supports a generalized version of this operator, of the form IS_SAME_TYPE_AS (*exp1,exp2*), where the expressions *exp1* and *exp2* aren't limited to being scalar. This generalized version is effectively equivalent to the expression IS_T1 (*exp2*), where $T1$ is $DT(exp1)$—assuming for definitional purposes here that the expression IS_T1 (*exp2*) is syntactically valid—and thus returns TRUE if and only if $MST(exp2)$ is some subtype of $DT(exp1)$.

Note: It might be desirable to support negated forms of these operators, too—IS_NOT_T (*exp*) and IS_NOT_SAME_TYPE_AS (*exp1,exp2*)—with the obvious semantics.

Examples: 1. With reference to Fig. 2, let E be a variable of declared type and current most specific type both ELLIPSE; then IS_PLANE_FIGURE (E) and IS_ELLIPSE (E) both return TRUE and IS_CIRCLE (E) returns FALSE. 2. With reference to Fig. 3, let RE be a variable of declared type RECTANGLE and current most specific type SQUARE; then IS_SQUARE (RE), IS_RECTANGLE (RE), IS_RHOMBUS (RE), and IS_PARALLELOGRAM (RE) all return TRUE. 3. With reference to Fig. 5, let ERV be a relvar of declared type ER and current most specific type CS, and let ESV be a relvar of declared type and most specific type both ES; then IS_SAME_TYPE_AS (ERV,ESV) returns TRUE.

———— ♦ ♦ ♦ ♦ ♦ ————

join (*With inheritance*) *See* dyadic relational operators.

joinable (*With inheritance*) 1. (*Dyadic case*) Relations *r1* and *r2* are joinable if and only if attributes with the same name are such that their types have a common supertype (i.e., those types belong to the same type lattice, q.v.). 2. (*N-adic case*) Relations $r1, r2, ..., rn$ ($n \geq 0$) are joinable—sometimes *n*-way joinable, for emphasis—if and only if for all *i* and *j*, relations *ri* and *rj* are joinable ($1 \leq i \leq n,\ 1 \leq j \leq n$).

———— ♦ ♦ ♦ ♦ ♦ ————

late binding Run time binding, q.v.

lattice Let *s* be a set, and let a partial ordering be defined on *s*. Then the combination of *s* and that partial ordering is a lattice if and only if every two elements of the set have both a least upper bound, q.v., and a greatest lower bound, q.v., with respect to that ordering. *Note:* It follows from this definition that a set of cardinality either one or zero can always be regarded as a lattice.
    Examples: See the examples under type lattice.

leaf Abbreviation for leaf type.

leaf type A type with no immediate subtype other than the pertinent minimal type, q.v.
    Examples: 1. In Fig. 2, CIRCLE and SQUARE are leaf types. What's more, they're disjoint (see further discussion below). 2. In Figs. 3 and 4, SQUARE is the only leaf type. 3. In Fig. 5, type CS is the only leaf type.
    Note: Let *T1* and *T2* be distinct leaf types from the same type lattice, q.v. If those types are scalar or tuple types, they're certainly disjoint; by contrast, if they're relation types, they're not disjoint. With reference to Fig. 2, for instance, let *T1* and *T2* be the relation types RELATION {PF CIRCLE} and RELATION {PF SQUARE}, respectively. Then *T1* and *T2* overlap because they both contain the (empty) relation RELATION {PF *omega*} { }. In fact, every type in that same type lattice—even the minimal type RELATION {PF *omega*}—contains that same empty relation as a value.

least specific common subtype   Let *T1, T2, ..., Tm* ($m \geq 0$) be types from the same type lattice, q.v. Then type *T'* is the least specific common subtype for types *T1, T2, ..., Tm* if and only if it's a common subtype (q.v.) for those types and no proper supertype of *T'* is also a common subtype for those types. *Note:* It can be shown—see the *Manifesto* book—that, given types *T1, T2, ..., Tm*, the corresponding least specific common subtype *T'* always exists and is unique (though it might be one of those specified types *T1, T2, ..., Tm*, or even the pertinent minimal type, q.v.); in fact, it's the greatest lower bound, q.v., of types *T1, T2, ..., Tm*. It can also be shown—again, see the *Manifesto* book—that whenever a value is of each of types *T1, T2, ..., Tm*, it's also of type *T'* (hence the alternative, and sometimes preferred, names *intersection type* and *intersection subtype*). Note too that (a) if *m* = 1, then the set of types *T1, T2, ..., Tm* reduces to just *T1*, and *T1* itself is the least specific common subtype for that set; (b) if *m* = 0, then the set of types *T1, T2, ..., Tm* is empty, and the least specific common subtype is the pertinent maximal type. *Contrast* **least specific common supertype; most specific common subtype; most specific common supertype.**

   Examples: 1. With reference to Fig. 2, the least specific common subtype for types PLANE_FIGURE, POLYGON, and RECTANGLE is RECTANGLE, and the least specific common subtype for ELLIPSE and SQUARE is *omega*. 2. With reference to Fig. 3, the least specific common subtype for types RECTANGLE and RHOMBUS is SQUARE. 3. With reference to Fig. 4, the least specific common subtype for types KITE and CYCLIC QUADRILATERAL is RIGHT KITE. Note that SQUARE is also a common subtype in this example, but it's not the least specific one (i.e., it's not the intersection type as such).

   Note: Of course, it's always possible that the type designer could make a mistake and omit the definition of some intersection type that's logically required. For example, with reference to Fig. 3, the designer might specify types RECTANGLE and RHOMBUS as immediate subtypes of type PARALLELOGRAM and forget that some parallelograms are both a rectangle and a rhombus. The consequences of such violations (violations of the prescriptions of the model, that is) will be unpredictable, in general. Although this fact is of no concern from the point of view of the model—a violation is simply a violation, and there's no need as far as the model is concerned to spell out what the consequences might be—in practice it's to be hoped that some kind of mechanical aid would be available to help avoid such errors.

least specific common subtype (relation types)   Let *T1, T2, ..., Tm* ($m \geq 0$) be relation types from the same type lattice, q.v.; by definition, then, those types all have the same attribute names, say *A1, A2, ..., An* ($n \geq 0$). Let the type of attribute *Aj* (*j* = 1, 2, ..., *n*) within type *Ti* (*i* = 1, 2, ..., *m*) be *Tij*. Then type *T'* = RELATION {<*A1,T01'*>,<*A2,T02'*>,...,<*An,T0n'*>} is the least specific common subtype for types *T1, T2, ..., Tm* if and only if, for all *j* (*j* = 1, 2, ..., *n*), type *T0j'* is the least specific common subtype for types *T1j, T2j, ..., Tmj*. *See also* **least specific common subtype;** *contrast* **least specific common supertype (relation types); most specific common subtype (relation types); most specific common supertype (relation types).**

   Example: With reference to Fig. 5, the least specific common subtype for relation types CR and ES is relation type CS.

least specific common subtype (tuple types) Let *T1, T2, ..., Tm* (*m* ≥ 0) be tuple types from the same type lattice, q.v.; by definition, then, those types all have the same attribute names, say *A1, A2, ..., An* (*n* ≥ 0). Let the type of attribute *Aj* (*j* = 1, 2, ..., *n*) within type *Ti* (*i* = 1, 2, ..., *m*) be *Tij*. Then type *T'* = TUPLE {<*A1,T01'*>,<*A2,T02'*>,...,<*An,T0n'*>} is the least specific common subtype for types *T1, T2, ..., Tm* if and only if, for all *j* (*j* = 1, 2, ..., *n*), type *T0j'* is the least specific common subtype for types *T1j, T2j, ..., Tmj*. *See also* least specific common subtype; *contrast* least specific common supertype (tuple types); most specific common subtype (tuple types); most specific common supertype (tuple types).

    Example: With reference to Fig. 5, the least specific common subtype for tuple types ER and ES is tuple type ES.

least specific common supertype Let *T1, T2, ..., Tm* (*m* ≥ 0) be types from the same type lattice, q.v. Then type *T* is the least specific common supertype for types *T1, T2, ..., Tm* if and only if it's the maximal type with respect to the type lattice in question. *Note:* Informally, least specific common supertypes are sometimes defined to exclude the pertinent maximal type, in which case the term is taken to apply to the pertinent root type. With reference to Fig. 4, for example, the least specific common supertype for types RECTANGLE and RHOMBUS is either type *alpha*, q.v., or (if maximal types are excluded) type QUADRILATERAL. *Contrast* least specific common subtype; most specific common subtype; most specific common supertype.

least specific common supertype (relation types) *See* least specific common supertype.

least specific common supertype (tuple types) *See* least specific common supertype.

least specific type Let value *x* be of type *T* and not of any proper supertype of *T*; then *T* is the least specific type of *x*. Note that *T* is necessarily a maximal type (and is thus unique). Further, let *exp* be an expression. Then *exp* has the same least specific type as the value it denotes. *Note:* Informally, least specific types are sometimes defined to exclude the pertinent maximal type, thus: Let *x* be of type *T* and not of any proper supertype of *T* (apart from the pertinent maximal type, q.v.); then *T*—which is necessarily a root type and is thus unique—is the least specific type of *x*. *Contrast* most specific type.

    Examples: 1. Let *x* be a value of any of the types shown in Fig. 2. Then the least specific type of *x* is either *alpha* or (if maximal types are excluded) PLANE_FIGURE. 2. Let *x* be a relation of any of the types shown in Fig. 5. Then the least specific type of *x* is RELATION {E *alpha*, R *alpha*} or (if maximal types are excluded) type ER = RELATION {E ELLIPSE, R RECTANGLE}. 3. The least specific type of the sole tuple of type TUPLE { }—viz., the 0-tuple—is TUPLE { } itself. 4. The least specific type of any relation—necessarily either TABLE_DUM or TABLE_DEE—of type RELATION { } is RELATION { } itself.

least specific type (relation types) *See* least specific type.

least specific type (tuple types) *See* least specific type.

least upper bound Let *s* be a set; let a partial ordering be defined on *s*; and let *s'* be a subset of *s*. Then *x* is an upper bound for *s'* if and only if *x* ∈ *s* and *x* is greater than or equal to every element of *s'* with respect to the specified ordering. Moreover, if there do exist any such *x*'s, it's easy to show there must be a smallest one, and that smallest *x* is the least upper bound (LUB) for *s'* with respect to the specified ordering. (Note that the LUB for *s'* might or might not itself be contained within *s'*.) *See also* lattice.
    Examples: See the examples under type lattice.

Liskov Substitution Principle A principle frequently claimed as the origin of the notion of substitutability, q.v. Unfortunately the paper usually cited as the source for this principle— Barbara Liskov and Jeannette Wing, "A Behavioral Notion of Subtyping," *ACM Transactions on Programming Languages and Systems 16*, No. 6, November 1994—appears not to contain any precise statement of the principle as such. The closest it gets seems to be as follows:

> [Objects] of the subtype ought to behave the same as those of the supertype as far as anyone or any program using supertype objects can tell.

The term *objects* here refers to objects in the OO sense, of course; note, therefore, that the definition, if definition it is, fails to distinguish adequately between value and variable substitutability (*see Principle of Value Substitutability, Principle of Variable Substitutability*). Unfortunately, the same appears to be true of OO writings in general.

LSP Liskov Substitution Principle.

LUB Least upper bound.

————— ♦♦♦♦♦ —————

***Manifesto* model** Term used in this part of the dictionary to refer to the model of type inheritance described in the book *Databases, Types, and the Relational Model: The Third Manifesto* (3rd edition), by C. J. Date and Hugh Darwen (Addison-Wesley, 2007), as revised and extended in the book *Database Explorations: Essays on The Third Manifesto and Related Topics*, by C. J. Date and Hugh Darwen (Trafford, 2010). See the *Manifesto* website *www.thethirdmanifesto.com.* Perhaps the most salient feature of the model in question—in sharp contrast to other approaches to inheritance described in the literature—is that, in that model, value *v* is of type *T* if and only if *v* satisfies the type constraint for *T*. In particular, therefore, absurdities such as circular noncircles (q.v.) and noncircular circles (q.v.) can't occur. *Note:*

The type constraint for type *T* defines the set of values that make up that type *T* (see Part I of this dictionary). For further discussion, *see* CONSTRAINT; IS; specialization constraint.

maximal supertype (SQL)   SQL term for a root type. (Oddly enough, the SQL term for a leaf type isn't "minimal subtype" but "leaf type.") Note that the concepts of maximal type and minimal type as defined elsewhere in this part of the dictionary are absent from SQL.

maximal type   A type with no immediate supertype. Every type lattice (q.v.) has exactly one maximal type. For scalar types, the unique maximal type is *alpha*; for tuple and relation types, *see* maximal type (tuple types) and maximal type (relation types), respectively.

maximal type (relation types)   Let *T* be a relation type with heading {<*A1,T1*>, <*A2,T2*>, ..., <*An,Tn*>} (*n* ≥ 0). Then type *T_alpha* = RELATION {<*A1,T1_alpha*>, <*A2,T2_alpha*>, ..., <*An,Tn_alpha*>} is the maximal type with respect to relation type *T* (in fact, it's the maximal type with respect to the pertinent type lattice, q.v.) if and only if, for all *i* (*i* = 1, 2, ..., *n*), type *Ti_alpha* is the maximal type with respect to type *Ti*.
    Examples: 1. For the relation types shown in Fig. 5, the maximal type is RELATION {E *alpha*, R *alpha*}. 2. Let *T* be the relation type RELATION { }. Then the maximal type with respect to *T* is *T* itself (the only type in the pertinent type lattice), and it contains exactly two values: namely, TABLE_DUM and TABLE_DEE.

maximal type (tuple types)   Let *T* be a tuple type with heading {<*A1,T1*>, <*A2,T2*>, ..., <*An,Tn*>} (*n* ≥ 0). Then type *T_alpha* = TUPLE {<*A1,T1_alpha*>, <*A2,T2_alpha*>, ..., <*An,Tn_alpha*>} is the maximal type with respect to tuple type *T* (in fact, it's the maximal type with respect to the pertinent type lattice, q.v.) if and only if, for all *i* (*i* = 1, 2, ..., *n*), type *Ti_alpha* is the maximal type with respect to type *Ti*.
    Examples: 1. For the tuple types shown in Fig. 5, the maximal type is TUPLE {E *alpha*, R *alpha*}. 2. Let *T* be the tuple type TUPLE { }. Then the maximal type with respect to *T* is *T* itself (the only type in the pertinent type lattice), and it contains exactly one value: namely, the 0-tuple.

minimal subtype (SQL)   *See* maximal supertype (SQL).

minimal type   A type with no proper subtype. Every type lattice (q.v.) has exactly one minimal type. For scalar types, the unique minimal type is *omega*; for tuple and relation types, *see* minimal type (tuple types) and minimal type (relation types), respectively.

minimal type (relation types)   Let *T* be a relation type with heading {<*A1,T1*>, ..., <*An,Tn*>} (*n* ≥ 0). Then type *T_omega* = RELATION {<*A1,T1_omega*>, <*A2,T2_omega*>, ..., <*An,Tn_omega*>} is the minimal type with respect to relation type *T* (in fact, it's the minimal type with respect to the pertinent type lattice, q.v.) if and only if, for all i ($i = 1, 2, ..., n$), type *Ti_omega* is the minimal type with respect to type *Ti*.

Examples: 1. For the relation types shown in Fig. 5, the minimal type is RELATION {E *omega*, R *omega*}. Note that this type contains exactly exactly one value: namely, the empty relation of that type. 2. Let *T* be the relation type RELATION { }. Then the minimal type with respect to *T* is *T* itself (the only type in the pertinent type lattice), and it contains exactly two values: namely, TABLE_DUM and TABLE_DEE.

minimal type (tuple types) Let *T* be a tuple type with heading {<*A1,T1*>, <*A2,T2*>, ..., <*An,Tn*>} ($n \geq 0$). Then type *T_omega* = TUPLE {<*A1,T1_omega*>, <*A2,T2_omega*>, ..., <*An,Tn_omega*>} is the minimal type with respect to tuple type *T* (in fact, it's the minimal type with respect to the pertinent type lattice, q.v.) if and only if, for all i ($i = 1, 2, ..., n$), type *Ti_omega* is the minimal type with respect to type *Ti*.

Examples: For the tuple types shown in Fig. 5, the minimal type is TUPLE {E *omega*, R *omega*}; note that this type is empty (there are no tuples of this type). However, minimal tuple types aren't necessarily empty. For example, let *T* be the tuple type TUPLE { }. Then the minimal type with respect to *T* is *T* itself (the only type in the pertinent type lattice), and it contains exactly one value: namely, the 0-tuple.

model of a relation variable Let relation variable (relvar) *V* be of declared type *T*, and let it have attributes *A1, A2, ..., An* ($n \geq 0$). Because of value substitutability, q.v., the value *v* assigned to *V* at any given time can have any subtype *T'* of type *T* as its most specific type. *V* can therefore be modeled as a named set, containing *n* named ordered triples of the form <*DTi,MSTi,vi*> ($i = 1, 2, ..., n$), where:

- The name of the set is the name of the relvar, *V*.

- The name of each triple is the name of the corresponding attribute.

- *DTi* is the name of the declared type of attribute *Ai*.

- *MSTi* is the name of the most specific type for, or of, attribute *Ai*. That most specific type is the most specific common supertype of the most specific types of the values in *vi*—see the explanation of *vi* in the next bullet item below. (Actually *MSTi* is uniquely determined by *vi* and so could be omitted from the model, but it's convenient to include it.)

- Let the body of the current value of *V* consist of *m* tuples ($m \geq 0$); label those tuples (in some arbitrary sequence) "tuple 1," "tuple 2," ..., "tuple *m*"; then *vi* is a sequence of *m* values (not necessarily all distinct), being the *Ai* values from tuple 1, tuple 2, ..., tuple *m* (in that order). Note that those *Ai* values are all of type *MSTi*.

Note: The notation $DT(Ai)$, $MST(Ai)$, $v(Ai)$ is used elsewhere in this dictionary to refer to the DTi, $MSTi$, vi components, respectively, of the Ai component of this model of relvar V. Also, the notation $DT(V)$, $MST(V)$, $v(V)$ is used to refer to the overall declared type, overall most specific type, and overall current value components, respectively, of this model of relvar V.

model of a relational expression Let *exp* be a relational expression. Then the notation $DTi(V)$, $MSTi(V)$, $vi(V)$ introduced under **model of a relation variable** can be extended in an obvious way to allow $DTi(exp)$, $MSTi(exp)$, $vi(exp)$ to be used to refer to the DTi, $MSTi$, vi components, respectively, of the Ai component of the model of the relation denoted by the expression *exp*. Similarly, the notation $DT(V)$, $MST(V)$, $v(V)$ introduced under **model of a relation variable** can be extended in an obvious way to allow $DT(exp)$, $MST(exp)$, $v(exp)$ to be used to refer to the overall DT, MST, v components of the model of the relation denoted by the expression *exp*.

model of a scalar expression Let *exp* be a scalar expression. Then the notation $DT(V)$, $MST(V)$, $v(V)$ introduced under **model of a scalar variable** can be extended in an obvious way to allow $DT(exp)$, $MST(exp)$, $v(exp)$ to be used to refer to the DT, MST, v components of the model of the scalar value denoted by the expression *exp*.

model of a scalar variable Let scalar variable V be of declared type T. Because of value substitutability, q.v., the value v assigned to V at any given time can have any nonempty subtype T' of type T as its most specific type. V can therefore be modeled as a named ordered triple of the form $<DT,MST,v>$, where:

■ The name of the triple is the name of the variable, V.

■ DT is the name of the declared type for variable V.

■ MST is the name of the most specific type for, or of, variable V. (Actually MST is uniquely determined by v—*see* **most specific type**—and so the MST component of V could be omitted from the model, but it's convenient to include it.)

■ v is a value of most specific type MST—the current value for, or of, variable V.

Note: The notation $DT(V)$, $MST(V)$, $v(V)$ is used elsewhere in this dictionary to refer to the DT, MST, v components, respectively, of this model of scalar variable V.

model of a tuple expression Let *exp* be a tuple expression. Then the notation $DTi(V)$, $MSTi(V)$, $vi(V)$ introduced under **model of a tuple variable** can be extended in an obvious way to allow $DTi(exp)$, $MSTi(exp)$, $vi(exp)$ to be used to refer to the DTi, $MSTi$, vi components, respectively, of the Ai component of the model of the tuple denoted by the expression *exp*.

Similarly, the notation $DT(V)$, $MST(V)$, $v(V)$ introduced under **model of a tuple variable** can be extended in an obvious way to allow $DT(exp)$, $MST(exp)$, $v(exp)$ to be used to refer to the overall DT, MST, v components of the model of the tuple denoted by the expression *exp*.

model of a tuple variable Let tuple variable (tuplevar) V be of declared type T, and let the heading of T have attributes $A1$, $A2$, ..., An $(n \geq 0)$. Because of value substitutability, q.v., the value v assigned to V at any given time can have any nonempty subtype T' of type T as its most specific type. V can therefore be modeled as a named set of named ordered triples of the form $<DTi,MSTi,vi>$ $(i = 1, 2, ..., n)$, where:

- The name of the set is the name of the tuplevar, V.

- The name of each triple is the name of the corresponding attribute.

- DTi is the name of the declared type of attribute Ai.

- $MSTi$ is the name of the most specific type for, or of, attribute Ai. (Actually $MSTi$ is uniquely determined by vi—see below—and so could be omitted from the model, but it's convenient to include it.)

- vi is a value of most specific type $MSTi$—the current value for, or of, attribute Ai.

Note: The notation $DT(Ai)$, $MST(Ai)$, $v(Ai)$ is used elsewhere in this dictionary to refer to the DTi, $MSTi$, vi components, respectively, of the Ai component of this model of tuplevar V. Also, the notation $DT(V)$, $MST(V)$, $v(V)$ is used to refer to the overall declared type, overall most specific type, and overall current value components, respectively, of this model of tuplevar V.

model of a variable *See* model of a relation variable; model of a scalar variable; model of a tuple variable.

model of an expression *See* model of a relational expression; model of a scalar expression; model of a tuple expression.

most specific common subtype Let $T1$, $T2$, ..., Tm $(m \geq 0)$ be types from the same type lattice, q.v. Then type T' is the most specific common subtype for types $T1$, $T2$, ..., Tm if and only if it's the minimal type with respect to the type lattice in question. *Note:* Informally, most specific common subtypes are sometimes defined to exclude the pertinent minimal type, in which case the term is taken to apply to the pertinent leaf type (but only if every type in the given set of types $T1$, $T2$, ..., Tm overlaps every other—for otherwise no such leaf type exists). With reference to Fig. 4, for example, the most specific common subtype for types KITE and CYCLIC QUADRILATERAL is either type *omega*, q.v., or (if minimal types are excluded) type

SQUARE. (Note that RIGHT KITE is also a common subtype in this example, but it's not the most specific one.) By contrast, with reference to Fig. 2, the most specific common subtype for types ELLIPSE and RECTANGLE either is type *omega* or (if minimal types are excluded) doesn't exist. *Contrast* least specific common subtype; least specific common supertype; most specific common supertype.

most specific common subtype (relation types) *See* most specific common subtype.

most specific common subtype (tuple types) *See* most specific common subtype.

most specific common supertype Let *T1, T2, ..., Tm* ($m \geq 0$) be types from the same type lattice, q.v. Then type *T* is the most specific common supertype for types *T1, T2, ..., Tm* if and only if it's a common supertype (q.v.) for those types and no proper subtype of *T* is also a common supertype for those types. *Note:* It can be shown—see the *Manifesto* book—that, given types *T1, T2, ..., Tm,* the corresponding most specific common supertype *T* always exists and is unique (though it might be one of those specified types *T1, T2, ..., Tm,* or even the pertinent maximal type, q.v.); in fact, it's the least upper bound, q.v., of types *T1, T2, ..., Tm.* Note too that (a) if *m* = 1, then the set of types *T1, T2, ..., Tm* reduces to just *T1,* and *T1* itself is the most specific common supertype for that set; (b) if *m* = 0, then the set of types *T1, T2, ..., Tm* is empty, and the most specific common supertype is the pertinent minimal type. *Contrast* least specific common subtype; least specific common supertype; most specific common subtype.

 Examples: 1. With reference to Fig. 2, the most specific common supertype for types SQUARE and POLYGON is POLYGON, and the most specific common supertype for ELLIPSE and SQUARE is PLANE_FIGURE. 2. With reference to Fig. 3, the most specific common supertype for types RECTANGLE and RHOMBUS is PARALLELOGRAM. 3. With reference to Fig. 4, the most specific common supertype for types RIGHT KITE and RHOMBUS is KITE. Note that QUADRILATERAL is also a common supertype in this example, but it's not the most specific one.

 Note: As mentioned under **intersection type**, whereas least specific common subtypes are always intersection types, most specific common supertypes aren't necessarily union types, because there might reasonably be cases in which the most specific common supertype contains values that aren't values of any of its immediate subtypes. In Fig. 3, for example, the most specific common supertype for types RECTANGLE and RHOMBUS is PARALLELOGRAM, yet there certainly exist parallelograms that are neither rectangles nor rhombuses (rhombi, if you prefer).

most specific common supertype (relation types) Let *T1, T2, ..., Tm* ($m \geq 0$) be relation types from the same type lattice, q.v.; by definition, then, those types all have the same attribute names, say *A1, A2, ..., An* ($n \geq 0$). Let the type of attribute *Aj* (*j* = 1, 2, ..., *n*) within type *Ti* (*i* = 1, 2, ..., *m*) be *Tij*. Then type *T* = RELATION {<*A1,T01*>,<*A2,T02*>, ...,<*An,T0n*>} is the most specific common supertype for types *T1, T2, ..., Tm* if and only if, for all *j* (*j* = 1, 2, ..., *n*), type

T0j is the most specific common supertype for types *T1j*, *T2j*, ..., *Tmj*. *See also* most specific common supertype; *contrast* least specific common subtype (relation types); least specific common supertype (relation types); most specific common supertype (tuple types).

Example: With reference to Fig. 5, the most specific common supertype for (e.g.) relation types CR and ES is relation type ER.

most specific common supertype (tuple types)   Let *T1*, *T2*, ..., *Tm* ($m \geq 0$) be tuple types from the same type lattice, q.v.; by definition, then, those types all have the same attribute names, say *A1*, *A2*, ..., *An* ($n \geq 0$). Let the type of attribute *Aj* (j = 1, 2, ..., *n*) within type *Ti* (i = 1, 2, ..., *m*) be *Tij*. Then type *T* = TUPLE {<*A1,T01*>,<*A2,T02*>,...,<*An,T0n*>} is the most specific common supertype for types *T1*, *T2*, ..., *Tm* if and only if, for all *j* (j = 1, 2, ..., *n*), type *T0j* is the most specific common supertype for types *T1j*, *T2j*, ..., *Tmj*. *See also* most specific common supertype; *contrast* least specific common subtype (tuple types); least specific common supertype (tuple types); most specific common supertype (relation types).

Example: With reference to Fig. 5, the most specific common supertype for (e.g.) tuple types ER and ES is tuple type ER.

most specific type   Let value *x* be of type *T* and not of any proper subtype of *T*; then *T* is the most specific type of *x* (and the set of types possessed by *x* is, precisely, the set of all supertypes of *T*). Note that *T* isn't necessarily a minimal type, nor even a leaf type. For scalar types, in fact, it can't possibly be the sole minimal type, which is type *omega*; for tuple types, it might be the corresponding minimal type, but only if that type is nonempty, which it usually won't be; for relation types, it'll be the corresponding minimal type if and only if *x* is an empty relation. *See* most specific type (relation types); most specific type (tuple types).

Further, let *exp* be an expression. Then *exp* has the same most specific type as the value it denotes. Observe that most specific types are (a) unique; (b) not known until run time (in general). *Contrast* least specific type.

Example: With reference to Fig. 3, if *x* is of type SQUARE and not of any proper subtype of SQUARE (in fact, of course, SQUARE doesn't have any proper subtypes in the case at hand), then the most specific type of *x* is SQUARE, and the set of types possessed by *x* is SQUARE, RECTANGLE, RHOMBUS, PARALLELOGRAM, and *alpha*.

Note: Elsewhere in this dictionary, the most specific type of *x* is denoted *MST(x)*; likewise, the most specific type of *exp* is denoted *MST(exp)*. Note further that an important special case occurs when the expression *exp* consists of a simple variable reference, *V*; in this case, it's usual to refer to *MST(V)* as the most specific type of the variable *V* as such, as well as of the expression consisting of a reference to that variable.

most specific type (relation types)   Let relation *x* be of type *T* and not of any proper subtype of *T*; then *T* is the most specific type of *x* (and the set of types possessed by *x* is, precisely, the set of all supertypes of *T*). Note that *T* isn't necessarily a minimal type, nor even a leaf type. Further, let *exp* be a relational expression. Then *exp* has the same most specific type as the relation it denotes. Observe that most specific relation types are (a) unique; (b) not known until run time (in general). *See also* **most specific type**; *contrast* **least specific type (relation types)**.

Note: It follows from the foregoing definitions that if *T* is the most specific type for some relation *x* and *A* is some attribute within *T*, then the type of *A* within *T* is the most specific common supertype of the most specific types of all of the *A* values in *x*. By way of example, let relation *x* be as follows:

E : ELLIPSE	R : RECTANGLE
e1 : circle	*r1 : rectangle*
e2 : ellipse	*r2 : square*
e3 : circle	*r3 : square*

(Most specific types are shown in lowercase italics.) The most specific type of this relation is RELATION {E ELLIPSE, R RECTANGLE}—not, as might intuitively have been thought, RELATION {E CIRCLE, R SQUARE}. For if we were to define this latter to be the most specific type of *x*, then certain tuples in *x* would have attribute values "of the wrong type"; for example, the *<e2,r2>* tuple would contain an E value of type ELLIPSE and not CIRCLE, and we would have a "noncircular circle" (q.v.) on our hands.

Two further examples: The most specific type of the empty relation of type RELATION {E ELLIPSE, R RECTANGLE} is RELATION {E *omega*, R *omega*}; the most specific type of any relation—necessarily either TABLE_DUM or TABLE_DEE—of type RELATION { } is RELATION { } itself.

Note: Elsewhere in this dictionary, the most specific type of relation *x* is denoted *MST(x)*; likewise, the most specific type of the relational expression *exp* is denoted *MST(exp)*, and the most specific type of attribute *A* of relation *x* is denoted *MST(A)*. Note further that an important special case occurs when the expression *exp* consists of a simple relation variable (relvar) reference, *V*; in this case, it's usual to refer to *MST(V)* as the most specific type of the relvar *V* as such, as well as of the expression consisting of a reference to that relvar.

most specific type (tuple types)   Let tuple *x* be of type *T* and not of any proper subtype of *T*; then *T* is the most specific type of *x* (and the set of types possessed by *x* is, precisely, the set of all supertypes of *T*). Note that *T* isn't necessarily a minimal type (in fact it can't be, unless that minimal type is nonempty), nor even a leaf type. Further, let *exp* be a tuple expression. Then *exp* has the same most specific type as the tuple it denotes. Observe that most specific tuple types are (a) unique; (b) not known until run time (in general). *See also* **most specific type**; *contrast* **least specific type (tuple types)**.

Note: It follows from the foregoing definitions that if *T* is the most specific type for some tuple *x* and *A* is some attribute within *T*, then the type of *A* within *T* is just the type of the *A* value in *x*. By way of example, let tuple *x* be as follows:

E : CIRCLE	R : SQUARE
e3 : circle	*r3 : square*

(Attribute value most specific types are shown in lowercase italics.) As the heading indicates, the most specific type of this tuple is TUPLE {E CIRCLE, R SQUARE}.

By way of another example, the most specific type of the sole tuple of type TUPLE { }—viz., the 0-tuple—is TUPLE { } itself.

Note: Elsewhere in this dictionary, the most specific type of tuple *x* is denoted *MST(x)*; likewise, the most specific type of the tuple expression *exp* is denoted *MST(exp)*, and the most specific type of attribute *A* of tuple *x* is denoted *MST(A)*. Note further that an important special case occurs when the expression *exp* consists of a simple tuple variable reference, *V*; in this case, it's usual to refer to *MST(V)* as the most specific type of the tuple variable *V* as such, as well as of the expression consisting of a reference to that variable.

MST (...)   Most specific type of. *See* model of a variable; model of an expression; most specific type.

multiple inheritance   A form of inheritance in which a proper subtype can have any number, *n* say, of immediate supertypes (*n* > 1). *Contrast* single inheritance (but single inheritance is, of course, just that degenerate case of multiple inheritance for which the condition *n* > 1 is relaxed). Note that tuple inheritance and relation inheritance are necessarily multiple, and scalar inheritance is too if type *omega* is taken into account (since type *omega* is a subtype of every scalar type).

Examples: See Figs. 3, 4, and 5.

———— ◆◆◆◆◆ ————

noncircular circle   A contradiction in terms, typical of the logical absurdities that can and do occur if S by C, q.v., and G by C, q.v., aren't supported, and used as a convenient shorthand to refer to such absurdities in general. To spell out the details of this particular solecism: Consider the type hierarchy of Fig. 2; however, let's agree for simplicity to ignore all of the types in that figure apart from types ELLIPSE and CIRCLE. Then a noncircular circle is something the system thinks is a circle but actually isn't—i.e., it's a value whose most specific type as far as the system is concerned is CIRCLE and yet has different semiaxis lengths, and thus logically ought to have most specific type ELLIPSE. *Note:* Noncircular circles and suchlike solecisms can't occur in the *Manifesto* model. *See also* circular noncircle.

nondummy type   A regular type (the term *nondummy type* is sometimes used for emphasis).

noninstantiable type   Term sometimes used in OO contexts to mean a union type. The name presumably derives from the fact that such a type has no "instances," where the term "instances" presumably means—at least in this context—values whose most specific type is the type in question (it has nothing to do with instance variables, q.v., nor with instantiation in the sense of logic). Note, however, that elsewhere in those same OO contexts that same term *instance* is certainly taken to include variables, etc., as well as values as such; in fact, it's often used a synonym for *object*. *Contrast* **instantiable type**.

nonunion type   A regular type that isn't a union type; equivalently, a scalar type such that there exists at least one value with most specific type the type in question. The term *nonunion type* is sometimes used for emphasis.

   Examples: See the examples under **union type**.

omega   The minimal scalar type. Type *omega* (a) contains no values at all, (b) has no immediate subtype, and (c) is an immediate subtype for every scalar leaf type (with respect to the set of available types, q.v., in the case of property (c)). No scalar type other than type *omega* possesses any of properties (a), (b), or (c). Note that, by definition, type *omega* is system defined; unique; primarily conceptual in nature; a dummy type, q.v. (and in fact a union type, q.v., albeit vacuously so); and not a leaf type, q.v. Note further that the type constraint for *omega* is simply FALSE; the expression IS_*omega* (*exp*), where *exp* is a scalar expression, always evaluates to FALSE; and the expression TREAT_AS_*omega* (*exp*), where *exp* is a scalar expression always fails (or would always fail, rather, since the expression is clearly a contradiction in terms and might well not be recognized as legitimate). *See also* **T_omega**.

   It's worth pointing out that type *omega* inherits every read-only operator that applies to scalar values, but vacuously so (since those operators can never be invoked on any value of the type). A similar remark applies to type constraints also.

operator inheritance   *See* **type inheritance**.

operator version   Same as implementation version.

overlapping types   Types *T1* and *T2* overlap if and only if there exists at least one value that's common to both. (Observe in particular, therefore, that an empty type doesn't overlap with anything, not even itself). Note that the foregoing definition is equivalent to saying *T1* and *T2* have a nonempty common subtype—and if they do have a nonempty common subtype, they necessarily have a nonempty common supertype also, though the converse is false. Note too that types can't possibly overlap if they're not from the same type lattice, q.v. *Contrast* **disjoint types**.

overloading   (*With inheritance*) In an inheritance context, the term *overloading* is sometimes used to mean inclusion polymorphism, q.v. This particular usage is strongly deprecated, however, because there's an important logical difference between the two concepts, a difference that can be characterized as follows:

■ Inclusion polymorphism means there's just one operator, with several distinct implementation versions under the covers, but the user doesn't need to know the versions in question are in fact distinct—as far as the user is concerned, there's just the one operator.

■ Overloading polymorphism means there are several distinct operators with the same name, and the user does need to know the operators in question are in fact distinct.

overriding   (*With inheritance*) In an inheritance context, overriding is often confused with either overloading or inclusion polymorphism or both, though it shouldn't be. For example (from Douglas K. Barry, *The Object Database Handbook: How to Select, Implement, and Use Object-Oriented Databases*, Wiley Publishing, 1996—italics in the original):

> The object model allows ... multiple use of the same method, which is called *overloading*. The overloaded definition of Display in the [subclass] *overrides* the definition of Display in the [superclass] because it is lower in the class hierarchy.

And elsewhere in the same book:

> *Overriding:* Where a method for a subclass adds to or replaces a method of its superclass.

Incidentally, these quotes seem to embrace the idea that changing semantics, q.v., is a virtue. They also seem to be confused over the difference between a model and its implementation, though in fact this latter is a criticism that can be leveled at OO writings in general.

parent type   Term occasionally used to mean an immediate supertype.

possrep inheritance   Let scalar type T be an immediate supertype of scalar type T'. Then every possrep for values of type T is necessarily, albeit implicitly, a possrep for values of type T' as well. (With reference to Fig. 2, for example, circles are ellipses and so, by definition, "possibly representable"—like ellipses in general—in terms of their major and minor semiaxis lengths and their center.) Thus, possreps might be regarded as further "properties" that are inherited by subtypes from supertypes in general. However, such an inherited possrep isn't regarded as an explicitly declared one in the sense explained under **possible representation** in Part I of this dictionary, because to regard it as such would lead to a contradiction concerning inheritance of update operators (inheritance of THE_ pseudovariables, to be specific—again, see

Part I of this dictionary). Thus, to say that type T' inherits a possrep from type T is only a manner of speaking—it doesn't carry any formal weight. *Contrast* derived possrep.

Example: With reference to Fig. 2 again, type CIRCLE inherits a possrep with components A, B, and CTR from its immediate supertype ELLIPSE. Now, if that possrep were a declared one, an assignment such as this one to a variable C of declared type CIRCLE—

```
THE_A ( C ) := LENGTH ( 5.0 ) ;
```

—would have to be legal. But assignments like this one, if permitted, are exactly what give rise to noncircular circles (q.v.) and the like, which is why they're prohibited (at least in the *Manifesto* model). It follows that inherited possreps can't be considered declared ones.

Principle of Read-Only Operator Inheritance Let Op be a read-only operator, let P be a parameter to Op, and let T be the declared type of P. Then the declared type of the argument expression, and hence the most specific type of the argument as such, corresponding to P in an invocation of Op can be any nonempty subtype T' of T. In other words, the operator Op applies to values of type T and therefore, necessarily, to values of type T'—*The Principle of Read-Only Operator Inheritance*. It follows that such operators are polymorphic, since they apply to values of several different types—*The Principle of Read-Only Operator Polymorphism* (where the kind of polymorphism involved is, specifically, inclusion polymorphism, q.v.). It further follows that wherever a value of type T is permitted, a value of any subtype of T is also permitted—*The Principle of Value Substitutability*. *Note:* If Op is an update operator and P is a parameter to Op that isn't subject to update, then Op behaves as if it were a read-only operator as far as P is concerned, and all relevant aspects of this definition therefore apply directly, mutatis mutandis.

Example: See the example under **argument** involving the read-only version of the MOVE operator.

Principle of Read-Only Operator Polymorphism *See Principle of Read-Only Operator Inheritance.*

Principle of Update Operator Inheritance Let Op be an update operator, let P be a parameter to Op that's subject to update, and let T be the declared type of P. Then it might or might not be the case that the declared type of the argument expression (which must in fact be a variable reference specifically), and hence the most specific type of the argument (a variable) as such, corresponding to P in an invocation of Op can be some nonempty proper subtype T' of type T. It follows that for each such update operator Op and for each parameter P to Op that's subject to update, it's necessary to state explicitly for which proper subtypes T' of the declared type T of parameter P operator Op is inherited—*The Principle of Update Operator Inheritance*. (And if update operator Op isn't inherited in this way by type T', it isn't inherited by any proper subtype of type T' either. *See* **signature** for further discussion.) Update operators are thus only conditionally polymorphic—*The Principle of Update Operator Polymorphism*. Thus, if Op is an update operator and P is a parameter to Op that's subject to update and T' is a proper subtype of the declared type *T* of *P* for which *Op* is inherited, then by definition it's possible to invoke *Op* with an argument expression (actually a variable reference) corresponding to parameter *P* that's of declared type *T'*—*The Principle of Variable Substitutability.*

Examples: To see why it makes no sense for update operators to be inherited unconditionally, let variables R and S be of declared types RECTANGLE and SQUARE, respectively (see Fig. 2). Clearly, then, it's possible—speaking rather loosely—to change the height of R without changing its width; more precisely, it's possible to update R in such a way as to replace the current rectangle value *r1* by a new rectangle value *r2* that has the same width as *r1* but a different height. Equally clearly, it's not possible to do the same thing to S, because squares must always have equal height and width. In other words, a certain update operator ("change the height but not the width") is effectively defined for type RECTANGLE but not for type SQUARE.

So update operator inheritance has to be conditional; in other words, which update operators are inherited by which subtypes must be specified explicitly (*see* **signature**). For example, with reference to Fig. 2 once again, we might reasonably specify the following:

- The update operators that apply to variables of declared type ELLIPSE are (a) assignment to THE_A, THE_B, and THE_CTR and (b) the update form of MOVE (see the examples under **signature**).

- The update operators that apply to variables of declared type CIRCLE are (a) assignment to THE_CTR and THE_R and (b) the update form of MOVE.

And if we were to define, as we did in the examples under **argument**, type CIRCLE to have a proper subtype O_CIRCLE (where an "O-circle" is a circle with center the origin), then:

- The only update operator that applies to variables of declared type O_CIRCLE is assignment to THE_R.

Of course, the operators referred to above as assignments to some THE_ operator are all defined automatically anyway, by virtue of the fact that corresponding possreps have been explicitly declared for the pertinent types. *See* **automatic definition**.

Note: Despite the foregoing, some writers still argue that update operators, like read-only operators, should be inherited unconditionally, and some languages and systems do indeed behave that way. But it's precisely such behavior that leads to logical absurdities such as circular noncircles, q.v., and noncircular circles, q.v. (not to mention the almost total lack of type constraint support found in SQL in particular!). For further discussion, see the *Manifesto* book.

Principle of Update Operator Polymorphism   *See Principle of Update Operator Inheritance.*

Principle of Value Substitutability   The principle that wherever a value of type *T* is permitted, a value of any subtype of *T* can be substituted. *See Principle of Read-Only Operator Inheritance.*

Principle of Variable Substitutability   The principle that wherever a variable of declared type *T* is permitted, a variable of declared type some nonempty subtype of *T* can be substituted—but only if such substitution makes sense. *See Principle of Update Operator Inheritance.*

proper subtype   Type *T′* is a proper subtype of type *T* if and only if (a) it's a subtype of *T* and (b) *T* and *T′* are distinct. *See also* immediate subtype; proper supertype. *Note:* If *T* and *T′* are scalar types, then there must be at least one value of type *T* that's not a value of type *T′* (*see* example value, second definition). As for tuple and relation types, the same will be true so long as none of type *T*'s attributes is of some empty type.
   Examples: 1. With reference to Fig. 2, type SQUARE is a proper subtype of type POLYGON. Note in particular that there do exist polygons (i.e., values of type POLYGON) that aren't squares (i.e., values of type SQUARE). 2. Here by contrast is an example involving two relation types, one a proper subtype of the other, such that the proper subtype isn't a proper subset:

```
RELATION { E omega , R RECTANGLE }

RELATION { E omega , R omega }
```

Neither of these types is empty, despite the fact that they both have at least one attribute of an empty type; in fact, they both contain exactly one value, viz., the empty relation of most specific type RELATION {E *omega*, R *omega*}. 3. Similarly, given the following tuple types—

```
TUPLE { E omega , R RECTANGLE }
TUPLE { E omega , R omega }
```

—again one type is a proper subtype, but not a proper subset, of the other; in this case, however, both types are empty.

proper supertype   Type *T* is a proper supertype of type *T′* if and only if (a) it's a supertype of *T′* and (b) *T* and *T′* are distinct. *See also* immediate supertype; proper subtype. *Note:* If *T* and *T′* are scalar types, then there must be at least one value of type *T* that's not a value of type *T′* (*see* example value, second definition). As for tuple and relation types, the same will be true so long as none of type *T*'s attributes is of some empty type.
   Examples: See the examples under **proper subtype** (note that *T* is a proper supertype of *T′* if and only if *T′* is a proper subtype of *T*).

properties   Term used informally and generically to refer to the type constraints and read-only operators (sometimes update operators as well, depending on context) that apply to some given type *T*—in other words, anything that will or might be inherited by an immediate subtype *T'* of the given type *T*. *Note:* The term *properties* is sometimes used, even more informally, to include possreps (q.v.) as well, since any possrep that applies to type *T* necessarily applies to type *T'* as well and so can be thought of—but only informally—as also being inherited by *T'* from *T* (*see* **possrep inheritance**).

———— ♦ ♦ ♦ ♦ ♦ ————

R : **IS_SAME_TYPE_AS**   *See R* : IS_*T*.

R : **IS_*T***   Let *R* be a relational expression, let *A* be a scalar attribute of the relation *r* denoted by *R*, let *T* be a scalar type, and let *DT*(*A*) and *T* overlap (this is a compile time check). Then the expression *R* : IS_*T* (*A*)—or some logical equivalent to that expression—returns a relation with (a) heading the same as that of *r*, except that *DT*(*A*) in that heading is *T*, and (b) body consisting of those tuples of *r* in which *v*(*A*) is of type *T*, except that *DT*(*A*) in each of those tuples is *T*. *Note:* **Tutorial D** also supports a generalized version of this operator of the form *R* : IS_SAME_TYPE_AS (*exp*,*A*), where *DT*(*exp*) and *DT*(*A*) aren't limited to being scalar. This generalized version is effectively equivalent to *R* : IS_*T* (*A*), where *T* is *DT*(*exp*)—assuming for definitional purposes here that the expression *R* : IS_*T* (*A*) is syntactically valid.

Examples: Let relvar R have an attribute E of declared type ELLIPSE. Then (assuming the obvious operator precedence) the expression

```
R : IS_CIRCLE ( E ) WHERE THE_R ( E ) > LENGTH ( 2.0 )
```

returns a relation with (a) heading the same as that of R, except that the type of attribute E in that result is CIRCLE instead of ELLIPSE, and (b) body consisting of just those tuples from R in which the E value is of type CIRCLE and the radius for the circle in question has length greater than two. Note that, by contrast, the expression

```
R WHERE THE_R ( E ) > LENGTH ( 2.0 )
```

is invalid (it fails on a compile time type error), since THE_R is not defined for values of type ELLIPSE. Note too that the valid version—R : IS_CIRCLE (E) WHERE ... — is almost but not quite equivalent to the following:

```
R WHERE CASE
          WHEN IS_CIRCLE ( E ) THEN
               THE_R ( TREAT_AS_CIRCLE ( E ) ) > LENGTH ( 2.0 )
          WHEN NOT ( IS_CIRCLE ( E ) ) THEN FALSE
        END CASE
```

The difference is that this latter expression yields a relation with the same heading as R, rather than one in which the type of attribute E is CIRCLE. More generally, however, the expression

```
R : IS_T ( A )
```

is equivalent to, and is therefore shorthand for, the following:

```
( R WHERE IS_T ( A ) ) : TREAT_AS_T ( A )
```

Moreover, this latter expression is shorthand too (*see R*: TREAT_AS_*T*).

By way of another example, consider the relation types shown in Fig. 5. Let relvar R have an attribute X of declared type ER and let ESV be a variable of declared type and current most specific type both ES; then the expression

```
R : IS_SAME_TYPE_AS ( ESV , X )
```

returns a relation with (a) heading the same as that of R, except that the type of attribute X in that result is ES instead of ER, and (b) body consisting of just those tuples from R in which the X value is of type ES.

R: **TREAT_AS_*T*** Let *R* be a relational expression, let *A* be a scalar attribute of the relation *r* denoted by *R*, let *T* be a scalar type, and let *DT*(*A*) and *T* overlap (this is a compile time check). Then the expression *R* : TREAT_AS_*T* (*A*)—or some logical equivalent to that expression— either raises a run time type error (if *MST*(*A*) isn't some subtype of type *T*) or returns a relation identical to *r* except that the type of attribute *A* in that relation is *T* (otherwise). *Note:* **Tutorial D** supports a generalized form of this operator, *R* : TREAT_AS_SAME_TYPE_AS (*exp,A*), where *DT*(*exp*) and *DT*(*A*) aren't limited to being scalar. This generalized form is effectively equivalent to *R* : TREAT_AS_*T* (*A*), where *T* is *DT*(*exp*)—assuming for definitional purposes here that the expression *R* : TREAT_AS_*T* (*A*) is syntactically valid.

Examples: Let relvar R have an attribute E of declared type ELLIPSE. Then the expression

```
R : TREAT_AS_CIRCLE ( E )
```

either raises a run time type error (if any tuple in R has an E value of most specific type some proper supertype of CIRCLE), or returns a relation identical to the current value of R (otherwise), except that the type of attribute E in that result is CIRCLE instead of ELLIPSE. In other words, the expression shown is shorthand for the following:

```
EXTEND R : { E := TREAT_AS_CIRCLE ( E ) }
```

By way of another example, consider the relation types shown in Fig. 5. Let relvar R have an attribute X of declared type ER and let ESV be a variable of declared type and current most specific type both ES; then the expression

```
R : TREAT_AS_SAME_TYPE_AS ( ESV , X )
```

either raises a run time type error (if any tuple in R has an X value of most specific type some supertype of ES), or returns a relation identical to the current value of R (otherwise), except that the type of attribute X in that result is ES instead of ER. In other words, the expression shown is shorthand for the following:

```
EXTEND R : { X := TREAT_AS_SAME_TYPE_AS ( ESV , X ) }
```

receiver parameter   *See* selfish method.

recursively defined type   (*With inheritance*) A type defined in terms of itself. Let T be a scalar type, and let $S(1)$, $S(2)$, ... be a sequence of sets defined as follows:

$S(1) = \{\, t : t$ is the declared type of some scalar component,
            or of some attribute of some tuple valued or relation valued component,
            of some possrep for $T \}$

$S(i) \;= \{\, t : t$ is the declared type of some scalar component,
            or of some attribute of some tuple valued or relation valued component,
            of some possrep for some type in $S(i-1) \}$
     $(i > 1)$

If there exists some n $(n > 0)$ such that some subtype or supertype of T is a member of $S(n)$, then T is recursively defined.

As for tuple and relation types: Let H be a heading, and let $S(1)$, $S(2)$, ... be a sequence of sets defined as follows:

$S(1) = \{\, t : t$ is the declared type of some attribute in $H \}$

$S(i) \;= \{\, t : t$ is the declared type of some component of some possrep for some scalar type,
            or of some attribute of some tuple or relation type, in $S(i-1) \}$
     $(i > 1)$

If there exists some n $(n > 0)$ such that some subtype or supertype of either TUPLE H or RELATION H is a member of $S(n)$, then the heading H is recursively defined (and any tuple or relation type with heading H is therefore recursively defined as well).

The relational model currently prohibits recursively defined types.

regular root type   A type that's both (a) a regular (and hence necessarily scalar) type and (b) a root type.

regular type   A scalar type that's not a dummy type. Note that the concept of dummy vs. regular types doesn't really apply to nonscalar types. For further discussion, *see* **dummy type**.

relation assignment   *See* relational assignment.

relation comparison   *See* relational comparison.

relation equality   *See* relational equality.

relation subtype   *See* subtype (relation types).

relation supertype   *See* supertype (relation types).

relation type inheritance   A form of inheritance in which the types are relation types specifically. Note that relation type inheritance is necessarily multiple; note too that it has nothing to do with subtables and supertables, q.v.
    Example: See Fig. 5.

relational assignment   *(With inheritance)* Let R and r be a relvar and a relation, respectively, such that the most specific type $MST(r)$ of r is some subtype of the declared type $DT(R)$ of R. Then (and only then) r can be assigned to R; the assignment has the effect of setting $v(R)$ equal to r and $MST(R)$ equal to $MST(r)$. *Note:* In order for the assignment to be syntactically valid, the declared type $DT(rx)$ of the expression rx used to denote relation r must be some subtype of the declared type $DT(R)$ of relvar R (this condition is implied by the fact that $MST(r)$ is required to be some subtype of $DT(R)$, and is a compile time check).
    Examples: Let relvars RE and RC be of declared types RELATION {E ELLIPSE} and RELATION {E CIRCLE}, respectively, and consider the following assignment:

```
RE := RC ;
```

In this example, compile time type checking succeeds ($DT(RC)$ is a subtype of $DT(RE)$), and at run time $v(RE)$ and $MST(RE)$ are set equal to $v(RC)$ and $MST(RC)$, respectively.
    Now consider this assignment:

```
RC := RE ;
```

This example raises a compile time type error, because $DT(RE)$ isn't a subtype of $DT(RC)$. By contrast, if the expression RE in this example were to be replaced by the expression TREAT_AS_SAME_TYPE_AS (RC,RE), then compile time type checking would succeed; however, this latter expression will raise a type error—a run time type error, of course—if $MST(RE)$ isn't some subtype of RELATION {E CIRCLE} at run time (*see* TREAT).

relational comparison   *(With inheritance)* A boolean expression of the form $(rx1)$ *theta* $(rx2)$, where (a) $rx1$ and $rx2$ are relational expressions and (b) *theta* is any comparison operator that makes sense for relations ("=", "≠", "⊆", etc.). *Note:* If *theta* is "=" or "≠", then, in order for the comparison to be syntactically valid, the declared types *DT(rx1)* and *DT(rx2)* must overlap (this is a compile time check). Also, the parentheses enclosing *rx1* and *rx2* in the comparison might not be needed in practice.

relational equality   *(With inheritance)* Let *r1* and *r2* be relations such that the most specific types *MST(r1)* and *MST(r2)* overlap. Then *r1* and *r2* can be compared for equality; the comparison returns TRUE if and only if *r1* is equal to *r2* (in which case *MST(r1)* is equal to *MST(r2)* also). *Note:* In order for the comparison to be syntactically valid, the declared types *DT(rx1)* and *DT(rx2)* of the expressions *rx1* and *rx2* used to denote *r1* and *r2*, respectively, must overlap (this condition is implied by the fact that *MST(rx1)* and *MST(rx2)* are required to overlap, and is a compile time check).

result covariance   Let *Op* be a read-only operator and let *T* be the declared type of the result as specified in some invocation signature for *Op* (*see* **signature**). Then an invocation of *Op* whose arguments are of types as specified in that invocation signature can return a result whose most specific type is any nonempty subtype of *T*. *Contrast* **argument contravariance.**

    Examples: First, observe that result covariance as just defined is essentially just a consequence of *The Principle of Value Substitutability*; that is, just as a reference to a variable of declared type *T* can denote a value of any nonempty subtype of *T* (in general), so also an invocation of an operator with declared type *T* can denote a value of any nonempty subtype of *T* (in general). But, although the definition given above does capture the essence of the concept, there's quite a lot more to be said on the subject of result covariance in general. First, here for interest is a definition from the OO literature (it's taken from Elisa Bertino and Lorenzo Martino, *Object-Oriented Database Systems: Concepts and Architectures*, Addison-Wesley, 1993, but is somewhat paraphrased here):

> A type *T'* is a subtype of a type *T* if ... for each method *M* of *T* there is a corresponding method *M'* of *T'* such that ... if there is a result, then the type of the result of *M'* is a subtype of the type of the result of *M* (*rule of covariance in results*).

    Now, this definition can be criticized on a number of grounds. First of all, as pointed out in connection with some related text under **argument contravariance,** it seems to be circular—it defines what it means for some type to be a subtype of another in terms of the concept of some type being a subtype of another. Second, it seems to be insisting—though it's hard to be sure— that the result of *M'*, if there is one, *must* be of some (apparently proper) subtype of the type of the result of *M*: surely an undesirable state of affairs in practice. Third, it seems to be saying that *T'* is a subtype of *T* if substitutability applies, whereas the *Manifesto* model says that substitutability applies if *T'* is a subtype of *T*.

    Be that as it may, consider by way of a simple example the type hierarchy of Fig. 2 and the following operator definition:

```
OPERATOR COPY ( E ELLIPSE ) RETURNS ELLIPSE ;
    RETURN E ;
END OPERATOR ;
```

An invocation of this operator will return either a circle or just an ellipse, depending on whether its argument is a circle or just an ellipse. In this example, then, the type—the most specific type, that is—of the result clearly "covaries" with the type of the sole argument (whence the term *result covariance*, presumably). So far, so good. But what about the following example?

```
OPERATOR EORC ( B BOOLEAN ) RETURNS ELLIPSE ;
    RETURN ( IF B THEN ELLIPSE ( ... )
                  ELSE CIRCLE  ( ... ) END IF ) ;
END OPERATOR ;
```

An invocation of this operator will return either a circle or just an ellipse, depending on the value, not the type, of its argument. In this example, then, we obviously can't say the type of the result covaries with the type, as such, of the argument. What's more, it would surely be a little odd to think of it as covarying with the *value* of the argument, since the mapping between argument values and result types could in principle be arbitrarily complex—much more complex, surely, than the simple term "covarying" could reasonably be expected to signify.

For a third example, consider the operator MOVE (read-only version), with invocation signatures as follows (*see* **signature**):

```
( ELLIPSE , RECTANGLE ) RETURNS ELLIPSE
( ELLIPSE , SQUARE    ) RETURNS ELLIPSE
( CIRCLE  , RECTANGLE ) RETURNS CIRCLE
( CIRCLE  , SQUARE    ) RETURNS CIRCLE
```

Here the result type does covary with the type of the first argument but not with that of the second.

The net of the foregoing discussion is that—unlike the concept of argument contravariance, q.v.—the concept of result covariance is both necessary and desirable; in fact, it's a logical consequence of *The Principle of Value Substitutability*, q.v. However, the term *result covariance* as such is inappropriate, and logically unnecessary, and in some ways quite misleading.

RETURNS   (*With inheritance*) *See* **signature**.

reuse   *See* **code reuse**.

root   Abbreviation for root type.

root type A type with no immediate supertype other than the pertinent maximal type, q.v. Distinct root types are disjoint.

    Examples: In Fig. 2, PLANE_FIGURE is the only root type; in Fig. 3, PARALLELOGRAM is the only root type; in Fig. 4, QUADRILATERAL is the only root type; in Fig. 5, ER is the only root type. No two of these root types overlap.

run time binding As noted under binding, the term *binding* is used in the inheritance context to refer to the process of determining which implementation version of a given operator is to be executed in response to a given invocation of the operator in question. Such binding can be done at compile time or run time or both. Run time binding in particular (at least as that term is understood in the *Manifesto* model) can be defined thus: Given some invocation of some operator *Op*, it's the process of finding, at run time, the unique invocation signature for *Op*—*see* signature—for which the declared types of the parameters exactly match the most specific types of the corresponding arguments to that invocation, thereby causing the unique corresponding implementation version, q.v., of *Op* to be invoked. *Note:* In principle, binding can always be done at compile time—run time binding is logically unnecessary (though it might lead to better performance). *See* implementation version for further discussion; *see also* compile time binding.

run time type checking Checking at run time that the types of the arguments to an invocation of some operator conform to that operator's parameter type requirements, as specified by that operator's specification signature. *Note:* In the *Manifesto* model, such checking reduces to a single special case (all other type checking can be done at compile time): namely, checking at run time that the most specific type of the argument to a TREAT invocation is some subtype of the specified target type. *Contrast* compile time type checking.

    Examples: See the examples under TREAT.

run time type error The error that occurs if run time type checking (q.v.) fails. In the *Manifesto* model, such errors can occur only in the context of TREAT, q.v.

———— ♦♦♦♦♦ ————

S by C Specialization by constraint.

scalar subtype *See* subtype.

scalar supertype *See* supertype.

SELF *See* selfish method.

selfish method A method in the OO sense for which one parameter—the distinguished, receiver, or target parameter—is singled out for special semantic treatment (and special syntactic treatment also, necessarily), instead of all parameters being treated equally. The special treatment in question consists in using the argument corresponding to the distinguished parameter, and no other arguments, to control the binding process—i.e., to determine the implementation version, q.v., to be invoked. The term *selfish method* derives from the fact that the distinguished parameter is typically unnamed and thus has to be referenced within the method's implementation code in some ad hoc way, typically by means of the keyword SELF.

Note: In practice, OO methods are usually assumed to be selfish in the foregoing sense. For example, here's a quote from Douglas K. Barry, *The Object Database Handbook: How to Select, Implement, and Use Object-Oriented Databases* (Wiley Publishing, 1996):

> [Polymorphism is a] mechanism that selects a method based on the type of the target operand.

(Note the last eight words in particular.) And it's worth pointing out that selfish methods do make the binding process simpler than it would otherwise be (simpler, that is, than the binding process as defined elsewhere in this part of the dictionary). But "simpler" here really means simpler for the system, whose job it is to perform the actual binding; unfortunately, it's easy to see by contrast that it can have the effect of making matters much more complicated for the person whose job it is to write the code for the various implementation versions of the operator in question. See the *Manifesto* book for detailed arguments in support of this position.

set of available types   *See* available types.

signature   (*With inheritance*) Let Op be a read-only operator, with parameters $P1, P2, ..., Pn$ (and no others). Also, let parameter Pi have declared type DTi ($i = 1, 2, ..., n$)—but note immediately that a large part of the point of the discussion that follows is to make this remark, concerning parameter declared types, much more precise. In an invocation of Op, then, the argument Ai corresponding to parameter Pi can have as its most specific type $MSTi$ any nonempty subtype of DTi. (It follows a fortiori that the expression Xi denoting argument Ai can have as its declared type any type that's simultaneously a subtype of DTi and a supertype of $MSTi$.) Conceptually, therefore, Op has a specification signature, denoting that operator as perceived by the user, and a set of invocation signatures, where:

■ The specification signature consists of the operator name, the parameter declared types $PDT1, PDT2, ..., PDTn$, and the result declared type RDT.

■ Each invocation signature consists of one possible combination of argument expression declared types $ADT1, ADT2, ..., ADTn$, together with the declared type $IRDT$ of the result—necessarily a subtype of RDT—produced by an invocation of Op with arguments of most specific types equal to the declared types $ADT1, ADT2, ..., ADTn$, respectively, specified in the invocation signature in question.

Note: Under the covers, each distinct invocation signature will be associated with exactly one implementation version of *Op*, though a given implementation version might be associated with any number of distinct invocation signatures. *See* binding; implementation version.

Note, therefore, that (to repeat) *Op* has exactly one specification signature, plus exactly one invocation signature for each possible combination of argument expression declared types. (At least, that's what the model says, though certain obvious shorthands are likely to be available in concrete syntax—see further discussion below.)

Example: Consider the read-only version of the operator MOVE (mentioned in the examples under **argument** and elsewhere), which moves a specified ellipse such that it becomes centered on the center of a specified rectangle. Abstractly, that operator might have a specification signature that looks like this:

```
MOVE ( ELLIPSE , RECTANGLE ) RETURNS ELLIPSE
```

As far as the user is concerned, in other words, MOVE is an operator that takes an ellipse and a rectangle as arguments and returns an ellipse as result—and the following implementation code, repeated from the examples under **argument**, supports that understanding (CTR here is a read-only operator that returns the center of its rectangle argument):

```
OPERATOR MOVE ( E ELLIPSE , R RECTANGLE ) RETURNS ELLIPSE ;
    RETURN ELLIPSE ( THE_A ( E ) , THE_B ( E ) , CTR ( R ) ) ;
END OPERATOR ;
```

Because of value substitutability, however (q.v.), a given MOVE invocation can have a value of any nonempty subtype of ELLIPSE as its first argument and a value of any nonempty subtype of RECTANGLE as its second argument. Thus, we see from Fig. 2 that the first argument can have most specific type either ELLIPSE or CIRCLE, and the second argument can have most specific type either RECTANGLE or SQUARE. Moreover, if the first argument is in fact a circle and not just an ellipse, the result will clearly be a circle too. At least abstractly, then, MOVE will have four distinct invocation signatures that might look like this:

```
( ELLIPSE , RECTANGLE ) RETURNS ELLIPSE
( ELLIPSE , SQUARE    ) RETURNS ELLIPSE
( CIRCLE  , RECTANGLE ) RETURNS CIRCLE
( CIRCLE  , SQUARE    ) RETURNS CIRCLE
```

Thus, e.g., if C and R are variables of declared types CIRCLE and RECTANGLE, respectively, then the declared type of the expression MOVE (C,R) is CIRCLE.

In **Tutorial D**, invocation signatures are defined by means of the RETURNS clause, q.v. For example, here again is the definition of MOVE as a read-only operator, now shown complete:

```
OPERATOR MOVE ( E ELLIPSE , R RECTANGLE )
          RETURNS
             CASE
                WHEN IS_ELLIPSE ( E ) AND IS_RECTANGLE ( R ) THEN ELLIPSE
                WHEN IS_ELLIPSE ( E ) AND IS_SQUARE    ( R ) THEN ELLIPSE
                WHEN IS_CIRCLE  ( E ) AND IS_RECTANGLE ( R ) THEN CIRCLE
                WHEN IS_CIRCLE  ( E ) AND IS_SQUARE    ( R ) THEN CIRCLE
             END CASE ;
     RETURN ELLIPSE ( THE_A ( E ) , THE_B ( E ) , CTR ( R ) ) ;
END OPERATOR ;
```

Observe that the specification signature as such is now effectively defined by means of the combination of the operator name, the parameter declared types, and that particular one of the invocation signatures that has argument declared types all equal to the corresponding parameter declared types—in other words, the first of the invocation signatures shown, in the case at hand. However, observe further that (a) the CASE expression in the RETURNS specification is evaluated at compile time, not run time (to be specific, it's evaluated whenever the compiler processes a MOVE invocation); hence, (b) the various "IS_" operator invocations in that CASE expression are also evaluated at compile time, and (c) those "IS_" operator invocations therefore return TRUE if and only if the corresponding *declared* types are as indicated. In other words, those "IS_" operators aren't the usual operators of those names, which return TRUE if and only if their operands have the indicated types at *run* time. If this state of affairs is considered undesirable, it could perhaps be avoided by insisting that the various WHEN clauses appear in an appropriate sequence, as here:

```
OPERATOR MOVE ( E ELLIPSE , R RECTANGLE )
          RETURNS
             CASE
                WHEN IS_CIRCLE  ( E ) AND IS_SQUARE    ( R ) THEN CIRCLE
                WHEN IS_CIRCLE  ( E ) AND IS_RECTANGLE ( R ) THEN CIRCLE
                WHEN IS_ELLIPSE ( E ) AND IS_SQUARE    ( R ) THEN ELLIPSE
                WHEN IS_ELLIPSE ( E ) AND IS_RECTANGLE ( R ) THEN ELLIPSE
             END CASE ;
     RETURN ELLIPSE ( THE_A ( E ) , THE_B ( E ) , CTR ( R ) ) ;
END OPERATOR ;
```

With this revised sequence, it will still be the case that the "IS_" operator invocations are evaluated at compile time and so are interpreted in terms of declared types, but the results they return will be the same as if they were interpreted in terms of most specific types at run time.

Now, we've said that if C and R are variables of declared types CIRCLE and RECTANGLE, respectively, then the declared type of the expression MOVE (C,R) is CIRCLE. Moreover, the RETURNS clause means the compiler is aware of such matters, as just explained. As a consequence, various TREAT invocations that might otherwise have been needed won't be needed after all. For example, given C and R as above, we can write

```
C := MOVE ( C , R ) ;
```

instead of what we would otherwise have had to write:

```
C := TREAT_AS_CIRCLE ( MOVE ( C , R ) ) ;
```

Note: As pointed out in Part I of this dictionary, few writers (or languages or systems, come to that) seem to distinguish properly—or at all—between specification and invocation signatures. As the foregoing example suggests, however, languages and systems that fail to make this distinction will probably require more TREAT invocations than ones that do make it.

To return to the question of concrete syntax: As already suggested, certain obvious shorthands are surely possible in practice. For example, the RETURNS clause in the foregoing MOVE example might reasonably be abbreviated to just:

```
RETURNS IF IS_CIRCLE ( E ) THEN CIRCLE ELSE ELLIPSE END IF
```

Another possible shorthand is illustrated by the following self-explanatory example:

```
RETURNS SAME_TYPE_AS ( E )
```

Now suppose, as we did in the examples under **argument**, that type CIRCLE has a proper subtype O_CIRCLE (where an "O-circle" is a circle with center the origin):

```
TYPE O_CIRCLE
     IS { CIRCLE
          CONSTRAINT THE_CTR ( CIRCLE ) = POINT ( 0.0 , 0.0 )
          POSSREP { R = THE_R ( CIRCLE ) } } ;
```

Conceptually, then, the read-only version of MOVE will now require six invocation signatures, thus (note the last two in particular):

```
( ELLIPSE   , RECTANGLE ) RETURNS ELLIPSE
( ELLIPSE   , SQUARE    ) RETURNS ELLIPSE
( CIRCLE    , RECTANGLE ) RETURNS CIRCLE
( CIRCLE    , SQUARE    ) RETURNS CIRCLE
( O_CIRCLE , RECTANGLE ) RETURNS CIRCLE
( O_CIRCLE , SQUARE    ) RETURNS CIRCLE
```

Here's a possible RETURNS clause shorthand:

```
RETURNS
    CASE
        WHEN IS_CIRCLE  ( E ) THEN CIRCLE
        WHEN IS_ELLIPSE ( E ) THEN ELLIPSE
    END CASE
```

Here we're assuming further that the compile time version of IS_CIRCLE will return TRUE if the declared type of E is *any subtype of* CIRCLE (including O_CIRCLE in particular). *Note:*

The second of these WHEN specifications might be simplified to just ELSE ELLIPSE—see the paragraph immediately following. (Alternatively, the entire CASE expression might be replaced by IF IS_CIRCLE(E) THEN CIRCLE ELSE ELLIPSE END IF.)

One final example, to illustrate yet another possibility: Suppose (a) read-only operator *Op* has a specification signature involving two parameters X and Y, both of declared type ELLIPSE; (b) result declared types are defined (via appropriate invocation signatures) corresponding to the argument expression declared type combinations ELLIPSE / ELLIPSE, ELLIPSE / CIRCLE, and CIRCLE / ELLIPSE (only); and (c) *Op* is invoked with the argument expression declared type combination CIRCLE / CIRCLE. That invocation doesn't match any of the specified invocation signatures exactly—so what's its declared type? The simplest solution to this problem (perhaps not the only one) is to allow the CASE expression that specifies the various invocation signatures to include an appropriate ELSE clause, as here:

```
CASE
   WHEN IS_ELLIPSE ( X ) AND IS_CIRCLE  ( Y ) THEN ...
   WHEN IS_CIRCLE  ( X ) AND IS_ELLIPSE ( Y ) THEN ...
   WHEN IS_ELLIPSE ( X ) AND IS_ELLIPSE ( Y ) THEN ...
   ELSE ...
END CASE
```

So much for the read-only case; we turn now to the question of signatures for update operators. Here (again repeated from the examples under **argument**) is MOVE as an update operator:

```
OPERATOR MOVE ( E ELLIPSE , R RECTANGLE ) UPDATES { E } ;
   THE_CTR ( E ) := CTR ( R ) ;
END OPERATOR ;
```

Now there's no question of specifying the declared type of the result of invoking the operator, because update operator invocations don't have a result. But signatures are still required for purposes of binding, q.v., and type checking, q.v., as well as for defining the user's perception of the operator. Thus, the specification signature in the example might look like this:

```
MOVE ( ELLIPSE , RECTANGLE )
```

And the invocation signatures might look like this:

```
( ELLIPSE , RECTANGLE )
( ELLIPSE , SQUARE    )
( CIRCLE  , RECTANGLE )
( CIRCLE  , SQUARE    )
```

Of course, the specification signature, though probably not the invocation signatures, would additionally need to indicate that MOVE invocations update the argument corresponding to their first parameter, but we omit any such indication here for simplicity (*see* UPDATES in

Part I of this dictionary). More to the point, note that even if circles have "O-circles" as a proper subtype, then—as explained under **argument**—that first argument can't be of type O_CIRCLE, because the center of an O-circle is always the origin and can't be changed. Thus, there are now no invocation signatures (not even purely conceptual ones) showing the type of the first parameter as O_CIRCLE. As far as the first parameter is concerned, in other words (the parameter that's subject to update), the update form of MOVE is defined for type ELLIPSE, is inherited by type CIRCLE, but isn't inherited by type O_CIRCLE. (As noted under *Principle of Update Operator Inheritance*, if O_CIRCLE had any nonempty proper subtypes, it wouldn't inherited by those either, a fortiori.) Some syntactic construct for expressing such a state of affairs is thus necessary—perhaps as illustrated here:

```
OPERATOR MOVE ( E ELLIPSE , R RECTANGLE ) UPDATES { E }
                                    NOT ( IS_O_CIRCLE ( E ) ) ;
    THE_CTR ( E ) := CTR ( R ) ;
END OPERATOR ;
```

So let *Op* be an update operator, with parameters *P1*, *P2*, ..., *Pn* (and no others), and let parameter *Pi* have declared type *PDTi* ($i = 1, 2, ..., n$). If *Pi* isn't subject to update, then *Op* behaves as if it were a read-only operator as far as *Pi* is concerned, and the previous discussion of the read-only case applies directly, mutatis mutandis. But if *Pi* is subject to update, then the argument *Ai* corresponding to *Pi* in an invocation of *Op* must be a variable specifically, and it might or might not be allowed to have some given subtype of *PDTi* as its most specific type (and a fortiori as its declared type, too). Thus, *Op* has a specification signature, denoting that operator as perceived by the user, and a set of invocation signatures. The specification signature consists of the operator name, the parameter declared types *PDT1*, *PDT2*, ..., *PDTn*, and an indication as to which parameters are subject to update. Each invocation signature consists of one possible combination of argument expression declared types *ADT1*, *ADT2*, ..., *ADTn*.

Note finally that no two distinct operators can have specification signatures with the same operator name and the same sequence of parameter declared types *PDT*. Moreover, let *S* be a set of types with a nonempty common subtype. Then no two distinct operators can have specification signatures that differ only in that, for some *i, j*, ..., *k*, the declared types of their *i*th parameters are distinct members of *S*, the declared types of their *j*th parameters are distinct members of *S*, ..., and the declared types of their *k*th parameters are distinct members of *S*.

single inheritance   A form of inheritance in which each proper subtype has exactly one immediate supertype. *Contrast* **multiple inheritance**.
   Examples: See Fig. 2.

specialization   Let types *T″*, *T′*, and *T* be such that *T″* is a subtype of *T′* and *T′* is a subtype of *T*, and let *v″* be a value of most specific type *T″*. Also, let *V* be a variable of declared type *T*, and let the current most specific type *MST(V)* of *V* be *T′*. Finally, let the value *v″* be assigned to *V*. Then the current most specific type of *V* is now *T″*; in other words, *MST(V)* has been specialized—sometimes further specialized, for emphasis—from *T'* to *T''*. (Of course, *T'* and *T''* might in fact be one and the same, and so might *T* and *T'*, but in general they won't be.) *Contrast* generalization; specialization by constraint.

Example: With reference to Fig. 2, let variables E and C be of declared types ELLIPSE and CIRCLE, respectively. Moreover, let their current most specific types be ELLIPSE and CIRCLE, respectively, as well. Now consider this assignment:

```
E := C ;
```

This assignment has the effect of changing ("specializing") the most specific type of E—or, loosely, just specializing E—"down" from ELLIPSE to CIRCLE; in other words, *MST*(E) is now CIRCLE. More precisely, after the assignment, *MST*(E) is the same as *MST*(C), which in principle might be some nonempty proper subtype of CIRCLE—though not in the case at hand, because type CIRCLE doesn't have any proper subtypes apart from type *omega*, q.v. But if (as in the examples under **argument**) type CIRCLE has a proper subtype O_CIRCLE (where an "O-circle" is a circle with center the origin), and C currently contains an O-circle, then after the foregoing assignment *MST*(E) will be O_CIRCLE.

Note: The foregoing definition and example explain how the *Manifesto* model works, and probably how most other systems work too. (Indeed, if they don't, then the result will be a circular noncircle, q.v.) For further details, see the discussion under **specialization by constraint**.

specialization by constraint Let *S* be a selector of declared type *T*, and let *exp* be an expression denoting an invocation of *S* (so *DT*(*exp*) = *T*). Let *v* be the value returned by *exp* (so *v*(*exp*) = *v*). Further, let *v* satisfy the type constraint for subtype *T'* of *T* (and not for any proper subtype of *T'*). Then the most specific types *MST*(*v*) and *MST*(*exp*) of *v* and *exp*, respectively, are both *T'*. (Of course, *T* and *T'* might in fact be one and the same, but in general they won't be.) *Contrast* generalization by constraint; specialization; see also **specialization constraint**; **specialization via constraints**.

Examples: Assume for simplicity that the only types we have to deal with are ELLIPSE and CIRCLE (see Fig. 2). Here once again are the type definitions for those types:

```
TYPE ELLIPSE
     IS { PLANE_FIGURE
          POSSREP { A LENGTH , B LENGTH , CTR POINT
                    CONSTRAINT A ≥ B } } ;

TYPE CIRCLE
     IS { ELLIPSE
          CONSTRAINT THE_A ( ELLIPSE ) = THE_B ( ELLIPSE )
          POSSREP { R   = THE_A   ( ELLIPSE ) ,
                    CTR = THE_CTR ( ELLIPSE ) } } ;
```

Note in particular the CONSTRAINT specification for type CIRCLE, which says among other things (and speaking a trifle loosely) that the semiaxis lengths *a* and *b* are supposed to be equal for a circle. But what does it say precisely? Let *e* be a value of type ELLIPSE, and let *a* and *b* be the corresponding semiaxis lengths. Then there are four possibilities:

1. If $a = b$, then *e* is of type CIRCLE.
2. If *e* is of type CIRCLE, then $a = b$.
3. Neither 1 nor 2.
4. Both 1 and 2.

Clearly, possibility 1 permits—or at least fails to prohibit—"noncircular circles" (i.e., values *e* of type CIRCLE that don't have $a = b$). Likewise, possibility 2 permits "circular noncircles" (i.e., values *e* of type ELLIPSE and not type CIRCLE that do have $a = b$), and possibility 3 permits both "noncircular circles" and "circular noncircles," in which case there doesn't seem to be any point in specifying the constraint at all. (Note, however, that this latter case is exactly the one "supported" by SQL!—see the further remarks on this point near the end of the present entry.) Thus, possibility 4 appears to be the only sensible option; certainly it's the only one that corresponds to mathematical reality, which is why it's the one adopted in the *Manifesto* model. And it follows immediately that the system must support specialization by constraint. By way of example, consider the following selector invocation:

```
ELLIPSE ( LENGTH ( 5.0 ) , LENGTH ( 5.0 ) , POINT ( ... ) )
```

The value denoted by this expression is an ellipse with $a = b$ and is thus a circle, and is therefore—at least in the *Manifesto* model—of type CIRCLE. Thus, specialization by constraint (S by C for short) implies, as the original definition states, that certain selector invocations will produce results whose most specific type is some proper subtype of the specified target type. Of course, ultimately, the only way any expression can yield a result value of any type is via some selector invocation. It follows that S by C must be implemented as part of the implementation of the pertinent selector (conceptually, at any rate, though various optimizations are possible in practice, as explained in the *Manifesto* book).

By way of another example, let the current value of variable E be an ellipse with $a = 4$ and $b = 3$, and consider the following assignment:

```
THE_A ( E ) := LENGTH ( 3.0 ) ;
```

The expanded form of this assignment is:

```
E := ELLIPSE ( LENGTH ( 3.0 ) , THE_B ( E ) , THE_CTR ( E ) ) ;
```

Since THE_B(E) = 3.0, the selector invocation on the right side here returns a circle, not "just an ellipse," and that circle is then assigned to the variable E. Loosely, we can say that the type—meaning, more precisely, the most specific type *MST*(E)—of variable E has been changed "down," or specialized, from ELLIPSE to CIRCLE.

Now suppose the foregoing assignment is followed by this one:

```
THE_B ( E ) := LENGTH ( 2.5 ) ;
```

Expanded form:

```
E := ELLIPSE ( THE_A ( E ) , LENGTH ( 2.5 ) , THE_CTR ( E ) ) ;
```

Since THE_A(E) = 3.0, the selector invocation on the right side here returns "just an ellipse" (i.e., an ellipse that's not a circle), and that ellipse is then assigned to the variable E. In other words, generalization by constraint (G by C) has occurred, and the most specific type *MST*(E) of variable E is now ELLIPSE again. Loosely, we can say that the type—meaning, more precisely, the most specific type *MST*(E)—of variable E has been changed "up," or generalized, from CIRCLE to ELLIPSE.

So S by C and G by C together support changing types both up and down— and hence "sideways," too. Suppose type ELLIPSE has another immediate subtype NONCIRCLE, with the obvious semantics (i.e., ELLIPSE is now a union type, q.v., and every ellipse is either a circle or a noncircle and not both). Let the current value of variable E be an ellipse with $a = 4$ and $b = 3$, and hence in fact a noncircle. Then the following assignment—

```
THE_A ( E ) := LENGTH ( 3.0 ) ;
```

—will assign a circle (of radius length 3) to E, and will thus effectively also change the type— meaning, more precisely, the most specific type *MST*(E)—of variable E "sideways," from NONCIRCLE to CIRCLE.

What about S by C for tuple and relation types? Well, if S by C is performed as described above for scalar types, it'll happen automatically for tuple and relation types too, and nothing more needs to be said about the matter. What's more, the same goes for G by C too, mutatis mutandis.

Note: Most languages and systems (including SQL systems in particular) that support inheritance at all don't actually support either S by C or G by C. Thus, SQL in particular does permit "noncircular circles" and "circular noncircles" (in fact, as noted under *Principle of Update Operator Inheritance*, as well as under **type constraint** in Part I of this dictionary, SQL doesn't support much in the way of type constraints at all). It's also worth mentioning that changing types up, down, or sideways is a much more complex business—it might even be impossible—in systems that fail to support S by C and G by C. Finally, many further advantages also accrue if and only if S by C and G by C are supported; however, further details are beyond the scope of this dictionary (they can be found in the *Manifesto* book).

specialization constraint   Let *T* be a regular type (and hence, necessarily, a scalar type), and let *T′* be a nonempty immediate subtype of *T*. Then the type constraint for type *T′* will specify that, in order for some given value to be of type *T′*, that value must be of type *T* and must additionally satisfy some further constraint. That type constraint is the specialization constraint for type *T'*. For further discussion and examples, *see* IS. *Note:* As indicated under **proper subtype**, in practice there'll always be at least one value of type *T* that's not of type *T'*. *See* **example value**, second definition.

specialization via constraints   A term found in the OO literature, possibly related to—but not to be confused with—specialization by constraint, q.v. The following definition is taken from Stanley B. Zdonik and David Maier, "Fundamentals of Object-Oriented Databases," in *Readings in Object-Oriented Database Systems* (Zdonik and Maier, eds.; Morgan Kaufmann, 1990):

> *Specialization via constraints* happens whenever the following is permitted:
>
> *B* subtype_of *A* and *T* subtype_of *S* and
> *f*(...*b:T*,...) returns *r:R* in Ops(*B*) and
> *f*(...*b:S*,...) returns *r:R* in Ops(*A*)
>
> That is, specialization via constraints occurs whenever the operation redefinition on a subtype constrains one of the arguments to be from a smaller value set than the corresponding operation on the supertype.

Note, however, that "operator redefinition on a subtype" apparently means (to use terminology defined elsewhere in this part of the dictionary) definition of a new implementation version, q.v. "Specialization via constraints" thus appears to mean nothing more than—to take a concrete example—that if *Op* is an operator that's defined to work on ellipses, and a version of *Op* is defined to work on ellipses that happen to be circles, then the argument to that version of *Op* must be a circle specifically and not just an ellipse. It's not really clear, therefore, that "specialization via constraints" has anything to do with the inheritance model, as such, at all (*but see* **three out of four "rule"**).

specification signature   (*With inheritance*) *See* **signature**.

static binding   Term sometimes used as a synonym for compile time binding, q.v.

static classification   Systems and languages (especially OO systems and languages) that use the term *class* to mean a type—see Part I of this dictionary—sometimes use the term *static classification* to refer to the process, or the result of the process, of determining at compile time the type(s) possessed by some object.

static dispatching / static despatching   Term sometimes used (especially OO systems and languages) as a synonym for compile time binding, q.v.

static type checking   Term sometimes used as a synonym for compile time type checking, q.v.

structural inheritance   A form of inheritance, supported in some OO systems, according to which if type T' is a subtype of type T, then T' inherits all of T's public instance variables. (It probably inherits T's private instance variables as well, but this latter is an implementation matter, not part of the model.) *Note:* The *Manifesto* model doesn't support structural inheritance at all (except, arguably, as discussed under inherited possrep). *See also* extends relationship; *contrast* behavioral inheritance.

subclass   Systems and languages that use the term *class*—see Part I of this dictionary—typically use the term *subclass* also, with a similar variety of interpretations.

subject routine determination   SQL term for binding.

substitutability   Value substitutability (q.v.) or variable substitutability (q.v.) or both, as the context demands. *See Principle of Read-Only Operator Inheritance; Principle of Update Operator Inheritance. Note:* In many ways, substitutability is the whole point of inheritance. One reason for wanting to support inheritance in the first place is that (for example) a program that works for ellipses might work for circles too, even if it was originally written with no thought for circles at all (*see* code reuse). And to the degree that such an objective might be attainable, it should be clear that it's substitutability that makes it so. *See also* coercion vs. substitutability.

substitutability vs. coercion   *See* coercion vs. substitutability.

subtable   *See* subtables and supertables.

subtables and supertables   A scheme—in fact, a specific concrete realization of the "extends relationship" concept, q.v.—according to which some table T' is defined to have all of the columns of some other table T, together with certain additional columns of its own. *Note:* We deliberately frame this definition in SQL terms—viz., tables, columns, and rows—instead of relational terms because SQL does at least support the "subtables and supertables" concept and the relational model doesn't (at least, not explicitly; see the discussion below, however, showing how relational views could be used to achieve comparable functionality).
    Example: Consider the following SQL tables (for definiteness, assume them to be base tables specifically):

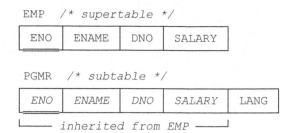

Observe that table EMP ("employees") has four columns; by contrast, table PGMR ("programmers") has just one column of its own, but is conceptually extended with four more columns, shown in the diagram above in italics, that it "inherits" from table EMP. (Note, therefore, that the *sub*table—a little counterintuitively, perhaps—has a *super*set of the columns of the supertable.) Column names are meant to be self-explanatory. Nonprogrammers have a row in EMP only, while programmers have a row in both tables (so every row in PGMR has a counterpart in EMP, but the converse is false). Here are some of the implications of this state of affairs for the usual SQL retrieval and update operations:

- *SELECT:* Retrieval from EMP behaves normally. Retrieval from PGMR behaves as if PGMR does actually contain columns ENO, ENAME, DNO, and SALARY (as well as column LANG, of course).

- *INSERT:* INSERT into EMP behaves normally. INSERT into PGMR effectively causes new rows to appear in both EMP and PGMR.

- *DELETE:* DELETE from EMP causes rows to disappear from EMP and (if the rows in question happen to correspond to programmers) from PGMR too. DELETE from PGMR causes rows to disappear from both EMP and PGMR.

- *UPDATE:* Updating columns ENO or ENAME or DNO or SALARY in EMP causes the same updates to be applied to any corresponding rows in PGMR. Updating those columns in PGMR causes the same updates to be applied to the corresponding rows in EMP. Updating column LANG in PGMR updates PGMR only.

Actually there are at least two further operations of an updating nature that a system supporting subtables and supertables would seem to need—viz., DELETE ONLY, q.v., and INSERT ONLY, q.v.—but no such operators are supported by SQL. What makes this omission a trifle odd is that such operators *would* be supported, in effect, if the tables were treated just as regular SQL tables instead of being bound together as a subtable / supertable pair. What makes it even odder is that the functionality, such as it is, of subtables and supertables, including the DELETE ONLY and INSERT ONLY functionality, could be achieved in its entirety by means of the conventional view mechanism! To be specific, suppose we define base tables EMP and EMP_LANG as follows (in outline):

```
EMP       ( ENO , ENAME , DNO , SALARY )

EMP_LANG ( ENO , LANG )
```

Suppose we also define PGMR as a view of these two base tables, with the following SQL expression as the necessary view defining expression:

```
EMP NATURAL JOIN EMP_LANG
```

Then tables EMP, EMP_LANG, and PGMR together not only provide all of the functionality of subtables and supertables, they also get around the lack of support for INSERT ONLY and DELETE ONLY (trivially so, in fact—those operators are simply no longer needed, being replaced by suitable INSERTs and DELETEs on table EMP_LANG).

Note carefully that the "subtables and supertables" scheme has nothing whatsoever to do with relation subtypes and supertypes, q.v. To be specific, let relation headings *EH* and *PH* correspond to tables EMP and PGMR in the obvious way; note in particular that *EH* has four attributes and *PH* either five or one, depending on your point of view. Whichever it is, type RELATION *PH* is clearly not a subtype of type RELATION *EH* in the sense of the *Manifesto* model, precisely because those two types have different headings. In particular, therefore, a value (a relation) of type RELATION *PH* isn't a value of type RELATION *EH*. Perhaps more to the point, a value (a tuple) of type TUPLE *PH* isn't a value of type TUPLE *EH*, either.

A more extensive description of the foregoing scheme and what's wrong with it (and why it's logically unnecessary anyway) can be found in the *Manifesto* book. Here we note just one further point, which is that, in general, which of tables *T* and *T'* is regarded as the subtable and which the supertable might depend on context. For example, consider an SQL version of the suppliers-and-parts database used as a running example throughout Part I of this dictionary. Suppose for the sake of the example that status information can be "missing" for certain suppliers. Then a good way to design the database, in SQL terms, would be to have two tables S and S' that look like this:

S

SNO	SNAME	STATUS	CITY

S'

SNO	SNAME	CITY

Table S corresponds to suppliers with a known status value, while table S' corresponds to suppliers for whom the status information is missing. And the point about this example—which illustrates, incidentally, a perfectly reasonable basis for dealing with the phenomenon of "missing information"—is that it would be quite natural to refer to S here as the supertable and S' as the subtable; but now the supertable has a superset of the columns of the subtable, instead of the other way around as in the "employees and programmers" example.

subtype   Type T' is a subtype of type T if and only if every value of type T' is a value of type T. Note that T and T' must be from the same type lattice, necessarily. *Note:* It follows from this definition that (a) every type is a subtype of itself (i.e., the "subtype of" relationship is reflexive), and (b) every subtype of T' is a subtype of T (i.e., the "subtype of" relationship is transitive). Note too that, by definition, read-only operators and type constraints ("properties") that apply to values of type T also apply to values of type T'. Note finally that there can't possibly be more values of type T' than there are of type T; this apparently trivial observation can be very helpful in pinpointing errors and clearing up confusions. (Indeed, it's worth stating explicitly, albeit rather loosely, that T' has a subset of type T's values but a superset of type T's properties.) *See also* supertype; *contrast* extends relationship.
   Examples (scalar types only): See Figs. 2-4.

subtype (relation types)   Let T and T' be relation types from the same type lattice, q.v.; by definition, then, those types have the same attribute names, say $A1, A2, ..., An$ $(n \geq 0)$. Then type T' is a subtype of type T if and only if, for all i $(i = 1, 2, ..., n)$, the type Ti' of attribute Ai within T' is a subtype of the type Ti of attribute Ai within T. Further, relation r is of some subtype of type T if and only if the heading of r is that of some subtype of T (in which case every tuple t in the body of r necessarily has a heading that's the heading of some subtype of the type of r). *See also* supertype (relation types).
   Examples: See Fig. 5.

subtype (tuple types)   Let T and T' be tuple types from the same type lattice, q.v.; by definition, then, those types have the same attribute names, say $A1, A2, ..., An$ $(n \geq 0)$. Then type T' is a subtype of type T if and only if, for all i $(i = 1, 2, ..., n)$, the type Ti' of attribute Ai within T' is a subtype of the type Ti of attribute Ai within T. Further, tuple t is of some subtype of type T if and only if the heading of t is the heading of some subtype of T. *See also* supertype (tuple types).
   Examples: See Fig. 5.

subtyping   Term sometimes used as a synonym for inheritance.

superclass   Systems and languages that use the term *class*—see Part I of this dictionary—typically use the term *superclass* also, with a similar variety of interpretations.

supertable   *See* subtables and supertables.

supertype   Type T is a supertype of type T' if and only if every value of type T' is a value of type T. Note that T and T' must be from the same type lattice, necessarily. *Note:* It follows from this definition that (a) every type is a supertype of itself (i.e., the "supertype of" relationship is reflexive), and (b) every supertype of T is a supertype of T' (i.e., the "supertype of" relationship is transitive). Note too that, by definition, read-only operators and type constraints ("properties") that apply to values of type T also apply to values of type T'. (Indeed, it's worth stating explicitly, albeit rather loosely, that T has a superset of type T''s values but a subset of type T''s properties.) *See also* subtype.
   Examples (scalar types only):   See Figs. 2-4.

supertype (relation types)   Let T and T' be relation types from the same type lattice, q.v.; by definition, then, those types have the same attribute names, say $A1, A2, ..., An$ ($n \geq 0$). Then type T is a supertype of type T' if and only if, for all i ($i = 1, 2, ..., n$), the type Ti of attribute Ai within T is a supertype of the type Ti' of attribute Ai within T'. Further, relation r is of some supertype of type T' if and only if the heading of r is that of some supertype of T' (in which case every tuple in the body of r necessarily has a heading that's both (a) the heading of some supertype of T' and (b) the heading of some subtype of the type of r). *See also* subtype (relation types).
   Examples: See Fig. 5.

supertype (tuple types)   Let T and T' be tuple types from the same type lattice, q.v.; by definition, then, those types have the same attribute names, say $A1, A2, ..., An$ ($n \geq 0$). Then type T is a supertype of type T' if and only if, for all i ($i = 1, 2, ..., n$), the type Ti of attribute Ai within T is a supertype of the type Ti' of attribute Ai within T'. Further, tuple t is of some supertype of type T' if and only if the heading of t is the heading of some supertype of T'. *See also* subtype (tuple types).
   Examples: See Fig. 5.

———— ♦ ♦ ♦ ♦ ♦ ————

T_alpha   Generic name for the maximal type in the type lattice, q.v., to which some specified type T belongs. *Note:* If T is scalar, the "$T\_$" prefix can be dropped, since all scalar types belong to the same type lattice and there's exactly one maximal scalar type, viz., *alpha*, q.v.

T_omega   Generic name for the minimal type in the type lattice, q.v., to which some specified type T belongs. *Note:* If T is scalar, the "$T\_$" prefix can be dropped, since all scalar types belong to the same type lattice and there's exactly one minimal scalar type, viz., *omega*, q.v.

target parameter   *See* selfish method.

target type   (*With inheritance*) 1. Let S be a selector for type T; then the target type for an invocation of S is T. 2. In the TREAT invocation TREAT_AS_T (...), the target type is T. 3. In the CAST invocation CAST_AS_*T* (...), the target type is *T*. *Note:* In all three of these cases, S by C (q.v.) implies that the most specific type of the result might be some nonempty proper subtype of the target type. However, the declared type of the result is the same as the target type in all cases.

three out of four "rule" In "Fundamentals of Object-Oriented Databases," by Stanley B. Zdonik and David Maier (in *Readings in Object-Oriented Database Systems*, Zdonik and Maier, eds., Morgan Kaufmann, 1990), the claim is made that at most three of the following four allegedly desirable features can be supported simultaneously: (a) substitutability, (b) compile time type checking, (c) mutability, and (d) "specialization via constraints" (q.v.). By way of illustration, consider the following code fragment (the example that follows is an edited version of one from Zdonik and Maier's own paper, revised to use **Tutorial D** syntax and types ELLIPSE and CIRCLE from Fig. 2):

```
VAR E ELLIPSE ;

E := CIRCLE ( LENGTH ( 2.0 ) , POINT ( ... ) ) ;
THE_A ( E ) := LENGTH ( 3.0 ) ;
```

The first line here defines E to be a variable of declared type ELLIPSE. The next line attempts to assign a circle to E; compile time type checking succeeds—feature (b)—and the assignment succeeds at run time because of feature (a), substitutability (value substitutability, to be precise). The last line is an illustration of mutability—feature (c)—and it attempts to change the length of the *a* semiaxis of the ellipse (actually a circle) in E; compile time type checking succeeds, but does the assignment succeed at run time? Zdonik and Maier claim, in effect, that it will fail if the system is aware that circles must have $a = b$; they therefore claim that, in order for the assignment to succeed, the system mustn't be told that circles do have $a = b$. In other words, they appear to be suggesting that it's better that such a constraint not be declared! (Apparently, they also regard declaring such a constraint as an example of "specialization via constraints"—feature (d)—though it's hard to see how that perception is consistent with their own definition of this latter concept, q.v. In fact, the constraint in question—the constraint, that is, that a circle is an ellipse with $a = b$—is basically just the pertinent specialization constraint, q.v.) Of course, if that constraint isn't declared, the assignment will indeed "succeed," but the effect will be that variable E now contains a "noncircular circle," q.v.

Note: In the *Manifesto* model, the assignment succeeds even though the constraint is declared (necessarily declared, in fact, as part of the definition of type CIRCLE). The point is, of course, that in that model G by C comes into play and the most specific type of the variable E after the assignment is ELLIPSE, not CIRCLE. In other words, the three out of four "rule" isn't a rule at all, in the *Manifesto* model (that's why the word "rule" is set in quotation marks here). Moreover, note also that:

- Feature (a), value substitutability, is logically implied by inheritance and is thus a sine qua non.

- Feature (b), compile time type checking, is highly desirable but can't be achieved 100 percent (*see* TREAT).

- Feature (c), mutability, is a sine qua non unless nothing is ever updated.

- Constraints of the kind under discussion—feature (d), apparently—are also a sine qua non if noncircular circles and the like are to be avoided.

See **four out of five rule** for further discussion.

One last point: It does seem to be the case in practice that most languages that provide inheritance support (including SQL in particular) do fail to support specialization constraints, q.v. The following quote from a paper by James Rumbaugh ("A Matter of Intent: How to Define Subclasses," *Journal of Object-Oriented Programming*, September 1996), tends to support this contention:

> Is SQUARE a subclass of RECTANGLE? ... Stretching the *x* dimension of a rectangle is a perfectly reasonable thing to do. But if you do it to a square, then the object is no longer a square. This is not necessarily a bad thing conceptually. When you stretch a square you *do* get a rectangle ... But ... most object-oriented languages do not want objects to change class ... [This] suggests [a] design principle for classification systems: *A subclass should not be defined by constraining a superclass.*

And Rumbaugh buttresses his conclusion with the following claim:

> It would be computationally infeasible to support a rule-based, intensional definition of class membership, because you would have to check the rules after each operation that affects an object.

(The phrase "rule-based, intensional definition of class membership" refers to S by C and G by C; it means, for example, that a given ellipse is a member of the class of circles if and only if it satisfies the rule that *a* = *b*.) But we reject this claim; we believe the computational aspects of S by C and G by C can be handled both simply and efficiently. See the *Manifesto* book for further discussion.

TREAT   Let *exp* be a scalar expression, let *T* be a nonempty scalar type, and let *DT*(*exp*) and *T* overlap (this is a compile time check). Then the expression TREAT_AS_*T* (*exp*)—or some logical equivalent to that expression—raises a run time type error, if *MST*(*exp*) isn't some subtype of *T*; otherwise, it returns a result *x* with *DT*(*x*) = *T*, *v*(*x*) = *v*(*exp*), and *MST*(*x*) = *MST*(*exp*). *Note:* **Tutorial D** additionally supports a generalized version of this operator of the form TREAT_AS_SAME_TYPE_AS (*exp1*,*exp2*), in which the expressions *exp1* and *exp2* aren't limited to being scalar. This generalized version is effectively equivalent to the expression

TREAT_AS_*T1* (*exp2*), where *T1* is *DT(exp1)*—assuming for definitional purposes that the expression TREAT_AS_*T1* (*exp2*) is syntactically valid.

Examples: First of all, here with reference to Fig. 2 are a couple of examples that illustrate the raison d'être for the TREAT operator. Let variables E and C be of declared types ELLIPSE and CIRCLE, respectively. Then the assignment

```
C := E ;
```

will fail on a compile time type error, even if we know that E will contain a circle at run time. Similarly, the expression THE_R (E) ("the radius of E") will also fail at compile time, even if we know, again, that E will contain a circle at run time. By contrast, consider this assignment:

```
C := TREAT_AS_CIRCLE ( E ) ;
```

This assignment won't fail at compile time, because the declared type of the expression TREAT_AS_CIRCLE (E) is CIRCLE; and if E does contain a circle at run time, the assignment will cause that circle to be assigned to C. (However, the TREAT invocation will raise a run time type error if E contains "just an ellipse" at run time.) Similarly, the expression THE_R (TREAT_AS_CIRCLE (E)) won't fail at compile time and—again, if E does contain a circle at run time—will return the length of the radius of that circle (but it'll raise a run time type error otherwise). In the *Manifesto* model, in fact, an attempt to TREAT a value to a type it doesn't possess is the only possible way a run time type error can ever occur.

Here are some more examples:

■ With reference to Fig. 3, let V be a variable of declared type RECTANGLE and current most specific type SQUARE; then the TREAT invocations TREAT_AS_SQUARE (V), TREAT_AS_RECTANGLE (V), TREAT_AS_RHOMBUS (V), and TREAT_AS_PARALLELOGRAM (V) all succeed at both compile time and run time.

■ With reference to Fig. 5, let ERV be a variable of declared type ER and current most specific type CS, and let ESV be a variable of declared type and most specific type both ES; then TREAT_AS_SAME_TYPE_AS (ERV,ESV) succeeds at both compile time and run time.

Note: The *Manifesto* model currently allows TREAT operator invocations to be used as pseudovariable references, but such "TREAT pseudovariables" don't actually seem to serve much purpose. For example, let variable E be of declared type ELLIPSE but current most specific type CIRCLE. Then the following assignment—

```
THE_R ( E ) := LENGTH ( 5.0 ) ;
```

—will fail at compile time. By contrast, the following assignment will succeed at both compile time and run time:

```
THE_R ( TREAT_AS_CIRCLE ( E ) ) := LENGTH ( 5.0 ) ;
```

However, this latter assignment is logically equivalent to this one:

```
E := CIRCLE ( LENGTH ( 5.0 ) , THE_CTR ( E ) ) ;
```

Thus, it's not clear that the TREAT pseudovariable has actually bought us anything in this example.

TREAT_AS_SAME_TYPE_AS   *See* TREAT.

TREAT expression   *See* TREAT.

TREAT pseudovariable   *See* TREAT.

tuple assignment   (*With inheritance*) Let T and t be a tuplevar and a tuple, respectively, such that the most specific type $MST(t)$ of t is some subtype of the declared type $DT(T)$ of T. Then (and only then) t can be assigned to T; the assignment has the effect of setting $v(T)$ equal to t and $MST(T)$ equal to $MST(t)$. *Note:* In order for the assignment to be syntactically valid, the declared type $DT(tx)$ of the expression tx used to denote tuple t must be some subtype of the declared type $DT(T)$ of tuplevar T (this condition is implied by the fact that $MST(t)$ is required to be some subtype of $DT(T)$, and is a compile time check).
Examples: Let tuplevars TE and TC be of declared types TUPLE {E ELLIPSE} and TUPLE {E CIRCLE}, respectively, and consider the following assignment:

```
TE := TC ;
```

In this example, compile time type checking succeeds ($DT(TC)$ is a subtype of $DT(TE)$), and at run time $v(TE)$ and $MST(TE)$ are set equal to $v(TC)$ and $MST(TC)$, respectively.
Now consider this assignment:

```
TC := TE ;
```

This example raises a compile time type error, because $DT(TE)$ isn't a subtype of $DT(TC)$. By contrast, if the expression TE in this example were to be replaced by the expression TREAT_AS_SAME_TYPE_AS (TC,TE), then compile time type checking would succeed; however, this latter expression will raise a type error (a run time type error, of course) if $MST(TE)$ isn't some subtype of TUPLE {E CIRCLE} at run time (*see* TREAT).

tuple comparison   (*With inheritance*) A boolean expression of the form (*tx1*) *theta* (*tx2*), where (a) *tx1* and *tx2* are tuple expressions whose most specific types *MST*(*tx1*) and *MST*(*tx2*) overlap and (b) *theta* is either "=" or "≠". *Note:* In order for the comparison to be syntactically valid, the declared types *DT*(*tx1*) and *DT*(*tx2*) must overlap (this condition is implied by the fact that *MST*(*tx1*) and *MST*(*tx2*) are required to overlap, and is a compile time check). Also, the parentheses enclosing *tx1* and *tx2* in the comparison might not be needed in practice.

tuple equality   (*With inheritance*) Let *t1* and *t2* be relations such that the most specific types *MST*(*t1*) and *MST*(*t2*) overlap. Then *t1* and *t2* can be compared for equality; the comparison returns TRUE if and only if *t1* is equal to *t2* (in which case *MST*(*t1*) is equal to *MST*(*t2*) also). *Note:* In order for the comparison to be syntactically valid, the declared types *DT*(*tx1*) and *DT*(*tx2*) of the expressions *tx1* and *tx2* used to denote *t1* and *t2*, respectively, must overlap (this condition is implied by the fact that *MST*(*t1*) and *MST*(*t2*) are required to overlap, and is a compile time check).

tuple subtype   *See* subtype (tuple types).

tuple supertype   *See* supertype (tuple types).

tuple type inheritance   A form of inheritance in which the types are tuple types specifically. Note that tuple type inheritance is necessarily multiple. *See* subtype (tuple types); supertype (tuple types).
   Example: See Fig. 5.

type checking   (*With inheritance*) *See* compile time type checking; run time type checking.

type constraint inheritance   *See* type inheritance.

type error   (*With inheritance*) The error that occurs if type checking fails (*see* compile time type checking; run time type checking). In the *Manifesto* model, such errors are detectable at compile time (except, sometimes, in the context of TREAT, q.v.).

type graph   A pictorial way of representing supertype / subtype relationships, applicable even when there's multiple inheritance involved (*contrast* type hierarchy). A type graph is a directed acyclic graph; more precisely, it's a graph *TG* consisting of a finite set *N* of nodes and a finite set *D* of directed arcs that together satisfy the following properties:

- *TG* is empty if and only if *N* is empty (in which case *D* is necessarily empty too).

- Each node is given the name of a type.

■ No two nodes have the same name. Also, no node is named either *T_alpha* (q.v.) or *T_omega* (q.v.) for any possible type *T*; by convention, the types with these names—which are primarily conceptual in nature anyway—aren't represented in the graph at all.

■ There's a directed arc from node *T* to node *T'* if and only if type *T* is an immediate supertype of type *T'*.

■ If there's a directed arc from node *T* to node *T'*, then node *T'* isn't reachable from node *T* via any other path, where (a) a path from node *T* to node *T'* is a sequence of *n* directed arcs *A1* (from *T* to *T1*, say), *A2* (from *T1* to *T2*, say), ..., *An* (from *T(n−1)*, say, to *T'*), where $n \geq 0$, and $n = 0$ implies *T* = *T'* (i.e., there's always a path from node *T* to itself); (b) a node *T'* is reachable from a node *T* if and only if there's a path from node *T* to node *T'*.

■ If the graph includes any nodes at all, then—because it's directed and acyclic—it necessarily contains at least one node that has no immediate supertype node. Such a node is called a root node (and the corresponding type is called a root type).

■ If the graph includes any nodes at all, then—again because it's directed and acyclic—it necessarily contains at least one node that has no immediate subtype node. Such a node is called a leaf node (and the corresponding type is called a leaf type).

■ If nodes *T1* and *T2* are distinct root nodes, then no node is reachable from both *T1* and *T2*.

■ If nodes *T1*, *T2*, *T'*, and *T"* are such that there exist paths from both *T1* and *T2* to both *T'* and *T"*, then there must exist a node *T* that's common to every such path.

It follows from the foregoing definition that any given type graph *TG* can be divided into a set of disjoint partitions—a nonempty set, unless *TG* itself is empty—such that (a) each partition in the set has exactly one root node and one or more leaf nodes, and (b) no type in any partition in the set overlaps any type in any other partition in the set. If such a partition has just one leaf node, then that partition forms a lattice; if it has more than one leaf node, it can be converted into a lattice by introducing the pertinent minimal type. Note, however, that the lattices in question aren't type lattices as such, q.v. (at least, not as this latter term is usually understood), because they don't contain the pertinent maximal type.

Note: Type graphs aren't part of the inheritance model as such—they're merely an intuitively convenient way of depicting supertype / subtype relationships, which are. (Type graphs play a role in the inheritance model analogous to that played by tables in the relational model: Tables aren't part of the relational model as such, they're merely an intuitively convenient way of depicting relations, which are.)

Examples: See Figs. 2-5. (Fig. 2 shows a type hierarchy, of course, which is a degenerate case; Figs. 3-5 show type graphs that aren't type hierarchies.)

type hierarchy A pictorial way of representing supertype / subtype relationships, applicable so long as there's no multiple inheritance involved (and hence applicable only to scalar types, and then only because type *omega* is ignored—see below). A type hierarchy is a directed acyclic graph; more precisely, it's a graph *TH* consisting of a finite set *N* of nodes and a finite set *D* of directed arcs that together satisfy the following properties:

- *TH* is empty if and only if *N* is empty (in which case *D* is necessarily empty too).

- Each node is given the name of a type.

- No two nodes have the same name. Also, no node is named either *alpha* or *omega*; by convention, the types with these names (which are primarily conceptual in nature anyway) aren't represented in the graph at all.

- Each arc connects exactly two distinct nodes and represents a directed path from one of those two nodes (the parent) to the other (the child). There's an arc from parent *T* to child *T'* if and only if type *T* is an immediate supertype of type *T'*.

- Each parent is connected to one or more children. Each child is connected to exactly one parent.

- Node *Y* is a descendant of node *X* if and only if it's a child of *X* or a child of a descendant of *X*. No node is a descendant of itself.

- Node *X* is an ancestor of node *Y* if and only if node *Y* is a descendant of node *X*. No node is an ancestor of itself.

- A node connected to no parent is a root node (and the corresponding type is called a root type). *Note:* If *TH* is nonempty, it has exactly one root node, otherwise it has no root node at all.

- A node connected to no children is a leaf node (and the corresponding type is called a leaf type).

Contrast **type graph**; *see also* **derived type hierarchy.**

    Note: Type hierarchies aren't part of the inheritance model as such—they're merely an intuitively convenient way of depicting supertype / subtype relationships, which are. (Type hierarchies play a role in the inheritance model analogous to that played by tables in the relational model: Tables aren't part of the relational model as such, they're merely an intuitively convenient way of depicting relations, which are.) Note further that type hierarchies are known in the literature by a variety of different names, the following among them:

- Class hierarchies (on the grounds that types are sometimes called classes, especially in an OO context)

- Generalization hierarchies (on the grounds that, e.g., an ellipse is a generalization of a circle)

- Specialization hierarchies (on the grounds that, e.g., a circle is a specialization of an ellipse)

- Inheritance hierarchies (on the grounds that, e.g., circles inherit properties from ellipses)

- "IS A" hierarchies (on the grounds that, e.g., every circle "is a" ellipse)

and so on (this isn't an exhaustive list).
Example: See Fig. 2.

type inheritance (*Expanded definition*) An organizing principle according to which one type can be defined as a subtype of one or more other types, called supertypes (of the type in question). If T' is a subtype of supertype T, then all values of type T' are also values of type T, and read-only operators and type constraints that apply to values of type T therefore also apply to—i.e., are "inherited by"—values of type T' (*see Principle of Read-Only Operator Inheritance*). However, values of type T' will have read-only operators and type constraints of their own that don't apply to values that are only of type T and not of type T'. As for variables of declared type T', they might or might not inherit update operators that apply to variables of type T (*see Principle of Update Operator Inheritance*). *See also* possrep inheritance.

Note: The foregoing definition of the term *type inheritance* is the definition the *Manifesto* model is based on. However, it has to be said there's no consensus in the literature on exactly what the term is supposed to mean. For example:

- From "The Object-Oriented Database System Manifesto," by Malcolm Atkinson, François Bancilhon, David DeWitt, Klaus Dittrich, David Maier, and Stanley Zdonik (Proc. 1st International Conference on Deductive and Object-Oriented Databases, Kyoto, Japan, Elsevier Science, 1990):

  [There] are at least four types of inheritance: *substitution* inheritance, *inclusion* inheritance, *constraint* inheritance, and *specialization* inheritance ... Various degrees of these four types of inheritance are provided by existing systems and prototypes, and we do not prescribe a specific style of inheritance. (Italics as in the original.)

■ From *An Introduction to Data Types,* by J. Craig Cleaveland (Addison-Wesley, 1986):

[Inheritance can be] based on [a variety of] different criteria and there is no commonly accepted standard definition.

The book then goes on to give eight possible interpretations. (Bertrand Meyer, in "The Many Faces of Inheritance: A Taxonomy of Taxonomy," *IEEE Computer 29*, No. 5, May 1996, gives twelve.)

■ From technical correspondence by Kenneth Baclawski and Bipin Indurkhya in *CACM 37*, No. 9, September 1994:

[A language merely] provides a set of [inheritance] mechanisms. While these mechanisms certainly restrict what one can do in that language and what views of inheritance can be implemented [in that language], they do not by themselves validate some view of inheritance or other. [Types,] specializations, generalizations, and inheritance are only concepts, and ... they do not have a universal objective meaning ... This [state of affairs] implies that how inheritance is to be incorporated into a specific system is up to the designers of [that] system, and it constitutes a policy decision that must be implemented with the available mechanisms.

And so on. *Caveat lector*.

type lattice   In general, a lattice, q.v., for which (a) the pertinent set is a set of types and (b) the necessary partial ordering is provided by the "is a subtype of" operator. In particular, the set of available types (q.v.) in any given situation can be considered as constituting a collection of disjoint lattices, as follows:

■ The set of all scalar types is a lattice; for any given pair of such types, the least upper bound and the greatest lower bound are, respectively, the most specific common supertype and the least specific common subtype (for that pair in each case). The least upper and greatest lower bounds for the lattice as a whole are the maximal scalar type *alpha* and the minimal scalar type *omega*, respectively.

■ Let *T* be a tuple type, with corresponding maximal and minimal types *T_alpha* and *T_omega*, respectively. Then the set of all subtypes of *T_alpha* and supertypes of *T_omega* is a lattice; for any given pair of such types, the least upper bound and the greatest lower bound are, respectively, the most specific common supertype and the least specific common subtype (for that pair in each case). The least upper and greatest lower bounds for the lattice as a whole are *T_alpha* and *T_omega*, respectively. Note that, by definition, all types belonging to the same tuple type lattice have the same attribute names.

■ Let *T* be a relation type, with corresponding maximal and minimal types *T_alpha* and *T_omega*, respectively. Then the set of all subtypes of *T_alpha* and supertypes of *T_omega* is a lattice; for any given pair of such types, the least upper bound and the greatest lower bound are, respectively, the most specific common supertype and the least specific common subtype (for that pair in each case). The least upper and greatest lower bounds for the lattice as a whole are *T_alpha* and *T_omega*, respectively. Note that, by definition, all types belonging to the same relation type lattice have the same attribute names.

The foregoing lattices are pairwise disjoint, in the sense that every type in the set of available types belongs to precisely one of them. Moreover, no type in any of the lattices in question overlaps any type in any other.

Let *T* be any type. Then the set of all subtypes of *T*, including both type *T* itself and type *T_omega*, can be regarded as a lattice in its own right. Likewise, the set of all supertypes of *T*, including both type *T* itself and type *T_alpha*, can also be regarded as a lattice in its own right. *Note:* That said, however, the unqualified term *type lattice* is almost invariably taken—in this dictionary in particular—to refer to one of the lattices described in the three bullet items above, unless the context demands otherwise.

Examples: The types shown in Fig. 4 (even without types *alpha* and *omega*), together with "is a subtype of" as the necessary partial ordering, constitute a type lattice. By way of illustration, consider types PARALLELOGRAM and ISOSCELES TRAPEZOID; these two types have their most specific common supertype TRAPEZOID as their least upper bound and their least specific common subtype RECTANGLE as their greatest lower bound. As another example, consider types RECTANGLE and RIGHT KITE; these two types have their most specific common supertype CYCLIC QUADRILATERAL as their least upper bound and their least specific common subtype SQUARE as their greatest lower bound.

type schema (*With inheritance*) Term sometimes used to refer to a collection of type definitions—especially if the types in question are involved in any subtype / supertype relationships. For example, the collection of type definitions for the set of six types shown in Fig. 2 could be regarded as constituting a type schema.

type testing *See* IS_*T*; *see also* *R* : IS_*T*.

typed table An SQL construct, highly intertwined with SQL's support for subtables and supertables, q.v., and REF types (see Part I of this dictionary), and deprecated for both of those reasons.

Note: The terminology of "typed tables" is quite inappropriate, because (a) all tables, not just "typed" ones, are effectively of some type anyway—though SQL fails to take advantage of, or indeed even recognize, this fact—and (b) if "typed table" *TT* is defined to be "of type *T*," then *TT* is in fact not of type *T*, and neither are its rows. (In particular, if the declared type of some parameter to some operator *Op* is *T*, no "typed table" *TT* can be passed as the corresponding argument to an invocation of that operator *Op*, and neither can any of its rows.) Further details are beyond the scope of this dictionary, but a brief discussion of such matters can be found in the book *An Introduction to Database Systems* (8th edition), by C. J. Date (Addison-Wesley, 2004).

———— ♦♦♦♦♦ ————

union   (*With inheritance*) *See* dyadic relational operators.

union type   A scalar type *T* such that every value *v* of type *T* has as its most specific type some proper and necessarily nonunion subtype of type *T* (i.e., there's no value *v* such that *MST*(*v*) is *T*). Dummy types, q.v., are an important special case. Note that—with the obvious exception of the special dummy type *omega*, q.v.—a union type must have at least two distinct immediate subtypes. Note too that the concept of union vs. nonunion types doesn't really apply to nonscalar types.

Examples: Consider first the following type schema, q.v. (based on a revised version of Fig. 2):

```
TYPE ELLIPSE UNION
    IS { PLANE_FIGURE
        POSSREP { A LENGTH , B LENGTH , CTR POINT
        CONSTRAINT A ≥ B } } ;

TYPE CIRCLE
    IS { ELLIPSE
        CONSTRAINT THE_A ( ELLIPSE ) = THE_B ( ELLIPSE )
        POSSREP { R   = THE_A    ( ELLIPSE ) ,
                CTR = THE_CTR ( ELLIPSE ) } } ;

TYPE NONCIRCLE
    IS { ELLIPSE
        CONSTRAINT THE_A ( ELLIPSE ) > THE_B ( ELLIPSE )
        POSSREP { A   = THE_A    ( ELLIPSE ) ,
                B   = THE_B  ( ELLIPSE ) ,
                CTR = THE_CTR ( ELLIPSE ) } } ;
```

Given these type definitions:

■ Type ELLIPSE is a union type and types CIRCLE and NONCIRCLE are nonunion types; what's more, every ellipse is either a circle or a noncircle (i.e., types CIRCLE and NONCIRCLE are disjoint).

■ Type ELLIPSE does have a declared possrep and hence a selector, but invoking that selector will never return a value of most specific type ELLIPSE. It also has THE_ operators, but such operators will never be applied to arguments of most specific type ELLIPSE.

- A variable of declared type ELLIPSE will always have most specific type some proper subtype of ELLIPSE.

- Invocation signatures can be defined having ELLIPSE as the declared type of their result. However, no operator invocation will ever return a value of most specific type ELLIPSE.

- Invocation signatures can also be defined having ELLIPSE as one of their argument types. However, no actual argument will ever have most specific type ELLIPSE.

- Let AREA_OF be an operator that applies to both circles and noncircles. Observe, then, that implementation code can be provided for that operator at the ELLIPSE level that will work for both circles and noncircles:

```
OPERATOR AREA_OF VERSION E_AREA ( E ELLIPSE ) RETURNS AREA ;
   RETURN 3.14159 * THE_A ( E ) * THE_B ( E ) ;
END OPERATOR ;
```

- The AREA_OF example gives some idea of the purpose of union types: They provide a way of defining operators, together with implementation code for those operators, that apply to values or variables of several different types, all of them proper subtypes of the union type in question.

A union type obviously can't be a leaf type. However, it would be possible to set up the type schema in such a way that all types except leaf types (and the pertinent minimal type or types) are union types. With reference to Fig. 2, for example, introducing type NONCIRCLE as above, together with types NONRECTANGLE and NONSQUARE (as immediate subtypes of types POLYGON and RECTANGLE, respectively, and with the intuitively obvious semantics) would have such an effect. "All most specific types must be leaf types" might thus be regarded as the extreme form of the idea of union types, and some writers have indeed advocated such a notion. The *Manifesto* model doesn't assume such an arrangement, but neither does it prohibit it.

Note that a nonunion type can have a union type (but not a dummy type) as a proper subtype. For example, type SQUARE might be a proper subtype of type RECTANGLE, where (a) RECTANGLE is a nonunion type and (b) SQUARE is divided into "big squares" and "small squares" and is therefore a union type.

Finally, what about tuple and relation union types? For simplicity, let's focus on tuple types specifically. Loosely speaking, then, a tuple type that includes an attribute of some union type will itself effectively be a union type also (even though, technically, the concept doesn't apply to tuple types). Similarly for relation types, mutatis mutandis.

———— ♦ ♦ ♦ ♦ ♦ ————

v (...)   Value of.

value of   *See* model of a variable; model of an expression.

value substitutability   Wherever a value of type *T* is permitted, a value of any subtype of *T* can be substituted. *See Principle of Value Substitutability.* Note that the concept of value substitutability is a logical consequence of the very notion of type inheritance. *Note:* Unfortunately, few writers (or languages or systems, come to that) seem to distinguish properly—or at all—between value substitutability and variable substitutability, q.v. But languages and systems that fail to make this distinction are very likely to permit such absurdities as circular noncircles (q.v.) and noncircular circles (q.v.).

variable substitutability   Wherever a variable of declared type *T* is permitted, a variable of declared type some nonempty subtype of *T* can be substituted—but only if such substitution makes sense. *See Principle of Variable Substitutability. Note:* Unfortunately, few writers (or languages or systems, come to that) seem to distinguish properly—or at all—between variable substitutability and value substitutability, q.v. But languages and systems that fail to make this distinction are very likely to permit such absurdities as circular noncircles (q.v.) and noncircular circles (q.v.).

version (operator)   Implementation version, q.v.

version signature   *See* implementation version.

Part III

Intervals

Examples in this part of the dictionary are based for the most part on a drastically revised version of the suppliers-and-parts database, involving suppliers and shipments only ("the suppliers-and-shipments database"). Sample values are shown in Fig. 6.

S_SINCE

SNO	SNO_SINCE	STATUS	STATUS_SINCE
S1	d04	20	d06
S2	d07	10	d07
S3	d03	30	d03
S4	d04	20	d08
S5	d02	30	d02

SP_SINCE

SNO	PNO	SINCE
S1	P1	d04
S1	P2	d05
S1	P3	d09
S1	P4	d05
S1	P5	d04
S1	P6	d06
S2	P1	d08
S2	P2	d09
S3	P2	d08
S4	P5	d05

S_DURING

SNO	DURING
S2	[d02:d04]
S6	[d03:d05]

SP_DURING

SNO	PNO	DURING
S2	P1	[d02:d04]
S2	P2	[d03:d03]
S3	P5	[d05:d07]
S4	P2	[d06:d09]
S4	P4	[d04:d08]
S6	P3	[d03:d03]
S6	P3	[d05:d05]

S_STATUS_DURING

SNO	STATUS	DURING
S1	15	[d04:d05]
S2	5	[d02:d02]
S2	10	[d03:d04]
S4	10	[d04:d04]
S4	25	[d05:d07]
S6	5	[d03:d04]
S6	7	[d05:d05]

Fig. 6: The suppliers-and-shipments database with both since and during relvars– sample values

The relvars illustrated in Fig. 6 are all base relvars. The predicates are as follows:

- Relvar S_SINCE: *Supplier SNO has been under contract ever since day SNO_SINCE (and not the day immediately before day SNO_SINCE) and will continue to be so until further notice, and has had status STATUS ever since day STATUS_SINCE (and not the day immediately before day STATUS_SINCE) and will continue to do so until further notice.*

- Relvar SP_SINCE: *Supplier SNO has been able to supply part PNO ever since day SINCE (and not the day immediately before day SINCE) and will continue to be so until further notice.*

- Relvar S_DURING: *DURING denotes a maximal interval of days throughout which supplier SNO was under contract.*

- Relvar S_STATUS_DURING: *DURING denotes a maximal interval of days throughout which supplier SNO had status STATUS.*

- Relvar SP_DURING: *DURING denotes a maximal interval of days throughout which supplier SNO was able to supply part PNO.*

Points arising:

- First of all, note the subtle change in semantics with respect to shipments in particular. In the original suppliers-and-parts database (with respect to relvar SP specifically), the term "shipments" referred to *actual* shipments—the specified supplier was actually supplying the specified part. By contrast, in the suppliers-and-shipments database (with respect to relvars SP_SINCE and SP_DURING specifically), the term refers to what might be called *potential* shipments—the specified supplier *is able to* supply the specified part, but might or might not actually be doing so at any given time.

- The symbols *d01*, *d02*, etc. in Fig. 6 can be read as "day 1," "day 2," etc., where day 1 immediately precedes day 2, day 2 immediately precedes day 3, and so on. The symbols in question can be thought of as shorthand for literals of type DATE (*see* DATE). *Note:* For simplicity, insignificant leading zeros are dropped from expressions such as "day 1." Also, the symbol *d99* ("day 99") is special—it's used to denote "the last day" (*see* end of time).

- Analogously, the symbols *t01*, *t02*, ..., *t99* (not illustrated in Fig. 6) stand for specific times;[1] they can be thought of as shorthand for literals of type TIME or some TIMESTAMP type (*see* TIME; TIMESTAMP), depending on context. Also, *t99*, like *d99*, is special (*see* bitemporal table (SQL); system time).

---

[1] In the context of an SQL period, however (*see* period), such symbols typically denote TO values.

■ Symbols of the form [*di:dj*] in Fig. 6 stand for intervals—to be specific, the interval from day *i* to day *j*, inclusive (*see* interval value). They can be thought of as shorthand for certain literals of type INTERVAL_DATE (*see* interval selector). Analogously, symbols of the form [*ti:tj*] (not illustrated in Fig. 6) also stand for certain intervals; they can be thought of as shorthand for certain literals of type INTERVAL_TIME or INTERVAL_ TIMESTAMP (again, *see* interval selector), depending on context. *Note:* More generally, symbols of the form [*b:e*]—*b* for begin and *e* for end—are used to stand for intervals whose contained points aren't necessarily temporal ones (they might be or they might not).

■ To say that (e.g.) DURING in relvar S_DURING denotes a "maximal" interval of days throughout which supplier SNO was under contract means that if there's a tuple in that relvar showing supplier S2 as under contract from, say, day 2 to day 4 inclusive—which indeed there is, in Fig. 6—then there isn't a tuple in that relvar showing that supplier as under contract on either day 1 or day 5. *See* maximal interval.

■ Use of the past tense in the predicates for relvars S_DURING, S_STATUS_DURING, and SP_DURING is merely a matter of convention. For example, the predicate for S_DURING refers to an interval throughout which the specified supplier *was* under contract (emphasis added). In general, however, intervals can refer to the past and/or the present and/or the future; thus, the predicate for S_DURING might more accurately be stated as follows: *DURING denotes a maximal interval of days throughout which supplier SNO was, is, or will be under contract.*

■ That said, the relvars illustrated in Fig. 6 are in fact subject to a variety of constraints that ensure among other things that the intervals in relvar S_DURING (also in relvars S_STATUS_DURING and SP_DURING) always refer to the past specifically. Unfortunately the constraints in question are a little complicated, and detailed discussion of them is beyond the scope of this dictionary; suffice it to say that one of the effects of those constraints is to ensure that there's no "overlap" between the since and during relvars. In other words (to spell the point out), no supplier is shown (a) as being under contract on some given day in both S_SINCE and S_DURING, or (b) as having some status on some given day in both S_SINCE and S_STATUS_DURING, or (c) as being able to supply some given part on some given day in both SP_SINCE and SP_DURING.

■ The previous point notwithstanding, Fig. 7 below does at least show a definition for the suppliers-and-shipments database that includes the constraints in question. For further discussion and explanation, including in particular an explanation of the various constraint names (BR12, etc.), see the book *Time and Relational Theory: Temporal Data in the Relational Model and SQL*, by C. J. Date, Hugh Darwen, and Nikos A. Lorentzos (Morgan Kaufmann, 2014).

```
VAR S_SINCE BASE RELATION
   { SNO SNO , SNO_SINCE DATE , STATUS INTEGER , STATUS_SINCE DATE }
     KEY { SNO } ;

VAR SP_SINCE BASE RELATION
   { SNO SNO , PNO PNO , SINCE DATE }
     KEY { SNO , PNO }
     FOREIGN KEY { SNO } REFERENCES S_SINCE ;

VAR S_DURING BASE RELATION
   { SNO SNO , DURING INTERVAL_DATE }
     USING ( DURING ) : KEY { SNO , DURING }
     USING ( DURING ) : FOREIGN KEY { SNO , DURING }
                                   REFERENCES S_STATUS_DURING ;

VAR S_STATUS_DURING BASE RELATION
   { SNO SNO , STATUS INTEGER , DURING INTERVAL_DATE }
     USING ( DURING ) : KEY { SNO , DURING } ;

VAR SP_DURING BASE RELATION
   { SNO SNO , PNO PNO , DURING INTERVAL_DATE }
     USING ( DURING ) : KEY { SNO , PNO , DURING } ;

CONSTRAINT BR12 IS_EMPTY
   ( ( S_SINCE JOIN S_DURING ) WHERE SNO_SINCE ≤ POST ( DURING ) ) ;

CONSTRAINT BR36
     WITH ( t1 := EXTEND S_SINCE : { DURING := INTERVAL_DATE
                                   ( [ SNO_SINCE : LAST_DATE ( ) ] ) } ,
            t2 := t1 { SNO , DURING } ,
            t3 := t2 UNION S_DURING ,
            t4 := EXTEND S_SINCE : { DURING := INTERVAL_DATE
                                   ( [ STATUS_SINCE : LAST_DATE ( ) ] ) } ,
            t5 := t4 { SNO , STATUS , DURING } ,
            t6 := t5 UNION S_STATUS_DURING ,
            t7 := t6 { SNO , DURING } ) :
     USING ( DURING ) : t3 = t7 ;

CONSTRAINT BR4 IS_EMPTY
   ( ( S_SINCE JOIN S_STATUS_DURING { SNO , DURING } )
                   WHERE STATUS_SINCE < POST ( DURING ) ) ;

CONSTRAINT BR5 IS_EMPTY
   ( ( S_SINCE JOIN S_STATUS_DURING )
             WHERE STATUS_SINCE = POST ( DURING ) ) ;

CONSTRAINT BR78 IS_EMPTY
   ( ( SP_SINCE JOIN SP_DURING ) WHERE SINCE ≤ POST ( DURING ) ) ;
```

Fig. 7: Complete definition for the database of Fig. 6 (part 1 of 2)

```
CONSTRAINT BR9
     WITH ( t1 := EXTEND S_SINCE : { DURING := INTERVAL_DATE
                                     ( [ SNO_SINCE : LAST_DATE ( ) ] ) } ,
            t2 := t1 { SNO , DURING } ,
            t3 := t2 UNION S_DURING ,
            t4 := EXTEND SP_SINCE : { DURING := INTERVAL_DATE
                                     ( [ SINCE : LAST_DATE ( ) ] ) } ,
            t5 := t4 { SNO , DURING } ,
            t6 := SP_DURING { SNO , DURING } ,
            t7 := t5 UNION t6 ) :
     USING ( DURING ) : t3 ⊇ t7 ;
```

Fig. 7 (cont.): Complete definition for the database of Fig. 6 (part 2 of 2)

Next, certain of the examples in what follows make use of a revised version of the suppliers-and-shipments database, with sample values as shown in Fig. 8. Exactly how the relvars of Fig. 8 are related to—in fact, are derived from—those of Fig. 6 is explained in the entry for COMBINED_IN, q.v., where the pertinent predicates can also be found.

S_DURING

SNO	DURING
S1	[d04:d99]
S2	[d02:d04]
S2	[d07:d99]
S3	[d03:d99]
S4	[d04:d99]
S5	[d02:d99]
S6	[d03:d05]

SP_DURING

SNO	PNO	DURING
S1	P1	[d04:d99]
S1	P2	[d05:d99]
S1	P3	[d09:d99]
S1	P4	[d05:d99]
S1	P5	[d04:d99]
S1	P6	[d06:d99]
S2	P1	[d02:d04]
S2	P1	[d08:d99]
S2	P2	[d03:d03]
S2	P2	[d09:d99]
S3	P2	[d08:d99]
S3	P5	[d05:d07]
S4	P2	[d06:d09]
S4	P4	[d04:d08]
S4	P5	[d05:d99]
S6	P3	[d03:d03]
S6	P3	[d05:d05]

S_STATUS_DURING

SNO	STATUS	DURING
S1	15	[d04:d05]
S1	20	[d06:d99]
S2	5	[d02:d02]
S2	10	[d03:d04]
S2	10	[d07:d99]
S3	30	[d03:d99]
S4	10	[d04:d04]
S4	25	[d05:d07]
S4	20	[d08:d99]
S5	30	[d02:d99]
S6	5	[d03:d04]
S6	7	[d05:d05]

Fig. 8: Fig. 6 revised to use during relvars only

A Note on Redundancy

Take another look at Fig. 8; in particular, take a look at the tuples for supplier S6 in relvars S_DURING and S_STATUS_DURING. For convenience, we show those tuples again below (more precisely, we show the S_DURING and S_STATUS_DURING relation values from the figure, restricted in each case to just the tuples for supplier S6):

S_DURING

SNO	DURING
S6	[d03:d05]

S_STATUS_DURING

SNO	STATUS	DURING
S6	5	[d03:d04]
S6	7	[d05:d05]

   Observe now that the information represented explicitly in S_DURING to the effect that supplier S6 was under contract throughout the interval from day 3 to day 5, inclusive, is represented implicitly in S_STATUS_DURING as well. (More precisely, one of the tuples for supplier S6 in S_STATUS_DURING tells us that that supplier had some status on days 3 and 4, and the other tells us that that same supplier had some status on day 5 as well—from which it follows that supplier S6 must indeed have been under contract throughout those three days.) And, of course, similar remarks apply to every individual supplier; we chose supplier S6 just by way of example. In other words, relvar S_DURING is 100% redundant in the design of Fig. 8! Indeed, given that whenever the database shows a supplier as being under contract, it must also show that supplier as having some status, it should be intuitively obvious that S_DURING is indeed redundant as claimed.

   As noted in Part I of this dictionary, however, redundancy in the database shouldn't be a problem so long as it's controlled, meaning it's guaranteed never to lead to any formal inconsistencies. In order to ensure that the particular redundancy under discussion is controlled in this sense, what's needed is for a certain constraint to be stated and enforced—to be precise, a certain *foreign U_key constraint* (q.v.) from S_DURING to S_STATUS_DURING, which will ensure that for every day on which, according to S_DURING, a given supplier is under contract, there'll be a tuple that effectively asserts the same thing in S_STATUS_DURING.[2]

   Of course, the obvious question is: If S_DURING is indeed redundant as described, why do we include it in our design at all? The answer is: We do so in order to avoid a certain degree of awkwardness, arbitrariness, and asymmetry that would otherwise occur. Further specifics are beyond the scope of this brief discussion; suffice it to say that S_DURING plays a role with respect to the design of Fig. 8 that's analogous, somewhat, to the role played by E-relvars in an RM/T design (see Part I of this dictionary).

---

[2] As a matter of fact there's an analogous constraint from S_STATUS_DURING to S_DURING as well, and the two foreign U_key constraints can therefore be combined into a *U_equality dependency*, q.v. *See* foreign U_key for further discussion.

Note: Remarks analogous to the foregoing apply to the design of Fig. 6 as well, though the specifics are a little more complicated. Again, for detailed discussion see the book *Time and Relational Theory: Temporal Data in the Relational Model and SQL*, by C. J. Date, Hugh Darwen, and Nikos A. Lorentzos (Morgan Kaufmann, 2014).

A Note on SQL

This part of the dictionary contains rather more definitions, examples, and discussions having to do with SQL specifically than Parts I and II did. The reason is that the pertinent features of SQL were added to the standard only comparatively recently, as part of SQL:2011 (see Part I of this dictionary), and for the most part they haven't yet found their way into commercial products. For that reason, they're likely to be unfamiliar to most readers. *Note:* Those SQL examples in particular make use of the database shown in Fig. 9 (a variation on the database of Fig. 8). Tables S_FROM_TO, S_STATUS_FROM_TO, and SP_FROM_TO in that database are all base tables. Note in particular that those tables involve no intervals, as such, at all—they have *periods* instead, q.v., made up of column pairs (DFROM and DTO, in the figure). In the body of the dictionary, we use SQL-style expressions of the form PERIOD (*f,t*) to denote such periods.

S_FROM_TO

SNO	DFROM	DTO
S1	d04	d99
S2	d02	d05
S2	d07	d99
S3	d03	d99
S4	d04	d99
S5	d02	d99
S6	d03	d06

SP_FROM_TO

SNO	PNO	DFROM	DTO
S1	P1	d04	d99
S1	P2	d05	d99
S1	P3	d09	d99
S1	P4	d05	d99
S1	P5	d04	d99
S1	P6	d06	d99
S2	P1	d02	d05
S2	P1	d08	d99
S2	P2	d03	d04
S2	P2	d09	d99
S3	P2	d08	d99
S3	P5	d05	d08
S4	P2	d06	d10
S4	P4	d04	d09
S4	P5	d05	d99
S6	P3	d03	d04
S6	P3	d05	d06

S_STATUS_FROM_TO

SNO	STATUS	DFROM	DTO
S1	15	d04	d06
S1	20	d06	d99
S2	5	d02	d03
S2	10	d03	d05
S2	10	d07	d99
S3	30	d03	d99
S4	10	d04	d05
S4	25	d05	d08
S4	20	d08	d99
S5	30	d02	d99
S6	5	d03	d05
S6	7	d05	d06

Fig. 9: SQL analog of Fig. 8

As for the predicates for these SQL tables, see the entry for **table predicate (SQL)**.

A Note on Tutorial D

The current version of **Tutorial D** as defined in the book *Database Explorations: Essays on The Third Manifesto and Related Topics*, by C. J. Date and Hugh Darwen (Trafford, 2010), has no support for intervals. However, the book mentioned a couple of times already, *Time and Relational Theory: Temporal Data in the Relational Model and SQL*, by Date, Darwen, and Lorentzos, contains some proposals for extending the language to incorporate such support, and the name "**Tutorial D**" in this part of the dictionary should be understood as referring to a version of the language that has been extended in accordance with the proposals in that book.

———— ♦ ♦ ♦ ♦ ♦ ————

adding temporal support   *See* temporal upward compatibility.

AFTER   One of Allen's operators, q.v. Let $i1 = [b1{:}e1]$ and $i2 = [b2{:}e2]$ be intervals of the same type. Then $i1$ AFTER $i2$ is true if and only if $b1 > e2$ is true.
    Examples: Let $i1$ and $i2$ be $[d08{:}d10]$ and $[d02{:}d03]$, respectively; then $i1$ AFTER $i2$ is true. By contrast, if $i1$ and $i2$ are $[d08{:}d10]$ and $[d02{:}d08]$, respectively, then $i1$ AFTER $i2$ is false. Observe that $i1$ AFTER $i2$ and $i2$ BEFORE $i1$ are equivalent (i.e., $i1$ AFTER $i2$ is true if and only if $i2$ BEFORE $i1$ is true).
    Note: SQL uses the keyword SUCCEEDS in place of AFTER. For example, let $p1$ and $p2$ be the SQL periods PERIOD $(d08,d11)$ and PERIOD $(d02,d04)$, respectively; then the SQL expression $p1$ SUCCEEDS $p2$ is true.

Allen's operators   A set of operators for comparing two intervals of the same type to see whether they're equal, whether they overlap, and so on. The operators are referred to collectively as Allen's operators because most of them—not all—were first proposed by James F. Allen in "Maintaining Knowledge about Temporal Intervals" (*CACM 26*, No. 11, November 1983). The following table lists the Allen operators defined in this dictionary and shows their direct SQL analogs, where such analogs exist ($p1$ and $p2$ denote SQL periods):

Operator	SQL analog
equality	*p1* EQUALS *p2*
includes	*p1* CONTAINS *p2*
properly includes	
is included in	
is properly included in	
AFTER	*p1* SUCCEEDS *p2*
BEFORE	*p1* PRECEDES *p2*
BEGINS	
ENDS	
DISJOINT	
OVERLAPS	*p1* OVERLAPS *p2*
MEETS	*p1* IMMEDIATELY PRECEDES *p2* OR
	p1 IMMEDIATELY SUCCEEDS *p2*
MERGES	

Note: Despite the title of Allen's paper, the operators don't apply just to temporal intervals as such. Also, (a) the operators defined in this dictionary aren't the only ones possible, but they're probably the most useful ones in practice; (b) the names used in this dictionary to refer to those operators—and indeed the definitions too—do sometimes differ (deliberately, of course) from the ones originally proposed by Allen.

application time SQL term for stated time, q.v. An SQL base table can have at most one application time period (*see* period). However, such periods don't "carry through" operational expressions; thus, no SQL table other than a base table has, or can have, any application time period at all.

Examples: Each of the tables in Fig. 9 has an application time period, represented by the (DFROM,DTO) column pair in the table in question. By contrast, the table resulting from, e.g., the SQL expression

```
SELECT *
FROM    S_FROM_TO
```

has no application time period at all, even though it's essentially identical to the current value of table S_FROM_TO, and in particular does have a (DFROM,DTO) column pair. *See* period for further discussion and explanation.

application time period *See* application time.

BEFORE One of Allen's operators, q.v. Let *i1* = [*b1*:*e1*] and *i2* = [*b2*:*e2*] be intervals of the same type. Then *i1* BEFORE *i2* is true if and only if *e1* < *b2* is true.

Examples: Let *i1* and *i2* be [*d02:d03*] and [*d08:d10*], respectively; then *i1* BEFORE *i2* is true. By contrast, if *i1* and *i2* are [*d02:d08*] and [*d08:d10*], respectively, then *i1* BEFORE *i2* is false. Observe that *i1* BEFORE *i2* and *i2* AFTER *i1* are equivalent (i.e., *i1* BEFORE *i2* is true if and only if *i2* AFTER *i1* is true).

Note: SQL uses the keyword PRECEDES in place of BEFORE. For example, let *p1* and *p2* be the SQL periods PERIOD (*d02,d04*) and PERIOD (*d08,d11*), respectively; then the SQL expression *p1* PRECEDES *p2* is true.

BEGIN   *See* begin point.

begin point   The begin point of the interval *i* = [*b:e*], denoted BEGIN (*i*), is the point *b*. *Note:* SQL has no support for the BEGIN operator as such. Rather, if *p* denotes the SQL period PERIOD (*f,t*), then the SQL expression *f* is effectively equivalent to the hypothetical SQL expression "BEGIN (*p*)." *See* period for further explanation.

beginning of time   *See* timeline.

BEGINS   One of Allen's operators, q.v. Let *i1* = [*b1:e1*] and *i2* = [*b2:e2*] be intervals of the same type. Then *i1* BEGINS *i2* is true if and only if *b1* = *b2* and *e1* ≤ *e2* are both true.

Examples: Let *i1* and *i2* be [*d02:d05*] and [*d02:d10*], respectively; then *i1* BEGINS *i2* is true. By contrast, if *i1* and *i2* are [*d02:d05*] and [*d01:d10*], respectively, then *i1* BEGINS *i2* is false.

Note: SQL has no direct support for the BEGINS operator. However, if *p1* and *p2* denote the SQL periods PERIOD (*f1,t1*) and PERIOD (*f2,t2*), respectively, then the SQL expression *f1* = *f2* AND *t1* ≤ *t2* is effectively equivalent to the hypothetical SQL expression "*p1* BEGINS *p2*." *See* period for further explanation.

bitemporal   An informal and somewhat deprecated term used to characterize a heading (or a tuple, or a relation, or a relvar, or an SQL row or table) having exactly two temporal components, one representing stated time, q.v., and the other logged time, q.v. *Note:* Actually it's not so much the term as such, but rather the concept denoted by that term, that's deprecated. Indeed, the term as such can be useful in referring to that otherwise deprecated concept.

Example: Consider the following tuple:

SNO	DURING	X_DURING
S2	[*d02:d04*]	[*t50:t75*]

This tuple is bitemporal; the intended interpretation—deliberately stated a little loosely here—is "From time *t50* to time *t75*, inclusive, the database said that supplier S2 was under contract from day 2 to day 4, inclusive." In other words, attribute DURING denotes the stated time for a certain proposition (viz., "Supplier S2 was under contract," in the case at hand), and attribute X_DURING denotes the logged time for another, different, proposition (viz., "Supplier S2 was under contract from day 2 to day 4, inclusive," in the case at hand).

So much for the basic idea. Unfortunately, the term and the concept both have their origins in a nonrelational approach to temporal data—an approach in which time is regarded as special, and intervals like [*d02:d04*] and [*t50:t75*] are represented not by regular relational attributes as in the foregoing example, but rather in some special and ad hoc kind of way. And it's generally assumed in such nonrelational approaches that data can never be "more than" bitemporal, meaning that a given heading (or tuple, or relation, etc.) can never involve more than one "stated time" component and/or more than one "logged time" component. What are the implications? Well, consider the following two perfectly reasonable tuples (each of which might perhaps be characterized as "unitemporal"):

PERSON	DAYS
p	[Sun:Thu]

PERSON	HOURS
p	[1030:1830]

The intended interpretations are "Person *p* works on Sunday to Thursday" and "Person *p* works from 10:30 am to 6:30 pm." Observe that each of these tuples has just one temporal attribute, each representing a certain "stated time." So what happens if these two tuples are joined together? Clearly, the result is:

PERSON	DAYS	HOURS
p	[Sun:Thu]	[1030:1830]

But this tuple has two "stated time" temporal attributes, and is thus not legal under a scheme in which tuples are limited to being at most bitemporal—meaning, to repeat, that they can have at most one stated time component and/or at most one logged time component.

By way of another example, here are two more "unitemporal" tuples:

PERSON	PRIMARY
p	[1946:1951]

PERSON	SECONDARY
p	[1951:1959]

The intended interpretations are "Person *p*'s primary education lasted from 1946 to 1951" and "Person *p*'s secondary education lasted from 1951 to 1959." And here's the bitemporal tuple that results if these two tuples are joined together:

PERSON	PRIMARY	SECONDARY
p	[1946:1951]	[1951:1959]

bitemporal table (SQL)   Unofficial but useful term for an SQL table (necessarily a base table) having both an application time period, q.v. (necessarily unique), and a system time period, q.v. (also necessarily uniqe).

Example: Suppose we want to keep system time information as well as application time information for suppliers and their status values. Then instead of table S_STATUS_FROM_TO as illustrated in Fig. 9 (and as defined in the examples under **period**, q.v.), we might define a bitemporal table BS_STATUS_FROM_TO as shown here:

```
CREATE TABLE BS_STATUS_FROM_TO
 ( SNO     SNO      NOT NULL ,
   STATUS  INTEGER  NOT NULL ,
   DFROM   DATE     NOT NULL ,
   DTO     DATE     NOT NULL ,
   PERIOD FOR DPERIOD ( DFROM , DTO ) ,
   UNIQUE ( SNO , DPERIOD WITHOUT OVERLAPS ) ,
   FOREIGN KEY ( SNO , PERIOD DPERIOD )
          REFERENCES BS_FROM_TO ( SNO , PERIOD DPERIOD ) ,
   XFROM   TIMESTAMP(12) GENERATED ALWAYS AS ROW START NOT NULL ,
   XTO     TIMESTAMP(12) GENERATED ALWAYS AS ROW END   NOT NULL ,
   PERIOD FOR SYSTEM_TIME ( XFROM , XTO ) )
   WITH SYSTEM VERSIONING ;
```

See the examples under **period** and **system time** for further explanation, in particular regarding queries on tables like BS_STATUS_FROM_TO. (Updates are discussed below, though again further explanation can be found under **system time**. Here we just note that the system time columns XFROM and XTO can't be directly updated by the user.)

Note: The FOREIGN KEY specification in the foregoing definition assumes the existence of another bitemporal table called BS_FROM_TO, with the obvious definition and semantics. For simplicity, however, we ignore foreign keys in the discussion of updates below. However, we note for the record that, while SQL does indeed call the constructs in question "foreign keys," it would be closer to the truth, though still not entirely accurate, to refer to them as *foreign U_keys*, q.v. *See* **foreign key (SQL)** for further explanation.

Table BS_STATUS_FROM_TO is initially empty, of course. Suppose we now execute the following INSERT:

```
INSERT INTO BS_STATUS_FROM_TO ( SNO , STATUS , DFROM , DTO )
       VALUES ( SNO('S2') , 5 , d02 , d05 ) ;
```

Further, suppose this INSERT statement is executed at time *t11* by the system clock (*see* **system time**). Then the row that's actually inserted looks like this:

SNO	STATUS	DFROM	DTO	XFROM	XTO
S2	5	*d02*	*d05*	*t11*	*t99*

In other words, the system automatically appends (a) an XFROM value denoting the time of the update, and (b) an XTO value of *t99* denoting "the end of time," to the row before inserting it. Thus, the row that's actually inserted effectively says: "During the interval [*t11*:*t99*), the database said that supplier S2 had status 5 during the interval [*d02*:*d05*)." *Note:* In accordance with SQL conventions, these intervals are given in closed:open style, q.v.

Now suppose we execute the following UPDATE statement at time *t22* by the system clock:

```
UPDATE  BS_STATUS_FROM_TO
FOR     PORTION OF DPERIOD FROM d03 TO d04
SET     STATUS = 10
WHERE   SNO = SNO('S2') ;
```

After this UPDATE, the table looks like this:

SNO	STATUS	DFROM	DTO	XFROM	XTO
S2	5	*d02*	*d05*	*t11*	*t22*
S2	5	*d02*	*d03*	*t22*	*t99*
S2	10	*d03*	*d04*	*t22*	*t99*
S2	5	*d04*	*d05*	*t22*	*t99*

In other words, the table now says "During the interval [*t11*:*t22*), the database said that supplier S2 had status 5 during the interval [*d02*:*d05*); during the interval [*t22*:*t99*), it said that supplier S2 had status 5 during the intervals [*d02*:*d03*) and [*d04*:*d05*), but status 10 during the interval [*d03*:*d04*)."

Now suppose we execute the following DELETE statement at time *t33* by the system clock:

```
DELETE
FROM    BS_STATUS_FROM_TO
FOR     PORTION OF DPERIOD FROM d03 TO d05
WHERE   SNO = SNO('S2') ;
```

Now the table looks like this:

SNO	STATUS	DFROM	DTO	XFROM	XTO
S2	5	*d02*	*d05*	*t11*	*t22*
S2	5	*d02*	*d03*	*t22*	*t99*
S2	10	*d03*	*d04*	*t22*	*t33*
S2	5	*d04*	*d05*	*t22*	*t33*

Thus, the table now says "During the interval [*t11*:*t22*), the database said that supplier S2 had status 5 during the interval [*d02*:*d05*); during the interval [*t22*:*t33*), it said that supplier S2 had status 5 during the interval [*d04*:*d05*) but status 10 during the interval [*d03*:*d04*); and during the interval [*t22*:*t99*), it said that supplier S2 had status 5 during the interval [*d02*:*d03*)."

Finally, we execute the following DELETE statement at time *t44*:

```
DELETE
FROM    BS_STATUS_FROM_TO
WHERE   SNO = SNO('S2') ;
```

Then the final version of the table looks like this:

SNO	STATUS	DFROM	DTO	XFROM	XTO
S2	5	*d02*	*d05*	*t11*	*t22*
S2	5	*d02*	*d03*	*t22*	*t44*
S2	10	*d03*	*d04*	*t22*	*t33*
S2	5	*d04*	*d05*	*t22*	*t33*

The table now says "During the interval [*t11*:*t22*), the database said that supplier S2 had status 5 during the interval [*d02*:*d05*); during the interval [*t22*:*t33*), it said that supplier S2 had status 5 during the interval [*d04*:*d05*) but status 10 during the interval [*d03*:*d04*); and during the interval [*t22*:*t44*), it said that supplier S2 had status 5 during the interval [*d02*:*d03*)."

boundary column (SQL) *See* period.

boundary point Let *i* be the interval [*b*:*e*]. Then the begin point *b* and the end point *e* of *i* are sometimes said to be the boundary points of *i*. The term is fuzzy, however (and best avoided for that reason, unless the context makes the intended meaning clear), because it's also used to refer:

- If *i* is expressed using closed:open style as [*b*:*es*), to the specified points *b* and *es*;

- If *i* is expressed using open:closed style as (*pb*:*e*], to the specified points *pb* and *e*;

- If *i* is expressed using open:open style as (*pb*:*es*), to the specified points *pb* and *es*.

See interval selector for further explanation.

boundary value (SQL)   *See* period.

business time   Term used in certain DBMS products as a synonym for stated time, q.v.

———— ♦ ♦ ♦ ♦ ♦ ————

cardinality   (*Of an interval*) The number of points in the interval in question. *See also* COUNT; duration; length.

chronon   A "time quantum"; the smallest unit of time capable of representation in a given system (and hence the smallest possible time point, q.v., capable of representation in the system in question as well, a fortiori). *Contrast* time point.

chronon timeline   *See* timeline.

circumlocution problem   A problem that can arise in connection with relvars with interval attributes, absent suitable controls: specifically, the problem that two tuples appearing in such a relvar at the same time might together represent propositions that could better be represented by a single tuple. For example, suppose with reference to either Fig. 6 or Fig. 7 that the following tuples were both to appear in relvar S_STATUS_DURING at the same time:

SNO	STATUS	DURING
S4	25	[*d05:d05*]

SNO	STATUS	DURING
S4	25	[*d06:d07*]

Clearly, the propositions represented by these tuples could alternatively (and better) be represented by a single tuple, thus:

SNO	STATUS	DURING
S4	25	[*d05:d07*]

Formally, the problem illustrated by this example is that the two original tuples (a) agree on their SNO and STATUS values and (b) have DURING values *i1* and *i2* such that *i1* MEETS *i2* is true (*see* MEETS). Note that if those original tuples were indeed both allowed to appear, then the relvar would be in violation of its own predicate, because neither [*d05:d05*] nor [*d06:d07*] would be a maximal interval, q.v., of days during which supplier S4 had status 25. (In fact, it's not entirely clear that the relvar would even have a proper relvar predicate, if those original tuples were both allowed to appear. *See* **table predicate (SQL)** for further discussion.) Note finally that enforcing a constraint to the effect that {SNO,DURING} is a key for S_STATUS_DURING—which it is—isn't sufficient to prevent the foregoing problem from occurring. *See* **PACKED ON** for further discussion.

closed   (*Of an interval*) *See* **interval** selector; interval value.

closed:closed   (*Of an interval*) *See* **interval** selector.

closed:open   (*Of an interval*) *See* **interval** selector.

coalescing   Term sometimes used as a synonym for packing, q.v. (or for an operation of the same general nature as packing). *Note:* SQL supports an operator it calls COALESCE, but that operator has nothing to do with coalescing as here defined. An example of the use of that SQL operator can be found under **summarization** in Part I of this dictionary.

COLLAPSE   *See* **collapsed form.** *Note:* SQL has no direct support for the COLLAPSE operator.

collapsed form   1. (*Sets of intervals*) Let x be a set of intervals all of the same type T. Then the expression COLLAPSE (x) denotes the collapsed form of x, and it returns the unique set y of intervals (necessarily also all of that same type T) such that (a) x and y have the same expanded form, q.v., and (b) no two distinct intervals $i1$ and $i2$ in y are such that $i1$ MERGES $i2$ is true (*see* **MERGES**); equivalently, no two distinct intervals $i1$ and $i2$ in y are such that $i1$ UNION $i2$ is defined—*see* **union (interval theory).** Observe that y can be computed from x by successively replacing pairs of intervals in x by their union until no further such replacements are possible. Observe further that no two distinct intervals $i1$ and $i2$ in y are such that $i1$ INTERSECT $i2$ is defined—*see* **intersection (interval theory).** Observe finally that if the cardinality of x is either zero or one, then COLLAPSE (x) is equal to x. 2. (*Unary relations*) Let x be a unary relation whose sole attribute is of some interval type. Then the expression COLLAPSE (x) denotes the collapsed form of x, and it returns the unique relation y of the same type as x such that (a) x and y have the same expanded form and (b) no two distinct tuples $t1$ and $t2$ in y are such that the intervals $i1$ and $i2$ contained in $t1$ and $t2$, respectively, are such that $i1$ MERGES $i2$ is true. 3. (*Nullary relations*) Let x be a nullary relation (i.e., let x be either TABLE_DUM or TABLE_DEE). Then the expression COLLAPSE (x) denotes the collapsed form of x, and it returns the relation x itself (i.e., each of TABLE_DUM and TABLE_DEE is its own collapsed form). *Contrast* **expanded form.**
      Example (second definition only): Let relation x look like this:

```
DURING

[d06:d09]
[d04:d08]
[d05:d10]
[d01:d01]
```

Then *y* = COLLAPSE (*x*) looks like this:

```
DURING

[d01:d01]
[d04:d10]
```

Note: The relational version of COLLAPSE is actually a special case of PACK (*see* packed form). To be specific, (a) if relation *x* has just one attribute, say *A*, and that attribute is interval valued, then COLLAPSE (*x*) and PACK *x* ON (*A*) are equivalent; moreover, (b) if relation *x* has no attributes at all, then COLLAPSE (*x*) and PACK *x* ON ( )—the packing here necessarily being on no attributes at all—are also equivalent.

Here for the record is a more formal version of the first (only) of the foregoing definitions. Again let *x* be a set of intervals all of the same type *T*; also, let the underlying point type for *T* be *PT*. Let *p* be a point of type *PT*, and let *i* = [*b:e*], *i1* = [*b1:e1*], *i2* = [*b2:e2*], and *j* be intervals of type *T*. Then *y* = COLLAPSE (*x*) can be defined thus:

```
y ≝ { i : FORALL p ∈ i ( EXISTS j ∈ x ( p ∈ j ) )
          AND
          EXISTS i1 ∈ x ( EXISTS i2 ∈ x
             ( b = b1 AND e = e2 AND b1 ≤ b2 AND e1 ≤ e2
               AND
               IF b2 ≠ FIRST_PT ( ) THEN
                  IF e1 < PRE̅ ( i2 ) THEN
                     FORALL p ∈ ( e1 : b2 )
                        ( EXISTS j ∈ x ( p ∈ j ) ) END IF END IF
          AND
          FORALL p ∈ i
             ( IF p ≠ FIRST_PT ( ) THEN
                  NOT EXIST̅S j ∈ x ( PRE ( i ) ∈ j ) END IF
               AND
               IF p ≠ LAST_PT ( ) THEN
                  NOT EXIST̅S j ∈ x ( POST ( i ) ∈ j ) END IF ) ) ) }
```

COMBINED_IN   A syntactic shorthand, intended to make certain operations on a temporal database (to be specific, certain queries, constraints, and updates) easier to formulate. By way of example, consider shipments. Given the database of Fig. 6, it should be intuitively obvious that certain operations on shipments—both read-only and update operations, in general—will need to refer to two distinct relvars (viz., SP_SINCE and SP_DURING), because shipment information is split across those two relvars in that database. By contrast, it should also be intuitively obvious that analogous operations on the database of Fig. 8 will need to refer to just one relvar (viz., SP_DURING), and hence that these latter operations stand a chance of being conceptually simpler, or at least superficially easier to understand, than their counterparts on Fig. 6. So the idea is that the relvars illustrated in Fig. 8 might be defined as appropriate views of the ones illustrated in Fig. 6, thereby allowing users to operate in terms of Fig. 8 even if the underlying database looks like Fig. 6.

With the foregoing in mind by way of motivation, therefore, consider the following expression:

```
WITH ( t1 := EXTEND S_SINCE : { DURING :=
                    INTERVAL_DATE ( [ SNO_SINCE : LAST_DATE ( ) ] ) } ,
       t2 := t1 { SNO , DURING } ) :
t2 UNION S_DURING
```

Given the sample values for S_SINCE and S_DURING shown in Fig. 6, this expression evaluates to the relation shown as the sample value for S_DURING in Fig. 8. (The expression INTERVAL_DATE (...) in line 2 is an interval selector invocation, and the subexpression LAST_DATE ( ) within that selector invocation denotes "the last day," which is shown as *d99* in Figs. 6 and 8.) In analogous fashion, given the sample values shown in Fig. 6 for S_SINCE, S_STATUS_DURING, SP_SINCE, and SP_DURING, (a) the expression

```
WITH ( t1 := EXTEND S_SINCE : { DURING :=
                    INTERVAL_DATE ( [ STATUS_SINCE : LAST_DATE ( ) ] ) } ,
       t2 := t1 { SNO , STATUS , DURING } ) :
t2 UNION S_STATUS_DURING
```

evaluates to the relation shown as the sample value for S_STATUS_DURING in Fig. 8, and (b) the expression

```
WITH ( t1 := EXTEND SP_SINCE : { DURING :=
                    INTERVAL_DATE ( [ SINCE : LAST_DATE ( ) ] ) } ,
       t2 := t1 { SNO , PNO , DURING } ) :
t2 UNION SP_DURING
```

evaluates to the relation shown as the sample value for SP_DURING in Fig. 8. It follows that the design illustrated in Fig. 8 can indeed be defined as views of the design illustrated in Fig. 6. What's more (to spell the point out), the design of Fig. 6 consists of a mixture of since and during relvars, whereas the design of Fig. 8 consists of during relvars only.

The design of Fig. 8 is thus "simpler," in a sense, than the design of Fig. 6. On the other hand, the design of Fig. 8 suffers, as the design of Fig. 6 does not, from the fact that we have to show a specific and arguably artificial time point (viz., "the end of time," *d99*) as the end point for any interval for which the actual end point is unknown. Thus, the design of Fig. 8 effectively requires us to put information into the database that we know is false, or at best ambiguous. Observe in particular that we can't tell the difference in that design between an appearance of *d99* that means what it says—i.e., day 99 as such—and one that's just some kind of code for *until further notice* (q.v.). In fact, that design constitutes a violation of *The Closed World Assumption* (see Part I of this dictionary), unless the relvar predicates are carefully—and rather awkwardly—reformulated in such a way as to ensure adherence to the letter, if not the spirit, of that assumption. Here are such reformulated predicates (but observe that these reformulations, complicated though they undoubtedly are, still fail to get round the ambiguity problem):

- Relvar S_DURING: *If END (DURING) is "the end of time," then supplier SNO has been under contract ever since day BEGIN (DURING) (and not the day immediately before day BEGIN (DURING)) and will continue to be so until further notice; otherwise DURING denotes a maximal interval of days throughout which supplier SNO was under contract.*

- Relvar S_STATUS_DURING: *If END (DURING) is "the end of time," then supplier SNO has had status STATUS ever since day BEGIN (DURING) (and not the day immediately before day BEGIN (DURING)) and will continue to do so until further notice; otherwise DURING denotes a maximal interval of days throughout which supplier SNO had status STATUS.*

- Relvar SP_DURING: *If END (DURING) is "the end of time," then supplier SNO has been able to supply part PNO ever since day BEGIN (DURING) (and not the day immediately before day BEGIN (DURING)) and will continue to be so until further notice; otherwise DURING denotes a maximal interval of days throughout which supplier SNO was able to supply part PNO.*

The complexity of these predicates notwithstanding, it's still the case that designs like that of Fig. 8 can make life easier for the user in certain ways. Hence the notion of COMBINED_IN specifications. The basic idea is that, given a design like that of Fig. 6, it should be possible to get the DBMS to produce a design like that of Fig. 8 automatically in response to such specifications. For example, specifying

```
COMBINED_IN ( CSP_DURING )
```

in connection with relvars SP_SINCE and SP_DURING as illustrated in Fig. 6 (and as defined in Fig. 7) should be sufficient for the system to define, automatically, a view called CSP_DURING that looks like relvar SP_DURING as illustrated in Fig. 8.

Now, the effect of the COMBINED_IN specification in the foregoing example, and indeed the effect of COMBINED_IN specifications in general (at least as so far discussed), can be regarded as undoing certain horizontal decompositions, q.v. In practice, however, we would want to be able to undo certain vertical decompositions, q.v., as well. Unfortunately, Figs. 6-8 are a little too simple to illustrate this point, so let's extend our running example (just for the sake of the present discussion) as follows. First, let's extend relvar S_SINCE to add two more attributes, CITY and CITY_SINCE. Here's a sample value:

SNO	SNO_SINCE	STATUS	STATUS_SINCE	CITY	CITY_SINCE
S1	d04	20	d06	Athens	d06
S2	d07	10	d07	Paris	d07
S3	d03	30	d03	Paris	d03
S4	d04	20	d08	Madrid	d10
S5	d02	30	d02	Athens	d02

The predicate for this revised version of S_SINCE is as follows:

> *Supplier SNO has been under contract ever since day SNO_SINCE (and not the day immediately before day SNO_SINCE) and will continue to be so until further notice; has had status STATUS ever since day STATUS_SINCE (and not the day immediately before day STATUS_SINCE) and will continue to do so until further notice; and has been located in city CITY ever since day CITY_SINCE (and not the day immediately before day CITY_SINCE) and will continue to be so until further notice.*

Second, let's also introduce an additional base relvar, S_CITY_DURING, with attributes SNO, CITY, and DURING, and predicate as follows:

> *DURING denotes a maximal interval of days throughout which supplier SNO was located in city CITY.*

Here's a sample value:

SNO	CITY	DURING
S1	London	[d04:d05]
S2	Rome	[d02:d04]
S4	Athens	[d04:d04]
S4	Oslo	[d05:d07]
S4	London	[d08:d09]
S6	Madrid	[d03:d05]

Given these additions to the database of Figs. 6-7, we can now certainly define views CS_DURING, CS_STATUS_DURING, and CS_CITY_DURING, more or less as already discussed. However, there's still a problem—the design is still vertically decomposed, implying that information regarding individual suppliers is still split across more than one relvar. What we need to do is combine those relvars into one (another view, of course), which we can do using U_join (q.v.):

```
USING ( DURING ) : JOIN { CS_DURING , CS_STATUS_DURING , CS_CITY_DURING }
```

The predicate for the result of this U_join is as follows:

> *If END (DURING) is "the end of time," then supplier SNO (a) has been under contract, (b) has had status STATUS, and (c) has been located in city CITY, ever since day BEGIN (DURING) (and not the day immediately before day BEGIN (DURING)) and will continue to be or do so until further notice; otherwise DURING denotes a maximal interval of days throughout which supplier SNO (a) was under contract, (b) had status STATUS, and (c) was located in city CITY.*

Note: Given the fact that (as pointed out, in effect, in the section "A Note on Redundancy" in the introduction to this part of the dictionary) there'll be a foreign U_key constraint from CS_DURING to CS_STATUS_DURING that guarantees that for every day on which a given supplier is under contract according to CS_DURING, there'll be a tuple that effectively asserts the same thing in CS_STATUS_DURING, there's actually no need to include CS_DURING in the foregoing U_join. The reason is that—assuming that this foreign U_key constraint is enforced, of course—the value of CS_DURING will be equal at all times to the U_projection (q.v.) on {SNO,DURING} of CS_STATUS_DURING at the time in question, and so nothing will be either gained or lost if CS_DURING is included. (In fact, the value of CS_DURING will be equal at all times to the U_projection, q.v., on {SNO,DURING} of CS_CITY_DURING at the time in question as well, for essentially analogous reasons.)

Incidentally, it's precisely because the value of CS_DURING is equal at all times to the U_projection on {SNO,DURING} of CS_STATUS_DURING at the time in question that Figs. 6-8 are too simple to illustrate the point under discussion (the point, that is, that we sometimes need to be able to undo vertical as well as horizontal decomposition).

Note finally that, precisely because of the existence of that (necessary) foreign U_key constraint from CS_DURING to CS_STATUS_DURING—equivalently, from the Fig. 8 version of S_DURING to the Fig. 8 version of S_STATUS_DURING—the predicate for either CS_STATUS_DURING or the Fig. 8 version of S_STATUS_DURING might more accurately be stated thus:

> *If END (DURING) is "the end of time," then supplier SNO has been under contract and has had status STATUS ever since day BEGIN (DURING) (and not the day immediately before day BEGIN (DURING)) and will continue to be or do so until further notice; otherwise DURING denotes a maximal interval of days throughout which supplier SNO was under contract and had status STATUS.*

(The additional text has to do with the supplier in question being under contract.) Analogous remarks apply to CS_CITY_DURING (and to S_CITY_DURING as well, if such a relvar were to be added to the database of Fig. 8).

containment   (*Expanded definition*) Generally, the relationship between a container and the things it contains; in particular, the relationship between an interval and its points. Let p be a point of type T and let i be an interval of type INTERVAL_T. Then the expression $p \in i$ (pronounced "p belongs to i" or "p is contained in i" or, more simply, just "p [is] in i") is true if and only if BEGIN $(i) \leq p$ and $p \leq$ END (i) are both true. Also, the expression $i \ni p$ (pronounced "i contains p") is true if and only if $p \in i$ is true. *See* **interval value.**

    Note: SQL uses the keyword CONTAINS in place of "$\ni$" (it doesn't support "$\in$"). Since it also uses that same keyword in place of "$\supseteq$" (*see* **interval inclusion**), it follows that CONTAINS in SQL is overloaded. Of course, although SQL has no direct support for the "$\in$" operator as such, if p denotes the SQL period PERIOD (f,t) and x is an expression of the underlying datetime type, then the SQL expression $x \geq f$ AND $x < t$ is effectively equivalent to the hypothetical SQL expression "$x \in p$." *See* **period** for further explanation.

continuity assumption   Let T be a point type, q.v. Barring explicit statements to the contrary, then, T is generally assumed to be an ordinal type, q.v., meaning among other things that an associated successor function, q.v., is assumed to exist. However, it might be possible to drop that assumption of ordinality (albeit at the cost of an increase in complexity, with little if any accompanying increase in functionality), and doing so is referred to, somewhat inappropriately, as "adopting the continuity assumption." The book *Time and Relational Theory: Temporal Data in the Relational Model and SQL*, by Date, Darwen, and Lorentzos, explores this possibility in some detail. *Contrast* **discreteness assumption.**

    Note: The term *continuity assumption* derives from the fact that a point type without a successor function behaves in some respects like the real number line (see Part I of this dictionary)—which is certainly continuous—and hence that an interval defined on such a point type behaves like a section of that line. (Note that most people would surely agree that time in particular does feel as if it were continuous in this sense.) But continuity as such isn't the real issue here; rather, the real issue is the lack of a successor function. For example, consider the rational numbers (see Part I of this dictionary), which differ from the real numbers in that they don't form a continuum, and yet resemble the real numbers in that they're "everywhere dense" and so have no successor function. (To say the rational numbers are everywhere dense is to say that if p and q are rational numbers such that $p < q$, then there's an infinite number of rational numbers r such that $p < r < q$.) Thus, the problem with using rational numbers as a point type isn't that they're continuous—they're not—but rather that they have no successor function; i.e., if r is a rational number, there's no rational number r' that can be considered the immediate successor of r.

contradiction problem   A problem that can arise in connection with relations with interval attributes, absent suitable controls: specifically, the problem that two tuples appearing in such a relvar at the same time might represent propositions that can't both be true at the same time. For example, suppose with reference to either Fig. 6 or Fig. 7 that the following tuples were both to appear in relvar S_STATUS_DURING at the same time:

SNO	STATUS	DURING
S4	25	[d05:d06]

SNO	STATUS	DURING
S4	30	[d06:d07]

Note that if these tuples were indeed both allowed to appear, the relvar would be in violation of its own predicate (because taken together, these tuples show among other things that supplier S4 had status both 25 and 30 on day 6, an impossible state of affairs). Note too that enforcing a constraint to the effect that {SNO,DURING} is a key for S_STATUS_DURING—which it is—isn't sufficient to prevent the foregoing problem from occurring. *See* WHEN / THEN for further discussion.

COUNT (*Of an interval*) Given an interval *i*, the expression COUNT (*i*) returns the number of points in that interval. *See also* **cardinality**; **duration**; **length**. *Note:* SQL has no direct support for the COUNT operator. However, if *p* denotes the SQL period PERIOD (*f,t*), then the SQL expression CAST ((*t* $-$ *f*) AS INTEGER) is effectively equivalent to the hypothetical SQL expression "COUNT (*p*)." *See* **period** for further explanation.

current relation Informal term sometimes used to refer to the value of a current relvar, q.v.

current relvar Informal term sometimes used to refer to a since relvar, q.v. However, the term is deprecated, somewhat, because such relvars aren't limited to containing information that pertains only to the current state of affairs. Indeed, they certainly contain (in general) both implicit and explicit information about the past as well as implicit information about the future, and depending on circumstances they might even contain explicit information about the future as well.

Example: Consider the sample value shown for relvar S_SINCE in Fig. 6. If we make the reasonable assumption that all of the since attribute values in that relation denote either dates in the past or (at the most recent) the date today, then it's clear that (a) today is at least day 8 and (b) any since attribute value that's earlier than day 8 represents explicit information about the past. For example, supplier S1 was under contract on day 4 (explicit information about the past); also, supplier S1 was under contract throughout the interval from day 5 to day 7 inclusive (implicit information about the past). Moreover, supplier S1 will remain under contract until further notice (implicit information about the future). And if we know that (say) supplier S8 will be placed under contract on day *dc*, where *dc* is in the future, and we insert a tuple into S_SINCE to say as much, then that relvar will now contain explicit information about the future as well.

current row (SQL) *See* **system time**.

cyclic point type *See* **point type**.

—————— ♦ ♦ ♦ ♦ ♦ ——————

DATE   A point type, assumed for the purposes of this dictionary to be system defined and to have values consisting of calendar dates, accurate to the day. In other words, the scale, q.v., is one day, and the successor function is basically "next day," meaning "add one day to the specified date" (i.e., it's a function that, given a specified DATE value *d*, returns the DATE value that's the immediate successor of *d* according to conventional calendar ordering).

Examples: Here's an example of a DATE literal in **Tutorial D**:

```
DATE ( '2014/8/25' )
```

("August 25th, 2014"). As noted in the introduction to this part of the dictionary, symbols such as *d01*, *d02*, etc. in examples elsewhere can be thought of as shorthand for such literals. *Note:* An SQL version of the literal shown above would look like this:

```
DATE '2014-8-25'
```

datetime arithmetic (SQL)   SQL's support for dates and times is quite extensive (details can be found in, e.g., the book *A Guide to the SQL Standard*, by C. J. Date and Hugh Darwen, 4th edition, Addison-Wesley, 1997). For the purposes of this dictionary, however, it's sufficient to note that (a) the support in question includes support for datetime arithmetic expressions of the form *dx* ± *ix*, where *dx* is an expression denoting an SQL-style date and *ix* is an SQL expression denoting an SQL-style interval (in other words, a duration, q.v.), and also that (b) expressions of that form *dx* ± *ix* can effectively be used as successor and predecessor function invocations (*see* **successor; predecessor**). Here are some examples of such "SQL successor function invocations" ("SQL predecessor function invocations" are analogous, of course—see further discussion below):

```
DV + INTERVAL '1' DAY

DV + INTERVAL '30' DAY

DV + INTERVAL '1' MONTH
```

In these examples, DV is an SQL variable of type DATE and the three subexpressions INTERVAL '1' DAY, INTERVAL '30' DAY, and INTERVAL '1' MONTH are SQL literals, each of type INTERVAL. (More precisely, the first of these literals denotes "zero years, zero months, one day"; the second denotes "zero years, zero months, 30 days"; and the third denotes "zero years, one month, zero days.") Suppose the current value of DV is the date July 31st, 2014. Then the first of the foregoing expressions returns August 1st, 2014; the second returns August 30th, 2014; and the third returns August 31st, 2014.

There's a trap for the unwary here, however. Suppose in the foregoing examples that the current value of DV is the date August (not July) 31st, 2014. Then the first expression returns

September 1st, 2014; the second returns September 30th, 2014; but the third fails, because September 31st, 2014 isn't a legitimate date. In general, adding an interval to a date is performed by adding the day component first, then the months component, and then the years component; but it's important to understand that while any of these individual additions can cause a carry forward to affect the next component, they never have any effect backward on the previous one.

Subtraction is performed analogously, except that carries to the next component are replaced by borrows from that component. Thus, for example, if again the current value of DV is the date August 31st, 2014, then the expression

```
DV - INTERVAL '1' MONTH
```

returns July 31st, 2014 (but would fail if the current value of DV were, say, the date March 31st, 2014), while the expression

```
DV - INTERVAL '30' DAY
```

returns August 1st, 2014.

denseness constraint A constraint to the effect that some specified condition must be satisfied at every point within some interval (q.v.). Such constraints typically arise if the intervals in question are temporal intervals specifically.

Example: Suppose the database shows supplier S2 as being under contract throughout the interval from day 2 to day 4. Then it must also show supplier S2 as having some status throughout the interval from day 2 to day 4, and this latter is a denseness constraint.

Note: It so happens in the foregoing example that the converse holds true as well: If the database shows supplier S2 as having some status throughout the interval from day 2 to day 4, then it must also show supplier S2 as being under contract throughout the interval from day 2 to day 4 (*see* U_equality dependency). By way of an example in which no such converse holds, note that if the database shows a given supplier as being able to supply some part throughout some interval, then it must certainly show that supplier as being under contract throughout that same interval, but the converse is false—if the database shows a given supplier as being under contract throughout some interval, it doesn't necessarily have to show that supplier as being able to supply some part throughout that same interval. For example, Fig. 6 shows supplier S5 as having been under contract since day 2, but it doesn't show supplier S5 as ever having been able to supply any parts at all. For further discussion, *see* foreign U_key.

difference (interval theory) Let $i1 = [b1:e1]$ and $i2 = [b2:e2]$ be intervals of the same type. Then:

- If (a) $i1$ and $i2$ are disjoint, or (b) $i1$ contains either $b2$ or $e2$ but not both, or (c) exactly one of $i2$ BEGINS $i1$ and $i2$ ENDS $i1$ is true—in other words, if either $b1 < b2$ and $e1 \le e2$ are both true or $b1 \geq b2$ and $e1 > e2$ are both true—then (and only then) the expression $i1$ MINUS $i2$ denotes the difference between $i1$ and $i2$ (in that order), and it returns either $[b1:$MIN$\{$PRE$(i2),e1\}]$ if $b1 < b2$ and $e1 \leq e2$ are both true, or $[$MAX$\{$POST$(i2),b1\}:e1]$ if $b1 \geq b2$ and $e1 > e2$ are both true (*see* POST; PRE).

■ Otherwise $i1$ MINUS $i2$ is undefined.

Observe that the foregoing definition guarantees that the result (when it's defined) isn't just some set of points but is, rather, an interval specifically. *Note:* SQL has no direct support for the interval difference operator.

Example: Let $i1$ and $i2$ be $[d02:d07]$ and $[d04:d10]$, respectively. Then $i1$ MINUS $i2$ is $[d02:d03]$. By contrast, let $i1$ and $i2$ be $[d02:d14]$ and $[d04:d10]$, respectively; then $i1$ MINUS $i2$ is undefined.

discreteness assumption   Let T be a point type, q.v. Barring explicit statements to the contrary, then, T is generally assumed to be an ordinal type, q.v., meaning among other things that an associated successor function, q.v., is assumed to exist. That assumption (viz., that a successor function exists) is referred to, somewhat inappropriately, as "adopting the discreteness assumption." *Contrast* continuity assumption.

Note: The term *discreteness assumption* derives from the fact that values of a point type with a successor function are certainly discrete. But discreteness as such isn't the real issue; rather, the real issue is whether a successor function exists. For example, consider the rational numbers, which are certainly discrete and yet have no successor function (in other words, if r is a rational number, there's no rational number r' that can be considered the immediate successor of r). Thus, the problem with using rational numbers as a point type isn't that they're not discrete—they are—but rather that they have no successor function.

DISJOINT   One of Allen's operators, q.v. Let $i1$ and $i2$ be intervals of the same type. Then $i1$ DISJOINT $i2$ is true if and only if $i1$ OVERLAPS $i2$ is false.

Examples: Let $i1$ and $i2$ be $[d02:d03]$ and $[d08:d10]$, respectively; then $i1$ DISJOINT $i2$ is true. By contrast, if $i1$ and $i2$ are $[d02:d08]$ and $[d08:d10]$, respectively, then $i1$ DISJOINT $i2$ is false. Observe that DISJOINT is commutative—that is, $i1$ DISJOINT $i2$ and $i2$ DISJOINT $i1$ are equivalent (so $i1$ DISJOINT $i2$ is true if and only if $i2$ DISJOINT $i1$ is true).

Note: SQL has no direct support for the DISJOINT operator. However, if $p1$ and $p2$ denote SQL periods, then the SQL expression NOT ($p1$ OVERLAPS $p2$) is effectively equivalent to the hypothetical SQL expression "$p1$ DISJOINT $p2$" (or to the equally hypothetical SQL expression "$p1$ NOT OVERLAPS $p2$"). *See* period for further explanation.

disjoint U_INSERT   *See* U_INSERT.

disjoint U_UNION   *See* U_disjoint union.

duration   A length of time expressed as an integral number of time points, not anchored at any specific time point (e.g., three days; 90 minutes; two hours); equivalently, the number of points contained in some given temporal interval. See also **cardinality; COUNT; length**.

during   Term much used in connection with temporal data; if some specified condition c holds "during" some specified temporal interval i, it means condition c holds throughout (i.e., at every time point within) interval i. *Note:* The term is often used, in this dictionary in particular, in a more restrictive sense, according to which the condition in question holds throughout and not immediately before and not immediately after the interval in question—in which case the interval in question is said to be maximal. *See* **maximal interval** for further discussion.

during attribute   Term used informally to refer to an attribute of some temporal interval type.
    Examples: The DURING attributes in relvars S_DURING, S_STATUS_DURING, and SP_DURING in the suppliers-and-shipments database of either Fig. 6 or Fig. 8.

during relation   Term used informally to refer to a relation one of whose attributes is of some temporal interval type (especially a relation that's the current value of some during relvar, q.v.).
    Examples: The current values of relvars S_DURING, S_STATUS_DURING, and SP_DURING in the suppliers-and-shipments database of either Fig. 6 or Fig. 8.

during relvar   Term used informally to refer to a relvar that (a) isn't a since relvar, q.v., and (b) has a predicate that can reasonably be formulated in such a way as to include one or more qualifications of the form "during interval i" (and thus has one or more attributes of some temporal interval type); very loosely, a relvar that contains historical information.
    Examples: Relvars S_DURING, S_STATUS_DURING, and SP_DURING in the suppliers-and-shipments database of either Fig. 6 or Fig. 8.

————— ♦♦♦♦♦ —————

END   *See* end point.

end of time   *See* timeline.

end point   The end point of the interval $i = [b:e]$, denoted END (i), is the point e. *Note:* SQL has no support for the END operator as such. Rather, if p denotes the SQL period PERIOD (f,t)—and if we assume for definiteness that f and t are of type DATE and the scale, q.v., is one day—then the SQL expression t – INTERVAL '1' DAY is effectively equivalent to the hypothetical SQL expression "END (p)." For further explanation and discussion, *see* **datetime arithmetic (SQL); period**.

ENDS   One of Allen's operators, q.v. Let *i1* = [*b1*:*e1*] and *i2* = [*b2*:*e2*] be intervals of the same type. Then *i1* ENDS *i2* is true if and only if *b1* ≥ *b2* and *e1* = *e2* are both true.

   Examples: Let *i1* and *i2* be [*d08*:*d10*] and [*d04*:*d10*], respectively; then *i1* ENDS *i2* is true. By contrast, if *i1* and *i2* are [*d08*:*d11*] and [*d06*:*d10*], respectively, then *i1* ENDS *i2* is false.

   Note: SQL has no direct support for the ENDS operator. However, if *p1* and *p2* denote the SQL periods PERIOD (*f1*,*t1*) and PERIOD (*f2*,*t2*), respectively, then the SQL expression *f1* ≥ *f2* AND *t1* = *t2* is effectively equivalent to the hypothetical SQL expression "*p1* ENDS *p2*." *See* period for further explanation.

equality   (*Of intervals*) *See* interval equality.

EXPAND   *See* expanded form. *Note:* SQL has no direct support for the EXPAND operator.

expanded form   1. (*Sets of intervals*) Let *x* be a set of intervals all of the same type *T*. Then the expression EXPAND (*x*) denotes the expanded form of *x*, and it returns the unique set *y* of unit intervals [*p*:*p*] (necessarily also all of that same type *T*) such that *p* is a point in some interval in *x*—*see* unit interval. Observe that no two distinct intervals *i1* and *i2* in *y* are such that *i1* INTERSECT *i2* is defined—*see* intersection (interval theory). Observe further that if the cardinality of *x* is zero, then EXPAND (*x*) is equal to *x*; if the cardinality of *x* is one, then EXPAND (*x*) is equal to *x* if and only if the sole interval in *x* is a unit interval specifically. 2. (*Unary relations*) Let *x* be a unary relation whose sole attribute is of some interval type. Then the expression EXPAND (*x*) denotes the expanded form of *x*, and it returns the unique relation *y* of the same type as *x* such that tuple *t*, containing interval *i*, appears in *y* if and only if *i* is a unit interval [*p*:*p*] and *p* appears in some interval in some tuple in *x*. 3. (*Nullary relations*) Let *x* be a nullary relation (i.e., let *x* be either TABLE_DUM or TABLE_DEE). Then the expression EXPAND (*x*) denotes the expanded form of *x*, and it returns the relation *x* itself (i.e., each of TABLE_DUM and TABLE_DEE is its own expanded form). *Contrast* collapsed form.

   Example (second definition only): Let relation *x* look like this:

DURING
[*d06*:*d09*]
[*d04*:*d08*]
[*d05*:*d10*]
[*d01*:*d01*]

Then *y* = EXPAND (*x*) looks like this:

```
┌─────────────────────┐
│ DURING              │
╞═════════════════════╡
│ [d01:d01]           │
│ [d04:d04]           │
│ [d05:d05]           │
│ [d06:d06]           │
│ [d07:d07]           │
│ [d08:d08]           │
│ [d09:d09]           │
│ [d10:d10]           │
└─────────────────────┘
```

Note: The relational version of EXPAND is actually a special case of UNPACK (*see* unpacked form). To be specific, (a) if relation *x* has just one attribute, say *A*, and that attribute is interval valued, then EXPAND (*x*) and UNPACK *x* ON (*A*) are equivalent; moreover, (b) if relation *x* has no attributes at all, then EXPAND (*x*) and UNPACK *x* ON ( )—the unpacking here necessarily being on no attributes at all—are also equivalent.

Here for the record is a more formal version of the first (only) of the foregoing definitions. Again let *x* be a set of intervals all of the same type *T*, and let *i* and *j* be intervals of that same type *T*. Then *y* = EXPAND (*x*) can be defined thus:

$$y \stackrel{\text{def}}{=} \{ \ i \ : \ b = e \ \text{AND EXISTS} \ j \in x \ (\ b \in j \ ) \ \}$$

——— ♦♦♦♦♦ ———

FIRST_*T* *See* beginning of time; FIRST (in Part I of this dictionary); ordinality; point type. *Note:* SQL has no support for the FIRST_*T* operator as such, but an appropriate literal can be used in its place. In the case of point type DATE, for example, SQL's analog of the expression FIRST_DATE ( ) is the following literal:

```
DATE '0001-01-01'
```

Note, however, that SQL requires the user to know the actual value involved, which the expression FIRST_*T* ( ) doesn't.

folding Term sometimes used as a synonym for packing, q.v. (or for an operation of the same general nature as packing).

FOR PORTION OF (SQL) *See* PORTION.

FOR SYSTEM TIME (SQL) *See* system time.

foreign key   (*Expanded definition*) A foreign key in the relational sense means exactly what it always did mean (see Part I of this dictionary); however, such a foreign key can, and now should, be regarded as a degenerate special case of a foreign U_key, q.v.

foreign key (SQL)   Consider the following CREATE table statements (repeated from the examples under **period** but simplified slightly here) for the SQL tables S_FROM_TO and SP_FROM_TO from Fig. 9:

```
CREATE TABLE S_FROM_TO
     ( SNO   SNO  NOT NULL ,
       DFROM DATE NOT NULL ,
       DTO   DATE NOT NULL ,
       PERIOD FOR DPERIOD ( DFROM , DTO ) ,
       UNIQUE ( SNO , DPERIOD WITHOUT OVERLAPS ) ;

CREATE TABLE SP_FROM_TO
     ( SNO   SNO  NOT NULL ,
       PNO   PNO  NOT NULL ,
       DFROM DATE NOT NULL ,
       DTO   DATE NOT NULL ,
       PERIOD FOR DPERIOD ( DFROM , DTO ) ,
       UNIQUE ( SNO , PNO , DPERIOD WITHOUT OVERLAPS ) ,
       FOREIGN KEY ( SNO , PERIOD DPERIOD )
             REFERENCES S_FROM_TO ( SNO , PERIOD DPERIOD ) ) ;
```

Observe in particular that, first, the combination (SNO,DPERIOD) is defined to be a "key" for table S_FROM_TO, thanks to the specification UNIQUE (SNO, DPERIOD WITHOUT OVERLAPS); second, that same combination (SNO,DPERIOD) is defined to be a "foreign key" in table SP_FROM_TO, thanks to the specification FOREIGN KEY (SNO, PERIOD DPERIOD), matching that "key" in table S_FROM_TO. *Note:* For present purposes, let's agree to ignore both the WITHOUT OVERLAPS specification, q.v., in the "key" definition and the keyword—effectively just a noiseword—PERIOD in the "foreign key" definition. However, note that (as the discussion below makes clear) (a) the "key" in question isn't a true relational key and (b) the "foreign key" in question isn't a true relational foreign key either, which is why the terms are set in quotation marks here.

Now, it's actually quite difficult to explain the semantics of the foregoing specifications properly in purely SQL terms, because SQL has nothing analogous to the crucial UNPACK operator. However, if we overlook that omission, we can say, loosely, that what the specifications mean is this: If we unpack each of the tables on DPERIOD, then (SNO,DPERIOD) will be a key for the unpacked form of S_FROM_TO and (SNO,DPERIOD) will be a matching foreign key in the unpacked form of SP_FROM_TO. But then, noting that the symbol *DPERIOD* is little more than a shorthand name for columns DFROM and DTO taken in combination, we see that the "key" in question isn't a true relational key, because it's reducible (either DFROM or DTO could be dropped, and what remained would still have the necessary uniqueness property). In fact, that "key" is really a proper superkey. And for essentially similar reasons, the matching "foreign key" isn't a true relational foreign key, either.

(Actually, even before the introduction of temporal support into SQL in the 2011 version of the standard, it was the case that SQL explicitly allowed "keys" and corresponding "foreign keys" to be defined that were clearly reducible. So SQL's departures from relational theory in this area aren't really new; in particular, they aren't limited to the temporal context as such.)

foreign U_key Let *ACL* be a commalist of attribute names such that every attribute mentioned (a) is interval valued and (b) is common to relvars *R1* and *R2* (*R1* and *R2* not necessarily distinct), and let those relvars be kept packed on *ACL*. Let *R1'* be a relvar whose value at any given time is equal to the value of UNPACK *R1* ON (*ACL*) at the time in question; likewise, let *R2'* be a relvar whose value at any given time is equal to the value of UNPACK *R2* ON (*ACL*) at the time in question. Let *K* be a key in *R1'* and let *FK* be a matching foreign key in *R2'*. Then (and only then) *K* is a U_key (q.v.) in *R1*, and *FK* is a matching foreign U_key in *R2* (where the U_key and foreign U_key in question must both be understood as being with respect to *ACL*). *Note:* If *ACL* is empty, the U_key *K* in *R1* reduces to a regular key and the foreign U_key *FK* in *R2* reduces to a regular foreign key.

Examples: With reference to Fig. 8 (but *not* Fig. 6), {SNO,DURING} in relvar SP_DURING is a foreign U_key matching the U_key {SNO,DURING} in relvar S_DURING (where the foreign U_key and matching U_key must both be understood as being with respect to DURING). Thus, the definitions of those two relvars might look like this:

```
VAR S_DURING BASE RELATION
   { SNO      SNO ,
     DURING INTERVAL_DATE }
   USING ( DURING ) : KEY { SNO , DURING } ;

VAR SP_DURING BASE RELATION
   { SNO      SNO ,
     PNO      PNO ,
     DURING INTERVAL_DATE }
   USING ( DURING ) : KEY { SNO , PNO , DURING }
   USING ( DURING ) : FOREIGN KEY { SNO , DURING } REFERENCES S_DURING ;
```

Note the last line here in particular: It's what defines {SNO,DURING} to be a foreign U_key in relvar SP_DURING, matching the U_key involving those same attributes (SNO and DURING) in relvar S_DURING.

By way of another example, again with reference to Fig. 8 but not Fig. 6 (and again with respect to DURING throughout), {SNO,DURING} in relvar S_STATUS_DURING is a foreign U_key matching the U_key {SNO,DURING} in relvar S_DURING. In this case, however, the converse is true as well—{SNO,DURING} in relvar S_DURING is a foreign U_key matching the U_key {SNO,DURING} in relvar S_STATUS_DURING. In other words, S_DURING and S_STATUS_DURING are together subject to the following U_EQD (q.v.):

```
CONSTRAINT U_EQDX USING ( DURING ) :
                  S_DURING = S_STATUS_DURING { SNO , DURING } ;
```

(This point was previously mentioned in a footnote in the section "A Note on Redundancy" in the introduction to this part of the dictionary.)

   Note: There's no requirement that relvars *R1* and *R2* in the foregoing definition be base relvars specifically; for example, there might be a foreign U_key constraint from a base relvar to a view, or from a view to a base relvar, or from one view to another. In fact (speaking a little loosely), **Tutorial D** allows foreign U_key constraints to be specified between arbitrary relational expressions (*see* foreign U_key constraint).

foreign U_key constraint   A generalized form of foreign key constraint (see Part I of this dictionary) in which the roles of the pertinent key and matching foreign key are played by a U_key (q.v.) and matching foreign U_key (q.v.), respectively. Note that (as noted under foreign U_key) **Tutorial D** allows foreign U_key constraints to be specified not just for relvars as such, base or otherwise, but in fact for arbitrary relational expressions.

FROM value (SQL)   *See* period.

fully packed   Let relation *r* have interval attributes *A1*, *A2*, ..., *An* (and no others). Then the somewhat informal term *fully packed form of r* refers to any relation obtained by packing *r* on attributes *A1*, *A2*, ..., *An* in some order. (Note that different orders will give rise to different fully packed versions, in general. *Contrast* fully unpacked.) An analogous definition applies to relvars also, mutatis mutandis.

fully temporal   Term used informally to characterize a during relvar, q.v., in contrast to a since relvar, q.v. *Contrast* semitemporal.

fully unpacked   Let relation *r* have interval attributes *A1*, *A2*, ..., *An* (and no others). Then the somewhat informal term *fully unpacked form of r* refers to the relation obtained by unpacking *r* on attributes *A1*, *A2*, ..., *An* in some order. (Note that different orders will always give rise to the same fully packed version. *Contrast* fully packed.) An analogous definition applies to relvars also, mutatis mutandis.

———— ♦ ♦ ♦ ♦ ♦ ————

granularity   Informal term sometimes used to refer to the "size," or scale (q.v.), of a value of some given point type, or equivalently to the "size" of the gap between one such value and its successor according to the pertinent ordering. *See* scale for further discussion.

   Example: For the time points involved in the stated times (q.v.) in the various versions of the suppliers-and-shipments database (see Figs. 6-9), the granularity is one day. In other words, we're ignoring in this context the fact that a day is made up of hours, which are made up of minutes, etc. Such notions can be expressed only by recourse to finer levels of granularity, or in other words finer scales.

granule Informal term sometimes used as a synonym for point, q.v. *See* scale for further discussion; *contrast* chronon.

———— ♦ ♦ ♦ ♦ ♦ ————

historical relation Informal term sometimes used to refer to the value of a historical relvar, q.v.

historical relvar Informal term sometimes used to refer to a during relvar, q.v. However, the term is deprecated, somewhat, because such relvars aren't limited to containing information that pertains only to some historical state of affairs—depending on circumstances, they might contain information that pertains to past and/or current and/or even future states of affairs.

Example: Consider the relation shown as a sample value for relvar S_DURING in Fig. 8. If we make the reasonable assumption that at least some of the BEGIN (DURING) values in that relation denote dates in the past, then that relation clearly contains information concerning the current state of affairs; for example, the sole tuple for supplier S1, with DURING value [*d04*:*d99*], presumably shows that supplier as currently being under contract, since that *d99* really means *until further notice*, q.v. (see the discussion under COMBINED_IN). Indeed, and for the same reason, that tuple also contains information about the future, at least implicitly. What's more, if we know that (say) supplier S8 will be placed under contract on day *dc*, where *dc* is in the future, and we insert a tuple into S_DURING to say as much, then that relvar will now contain explicit information about the future as well.

historical row (SQL) *See* system time.

horizontal decomposition (*Of temporal relvars*) Informal term used to refer to the decomposition of a temporal relvar into a combination of since relvars, q.v., and during relvars, q.v.

Example: The relvars of Fig. 6 can be regarded as the result of applying horizontal decomposition to the relvars of Fig. 8. Note that Fig. 8 contains during relvars only, but those during relvars aren't purely historical, because they contain information that pertains to the current state of affairs (as well as to the future, at least implicitly if not explicitly). By contrast, Fig. 6 contains a mixture of since and during relvars, and those during relvars, by contrast, contain historical information only—information that pertains to the current state of affairs has been moved into the since relvars. (Note, however, that those since relvars also contain implicit information regarding both the past and the future, and they might even contain explicit information regarding the future as well. *See* current relvar.)

———— ♦ ♦ ♦ ♦ ♦ ————

included U_DELETE *See* U_DELETE.

included U_difference   *See* U_included difference.

included U_MINUS   *See* U_included difference.

inclusion   (*Of intervals*) *See* interval inclusion.

inheritance (interval types)   Let *IT* be the interval type INTERVAL_*T*, with underlying point type *T* (*see* interval type). In general, then, *IT* has no proper subtypes; that is, the concept of inheritance doesn't really apply to interval types. For suppose, contrariwise, that interval type *IT* has a proper subtype *IT'* (where *IT'* is INTERVAL_*T'* for some point type *T'*, $T' \neq T$). Let $i' = [b':e']$ be an interval of type *IT'* such that $b' \neq e'$. Since *IT'* is a subtype of *IT*, i' must be an interval of type *IT* as well. But i' can't possibly be an interval of type *IT*—not even if *T'* is a proper subtype of *T*, in which case b' and e' are certainly both values of type *T*—because the points in i' are determined by the successor function for *T'*, which (since *T* and *T'* are distinct) is distinct from the successor function for *T*, by definition. Thus, *IT'* can't be a proper subtype of *IT* after all.

Example: Let *T* and *T'* be INTEGER and EVEN_INTEGER, respectively, with the obvious semantics (so the interval types *IT* and *IT'* are INTERVAL_INTEGER and INTERVAL_EVEN_INTEGER, respectively). Note in particular that *T'* here is definitely a proper subtype of *T*. Now consider the intervals $i = [2:6]$ and $i' = [2:6]$, of types *IT* and *IT'*, respectively. Then i and i' aren't the same interval, even though they have the same begin and end points, because i contains the points 2, 3, 4, 5, 6 while i' contains only the points 2, 4, 6. Thus, i' isn't a value of type *IT*, and so *IT'* isn't a proper subtype of *IT*.

Given the above, it follows that we can refer unambiguously to *the* type of any given interval (where the type in question is basically just the corresponding declared type). *See* interval type.

Note: The foregoing remarks are broadly true, but there are a couple of minor exceptions —pathological cases, really—that ought at least to be mentioned. First, if *T'* is empty, then *IT'* is a subtype of all possible interval types (in fact, it's a *proper* subtype of all such types except for itself); however, *IT'*, like *T'*, is empty in this case. Second, if *T'* is a singleton type whose sole value is a value of type *T*, then *IT'* is a proper subtype of *IT* after all, but it contains just one interval (necessarily a unit interval).

inheritance (point types)   Elsewhere in this dictionary, the definition of what it means for a type to be usable as a point type (q.v.) includes the requirement that the type in question must have a unique successor function. However, consider the point type DATE; surely there are several different successor functions that might make sense for that type—for example, "next week," "next business day," "next month," and so on? Type inheritance provides a solution to this apparent dilemma. For example, we might define proper subtypes of type DATE called WDATE, BDATE, and MDATE, representing dates measured in weeks, business days, and months, respectively. Each of these types will have its own associated set of operators, including its own successor function in particular. Further details are beyond the scope of this dictionary, except to note that remarks analogous to the foregoing apply to types TIME and TIMESTAMP as well, obviously enough.

Note: To the extent that SQL addresses the foregoing requirement—i.e., the need to support several distinct successor functions for the same point type—it does so not by means of inheritance but by means of its regular datetime arithmetic facilities, q.v. For example, if DV is an SQL variable of type DATE, then

```
DV + INTERVAL '1' DAY
```

returns the next day, and

```
DV + INTERVAL '1' MONTH
```

returns the next month. (By contrast, more specialized requirements such as "next week" and "next business day" aren't directly supported at all.) *See* **datetime arithmetic (SQL)** for further discussion.

intersection (interval theory)   Let $i1 = [b1:e1]$ and $i2 = [b2:e2]$ be intervals of the same type. Then:

- If $i1$ OVERLAPS $i2$ is true, then (and only then) the expression $i1$ INTERSECT $i2$ denotes the intersection of $i1$ and $i2$, and it returns $[MAX\{b1,b2\}:MIN\{e1,e2\}]$.

- Otherwise $i1$ INTERSECT $i2$ is undefined.

Observe that the foregoing definition guarantees that the result (when it's defined) isn't just some set of points but is, rather, an interval specifically. *Note:* SQL has no direct support for the interval intersection operator.

Example: Let $i1$ and $i2$ be $[d02:d07]$ and $[d04:d10]$, respectively. Then $i1$ INTERSECT $i2$ is $[d04:d07]$. By contrast, let $i1$ and $i2$ be $[d02:d04]$ and $[d07:d10]$, respectively; then $i1$ INTERSECT $i2$ is undefined. Incidentally, note that interval intersection, like set theory intersection—like the intersection operator of the relational algebra also, come to that—does have a corresponding identity value: viz., the universal interval of the applicable type, q.v. Note further that the operator is both commutative and associative.

interval   An interval value, q.v. Be aware, however, that SQL uses the term *interval* to mean a duration, q.v. The SQL term for an interval as such—or, rather, for SQL's analog of an interval as such—is *period*, q.v.

interval (SQL)   A duration, q.v.

interval attribute   An attribute of some interval type; an interval valued attribute.

interval comparison   *See* Allen's operators.

interval difference   *See* difference (interval theory).

interval equality   One of Allen's operators, q.v. Let $i1 = [b1:e1]$ and $i2 = [b2:e2]$ be intervals of the same type. Then $i1$ is equal to $i2$ ("$i1 = i2$") if and only if $b1 = b2$ and $e1 = e2$ are both true. In other words, intervals $i1$ and $i2$ (necessarily of the same type) are equal if and only if they're the very same interval, meaning they have the same begin point and the same end point, and hence the same contained points as well.

    Note: SQL uses the keyword EQUALS in place of the symbol "=". Let $p1$ and $p2$ be the SQL periods PERIOD $(f1,t1)$ and PERIOD $(f2,t2)$, respectively; then the SQL expression $p1$ EQUALS $p2$ is true if and only if $f1 = f2$ and $t1 = t2$ are both true. Oddly enough, however, while the hypothetical SQL expression "PERIOD $(f1,t1)$ = PERIOD $(f2,t2)$"—note the explicit "=" symbol—is illegal, the simpler and more succinct expression $(f1,t1) = (f2,t2)$ is not only legal but means exactly the same as PERIOD $(f1,t1)$ EQUALS PERIOD $(f2,t2)$. *See* period for further explanation.

interval expression   An expression denoting an interval. Interval selector invocations (and hence interval literals) are an important special case.

interval inclusion   One of Allen's operators, q.v. Let $i1 = [b1:e1]$ and $i2 = [b2:e2]$ be intervals of the same type. Then $i1$ includes $i2$ ("$i1 \supseteq i2$") if and only if $b1 \le b2$ and $e1 \ge e2$ are both true. Also, $i2$ is included in $i1$ ("$i2 \subseteq i1$") if and only if $i1 \supseteq i2$ is true. *See also* proper interval inclusion.

    Examples: Let $i1$ and $i2$ be $[d02:d10]$ and $[d04:d08]$, respectively; then $i1 \supseteq i2$ is true. By contrast, if $i1$ and $i2$ are $[d02:d04]$ and $[d04:d08]$, respectively, then $i1 \supseteq i2$ is false. Note that interval $i1$ is equal to interval $i2$ ("$i1 = i2$") if and only if each includes the other. Note too that every interval is included in itself. Note finally that the term *interval inclusion* is usually taken, a trifle arbitrarily, to refer to the operator "$\subseteq$" specifically, not the operator "$\supseteq$".

    Note: SQL supports "$\supseteq$" (for which it uses the keyword CONTAINS, which is thereby overloaded—*see* containment) but not "$\subseteq$". However, if $p1$ and $p2$ denote the SQL periods PERIOD $(f1,t1)$ and PERIOD $(f2,t2)$, respectively, then the SQL expression $f1 \ge f2$ AND $t1 \le t2$ is effectively equivalent to the hypothetical SQL expression "$p1 \subseteq p2$." *See* period for further explanation.

interval intersection   *See* intersection (interval theory).

interval literal   A literal that denotes an interval.

Examples: See the examples under interval selector.

interval selector Let INTERVAL_*T* be an interval type; then the (unique) corresponding selector is an operator that allows an interval of that type to be selected or specified by supplying, either directly or indirectly (see further discussion below), the begin and end points of the interval in question. More precisely, let INTERVAL_*T* be an interval type, with underlying point type *T*. Corresponding to that interval type, then, there's exactly one corresponding selector (having the same name as the type, in **Tutorial D**), such that (a) the sole argument to any given invocation of that selector is a pair of values of type *T*, separated by a colon and enclosed in brackets or parentheses or a mixture (again, see further discussion below); (b) every interval of that interval type is producible by means of some invocation of that selector in which those values of type *T* are represented by literals; and (c) every successful invocation of that selector produces an interval of that interval type.

As the foregoing paragraph suggests (and as explained further under interval value), there are actually four different ways, or styles, available for representing an interval in concrete syntax (at least in general, but note the exceptions indicated below):

- The *closed:closed* style, or syntax, uses brackets "[" and "]", and it represents the given interval directly in terms of its begin and end points *b* and *e*. In other words, the syntax "[*b*:*e*]" denotes the interval stretching from the begin point *b* to the end point *e* ($b \leq e$), inclusive. For example, consider the interval type INTERVAL_DATE, where the underlying point type is DATE (i.e., calendar dates accurate to the day). Then the expression

```
INTERVAL_DATE ( [ d04 : d10 ] )
```

constitutes an invocation of the INTERVAL_DATE selector, and it denotes the interval of type INTERVAL_DATE whose contained points are precisely the dates *d04*, *d05*, *d06*, *d07*, *d08*, *d09*, and *d10*. *Note:* Expressions such as [*d04:d10*], much used elsewhere in this dictionary, can be thought of as informal shorthand for an interval selector invocation of the foregoing form. Note also that, other things being equal, this dictionary does tend to favor the closed:closed style.

- The *closed:open* style or syntax uses an opening bracket "[" and a closing parenthesis ")", and it represents the given interval in terms of its begin point *b* together with the immediate successor *es* of its end point *e*. In other words, the syntax "[*b*:*es*)" denotes the interval stretching from the begin point *b* to the end point *e* ($b \leq e$), inclusive, where *e* is the immediate predecessor of *es*. For example, the interval selector invocation

```
INTERVAL_DATE ( [ d04 : d11 ) )
```

denotes the same interval as in the closed:closed example above. *Note:* Expressions such as [*d04:d11*) can be thought of as informal shorthand for an interval selector invocation of the foregoing form. Note too, however, that an interval for which *e* is "the end of time" can't be expressed using closed:open style.

■ The *open:closed* style or syntax uses an opening parenthesis "(" and a closing bracket "]", and it represents the given interval in terms of the immediate predecessor *pb* of its begin point *b*, together with its end point *e*. In other words, the syntax "(*pb:e*]" denotes the interval stretching from the begin point *b* to the end point *e* ($b \leq e$), inclusive, where *b* is the immediate successor of *pb*. For example, the interval selector invocation

```
INTERVAL_DATE ( ( d03 : d10 ] )
```

again denotes the same interval as in the previous examples. *Note:* Expressions such as (*d03:d10*] can be thought of as informal shorthand for an interval selector invocation of the foregoing form. Note too, however, that an interval for which *b* is "the beginning of time" can't be expressed using open:closed style.

■ Finally, the *open:open* style or syntax uses parentheses "(" and ")", and it represents the given interval in terms of the immediate predecessor *pb* of its begin point *b* together with the immediate successor *es* of its end point *e*. In other words, the syntax "(*pb:es*)" denotes the interval stretching from the begin point *b* to the end point *e* ($b \leq e$), inclusive, where *b* is the immediate successor of *pb* and *s* is the immediate predecessor of *es*. For example, the interval selector invocation

```
INTERVAL_DATE ( ( d03 : d11 ) )
```

again denotes the same interval as in the previous examples. *Note:* Expressions such as (*d03:d11*) can be thought of as informal shorthand for an interval selector invocation of the foregoing form. Note too, however, that an interval for which *b* is "the beginning of time" or *e* is "the end of time" can't be expressed using open:open style.

Of course, all of the foregoing examples illustrate, not incidentally, the syntax used for interval selectors in **Tutorial D** specifically. Other syntactic styles might be possible, but they must be logically equivalent to the **Tutorial D** style. Note in particular that other separators— e.g., commas, hyphens—are typically used in the literature; **Tutorial D** uses colons because commas can make intervals look like subscripts and hyphens can look like minus signs.

Note: Assuming *d03*, *d04*, etc., are all DATE literals, all of the selector invocations shown above are in fact themselves literals in turn (interval literals, that is). Here by contrast is an interval selector invocation that's not a literal:

```
INTERVAL_DATE ( [ FIRST_DATE ( ) : LAST_DATE ( ) ] )
```

This expression returns the interval of type INTERVAL_DATE whose begin and end points are the beginning of time and the end of time, respectively (accurate to the day in each case). *See* FIRST_*T*; LAST_*T*; timeline; *see also* universal interval.

interval type   Let *T* be a point type, q.v.; then (and only then) INTERVAL_*T* denotes an interval type—in fact, the sole interval type—whose values are, precisely, all possible intervals of the form [*b*:*e*], where *b* and *e* are values of type *T* and $b \leq e$. *Note:* **Tutorial D** provides nothing analogous to a TYPE statement, q.v., for defining interval types. Instead, such types can be defined only by invoking the interval type generator, q.v. It follows that, in **Tutorial D** at any rate, interval types always have names of the form INTERVAL_*T*. It also follows that there's no way to define, e.g., an interval type consisting solely of all possible unit intervals of the form [*p*:*p*] for all possible values *p* of type INTEGER.
  Examples: 1. Type INTERVAL_INTEGER is an interval type whose underlying point type is INTEGER; thus, values of this interval type are intervals of the form [*b*:*e*], where *b* and *e* are values of type INTEGER (for which the successor function is just "add one") such that $b \leq e$. 2. Type INTERVAL_MONEY is an interval type whose underlying point type is MONEY, which is (let's assume) a type that represents monetary amounts measured in dollars and cents; thus, values of this interval type are intervals of the form [*b*:*e*], where *b* and *e* are values of type MONEY (for which the successor function is "add one cent") such that $b \leq e$. 3. Type INTERVAL_DATE is an interval type—used several times in the suppliers-and-shipments databases of Figs. 6-8—whose underlying point type is DATE; thus, values of this interval type are intervals of the form [*b*:*e*], where *b* and *e* are values of type DATE (for which the successor function is "add one day") such that $b \leq e$.

interval type generator   The operator used to generate specific interval types (q.v.), denoted INTERVAL in **Tutorial D**. If *T* is a point type (q.v.), then the corresponding interval type—i.e., the corresponding invocation of the INTERVAL type generator—is denoted INTERVAL_*T* in **Tutorial D**.
  Examples: See the examples under interval type.

interval type inheritance   *See* inheritance (interval types).

interval union   *See* union (interval theory).

interval value   Let *T* be a point type, q.v. Then an interval value *i* (or just interval *i* for short) of type INTERVAL_*T* is a value for which two monadic operators, BEGIN and END, and one dyadic operator, "∈", are defined, such that (a) BEGIN (*i*) and END (*i*) both return a value of type *T* (viz., the begin point and the end point, respectively, of interval *i*); (b) BEGIN (*i*) ≤ END (*i*); and (c) if *p* is a value of type *T*, then $p \in i$ is true if and only if BEGIN (*i*) $\leq p$ and

$p \leq$ END (i) are both true. Observe that intervals are never empty (i.e., every interval contains at least one point).

Let interval i have begin point b and end point e, respectively. Then, thanks to the availability of the successor function, q.v., we can say that interval i consists of a sequence—not just a set—of contiguous points: viz., the sequence b, $b+1$, $b+2$, ..., e. (Here we're using—very informally!—the notation $b+1$ to denote the successor of b, $b+2$ to denote the successor of $b+1$, and so on.)

Now consider the informal phrase "the interval from day 4 to day 10." What interval exactly is intended by such a phrase? It's clear that the interval in question contains days 5, 6, 7, 8, and 9—but what about days 4 and 10 themselves? It turns out that if some interval i is described as stretching "from x to y," sometimes we want to consider the points x and y as part of that interval i and sometimes we don't. If we do want to consider x as part of i, we say i is closed at its beginning, otherwise we say it's open at its beginning. Likewise, if we want to consider y as part of i, we say i is closed at its end, otherwise we say it's open at its end.

Conventionally, therefore (albeit informally), we denote an interval by a pair of points x and y separated by a colon, preceded by an opening bracket or parenthesis and followed by a closing bracket or parenthesis. We use a bracket where we want the closed interpretation, a parenthesis where we want the open one. Thus, there are four distinct ways to denote, e.g., the specific interval that runs from the begin point *d04* to the end point *d10*, inclusive:

```
[d04:d10]
[d04:d11)
(d03:d10]
(d03:d11)
```

See **interval selector** for further discussion.

Examples: Intervals don't necessarily have to be temporal in nature. Here are some examples of ones that aren't:

- Tax brackets are represented by taxable income ranges—i.e., intervals whose contained points are money values.

- Machines are built to operate within certain temperature and voltage ranges—i.e., intervals whose contained points are temperatures and voltages, respectively.

- Animals vary in the range of frequencies of light and sound waves to which their eyes and ears are receptive.

- Various natural phenomena occur and can be measured in ranges in depth of soil or sea or height above sea level.

And so on.

interval valued attribute   An attribute whose type is some interval type.

key   (*Expanded definition*) A key in the relational sense means exactly what it always did mean (see Part I of this dictionary); however, such a key can, and now should, be regarded as a degenerate special case of a U_key, q.v.

key (SQL)   *See* foreign key (SQL).

LAST_*T*   *See* end of time; LAST (in Part I of this dictionary); ordinality; point type. *Note:* SQL has no support for the LAST_*T* operator as such, but an appropriate literal can be used in its place. In the case of point type DATE, for example, SQL's analog of the expression LAST_DATE ( ) is the following literal:

```
DATE '9999-12-31'
```

Note, however, that SQL requires the user to know the actual value involved, which the expression LAST_*T* ( ) doesn't.

length   (*Of an interval*) The number of points in the interval in question. *See also* cardinality; COUNT; duration.

logged time   (*Of a proposition*) The time or times, represented as a set of temporal intervals (preferably in packed form), when the database said the proposition in question was true. *Note:* Other terms that might be used for this concept include *system time*, q.v. (this is the SQL term); *system stated time*; *system asserted time*; and *transaction time*, q.v. (this is the term most often encountered in the literature). Note that, by definition, logged times (a) always refer strictly to the past and (b) can't be updated. (The reason they can't be updated is that they represent history as such, not just somebody's beliefs about history; the latter can and typically do change from time to time, but history as such is immutable.)

    Example: Let today be day 75. Then the logged time relvar (q.v.) S_DURING_LOG corresponding to relvar S_DURING (with sample value as shown in Fig. 6) might currently look like this:

SNO	DURING	X_DURING
S2	[d02:d04]	[d04:d07]
S2	[d02:d04]	[d10:d20]
S2	[d02:d04]	[d50:d75]
S6	[d02:d05]	[d15:d25]
S6	[d03:d05]	[d26:d75]
S1	[d01:d01]	[d20:d30]
S1	[d05:d06]	[d40:d50]

In other words:

- For the proposition *The interval [d03:d05] is a maximal interval of days throughout which supplier S6 was under contract*, the logged time is {[d26:d75]}.

- For the proposition *The interval [d02:d04] is a maximal interval of days throughout which supplier S2 was under contract*, the logged time is {[d04:d07], [d10:d20], [d50:d75]}.

- For the proposition *Supplier S1 was under contract throughout some interval*, the logged time is {[d20:d30], [d40:d50]}. Note that the proposition in question in this example was never represented as such in the database, but is, rather, a proposition derived from those that were.

- For the proposition *Supplier S6 was under contract throughout some interval*, the logged time is {[d15:d75]}. Note the packing involved in this example; note too that (as with the previous example) the proposition in question was never represented as such in the database but is, rather, a proposition derived from those that were.

And so on. *Note:* The foregoing example shows X_DURING intervals as measured in days, for reasons of simplicity. In practice, of course, they would surely be based on some much smaller unit—microseconds, perhaps, or something even smaller. In fact, they're probably based on readings from the system clock, q.v. (at least conceptually).

logged time relvar Let *rx* be a relational expression (typically but not necessarily a simple relvar reference *R*). Then the logged time relvar for *rx* is a relvar—automatically maintained by the DBMS as, in effect, an appropriately fully packed view of appropriate portions of the log— that shows, for every tuple *t* that has ever appeared in the fully unpacked form of the result of evaluating *rx*, the time or times when that tuple *t* did in fact appear in that fully unpacked form.

———— ♦ ♦ ♦ ♦ ♦ ————

maximal interval   Let *P* be a predicate whose sole parameter is of some interval type. Then interval *i* is maximal with respect to *P* if and only if *i* satisfies *P* and no *j* such that $j \supset i$ satisfies *P*. *Note:* The qualifier "with respect to *P*" can be omitted if *P* is understood.

    Example (repeated from the introduction to this part of the dictionary, but elaborated here): Consider the predicate for relvar S_DURING (first version, as illustrated in Fig. 6):

> *DURING denotes a maximal interval of days throughout which supplier SNO was under contract.*

This predicate is dyadic (it involves two parameters, DURING and SNO). However, we can derive a set of monadic predicates from it, one for each SNO value appearing in some currently true instantiation of the dyadic predicate—which is to say, one for S2 and one for S6, given the sample value for relvar S_DURING shown in Fig. 6:

- *DURING denotes a maximal interval of days throughout which supplier S2 was under contract. Note:* This predicate applies to the result of the restriction expression S_DURING WHERE SNO = SNO('S2').

- *DURING denotes a maximal interval of days throughout which supplier S6 was under contract. Note:* This predicate applies to the result of the restriction expression S_DURING WHERE SNO = SNO('S6').

    Each of these monadic predicates is a partial instantiation (see Part I of this dictionary) of the original dyadic predicate. For definiteness, let's concentrate on the first one. Essentially, what that first one means is that if there's a tuple in the relvar showing supplier S2 was under contract throughout the interval [*d02:d04*]—which indeed there is, in Fig. 6—then there isn't a tuple in that relvar showing that supplier S2 was under contract on either day 1 or day 5. In other words, there's no interval *j* that contains either day 1 or day 5 such that "Supplier S2 was under contract throughout interval *j*" is true, and the interval [*d02:d04*] is thus maximal with respect to the predicate *DURING denotes an interval of days throughout which supplier S2 was under contract.*

MEETS   One of Allen's operators, q.v. Let *i1* = [*b1:e1*] and *i2* = [*b2:e2*] be intervals of the same type. Then *i1* MEETS *i2* is true if and only if *b2* = POST (*i1*) is true or *b1* = POST (*i2*) is true (*see* POST); equivalently, *i1* MEETS *i2* is true if and only if *e1* = PRE (*i2*) is true or *e2* = PRE (*i1*) is true (*see* PRE).

    Examples: Let *i1* and *i2* be [*d02:d03*] and [*d04:d10*], respectively; then *i1* MEETS *i2* is true. By contrast, if *i1* and *i2* are [*d02:d04*] and [*d04:d10*], respectively, then *i1* MEETS *i2* is false. Observe that MEETS is commutative—that is, *i1* MEETS *i2* and *i2* MEETS *i1* are equivalent (so *i1* MEETS *i2* is true if and only if *i2* MEETS *i1* is true).

Note: SQL uses a combination of the keywords IMMEDIATELY PRECEDES and IMMEDIATELY SUCCEEDS in place of MEETS. For example, let *p1* and *p2* be the SQL periods PERIOD (*d02,d04*) and PERIOD (*d04,d11*), respectively; then the SQL expression

```
p1 IMMEDIATELY PRECEDES p2
```

is true, and so is

```
p2 IMMEDIATELY SUCCEEDS p1
```

Hence

```
p1 IMMEDIATELY PRECEDES p2 OR p1 IMMEDIATELY SUCCEEDS p2
```

is true too, a fortiori, and so of course is

```
p2 IMMEDIATELY PRECEDES p1 OR p2 IMMEDIATELY SUCCEEDS p1
```

(and these two latter expressions are both effectively equivalent to either of the hypothetical SQL expressions "*p1* MEETS *p2*" and "*p2* MEETS *p1*").

Oddly enough, however, while the hypothetical SQL expression "PERIOD (*f1,t1*) MEETS PERIOD (*f2,t2*)" is illegal, the simpler—and much more succinct!—expression *t1* = *f2* OR *t2* = *f1* is not only legal but means exactly the same as

```
p1 IMMEDIATELY PRECEDES p2 OR p1 IMMEDIATELY SUCCEEDS p2
```

See period for further explanation.

MERGES   One of Allen's operators, q.v. Let *i1* and *i2* be intervals of the same type. Then *i1* MERGES *i2* is true if and only if *i1* MEETS *i2* is true or *i1* OVERLAPS *i2* is true (*see* MEETS; OVERLAPS).

Examples: Let *i1* and *i2* be [*d02:d04*] and [*d05:d10*], respectively; then *i1* MERGES *i2* is true. Likewise, if *i1* and *i2* are [*d02:d04*] and [*d03:d10*], respectively; then *i1* MERGES *i2* is true. By contrast, if *i1* and *i2* are [*d02:d06*] and [*d08:d10*], respectively, then *i1* MERGES *i2* is false. Observe that MERGES is commutative—that is, *i1* MERGES *i2* and *i2* MERGES *i1* are equivalent (so *i1* MERGES *i2* is true if and only if *i2* MERGES *i1* is true).

Note: SQL has no direct support for the MERGES operator. However, if *p1* and *p2* denote SQL periods, then the SQL expression

```
p1 OVERLAPS p2 OR
p1 IMMEDIATELY PRECEDES p2 OR
p1 IMMEDIATELY SUCCEEDS p2
```

is effectively equivalent to either of the hypothetical SQL expressions "*p1* MERGES *p2*" and "*p2* MERGES *p1*." *See* period for further explanation.

moving point *now* Term frequently used in the temporal database literature to refer to the present time (i.e., "the time right now"). *Note:* Suggestions are frequently encountered in the literature to the effect that "the moving point *now*" should somehow be capable of explicit representation as such within a relation (see, e.g., James Clifford, Curtis Dyreson, Tomás Isakowitz, Christian S. Jensen, and Richard T. Snodgrass, "On the Semantics of 'Now' in Databases," *ACM TODS 22*, No. 2, June 1997). But relations are values and "the moving point *now*" is a variable, and the idea that values might contain variables is a logical absurdity. (To see that "the moving point *now*" is indeed a variable, observe that the value denoted by that phrase is always changing—in fact, of course, it's always increasing—and if some object *x* denotes different values at different times, then that object *x* is a variable by definition.) Indeed, it's precisely because "the moving point *now*," as such, can't be represented within a relation that horizontal decomposition, q.v., is recommended as an approach to temporal database design. *See also* NOW; *until further notice*.

——— ♦ ♦ ♦ ♦ ♦ ———

NEXT_*T* The successor function for point type *T*. *See* NEXT (in Part I of this dictionary); ordinality; point type. *Note:* SQL has no support for this operator as such; instead, an expression involving explicit datetime arithmetic, such as DV + INTERVAL '1' DAY, has to be used. For further explanation and discussion, *see* datetime arithmetic (SQL); period.

nontemporal database A database that's not a temporal database, q.v.. Sometimes referred to as a snapshot database (but this term is deprecated on account of possible confusion with other uses of the term *snapshot*—see Part I of this dictionary).

NOT U_MATCHING *See* U_semidifference.

NOW A construct, or marker, proposed in certain nonrelational approaches to temporal data for representing the present time (*see* moving point *now*). However, the construct in question is a variable, not a value; it follows that a "type" that contains such a construct isn't a type, a "tuple" that contains such a construct isn't a tuple, a "relation" that contains such a construct isn't a relation, and a "relvar" that contains such a construct isn't a relvar. It further follows that the NOW construct as usually understood does serious violence to the relational model, and this dictionary therefore has very little more to say regarding that construct or matters related to it.

——— ♦ ♦ ♦ ♦ ♦ ———

open (*Of an interval*) *See* interval selector; interval value.

open:closed *See* interval selector.

open:open (*Of an interval*) *See* interval selector.

ordinality That which distinguishes an ordinal type from one that's merely ordered (see Part I of this dictionary). Let *T* be an ordered type, and let *Ord* be the pertinent ordering. Then *T* is said to possess the property of ordinality if and only if (a) a first and a last value of the type, denoted FIRST_*T* ( ) and LAST_*T* ( ), respectively, exist with respect to *Ord*, and (b) a successor function, denoted NEXT_*T* (*p*) and returning the (unique) immediate successor of *p* with respect to *Ord*, is defined for every value *p* of type *T* except for *p* = LAST_*T* ( ). Moreover, that successor function must be such that (a) if *p1* ≠ *p2* then NEXT_*T* (*p1*) ≠ NEXT_*T* (*p2*), and (b) there's exactly one value of type *T*, viz., FIRST_*T* ( ), that's not equal to NEXT_*T* (*p*) for any *p*. *Note:* Throughout definitions and examples in this part of the dictionary, intervals are assumed to be defined over an ordinal type, unless the context demands otherwise.

OVERLAPS One of Allen's operators, q.v. Let *i1* = [*b1:e1*] and *i2* = [*b2:e2*] be intervals of the same type. Then *i1* OVERLAPS *i2* is true if and only if *b1* ≤ *e2* and *b2* ≤ *e1* are both true.

   Examples: Let *i1* and *i2* be [*d02:d05*] and [*d04:d10*], respectively; then *i1* OVERLAPS *i2* is true. By contrast, if *i1* and *i2* are [*d02:d03*] and [*d04:d10*], respectively, then *i1* OVERLAPS *i2* is false. Observe that OVERLAPS is commutative—that is, *i1* OVERLAPS *i2* and *i2* OVERLAPS *i1* are equivalent (so *i1* OVERLAPS *i2* is true if and only if *i2* OVERLAPS *i1* is true).

   Note: SQL supports the OVERLAPS operator directly. For example, let *p1* and *p2* be the SQL periods PERIOD (*d02,d06*) and PERIOD (*d04,d11*), respectively; then the SQL expressions *p1* OVERLAPS *p2* and *p2* OVERLAPS *p1* are both true.

————— ♦ ♦ ♦ ♦ ♦ —————

PACK *See* packing. *Note:* SQL has no direct support for the PACK operator.

packed constraint Same as PACKED ON constraint.
   Example: See the example under PACKED ON.

packed form 1. Let relation *r* have interval attributes *A1*, *A2*, ..., *An* (*n* ≥ 0). Then *r* is in packed form with respect to *A1*, *A2*, ..., *An* (in that order, if *n* > 1) if and only if *r* is equal to the result of evaluating the expression PACK *r* ON (*A1,A2,...,An*). 2. Let relvar *R* have interval attributes *A1*, *A2*, ..., *An* (*n* ≥ 0). Then *R* is in packed form with respect to *A1*, *A2*, ..., *An* (in that order, if *n* > 1) if and only if every relation *r* that can ever be assigned to *R* is in packed form with respect to *A1*, *A2*, ..., *An* (in that order, if *n* > 1). *Note:* The phrase *packed form with* *respect to A1, A2, ..., An* can be abbreviated to just *packed form* if the attributes *A1, A2, ..., An* (in that order, if *n* > 1) are understood. *See* packing for further discussion; *see also* PACKED ON.

Examples: 1. The relation shown as the current value of relvar S_STATUS_DURING in Fig. 6 is in packed form with respect to attribute DURING, because whenever two tuples in that relation have the same SNO and STATUS values, their DURING values *i1* and *i2* are such that *i1* MERGES *i2* is false. The same goes for the relation shown as the current value of relvar S_STATUS_DURING in Fig. 8. 2. The two versions of relvar S_STATUS_DURING itself— both the one illustrated in Fig. 6 and the one illustrated in Fig. 8—are themselves in packed form with respect to DURING, because their definitions both at least implicitly include the specification PACKED ON (DURING) (*see* U_key).

PACKED ON   A specification used in **Tutorial D** as part of a relvar definition to impose a constraint to the effect that the pertinent relvar is to be kept in a certain packed form. Let *ACL* be a commalist of attribute names such that every attribute mentioned (a) is an attribute of the same relvar *R* and (b) is interval valued. Then the specification PACKED ON (*ACL*)—part of the definition of relvar *R*—ensures that any attempt to update *R* will fail if the result isn't in packed form with respect to *ACL*, and thereby further ensures that *R* won't suffer from either the circumlocution problem (as defined elsewhere in this part of the dictionary) or the redundancy problem (again as defined elsewhere in this part of the dictionary) with respect to *ACL*. *Note:* In practice, PACKED ON specifications will usually be implicit (*see* U_key).

Example: Consider relvar S_STATUS_DURING (either the Fig. 6 version or the Fig. 8 version, it makes no difference). Here's a possible definition for that relvar (irrelevant details omitted):

```
VAR S_STATUS_DURING BASE RELATION
   { SNO SNO , STATUS INTEGER , DURING INTERVAL_DATE }
     PACKED ON ( DURING ) ... ;
```

The effect of the PACKED ON specification here is to ensure that any attempt to update S_STATUS_DURING in such a way as to leave that relvar less than fully packed on DURING will fail. (Similar PACKED ON constraints can and should also be specified for relvars S_DURING and SP_DURING.) *Note:* A variety of U_update operators, q.v., are available to help with the process of updating a relvar to which a PACKED ON constraint applies.

The specification PACKED ON (*ACL*) on relvar *R* is trivial—i.e., has no effect—if *ACL* is empty or if the set of attributes of *R* not included in *ACL* is a superkey for *R*.

packing   1. (*Single-attribute PACK*) Let relation *r* have an interval attribute *A*. Then (and only then) the expression PACK *r* ON (*A*) denotes the packing of *r* on *A*, and it's equivalent to the following:

```
WITH ( r1 := r GROUP { A } AS X ,
       r2 := EXTEND r1 : { X := COLLAPSE ( X ) } ) :
r2 UNGROUP X
```

2. (*Multiattribute PACK*): Let relation *r* have interval attributes *A1, A2, ..., An* (*n* > 1). Then (and only then) the expression PACK *r* ON (*A1, A2, ..., An*) denotes the packing of *r* on *A1, A2, ..., An*, in that order, and it's equivalent to the following—

```
PACK ( ... ( PACK ( PACK r' ON ( A1 ) ) ON ( A2 ) ) ... ) ON ( An )
```

—where *r'* is the fully unpacked form of *r* (in other words, *r'* is the relation denoted by the expression UNPACK *r* ON (*A1, A2, ..., An*)). 3. (*Nullary PACK*) Let *r* be a relation. Then (and only then) the expression PACK *r* ON ( ) denotes the packing of *r* on no attributes, and it returns relation *r* itself.

    Examples: 1. Let relation *r* be as follows:

SNO	DURING
S2	[d02:d04]
S2	[d03:d05]
S4	[d02:d05]
S4	[d04:d06]
S4	[d09:d10]

Then packing *r* on DURING yields:

SNO	DURING
S2	[d02:d05]
S4	[d02:d06]
S4	[d09:d10]

2. Let relation *r* be as follows:

A1	A2
[P2:P4]	[d01:d04]
[P3:P5]	[d01:d04]
[P2:P4]	[d05:d06]
[P2:P4]	[d06:d09]

Then packing *r* on (A1,A2) yields:

A1	A2
`[P2:P5]`	`[d01:d04]`
`[P2:P4]`	`[d05:d09]`

By contrast, packing *r* on (A2,A1) yields:

A1	A2
`[P2:P4]`	`[d01:d09]`
`[P5:P5]`	`[d01:d04]`

Observe that these latter two results are logically distinct.

period SQL analog of an interval. Note, however, that SQL has no analog of the interval type generator, q.v. (i.e., there's no period type generator); in fact, it doesn't actually have any period types as such. Instead, SQL periods are represented by explicit (FROM,TO) pairs—specifically, pairs of column values, in the case of a period that happens to be part of an SQL table—and they're always understood, implicitly, to be represented in closed:open style (despite the fact that they're represented in concrete syntax with an opening parenthesis, not a bracket). Thus, e.g., the SQL period PERIOD (*d04,d11*), with FROM value *d04* and TO value *d11*, consists precisely of the points *d04*, *d05*, *d06*, *d07*, *d08*, *d09*, and *d10*—in other words, it corresponds to the closed:closed interval [*d04:d10*]. Note too that (as indeed the term *period* tends to suggest) SQL's periods are quite specifically temporal in nature; SQL has nothing corresponding to the general purpose interval abstraction as discussed elsewhere in this dictionary. Also, precisely because SQL periods are represented in closed:open style, there's no way "the end of time" can actually be contained in such a period. In particular, if (as in several examples in Fig. 9) some period has a TO value of *d99*, then the last day that's actually contained in the period in question is that day's immediate predecessor—denoted symbolically *d98*—which of course isn't "the end of time."

Let *p* be the SQL period PERIOD (*f,t*), where *f* and *t* are SQL datetime values (see further discussion below). Then *f* and *t* are the boundary values for *p*. Further, if *p* happens to be part of an SQL table, then the columns of that table corresponding to *f* and *t* are the boundary columns for *p*.

Note: Actually, SQL supports two kinds of periods, representing application time (q.v.) and system time (q.v.), respectively. The remainder of this entry assumes, where it makes any difference, that the periods in question are application time periods specifically. The special considerations (such as they are) that apply to system time periods are discussed under **system time**, q.v.

Examples: Here first is a possible definition—i.e., a CREATE TABLE statement—for the base table S_FROM_TO as illustrated in Fig. 9 (irrelevant details omitted):

```
CREATE TABLE S_FROM_TO
    ( SNO    SNO   NOT NULL ,
      DFROM DATE NOT NULL ,
      DTO    DATE NOT NULL ,
      PERIOD FOR DPERIOD ( DFROM , DTO ) ,
      UNIQUE ( SNO , DPERIOD WITHOUT OVERLAPS ) ... ) ;
```

The specification PERIOD FOR DPERIOD (DFROM, DTO) means that columns DFROM and DTO taken together represent an application time period, called DPERIOD, for table S_FROM_TO. The UNIQUE specification means that (a) the combination (SNO,DPERIOD) constitutes a proper superkey for that table—note that it's explicitly not a key as such because, as explained under **foreign key (SQL)**, it's not irreducible (see Part I of this dictionary)—and (b) if two rows of that table have the same SNO value, then their DPERIOD values can't overlap, thanks to the qualification WITHOUT OVERLAPS. *Note:* WITHOUT OVERLAPS prevents the table from suffering from the redundancy and contradiction problems but not from the circumlocution problem (where the terms *redundancy problem, contradiction problem*, and *circumlocution problem* are each to be understood as defined elsewhere in this part of the dictionary, and where the problems in question are to be understood as with respect to DPERIOD in each case). Unfortunately, the fact that the table is subject to the circumlocution problem seems to mean the table isn't properly relational, because it doesn't seem to have anything corresponding to a proper relvar predicate. *See* **table predicate (SQL)** for further discussion of this point.

Here now are the CREATE TABLE statements for all three of the base tables illustrated in Fig. 9, now shown complete:

```
CREATE TABLE S_FROM_TO
    ( SNO    SNO   NOT NULL ,
      DFROM DATE NOT NULL ,
      DTO    DATE NOT NULL ,
      PERIOD FOR DPERIOD ( DFROM , DTO ) ,
      UNIQUE ( SNO , DPERIOD WITHOUT OVERLAPS ) ,
      FOREIGN KEY ( SNO , PERIOD DPERIOD )
            REFERENCES S_STATUS_FROM_TO ( SNO , PERIOD DPERIOD ) ) ;

CREATE TABLE S_STATUS_FROM_TO
    ( SNO     SNO       NOT NULL ,
      STATUS INTEGER NOT NULL ,
      DFROM   DATE      NOT NULL ,
      DTO     DATE      NOT NULL ,
      PERIOD FOR DPERIOD ( DFROM , DTO ) ,
      UNIQUE ( SNO , DPERIOD WITHOUT OVERLAPS ) ,
      FOREIGN KEY ( SNO , PERIOD DPERIOD )
            REFERENCES S_FROM_TO ( SNO , PERIOD DPERIOD ) ) ;
```

```
CREATE TABLE SP_FROM_TO
    ( SNO    SNO   NOT NULL ,
      PNO    PNO   NOT NULL ,
      DFROM DATE NOT NULL ,
      DTO    DATE NOT NULL ,
      PERIOD FOR DPERIOD ( DFROM , DTO ) ,
      UNIQUE ( SNO , PNO , DPERIOD WITHOUT OVERLAPS ) ,
      FOREIGN KEY ( SNO , PERIOD DPERIOD )
                REFERENCES S_FROM_TO ( SNO , PERIOD DPERIOD ) ) ;
```

Observe in particular that each of tables S_FROM_TO and S_STATUS_FROM_TO has a "foreign key" that references the other (and table SP_FROM_TO has a "foreign key" that references S_FROM_TO, but not the other way around). *Note: Foreign key* is indeed what SQL calls the constructs in question, but it would be closer to the truth, though still not entirely accurate, to refer to them as *foreign U_keys*, q.v. *See* **foreign key (SQL)** for further explanation. Note too that, precisely because each of the tables does have a "foreign key" that references the other, updates to either table will often need to be accompanied by updates to the other. Unfortunately, however, SQL lacks support for the multiple assignment operator that's needed in order to perform such double updates properly (see Part I of this dictionary).

Now, since SQL has no period types, it also has no period variables. A fortiori, therefore, it has no period variable references, nor more generally does it have period expressions—i.e., expressions that return a period value—of any kind. But it does have a construct that might be thought of, informally, as a kind of "period selector," and, as a special case of that construct, it does support a kind of "period literal." However, these constructs can appear in just one context where it might have been expected that a column reference would be allowed: To be specific, they can appear in what SQL calls a *period predicate*, q.v., where they can be used to denote an operand, or both operands, to one of Allen's operators. The syntax is PERIOD (*f,t*), where *f* and *t* are expressions both of the same SQL type, viz., either DATE or one of SQL's TIMESTAMP types (these are the only point types that SQL supports).

Here now is a simple SQL query against table S_FROM_TO:

```
SELECT DISTINCT SNO
FROM    S_FROM_TO
WHERE   PERIOD ( DFROM , DTO ) OVERLAPS
        PERIOD ( DATE '2012-12-01' , DATE '2013-01-01' )
```

Observe that the OVERLAPS operands in this example are denoted by constructs—SQL calls them *period predicands*—that do look something like hypothetical "period selector" invocations, and the second in particular does look something like a hypothetical "period literal."

Note: In the common special case where a period predicand denotes a period that's explicitly defined to be part of some SQL table (necessarily a base table), the corresponding period name can be used in place of the corresponding "period selector invocation." Thus, the WHERE clause in the foregoing example can be simplified slightly as indicated here:

```
SELECT DISTINCT SNO
FROM    S_FROM_TO
WHERE   DPERIOD OVERLAPS
        PERIOD ( DATE '2012-12-01' , DATE '2013-01-01' )
```

Note finally that periods don't "carry through" operational expressions; thus, no SQL table other than a base table contains, or can contain, any periods at all. Thus, for example, the following attempted query—

```
SELECT *
FROM    S_FROM_TO NATURAL JOIN SP_FROM_TO
WHERE   DPERIOD OVERLAPS
        PERIOD ( DATE '2012-12-01' , DATE '2013-01-01' )
```

—fails on a syntax error, because the result of the join has no period called DPERIOD (in fact, it has no period at all). However, the desired effect can be obtained by replacing the reference to DPERIOD in the WHERE clause by an appropriate "period selector invocation," thus:

```
SELECT *
FROM    S_FROM_TO NATURAL JOIN SP_FROM_TO
WHERE   PERIOD ( DFROM , DTO ) OVERLAPS
        PERIOD ( DATE '2012-12-01' , DATE '2013-01-01' )
```

PERIOD FOR (SQL) *See* period; *see also* system time.

period literal (SQL) *See* period.

period name (SQL) Periods in SQL are named if and only if the period in question is represented by a column pair in some SQL base table. Such names can be used (a) in a period predicate to denote a period predicand (*see* period); (b) in a FOR PORTION OF specification, q.v. (but only if the period name in question denotes an application time period, q.v., not a system time period); (c) in SQL "key" and "foreign key" specifications, q.v. (again, only if the period name in question denotes an application time period, q.v., not a system time period); (d) nowhere else.

period predicand (SQL) *See* period.

period predicate (SQL) A boolean expression, representing the SQL analog of an invocation of one of Allen's operators, q.v.

period selector (SQL) *See* period.

point A value of some point type, q.v.; a point value.

point attribute An attribute of some point type, q.v.; a point valued attribute.

point extractor An operator for extracting the single point *p* from the unit interval [*p:p*].

Example: The following expression extracts the single DATE value (viz., *d03*) from the unit interval that's the DURING value in the tuple for supplier S2 and part P2 in the relation that's shown as the sample value for relvar SP_DURING in Fig. 6:

```
POINT FROM
     ( DURING FROM
            ( TUPLE FROM
                  ( SP_DURING WHERE SNO = SNO('S2')
                             AND  PNO = PNO('P2') ) ) )
```

A run-time error will occur if the interval expression that denotes the POINT FROM argument doesn't evaluate to an interval of cardinality exactly one (i.e., a unit interval).

POINT FROM **Tutorial D** syntax for a point extractor, q.v. *Note:* SQL has no support for the POINT FROM operator as such. But if *p* denotes the SQL period PERIOD (*f,t*), where *t* is in fact the immediate successor of *f*, then *p* is effectively a "unit period," and the SQL expression *f* is then effectively equivalent to the hypothetical SQL expression "POINT FROM (*p*)." However, it's the user's responsibility in such a situation to ensure that period *p* does indeed contain just one point—no exception will be raised if it doesn't. *See* **period** for further explanation.

point type A type—usually assumed to be an ordinal type (see Part I of this dictionary)—over which an interval type, q.v, can be defined. In other words, let *T* be a type for which all of the following are defined: (a) a total ordering, according to which the operator "≤" is defined for every pair of values *v1* and *v2* of type *T*, such that if *v1* and *v2* are distinct, exactly one of the comparisons *v1* < *v2* and *v2* < *v1* returns TRUE; (b) niladic FIRST_*T* and LAST_*T* operators, which return the smallest (first) and largest (last) value of type *T*, respectively, according to the aforementioned ordering; and (c) monadic NEXT_*T* and PRIOR_*T* operators, which return the successor (if it exists) and predecessor (if it exists), respectively, of any given value of type *T* according to the aforementioned ordering. Then *T* is an ordinal type, and it's usable as a point type. *Note:* NEXT_*T* and PRIOR_*T* are the successor function and predecessor function, respectively, for type *T*. The only value of type *T* for which NEXT_*T* is undefined is the value denoted by LAST_*T* ( ); similarly, the only value of type *T* for which PRIOR_*T* is undefined is the value denoted by FIRST_*T* ( ).

Examples: 1. Type INTEGER (the scale is unity, and the successor function is "add one"). 2. Type MONEY, which we assume for the sake of the example is a type that represents monetary amounts measured in dollars and cents (the scale is one cent, and the successor function is "add one cent"). 3. Type DATE (the scale is one day, and the successor function is "add one day").

Note: The foregoing definition gives a set of conditions on type *T* that are certainly sufficient for that type to be usable as a point type. However, those conditions might not all be necessary. For example, it might be possible to drop conditions (b) and (c), which together constitute the property of ordinality, q.v. (*see* **continuity assumption**). Alternatively, it might be possible to replace the linear ordering required by condition (a) by a cyclic ordering, thereby making the type in question a cyclic point type. (An example of this possibility is provided by days of the week, where the available values can be thought of as being arranged around the circumference of a circle, such that every value has both a successor and a predecessor and there's no first or last value.) Further details of such possibilities are beyond the scope of this dictionary.

Note finally that the definition implicitly requires the successor function for a given point type to be unique. So what about a point type such as DATE for which (it would appear) several different successor functions might make sense—for example, "next week," "next business day," "next month," and so on? One possible approach to such questions consists in defining a series of proper subtypes of the type in question, each with its own unique successor function. *See* inheritance (point types) for further discussion of this possibility.

point type (SQL)   *See* period.

point type inheritance   *See* inheritance (point types).

point value   A value of some point type; hence, a value that can be contained within some interval.

PORTION   An auxiliary operator, available for use in conjunction with certain other operators on a relation or relvar having at least one interval attribute, that simplifies the process of accessing just a certain "portion" of the relation or relvar in question. The portion in question can be thought of as the result of (a) picking out those tuples of the relation or relvar in question for which the value of a specified interval attribute overlaps a specified interval; (b) unpacking the set of tuples so identified on the specified attribute; (c) picking out the tuples in the result of that unpacking whose interval value is included in the specified interval; and then (d) (re)packing this latter set of tuples on the specified attribute. *Note:* The foregoing definition is deliberately somewhat simplified, in that it assumes there's just one interval attribute and just one specified interval. Details of the general case are beyond the scope of this dictionary.

Examples: First a retrieval example. Given the sample value shown for SP_DURING in Fig. 6, the expression

```
SP_DURING PORTION { DURING { INTERVAL_DATE ( [ d06 : d08 ] ) } }
```

yields:

SNO	PNO	DURING
S3	P5	[d06:d07]
S4	P2	[d06:d08]
S4	P4	[d06:d08]

To see how this example works, observe that the given expression, using PORTION, can be regarded as shorthand for the following:

```
WITH ( i0 := INTERVAL_DATE ( [ d06 : d08 ] ) ,
       t1 := SP_DURING WHERE DURING OVERLAPS i0 ,
       t2 := UNPACK t1 ON ( DURING ) ,
       t3 := t2 WHERE DURING ⊆ i0 ) :
PACK t3 ON ( DURING )
```

(The final PACK step has no effect in this example, but it's necessary in the general case.)
Here now is a DELETE example:

```
DELETE SP_DURING WHERE SNO = SNO('S4') :
       PORTION { DURING { INTERVAL_DATE ( [ d08 : d13 ] ) } } ;
```

The effect of this DELETE, loosely speaking, is to remove from relvar SP_DURING any representation of the proposition "Supplier S4 was able to supply some part from day 8 to day 13." Here's the result, given the sample values shown in Fig. 8 (only tuples for supplier S4 shown):

SNO	PNO	DURING
..	..	....
S4	P2	[d06:d07]
S4	P4	[d04:d07]
S4	P5	[d05:d07]
S4	P5	[d14:d99]
..	..	....

In general, the DELETE statement

```
DELETE R WHERE bx : PORTION { A { ix } } ;
```

can be regarded as shorthand for the following:

```
WITH ( t1 := R WHERE ( bx ) AND A OVERLAPS ( ix ) ,
       t2 := R MINUS t1 ,
       t3 := UNPACK t1 ON ( A ) ,
       t4 := t3 WHERE NOT ( A ⊆ ( ix ) ) ,
       t5 := t2 UNION t4 ) :
R := PACK t5 ON ( A ) ;
```

(Once again, in the case of the particular DELETE example shown earlier, the final PACK step actually has no effect, but it's necessary in the general case.)

Finally, here's an UPDATE example (note that PORTION makes sense with DELETE and UPDATE but not with INSERT). The following statement has the effect of replacing the proposition "Supplier S2 was able to supply part P1 on day 3" by the proposition "Supplier S2 was able to supply part P1 on day 5":

```
UPDATE SP_DURING WHERE SNO = SNO('S2')
                 AND   PNO = PNO('P1') :
     PORTION { DURING { INTERVAL_DATE ( [ d03 : d03 ] ) } } :
   { DURING := INTERVAL_DATE ( [ d05 : d05 ] ) } ;
```

In this example, assuming the initial value of relvar SP_DURING is as shown in either Fig. 6 or Fig. 8, the final PACK step does have some effect. (Details of the expanded form of UPDATE with PORTION are omitted here for simplicity, but they follow the same general pattern as that already shown for DELETE with PORTION.)

Turning now to SQL: SQL does support PORTION, but (a) it does so only in conjunction with DELETE and UPDATE, not with retrieval; (b) that support is limited to operating in terms of just one period in the target table—necessarily so, given that SQL allows at most one application time period per table—and just one overlapping period; (c) as in fact the previous point suggests, the period in the target table must be an application time period, not a system time period, q.v.; and (d) in the case of UPDATE, the SET clause isn't allowed to assign to the application time period boundary columns. *Note:* As a consequence of point (d) here, the UPDATE example shown above has no direct SQL counterpart. However, the earlier DELETE example does. Here it is:

```
DELETE
FROM   SP_FROM_TO FOR PORTION OF DPERIOD FROM d08 TO d14
WHERE  SNO = SNO('S4') ;
```

By the way, suppose we now execute the following SQL INSERT (which can be regarded, a trifle loosely, as a partial inverse of the foregoing SQL DELETE):

```
INSERT INTO SP_FROM_TO ( SNO , PNO , DFROM , DTO )
       VALUES ( SNO('S4') , PNO('P5') , d08 , d14 ) ;
```

Here's the result (rows for S4 only):

SNO	PNO	DFROM	DTO
..	..	. . .	. . .
S4	P2	*d06*	*d08*
S4	P4	*d04*	*d08*
S4	P5	*d05*	*d08*
S4	P5	*d08*	*d14*
S4	P5	*d14*	*d99*
..	..	. . .	. . .

The point about this example, of course, is that the three rows for S4 and P5 in the result are *not* automatically packed together into one, in SQL. *See* table predicate (SQL); *see also* U_INSERT.

POST   Let *i* be the interval [*b:e*]. Then if *e* is the last value of the point type underlying the type of interval *i*, POST (*i*) is undefined; otherwise it returns the immediate successor (informally denoted "*e*+1") of *e*. *Note:* SQL has no support for the POST operator as such. Rather, if *p* denotes the SQL period PERIOD (*f,t*), then the SQL expression *t* is effectively equivalent to the hypothetical SQL expression "POST (*p*)." *See* period for further explanation.

PRE   Let *i* be the interval [*b:e*]. Then if *b* is the first value of the point type underlying the type of interval *i*, PRE (*i*) is undefined; otherwise it returns the immediate predecessor (informally denoted "*b*-1") of *b*. *Note:* SQL has no support for the PRE operator as such. Rather, if *p* denotes the SQL period PERIOD (*f,t*)—and if we assume for definiteness that *f* and *t* are of type DATE and the scale, q.v., is one day—then the SQL expression

```
f - INTERVAL '1' DAY
```

(which will fail, of course, if *f* is "the beginning of time") is effectively equivalent to the hypothetical SQL expression "PRE (*p*)." For further explanation and discussion, *see* datetime arithmetic (SQL); period.

predecessor   Let *p* be a value of point type *T* (*p* ≠ FIRST_*T* ( )); then the predecessor of *p* (informally denoted "*p*-1") is the point that's the immediate predecessor of *p* with respect to the ordering associated with *T*. *Note:* The term "predecessor of *p*" is always used to mean the immediate predecessor of *p* specifically, though the explicit qualifier *immediate* is sometimes used for emphasis.

predecessor function (SQL)   *See* datetime arithmetic (SQL).

predecessor function / predecessor operator   *See* point type.

PRIOR_*T* The predecessor function for point type *T*. *See* ordinality; PRIOR (in Part I of this dictionary); point type. *Note:* SQL has no support for this operator as such; instead, an expression involving explicit datetime arithmetic, such as DV − INTERVAL '1' DAY, has to be used. For further explanation and discussion, *see* datetime arithmetic (SQL); period.

proper interval inclusion One of Allen's operators, q.v. Let *i1* and *i2* be intervals of the same type. Then *i1* properly includes *i2* ("*i1* ⊃ *i2*") if and only if *i1* includes *i2* and *i1* ≠ *i2*. Also, *i2* is properly included in *i1* ("*i2* ⊂ *i1*") if and only if *i1* ⊃ *i2* is true.

    Examples: Let *i1* and *i2* be [*d02:d10*] and [*d04:d08*], respectively; then *i1* ⊃ *i2* is true. By contrast, if *i1* and *i2* are [*d02:d07*] and [*d04:d08*], respectively, then *i1* ⊃ *i2* is false. Note that no interval is properly included in itself. Note too that the term *proper interval inclusion* is usually taken, a trifle arbitrarily, to refer to the operator "⊂" specifically, not the operator "⊃".

    Note: SQL has no direct support for proper interval inclusion. However, if *p1* and *p2* denote the SQL periods PERIOD (*f1,t1*) and PERIOD (*f2,t2*), respectively, then (e.g.) the SQL expression (*f1* ≥ *f2* AND *t1* < *t2*) OR (*f1* > *f2* AND *t1* ≤ *t2*) is effectively equivalent to the hypothetical SQL expression "*p1* ⊂ *p2*." *See* period for further discussion.

———— ◆ ◆ ◆ ◆ ◆ ————

redundancy problem A problem that can arise in connection with relations with interval attributes, absent suitable controls: specifically, the problem that two tuples appearing in such a relvar at the same time might effectively imply the same proposition. For example, suppose with reference to either Fig. 6 or Fig. 8 that the following tuples were both to appear in relvar S_STATUS_DURING at the same time:

SNO	STATUS	DURING
S4	25	[*d05:d06*]

SNO	STATUS	DURING
S4	25	[*d06:d07*]

These two tuples both imply among other things the proposition "Supplier S4 had status 25 on day 6." Clearly, it would be better if the two tuples were replaced by the following single tuple:

SNO	STATUS	DURING
S4	25	[*d05:d07*]

    Formally, the problem illustrated by this example is that the two original tuples (a) agree on their SNO and STATUS values and (b) have DURING values *i1* and *i2* such that *i1* OVERLAPS *i2* is true (*see* OVERLAPS). Note that if those original tuples were indeed both allowed to appear, the relvar would be in violation of its own predicate, because neither [*d05:d06*] nor [*d06:d07*] would in fact be a maximal interval, q.v., of days during which supplier S4 had status 25. Note too that enforcing a constraint to the effect that {SNO,DURING} is a key for S_STATUS_DURING—which it is—isn't sufficient to prevent the foregoing problem from occurring. *See* PACKED ON for further discussion.

———— ♦♦♦♦♦ ————

scale (*Of a point type*) Same as granularity. The term *scale* is preferred, in part because it has a precise definition (see Part I of this dictionary), which *granularity* seems not to have.

  Note: Scales aren't necessarily uniform. For example, let type MDATE represent calendar dates measured in months—*see* inheritance (point types). Then the associated successor function NEXT_MDATE will add 28, 29, 30, or 31 days to its MDATE argument, depending on which particular month of which particular year that argument happens to denote. (Observe, incidentally, that—as pointed out under datetime arithmetic (SQL)—the same is not true of the SQL expression DV + INTERVAL '1' MONTH, where DV is of type DATE. For example, if the current value of DV happens to be August 31st, then an error will occur, because September 31st isn't a legitimate date.)

semitemporal Term used informally to characterize a since relvar, q.v., in contrast to a during relvar, q.v. *Contrast* fully temporal.

since Term much used in connection with temporal data; if some specified condition *c* holds "since" some specified time point *p*, it means condition *c* holds throughout (i.e., at every time point within) the interval from *p* to "the end of time" inclusive. *See* until further notice. *Note:* The term is often used—in this dictionary in particular—in a more restrictive sense, according to which the condition in question holds throughout and not immediately before the interval in question, in which case the interval in question is said to be maximal. *See* maximal interval for further discussion.

since attribute Term used informally to refer to an attribute of some temporal point type.
  Examples: Attributes SNO_SINCE and STATUS_SINCE in relvar S_SINCE, and attribute SINCE in relvar SP_SINCE, in the suppliers-and-shipments database of Fig. 6.

since relation Term used informally to refer to a relation one of whose attributes is of some temporal point type (especially a relation that's the current value of some since relvar, q.v.).
  Examples: The current values of relvars S_SINCE and SP_SINCE in the suppliers-and-shipments database of Fig. 6.

since relvar Term used informally to denote a relvar that (a) isn't a during relvar, q.v., and (b) has a predicate that can reasonably be formulated in such a way as to include one or more qualifications of the form "since time *t*" (and thus has one or more attributes of some temporal point type); very loosely, a relvar that contains current information.

Examples: Relvars S_SINCE and SP_SINCE in the suppliers-and-shipments database of Fig. 6.

sixth normal form   (*Expanded definition*) Relvar *R* is in sixth normal form, 6NF, if and only if it can't be nonloss decomposed at all, other than trivially—i.e., if and only if the only JDs to which it's subject are trivial ones. *Note:* The foregoing definition of what it means for a given relvar to be in 6NF is identical to the one given in Part I of this dictionary. However, (a) the term *JD* must now be understood to include U_JDs, q.v., in particular, and (b) the term *nonloss decomposed* must now be understood in terms of U_projection, q.v. (the decomposition operator) and U_join, q.v. (the corresponding recomposition operator), rather than just regular projection and regular join. *See* vertical decomposition.

Examples: In Figs. 6 and 8, relvars S_DURING, S_STATUS_DURING, and SP_DURING are all in 6NF. By contrast, in Fig. 6, relvar S_SINCE isn't (though SP_SINCE is).

Note, incidentally, that the SQL analog of relvar S_STATUS_DURING—viz., base table S_STATUS_FROM_TO (see Fig. 9)—isn't in 6NF, because the following join dependencies—

```
⋈ { { SNO , DFROM , DTO } , { SNO , DFROM , STATUS } }

⋈ { { SNO , DTO , DFROM } , { SNO , DTO , STATUS } }
```

—both hold in that table. These JDs are clearly nontrivial, and the table is thus not in 6NF (though it is in 5NF).

snapshot database   Deprecated term for a nontemporal database, q.v.

snapshot of the database   Deprecated term for a database value—especially a value of some temporal database.

snapshot query   Informal and somewhat deprecated term for a query on a temporal database whose result represents the state of affairs as it was at some specified time.

Example: Consider the query "Get (SNO, STATUS, PNO, DURING) tuples such that supplier SNO (a) had status STATUS, and (b) was able to supply part PNO, throughout interval DURING, where DURING contains day 4." Here's a possible formulation of this query against the database of Fig. 8:

```
( USING ( DURING ) : S_STATUS_DURING JOIN SP_DURING ) WHERE d04 ∈ DURING
```

Let's agree to refer to this expression as *exp* (note, incidentally, that *exp* involves a U_join followed by a regular restriction, not a U_restriction). Then the expression

```
( exp ) { ALL BUT DURING }
```

is a snapshot query—it returns a "snapshot" of a certain portion of the database as of a certain point in time (day 4, in the case at hand).

stated time   (*Of a proposition*)   The time or times, represented as a set of temporal intervals (preferably in packed form), when, according to what the database currently says (which is to say, according to what we currently believe), the proposition in question is, was, or will be true. *Note:* Other terms that might be used for this concept include *user stated time* (to emphasize the point that it's some user, not the system, that did the stating); *user time*; *asserted time*; *user asserted time*; *application time*, q.v. (this is the term used in the SQL standard); *business time*, q.v.; and *valid time*, q.v. (this is the term most often encountered in the literature).

   Example: In Fig. 6, the stated time for the proposition *Supplier S2 is, was, or will be under contract* is {[*d02:d04*],[*d07:d99*]}. Note carefully that the proposition in this example—the proposition, that is, to which the specified stated time applies—isn't currently represented in the database; rather, the proposition that *is* represented in the database is the proposition *Supplier S2 is, was, or will be under contract during certain intervals* (where the "certain intervals" in question are [*d02:d04*] and [*d07:d99*], of course). Note, however, that those "certain intervals" aren't mentioned in the proposition to which the specified stated time applies; rather, they *are* the stated time for that proposition. And an analogous remark applies to the stated time concept in general; that is, stated times in general apply to some proposition that's not actually represented in the database.

   Note: In the relational approach to temporal data espoused in this dictionary, stated times are represented by regular relational attributes in the usual way. Precisely for that reason, there's very little need to use a special term ("stated times") for them at all. In nonrelational approaches, by contrast (see, e.g., the approach adopted in the SQL standard), stated times are treated as special—in particular, they're typically not represented by regular relational attributes in the usual way—and the need for some kind of special term to refer to them thus becomes somewhat more pressing. Note, incidentally, that not representing stated times by regular relational attributes in the usual way means the approach in question is indeed nonrelational; in fact, such an approach is in clear violation of *The Information Principle* (see Part I of this dictionary).

successor   Let *p* be a value of point type *T* ($p \neq$ LAST_*T* ( )); then the successor of *p* (informally denoted "*p*+1") is the point that's the immediate successor of *p* with respect to the ordering associated with *T*. *Note:* The term "successor of *p*" is always used to mean the immediate successor of *p* specifically, though the explicit qualifier *immediate* is sometimes used for emphasis.

successor function (SQL)   *See* datetime arithmetic (SQL).

successor function / successor operator *See* point type.

system clock *See* logged time; system time.

system time SQL term for logged time, q.v. Note, however, that system times in SQL are kept as part of the table to which they pertain, whereas—at least in the approach advocated in *Time and Relational Theory: Temporal Data in the Relational Model and SQL*, by Date, Darwen, and Lorentzos—logged times are kept in distinct logged time relvars, q.v. An SQL base table can have at most one system time period (*see* period). However, such periods don't "carry through" operational expressions; thus, no SQL table other than a base table has, or can have, any system time period at all (*see* period for further discussion and explanation).

Example: Suppose we want to keep system time information, but (for simplicity) not application time information, for suppliers and their status values. Then instead of table S_STATUS_FROM_TO as defined in the examples under period (and as illustrated in Fig. 9), we might define a table XS_STATUS_FROM_TO that looks like this:

```
CREATE TABLE XS_STATUS_FROM_TO
     ( SNO    SNO     NOT NULL ,
       STATUS INTEGER NOT NULL ,
       XFROM  TIMESTAMP(12) GENERATED ALWAYS AS ROW START NOT NULL ,
       XTO    TIMESTAMP(12) GENERATED ALWAYS AS ROW END   NOT NULL ,
       PERIOD FOR SYSTEM_TIME ( XFROM , XTO ) ,
       UNIQUE ( SNO ) ,
       FOREIGN KEY ( SNO ) REFERENCES XS_FROM_TO ( SNO ) )
     WITH SYSTEM VERSIONING ;
```

Points arising:

■ Table XS_STATUS_FROM_TO has just two "regular" columns, SNO and STATUS. These are the only columns the user can update directly (see below).

■ The system time period, which (as usual in SQL) is implicitly represented in closed:open style, has the required name SYSTEM_TIME. The PERIOD FOR SYSTEM_TIME specification defines columns XFROM and XTO to be the boundary columns for that period. Those columns must both be of the same type (either DATE—which is unlikely— or some specific TIMESTAMP type). Purely for definiteness, the example shows them as being of type TIMESTAMP(12), meaning times that are accurate to the picosecond (one picosecond = 10^{-12} seconds).

■ The specifications GENERATED ALWAYS AS ROW START (on XFROM) and GENERATED ALWAYS AS ROW END (on XTO) are required.

■ The UNIQUE and FOREIGN KEY specifications effectively assume the table contains the two regular columns SNO and STATUS only. *Note:* The FOREIGN KEY specification in particular assumes the existence of an analogous table called XS_FROM_TO, with the obvious definition and semantics. For simplicity, however, foreign keys are ignored in the discussion of updates below. Note, however, that while SQL does indeed call the constructs in question "foreign keys," it would be closer to the truth, though still not entirely accurate, to refer to them as *foreign U_keys*, q.v. *See* **foreign key (SQL)** for further explanation.

■ The specification WITH SYSTEM VERSIONING is optional, but it seems unlikely that it would ever be omitted in practice (and details of what happens if it's omitted are therefore omitted from this dictionary). If it's not omitted, the table is said to be a system versioned table.

Table XS_STATUS_FROM_TO is initially empty, of course. Suppose we now execute the following INSERT:

```
INSERT INTO XS_STATUS_FROM_TO ( SNO , STATUS )
       VALUES ( SNO('S1') , 20 ) ;
```

Further, suppose this INSERT statement is executed at time *t02* by the system clock. Then the row that's actually inserted looks like this:

SNO	STATUS	XFROM	XTO
S1	20	*t02*	*t99*

In other words, the system automatically inserts the timestamp *t02* in the XFROM position and "the end of time" timestamp *t99* in the XTO position. (Of course, system times are supposed always to be times in the past—*see* **logged time**—but that "end of time" timestamp *t99* doesn't really mean the end of time as such, it means "until further notice," q.v. Though it should be noted that the concept of "until further notice" doesn't really make much sense in this context either, given the intended semantics for the concept of logged time. Perhaps it would be better to say of such appearances of *t99* that they denote, not "until further notice," but rather "the time right now," meaning the time when the update occurred.)

Note: The foregoing explanation is somewhat simplified. To be more specific, the SQL standard doesn't actually mention the system clock as such; instead, it says there's something called *the transaction timestamp*, which (a) is required to remain constant throughout the life of the transaction in question, (b) is used as the source for system time values in general, and (c) is presumably distinct for distinct transactions, though the standard doesn't actually seem to come out and say as much. This state of affairs notwithstanding, the remainder of this entry continues to talk in terms of the system clock as such, for reasons of definiteness and simplicity.

Now suppose we execute the following UPDATE statement:

```
UPDATE XS_STATUS_FROM_TO
SET     STATUS = 25
WHERE   SNO = SNO('S1') ;
```

Further, suppose this UPDATE statement is executed at time *t06* by the system clock. After the UPDATE, then, the table looks like this:

SNO	STATUS	XFROM	XTO
S1	25	*t06*	*t99*
S1	20	*t02*	*t06*

In other words, the UPDATE (a) inserts a new row for supplier S1 with STATUS value 25, XFROM value *t06*, and XTO value *t99*, and (b) replaces the old row for supplier S1 by a row that's identical to that old row except that the XTO value is *t06* instead of *t99*.

Finally, suppose we subsequently execute the following DELETE statement:

```
DELETE
FROM    XS_STATUS_FROM_TO
WHERE   SNO = SNO('S1') ;
```

Further, suppose this DELETE statement is executed at time *t45* by the system clock. After the DELETE, then, the table looks like this:

SNO	STATUS	XFROM	XTO
S1	25	*t06*	*t45*
S1	20	*t02*	*t06*

In other words, the DELETE doesn't actually delete anything; instead, it simply replaces the XTO value in the "current row" for supplier S1 by *t45*. *Note:* The current row for supplier S1 is, of course, the row for supplier S1 in which the XTO value is *t99*. After the DELETE, there's no current row for supplier S1 at all. More generally, current rows are the only ones that can be updated—once a "historical" row gets into the table, it's there forever, and it never changes.

Turning now to queries: By default, queries on a system versioned table apply only to the current rows. Thus, if table XS_STATUS_FROM_TO currently looks like this—

SNO	STATUS	XFROM	XTO
S1	25	*t06*	*t99*
S1	20	*t02*	*t06*

—then the query

```
SELECT STATUS
FROM   XS_STATUS_FROM_TO
WHERE  SNO = SNO('S1')
```

returns the following result:

STATUS
25

To query historical rows, or more generally to query both current and historical rows, we can qualify the pertinent table reference (in the FROM clause) by a FOR SYSTEM_TIME specification, as in this example:

```
SELECT STATUS , XFROM , XTO
FROM   XS_STATUS_FROM_TO FOR SYSTEM_TIME AS OF t04
WHERE  SNO = SNO('S1')
```

Here's the result:

STATUS	XFROM	XTO
20	*t02*	*t06*

Note that, although this result does have XFROM and XTO columns, it doesn't have a system time period as such—like application time periods, q.v., system time periods don't "carry through" operational expressions. See **period** for further discussion of this and related matters.

The following FOR SYSTEM_TIME options are supported (*t*, *t1*, and *t2* are expressions denoting values of the same type, either type DATE—which is unlikely—or some specific TIMESTAMP type):

■ `FOR SYSTEM_TIME AS OF t`

Selects rows whose system time period contains *t*.

■ `FOR SYSTEM_TIME FROM t1 TO t2`

Selects rows whose system time period overlaps the closed:open period [*t1:t2*).

■ FOR SYSTEM_TIME BETWEEN *t1* AND *t2*

Selects rows whose system time period overlaps the closed:closed period [*t1:t2*]. Note that here for once SQL does make use of the closed:closed style, albeit implicitly.

system time period (SQL)   *See* system time.

system versioned table (SQL)   *See* system time.

———— ♦♦♦♦♦ ————

table predicate (SQL)   As noted elsewhere (*see* period), the fact that SQL has no direct way of preventing tables from being subject to the circumlocution problem, q.v., appears to mean that such tables aren't properly relational, because they don't seem to have anything corresponding to a proper relvar predicate.   To illustrate the point, consider table SP_FROM_TO (see Fig. 9). Note in particular that this table isn't guaranteed to be kept packed on DPERIOD.   So here's the obvious first attempt at a predicate—call it *P*—for this table:

> *If DTO is "the end of time," then supplier SNO has been able to supply part PNO ever since day DFROM (and not the day immediately before day DFROM) and will continue to be so until further notice; otherwise supplier SNO was able to supply part PNO throughout the period ("period p") from day DFROM to the day that's the immediate predecessor of day DTO, inclusive.*

Note that we can't extend this predicate by adding *and not throughout any period that properly includes period p*, precisely because the table isn't guaranteed to be kept packed on DPERIOD. (Though it is at least true that there can't be more than one row for any given combination of a supplier number, a part number, and some specific day, thanks to the applicable WITHOUT OVERLAPS constraint, q.v.)

Now, Fig. 9 shows SP_FROM_TO as containing a row—call it *r*—indicating that supplier S4 was able to supply part P4 throughout the interval [*d04:d08*] (or PERIOD (*d04,d09*), in SQL notation).   However, there are numerous ways of splitting that interval [*d04,d08*] up into smaller, nonoverlapping intervals.   Here are just a few of them:

■ [*d04:d04*]   [*d05:d05*]   [*d06:d06*]   [*d07:d07*]   [*d08:d08*]

■ [*d04:d04*]   [*d05:d05*]   [*d06:d06*]   [*d07:d08*]

■ [*d04:d05*]   [*d06:d06*]   [*d07:d07*]   [*d08:d08*]

■ [*d04:d05*]   [*d06:d07*]   [*d08:d08*]

■ [*d04:d06*]   [*d07:d08*]

And so on. It follows that it would be possible, without violating the WITHOUT OVERLAPS constraint, to replace row *r* by several different rows, and to do so, moreover, in several different ways. And every such possible replacement row—call it *r'*—would represent a true instantiation of predicate *P*. By *The Closed World Assumption* (q.v.), therefore, predicate *P* can't possibly be right—because that assumption, translated into SQL terms, says that row *r* appears in table *T* at time *t* **if and only if** *r* satisfies the predicate for *T* at time *t* (boldface for emphasis). In the case at hand, however, table SP_FROM_TO clearly isn't going to contain all of those possible rows *r'* at the same time—in fact it can't possibly do so, thanks to the WITHOUT OVERLAPS constraint—and so predicate *P* clearly isn't sufficient, in and of itself, to pin down just which rows do or don't appear in that table at any given time.

Here's another predicate we might consider (let's call it *P'*):

If DTO is "the end of time," then supplier SNO has been able to supply part PNO ever since day DFROM (and not the day immediately before day DFROM) and will continue to be so until further notice; otherwise supplier SNO was able to supply part PNO throughout the period ("period p") from day DFROM to the day that's the immediate predecessor of day DTO, inclusive, and hence—but only implicitly—throughout every period properly included in period p.

But predicate *P'* doesn't do the job either. To be specific, it's true—as it was with the previous attempt, predicate *P*—that if row *r* appears in the table, then row *r* necessarily satisfies this predicate; by contrast, however, it *isn't* true that if row *r* satisfies this predicate, then row *r* necessarily appears in the table.

So it seems to be quite difficult—in fact, it seems to be impossible (?)—to come up with a predicate that exactly characterizes table SP_FROM_TO. If such is indeed the case, then (to generalize from the example) it seems that certain SQL tables fail to correspond to any well defined predicate; equivalently, certain real world situations seem to be representable by a given SQL table in many different ways. This state of affairs would appear to constitute a rather serious departure from relational principles. (Of course, the same criticism would apply to relvars in **Tutorial D** as well, if they permitted the same kind of circumlocution.)

temporal Many concepts from conventional database theory have, or can be given, extended interpretations in the context of relations and relvars with interval attributes. Thus, the terminology used to refer to the concepts in question needs some corresponding extension as well; for example, the familiar term *join* is extended to *U_join*, q.v. Unfortunately, much of the literature uses the qualifier *temporal* for this purpose, as in (for example) *temporal join*; *temporal restriction*; *temporal projection*; *temporal FD*; *temporal MVD*; *temporal key*; *temporal superkey*; *temporal BCNF*; *temporal 3NF*; *temporal 4NF*; and so on. But the concepts denoted by these terms are by no means limited to applying only to temporal data as such, and use of the qualifier *temporal* in such contexts is therefore deprecated. *See also* **temporal operator**.

temporal database   A database containing at least one temporal relvar, q.v.
   Example: The suppliers-and-shipments database of either Fig. 6 or Fig. 8.

temporal interval type   An interval type defined over some temporal point type, q.v.

temporal operator   Deprecated term sometimes used to refer to any of the U_ operators
(U_JOIN, U_MINUS, etc.), q.v. Such terminology is deprecated because the operators aren't
limited to operating on temporal data as such. *See* **temporal** for further discussion.

temporal point type   A type such as DATE or TIME or TIMESTAMP, whose values represent
points in time ("time points") as such.

temporal relation   A relation whose heading contains at least one attribute of some temporal
type; in particular, the value of a given temporal relvar at a given time.
   Examples: With reference to Fig. 6, the relations that are the values of relvars S_SINCE
and S_DURING at any given time.

temporal relvar   A relvar whose heading contains at least one attribute of some temporal type
(implying that the corresponding predicate has at least one parameter of some temporal type); a
since relvar or a during relvar.

temporal type   Either a temporal point type or a temporal interval type.

temporal upward compatibility   The idea that it should be possible to convert a nontemporal
database into a temporal one by just "adding temporal support," while allowing existing
nontemporal applications to run unchanged against the now temporal database. In other words,
suppose we're given some nontemporal database *DB*, together with a set of applications that run
successfully on that database, and suppose we now want *DB* to evolve to include some temporal
features. Then it would be nice if we could add those features in such a way that those existing
applications can continue to run unchanged, and produce correct results, on that temporal version
of *DB*. If this goal is met, then temporal upward compatibility has been achieved.
   Unfortunately, it seems impossible to achieve such a goal without doing serious violence to
the relational model. What's more—and what might be more important in practice—it's easy to
see that such a goal is quite unrealistic (see "An Overview and Analysis of Proposals Based on
the TSQL2 Approach," by Hugh Darwen and C. J. Date, in *Date on Database: Writings
2000-2006*, Apress, 2006). The whole idea is thus now somewhat discredited.

TIME   A point type, assumed for the purposes of this dictionary to be system defined and to
have values that represent times of the day on a 24 hour clock, accurate to the second. In other
words, the scale, q.v., is one second, and the successor function is basically "next second,"
meaning "add one second to the given time" (i.e., it's a function that, given a TIME value *t*,

returns the TIME value that's the immediate successor of *t* according to conventional clock ordering). *Note:* Type TIME might very reasonably be not just a regular or "linear" point type but a cyclic one (*see* cyclic point type), though it isn't in SQL. Further details (of cyclic point types of any kind) are beyond the scope of this dictionary.

Examples: Here's an example of a TIME literal in **Tutorial D**:

```
TIME ( '18:33:45' )
```

("33 minutes and 45 seconds past 6:00 pm"). As noted in the introduction to this part of the dictionary, symbols such as *t01*, *t02*, etc. used in examples elsewhere can be thought of as shorthand for such literals (or—more likely, perhaps—possibly for literals of type some TIMESTAMP type, q.v.). *Note:* An SQL version of the literal shown above would look like this:

```
TIME '18:33:45'
```

time point   A value of some temporal point type, such as DATE or TIME or TIMESTAMP; a granule, q.v. The smallest possible time point is the chronon, q.v.

time quantum   A chronon, q.v.

timeline   Let *T* be a temporal point type. Then the set of all values of type *T*, in sequence according to the ordering associated with that type, can be regarded as the timeline corresponding to type *T* (equivalently, as the timeline whose scale is the scale associated with type *T*). The values returned by FIRST_*T* ( ) and LAST_*T* ( ) can be regarded as "the beginning of time" and "the end of time," respectively, with respect to type *T*, or equivalently with respect to that particular timeline or that particular scale.

Examples: 1. Let *T* be type DATE, q.v. Then the corresponding timeline is measured in days (i.e., the scale is one day); the beginning of time with respect to that timeline is "the first day," which is returned by FIRST_DATE ( ), and the end of time with respect to that timeline is "the last day," which is returned by LAST_DATE ( ). *Note:* As far as the SQL type DATE is concerned, the beginning of time is DATE '0001-01-01' and the end of time is DATE '9999-12-31' (both values given here in the form of SQL DATE literals, which by definition are accurate to the day). Note, however, that SQL does also support finer granularities with its various TIMESTAMP types. 2. Let *T* be type TIMESTAMP, q.v. Then the corresponding timeline—the chronon timeline—is measured in chronons (i.e., the scale is one chronon); the beginning of time with respect to that timeline is "the first chronon" (returned by FIRST_TIMESTAMP ( )), and the end of time with respect to that timeline is "the last chronon" (returned by LAST_TIMESTAMP ( )). *See* TIMESTAMP for further discussion.

TIMESTAMP   A point type, assumed for the purposes of this dictionary to be system defined and to have values that represent points on the chronon timeline. In other words, the scale, q.v., is one chronon, and the successor function is basically "next chronon," meaning "add one chronon to the given timestamp" (i.e., it's a function that, given a TIMESTAMP value *ts*, returns the TIMESTAMP value that's the immediate successor of *ts* on the chronon timeline). *Note:* If timestamps of some coarser scale are needed (say milliseconds), the mechanism sketched under inheritance (point types) can be used to achieve the desired effect.

Examples: Here's an example of a TIMESTAMP literal in **Tutorial D**:

```
TIMESTAMP ( '2014/8/25 18:33:45' )
```

("33 minutes and 45 seconds past 6:00 pm, August 25th, 2014"; we're assuming for simplicity in this example that the digits representing fractional parts of a second are all zeros and can therefore be omitted). As noted in the introduction to this part of the dictionary, symbols such as *t01, t02*, etc. used in examples elsewhere can be thought of as shorthand for such literals (or— less likely, perhaps—possibly for literals of type TIME, q.v.). *Note:* An SQL version of the literal shown above would look like this:

```
TIMESTAMP '2014-8-25 18:33:45'
```

Be aware, however, that SQL's TIMESTAMP "type" isn't really a type at all (in particular, it's not the specific point type that's defined in the present entry); rather, it's a type generator.

TO value (SQL)   *See* period.

transaction time   The original term, much used in the literature, for logged time, q.v. Note, however, that transaction times are usually assumed in the literature to be part of the table (or relvar) to which they apply, and further that the table (or relvar) in question is usually assumed to be a base one specifically; in other words, there's usually no distinct "transaction time table" (or relvar), and transaction times are usually assumed to be associated with base tables (or relvars) specifically. *Contrast* logged time relvar.

transaction timestamp (SQL)   *See* system time.

TUC   Temporal upward compatibility.

———— ♦♦♦♦♦ ————

U_   A prefix (short for USING), used generically to refer to a variety of operators and other constructs that are useful in connection with relations (and/or relvars) with interval attributes. By way of example, here's a slightly simplified and abbreviated definition for the operator U_MINUS, q.v.: Let *ACL* be a commalist of attribute names in which every attribute mentioned (a) is common to relations *r1* and *r2* and (b) is of some interval type. Then (and only then)

USING (*ACL*) : *r1* MINUS *r2* denotes the U_difference with respect to *ACL* between *r1* and *r2* (in that order), and it's shorthand for the following:

```
WITH ( t1 := UNPACK r1 ON ( ACL ) ,
       t2 := UNPACK r2 ON ( ACL ) ,
       t3 := t1 MINUS t2 ) :
PACK t3 ON ( ACL )
```

Points arising from this definition (but note that the following points apply to U_ operators and U_ constructs in general, mutatis mutandis, not just to U_MINUS as such, and hence should be considered an implicit part of every "U_..." entry in this dictionary):

- The qualification "with respect to *ACL*" can be omitted from the definition if the commalist *ACL* is understood.

- Suppose *ACL* contains the names of *all* of the interval valued attributes that are common to *r1* and *r2*. In general, then, there'll be a distinct U_difference between *r1* and *r2* (in that order) for each distinct permutation of the attributes in each distinct subset of *ACL*.

- Suppose *ACL* is empty. Then (a) the prefix "USING (*ACL*)" reduces to just "USING ( )" and can be omitted from the concrete syntax (together with the colon separator), and (b) the U_MINUS operation reduces to its regular, or conventional, "non U_" counterpart. In other words, regular MINUS is a special case of U_MINUS.

Note: SQL has no direct support for U_MINUS, nor indeed for any U_ operators or other U_ constructs.

U_ operator *See* U_.

U_assignment Let *ACL* be a commalist of attribute names such that every attribute mentioned (a) is interval valued and (b) is common to relvar *R* and relation *r*. Then (and only then) USING (*ACL*) : *R := r* denotes the U_assignment of relation *r* to relvar *R* with respect to *ACL*, and it's equivalent to the following:

```
R := PACK r ON ( ACL )
```

Note: Explicit U_assignment is defined mainly for completeness; in practice, updates are much more likely to be done by means of U_INSERT and/or U_DELETE and/or U_UPDATE, q.v. *See also* PORTION.

U_comparison Let relations *r1* and *r2* be of the same type *T*, and let *ACL* be a commalist of attribute names in which every attribute mentioned (a) is one of type *T*'s component attributes and (b) is of some interval type. Then (and only then) the expression USING (*ACL*) : *r1* theta *r2* (where *theta* is any of the regular relational comparison operators "=", "≠", "⊆", "⊂", "⊇", or "⊃") denotes a U_comparison with respect to *ACL* between *r1* and *r2*, and it's equivalent to the following:

```
( UNPACK r1 ON ( ACL ) ) theta ( UNPACK r2 ON ( ACL ) )
```

Example: Let *r1* and *r2* be as follows:

r1

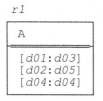

r2

Then *r1* = *r2* is obviously false, but USING (A) : *r1* = *r2* is true. *Note:* When (as in this example) *theta* is "=", the U_comparison reduces to U_equality, q.v.

U_COMPOSE   *See* U_composition.

U_composition   1. (*Dyadic case*) Let relations *r1* and *r2* be joinable, and let *ACL* be a commalist of attribute names in which every attribute mentioned (a) is an attribute of both *r1* and *r2* and (b) is of some interval type. Then (and only then) the expression USING (*ACL*) : *r1* COMPOSE *r2* denotes the U_composition with respect to *ACL* of *r1* and *r2*, and it's equivalent to the following:

```
WITH ( t1 := UNPACK r1 ON ( ACL ) ,
       t2 := UNPACK r2 ON ( ACL ) ,
       t3 := t1 COMPOSE t2 ) :
PACK t3 ON ( ACL )
```

2. (*N-adic case*) Let relations *r1*, *r2*, ..., *rn* (*n* ≥ 0) be *n*-way joinable, and let *ACL* be a commalist of attribute names in which every attribute mentioned (a) is an attribute of each of *r1*, *r2*, ..., *rn*, and (b) is of some interval type. Then (and only then) the expression USING (*ACL*) : COMPOSE {*r1,r2,...,rn*} denotes the U_composition with respect to *ACL* of *r1*, *r2*, ..., *rn*, and it's equivalent to the following:

```
WITH ( t1 := UNPACK r1 ON ( ACL ) ,
       t2 := UNPACK r2 ON ( ACL ) ,
       ...................... ,
       tn := UNPACK rn ON ( ACL ) ,
       tz := COMPOSE { t1 , t2 , ... , tn } ) :
PACK tz ON ( ACL )
```

U_DELETE   1. Let *R* be a relvar and let *ACL* be a commalist of attribute names in which every attribute mentioned (a) is one of *R*'s component attributes and (b) is of some interval type. Then (and only then) USING (*ACL*) : DELETE *R* WHERE *bx* denotes a U_DELETE WHERE (with respect to *ACL* and *bx*) on *R*, and it's equivalent to the following:

```
R := USING ( ACL ) : R WHERE NOT ( bx )
```

2. Let relvar *R* and relation *r* be of the same type *T*, and let *ACL* be a commalist of attribute names in which every attribute mentioned (a) is one of type *T*'s component attributes and (b) is of some interval type. Then (and only then) USING (*ACL*) : DELETE *R r* denotes the U_DELETE (with respect to *ACL*) of *r* from *R*, and it's equivalent to the following:

```
R := USING ( ACL ) : R MINUS r
```

Note: Because operations of the form USING (*ACL*) : DELETE *R* WHERE *bx* are so much more common in practice than ones of the form USING (*ACL*) : DELETE *R r*, the unqualified name "U_DELETE" is usually taken to refer to a U_DELETE WHERE operation rather than a U_DELETE as such. *Caveat lector.* Note too that an "included" version of U_DELETE ("included U_DELETE") is also defined (*see* **included DELETE** in Part I of this dictionary). The syntax is as for U_DELETE—not U_DELETE WHERE—except that I_DELETE appears in place of DELETE; likewise, the expansion is as for U_DELETE, except that I_MINUS appears in place of MINUS.

Examples: Consider a request to remove from the database of Fig. 8 the proposition "Supplier S4 was able to supply part P4 on days 5, 6, and 7." Here's a formulation using U_DELETE WHERE:

```
USING ( DURING ) :
DELETE SP_DURING WHERE SNO = SNO('S4') AND PNO = PNO('P4')
                 AND DURING ⊆ INTERVAL_DATE ( [ d05 : d07 ] )
```

Here by contrast is a formulation using U_DELETE without a WHERE:

```
USING ( DURING ) :
DELETE SP_DURING
       RELATION { TUPLE { SNO SNO('S4') , PNO PNO('P4') ,
                          DURING INTERVAL_DATE ( [ d05 : d07 ] } }
```

Note: In fact, however, this particular update can alternatively be achieved using a regular DELETE with a PORTION specification (i.e., without using U_DELETE at all):

```
DELETE SP_DURING WHERE SNO = SNO('S4') AND PNO = PNO('P4') :
       PORTION { DURING { INTERVAL_DATE ( [ d05 : d07 ] ) } } ;
```

U_DELETE WHERE   *See* U_DELETE.

U_difference   Let relations *r1* and *r2* be of the same type *T*, and let *ACL* be a commalist of attribute names in which every attribute mentioned (a) is one of type *T*'s component attributes and (b) is of some interval type. Then (and only then) the expression USING (*ACL*) : *r1* MINUS *r2* denotes the U_difference with respect to *ACL* between *r1* and *r2* (in that order), and it's equivalent to the following:

```
WITH ( t1 := UNPACK r1 ON ( ACL ) ,
       t2 := UNPACK r2 ON ( ACL ) ,
       t3 := t1 MINUS t2 ) :
PACK t3 ON ( ACL )
```

Example: Given the sample values shown for relvars S_DURING and SP_DURING in Fig. 8, the expression

```
USING ( DURING ) : S_DURING MINUS SP_DURING { SNO , DURING }
```

yields:

SNO	DURING
S2	[d07:d07]
S3	[d03:d04]
S5	[d02:d99]
S6	[d04:d04]

U_disjoint union   Let relations *r1* and *r2* be of the same type *T*, and let *ACL* be a commalist of attribute names in which every attribute mentioned (a) is one of type *T*'s component attributes and (b) is of some interval type. Then (and only then) the expression USING (*ACL*) : *r1* D_UNION *r2* denotes the U_disjoint union with respect to *ACL* of *r1* and *r2*, and it's equivalent to the following:

```
WITH ( t1 := UNPACK r1 ON ( ACL ) ,
       t2 := UNPACK r2 ON ( ACL ) ,
       t3 := t1 D_UNION t2 ) :
PACK t3 ON ( ACL )
```

Note: An *n*-adic version of this operator could also be defined if desired.

U_EQD   U_equality dependency.

U_equality   *See* U_comparison.

U_equality dependency An expression of the form USING (*ACL*) : *rx* = *ry*, where *rx* and *ry* are relational expressions of the same type and *ACL* is a commalist of attribute names such that every attribute mentioned (a) is interval valued and (b) is common to the relations denoted by *rx* and *ry*. It can be read as "The relations obtained by unpacking *rx* and *ry* on *ACL* are equal." An important special case is as follows: Let *R1* and *R2* be relvars, not necessarily distinct. Let *X1* and *X2* be subsets of the heading of *R1* and the heading of *R2*, respectively, such that there exists a possibly empty set of attribute renamings on *R1* that maps *X1* into *X1'*, say, where *X1'* and *X2* contain exactly the same attributes (in other words, *X1'* and *X2* are in fact one and the same). Further, let *R1* and *R2* be subject to the constraint that, at all times, (a) every tuple *t1* in the result of unpacking *R1* on *ACL* has an *X1'* value that's the *X2* value for at least one tuple *t2* in the result of unpacking *R2* on *ACL* at the time in question, and (b) every tuple *t2* in the result of unpacking *R2* on *ACL* has an *X2* value that's the *X1'* value for at least one tuple *t1* in the result of unpacking *R1* on *ACL* at the time in question. Then that constraint is a U_equality dependency (U_EQD for short)—very loosely, a U_EQD "on" relvars *R1* and *R2*.

Example: The suppliers-and-shipments database (either the Fig. 6 or the Fig. 8 version) is subject to the constraint that whenever a supplier is under contract, that supplier must have some status and vice versa. Here's a formulation of that constraint for the database of Fig. 8:

```
CONSTRAINT U_EQDX USING ( DURING ) :
            S_DURING = S_STATUS_DURING { SNO , DURING } ;
```

This constraint is a U_EQD "on" S_DURING and S_STATUS_DURING; in effect, it says that each of S_DURING and S_STATUS_DURING has a foreign U_key, q.v., that references the other, where the foreign U_keys in question are both defined with respect to DURING.

U_exclusive union 1. (*Dyadic case*) Let relations *r1* and *r2* be of the same type *T*, and let *ACL* be a commalist of attribute names in which every attribute mentioned (a) is one of type *T*'s component attributes and (b) is of some interval type. Then (and only then) the expression USING (*ACL*) : *r1* XUNION *r2* denotes the U_exclusive union with respect to *ACL* of *r1* and *r2*, and it's equivalent to the following:

```
WITH ( t1 := UNPACK r1 ON ( ACL ) ,
       t2 := UNPACK r2 ON ( ACL ) ,
       t3 := t1 XUNION t2 ) :
PACK t3 ON ( ACL )
```

2. (*N-adic case*) Let relations *r1*, *r2*, ..., *rn* (*n* ≥ 0) be all of the same type *T*, and let *ACL* be a commalist of attribute names in which every attribute mentioned (a) is one of type *T*'s component attributes and (b) is of some interval type. Then (and only then) the expression USING (*ACL*) : XUNION {*r1,r2,...,rn*} denotes the U_exclusive union with respect to *ACL* of *r1*, *r2*, ..., *rn*, and it's equivalent to the following:

```
WITH ( t1 := UNPACK r1 ON ( ACL ) ,
       t2 := UNPACK r2 ON ( ACL ) ,
       . . . . . . . . . . . . . . . . . . . . . . . ,
       tn := UNPACK rn ON ( ACL ) ,
       tz := XUNION { t1 , t2 , ... , tn } ) :
PACK tz ON ( ACL )
```

U_EXTEND *See* U_extension.

U_extension Let *r* be a relation, and let *ACL* be a commalist of attribute names in which every attribute mentioned (a) is an attribute of *r* and (b) is of some interval type. Then (and only then) the expression USING (*ACL*) : EXTEND *r* : {*A* := *exp*} denotes a U_extension with respect to *ACL* of *r*, and it's equivalent to the following:

```
WITH ( t1 := UNPACK r ON ( ACL ) ,
       t2 := EXTEND t1 : { A := exp } ) :
PACK t2 ON ( ACL )
```

Examples: Let relation *r* contain just two tuples, as follows (note, incidentally, that this relation is neither packed nor unpacked on DURING):

SNO	DURING
S2	[d01:d05]
S2	[d03:d04]

Then the following expression returns a relation of cardinality five:

```
USING ( DURING )  : EXTEND r : { X := POINT FROM DURING }
```

Here's the result:

SNO	DURING	X
S2	[d01:d01]	d01
S2	[d02:d02]	d02
S2	[d03:d03]	d03
S2	[d04:d04]	d04
S2	[d05:d05]	d05

By contrast, the following expression returns a relation of cardinality one:

```
USING ( DURING )  : EXTEND r : { Y := COUNT ( DURING ) }
```

Here's the result:

SNO	DURING	Y
S2	[*d01:d05*]	1

U_GROUP *See* U_grouping.

U_grouping Let *r* be a relation, let *ACL* be a commalist of attribute names in which every attribute mentioned (a) is an attribute of *r* and (b) is of some interval type, let *BCL* be a commalist of attribute names in which every attribute mentioned is an attribute of *r* not mentioned in *ACL*, and let *X* be an attribute name that's distinct from that of every attribute of *r* apart possibly from those attributes mentioned in *BCL*. Then (and only then) the expression USING (*ACL*) : *r* GROUP {*BCL*} AS *X* denotes a U_grouping with respect to *ACL* of *r* on *BCL*, and it's equivalent to the following:

```
WITH ( t1 := UNPACK r ON ( ACL ) ,
       t2 := t1 GROUP { BCL } AS X ) :
PACK t2 ON ( ACL )
```

Example: Let relation *r* be as follows:

SNO	PNO	DURING
S2	P1	[*d08:d10*]
S2	P2	[*d09:d10*]
S4	P2	[*d07:d09*]
S4	P4	[*d07:d08*]

Then the expression

```
USING ( DURING ) : r GROUP { PNO } AS PNO_REL
```

yields the following result:

SNO	DURING	PNO_REL
S2	[*d08:d08*]	PNO ─── P1
S2	[*d09:d10*]	PNO ─── P1 P2

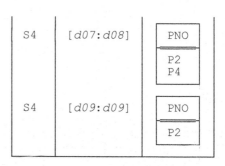

U_included difference   Let relations *r1* and *r2* be of the same type *T*, and let *ACL* be a commalist of attribute names in which every attribute mentioned (a) is one of type *T*'s component attributes and (b) is of some interval type. Then (and only then) the expression USING (*ACL*) : *r1* I_MINUS *r2* denotes the U_included difference with respect to *ACL* between *r1* and *r2* (in that order), and it's equivalent to the following:

```
WITH ( t1 := UNPACK r1 ON ( ACL ) ,
       t2 := UNPACK r2 ON ( ACL ) ,
       t3 := t1 I_MINUS t2 ) :
PACK t3 ON ( ACL )
```

U_INSERT   Let relvar *R* and relation *r* be of the same type *T*, and let *ACL* be a commalist of attribute names in which every attribute mentioned (a) is one of type *T*'s component attributes and (b) is of some interval type. Then (and only then) USING (*ACL*) : INSERT *R r* denotes the U_INSERT (with respect to *ACL*) of *r* into *R*, and it's equivalent to the following:

```
R := USING ( ACL ) : R UNION r
```

Note: A "disjoint" version of U_INSERT ("disjoint U_INSERT") is also defined (*see* disjoint INSERT in Part I of this dictionary). The syntax is as for U_INSERT, except that D_INSERT appears in place of INSERT; likewise, the expansion is as for U_INSERT, except that D_UNION appears in place of UNION.

Example: Let relvar SP_DURING be as shown in Fig. 6. Then the following U_INSERT—

```
USING ( DURING ) :
INSERT SP_DURING
       RELATION { TUPLE { SNO     SNO('S2') ,
                          PNO     PNO('P1') ,
                          DURING  INTERVAL_DATE ( [ d03 : d06 ] ) } } ;
```

—will yield the following result (the only change is in the tuple for S2 and P1):

SP_DURING

SNO	PNO	DURING
S2	P1	[d02:d06]
S2	P2	[d03:d03]
S3	P5	[d05:d07]
S4	P2	[d06:d09]
S4	P4	[d04:d08]
S6	P3	[d03:d03]
S6	P3	[d05:d05]

U_INTERSECT *See* U_intersection.

U_intersection 1. (*Dyadic case*) Let relations *r1* and *r2* be of the same type *T*, and let *ACL* be a commalist of attribute names in which every attribute mentioned (a) is one of type *T*'s component attributes and (b) is of some interval type. Then (and only then) the expression USING (*ACL*) : *r1* INTERSECT *r2* denotes the U_intersection with respect to *ACL* of *r1* and *r2*, and it's equivalent to the following:

```
WITH ( t1 := UNPACK r1 ON ( ACL ) ,
       t2 := UNPACK r2 ON ( ACL ) ,
       t3 := t1 INTERSECT t2 ) :
PACK t3 ON ( ACL )
```

2. (*N-adic case*) Let relations *r1*, *r2*, ..., *rn* (*n* ≥ 0) be all of the same type *T*, and let *ACL* be a commalist of attribute names in which every attribute mentioned (a) is one of type *T*'s component attributes and (b) is of some interval type. Then (and only then) the expression USING (*ACL*) : INTERSECT {*r1,r2,...,rn*} denotes the U_intersection with respect to *ACL* of *r1*, *r2*, ..., *rn*, and it's equivalent to the following:

```
WITH ( t1 := UNPACK r1 ON ( ACL ) ,
       t2 := UNPACK r2 ON ( ACL ) ,
       ....................... ,
       tn := UNPACK rn ON ( ACL ) ,
       tz := INTERSECT { t1 , t2 , ... , tn } ) :
PACK tz ON ( ACL )
```

Example (dyadic case): Given the sample values shown in Fig. 6, the expression

```
USING ( DURING ) : SP_DURING { SNO , DURING } INTERSECT
                   S_STATUS_DURING { SNO , DURING }
```

yields:

SNO	DURING
S2	[d02:d04]
S4	[d04:d07]
S6	[d03:d03]
S6	[d05:d05]

Note: U_intersection is a special case of U_join, q.v.

U_JD U_join dependency.

U_JOIN *See* U_join.

U_join 1. (*Dyadic case*) Let relations *r1* and *r2* be joinable, and let *ACL* be a commalist of attribute names in which every attribute mentioned (a) is an attribute of both *r1* and *r2* and (b) is of some interval type. Then (and only then) the expression USING (*ACL*) : *r1* JOIN *r2* denotes the U_join with respect to *ACL* of *r1* and *r2*, and it's equivalent to the following:

```
WITH ( t1 := UNPACK r1 ON ( ACL ) ,
       t2 := UNPACK r2 ON ( ACL ) ,
       t3 := t1 JOIN t2 ) :
PACK t3 ON ( ACL )
```

2. (*N-adic case*) Let relations *r1*, *r2*, ..., *rn* ($n \geq 0$) be *n*-way joinable, and let *ACL* be a commalist of attribute names in which every attribute mentioned (a) is an attribute of each of *r1*, *r2*, ..., *rn*, and (b) is of some interval type. Then (and only then) the expression USING (*ACL*) : JOIN {*r1*,*r2*,...,*rn*} denotes the U_join with respect to *ACL* of *r1*, *r2*, ..., *rn*, and it's equivalent to the following:

```
WITH ( t1 := UNPACK r1 ON ( ACL ) ,
       t2 := UNPACK r2 ON ( ACL ) ,
       ...................... ,
       tn := UNPACK rn ON ( ACL ) ,
       tz := JOIN { t1 , t2 , ... , tn } ) :
PACK tz ON ( ACL )
```

Example (dyadic case): With reference to Fig. 8, the expression

```
USING ( DURING ) : S_STATUS_DURING JOIN SP_DURING
```

is a possible formulation of the query "Get (SNO, STATUS, PNO, DURING) tuples such that DURING denotes a maximal interval of days throughout which supplier SNO (a) had status STATUS and (b) was able to supply part PNO."

Note: If *r1* and *r2* are of the same type, then U_join degenerates to U_intersection, q.v. *See also* U_TIMES.

U_join dependency Let *H* be a heading, and let *ACL* be a commalist of attribute names in which every attribute mentioned (a) is one of the attributes in *H* and (b) is of some interval type. Then a U_join dependency (U_JD) with respect to *ACL* and *H* is an expression of the form USING (*ACL*) : ✿{*X1,X2,...,Xn*}, such that the set theory union of *X1*, *X2*, ..., *Xn* is equal to *H*. *Note:* The phrase *U_JD with respect to ACL and H* can be abbreviated to *U_JD with respect to ACL* if *H* is understood; to *U_JD with respect to H* if *ACL* is understood; and to just *U_JD* if *ACL* and *H* are both understood.

Let relation *r* have heading *H* and let USING (*ACL*) : ✿{*X1,X2,...,Xn*} be a U_JD, *UJ* say, with respect to *ACL* and *H*. If *r* is U_equal to the U_join of its U_projections on *X1*, *X2*, ..., *Xn*, then *r* satisfies *UJ*; otherwise *r* violates *UJ*. *Note:* The U_equality comparison, the U_join, and the U_projections mentioned in this definition must all be with respect to *ACL* (i.e., they must all have a prefix of the form "USING (*ACL*) :").

Now let relvar *R* have heading *H*. Then *R* is subject to the U_JD *UJ*—equivalently, the U_JD *UJ* holds in *R*—if and only if every relation *r* that can ever be assigned to *R* satisfies that U_JD *UJ*. The U_JDs that hold in relvar *R* are the U_JDs of *R*, and they serve as constraints on *R*.

Note that U_JDs are defined with respect to some heading, not with respect to some relation or some relvar. Note too that from a formal point of view, a U_JD is just an expression: an expression that, when interpreted with respect to some specific relation, becomes a proposition that, by definition, evaluates to either TRUE or FALSE. Now, it's common informally to define USING (*ACL*) : ✿{*X1,X2,...,Xn*} to be a U_JD only if it actually holds in the pertinent relvar—but that definition leaves no way of saying a given U_JD fails to hold in some relvar, because, by that definition, a U_JD that fails to hold isn't a U_JD in the first place. Note finally that it's immediate from the definition that relvar *R* can be nonloss decomposed into its U_projections (using *ACL*) on *X1*, *X2*, ..., and *Xn* if and only if the U_JD USING (*ACL*) : ✿{*X1,X2,...,Xn*} holds in *R*.

U_key Let *ACL* and *K* be commalists of attribute names of relvar *R*, such that every attribute mentioned in *ACL* is also mentioned in *K*. Then (and only then) the specification

```
USING ( ACL ) : KEY { K }
```

—part of the definition of *R*—defines {*K*} to be a U_key for relvar *R*, and it's shorthand for all three of the following in combination:

```
PACKED ON ( ACL )
WHEN UNPACKED ON ( ACL ) THEN KEY { K }
KEY { K }
```

See PACKED ON; WHEN / THEN; *see also* foreign U_key.

   Examples: See the definitions of relvars S_DURING, S_STATUS_DURING, and SP_DURING in Fig. 7.

U_key constraint   A generalized form of key constraint (see Part I of this dictionary) in which the role usually played by a key as such is played by a U_key (q.v.) instead.

U_MATCHING   *See* U_semijoin.

U_MINUS   *See* U_difference.

U_operator   Same as U_ operator.

U_product   Let relations *r1* and *r2* have no attribute names in common; then (and only then) the expression USING ( ) : *r1* TIMES *r2* denotes the U_product of *r1* and *r2*. Note, however, that this expression simply and necessarily reduces to the regular cartesian product *r1* TIMES *r2*. *Note:* An *n*-adic version of this operator could also be defined if desired.

U_projection   Let *r* be a relation, let *ACL* be a commalist of attribute names in which every attribute mentioned (a) is an attribute of *r* and (b) is of some interval type, and let *BCL* be a commalist of attribute names such that every attribute mentioned in *ACL* is also mentioned in *BCL*. Then (and only then) the expression USING (*ACL*) : *r* {*BCL*} denotes the U_projection with respect to *ACL* of *r* on *BCL*, and it's equivalent to the following:

```
WITH ( t1 := UNPACK r1 ON ( ACL ) ,
       t2 := r2 { BCL } ) :
PACK t2 ON ( ACL )
```

Example: With reference to Fig. 8, the expression

```
USING ( DURING ) : SP_DURING { SNO , DURING }
```

is a possible formulation of the query "Get (SNO,DURING) pairs such that DURING designates a maximal interval of days during which supplier SNO was able to supply at least one part."

U_RENAME   *See* U_renaming.

U_renaming   Let *r* be a relation, let *ACL* be a commalist of attribute names in which every attribute mentioned (a) is an attribute of *r* and (b) is of some interval type, and let *r* have an attribute called *A*, not mentioned in *ACL*, and no attribute called *B*. Then (and only then) the expression USING (*ACL*) : *r* RENAME {*A* AS *B*} denotes an (attribute) U_renaming of *r*, and it's equivalent to the following:

```
WITH ( t1 := UNPACK r ON ( ACL ) ,
       t2 := t1 RENAME { A AS B } ) :
PACK t2 ON ( ACL )
```

Note: In fact, the foregoing expression reduces to just:

```
PACK ( r RENAME { A AS B } ) ON ( ACL )
```

U_restriction   Let *r* be a relation, let *ACL* be a commalist of attribute names in which every attribute mentioned (a) is an attribute of *r* and (b) is of some interval type, and let *bx* be a restriction condition on *r*. Then (and only then) the expression USING (*ACL*) : *r* WHERE *bx* denotes the U_restriction with respect to *ACL* of *r* according to *bx*, and it's equivalent to the following:

```
WITH ( t1 := UNPACK r ON ( ACL ) ,
       t2 := r WHERE bx ) :
PACK t2 ON ( ACL )
```

Examples: Suppose relvar S_DURING contains just two tuples, as follows:

SNO	DURING
S2	[d01:d03]
S2	[d05:d09]

Then the following expression—

```
USING ( DURING ) :
        S_DURING WHERE DURING ⊆ INTERVAL_DATE ( [ d03 : d07 ] )
```

—returns this result:

SNO	DURING
S2	[d03:d03]
S2	[d05:d07]

U_semidifference   Let relations *r1* and *r2* be joinable, and let *ACL* be a commalist of attribute names in which every attribute mentioned (a) is an attribute of both *r1* and *r2* and (b) is of some interval type. Then (and only then) the expression USING (*ACL*) : *r1* NOT MATCHING *r2* denotes the U_semidifference with respect to *ACL* between *r1* and *r2* (in that order), and it's equivalent to the following:

```
WITH ( t1 := UNPACK r1 ON ( ACL ) ,
       t2 := UNPACK r2 ON ( ACL ) ,
       t3 := t1 NOT MATCHING t2 ) :
PACK t3 ON ( ACL )
```

In other words, it's shorthand for:

```
USING ( ACL ) : ( r1 MINUS ( USING ( ACL ) : r1 MATCHING r2 ) )
```

(a U_difference in which the second operand is a U_semijoin).

U_semijoin   Let relations *r1* and *r2* be joinable, and let *ACL* be a commalist of attribute names in which every attribute mentioned (a) is an attribute of both *r1* and *r2* and (b) is of some interval type. Then (and only then) the expression USING (*ACL*) : *r1* MATCHING *r2* denotes the U_semijoin with respect to *ACL* of *r1* and *r2*, and it's equivalent to the following:

```
WITH ( t1 := UNPACK r1 ON ( ACL ) ,
       t2 := UNPACK r2 ON ( ACL ) ,
       t3 := t1 MATCHING t2 ) :
PACK t3 ON ( ACL )
```

In other words, it's shorthand for:

```
USING ( ACL ) : ( ( USING ( ACL ) : r1 JOIN r2 ) { ACL } )
```

(a U_projection of a U_join).

U_summarization   Let relations *r1* and *r2* be such that the heading of *r2* is some subset of that of *r1*, and let *ACL* be a commalist of attribute names in which every attribute mentioned (a) is an attribute of *r2* (and therefore of *r1* as well) and (b) is of some interval type. Then (and only then) the expression USING (*ACL*) : SUMMARIZE *r1* PER {*r2*} : { *B* := *exp* } denotes a U_summarization of *r1* (with respect to *ACL*) according to *r2*, and it's equivalent to the following:

```
WITH ( t1 := UNPACK r1 ON ( ACL ) ,
       t2 := UNPACK r2 ON ( ACL ) ,
       t3 := SUMMARIZE t1 PER ( t2 ) : { B := exp } ) :
PACK t3 ON ( ACL )
```

Example: With reference to Fig. 8, consider the following query: At any given time, if there are any shipments at all at that time, then there's some part number *pmax* such that, at that time, (a) at least one supplier is able to supply part *pmax*, but (b) no supplier is able to supply any part with a part number greater than *pmax*. So, for each part number that has ever been such a *pmax* value, get that part number together with the maximal interval(s) of days during which it actually was that *pmax* value. Here's a possible formulation:

```
USING ( DURING ) : SUMMARIZE SP_DURING PER ( SP_DURING { DURING } ) :
                                          { PMAX := MAX ( PNO ) }
```

Explanation: Relations *r1* and *r2* here are the current value of SP_DURING and the current value of the projection of SP_DURING on {DURING}, respectively. These relations are each unpacked on DURING. Then, each DURING value—by definition a unit interval— in the unpacked form of *r2* has appended to it the corresponding PMAX value, which is computed by examining all tuples with that DURING value in the unpacked form of *r1*; the result of this step is a relation with attributes DURING and PMAX. That relation is then packed on DURING.

U_SUMMARIZE   *See* U_summarization.

U_TIMES   *See* U_product.

U_UNGROUP   *See* U_ungrouping.

U_ungrouping   Let *r* be a relation, let *r* have a relation valued attribute *B*, and let *ACL* be a commalist of attribute names in which every attribute mentioned (a) is an attribute of *r* and (b) is of some interval type. Then (and only then) the expression USING (*ACL*) : *r* UNGROUP *B* denotes the U_ungrouping with respect to *ACL* of *r* on *B*, and it's equivalent to the following:

```
WITH ( t1 := UNPACK r ON ( ACL ) ,
       t2 := t1 UNGROUP B ) :
PACK t2 ON ( ACL )
```

Example: Let *r* be the relation shown as the result in the example under **grouping**. Then the expression

```
USING ( DURING ) : r UNGROUP PNO_REL
```

returns the relation used as input in that example.

U_UNION   *See* U_union.

U_union   1. (*Dyadic case*) Let relations *r1* and *r2* be of the same type *T*, and let *ACL* be a commalist of attribute names in which every attribute mentioned (a) is one of type *T*'s component attributes and (b) is of some interval type. Then (and only then) the expression USING (*ACL*) : *r1* UNION *r2* denotes the U_union with respect to *ACL* of *r1* and *r2*, and it's equivalent to the following:

```
WITH ( t1 := UNPACK r1 ON ( ACL ) ,
       t2 := UNPACK r2 ON ( ACL ) ,
       t3 := t1 UNION t2 ) :
PACK t3 ON ( ACL )
```

Note: In fact, the foregoing expression reduces to just:

```
PACK ( r1 UNION r2 ) ON ( ACL )
```

2. (*N-adic case*) Let relations *r1*, *r2*, ..., *rn* ($n \geq 0$) be all of the same type *T*, and let *ACL* be a commalist of attribute names in which every attribute mentioned (a) is one of type *T*'s component attributes and (b) is of some interval type. Then (and only then) the expression USING (*ACL*) : UNION {*r1,r2,...,rn*} denotes the U_union with respect to *ACL* of *r1*, *r2*, ..., *rn*, and it's equivalent to the following:

```
WITH ( t1 := UNPACK r1 ON ( ACL ) ,
       t2 := UNPACK r2 ON ( ACL ) ,
       ...................... ,
       tn := UNPACK rn ON ( ACL ) ,
       tz := UNION { t1 , t2 , ... , tn } ) :
PACK tz ON ( ACL )
```

Note: In fact, the foregoing expression reduces to just:

```
PACK ( UNION { r1 , r2 , ... , rn } ) ON ( ACL )
```

Example (dyadic case): Given the sample values shown in Fig. 6, the expression

```
USING ( DURING ) :
   ( S_STATUS_DURING WHERE SNO = SNO('S4') ) { SNO , DURING }
     UNION
   ( SP_DURING WHERE SNO = SNO('S4') ) { SNO , DURING }
```

(a U_union of two regular projections) yields:

SNO	DURING
S4	[*d04:d09*]

U_UPDATE   Let *R* be a relvar and let *ACL* be a commalist of attribute names in which every attribute mentioned (a) is one of *R*'s component attributes and (b) is of some interval type. Then (and only then)

```
USING ( ACL ) : UPDATE R WHERE bx : { attribute assignments }
```

denotes a U_UPDATE (with respect to *ACL* and *bx*) on *R*, and it's equivalent to the following:

```
WITH ( t1 := UNPACK R ON ( ACL ) ,
       t2 := t1 WHERE NOT ( bx ) ,
       t3 := t1 MINUS t2 ,
       t4 := EXTEND t3 : { attribute assignments } ,
       t5 := t2 UNION t4 ) :
R := PACK t5 ON ( ACL )
```

Example: Consider a request to update the database of Fig. 8 to replace the proposition "Supplier S4 was able to supply part P2 on day 9" by the proposition "Supplier S4 was able to supply part P2 on day 10": Here's a formulation using U_UPDATE:

```
USING ( DURING ) :
UPDATE SP_DURING WHERE SNO = SNO('S4') AND PNO = PNO('P2')
                 AND DURING = INTERVAL_DATE ( [ d09 : d09 ] ) :
            { DURING := INTERVAL_DATE ( [ d10 : d10 ] ) } ;
```

Note: In fact, however, this particular update can alternatively be achieved using a regular UPDATE with a PORTION specification (i.e., without using U_UPDATE at all):

```
UPDATE SP_DURING WHERE SNO = SNO('S4') AND PNO = PNO('P2') :
       PORTION { DURING { INTERVAL_DATE ( [ d09 : d09 ] ) } } :
       { DURING := INTERVAL_DATE ( [ d10 : d10 ] ) } ;
```

U_update   A U_assignment, U_INSERT, disjoint U_INSERT, U_DELETE, included U_DELETE, or U_UPDATE operation, q.v.

U_XUNION   *See* U_exclusive union.

unfolding   Term sometimes used as a synonym for unpacking, q.v. (or for an operation of the same general nature as unpacking).

union (interval theory)   Let $i1 = [b1:e1]$ and $i2 = [b2:e2]$ be intervals of the same type. Then:

■ If *i1* MERGES *i2* is true, then (and only then) the expression *i1* UNION *i2* denotes the union of *i1* and *i2*, and it returns $[\text{MIN}\{b1,b2\}:\text{MAX}\{e1,e2\}]$.

■ Otherwise *i1* UNION *i2* is undefined.

Observe that the foregoing definition guarantees that the result (when it's defined) isn't just some set of points but is, rather, an interval specifically. *Note:* SQL has no direct support for the interval union operator.

Example: Let *i1* and *i2* be [*d02:d07*] and [*d04:d10*], respectively. Then *i1* UNION *i2* is [*d02:d10*]. By contrast, let *i1* and *i2* be [*d02:d04*] and [*d07:d10*], respectively; then *i1* UNION *i2* is undefined. Incidentally, note that interval union, unlike set theory union (and unlike the union operator of the relational algebra also, come to that) has no corresponding identity value. (If it had one, it would be the empty interval of the applicable type, and intervals are never empty.) However, the operator is both commutative and associative.

unit interval   An interval containing exactly one point. In other words, the interval [*b*:*e*] is a unit interval if and only if *b* = *e*. *See also* **point** extractor.

unitemporal   *See* bitemporal.

universal interval   The interval containing all of the points of the pertinent point type; in other words, the interval

```
[ FIRST_T ( ) : LAST_T ( ) ]
```

(where *T* is the point type in question). *Note:* This definition needs some slight refinement in the case where the point type in question is cyclic. Further details are beyond the scope of this dictionary.

UNPACK   *See* unpacking. *Note:* SQL has no direct support for the UNPACK operator.

unpacked constraint   Term that might be used (but usually isn't) to mean a WHEN / THEN constraint, q.v.
    Examples: See the example under WHEN / THEN.

unpacked form   1. Let relation *r* have interval attributes *A1, A2, ..., An* ($n \geq 0$). Then *r* is in unpacked form with respect to *A1, A2, ..., An* if and only if *r* is equal to the result of evaluating the expression UNPACK *r* ON (*A1,A2,...,An*). 2. Let relvar *R* have interval attributes *A1, A2, ..., An* ($n \geq 0$). Then *R* is in unpacked form with respect to *A1, A2, ..., An* if and only if every relation *r* that can ever be assigned to *R* is in unpacked form with respect to *A1, A2, ..., An*. *Note:* The phrase *unpacked form with respect to A1, A2, ..., An* can be abbreviated to just *unpacked form* if the attributes *A1, A2, ..., An* are understood. *See* unpacking for examples and further discussion.

unpacking   1. (*Single-attribute UNPACK*) Let relation *r* have an interval attribute *A*. Then (and only then) the expression UNPACK *r* ON (*A*) denotes the unpacking of *r* on *A*, and it's equivalent to the following:

```
WITH ( r1 := r GROUP { A } AS X ,
       r2 := EXTEND r1 : { X := EXPAND ( X ) } ) :
r2 UNGROUP X
```

2. (*Multiattribute UNPACK*): Let relation *r* have interval attributes *A1, A2, ..., An* (*n* > 1). Then (and only then) the expression UNPACK *r* ON (*A1, A2, ..., An*) denotes the unpacking of *r* on *A1, A2, ..., An*, and it's equivalent to the following—

```
UNPACK ( ... ( UNPACK ( UNPACK r ON ( B1 ) ) ON ( B2 ) ) ... ) ON ( Bn )
```

—where the sequence of attribute names *B1, B2, ..., Bn* consists of some arbitrary permutation of the specified sequence of attribute names *A1, A2, ..., An*.

Examples: 1. Let relation *r* be as follows:

SNO	DURING
S2	[d02:d04]
S2	[d03:d05]
S4	[d02:d05]
S4	[d04:d06]
S4	[d09:d10]

Then the unpacked form of *r* looks like this (note that every DURING value in that unpacked form is a unit interval specifically):

SNO	DURING
S2	[d02:d02]
S2	[d03:d03]
S2	[d04:d04]
S2	[d05:d05]
S4	[d02:d02]
S4	[d03:d03]
S4	[d04:d04]
S4	[d05:d05]
S4	[d06:d06]
S4	[d09:d09]
S4	[d10:d10]

2. Let relation *r* be as follows:

A1	A2
[P1:P1]	[d08:d09]
[P1:P2]	[d08:d08]
[P3:P4]	[d07:d08]

Then unpacking *r* on A1 and A2 (in either order) yields:

A1	A2
[P1:P1]	[d08:d08]
[P1:P1]	[d09:d09]
[P2:P2]	[d08:d08]
[P3:P3]	[d07:d07]
[P3:P3]	[d08:d08]
[P4:P4]	[d07:d07]
[P4:P4]	[d08:d08]

until further notice   States of affairs that hold at the present time are often open ended; for example, a given supplier might be under contract and the date of termination of that contract might not currently be known. Such a state of affairs can thus be said to hold, or to be in effect, *until further notice*. Unfortunately, "until further notice," whatever else it might be, is most certainly not a value; as a consequence, it can't be explicitly recorded as such in a relation (nor in a relational database, a fortiori). In fact, it's precisely for this reason that horizontal decomposition, q.v., is recommended as the best way to do temporal database design. By contrast, in a design that consists of during relvars only, some artificial value—typically "the end of time," q.v.—will have to be used as the end point for any temporal interval for which the true end point is unknown.

——— ♦ ♦ ♦ ♦ ♦ ———

valid time   The original term, much used in the literature, for stated time, q.v.

vertical decomposition   (*Of temporal relvars*) Informal term used to refer to the decomposition (via U_projection, q.v.) of a during relvar that's not in sixth normal form, q.v., into a set of during relvars that are.
    Example: Relvars CS_DURING, CS_STATUS_DURING, and CS_STATUS_DURING, discussed under COMBINED_IN, might be regarded as the result of applying vertical decomposition to the relvar CS (not explicitly shown in that discussion) that's the U_join of those three relvars on DURING. That relvar CS isn't in sixth normal form, as the corresponding predicate makes clear:

> *If END (DURING) is "the end of time," then supplier SNO (a) has been under contract, (b) has had status STATUS, and (c) has been located in city CITY, ever since day BEGIN (DURING) (and not the day immediately before day BEGIN (DURING)) and will continue to be or do so until further notice; otherwise DURING denotes a maximal interval of days throughout which supplier SNO (a) was under contract, (b) had status STATUS, and (c) was located in city CITY.*

———— ♦♦♦♦♦ ————

WHEN / THEN A specification used in **Tutorial D** as part of a relvar definition to impose a constraint to the effect that if the pertinent relvar were to be kept in a certain unpacked form, then a certain attribute combination would constitute a key for the relvar in question (a regular key, that is, not a U_key, q.v.). Let *ACL* and *K* be commalists of attribute names of relvar *R*, such that every attribute mentioned in *ACL* is also mentioned in *K*, and let *X* be a commalist of all attribute names of *R* apart from those in *K*. Then the specification WHEN UNPACKED ON (*ACL*) THEN KEY {*K*}—part of the definition of relvar *R*—ensures that any attempt to update *R* will fail if the unpacked form of the result on *ACL* violates the functional dependency {*K*} → {*X*}, and thereby further ensures that *R* won't suffer from the contradiction problem (as defined elsewhere in this part of the dictionary) with respect to *ACL*. *Note:* In practice, WHEN / THEN specifications will usually be implicit (*see* U_key).

    Example: Consider relvar S_STATUS_DURING (either the Fig. 6 version or the Fig. 8 version, it makes no difference). Here's a possible definition for that relvar (irrelevant details omitted):

```
VAR S_STATUS_DURING BASE RELATION
   { SNO SNO , STATUS INTEGER , DURING INTERVAL_DATE }
     WHEN UNPACKED ON ( DURING ) THEN KEY { SNO , DURING } ... ;
```

The effect of the WHEN / THEN specification here is to ensure that any attempt to update S_STATUS_DURING in such a way as to cause the functional dependency {SNO,DURING} → {STATUS} to be violated in the unpacked form of that relvar on DURING will fail. *Note:* A variety of U_update operators, q.v., are provided in order to assist with the process of updating a relvar to which a WHEN / THEN constraint applies.

    The specification WHEN UNPACKED ON (*ACL*) THEN KEY {*K*} on relvar *R* is trivial— i.e., has no effect—if *ACL* is empty or if *K* is the entire heading of *R*.

when / then constraint A constraint—*see* WHEN / THEN—that prevents the contradiction problem (as defined elsewhere in this part of the dictionary) from occurring. *See also* U_key.

WITHOUT OVERLAPS (SQL) *See* period.

———— ♦♦♦♦♦ ————

Have it your way.

O'Reilly eBooks

- Lifetime access to the book when you buy through oreilly.com
- Provided in up to four, DRM-free file formats, for use on the devices of your choice: PDF, .epub, Kindle-compatible .mobi, and Android .apk
- Fully searchable, with copy-and-paste, and print functionality
- We also alert you when we've updated the files with corrections and additions.

oreilly.com/ebooks/

Safari Books Online

- Access the contents and quickly search over 7000 books on technology, business, and certification guides
- Learn from expert video tutorials, and explore thousands of hours of video on technology and design topics
- Download whole books or chapters in PDF format, at no extra cost, to print or read on the go
- Early access to books as they're being written
- Interact directly with authors of upcoming books
- Save up to 35% on O'Reilly print books

See the complete Safari Library at safaribooksonline.com

©2014 O'Reilly Media, Inc. O'Reilly logo is a registered trademark of O'Reilly Media, Inc. 14373

Get even more for your money.

Join the O'Reilly Community, and register the O'Reilly books you own. It's free, and you'll get:

- $4.99 ebook upgrade offer
- 40% upgrade offer on O'Reilly print books
- Membership discounts on books and events
- Free lifetime updates to ebooks and videos
- Multiple ebook formats, DRM FREE
- Participation in the O'Reilly community
- Newsletters
- Account management
- 100% Satisfaction Guarantee

Signing up is easy:

1. Go to: oreilly.com/go/register
2. Create an O'Reilly login.
3. Provide your address.
4. Register your books.

Note: English-language books only

To order books online:
oreilly.com/store

For questions about products or an order:
orders@oreilly.com

To sign up to get topic-specific email announcements and/or news about upcoming books, conferences, special offers, and new technologies:
elists@oreilly.com

For technical questions about book content:
booktech@oreilly.com

To submit new book proposals to our editors:
proposals@oreilly.com

O'Reilly books are available in multiple DRM-free ebook formats. For more information:
oreilly.com/ebooks

O'REILLY®

©2014 O'Reilly Media, Inc. O'Reilly logo is a registered trademark of O'Reilly Media, Inc. 14373

WITHDRAWN

CPSIA information can be obtained at www.ICGtesting.com
Printed in the USA
BVOW09s2349240116

434066BV00008B/44/P

31901059353815

9 781491 951736